CONFLICT AND COMMUNITY IN CORINTH

Conflict *and*

in

Community

Corinth

*A Socio-Rhetorical Commentary
on 1 and 2 Corinthians*

Ben Witherington III

WILLIAM B. EERDMANS PUBLISHING COMPANY
GRAND RAPIDS, MICHIGAN / CAMBRIDGE, U.K.

Wm. B. Eerdmans Publishing Co.
2140 Oak Industrial Drive N.E., Grand Rapids, Michigan 49505 /
P.O. Box 163, Cambridge 3 9PU U.K.
www.eerdmans.com

Printed in the United States of America

12 11   11 10

Library of Congress Cataloging-in-Publication Data

Witherington, Ben, 1951–
    Conflict and community in Corinth: a socio-rhetorical commentary on
1 and 2 Corinthians / Ben Witherington III.
      p.   cm.
    Includes bibliographical references and index.
    ISBN 978-0-8028-0144-9
    1. Bible. N.T. Corinthians — Commentaries. I. Title.
BS2675.3.W58   1994
227′.207 — dc20   94-19491
                                    CIP

Quotations from *Jesus the Sage: The Pilgrimage of Wisdom* by Ben Witherington III are copyright
© 1994 by Augsburg Fortress Publishers and used by permission.

Except as noted, all photos are by the author.

Contents

Contents   vii

Preface

Christianity is, like Islam and Judaism, a historical religion and thus not primarily a philosophical or theological construct. Specific events that took place in space and time — about 6 B.C. to A.D. 100 — and that involved particular people are foundational for the Christian faith, along with the words of particular people as they told of and interpreted these events. Therefore, when we examine the foundational documents of Christianity, we must take their historical character with absolute seriousness. The long-standing tendency to treat portions of the New Testament, particularly Paul's letters, as exercises in the history of ideas or as abstract collections of theological and ethical ideas divorced from their historical context and often even of their historical content does no justice to the character of these documents.

Paul was a pastor who wrote letters to address the specific problems of his converts. Many of these problems were essentially social in nature, though they had theological roots or ethical implications. Traditional commentaries on Paul's letters have too often neglected the social situations to which and out of which Paul wrote, with the result that the "theological and ethical principles" distilled from Paul for the modern Christian community are often difficult if not impossible to apply to our settings.

Of course Paul's letters cannot be reduced to nothing more than resources for understanding ancient social situations or to reflections of patterns of group behavior or problems. That would be to replace a theological or ethical reductionism with a sociological reductionism.

> Interest in the sociology of early Christianity is no attempt to limit reductionistically the reality of Christianity to social dynamic; rather it should be seen as an effort to guard against a reductionism from the other extreme,

a limitation of the reality of Christianity to an inner-spiritual, or objective-cognitive system. In short, sociology of early Christianity wants to put body and soul together again.[1]

While social dynamics may create a situation, they do not determine how Paul will respond as he speaks to the situation.[2] We are compelled to distinguish between social conditions and the theological intentions of the NT writers, including Paul.[3]

One aim of this commentary on 1 and 2 Corinthians is to show how use of the social sciences has shed new light on many NT texts and has helped us to understand more fully their content and historical context. Usually "exegetes focus their work on the ideas and images, the communication and form, of the text, whereas sociologists focus on behavior and social forms of the society."[4] Here we seek to bridge that gap and show that there is much to be learned about the text itself by allowing sociological insights to inform, reform, and expand traditional historical study of the text.[5]

1. R. Scroggs, "The Sociological Interpretation of the NT: The Present State of Research," *NTS* 26 (1980), pp. 164-79, here 165f.

2. Ibid., p. 167. The problem of reductionism arises when scholars attempt global explanations based on the analysis of only a certain kind of data using a certain kind of methodology. Since sociological methods focus on the typical, not the unique, not every aspect of behavior referred to in Paul's Corinthian correspondence, for instance, is explicable by use of these methods. A basic assumption is that behavior arises from the operation of social forces (as opposed to conscious cognitive interests) and that beliefs come into being to justify behavior. But we need not accept that beliefs are *always* generated in order to justify behavior, though there may be a *correlation* between behavior and belief structure. In fact, belief often engenders certain patterns of behavior as well as the converse.

We can also distinguish between experience, what happens to a person, and behavior, which I understand to involve conscious choice. Birth is an experience that all humans share, but it cannot be classified as a behavior. So, too, the three accounts in Acts of Paul's conversion/call to faith in Christ portray it as an unexpected and unsought experience, which then led to a change in Paul's beliefs and behavior.

3. So G. Theissen, *The Social Setting of Pauline Christianity: Essays on Corinth* (Philadelphia: Fortress, 1982), pp. 164-65: "Paul's own analysis of the conflict is informed by 'sociological' perceptions but at heart is derived from the theological sphere. . . . The social realities are interpreted, intensified, transcended." So we cannot ignore traditional concerns about Paul's theological views and concepts if we want to understand his writings.

4. R. A. Atkins, *Egalitarian Community: Ethnography and Exegesis* (Tuscaloosa: University of Alabama, 1991), p. 39.

5. There are many helpful introductions to sociological study of the NT. The best overall is clearly B. Holmberg's *Sociology and the NT* (Minneapolis: Fortress, 1990). H. C. Kee's *Knowing the Truth: A Sociological Approach to NT Interpretation* (Minneapolis: Fortress, 1989) makes a helpful contribution by introducing the student to a "sociology of knowledge." A. J. Malherbe's *Social Aspects of Early Christianity* (revised edition, Philadelphia: Fortress, 1983) was useful in initiating the discussion about the social level of the early Christians and issues related to the role that the household and its structure played

Since we have access to Paul's letters but not to their social contexts, it
is natural to give primary attention to the texts themselves. Sociological analysis of Paul's communities requires reading between or behind the lines of the
letters to reconstruct their social contexts.[6] Despite the conjectural nature of
such reconstructions, they are both necessary and extremely valuable, especially for understanding texts like 1 and 2 Corinthians.[7]

This commentary is called a "socio-*rhetorical* commentary"[8] because it
makes use of insights not just from the social sciences but also from study of
Greco-Roman rhetoric. Rhetorical criticism can be thought of as part of
literary criticism, but it has a decidedly historical interest. It tells us a great
deal about how the different NT authors structured their writings. Rhetoric
is by definition the art of persuasion, and particular literary devices and forms
were used in antiquity to persuade a hearer or reader to some position regarding the issue that the speaker or writer was addressing.[9] Attention to the
rhetorical dimension of Paul's letters has revealed how certain forms of argument or exhortation function in his letters, and thus how those forms ought
to be interpreted. Rhetorical criticism

> holds some promise for bridging biblical scholars' older, historical concerns
> and their newer, literary interests. . . . [It] is forthrightly interested in texts:
> defining their limits, exploring their construction and disposition, assessing

in the early years of Christianity. Of a more general and elementary nature is C. Osiek's
What Are They Saying about the Social Setting of the NT? (New York: Paulist, 1984).

6. Social description involves the cataloging of social institutions, customs, and
artifacts (the visible features of society), but scholars often go on to the stage of trying to
write social history, that is, examining the development, structure, and function of groups
over a period of time and looking for organized patterns and causes of behavior under the
assumption that behavior or even group structure can be explained from the working of
latent social forces (e.g., status inconsistency leading certain kinds of people to join the
Christian community). But see n. 2 above for a caution regarding this assumption.

7. The value of such reconstructions is seen in a number of recent studies. A good
place to begin is W. A. Meeks, *The First Urban Christians: The Social World of the Apostle
Paul* (New Haven: Yale University, 1983), and Theissen, *Social Setting.*

8. It appears that the term "socio-rhetorical" was first used by Vernon K. Robbins.
See his *Jesus the Teacher: A Socio-Rhetorical Interpretation of Mark* (Minneapolis: Fortress,
1992), pp. xixff.

9. The best brief introduction to Greco-Roman rhetoric is D. Watson, *Invention,
Arrangement, and Style: Rhetorical Criticism of Jude and 2 Peter* (Atlanta: Scholars, 1988),
pp. 1-28. For more detailed treatments see G. A. Kennedy, *NT Interpretation through Rhetorical Criticism* (Chapel Hill: University of North Carolina, 1984), and B. Mack, *Rhetoric
and the NT* (Minneapolis: Fortress, 1990).

The all too frequent view that ancient rhetoric was purely ornamental and made
little real contribution to culture in the Roman Empire (e.g., P. Veyne, *A History of Private
Life from Pagan Rome to Byzantium* I [Cambridge: Belknap, 1987], p. 22: Rhetoric "most
assuredly was not utilitarian; it contributed nothing to 'society'") is simply wrong.

their style, probing the salient issues that drive them in certain directions. . . . [It] attempts to understand more fully the overt and subtle relationships that exist between the form and content of texts, between those who generate and those who receive such texts. [It] . . . does not intend to be an ahistorical method of reading texts. Its *raison d'être* stems in large measure from the fact that rhetoric was a systematic, academic discipline taught and practiced throughout the Greco-Roman world.[10]

This commentary examines, then, both the social context and the rhetorical form of Paul's Corinthian correspondence as well as giving attention to insights from classical literature and Roman history and offering some of the usual linguistic and historical data of biblical commentaries. It thus distills the benefits of these new disciplines, placing them in the context of some older approaches, doing so for a general audience that includes college and seminary students, pastors, and lay persons. More detailed discussion for more advanced students and for scholars is confined mainly to footnotes and to sections of smaller type that come under the heading "A Closer Look."

Students of the NT in both college and seminary have repeatedly spoken to me of the desire and need for the modern Christian community to get back to the pristine character of the early *ekklēsia*.[11] I have always asked them "Which early community do you have in mind? Would you, for example, want your congregation to emulate the community in Corinth with all its problems as well as its promise?" I raise such questions not merely to provoke my students, but because there are better and worse ways of handling a text in order to bridge the gap between Paul's world and ours. In the concluding notes of several sections of this commentary I make suggestions regarding the relevance of various portions of these letters for the *ekklēsia* today. These comments are deliberately intended to be tentative, not definitive.

As an exegete I take very seriously the need to understand the Bible in its original historical context. Paul addressed specific people at a specific time in a language that they could understand. What he intended that the text mean must be the starting point for all responsible uses of the text today.[12] We are

10. C. C. Black, "Rhetorical Criticism and the NT," *Proceedings, Eastern Great Lakes and Midwest Bible Societies* 8 (1988), pp. 77-92, here p. 81.

11. In this commentary I use the Greek word *ekklēsia* rather than "church," its usual translation, because of some of the connotations that "church" has in our time.

12. It is a fundamental principle of the interpretation of the Bible that a document cannot mean something today that would contradict the thrust or trajectory of meaning that was originally intended by the writer. A letter of Paul, for example, may well have a larger *significance* or different *applications* today, but it ought not to be applied in a way that violates the apostle's *intended sense and meaning*. We must ask then what the text meant in its first-century context and then in light of that ask what it might mean for us here and now. Only so will we be faithful to the text and be guided and guarded by what it excludes

not free to rewrite his words simply because we seek a different or perhaps
less disturbing meaning. Because Paul is not available to be asked about what
he meant, careful historical study of the text and its context is necessary to
reconstruct the meaning of the text.[13]

But as a Christian minister I also believe that Paul's words are the Word
of God and if properly handled and interpreted can still meaningfully address
the *ekklēsia* today.[14] They cannot be simply transferred without care into the
late twentieth-century world.[15] We can no more modernize Paul than we can
turn the *ekklēsia* into a glorious anachronism. Paul did not seek to set up a
culture but to convey a Word that he believed could incarnate itself in a variety
of different cultures.[16] But cultural adaptability is not theological or ethical
malleability. Therefore, my occasional suggestions about the applicability of
the text do not seek either to fuse or to confuse the two horizons of Paul's
world and ours. They seek rather to build a bridge between those two horizons,
since I am convinced that the text is and ought to be treated as still normative
for the faith and practice of God's people today.[17]

---

and what it allows. It will be seen from this that I do not agree with some of the assumptions
of P. Ricoeur and of some practitioners of reader-response criticism concerning intention-
ality and the locus of meaning. Cf. B. Witherington, *Jesus the Sage: The Pilgrimage of Wisdom*
(Minneapolis: Fortress, 1994), ch. 4.

13. Meaning resides in the text and is placed there by the author by means of his or
her configuration of its words and phrases. Therefore, though the writer may be deceased,
his or her words and meaning can still live on without our trying to impose a modern
meaning on the text that violates the author's intended sense.

14. Here I would differ somewhat from J. C. Beker's approach in his stimulating
study *Heirs of Paul* (Minneapolis: Fortress, 1991), p. 100. I do not think it is our job to
bestow authoritative status on this or that text, or to withdraw such status because a text
seems to us no longer appropriate. The text's authority comes from its source, not from its
audience or from the current cultural matrix in which it is now a dialogue partner. The
task of the Christian exegete or preacher is to interpret and apply God's Word, not to create
a personal canon within the larger canon.

15. Paul addressed situations for which there is no analogy today. For example, his
advice to slaves in 1 Corinthians 7 presupposes the Roman institution of slavery. More
recent slavery, including that in the U.S., was different in many ways from ancient Roman
slavery. But there might be some general principles underlying Paul's advice that are still
of relevance, for example, his counsel not to become enslaved to other human beings.

Furthermore, we can easily name aspects of our culture that Paul never had to address
(e.g., the choices involved in modern medical ethics). But here again there may be general
principles in the text that we could learn to apply to new and different situations.

16. In addition, there are various aspects of Paul's gospel that, if they are to be heeded
today, require that we deinculturate ourselves, separate ourselves, that is, from cherished
Western cultural values, while being open to both the Word and the Spirit.

17. This is where I would part company with scholars such as E. Schüssler Fiorenza,
who has been rightly praised but also criticized by J. C. Beker: Although she "correctly
criticizes the androcentric legacy of the biblical and theological tradition and calls for its

Careful attention to the historical and social matrix of the Pauline communities makes it clear that the early *ekklesia* was far from perfect. As often as not, Paul was busy exhorting Christians to change their ways. If we believe that the Christian community of today should in some sense be biblically shaped and if we hold up the example of the Pauline communities, then we must say "go and do otherwise" at least as often as we say "go and do likewise."

One reason that we tend to commit the fallacy of idealism when we reflect on the early *ekklēsia* is that we have assumed that "the determining factors of the historical process are ideas and nothing else, and that all developments, conflicts and influences are at bottom developments of, and conflicts and influences between, ideas."[18] Such a false premise too often leads to the false conclusion that if we get our ideas about the faith right or if we emulate *"the pattern"* of the early *ekklēsia*,[19] then our Christian community will be what it ought to be.

But if we read Paul's letters carefully, they reveal that right living and proper social interaction both within the Christian community and with the larger world were at least as much of a concern as right thinking, and evidently the early Christians had difficulties with all these matters. Without denying the importance of ideas or the life of the mind, we must take more seriously the dialectic between ideas and social structures.

In some ways, there are no documents in the NT to illustrate better the help a socio-rhetorical approach can give to our understanding and application of the text than 1 and 2 Corinthians. Examining the conflict and the *koinōnia* in Corinth by means of this approach will enable us to see more clearly a part of the early *ekklēsia* as it truly was. For those of us striving to be the body of Christ today, I hope that we will see ourselves without illusions and will gain insights into how we might better be an *ekklēsia* about to enter its twenty-first century of existence.

BEN WITHERINGTON III

---

radical reconstruction, her hermeneutical proposals amount to a rejection of the normative character of the Bible" (*Heirs of Paul*, p. 121). She rejects the idea of timeless principles or practices in the Bible. I would say that there are both binding principles and binding practices (e.g., the celebration of the Lord's Supper).

18. As Holmberg, *Sociology and the NT*, p. 2, points out.

19. We cannot assume there was only one such discernible pattern. The NT data suggest that a variety of patterns of community structure existed and evolved during the course of the first century A.D.

Acknowledgments

I am especially grateful:

To Prof. W. J. McCoy for instilling in me a great love of ancient history and the Greek classics and inviting me to join his tour of Greece in 1992 and to Ms. Carolyn Phillips for giving me an appreciation of the Latin classics.

To Profs. C. K. Barrett and G. D. Fee, who first taught me the Corinthian correspondence.

To Dr. Bruce Winter, Warden of Tyndale House, for his assistance and kindness during my time in Cambridge and to Prof. Morna Hooker for sponsoring my Bye Fellowship at Robinson College, Cambridge University.

To Tim and Mary Anne Keyes for providing a nurturing home environment and *koinōnia* while I was in Cambridge.

To Profs. M. Hengel, P. Stuhlmacher, and O. Betz for their hospitality and help while I was in Tübingen doing research, and to Ken and Marcia Brewer for the same.

To my wife, Ann, and my children, Christy and David, who coped admirably with my absence during my sabbatical leave.

To Dr. Fred Finks for his continued support of my scholarly endeavors.

To Profs. Duane Watson and Margaret Mitchell among others for keeping me on the straight and narrow in regard to rhetoric.

To my various publishers, including Wm. B. Eerdmans, who have given me the opportunities to write about the subject I love the best, the New Testament, and to unite *eruditio et religio*.

Abbreviations

AJA	*American Journal of Archaeology*
ANRW	*Aufstieg und Niedergang der römischen Welt*
Apuleius	
Met.	*Metamorphoses*
Aristides	
Or.	*Orationes*
Aristotle	
Eth. Nic.	*Ethica Nicomachea*
Pol.	*Politica*
Rhet.	*Rhetorica*
ATR	*Anglican Theological Review*
BA	*Biblical Archaeologist*
BAGD	W. Bauer, W. F. Arndt, F. W. Gingrich, and F. Danker, *A Greek-English Lexicon of the NT and Other Early Christian Literature* (second ed., Chicago: University of Chicago, 1979)
BASOR	*Bulletin of the American Schools of Oriental Research*
CBQ	*Catholic Biblical Quarterly*
Cicero	
Brut.	*Brutus*
De Inv.	*De Inventione*
De Off.	*De Officiis*
De Orat.	*De Oratore*
Fin.	*De Finibus*
Tusc. Disp.	*Tusculan Disputations*
CII	*Corpus Inscriptionum Iudaicarum* (Rome, 1936-)

CIL   *Corpus Inscriptionum Latinarum* (Berlin, 1863-)
Clement of Alexandria
  Strom.   *Stromateis*
CTM   *Currents in Theology and Mission*
Demosthenes
  Ep.   *Epistulae*
Dionysius of Halicarnassus
  Ant. Rom.   *Antiquitates Romanae*
  Isoc.   *Isocrates*
Epictetus
  Diss.   *Dissertationes*
ETR   *Études théologiques et religieuses*
ETL   *Ephemerides theologicae Lovanienses*
Gaius
  Inst.   *Institutionum Commentarii Quattuor*
Herodotus
  Hist.   *History*
Horace
  Ep.   *Epodes*
  Sat.   *Satirae*
HTR   *Harvard Theological Review*
IG   *Inscriptiones Graecae* (1873-)
IGR   *Inscriptiones Graecae ad res Romanas pertinentes* (1906-)
ILS   H. Dessau, *Inscriptiones Latinae Selectae* (1892-1916)
Int   *Interpretation*
Isocrates
  Ep.   *Epistulae*
  Or.   *Orationes*
JAAR   *Journal of the American Academy of Religion*
JAC   *Jahrbuch für Antike und Christentum*
JBL   *Journal of Biblical Literature*
JETS   *Journal of the Evangelical Theological Society*
John Chrysostom
  Hom.   *Homilies*
Josephus
  Ant.   *Antiquitates Judaicae*
JRH   *Journal of Religious History*
JRS   *Journal of Roman Studies*
JSNT   *Journal for the Study of the NT*
Juvenal
  Sat.   *Satirae*

Lucian
   De Morte Pergr. *De Morte Peregrini*
   Sat.   *Satirae*
Maximus of Tyre
   Or.   *Orationes*
Neot   *Neotestamentica*
New Docs.   G. H. R. Horsley, ed., *New Documents Illustrating Early Christianity,* (4 vols.; North Ryde: Macquarrie University, 1981, 1982, 1983, 1987)
NovT   *Novum Testamentum*
NT   New Testament
NTS   *New Testament Studies*
OT   Old Testament
P. Oxy.   *The Oxyrhynchus Papyri,* ed. B. P. Grenfell, A. S. Hunt, et al. (1898-1972)
Petronius
   Sat.   *Satura*
Philo
   Abr.   *De Abrahamo*
   Agr.   *De Agricultura*
   Cher.   *De Cherubim*
   De Leg. Alleg. *De Legum Allegoriae*
   De Spec. Leg. *De Specialibus Legibus*
   Det.   *Quod Deterius Potiori Insidiari Soleat*
   Leg. ad Gaium *De Legatione ad Gaium*
   Mut.   *De Mutatione Nominum*
   Post.   *De Posteritate Caini*
   Vit. Mos.   *De Vita Mosis*
Philostratus
   Lives   *Lives of the Sophists*
Plato
   Alcib.   *Alcibiades*
   Prt.   *Protagoras*
   Rep.   *Republic*
Pliny (the Elder)
   Nat. Hist.   *Naturalis Historia*
Pliny (the Younger)
   Ep.   *Epistulae*
Plutarch
   Cor.   *Coriolanus*
   Lyc.   *Lycurgus*

Mor.	*Moralia*
Prof. Virt.	*De Profectu in Virtute*
Quaest. Conviv.	*Quaestiones Convivales*
Quaest. Rom.	*Quaestiones Romanae*
Suav. Viv.	*Non Posse Suaviter Vivi secundum Epicurum*
Vit. Caes.	*Vitae Parallelae: Caesar*
Quintilian	
Inst. Or.	*Institutio Oratio*
RB	*Revue biblique*
RevEx	*Review and Expositor*
Seneca	
De Ben.	*De Beneficiis*
De Clemen.	*De Clementia*
Ep.	*Epistulae*
Prov.	*De Providentia*
SIG	*Sylloge Inscriptionum Graecarum*, ed. W. Dittenberger (1915-24)
Strabo	
Geo.	*Geographia*
Tacitus	
Agr.	*Agricola*
Ann.	*Annales*
TDNT	*Theological Dictionary of the NT,* ed. G. Kittel and G. Friedrich (Grand Rapids: Eerdmans, 1964-76)
TrinJ	*Trinity Journal*
TynB	*Tyndale Bulletin*
ZNW	*Zeitschrift für die neutestamentliche Wissenschaft*

Introduction

Few figures in Christian history have been so beloved or so belittled as Paul. He has been cited as a strong advocate of both social change and the status quo on issues such as slavery and the roles of women in the *ekklēsia*. This bears witness to the complex figure that Paul was and to the profound and prolix character of his letters. Careful attention to the social and rhetorical dimensions of 1 and 2 Corinthians sheds a good deal of light on both the apostle and his agenda.

Paul the Greco-Roman Jew and Jewish Christian

Paul was the product of the confluence of three cultural orientations — Jewish, Hellenistic Greek, and Roman. It is easy to see why he would be so influenced by all three, since the evidence suggests

> that he was a Roman citizen, like his parents before him,
> that he was born in one of the centers of Hellenistic culture, that is, in the city of Tarsus in Asia Minor, and
> that he was a child of orthodox Jews who took or sent him to Jerusalem at an early age to study at the feet of the notable teacher Gamaliel and to become, himself, a Pharisaic teacher.[1]

---

1. Conclusions regarding some of these aspects of Paul's identity depend on how much stock we put in the historical veracity of texts such as Acts 22:3-25. It is my working hypothesis that Luke has his facts straight at this juncture, whatever disputes there may be

1

The Jewish influence is perhaps the most important for our discussion of Paul's rhetoric. W. C. Van Unnik argued forcefully that the evidence from Acts suggests that Paul was taken to Jerusalem at a very early age and raised there.[2] But does this rule out Paul receiving training in Greco-Roman rhetoric? The answer to this question is no, because even prominent teachers like Hillel before Paul's day were affected by the process of Hellenization that had swept the entire region centuries before, as is shown by the rhetorical patterns of Jewish argumentation of the time.[3] Half of Gamaliel's pupils are said to have been trained in the *sophia* ("wisdom") of the Greeks, which would include rhetoric. Paul could certainly have been one of those who received such training.[4] In addition, Pharisaism was to a real extent a proselytizing religion (cf. Mt. 23:15)[5] and as such needed forms of argumentation and persuasion in the *lingua franca* of the day, which was Koine Greek. With such arguments Pharisees could convince Diaspora Jews and even some Gentiles, especially those who were already synagogue adherents.

If Van Unnik was not correct, then Paul grew up not in Jerusalem but in Tarsus. But Tarsus was no cultural backwater, but rather a university town. In fact, many felt that the university there surpassed the universities in Athens or Alexandria in the study of philosophy and literature.[6] But whether Paul received his primary education in Tarsus or, as is more likely, in Jerusalem, he was in the upper one to two percent of the population in education. Only a distinct minority of families would have been able to provide the opportunities for education that Paul's letters indicate that he had. It is thus important not to underestimate any of his life influences. Paul owed a considerable intellec-

---

about other texts in Acts. C. Hemer, *The Book of Acts in the Setting of Hellenistic History* (Winona Lake: Eisenbrauns, 1989), pp. 181-89, has once again shown that there is good reason to believe that Luke was a rather reliable Hellenistic historian.

2. W. C. Van Unnik, *Tarsus or Jerusalem* (London: Epworth, 1962), pp. 8ff., points out that *anatethrammenos* in Acts 22:8 probably means "brought up," and in fact implies that all of Paul's formative education took place in Jerusalem. He demonstrates that the three perfect tense verbs in the sentence are often used together elsewhere to refer to birth, early nurture, and education (cf. Plato *Alcib.* I.122B; Philo *De Leg. Alleg.* I.31 para. 99; Plutarch *Quaest. Conviv.* 727B). Thus even Paul's preschool education under his parents or relatives took place in Jerusalem.

3. Cf. D. Daube, "Rabbinic Methods of Interpretation and Hellenistic Rhetoric," *HUCA* 22 (1949), pp. 239-62. Hillel's own teachers apparently first studied and taught in Alexandria, where, as Philo's work demonstrates, not only was rhetoric a staple of all education but declamation was a popular spectator sport (cf. *Worse Attacks the Better* 32-42). On the Greek of the rabbis in the synagogue and as part of a dialogue with Gentile synagogue adherents, see S. Lieberman, *Greek in Jewish Palestine* (New York: Jewish Theological Seminary, 1942), pp. 15ff.

4. E. A. Judge, "St. Paul and Classical Society," *JAC* 15 (1972), pp. 19-36, here p. 29.

5. Cf. A. Segal, "The Cost of Proselytism and Conversion," *Society of Biblical Literature 1988 Seminar Papers,* ed. D. J. Lull (Atlanta: Scholars Press, 1988), pp. 336-69.

6. So Strabo *Geo.* 14.5.13-14.

tual and personal debt to Greco-Roman culture and to Judaism, though it is fair to say that early Judaism had the strongest influence on him prior to his conversion to Christianity.[7]

Apparently Jews were not often granted Roman citizenship. So we may surmise that Paul's family must have provided some service to the empire to be granted this status. Perhaps they had made tents for the Roman army (cf. Acts 18:3). Paul's Roman citizenship ensured him free access to the whole Mediterranean and beyond and sometimes protected him from local injustices and prejudices (Acts 16:37). His citizenship may account for his somewhat positive view of the Roman Empire and its system of justice (Romans 13; 2 Thess. 2:7). In any case, he took advantage of Roman roads, Roman justice, and Roman order once he had become a missionary for Christ.

The diversity of Paul's background was good preparation for his role as *apostolos* ("apostle") to Gentiles. It likely provided him with a broader view of Jews and Greeks, women and men, and slaves and free persons (1 Cor. 9:19ff.) than would have been the case if he had been raised in more narrowly Jewish circles in a small Galilean or Judean village, as were some of the early Jewish Christians. Paul knew something of how to be the Jew to the Jew and the Greek to the Greek and this served him well once he found his Christian calling in life.

Paul's familiarity with the larger world of Greco-Roman culture is evident from his use of Greek ideas and from his occasional allusions to Greek poets and philosophers (e.g., 1 Cor. 15:33), though it is difficult to know how profound his knowledge of Greek and Roman philosophical writings was since these allusions are few and far between. Paul reflects more than a passing acquaintance with Cynic, Stoic, and Epicurean thought, though it is fair to say that they are not the main sources of his teaching.[8]

Paul was more clearly influenced by Greek rhetorical style, as we can see from the way that he forms and develops his whole letters, not just from use of occasional conventional rhetorical devices. We must, therefore, assume that he had had considerable Greek education. Rhetoric, unlike philosophy, was at the very heart of education, even secondary education, during the empire, and Paul is likely to have learned more rhetoric than philosophy in his schooling.[9]

---

7. A. D. Nock's summary in *St. Paul* (London: Lutterworth, 1938), p. 237, is reasonably apt: "The expression is externally Hellenic, but inwardly Jewish." Nock recognizes Paul's mastery of Greek with an "ear for rhythm" (p. 27), his use of the diatribe style, and his occasional rhetorical flourishes. But Nock also thinks that Paul did not use rhetoric and had "no social Gospel" (p. 180). Part of our purpose in this commentary is to show that Nock is wrong in regard to both rhetoric and social agenda. But he is right in saying that the predominant influence on Paul's *thought* was not pagan philosophy but the OT and early Jewish and Christian traditions.

8. Cf. A. J. Malherbe, *Paul and the Popular Philosophers* (Minneapolis: Fortress, 1989).

9. H. I. Marrou, *A History of Education in Antiquity* (New York: Sheed and Ward, 1956), pp. 194-205.

These larger cultural influences were filtered through a Jewish and scriptural orientation focused on issues such as the Law, the messiah, and eschatology[10] and, after Paul's experience on Damascus road, through a Jewish *Christian* orientation. Paul himself wrote, under some provocation, "What anyone else dares to boast about (I am speaking as a fool), I also dare to boast about. Are they Hebrews? So am I. Are they Israelites? So am I. Are they Abraham's descendents? So am I" (2 Cor. 11:21-22; cf. Phil. 3:4-6). Paul believed few could equal his pedigree.

Paul's teacher Gamaliel was one of the more broad-minded early Jewish teachers. But in his zeal against the fledgling *ekklēsia* Paul showed no such temperate character. Rather, he saw himself as a zealot for God's Law and enforcement of it. He adamantly opposed anyone who disputed that Jews should follow the same course (Gal. 1:13).

The Pharisees in general were attempting to extend the levitical standards of holiness, which are applied in the OT to the Israelite priesthood, to all Jews. They wished to organize all of life, every human activity, in accord with God's Word — including diet, clothing, and religious observances such as prayer, fasting, and tithing. The Pharisees accepted such ideas as the future resurrection of the righteous, eternal life, and eternal death, and unlike the Sadducees they believed in angels and spirits (Acts 23:8). Some also believed that everything happens through God's providence, though human beings also have moral responsibility. Some of these beliefs continued on in Paul's thinking as a Christian.

Even after Paul had become a Jewish Christian he still saw many advantages to being a Jew (cf. Rom. 11:1ff.; 3:1).[11] But Paul, whose Jewish name was

10. K.-W. Niebuhr rightly stresses that Paul was most shaped in his early and middle years by his Jewish origins and faith (*Heidenapostel aus Israel* [Tübingen: Mohr, 1992], pp. 158ff.).

11. Here I part company with D. Georgi and others. That Paul can and does deliberately distinguish himself from non-Christian Jews not only in Romans 9–11 but elsewhere in his letters and says that he is capable of relating to either Jew or Gentile on virtually equal footing (cf. 1 Corinthians 9) makes it clear that he sees himself as a third sort of person — not just a Jew but a Jewish Christian (cf. below, pp. 212-16). It is fundamental to his thinking that Jew and Gentile united in the Jewish messiah Jesus are true Israel. In his view, non-Christian Jews are at least temporarily broken off from the covenant community until the full number of Gentiles are converted. Then, according to Romans 11, Paul expects a great turning of Jews to Christ, apparently through an eschatological miracle at the end of human history, and that this turning will signal Christ's return and the great resurrection. Cf. B. Witherington, *Jesus, Paul and the End of the World* (Downers Grove: InterVarsity, 1992).

In short, Paul never envisions two different peoples of God coexisting at any point in human history. Thus, while it is true that he sees the Christian community as a development of early Judaism, he also believed that it was the true or only proper development of early Judaism. Paul was not an advocate of religious pluralism. Cf. B. W. Winter, "Theological and Ethical Responses to Religious Pluralism — 1 Cor. 8–10," *TynB* 41 (1990), pp. 209-44.

Saul,[12] also had reason to look back with regret on some of the things he did as an ardent Pharisee, particularly his persecution of the *ekklēsia*. This is at least part of why he later felt unworthy of the title *apostolos* (1 Cor. 15:9). In Gal. 1:13 Paul admits that he persecuted the church violently. He even went to foreign cities to try to persecute Christians because he felt that they were undermining the validity of Judaism, particularly that of the Law of Moses (Acts 26:11). He was probably in his early twenties or even younger when he began his campaigns against Christians, though it is difficult to tell whether or not he interrupted his studies under Gamaliel to fight Christians.

The Paul we meet in 1 Corinthians has been a Christian for as long as twenty years and so is not an immature Christian person. He has long since left his earlier life behind. He is an *apostolos* who has been fully engaged in missionary activities for perhaps more than a decade.[13] To further understand the apostle and his letters we need to reflect on his social world.

Roman Corinth[14]

The City and Its People

Corinth was, by any measure, one of the truly great cities of the Roman world. By the time Paul came to the city in the early 50s it was well on the way to becoming not only the largest but also the most prosperous city in all of Greece. But it had been destroyed in 146 B.C. by Roman forces led by the consul L. Mummius. As Cicero attested when he visited the site of classical Corinth between 79 and 77 B.C.,

---

12. Cf. T. J. Leary, "Paul's Improper Name," *NTS* 38 (1992), pp. 467-69; C. J. Hemer, "The Name of Paul," *TynB* 36 (1986), pp. 179-83. Probably *Paulos* was for Paul one of the three proper names that a Roman citizen would have. We do not know what the other two of these names were. According to Acts, Paul's name change did not occur with the Damascus road experience but when he began to reach out to the Roman world, specifically to Sergius Paulus; the way in which Acts 13:9 introduces the change may suggest that *Paulos* was a nickname, "the small one," rather than Paul's proper name. As Leary points out, once Paul became a missionary to the Gentiles an added reason not to use the name *Saulos* was that this word was used in Greek of the wanton style of walking of some prostitutes.

13. This means that most of the development in Paul's thought probably took place *before* any of his letters were written.

14. Cf. D. Engels, *Roman Corinth: An Alternative Model for the Classical City* (Chicago: University of Chicago, 1990), though there are some problems in judgment and in the use of statistics in this work. Cf. also J. Murphy-O'Connor, *St. Paul's Corinth: Texts and Archaeology* (Wilmington: Glazier, 1983); idem, "Corinth," *The Anchor Bible Dictionary*, ed. D. N. Freedman (New York: Doubleday, 1992), I, pp. 1134-39; S. E. Johnson, *Paul the Apostle and His Cities* (Wilmington: Glazier, 1987), pp. 94-105.

A reconstruction of the
forum of Roman Corinth

From N. Paphatzis, Ancient Corinth:
The Museums of Corinth,
Isthmia and Sicyon
(Athens: Ekdotike
Athenon, 1981).

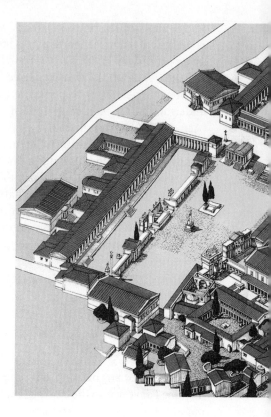

the city lay in ruins for a long time before anyone troubled with reconstruction (cf. *Tusc. Disp.* 3.53). It was Julius Caesar who, shortly before his death in March of 44 B.C., ordered that Corinth be rebuilt as a Roman colony.

This meant that the architecture of the city would take on a Roman look,[15] that it would be ruled by a Roman form of government with Roman officials, and that the city would be colonized by Romans — chiefly some of Caesar's veterans along with urban plebeians and freedmen and freedwomen from Rome itself and some Romanized Greeks (cf. Strabo 8.6.23; 17.3.15).[16]

---

15. Cf. Engels, *Roman Corinth,* p. 59.

16. One estimate suggests that over half the settlers in Corinth were freedmen and freedwomen (cf. T. B. Savage, *Power through Weakness: A Historical and Exegetical Study of the Ministry in 2 Corinthians* [dissertation, Cambridge, 1988], p. 44). On the rising status and increasing wealth of freed slaves during the first century A.D. see Seneca *Ep.* 27:5. One of the main factors in the rise to prominence of freed slaves was the establishment of the Imperial cult, in which freedmen were allowed to be officials. Some evidence suggests that over eighty-five percent of the officials in the cult of Augustus were freedmen (cf. *ILS* 607:3).

In part this was a way of rewarding veterans with land for their years of service, but it was also a shrewd means of removing disaffected and potentially volatile elements from Rome. There were some Greeks who had remained in and around Corinth living in the ruins, but once the colony was established they became resident aliens — *incolae* — and it was the colonists and their descendents who were counted as citizens *(cives)*. The *incolae* were not allowed to hold office, though apparently some of them could vote. In order to be a member of the local senate (the *decurio*), even a citizen had to meet either a stiff property qualification or be elected either an *aedile* (a city business manager) or a *duovir* (a chief magistrate).

Roman Corinth was certainly never simply a "Hellenistic" city. Taken as a whole, the architectural, artifactual, and inscriptional evidence points to a trend in the first century to Romanize the remains of the old city that went well beyond simply making Latin the official language and Roman law the rule of the city. There is evidence to suggest that the buildings of the rebuilt city were patterned on buildings in southern Italian cities (e.g., Pompeii), which were perhaps the homes of some of the veterans or freedmen and freedwomen who settled in Corinth.[17] Furthermore, there is evidence that significant quantities of Italian wares and goods were imported into Corinth, which again says something about the character of much of the population of Roman Corinth in the first five or six decades of the first century A.D.[18] The term "Greco-Roman" best describes Roman Corinth.[19]

As residents of a new city that was undergoing continual rebuilding and that was increasing in fame, the people of Corinth had both growing civic pride and individual pride (Plutarch *Mor.* 831A). All sorts of Corinthians, even slaves, are mentioned in inscriptions, often paid for and erected by and for themselves, that describe their contributions to building projects or their status in clubs *(collegia)*. The number of such inscriptions is staggering.[20] Corinth was a city where public boasting and self-promotion had become an art form.

The Corinthian people thus lived within an honor-shame cultural orientation, where public recognition was often more important than facts and where the worst thing that could happen was for one's reputation to be publicly tarnished. In such a culture a person's sense of worth is based on recognition by others of one's accomplishments, hence the self-promoting public inscriptions.

These cultural factors come into play over and over again in 1 and 2 Corinthians, where boasting, preening, false pride, and the like are topics that the apostle addresses repeatedly. Even though they were converted to a new religious orientation, the Corinthian Christians brought with them into the *ekklēsia* many of the primary social values gained over a life of living with a particular cultural orientation. Paul attempts in his letters to further his converts' resocialization by deinculturating them from some of their former primary values, chiefly by invoking certain eschatological ideas and the ethical implications of those ideas.[21]

---

17. Cf. J. B. Ward-Perkins, "From Republic to Empire," *JRS* 60 (1970), pp. 1-19; W. W. Cumer, "A Roman Tomb at Corinthian Kenchreai," *Hesperia* 40 (1971), pp. 205-31.

18. J. W. Hayes, "Roman Pottery from the South Stoa at Corinth," *Hesperia* 42 (1973), pp. 416-70, especially p. 470.

19. A. D. Litfin, *St. Paul's Theology of Proclamation: An Investigation of 1 Cor. 1–4 in Light of Greco-Roman Rhetoric* (dissertation, Oxford, 1983), p. 213: "More Greek than Rome, more Roman than Athens, if any city of the first century world deserved the hyphenated designation 'Greco-Roman' it must have been Corinth."

20. Cf., e.g., J. H. Kent, ed., *Corinth VIII/3: The Inscriptions 1926-50* (Princeton: ASCSA, 1966), n. 62 on slaves as outstanding members of a *collegium*. On self-promotion by others, mostly freedmen, cf. Kent, nn. 128, 155.

21. The conversion of an adult to a new religion is a form of *secondary* socialization (cf. P. L. Berger and T. Luckman, *The Social Construction of Reality* [New York: Doubleday, 1966], pp. 59ff.). Usually the values gained in primary socialization, that is, while growing up, remain throughout life. A dramatic *volte face* or change in life setting is usually necessary

In Paul's time, the city of Corinth was ultimately answerable to the Roman Senate because the district of Achaea, in which the city lay, had been renamed a senatorial province by Emperor Claudius in A.D. 44. Corinth, not Athens, was named the capital city of the region, possibly as early as 2 B.C. (Acts 18:12-17), and for several good reasons:

> Corinth's strategic position made it a center of trade,
> the city was also a manufacturing center,
> it was a major tourist attraction,
> and it was a center for religious pilgrimage.

Trade and Manufacturing

Corinth's site adjacent to the narrow isthmus separating the Aegean Sea from the Gulf of Corinth, and thus the Ionian Sea, and connecting the two major parts of Greece, allowed it to become a center for trade. As the geographer Strabo wrote,

> Corinth is called wealthy due to its commerce, since it is located on the Isthmus and is the master of two harbors,[22] one of which leads directly to Asia and the other to Italy. . . . The exchange of merchandise from both distant countries is made easier by the city's location. And, just as in early times, the seas around Sicily are not easy to navigate. . . . (*Geo.* 8.6.20)

Corinth was thus the central crossroads for Mediterranean trade going east and west and to a lesser degree for goods shipped from Egypt or elsewhere in northern Africa to points north of Corinth. For ships going east to west or west to east, it was far easier and safer not to make the six-day journey south around Greece but to unload at one of Corinth's two ports and have the goods carried to the other port, where they could be reloaded onto another ship, or onto the same ship if it was small enough to be dragged across the Isthmus on a road built especially for that purpose.

Corinth was also a manufacturing center. In classical times it had become

---

to redirect an adult's life orientation and pattern. Paul's converts remained where they were converted, e.g., in Corinth, and Paul encouraged them not to withdraw from the world totally. Deinculturation would have been difficult. Paul's basic strategy in Corinth was to emphasize that eschatological events of the past, present, and future had relativized the present world order and that the *schema* of this world was passing away (1 Cor. 7:31). Cf. pp. 178-81 below.

22. Lechaeum on the Gulf of Corinth to the west and Cenchaea on the Saronic Gulf to the east.

The Lechaion road as it comes into Roman Corinth

famous especially for its high tin bronze, called Corinthian bronze, and for the objects made from this bronze, which were much in demand in various places around the Mediterranean. It is less clear how much of this trade was revived in Roman Corinth. There was a bronze foundry, but it may have produced only objects for local use, not exports.[23] There were also prosperous pottery manufacturers and several schools of marble sculpture, including a workshop that specialized in the neo-Attic style during the second half of the first century A.D.

When Paul came to Corinth, the city had not yet reached its zenith as a manufacturing center, but it was already replacing some foreign goods

23. Cf. J. A. Wiseman, "Excavations in Corinth: The Gymnasium Area 1967-68," *Hesperia* 38 (1966), pp. 64-106. It appears that during the empire, so-called Corinthian bronze was manufactured elsewhere in the empire as well. As a caution against the arguments of J. Murphy-O'Connor, "Corinthian Bronze," *RB* 90 (1983), pp. 80-93, cf. E. G. Pemberton, "The Attribution of Corinthian Bronzes," *Hesperia* 50 (1981), pp. 101-11, who points out the paucity of evidence for Corinthian bronzeworkers in Roman Corinth, especially since the city seems at that time to have been primarily a merchant city, not a manufacturing city. On the foundry and use of bronze in the city see C. C. Matusch, "Corinthian Metal-Working: The Gymnasium Bronze Foundry," *Hesperia* 60 (1991), pp. 383-95; idem, "Corinthian Metalworking: An Inlaid Fulcrum Panel," *Hesperia* 60 (1991), pp. 525-28.

One of the northwest shops in Roman Corinth.
Paul may have practiced his trade in a place like this.

(including the Italian goods mentioned earlier) with comparable locally made products. During his stay in Corinth, Paul may have been among the artisans providing such locally made goods, and he probably had ample opportunity to ply his trade of making leather tents (cf. Acts 18:1-3).[24] There is evidence that by the end of the first century A.D. Roman Corinth had acquired a reputation for being the most competitive of all cities, even in economic matters. Apuleius suggests that it was a city of unprincipled profit-takers who would stop at little or nothing to outdo their rivals (*Met.* 10.19, 25). Corinth's ruthless competitive spirit is perhaps best symbolized by its position as the first Greek city to have Roman gladiatorial contests (Dio Chrysostom 31.121).

---

24. Probably not made of goat's hair cloth *(cilicium)*, as has often been thought. Most tents were made of leather. See R. F. Hock, *The Social Context of Paul's Ministry* (Philadelphia: Fortress, 1980), pp. 20ff.

Tourism

Periodic athletic contests were the basis of Corinthian tourism. The biennial Isthmian Games were second in fame only to the Olympic Games. The Romans revived the Isthmian Games at least as early as A.D. 3, and they were probably held in A.D. 49 and 51,[25] that is, at least once while Paul was in the city.[26] The quadrennial Imperial and Caesarean Games were also held in Corinth.

These games provided a great deal of short-term work and sales of, for instance, tents. It says something about Corinth that the city required a special elected official, the *agōnothetēs,* to run the games. And this official was by any normal means of measurement the most honored official in the city and thus in that sense the city's highest official.[27]

Women participated in the games, and it is possible that some of Paul's difficulties with women in Corinth were in part due to female Greek or Roman Christians used to a greater scope of activity in society than the apostle would allow in the Christian community.[28] There were also oratorical and musical contests at the games, and not long after Paul's time in Corinth Nero competed in these activities by playing the lyre (Suetonius *Nero* 22.53-55).

Religion

Corinth had long been visited by religious pilgrims coming to see the famous temple of Aphrodite on the mountain overlooking Corinth, the Acro-Corinth. Aphrodite was the goddess of love, beauty, and fertility, and prostitutes considered her their patroness. She was also a goddess of seafaring. Strabo informs us that in classical times this temple had many sacred prostitutes (*Geo.* 8.6.20c)

---

25. Cf. Kent, *Corinth VIII/3,* n. 31.

26. For a portrayal of the games see O. Broneer, "The Apostle Paul and the Isthmian Games," *BA* 25 (1962), pp. 2-31.

27. Cf. Kent, *Corinth VIII/3,* n. 30; B. D. Merritt, ed., *Corinth VIII/1: Results* (Princeton: ASCSA, 1931), n. 15.

28. On the degree of freedom enjoyed by Greek and Roman women, see B. Witherington, *Women in the Earliest Churches* (Cambridge: Cambridge University, 1988), ch. 1. On Paul's problems with women in Corinth, see A. C. Wire, *The Corinthian Women Prophets: A Reconstruction through Paul's Rhetoric* (Minneapolis: Fortress, 1990), though this work is flawed by too much "mirror-reading" and by the assumption that Paul was repressing an earlier more egalitarian and pneumatic form of Christianity. It is far more likely that Paul sought to Christianize values that these women already had from their social setting. There is no historical evidence of a Christian community in Corinth prior to Paul's missionary work there.

but it is not at all clear that the practice of *sacred* prostitution was revived on the same scale in Roman Corinth.[29]

Nevertheless, one should not underestimate the place of sexual expression, not only in some pagan religious festivals (cf. Apuleius *Met.* 10.20-22), but also in some pagan temple precincts.[30] It would be surprising if such activities did not take place in Corinth, especially in connection with the dinner parties *(convivia)* that were often held in the precincts of pagan temples (cf. Livy 23.18.12).[31] There is also evidence from Dio Chrysostom (near the end of the first century A.D.) that there were in Roman Corinth numerous *hetaerae,* who often served as companions of the well-to-do at meals (8.5-10).[32] 1 Cor. 10:7 is a meaningful warning only if Paul had good reason to assume that sexual play was a regular part of some meals in one or more of the pagan temples in Corinth.

Romans in general adopted and incorporated Greek gods and goddesses into their own religious practices, and apart from sometimes changing the names of the deities, they often did not significantly modify what they took over. This was especially so with the god or goddess that was the major religious attraction of a city. Before, during, and after Paul's day coins were minted in Roman Corinth with images of the temple of Aphrodite, in part as a form of advertisement. And given the connection of Aphrodite with prostitution, it is probable that the practice of sexual activity in some temple precincts in the city, perhaps even in Aphrodite's temples,[33] was continued.[34]

---

29. H. D. Saffrey, "Aphrodite à Corinthe. Reflexions sur une idée recue," *RB* 92 (1985), pp. 359-74, stresses that it is uncertain whether or not sacred prostitution was practiced even in classical Corinth. But Saffrey admits that Corinth clearly had a reputation for having many prostitutes (p. 373).

30. Cf. H. J. Mason, "Lucius at Corinth," *Phoenix* 25 (1971), pp. 160-65.

31. Cf. A. Booth, "The Age for Reclining and Its Attendent Perils," in *Dining in a Classical Context,* ed. W. J. Slater (Ann Arbor: University of Michigan, 1991), pp. 105-20. Booth notes that oratory was also often part of such feasts, and that sophists were often present. He notes (p. 105) that the chief enticements to Romanization were opportunities for cultivation of oratory, elegant banquets, use of the promenade and the toga, and participation in sexual play at such banquets (cf. Tacitus *Agr.* 21). Quintilian warns that a teacher of rhetoric should teach his charges about the dangers of such feasts, especially because of the possibility of more mature youths or men taking advantage of younger boys in such settings (*Inst. Or.* 2.2.14-15). On the dining facilities at the Asklepion in Corinth, see K. M. D. Dunbabin, "Triclinium and Stibadium," in *Dining in a Classical Context,* pp. 121-48, here p. 122.

32. Though Dio purports to be telling us about Diogenes's day, here and elsewhere the events he describes suit his own time, the second half of the first century A.D., better.

33. There were at least three temples of this goddess in Corinth.

34. Whether there were "sacred prostitutes" in the Roman period Aphrodite temple is a separate matter from the issue of sexual play in general at meals in temple precincts. I

The ancient temple (of Apollo?) in Corinth

Many also came to visit other religious shrines such as the temple of Apollo or, if one was seeking healing, the temple of Asklepios. There are few more startling sights for the modern tourist in Corinth than the numerous clay representations of body parts, including arms, legs, and genitalia, that ancient visitors to the Asklepion left behind in thanks to the god for healings.[35]

am arguing that it is very likely that hetaerae and prostitutes were present at some of the *convivia* held in homes and in temple precincts in Corinth.

There is no evidence that such earlier practices were dropped in Roman times, indeed quite the opposite. Engels, *Roman Corinth*, p. 226, n. 17, argues: "Strabo's statement (8.6.20) makes it clear that the cult of Aphrodite's sacred prostitutes belonged to the past and was not practiced in the Roman city." Strabo passed through Corinth in about 44 B.C., and if the first Roman colonists had arrived at all, they had hardly had time to revive and rebuild the city yet. He mentions in 8.6.21b, referring to a later visit in 29 B.C., that the temple of Aphrodite was small, but says nothing about changed religious practices. It appears that Engels, like Murphy-O'Connor, *St. Paul's Corinth*, pp. 55f., is attempting to exonerate Roman Corinth in reaction to the unduly lurid descriptions of Corinth in some works on the NT.

1 Cor. 10:7-8 does seem to allude to sexual play taking place after a meal in a pagan temple. Paul was apparently convinced that idolatry and immorality could be found in the same location in Corinth. But the city was probably morally neither better nor worse than other major cities of the empire.

35. Some have suggested that these objects were petitionary in character (i.e., they were a form of asking the god for a cure), though most classical scholars reject this

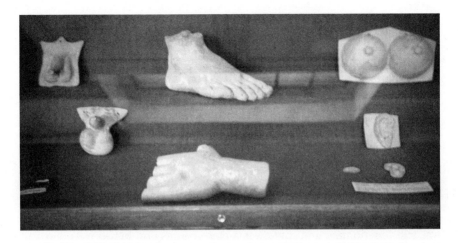

Body parts from molds found at the Asklepion in Corinth

Though the Asklepios sanctuary at Epidaurus was more important, the one at Corinth was significant. The three major elements in an Asklepion were a well or spring for purifications, a place for sleeping (the *abaton*), and the temple.[36] Asklepios was a god of not only physical but also emotional and mental health. His major sanctuaries included places for rest, exercise, and contemplation, including baths, theaters, gymnasia, libraries, and tree-lined gardens. They were in many ways similar to modern health resorts. Adjacent to the Asklepion in Corinth was the Lerna with its dining facilities and bath and fountain house. This environment made the Asklepion a popular location for public dining with friends in a relaxed atmosphere. Perhaps it was there that some Corinthian Christians were being invited to eat meat that had been offered to idols (1 Cor. 10:27f.).[37] The worship of Asklepios had many of the elements of worship of such pagan gods — processions, hymns, and sacrifices. Like that of Aphrodite, the cult of Asklepios was probably one of the most influential religious cults in shaping Corinthian thinking.

The goddess Hera Argaea, a goddess of marriage and especially of the

---

view. R. E. Oster, "Use, Misuse, and Neglect of Archaeological Evidence in Some Modern Works on 1 Corinthians," *ZNW* 83 (1992), pp. 52-73, warns rightly that it is not likely that ancient tourists saw the models of body parts and thus that it is quite unlikely that they were the inspiration for Paul's body imagery in 1 Corinthians 12. Cf. *New Doc.* 2, pp. 21-23, for an inscription dealing with healing in the cult of Asklepios.

36. See the report and drawings in M. Lang, *Cure and Cult in Ancient Corinth: A Guide to the Asklepion* (Princeton: ASCSA, 1971), pp. 1ff.

37. Murphy-O'Connor, *St. Paul's Corinth*, p. 163.

sexual life of women, had a temple in Roman Corinth near the marketplace. The most characteristic rite connected with this goddess was sacred marriage, but she was also associated with the ordinary sort of human marriage. Sacred marriage involved sexual union between two divine persons or one divine and one human person, with the union considered in some way sacral. The result was supposedly an increase in fertility or prosperity, which women might seek in such a cultic union. It is worth considering whether this might explain some of what we find in 1 Corinthians 7: Might some women have thought that a previous sacral union should not be defiled by a human union? Hera was often paired with Aphrodite but was also connected with childbirth and children and nurture of them. This might be behind the statement in 1 Cor. 7:14 concerning the holiness of children.

The oracle at Delphi was certainly past its heyday in Paul's time. But it was still functioning, and there was a close connection between Apollo and the oracle. There was a temple of Apollo in Corinth, and Delphi is only about 50 km. from Corinth. Apollo was the god of prophecy, and it is more than likely that the Corinthians would have understood prophecy in the light of this part of their context. Did then the Corinthian Christians understand Christian glossolalia and prophecy in terms of the practices at Delphi? Were male prophets in the church being interrupted by women who were asking the sorts of questions that were normally asked of the Delphic oracle — about childlessness, fate, prosperity, or the like (cf. 1 Cor. 14:34f.)?

There was also a temple of Tyche (fate or luck) in Corinth, and the Corinthian Christians apparently tended to be fatalistic, or at least believed in and depended on forces other than God to shape their lives. There was in Corinth also a statue of Tyche wearing a *corona muralis* (wall crown), which may shed some light on 2 Cor. 11:30-33.[38]

It is not clear what we should make of the apparently numerous dining facilities at the Corinthian temple of Demeter and Kore. The latest archaeological reports casts doubt on the earlier assumption that the issues addressed by Paul in 1 Corinthians 10 were focused on these facilities.[39] But these reports also show other possible points of contact with issues addressed in 1 Corinthi-

---

38. Cf. pp. 458-59 below.

39. Though reports by N. Bookides among others gave support to the conjecture that this is the location Paul had in mind when he wrote 1 Corinthians 10, Bookides's later work casts doubt on such a deduction, and so the matter must be approached with caution. Cf. Bookides and J. E. Fischer, "The Sanctuary of Demeter and Kore," *Hesperia* 41 (1972), pp. 283ff., and her most recent report given at the meeting on Roman Corinth, October, 1992, in Newcastle, England. It appears that W. L. Willis, *Idol Meat in Corinth: The Pauline Argument in 1 Corinthians 8 and 10* (Chico: Scholars, 1985) has ignored some of Bookides's warnings. The dining rooms at the Demeter sanctuary now appear mainly to be *under* the level of the Roman floor.

Statue of Kore with a sacred Eleusinian box on her head

ans 11–14. During Paul's time the shrine was apparently being revived.[40] Young girls apparently served there as priestesses as in other Greek Demeter shrines and may have worn a distinctive ceremonial hat.[41] There is evidence that secret rites, perhaps initiatory rites, were carried out in a room directly behind a dining room in a building in the shrine precincts (designated L-M:28 by archaeologists). At other Demeter shrines, such as at Eleusis, the Eleusian mysteries were celebrated (see the picture above). The god Dionysius was often connected with Demeter since both were fertility deities, which may

---

40. New buildings, including three small temples, were constructed at the shrine during the second half of the first century A.D.

41. Slightly earlier Hellenistic statues in Demeter shrines depict the priestess as wearing this ceremonial hat, the *polos*.

suggest a context for religious justification of sexual play at the shrine of Demeter.

Finally, lead curse tablets have been found under the floor of a Roman building on the site of the Demeter shrine that is believed to have been built during the second half of the first century A.D. All eleven curses that have been found are directed against women and include such invocations as "I adjure and implore you and I beg of you, Hermes of the underworld, [to grant] heavy curses." One tablet begins with "I consign and entrust Karpile Babbia . . . to the Fates, who exact justice. . . ." These tablets might have some bearing on the enigmatic *anathema Iēsou* ("Jesus be cursed!") passage in 1 Cor. 12:3.[42]

It is hardly surprising that Corinth, a Roman colony, assiduously cultivated its ties with the emperor and his family. For example, in A.D. 23 Livia was honored as divine Julia Augusta with a poetry contest, and this took place even before her death.[43] T. Claudius Dinippus, one of Paul's contemporaries serving as duovir in A.D. 52-53 in Corinth, was also priest of the rare cult of Britannic Victory, which celebrated the emperor's triumphs in Britain. During the Imperial Games the emperor was lauded with encomiums and other forms of ornamental rhetoric.[44] Most importantly, however, the imperial cult was strongly promoted in first-century Corinth,[45] and freedmen were given a prominent role in this cult and thereby gained social status. In order to be fully involved in the Christian *ekklēsia* it would surely have been necessary to give up whatever roles one had in other religious assemblies, including the imperial cult.

Corinth was a bustling and prosperous metropolis of perhaps seventy to eighty thousand inhabitants in Paul's day. As Engels has shown in great detail, it was primarily a service city, one that derived its wealth from the goods and services it provided to visitors, including religious pilgrims, sailors, merchants, soldiers, slave traders, and those who were in town for the games.[46] In many ways, Paul could not have picked a more appropriate place to plant the seeds of the gospel.

Paul's missionary strategy, at least by the late 40s, was to evangelize the urban cities, most of which lay on major Roman roads (e.g., Ephesus, the Roman colony of Philippi, Thessalonica, and Corinth). The image of Paul

42. On all these matters, cf. N. Bookides and R. S. Stroud, *Demeter and Persephone in Ancient Corinth* (Princeton: ASCSA, 1987), pp. 3ff.

43. Cf. Kent, *Corinth VIII/3*, p. 77.

44. Cf. Merritt, ed., *Corinth VIII/1*, n. 19.

45. The cult of the emperor is most easily dated to at least the reign of Nero, but it is likely that it existed long before then. Cf. J. K. Chow, *Patronage and Power: A Study of Social Networks in Corinth* (Sheffield: JSOT, 1992), pp. 57ff; pp. 295-98 below.

46. Engels, *Roman Corinth*, pp. 43ff.

racing breathlessly around the Roman Empire, never staying in one place more than a few days or weeks, is to a significant degree a false one. Acts 18:11 tells us that Paul stayed in Corinth for well over a year on his first visit there. Furthermore, 1 and 2 Corinthians suggest a stay long enough to establish a lively and complex community. Paul saw himself as a pioneer missionary whose chief task it was to start Christian communities in places where they had not previously existed (cf. 2 Cor. 10:14ff.). He tended and intended to stay in a location long enough to accomplish that task well.[47]

The Social Level of Paul and His Converts

Paul's Position and Presence

Paul may well have spent a considerable period of his time in Corinth at his work of tentmaking, since it would have allowed him to come into contact with all sorts of people, to support himself to a large extent, and thus to offer the gospel free of charge (cf. 1 Cor. 9:18).[48]

> We begin to realize that, far from being at the periphery of his life, tent-making was actually central to it. More than any of us has supposed, Paul was *Paul the tentmaker*. His trade occupied much of his time — from the years of his apprenticeship through the years of his life as a missionary for Christ, from before daylight through most of the day. Consequently, his trade in large measure determined his daily experiences and his social status. His life was very much that of the workshop, of artisan-friends like Aquila, Barnabas, and perhaps Jason; of leather, knives, and awls; of wearying toil; of being bent over a workbench like a slave and of working side by side with slaves; of thereby being perceived by others and by himself as slavish and humiliated; of suffering the artisan's lack of status and so being reviled and abused.[49]

---

47. Therefore, some readings of Acts can be misleading. Paul's travels after the "first missionary journey" should not be saddled with the designation "missionary journeys," since that term would seem to exclude Paul stopping in one place for a year and a half and practicing a trade in another place for two to three years (cf. Acts 19:10; 1 Cor. 16:8-9).

48. It may be that Paul gravitated to Aquila and Priscilla's house because they were members of the same trade association as Paul, that of the tentmakers. Such associations provided much natural fellowship, mutual support, and hospitality for travelers. Cf. R. Mac-Mullen, *Roman Social Relations 50 B.C. to A.D. 284* (New Haven: Yale University, 1974), pp. 73ff.

49. Hock, *Social Context*, p. 67.

Actually, this description by R. Hock seems to go a bit too far, since Paul himself in his catalogue of trials (2 Cor. 11:23ff.) makes clear that a good deal of his time was spent on travel and in contacts with Jews and Romans that led to punitive measures. He was not merely sitting in a workshop plying a trade.

But Paul did sometimes work with his hands and would have been seen by many as an artisan.[50] Well-to-do or aristocratic Romans, like Greeks, often had a low opinion of those who practiced a trade, and many of Paul's problems in Corinth seem to have been caused by the wealthy and the social climbers among Corinthian Christians who were upset at him for not meeting their expectations for a great orator and teacher. Corinth was a city where an enterprising person could rise quickly in society through the accumulation and judicious use of newfound wealth. It seems that in Paul's time many in Corinth were already suffering from a self-made-person-escapes-humble-origins syndrome.[51] Corinth was a magnet for the socially ambitious, since there were many opportunities for merchants, bankers, and artisans to gain higher social status and accumulate a fortune in this city refounded by freed slaves.

But a person visiting Paul's workshop would not have immediately concluded that he was nothing but a poor artisan, since Cynic philosophers were known to frequent workshops, and some of them were artisans before they became philosophers.[52] There is also considerable inscriptional evidence that many artisans and shopkeepers were quite proud of their work.[53] Along with being an artisan, Paul was a preacher, teacher, and missionary skilled in the use of Greco-Roman rhetoric in writing, as we can see from his letters.

---

50. The Thessalonian correspondence also suggests that Paul regularly practiced a trade, not only in Corinth. Furthermore, the reason given in 1 Thess. 2:5, 9 (that he might not be accused of greed or be a burden to anyone) seems similar to the reason given to the Corinthians. Cf. B. W. Winter, " 'If a Man Does Not Wish to Work . . . ': A Cultural and Historical Setting for 2 Thessalonians 3.6-16," *TynB* 40 (1989), pp. 303-15. Paul's acceptance of support from the Philippians and refusal of support from the Corinthians will be discussed below in the light of benefaction customs in Roman antiquity.

51. Cf. T. Savage, *Power through Weakness,* pp. 61ff.

52. Hock, *Social Context,* pp. 37ff. It should be noted that Paul continued to practice his trade. Furthermore, while it appears that he relied on the system of standing hospitality during his missionary travels, it would not be correct to paint him as being exactly like a traveling Cynic philosopher, who would beg for food or offer teaching in exchange for it. The sources suggest that some Cynics may have come from or taught in workshops, *not* that they worked and taught in workshops at the same time. The parallels between Paul and such peripatetic philosophers are informative to some degree, but they do not allow us to simply class Paul among the Cynics.

53. Cf. Petronius, *Sat.* 29; *CIL* 11.741; 6.9940; 6.9709; 1.1210. Grave inscriptions frequently include expressions of pride in one's profession.

The Corinthians, or possibly even Paul's opponents, observed, in fact, that his letters were weightier than his personal bodily presence and his oral rhetoric (2 Cor. 10:10), which was perhaps hampered by some physical disability.[54] They also apparently cared little for his deliberate self-humiliation, his assumption of a servant role, which was "an attitude in violent reaction to much that was central to the classical way of life, not excluding the smooth doctrines of moderation."[55] In a city where social climbing was a major preoccupation, Paul's deliberate stepping down in apparent status would have been seen by many as disturbing, disgusting, and even provocative.

The evidence is that Paul was well educated, and in that regard he would have been identified with and received by the well-to-do. His Roman citizenship would have worked in the same direction. But a number of other factors also mattered. Paul's standing in regard to all the variables that counted in social status — including also wealth, political influence, and family[56] — made him a person with considerable status inconsistency. At least in Corinth, that he was an artisan who practiced a trade, not a teacher or philosopher who accepted patronage, would have worked against his social status.[57] "The status opportunities Paul declined remain the measure of his potential professional standing, and of the expectation of his supporters for him. The extent of his renunciation helps to explain Paul's intense consciousness of debasement. He was stepping firmly down in the world."[58] An apparent result was that some considered him unsophisticated and unworthy of the status of *apostolos*.

54. During the time of the empire, increasing stress was placed on an orator's *parousia* ("presence"), that is, his appearance, gestures, voice, and delivery. Quintilian's words are almost a paraphrase of the Corinthians' complaints against Paul: Good delivery "is hampered by incurable speech impediments . . . , physical uncouthness may be such that no art can remedy it, while a weak voice is incompatible with first-rate excellence in delivery . . ." (11.3.12f.). On the crucial importance of delivery, cf. Cicero, *De Orat.* 3.56.213 and *Brut.* 38.142, where he says that Demosthenes regarded delivery as of the greatest significance.

55. Judge, "St. Paul and Classical Society," p. 36.

56. B. Holmberg, *Sociology and the New Testament* (Minneapolis: Fortress, 1990), pp. 56f.

57. As we shall see, patronage was one of the major problems the wealthier Corinthian Christians had with Paul. 2 Corinthians suggests that they were offended because he refused to be their client.

58. E. A. Judge, "The Social Identity of the First Christians," *JRH* 1 (1960), pp. 201-17, here p. 214. The Corinthians may also have complained about Paul's rhetoric because of his use of plain style "Roman" rhetoric, as opposed to the more florid Asiatic style.

The Corinthian Christians

Social Status

Discussion of the social level of Paul's Corinthian converts usually begins and frequently ends with 1 Cor. 1:26-28. Paul says there that *not many* of those to whom he is writing are "wise," "powerful," or "of noble birth." So some, though few, of the Corinthian Christians apparently *were* members of such high status groups. This group seems to have included one or two government officials (see pp. 33-34 below on Erastus).[59] Those whom Paul calls "powerful" might have been those with political power, but since 2 Corinthians deals with issues involved in benefaction, including the patron-client relationship, Paul is probably referring to the relatively wealthy with this term. In Greco-Roman society, "money is continually given by the powerful to their dependents, and this transfer of cash downwards in the social scale is the main instrument by which the status of the powerful is asserted."[60]

Though there were, according to Paul's testimony, few wealthy people in the Corinthian Christian community, their influence among the converts was probably well out of proportion to their numbers, since they could provide meeting places for the Christians in their homes (cf. 1 Cor. 16:15, 19). Furthermore, the "leisure, administrative skills, education, and affluence" of wealthy Christians "gave them enormous advantages for becoming the local, indigenous leaders in the congregations that Paul founded."[61]

That there were significant numbers of poor or relatively poor people among the converts is suggested by 1 Cor. 1:28 and 11:22. And there were domestic slaves in the congregation as well (1 Cor. 7:21-23). 1 Cor 16:2 and 2 Corinthians 8–9, on the other hand, suggest that Paul believed that there was disposable income or assets among his Corinthian converts. Therefore, the social level of the Corinthian Christians apparently varied from quite poor to rather well-off, though they probably did not include any Roman aristocrats, of which there were likely only a few in Corinth anyway.[62] "A Pauline congre-

---

59. Cf. A. J. Blasi, *Early Christianity as a Social Movement* (New York: Lang, 1988), pp. 56-60.

60. Judge, "Social Identity," p. 211. This comment will be very important for our understanding of 2 Corinthians.

61. O. C. Edwards, "Sociology as a Tool for Interpreting the NT," *ATR* 65 (1983), pp. 431-46, here p. 438. Edwards suggests that part of Paul's missionary strategy was to convert some villa owners so that the community would have meeting places.

62. G. Theissen, "Vers une theorie de l'histoire sociale du christanisme primitif," *ETR* 63 (1988), pp. 199-225, here 210f., still strongly argues that the majority of Corinthian converts came from the lower strata of Corinthian society. Further, he stresses that even the wealthy Corinthian Christians were "situant à la périphérie de la classe superieure locale"

gation generally reflected a fair cross-section of urban society,"[63] though on average the Corinthian Christians appear to have been better off than the members of some of Paul's other congregations, such as those in Macedonia, since he is willing to talk about the Corinthians having a surplus of assets (2 Cor. 8:1, 2, 14).[64]

But wealth was not the only means to high social status. The hierarchy of values in the Roman colonies also included family lineage, connections with Rome, and cultural sophistication.[65] It appears that some, at least, of the better-off Corinthian Christians were, like Paul, people with "a high ranking in one or more dimensions of status . . . accompanied by low rankings in other dimensions." They were thus "people of high status inconsistency," whose "achieved status [was] higher than their attributed status."[66]

They shared this "status inconsistency" with others of their city. Though ostensibly the basic division in Roman society was between the patricians or nobility who owned estates[67] and the plebeians,[68] Roman Corinth was a provincial city whose elite included freed slaves and veterans, with the latter

---

(p. 211). But this depends on what one means by "the superior class." There were many ways to achieve social prominence; one did not need to become a decurion to accomplish this, for even freedmen could be prominent in Corinth by gaining wealth and the influence that came with it. Furthermore, Corinth was in essence a freedman's city. The evidence suggests there was very little of the social elite that one would find in Rome, i.e., members of the imperial family or of the senatorial and equestrian classes. In fact, Tacitus could say of society in his own day (a few decades after Paul's ministry): "Freedmen supply most of the decurions, cohorts, most knights, and many senators" (*Ann.* 13.22). If there was a major division in Corinthian society, it may have been between enfranchised Romans or Roman citizens and the Greeks, Jews, and other foreigners who were not completely enfranchised.

63. W. Meeks, *The First Urban Christians: The Social World of the Apostle Paul* (New Haven: Yale University, 1983), pp. 70ff. So also A. J. Malherbe, *Social Aspects of Early Christianity* (revised edition, Philadelphia: Fortress, 1983), pp. 29ff.; Judge, "Social Identity," pp. 201-17. Probably there were few if any peasants or agricultural slaves from the surrounding regions involved in Christian congregations. Christianity was an urban phenomemon, and certainly Pauline Christianity was an urban phenomenon *by design.*

64. It may be that the majority of Paul's converts outside Corinth were poor. But one cannot conclude just on the basis of 1 Cor. 1:26-28 that the majority *in Corinth* were poor. Paul is not referring just to economic status in those verses. Probably the majority had an economic level somewhere between poverty and wealth. This may suggest that most were artisans, merchants, and the like. But the evidence clearly does not support the suggestion that the majority of early Christians, especially the Corinthians, were from the wealthy strata of society, much less from the upper classes (pace R. H. Smith, "Were the Early Christians Middle Class?" *CTM* 7 [1980], pp. 260-76).

65. MacMullen, *Roman Social Relations,* p. 122.

66. Meeks, *First Urban Christians,* p. 73.

67. One may also include Roman knights and members of the military hierarchy who retired to a patrician-like life.

68. I.e., all others, including merchants, freedmen, free men, and slaves.

perhaps dominant (Plutarch *Vit. Caes.* 47.8). Many of the city's top officials in Paul's day were the children of former slaves. Both the veterans and the freedmen gained status not by lineage or sophistication, but by mere accumulation of wealth and the power that it made possible.[69] Though some merchants and even some artisans were rather well-off and had high social aspirations, they had to form their own clubs in order to establish social bonding and identity. Such members of the *nouveau riche* were those most likely to affect culture by entertaining Sophists, preferring their more popular rhetoric of display and entertainment to serious discourse.[70]

Those whose status depended on newfound wealth played prominent roles not only in society at large, but undoubtedly also in the Christian assembly. Paul's words in 1 Cor. 1:26 would have been a pointed reminder to such status-hungry people of their origins. Some interpreters believe, in fact, that the status inconsistency of such people was at the root of the attraction that Christianity had for some Corinthians: This new religion gave them status in their own eyes that they had been unable to obtain in the larger society. But one would have to ask of this idea how much status could be gained by joining a minority monotheistic religion, one that cut one off from other aspects of society.[71]

Ethnic and Religious Background

It is clear that many of Paul's Corinthian converts were Gentiles. The urgent warnings in 1 Corinthians 10 against participating in feasts in pagan temples would not have been needed with a Jewish audience.

But there is clear evidence of Jews and Gentile synagogue adherents among the Corinthian Christians:

Paul refers to circumcised believers in Corinth (1 Cor. 7:18),
he may also allude to a mixed audience in Corinth (1 Cor. 1:22-24; 9:20-22),
he appeals to the Mosaic Law (1 Cor. 9:8-10; 14:34; 2 Cor. 3:4ff.),
he quotes the OT (e.g., 2 Cor. 6:2; 9:9; 10:17) in such a way as to assume

---

69. MacMullen, *Roman Social Relations,* pp. 108, 117.

70. See pp. 349-50 below and cf. Plutarch *Mor.* 543E-F on the popularity of the Sophists.

71. The motivation for joining a tiny minority religion that was socially diverse, relatively speaking, has seldom been discussed in any detail. More consideration should be given to the need probably felt by some to be part of a larger *familia* or to have *koinōnia*, especially among the *incolae*, those who were considered resident aliens, even if they were of Greek and Corinthian extraction. They could not have been entirely comfortable with being outsiders in their own culture and city. This sort of tension was often created in cities that had become Roman colonies. Perhaps this was a factor in the conversion of some of the Philippians as well as the Corinthians.

Menorah lintel and synagogue inscription from Roman Corinth, probably post–first century A.D. The inscription reads "Synagogue of the Hebrews."

that his audience will know and reflect on the larger contexts of some of these quotations,[72] and

his reference to the exodus generation in 1 Cor. 10:1-13 seems to assume that some of his audience will be conversant with specifically Jewish ways of interpreting and applying Scripture.

Therefore, it is plausible that a significant number of Jews and synagogue-attending Gentiles converted to the Christian faith in Corinth following the lead of Crispus, the synagogue leader in Corinth, who, according to Acts 18:8, was one of Paul's converts.

Philo, writing in the early 40s, tells us that there was a Jewish colony in

72. On this whole matter, cf. R. B. Hays, *Echoes of Scripture in Paul* (New Haven: Yale University, 1989).

Corinth (*Leg. ad Gaium* 281f.). Part of a lintel found in Corinth with the inscription "synagogue of the Hebrews" (see the photograph on p. 25)[73] confirms the existence of this colony. But both the lintel inscription and the Jewish votive lamps found in Corinth are from a period later than that of Paul. It could be that as a result of Claudius's expulsion of at least some Jews from Rome in A.D. 49 or 50, that is, shortly before Paul's arrival in Corinth, there was a larger than usual number of Jews there.[74] The view that Paul did not make it a practice to preach in synagogues when he was able and allowed to do so is made untenable by texts like 2 Cor. 10:24, not to mention the accounts in Acts.[75] Even more compelling is Paul's statement in 1 Cor. 9:20ff. that it was, indeed, his intention to win some Jews to Christ by relating to them in Jewish ways.[76]

---

73. Only a portion of the phrase remains: ". . . goge Hebr . . . ," but its interpretation seems clear enough. Cf. Murphy-O'Connor, *St. Paul's Corinth*, p. 78; J. A. Wiseman, "Corinth and Rome I: 228 B.C.–A.D. 267," *ANRW* II.7.1, pp. 438-548, here plate 5, n. 8.

74. That Claudius expelled some Jews from Rome at about this time is supported by Suetonius *Claudius* 25 and, from a much later date, Orosius *History* 7.6.15f. Orosius writes that Josephus placed this expulsion in Claudius's ninth year, i.e., January 49 to January 50. Unfortunately, we no longer have such a reference in the extant works of Josephus. Orosius also quotes Suetonius and does so in such a way as to indicate that he can probably be trusted to represent his sources accurately. There is also confirmation of this edict in Acts 18:2. B. Levick, *Claudius* (New Haven: Yale University, 1990), p. 121, reminds us that in 41 Claudius had already closed the synagogues due to disturbances, and there is no reason to doubt an expulsion in 49.

Suetonius says that the expulsion was due to riots caused *impulsore Chresto*. It has been traditionally been assumed that *Chresto* is a mistaken form of *Christus*, in which case it may have been a squabble over Christ in the Roman synagogues that precipitated the edict. But would Suetonius, writing in the second century, have gotten Christ's name wrong, since Christianity was by then fairly well known? Suetonius seems to think that *Chrestus* is alive in Rome and personally precipitating the expulsion by his agitation. S. Goranson ("Ebionites, Nazarenes, and the *Birkat Ha-Minim*," a paper given at the national meeting of the Society of Biblical Literature in 1989) argued that *Chrestus* was a slave or some other person leading a revolt in Rome and that this text thus provides us with no evidence of tensions in Rome between Jews and Jewish Christians or Gentile Christians. But this still leaves us with Acts 18:1-3. If Priscilla and Aquila were already Christians when they left Rome, we may, then, have some support for the traditional interpretation of Suetonius's words.

75. Paul himself says that the gospel is the power of salvation for the Jew *first* (Rom. 1:16). Should it surprise us, then, that when Paul went into a city that had not yet been evangelized he gravitated toward the synagogue first?

76. This in turn implies that he apparently felt no compulsion to be a practicing Jew in every respect. One suspects that he had laid aside those aspects of his heritage that would necessarily separate him from his main target audience, the Gentiles, i.e., strict adherence to food laws and to other practices concerning ritual purity. Perhaps Paul is vehement about moral purity in the Corinthian letters because his abandonment of Jewish ritual purity led some of his converts to conclude that Paul had adopted a Gentile view of sexual matters.

The fountain of Pirene in the center of Roman Corinth

As many as two-thirds of all Jews in Paul's day lived outside Palestine. About seven percent of the empire's population appears to have been Jewish. They ranged from very sectarian and separatist to very Hellenized, and also from rather wealthy to slaves, though there appear to have been fewer Jewish slaves than slaves of any other ethnic group.[77] The Jewish community of Corinth probably included a few Roman citizens, shipowners, ship workers, artisans, merchants, and slaves — the same social range as we have seen among Christians in the city.[78]

Jewish life in the Diaspora was centered around the synagogue, which required a quorum of ten Jewish men. The synagogue service focused on prayers and on reading, translating, and expounding of the Scriptures. The synagogue and its services were presided over by the *archisynagogos* (the office held by Crispus). Jewish religion in the Diaspora seems to have been somewhat more liberalized than in Palestine. Besides the use of the Greek OT, B. Brooten has argued that women had prominent roles in Diaspora synagogues.[79] Some

77. Jewish prisoners from the Jewish War were sent to Corinth by Vespasian in the 60s to do public work.

78. But see T. Rajak, "Was there a Roman Charter for the Jews," *JRS* 74 (1978), pp. 107-23.

79. B. Brooten, *Women Leaders in the Ancient Synagogues* (Atlanta: Scholars, 1982), pp. 1ff.

INTRODUCTION

of the data about some of the "mothers of the synagogue" indicates that they were synagogue patronesses, but in a liberal environment like Corinth other roles may have been possible as well. The case of Rufina the Jewess from Smyrna in Ionia[80] would seem to support such a possibility for at least as early as the second century A.D.

That some, at least, of the Gentile Christians had no prior link with Judaism seems likely in view of 1 Cor. 12:2 and the debacle over whether or not they might eat at idol feasts and still be Christians. To this one may add 1 Cor. 5:1ff: That incest took place, that it was of a sort that would shock even pagans, that it was known to the Corinthian Christians, and that they were doing nothing about it suggest that many if not most of Paul's Gentile converts had no preconversion connection with the synagogue, where such immorality was often condemned. At least the majority of them were not manifesting any typically Jewish or Christian reaction to the incident.

It may be that many of the Gentile Christians in Corinth were of Roman rather than Greek ancestry or background since there are more Latin names than Greek names among those named by Paul. But it is possible that some had Latin names by virtue of being freed by Romans, since the usual practice was to take the name of one's emancipator.

Social Diversity and Problems in the Christian Community

The diversity of socioeconomic levels and religious and ethnic backgrounds among Corinthian Christians was undoubtedly an underlying cause of several of the issues and problems that Paul addresses in 1 and 2 Corinthians. For example:

> The basis for the disagreement that arose in Corinth over participation in meals in temples (1 Corinthians 10) was probably economic as well as one of religious background, since only the relatively well-off were likely to have been regularly confronted with invitations to such meals.
> The larger issue of eating meat that had been sacrificed to idols (1 Corinthians 8) was apparently one of the issues dividing factions in the Corinthian Christian community, and these factions very likely had a basis in social and ethnic distinctions.[81]

80. Mentioned in inscriptions *CII* 741 and *IGR* IV, 1452; cf. Brooten, *Women Leaders,* p. 5.

81. G. D. Fee is convinced that the major tension dictating Paul's response is problems between himself and his whole Corinthian Christian audience, not among groups in Corinth. By contrast, Barrett and others, following F. C. Baur, have made much of "parties" in Corinth. They argue that those who favored Peter's version of Christianity, the "weak," poor Jewish Christians, rejected meat offered to idols. Paul identified with the "strong,"

At Christian fellowship meals the hosts may well have followed normal customs and served wealthy merchants in one room with one kind of food and the poor and slaves elsewhere, probably the atrium, with the leftovers. This may explain Paul's indignation in 1 Cor. 11:17-34.

And in 2 Corinthians Paul must address problems created by his refusal to accept the patronage of some of the wealthy Corinthian Christians.

So understanding social distinctions and customs is an essential part of understanding both letters.

Social tensions are inherent in any religious group that is missionary in character and seeks to construct strong boundaries between the believer and the world. These two tendencies pull in opposite directions — the former toward inclusiveness,[82] the latter toward exclusiveness. Paul's dilemma was to create a group with a clear sense of its moral and theological identity while at the same time incorporating a heterogeneous group of people: Jew and Gentile, male and female, slave and free.[83] 1 and 2 Corinthians were written, at least in part, to clarify what the church's social relations with the world as it existed in Roman Corinth could and should be. But to the Corinthians, it must have seemed as if Paul were sending mixed signals. Certain sorts of associations with the larger world were acceptable, while others were not. One could be like the Gentiles in what one ate, but not in where one ate.

---

mostly Gentile, wealthier members of congregation without such scruples about idol meat. I will argue that Barrett and others have the better of this argument.

According to G. Theissen's theory of love-patriarchalism (*The Social Setting of Pauline Christianity: Essays on Corinth* [Philadelphia: Fortress, 1982], pp. 106ff.), Paul appealed to the wealthy to practice Christian love in order to mitigate the harsher effects of the patriarchal structure of society, while leaving the structure basically intact. But this theory does not sufficiently distinguish between the structure of the Christian family and the structures of the Christian *ekklēsia*. We should not assume that the two were the same. Furthermore, Paul's approach in 1 Corinthians to the matter of social status and the model he presents of leadership, that of the enslaved sage, represents a strong attempt to reform certain kinds of patriarchal and hierarchial structures in society. Paul seems to have been more of a reformer, within the Christian assembly, of existing power structures than Theissen seems to think.

82. Groups that emphasize winning others by conversion are more likely to undergo "accommodation with the world" and "transformation . . . into a more church-like organization or 'denomination' (a new level of institutionalization)." So M. Y. MacDonald, *The Pauline Churches: A Socio-Historical Study of Institutionalisation in the Pauline and Deutero-Pauline Writings* (Cambridge: Cambridge University, 1988), p. 40.

83. That this was no small task should be evident since even today most local churches tend to cater to particular socioeconomic or ethnic groups.

Household Assemblies

After Paul's initial success and then rejection in a synagogue, it appears
that he preached mainly in private homes.

> An invitation to teach in someone's house would provide Paul with . . . a
> sponsor, an audience and credentials as a certain type of speaker corre-
> sponding to a certain kind of speaking event. Above all, speakers needed
> some type of social status or a recognized role. When Paul says "I baptized
> the household of Stephanas," it is probably correct to assume that the
> preaching which led up to these baptisms occurred not in a marketplace or
> a gymnasium, but in someone's house.[84]

And the Corinthian Christians apparently continued to meet in private
homes. The phrase "the *ekklēsia* in the house of" (Rom. 16:5; 1 Cor. 16:19; cf.
v. 15) apparently indicates a subgroup of the whole congregation in a given
city. The largest number that could have met in any of the homes of the wealthy
in Corinth was probably about fifty (see the drawing of a villa on p. 194).[85]
And it appears from 1 Cor. 14:23 and Rom. 16:23 that meetings of all Christians in a given city were the exception, not the norm. It is possible, therefore,
that some of the divisions in Corinth arose from divisions among household
assemblies.

How would outsiders — and the Corinthian Christians themselves —
have viewed the Christian congregations meeting in homes? Because early
Christianity had neither priests nor temples nor sacrifices, to the outsider a
household assembly would surely have seemed much more like a social club,
a society, or a group of students gathered around a great teacher teaching in
the home of his patron, than like a religious group.

Romans did carry on some religious activities in their homes. It is thus
tempting, especially in light of the use of family language in 1 and 2 Corinthians, to see the Corinthian house congregation as an extension of the household, with the head of the house also being the head of the assembly. Favoring
this view is that Gaius, Priscilla and Aquila, and perhaps Stephanas, Chloe,
and Phoebe were both the hosts and the leaders of the churches that met in
their homes.

84. S. K. Stowers, "Social Status, Public Speaking and Private Teaching: The Circumstances of Paul's Preaching Activity," *NovT* 26 (1984), pp. 59-82, here p. 68. While Paul did
not always preach in homes, he probably did so often. If his preaching was accompanied
by a meal, it would have been natural for the Corinthians to have seen Paul or Apollos as
yet another rhetorician brought in by a patron to provide the material for dinner conversation. Cf. S. M. Pogoloff, *Logos and Sophia: The Rhetorical Situation of First Corinthians*
(Atlanta: Scholars, 1992), pp. 237ff.

85. Murphy-O'Connor, *St. Paul's Corinth* (Wilmington, 1983).

A Corinthian statue showing typical Roman male attire — a tunic

The heads of Roman families would frequently encourage clubs or associations to meet in their homes. Some of these were essentially trade or professional associations. There were also burial societies, which in addition to the usual social functions also collected dues to help with expenses when a member died, a function that was especially necessary among the poor. Organized religion was not the focal point of these groups, though certain religious functions were important and necessary in them.[86] More important were simple bonding and socializing.

Probably the Corinthian household assemblies would have appeared to outsiders as clubs or societies meeting in homes.[87] This would especially be

86. Cf. below, pp. 241-47.

87. Justinian's *Digest* tells us (47.22.1) that provincial governors were not to allow societies to exist, except that the poor could have burial societies and were free to meet for the sake of religion. This rule comes from the reign of Septimus Severus, but even in the first century there was considerable concern on the part of Roman officials about illegal societies.

the case on occasions when dining was part of the Christian meeting. If the Christians themselves viewed their household assemblies as being like such *collegia*,[88] some of them might also have assumed that it was appropriate to operate the group according to the social conventions of the larger society. These associations had a clear hierarchical structure of deities, then patrons or leaders, and, finally, ordinary members, which on the surface at least would seem to parallel the structure of the Christian *ekklēsia* in Corinth.[89] It should not surprise us then that the Corinthians would revert to normal socializing and dining behavior at their meetings (cf. 1 Cor. 11:20-22). The major difference between the Christian house meetings and such societies was that the Christians gathered mainly for religious worship and fellowship, not ordinary socializing with a religious element. No doubt it took a while for some Corinthians to realize this.

From 1 Cor. 14:23 we discover that Christian household meetings were not closed meetings, unlike the meetings convened for the Isis rituals or by participants in the mystery religions. Strangers, including unbelievers, could drift into the Christian meeting. Perhaps some even showed up to get a free meal.

Two Prominent Members

Paul mentions fourteen males by name as Corinthian Christians in his letters. We must suppose that most of them were married, that most had children, and that some had slaves. As the Pauline household code shows (Col. 3:18–4:1), this was the normal structure of the comfortable family.[90] This indicates that the Corinthian Christian community included at least forty people. Because of his family background, education, and Roman citizenship, Paul would have naturally identified with those who were heads of such families or who were socially better off, people such as Erastus and Phoebe.

In Romans 16, Paul sends greetings from Corinth to Christians in another major urban center.[91] The last names that he mentions (v. 23) are

---

88. *Collegia,* unlike more exclusive groups, often included slaves as members and gave them a voice and authority that they did not have in society in general. The permission given by rulers for such societies to exist, though with restrictions, like the promotion of the roles of freedmen in the cult of the Emperor, was a means of forestalling strife and mitigating the sense of oppression that came with a highly stratified society.

89. Chow, *Patronage and Power,* pp. 65ff.

90. Witherington, *Women,* pp. 42ff.

91. It is probable that Romans 16 was sent to Rome, but Ephesus is also a possible address. It may be that the chapter was originally a separate document carried by Phoebe, hence the textual problems that one encounters in ch. 15 that suggest that Romans originally ended before ch. 16.

Pavement stone found near the theater in Corinth; the inscription indicates that Erastus the Aedile paid for the pavement out of his own funds

Photo courtesy of C. Kennedy

those of Gaius, who was his host in Corinth, Quartus "our brother," and, most importantly, Erastus, *ho oikonomos tēs poleōs*. This final greeting took on new significance when a pavement stone was found in front of the ancient theater in Corinth with an inscription reading "Erastus in return for aedileship laid [this] pavement at his own expense"[92] (see the photograph above). More recently a second inscription has been found that reads "The Vitelli, Frontinus, and Erastus [dedicate this] to. . . ."[93] The pavement inscription is probably from as early as the reign of Nero in view of the way the lettering is done. It seems unlikely that Paul would have drawn attention to the social status of the Erastus he names in Romans if Erastus were only a slave, even a public slave with civic responsibilities. This Erastus was more likely a freedman, or the son of a freedman, and socially prominent, like other famous freedmen of the period in Corinth such as Cn. Babbius Philinus. Paul was, after all, trying to curry favor with his Roman audience in preparation for a visit to their city.[94]

Could the Erastus of Romans 16 and of the inscriptions be the same person? The short answer is yes.[95] There is evidence that Greek *oikonomos* and

92. The inscription is fragmented and abbreviations are used, but the translation at this point is certain. The Latin is "Erastus pro aedilit[at]e s[ua] p[ecunia] stravit." See D. W. J. Gill, "Erastus the Aedile," *TynB* 40 (1989), pp. 293-301.

93. See A. D. Clarke, "Another Corinthian Erastus Inscription," *TynB* 42 (1991), pp. 146-51.

94. Contra R. L. Fox, *Pagans and Christians* (New York: Knopf, 1989), p. 293. Cf. D. W. J. Gill, "In Search of the Social Elite in the Early Church," *TynB* 44 (1992), pp. 323-38. On Philinus as an aedile and pontifex, see A. B. West, "Corinth: Latin Inscriptions 1898-1927," VIII/2 (Cambridge: ASCSA, 1931), numbers 132 and 122.

95. Paul may have met and converted Erastus while practicing his trade in the marketplace. It is harder to say what compromises Erastus may have had to make to maintain both his civic position and his Christian faith, especially in view of the second Erastus inscription. Pagan religion was inherently intertwined with serving as an official in a Roman colony.

agoranomos could both refer to the same office in a Roman colony — both as translations of Latin *aedilis*.[96] In view of his possession of such an office, the possibility that the Erastus mentioned in Romans 16 is *not* the same as the Erastus of the inscriptions seems slight.[97]

The office of aedile was just below that of duovir. The aedile's main tasks were to see to the maintenance of public streets, buildings, and marketplaces and to collect revenues from businesses in such places. He could also be a judge, and in places other than Corinth aediles were in charge of the local games. It was an important post, and in a wealthy city like Corinth one needed considerable wealth in money and property to obtain it. That the pavement inscription seems to have had room only for the man's *cognomen,* Erastus, may suggest he was a freedman. But this should not cause us to minimize his status. "Freedmen could . . . be extremely wealthy, hold high public office and become important benefactors,"[98] especially in a freedman's city like Roman Corinth.

Phoebe was a *diakonos* in the *ekklēsia* in Corinth's port city of Cenchreae. She is not mentioned in the Corinthian correspondence, but she has a prominent place in Rom. 16:1f. The term *diakonos* in Paul's letters does not necessarily denote the same office that "deacon" or in this case "deaconess" later represented. It is clear from 1 Cor. 3:5 and 2 Cor. 3:6; 6:4; 11:15; 11:23 that Paul used *diakonos* for leadership roles in the Christian community, since he applies it to himself and Apollos. It does not necessarily imply a role subordinate to other church offices, but it *does* imply a self-perception as one subordinate to God and as a servant to the *ekklēsia* that one has been called to serve. It is possible that it refers to someone who is a preacher and teacher, possibly even a traveling missionary.[99]

Paul also calls Phoebe a *prostatis,* which in view of the context in Romans 16 likely means "patroness," not "protector" or merely "helper."[100] There is clear evidence that women in the Roman world could assume the legal role of *prostatis*.[101] A papyrus document has been discovered that speaks of a woman becoming the *prostatis* of her fatherless son in 142 B.C. Furthermore, perhaps one-tenth of the patrons, protectors, or donors to *collegia* mentioned

96. H. J. Mason, *Greek Terms for Roman Institutions: A Lexicon and Analysis* (Toronto: Hakkert, 1974), pp. 71, 175f.
97. Though H. J. Cadbury, "Erastus of Corinth," *JBL* 50 (1931), pp. 42-58, disagrees.
98. Gill, "Erastus," p. 295.
99. Cf. E. Schüssler Fiorenza, *In Memory of Her: A Feminist Theological Reconstruction of Christian Origins* (New York: Crossroad, 1984), p. 171.
100. The evidence for such a translation from the Roman period is laid out in ample detail in *New Doc.* IV, pp. 241-44.
101. Noted in E. A. Judge, "Cultural Conformity and Innovation in Paul: Some Clues from Contemporary Documents," *TynB* 35 (1984), pp. 3-24, here p. 21.

in inscriptions are women. "As a general rule, then, women as benefactors should be imagined playing their part personally and visibly, out in the open."[102]

In view of the way Paul commends Phoebe, it seems likely that she carried his letter to the Roman Christians, that she was responsible also for reading and interpreting it, and that she was a patroness for Paul and for other Christians. He commends her to the Romans so that they will assist her in collecting funds, perhaps for Paul's planned missionary work in Spain.[103] The connection here between her socioeconomic position, which brought her social status, and her role as one of the *diakonoi* is important. It suggests that there were early Christians of relatively high social status who had the time, influence, and funds to take on active leadership roles in the Christian communities. It was easy and perhaps natural for them to assume some leadership roles, especially in view of the household context of the Christian gatherings. This adopting and adapting of the hierarchical household structure did not have to lead to an exclusively male leadership structure. In a home where a woman, for whatever reason, was the head of the household (e.g., Chloe in 1 Cor. 1:11), she might also become a leader, or the leader, of the *ekklēsia* meeting in her house.

The early *ekklēsia* probably did not begin with an ideal egalitarian structure and then descend into oppressive patriarchy. It began by taking up the patriarchal institutions of Greco-Roman home and society and re-forming them in a community context. Unfortunately, after the NT period, with the effective loss of an eschatological focus on the possible imminent return of Christ and in the heat of the struggle with various heresies, the reforming process was abandoned or exchanged for a conforming schema.[104]

The Literary World of Paul and His Converts

Paul wrote his letters as substitutes for oral communication. There is strong evidence that he intended his letters to be read aloud in congregational meetings:

102. R. MacMullen, "Women in Public in the Roman Empire," *Historia* 29 (1980), pp. 211f.

103. So R. Jewett, "Paul, Phoebe, and the Spanish Mission," in *The Social World of Formative Christianity and Judaism,* ed. J. Neusner (Philadelphia: Fortress, 1988), pp. 148-51.

104. Cf. the last chapter of Witherington, *Women in the Earliest Churches.*

The closing in 1 Cor. 16:20 refers to the practice of the holy kiss, which was part of early Christian worship.[105] This suggests that once the letter was read, the service was at or nearing completion.

At the end of Galatians Paul expects the addressees ("you" plural) to be able to see his handwriting at the end of the letter (Gal. 6:11), which again suggests that the letter was read to the assembled congregation.

The greetings at the ends of some of the letters imply a meeting of the group, where those named could hear the greetings. The evidence of Col. 4:16, whether written by Paul or another,[106] certainly reflects the practice in the Pauline churches.

This setting of the reception of the letters becomes important when we turn to the rhetorical form of Paul's letters to the Corinthians. Paul wrote much of what he wrote with the intention that it have a certain effect on the listening ear. The tendency to treat these documents simply as *texts* overlooks an important dimension of their intended function. Paul's letters conform to a significant degree to the general structure of other ancient letters. But he also chose to draw on the conventions of ancient Greco-Roman rhetoric in shaping his communications with his converts. So we will need to consider 1 and 2 Corinthians both as letters and in connection with the rhetorical conventions of Paul's day.

1 and 2 Corinthians as Letters

Letters in antiquity were, with rare exceptions (e.g., those of Cicero), not meant for the general public, much less for publication. They were considered inadequate though necessary substitutes for face-to-face oral communication (cf. Rom. 15:14-33; 1 Cor. 4:14-21; 1 Thess. 2:17–3:13; Gal. 4:12-20), and scholars have rightly begun to emphasize the oral character of Paul's letters. Furthermore, Paul's letters are, with the possible exception of Philemon, a more personal letter,[107] communications to groups. Each letter includes, therefore, what Paul is willing for an entire congregation to hear, or at least overhear where he singles out a member or group in the congregation.

Ancient letters from the 4th century B.C. to the 4th century A.D. could contain the following elements:[108]

105. Cf. S. Benko, *Pagan Rome and the Early Christians* (Bloomington: Indiana University, 1984), pp. 79ff.
106. It is my view that Paul wrote Colossians.
107. Even Philemon has a secondary audience, the *ekklēsia* that meets in Philemon's house and, more particularly, his family.
108. Cf. F. X. J. Exler, *The Form of the Ancient Greek Letter* (Chicago: Ares, 1976), pp. 23ff.

1. the name of the writer,
2. the name of the addressee,
3. a greeting,
4. the body of the letter, which included a thanksgiving or wish prayer, then an introductory formula, followed by the substance of the letter, sometimes followed by an eschatological conclusion or a travelogue,
5. ethical or practical advice, and
6. a conclusion with final greetings, benediction, and sometimes a description of how the letter was written.

Parts of the fourth and fifth of these elements are usually found in Paul's correspondence, but are uncommon in other ancient letters. The only letter of Paul's that does not contain a thanksgiving prayer of some sort is Galatians, where Paul could think of little to be thankful for in view of what was happening to his churches in Galatia. Most ancient letters were quite terse and to the point. Paul's letters are much longer than the average private letter of the first century.

Paul used scribes to write his letters, like other writers in antiquity. In Rom. 16:22 a scribe passes along his own greeting. At the end of some of his letters Paul indicates the point at which he takes up the pen to write a line himself and perhaps to add a characteristic signature (1 Cor. 16:21; Gal. 6:11; 2 Thess. 3:17).[109]

How much freedom did Paul give his scribes in composing his letters? Did he dictate word-for-word, did he give the sense and leave the formulation to the scribe, or did he sometimes perhaps even just instruct a secretary or friend like Silas or Timothy to write in his name without specifying the content of the letter? Some of the letters read like they are dictated documents expressing both the mind and very words of Paul. The sentence fragments in some of the letters may have resulted from Paul dictating too fast for a scribe to keep up. Even if Paul left the formulation of a letter to a scribe, perhaps giving him the main ideas, 2 Thess. 3:17 claims that Paul signed all his letters, likely reviewing the document first. If he did, it is not as important whether we have Paul's exact words in a particular letter, because we have his thoughts and directives.[110] The evidence suggests that Paul dictated most of his letters (e.g.,

---

109. On Quintilian's dislike for the usual practice of using scribes, see *Inst. Or.* 10.3.19f.

110. It may be of some importance that Sophists were regularly hired as scribes in order to compose letters in proper rhetorical form. Cf. A. Malherbe, *Ancient Epistolary Theorists* (Atlanta: Scholars, 1988), p. 3 (with notes); Philostratus *Lives* 590, 607. Might Paul have sometimes used Christian scribes who were trained in rhetoric? For example, when Paul stayed with Gaius in Corinth and was writing Romans (cf. Rom. 16:23), did he use Gaius's rhetorically trained household scribe, a convert named Tertius? This might also

1 and 2 Corinthians) verbatim. It was in extenuating circumstances, such as
when he was in prison, that he probably gave his scribes more freedom to
compose for him, after which he would read what they had written, make
changes, and then put his signature on the letter (such may have been the case
with Philippians). At any rate Paul's letters were too important as an expression
of his apostolic authority for him to allow anything inconsistent with his own
thinking or intent to remain in a document that he would ultimately endorse.

Paul's letters were carried by messengers who brought oral communications along with the letters. Perhaps Paul intended the messenger to be able
to explain or expand on some of the content of the letter being delivered.[111]
He may have chosen couriers such as Timothy or Titus who would be able to
read aloud a letter in a way that conformed to his own rhetorical strategy and
intent.

Paul's letters must be seen as part of a total communication effort that
included letters, oral instructions through messengers, and face-to-face communication, whether preaching, teaching, or some form of dialogue. The
dialogical character of many of the letters is evident, since parts of them are
given over to answering questions addressed to Paul. This is particularly true
of 1 and 2 Corinthians. Some have argued that in the first part of the body
of 1 Corinthians Paul responds to what he has heard orally about the situation
in Corinth (e.g., 5:1) and that in the second part he responds to matters that
the Corinthians have written about to him. But 11:18 shows that Paul is still
responding to oral reports in the later part of the letter. Furthermore, it is not
certain that *peri de* ("but concerning," 7:1, 25; 8:1; 12:1; 16:1) is anything more
than a topic marker at some points or that it necessarily indicates a subject
raised in a Corinthian letter to Paul. The context of each use of this formula
must be evaluated separately.[112]

Nevertheless, it is essentially correct to say that Paul's letters are "conversations in context"[113] and that they address specific matters of concern for
particular groups of Christians,[114] even while they include directives and
principles that can be applied in many other situations as well. There must be

---

explain why some of Paul's letters (e.g., Colossians) do not seem to have as much rhetorical
form.

111. This may be why in Rom. 16:1ff. Paul commends Phoebe and asks those in
Rome to receive her and help her in any way possible. Cf. E. R. Richards, *The Role of the
Secretary in the Letters of Paul* (Tübingen: Mohr, 1991), pp. 190ff.

112. Cf. M. M. Mitchell, "Concerning *peri de* in 1 Corinthians," *NovT* 31 (1989), pp.
229-56.

113. The phrase is borrowed from C. Roetzel's *The Letters of Paul: Conversations in
Context* (third edition, Louisville: Westminster/John Knox, 1991).

114. All of Paul's letters except Romans and Colossians are addressed to groups with
whom he already had a direct relationship.

a cautious balance between "treating Paul's letters as purely occasional, con-textual writings, directed only to specific situations, and as attempts to express a Christian understanding of life which has ramifications for theological ex-pression beyond the particular historical situation."[115] To a great extent Paul draws on not only preexisting mental resources but also preexisting forms in writing these letters. They are not purely ad hoc in character, though they do seek to persuade and thus to be "a word on target."[116]

Since all of Paul's letters are addressed to Christians, they do not repro-duce his missionary preaching, except where he alludes back to such preaching (as in 1 Corinthians 1 and 15). Furthermore, as letters, they do not provide a compendium of Paul's thought on any given subject. They are neither ex-amples of ivory tower theologizing nor rhetorical treatises composed as purely literary exercises. Paul was a pastor and a task theologian, and he wrote to meet specific needs, to deal with specific problems, and to encourage particular congregations. Some of his letters were written more for problem solving and others are more oriented toward encouraging progress in the faith.[117] The Corinthian correspondence definitely falls into the former of these two cate-gories.

1 and 2 Corinthians as Rhetoric

Study of the rhetorical form of Paul's letters is a discipline still being reborn, and any results that we come up with will necessarily be tentative and subject to further correction. Nevertheless, the evidence is considerable that Paul chose to cast his letters in rhetorical forms, that is, that he shaped them in accordance with formal oral speech, using rhetorical elements recognizable as such by his addressees. So it is important for us to understand the place that rhetoric occupied in his day.[118]

115. W. J. Doty, *Letters in Primitive Christianity* (Philadelphia: Fortress, 1973), p. 26.

116. So J. C. Beker, *Paul the Apostle: The Triumph of God in Life and Thought* (Philadelphia: Fortress, 1980); cf. pp. 351ff.

117. I owe this problem-progress distinction to A. Chapple, *Local Leadership in the Pauline Churches: Theological and Social Factors in Its Development* (dissertation, Durham, 1984), pp. 1ff.

118. For a basic introduction to rhetoric by a first-century practitioner of the art who sums up much of the developments that came before him, see Quintilian, *Institutio Oratoria*, books 4-10, most conveniently found in the Loeb Classical Library, tr. H. E. Butler (reprint, Cambridge: Harvard University, 1966).

Developments in Rhetoric in the Greco-Roman World

Early in the first century A.D. rhetoric became the primary discipline in Roman higher education.[119] It was not seen in the way we might view elocution lessons or speech exercises today. Rather, since eloquence was one of the main cultural objectives, rhetoric was "the crown and completion of any liberal education worthy of its name."[120]

Furthermore, rhetoric was not exclusive to just the wealthy or the well educated. Rhetors were found in all of the great cities of the Roman Empire, especially in university towns like Tarsus and even in strongly Jewish cities like Jerusalem. The broad popularity of rhetoric during the period of the Roman Empire is apparent from important literary works that lionize orators (e.g., Athenaeus's *Deipnosophists* and Philostratus's *Lives of the Sophists*) and from the examples of orators (e.g., Herodes Atticus) who became wealthy from their art and made major benefactions to cities like Corinth.[121] The art of the popular rhetors was widely imitated.[122] Furthermore, it not only served as a system of rules for the use of the spoken word but also shaped common ways of thinking in all fields of endeavor.[123]

The art of persuasion as it was originally used — and in many minds *rightly* used — flourished best in a democratic setting or in a voluntary society. There were three primary kinds of rhetoric: Deliberative rhetoric was the stuff of the assembly when it freely debated the proper course for the *polis* to take, forensic rhetoric was the form used in law courts, and epideictic rhetoric was most often used in funeral oratory or public speeches when some person or

---

119. Cf. S. F. Bonner, *Education in Ancient Rome: From the Elder Cato to the Younger Pliny* (Berkeley: University of California, 1977); D. L. Clark, *Rhetoric in Greco-Roman Education* (New York: Columbia University, 1957); M. L. Clarke, *Higher Education in the Ancient World* (London: Routledge and Kegan Paul, 1971). The rhetor came to be the one who dictated what would be taught in higher education (so P. A. Meador, "Quintilian and the *Institutio oratoria*," in *A Synoptic History of Classical Rhetoric*, ed. J. J. Murphy [Davis: Hermagoras, 1983], p. 151).

120. Marrou, *History of Education*, p. 196.

121. A papyrus fragment dating to about A.D. 110 reads in part: "Pay to Licinnius . . . the rhetor the amount due him for the speeches [in] which Aur[elius . . .] was honored . . . in the gymnasium in the Great Serapeion, four hundred drachmas of silver" (R. K. Sherk, *The Roman Empire* [Cambridge: Cambridge University, 1988], p. 195). This was more than a Roman soldier's annual pay according to Tacitus, *Ann.* 1.17. "Rhetoric played a powerful and persuasive role in first century Greco-Roman society. It was a commodity of which the vast majority of the population were either producers or, much more likely, consumers, and not seldom avid consumers . . ." (Litfin, *St. Paul's Theology*, p. 202). One did not have to be trained as a rhetor to appreciate hearing it or to develop a taste for it.

122. Cf. D. E. Aune, *The New Testament in its Literary Environment* (Philadelphia: Westminster, 1987), pp. 12f.

123. Cf. Marrou, *History of Education*, pp. 204f.

thing was being lauded or lambasted. But what happened when most of the remnants of democracy were snuffed out during the age of the empire? The rhetoric of flattery or polemics flourished while substantive or philosophical rhetoric fell on hard times.

In the empire, then, rhetoric of display and ornamentation came to the fore and forensic oratory continued to have a place in the courts. It is no accident that the handbooks of rhetoric such as Quintilian's focus especially on forensic rhetoric, since it was the major substantive form of rhetoric for the serious-minded user of rhetoric in daily life. Roman law and its system of jurisprudence encouraged young men seeking public success to pay special attention to forensic rhetoric.[124] While there might be deliberative speeches in assemblies, power usually dictated what would be concluded there.[125] But there were other occasions when deliberative rhetoric might be used, for example, when an ambassador needed to convince his audience of the proper decision regarding some course of action.

But stress had come to be placed on style and stylistic devices such as figures of speech, exclamations, and apostrophes and on wordplay and epigrams. Furthermore, while classical Aristotelian rhetoric had been chiefly the art of persuasion, by the time Quintilian wrote in the mid-90s of the first century A.D., he was willing to say that rhetoric had become the art of speaking well (*Inst. Or.* 2.15.1ff.).

Declamation, which at its best was a school exercise of practice on purely hypothetical topics, including trivial subjects such as the praiseworthiness of a flea or the shameful baldness of a man's head, became a form of public

---

124. Rhetoric was part of the training that wealthy males went through in preparation for public office, whether to be an aedile or a proconsul or simply a legal advocate or ambassador. This may be of some importance in discerning who was complaining about Paul's rhetoric or lack of rhetorical polish, namely, well-to-do Gentile men.

While there are a few isolated examples of women, such as Hortensia, the daughter of the famous rhetor Q. Hortensius Hortalus, delivering an oration, in her case to the triumvirs in 42 B.C., I know of no examples of women who were regularly practicing or professional rhetors. Hortensia no doubt gained her skills in the home, for it was not the normal practice for women to have "higher education," which means that even wealthy women lacked training in rhetoric beyond the progymnasta level. Cf. E. Cantarella, *Pandora's Daughters* (Baltimore: Johns Hopkins University, 1987), p. 141, 214, n. 12; Quintilian *Inst. Or.* 1.1.6.

125. Cf. Pogoloff, *Logos and Sophia*, p. 62: "In the Imperial period, rhetoric was particularly open to attack. Since opportunities for meaningful public address were greatly curtailed, rhetorical display was often reduced to showpieces, and Stoic philosophers claimed it had lost its content and become empty playing with style." The reduction of legislative freedom during the empire may be one reason for the attraction of another *ekklēsia* where debate and dialogue could still be carried on. The very term *ekklēsia* would have suggested to some that the Christian meeting was the place for such debates and the use of rhetoric, deliberative rhetoric in particular.

entertainment.[126] Rhetoric became an end in itself, mere ornamentation, elocution, and execution with an aim to please the crowd. This sort of rhetoric without serious content or intent, other than to play to and sway a crowd's emotions, was precisely the sort of nonthreatening and apolitical rhetoric that Roman society could encourage and enjoy.

Declamation, and especially the use of epideictic oratory, came to be associated with the revival of the Sophistic movement. This movement flourished, not just during the second-century A.D. period of the "second Sophistic," but already in the first half of the first century, so that by Paul's day it had already become something of a popular movement.[127] We will say more about sophistic rhetoric in the introduction to 2 Corinthians. One use of the term "Sophist," and this is the use of the term that we are concerned with here, was for any orator who emphasized style over substance and received pay for his work.[128]

In many circles Sophistic rhetoric was deplored as manipulation without substance. Philo called it shadowboxing (*Det.* 4). The long-standing use of rhetoric for more serious pedagogical, political, or philosophical ends continued, so that rhetoric was not, even during the empire, simply a matter of flattery, entertainment, or display of skills.[129] Rejection of mere declamation for its own sake, of Sophistic rhetoric in general, or of a florid Asiatic style as opposed to a plainer Atticizing style did not amount to a rejection of rhetoric in general. Greco-Roman rhetoric still involved content as well as form. "The entire hope of victory and the entire method of persuasion rest on proof and refutation, for when we have submitted our arguments and destroyed those

126. On the history and development of declamation during the empire see S. F. Bonner, *Roman Declamation in the Late Republic and Early Empire* (Liverpool: Liverpool University, 1949), pp. 26ff. Declamation was fundamentally consideration of a subject without any reference to specific circumstances, i.e., just the opposite of Paul's sort of rhetoric.

127. Cf. G. W. Bowersock, *Greek Sophists in the Roman Empire* (Oxford: Clarendon, 1969), p. 13; G. A. Kennedy, *The Art of Rhetoric in the Roman World* (Princeton: Princeton Uuniversity, 1972), p. 513; idem, *Classical Rhetoric* (Chapel Hill: University of North Carolina, 1980), p. 37.

128. Cf. C. P. Jones, *The Roman World of Dio Chrysostom* (Cambridge: Harvard University, 1978), p. 9, on the meanings of the word.

129. The distinction between primary rhetoric, which deals with real subjects, and secondary rhetoric or declamation (Kennedy, *Classical Rhetoric*, pp. 118f.; idem, *Art of Rhetoric*, p. 460) is important, especially since some first-century writers bemoaned the decline of eloquence during the empire. It was caused, they thought, by too much public declamation on esoteric topics and by the rise of Asianism, a florid eastern style of rhetoric. Seneca (*Ep.* 40:4) wrote that a philosopher's rhetoric should involve neither dragging out of words nor rushing headlong, since "speech that addresses itself to the truth should be simple and unadorned." Cf. Quintilian's opposition to declamation as an end in itself, which flourished in the first century A.D. (*Inst. Or.* 10.1.125-31).

of the opposition, we have, of course, completely fulfilled the speaker's function" (*Rhetorica ad Herennium* 1.9.19).[130] Teachers of rhetoric such as Isocrates and later Quintilian regularly made remarks like:

> Therefore, I would have the orator, while careful in his choice of words, be even more concerned about his subject matter. For as a rule the best words are essentially suggested by the subject matter and are discovered by their own intrinsic light. . . . It is with a more virile spirit that we should pursue eloquence, who, if only her whole body be sound, will never think it her duty to polish her nails and tie her hair. The usual result of over-attention to niceties of style is deterioration of our eloquence. (*Inst. Or.* 8. Pr. 21f.)

Modes and Functions of Greco-Roman Rhetoric

We have mentioned the three primary species of rhetoric — *forensic*, which was concerned with accusations and defense and thus focused on the past, *deliberative*, the true art of persuasion or dissuasion, which was future oriented, and *epideictic*, which was concerned with giving praise or blame in order to encourage agreement with or rejection of some value and was usually focused on the present. One could mix these types of rhetoric in a speech in order to convey a point.[131] For example, in the midst of urging a particular future course of action for a city, a rhetor might also have to defend himself and his previous record. In the course of his defense of Marcellus, Cicero also operates in a deliberative mode because he is implicitly, and at points almost explicitly, urging a future action, namely, regicide. Later epistolary theorists, such as pseudo-Libanius, recognized the "mixed" type of rhetorical letter,[132] and even among the church fathers, John Chrysostom saw in Galatians a mixture of two types of rhetoric.[133]

The function of a good deal of rhetoric was to arouse the emotions, which were divided into *pathos* and *ēthos*. The former included the stronger feelings such as anger, fear, and pity, the latter the gentler emotions, such as

---

130. Cf. Pogoloff, *Logos and Sophia*, pp. 45ff. Some NT scholars falsely assume that rhetoric has to do only with the form or style of a speech or letter.

131. Cf. Kennedy, *Classical Rhetoric*, p. 74 on the insertion of epedeictic material in judicial or deliberative speeches in order to win the audience's goodwill or to discredit an opponent.

132. Cf. Malherbe, *Ancient Epistolary Theorists*, pp. 66f. The last type mentioned is *mixte*.

133. See his commentary on Galatians at 6:18. I owe some of the examples in this paragraph to Janet Fairweather of the classics faculty at Cambridge University. On mixed rhetoric, cf. also Dionysius of Halicarnassus, *Vol. 6, Opuscula II*, ed. H. Usener and L. Radermacher (Leipzig: Teubner, 1933), in the treatise *peri eschēmatismenon*. One may also wish to consider Demosthenes' famous speech *De Corona*.

the capacity for laughter. Quintilian tells us that humor includes speaking in such a way that one refutes, reproves, or generally makes light of an opponent's argument; saying things that on the surface appear absurd or paradoxical; and using words in unusual senses (cf. *Inst. Or.* 6.2f.). According to the usual order, a speech attempted first to establish the speaker's or writer's *ēthos* or character. Then *logos*, the act of actual persuasion or argumentation, would come into play. Finally the speech or letter would turn to *pathos*, to what the rhetor hoped to arouse in the audience.[134]

The arrangement of a rhetorical piece usually broke down into either four or six parts:

> The *exordium* is the beginning part and is aimed at making the audience open and indeed well-disposed toward what follows.
> The *narratio* then explains the nature of the disputed matter.
> The *partitio* or *propositio*, which follows the *narratio* or is included in it, is where the essential proposition(s) of the speaker and perhaps also of the opponent are laid out.
> The *probatio* brings in arguments to support the speaker's case.
> In the *refutatio*, which is often included in the *probatio*, the opponent's arguments are disproved or weakened.
> Finally, the *peroratio* recapitulates the main points of the *probatio*, attempting to arouse the audience's emotions in favor of the speaker's viewpoint by amplifying what has been said before.

What primarily determines the character of a piece of rhetoric was not whether it has all the elements of the standard textbook arrangement of a speech. One or more of these elements were often omitted in actual speeches and in all the elements the speaker attended to the matters of *ēthos*, *logos*, and *pathos*. What does determine the character of a speech is whether its *function* is primarily to persuade the audience in regard to some future action, to defend some past course of action, or to offer praise or blame about something in the present.

Paul's Use of Rhetoric

Since reading was almost always done aloud, the difference between reading and speaking was often small. "The categories of eloquence were imposed on every form of mental activity," including the writing of letters. "Hellenistic culture was above all things a rhetorical culture, and its typical literary form was the public lecture."[135] The same can be said of Greco-Roman culture.

---

134. Cf. Kennedy, *Classical Rhetoric*, pp. 68ff.
135. Marrou, *History of Education*, p. 195. Ancient writers did, of course, distinguish

Letters in the hands of a Cicero or a Paul became surrogates for and extensions of oral speech, especially of dialogues, and the rhetorical conventions of public speech and discourse were carried over into such letters.[136] Rhetoric gave Paul a means to relate to and impress his Corinthian audience. Even those with little education had heard speeches that followed the conventions of rhetoric and were able to appreciate much of Paul's artistry.

Of course letters cannot include some features that were, especially during the empire, deemed very important in rhetoric — inflection, gestures, volume, and overt emotional display — unless they are, in fact, delivered as speeches. It does appear that Paul gave attention in the composition of his letters to various aural devices, such as alliteration, assonance, and rhythm, meant to affect the ear and aid persuasion. Furthermore, though it is only a conjecture, I suspect that Paul entrusted his letters to coworkers because he knew that they could read and speak Greek well, expound on points the audience did not fully understand (which required that the person in question know the mind of Paul rather intimately), and catch and express the various shades of tone in the written record of Paul's voice, including irony, sarcasm, love, compassion — who could, in short, be not merely letter carriers, but also the rhetorical deliverers of his communications. In this way the oral aspects of the communication would not be entirely lost, and persuasion was more likely to be accomplished.

There were both formal and material reasons for Paul to use rhetoric. He wished to speak in such a manner that his audience would hear and heed his message. His use of rhetoric shows that "precisely when the question is one of changing other people's lives the very content of the gospel demands a 'method' of effecting such changes which is directly opposed to any use of force. . . . It is that of speaking *to* them in ways that do not encroach upon their independence."[137] That Paul used rhetoric with his converts indicates his commitment to the Christian community as a society that should be led by

---

between the average letter and a speech (cf. Aristotle *Rhetoric* 3.12.1; Pliny *Letters* 5:8; Demetrius *On Style* 223.25-28), but Quintilian informs us that letters that were in effect meant for proclamation, and thus were to a large extent written-out speeches, were closer to speeches in character (*Inst. Or.* 12.10.53-55). Paul has blended letter and speech conventions, so that apart from the epistolary opening and closing of a Pauline letter, one can evaluate the letter in terms of rhetorical conventions. In short, the thanksgiving section and the body of the letter can be evaluated in this way.

136. Later epistolary theorists stressed that letters should not take on a Sophistic or ornamental character, but should be written in a plainer, less elaborate style (e.g., avoiding long rhetorically impressive periods and Atticism). Cf. on Philostratus of Lemnos in Malherbe, *Ancient Epistolary Theorists*, p. 43.

137. T. Engsberg-Petersen, "The Gospel and Social Practice according to 1 Corinthians," *NTS* 36 (1990), pp. 557-84, here pp. 572f.

means of persuasion whenever possible and commanded only when necessary.[138]

Paul used the conventions of rhetoric and thus sought *by all means* to
win people to Christ (1 Cor. 9:19-22). But he also resolved not to declaim the
gospel (2:1), that is, not to use Sophistic or ornamental rhetoric in his missionary preaching, lest the audience focus on form rather than content. Perhaps this also meant that he used the Attic or Roman plain style, rather than
the more verbose Asiatic style, in preaching. In fact, as we will argue in this
commentary, Paul lampoons Sophistic or ornamental rhetoric at crucial points
in his letters to the Corinthians, using the very rhetorical weapons of his
opponents and thus turning their forms of argumentation against them.[139]
This becomes evident in 2 Corinthians 10–13, but there are pointers in this
direction even as early as 1 Cor. 4:6.

In 1 Corinthians Paul's primary task was to reconcile members of a
faction-ridden congregation to each other. In 2 Corinthians he needed to
reconcile the Corinthians to himself by means of a spirited defense of the
legitimacy and practices of his ministry for and with them. He did not hesitate
to use various kinds of persuasion to achieve his aims. 1 Corinthians is
deliberative rhetoric, but there is a semi-forensic cast to ch. 9 and an epideictic
character to ch. 13, both of which are "digressions" from the main trajectory
of the argument, though they have direct relevance for the larger argument.
2 Corinthians by contrast is forensic rhetoric, Paul's defense of his ministry,
though it has a major deliberative digression in 6:14–7:1. 2 Corinthians 8–9
has a deliberative form but serves the larger forensic purpose.

Probably Paul envisioned the reading of 1 Corinthians in the Christian
assembly as a substitute for the deliberative discourse he would have delivered

138. For a detailed and rhetorically sensitive analysis of the formal characteristics of
Pauline argumentation, such as his use of antithesis, typology, standard topoi, aphorisms,
analogies, arguments *a fortiori* and *ad hominem, ēthos* and *pathos,* diatribe style, ellipsis,
paradox, and irony, see F. Siegert, *Argumentation bei Paulus gezeigt an Röm 9–11* (Tübingen:
Mohr, 1985), pp. 181-241.

139. In terms of strategy, one's approach to a new audience and to an audience
already won over to essential parts of one's agenda are quite different. It is possible that in
his missionary preaching Paul used only plain unvarnished truth, while in his letters to
churches he used rhetoric. But as B. Winter, J. Neyrey, and others have pointed out, Acts
portrays Paul as using forensic rhetoric to defend himself in public, and one would need
to ask why this is so were there not some basis in fact for such a portrayal. Furthermore,
Paul's statement that he became the Greek to the Greek (1 Cor. 9:21) implies that he might
have used rhetoric to make a good first impression on rhetorically sophisticated audiences.
It does not follow from 2 Cor. 10:10 that Paul did not use rhetoric in his preaching, though
he may have appeared to have been an amateur due to his appearance, voice, or oral skills.
And even 2 Cor. 11:6 is apparently hypothetical, not an actual admission of rhetorical
ineptness.

in person, just as 2 Corinthians is an impassioned defense of his ministry that had to be delivered in absentia. That he used deliberative rhetoric, even with a troubled community, suggests that he believed the Corinthian Christian community had a future and that it needed to make decisions pertaining to that future. It was probably no accident that Paul chose the term *ekklēsia* for the gathering of his converts together. This was the familiar term for a public assembly where in ancient times deliberative discourse was heard and debated. It was not a technical term for a religious gathering, much less a Christian one. Paul may have envisioned the Christian assembly as somewhat like those other forums that nurtured freedom and that at their best worked by means of the willing consent of the participants.

The cultural expectation in regard to rhetoric was that the audience should judge the quality of the oratory. In Sophistic rhetoric this principle was extended so far that rhetoric came to be understood as the art of being able to please the audience or sway their emotions by catering to their predilections. It appears that the Corinthians felt they had the right to judge Paul and his message and were evaluating him by the same criteria by which popular orators and teachers were judged. Paul disputed this right, especially in 2 Corinthians, and sought to make clear that he was answerable only to God. He was swimming upstream on this point: As Tacitus noted (*Dialogus* 19.5), many audiences were highly adept at evaluating rhetoric and almost everyone knew some rhetoric. Most relished the opportunity to be judge and jury, like the crowds in the Roman arena passing final judgment over whether a combatant deserved to live or die. In a culture where public reputation was of great importance, a crowd could make or break the career of an orator.

As we examine further the rhetorical structures of 1 and 2 Corinthians,[140] we will follow the normal procedure in studying a rhetorical document by looking for discrete rhetorical units marked by evidence of *inclusio*, evidence, that is, of the beginning and end of each unit. We will also be concerned to discern the rhetorical situation of each letter — the *exigence* of the letter,

---

140. Often we will be following M. M. Mitchell's exposition (*Paul and the Rhetoric of Reconciliation* [Tübingen: Mohr, 1991]), though with some differences at certain points. I reject her strictures in regard to the impossibility of individual parts of a letter reflecting all the parts of the arrangement. While it is correct to say that there is usually a macro-argument and dominant character that directs the course of a whole Pauline letter, nevertheless individual subarguments may manifest in miniature the various parts of rhetorical arrangement. This is so because Paul's letters are not simply equivalent to *a* speech on *a* subject, as was commonly the case in regard to declamations, but purposeful letters often addressing a *variety* of subjects, using a variety of arguments. Even so, the variety of arguments used in 1 Corinthians, except perhaps for ch. 13, all manifest a character that is basically deliberative, while, apart from the digressions, 2 Corinthians is basically forensic in character. And even in the digressions the larger deliberative or forensic purposes of the respective documents are furthered in several ways.

that is, the problem that prompted Paul to respond with this particular rhetorical composition. Considerations of style, "invention" (Paul's development of his arguments), and the effectiveness of the rhetorical composition will also come into play.

Socio-Rhetorical Resources on 1 and 2 Corinthians: An Annotated Bibliography

This bibliography makes no pretense of being exhaustive, but attempts to give the reader adequate resources from both the older and newer disciplines of biblical studies as well as resources from classical studies to aid a proper understanding of 1 and 2 Corinthians.

One may wish to begin with the brief but helpful survey articles by M. M. Mitchell and H. D. Betz on 1 and 2 Corinthians respectively in the *The Anchor Bible Dictionary,* ed. D. N. Freedman (Garden City: Doubleday, 1992) I, 1139-53. Both articles helpfully integrate rhetorical matters into the general discussion, but Betz's article has the drawback of relying on excessive mirror-reading to reconstruct multiple letters from 2 Corinthians.

Of the numerous standard commentaries on 1 and 2 Corinthians, few of those written in the last fifty years evaluate the material in terms of rhetoric or the social sciences. C. Senft, *La Premiere Èpître de Saint-Paul aux Corinthiens* (Neuchâtel: Delachaux & Niestle, 1979) shows some familiarity with rhetorical issues raised in the older commentaries, especially those in German. Of the older commentaries by authors trained in classics and sensitive to the rhetorical dimensions of Paul's letters, see especially J. B. Lightfoot, *Notes on the Epistles of Saint Paul* (Winona Lake: Alpha Publications, reprint), pp. 139-235; H. Windisch, *Der zweite Korintherbrief* (Göttingen: Vandenhoeck and Ruprecht, 1924); and J. Weiss, *Der erste Korintherbrief* (Göttingen: Vandenhoeck and Ruprecht, 1925).

Archaeology

At the outset the helpful essay by R. E. Oster, " Use, Misuse, and Neglect of Archaeological Evidence in Some Modern Works on 1 Corinthians," *ZNW* 83 (1992), pp. 52-73, should be read in order to see what may and may not be discerned by means of archaeological research. The student who wishes to study in depth the history of the archaeology of Roman Corinth will need to work through the many years of field reports which appear nearly every year in the journal *Hesperia.* Some of the more salient reports are mentioned below.

In addition, numerous other articles and resources have apppeared in various journals and collections of sources, especially the *American Journal of Archaeology* and *Biblical Archaeologist*. Helpful collections of inscriptions are in the *CIG* (*Corpus Inscriptionum Graecarum*, ed. A. Boeckh [1825-77]), the *CIL* (*Corpus Inscriptionum Latinarum* [1863-]), in the *SIG* (*Sylloge Inscriptionum Graecarum et Latinarum Macedoniae*, ed. W. Dittenberger [4 vols.; Leipzig: Hirzel, 1915-24]), in the *IGR* (*Inscriptiones Graecae ad Res Romanas Pertinentes* [Chicago: Ares, 1975]), and in the *ILS* (*Inscriptiones Latinae Selectae*, ed. H. Dessau [3 vols.; Berlin: Weidmann, 1954-55]).

Of direct relevance to Corinth are B. D. Merritt, ed., *Corinth: Results* VIII/1 (Princeton: ASCSA, 1931), and J. H. Kent, ed., *The Inscriptions, 1926-1950*, VIII/3 (Princeton: ASCSA, 1966). For a helpful review of Kent see D. J. Geegan in *AJA* 71 (1967), pp. 422-24. Geegan agrees with Kent that Latin was used almost exclusively in Corinth until the reign of Hadrian, except in inscriptions having to do with the Isthmian games. For the Latin inscriptions see A. B. West, *Corinth: Latin Inscriptions 1898-1927* VIII/2 (Cambridge: ASCSA, 1931).

For an excellent collection of documents and inscriptions in English from the NT era, see R. K. Sherk, ed., *The Roman Empire: Augustus to Hadrian* (Cambridge: Cambridge University, 1988). New light from the papyri can be found in G. H. R. Horsley, ed., *New Documents Illustrating Early Christianity*, Vols. 1-4 (North Ryde: Macquarrie University, 1981, 1982, 1983, 1987), and there are still insights to be gained from reading A. Deissmann, *Light from the Ancient East* (Grand Rapids: Baker, reprint). A helpful collection of texts specifically on Corinth can be found in J. Murphy-O'Connor, *St. Paul's Corinth: Texts and Archaeology* (Wilmington: Glazier, 1983), but there are some inaccuracies about the archaeology of Roman Corinth (e.g., on the issue of Corinthian bronze).

J. A. Wiseman, "Corinth and Rome I: 228 b.c.–a.d. 267," *ANRW* II/7/1 (Berlin: de Gruyter, 1979), pp. 497-531, gives a seminal overview of the physical archaeology of Corinth. See also J. Murphy-O'Connor, "Corinth," in *The Anchor Bible Dictionary*, ed. D. N. Freedman (Garden City: Doubleday, 1992) I, pp. 1134-39; H. J. Cadbury, "Erastus of Corinth," *JBL* 50 (1931), pp. 42-58; W. A. MacDonald, "Archaeology and St. Paul's Journeys in Greek Lands Part III — Corinth," *BA* 5 (1942), pp. 36-48; O. Broneer, "Hero Cults in the Corinthian Agora," *Hesperia* 11 (1942), pp. 128-61; *idem*, "Corinth: Center of St. Paul's Missionary Work in Greece," *BA* 14 (1951), pp. 78-96; D. C. Spitzer, "Roman Relief Bowls from Corinth," *Hesperia* 11 (1942), pp. 162-92; O. Broneer, "The Apostle Paul and the Isthmian Games," *BA* 25 (1962), pp. 2-31; J. A. Wiseman, "Excavations in Corinth, the Gymnasium Area 1967-68," *Hesperia* 38 (1969), pp. 64-106 (one of the most extensive underground water systems in the world was found in Corinth); N. Bookides, C. K. Williams, and

J. E. Fischer, "The Sanctuary of Demeter and Kore on Acro-Corinth," *Hesperia* 43 (1974), pp. 267-307; G. R. Bugh, "An Emendation to the Prosopography of Roman Corinth," *Hesperia* 48 (1979), pp. 45-53; C. K. Williams and O. H. Zervos, "Corinth 1981: East of the Theater," *Hesperia* 51 (1982), pp. 115-63; D. R. Jordan and A. J. S. Spawforth, "A New Document from the Isthmian Games," *Hesperia* 51 (1982), pp. 65-68; J. Murphy-O'Connor, "Corinthian Bronze," *RB* 90 (1983), pp. 80-93; J. Murphy-O'Connor, "The Corinth That Paul Saw," *BA* 47 (1984), pp. 147-59; C. K. Williams and O. H. Zervos, "Corinth 1983. The Route to Sikyon," *Hesperia* 53 (1984), pp. 83-122; E. J. Milleker, "Three Heads of Serapis from Corinth," *Hesperia* 54 (1985), pp. 121-35; D. W. J. Gill, "Erastus the Aedile," *TynB* 40 (1989), pp. 293-301; M. T. Boatwright, "Theaters in the Roman Empire," *BA* 53 (1990), pp. 184-92; C. K. Williams and O. H. Zervos, "Excavations at Corinth 1989: The Temenos of Temple E," *Hesperia* 59 (1990), pp. 325-69; C. M. Edwards, "Tyche at Corinth," *Hesperia* 59 (1990), pp. 529-42 (a first-century-A.D. statue of Tyche; A. D. Clarke, "Another Corinthian Erastus Inscription," *TynB* 42 (1991), pp. 146-51; C. C. Mattusch, "Corinthian Metal-Working: The Gymnasium Bronze Foundry," *Hesperia* 60 (1991), pp. 383-95; C. K. Williams and O. H. Zervos, "Corinth 1990: Southeast Corner of Temenos E," *Hesperia* 60 (1991), pp. 1-58; C. C. Mattusch, "Corinthian Metalworking: An Inlaid Fulcrum Panel," *Hesperia* 60 (1991) pp. 525-28.

J. B. Ward-Perkins, "From Republic to Empire: Reflections on the Early Provincial Architecture of the Roman West," *Journal of Roman Studies* 60 (1970), pp. 1-19, argues that the *macellum* in Corinth follows the architectural style found in certain Roman cities other than the capital such as Pompeii, which may suggest that the Romans in Corinth came from southern Italy (cf. p. 19). J. H. Oliver, "The Epistle of Claudius Which Mentions the Proconsul Junius Gallio," *Hesperia* 40 (1971), pp. 239f., gives the whole restored text of the letter and argues that Gallio was still proconsul in A.D. 52. W. W. Cumer, "A Roman Tomb at Corinthian Kenchreai," *Hesperia* 40 (1971), pp. 205-31: the strong Roman character of the tomb shows how powerful was the feeling for traditional Italian design (p. 231). N. Bookides and J. E. Fischer, "The Sanctuary of Demeter and Kore on Acro-Corinth," *Hesperia* 41 (1972), pp. 283-331, give possible evidence of dining couches in an area adjoining the temple of Demeter. J. A. Wiseman, "The Gymnasium Area at Corinth 1969-70," *Hesperia* 41 (1972), pp. 1-42, discusses Roman terra-cotta lamps imported from Italy, evidence for the Roman bath built in the first century A.D., Jewish or possibly Jewish Christian inscriptions on lamps that refer to deceased humans as angels. He thus gives solid literary evidence of Jews in Corinth, though from a post-NT era. According to J. W. Hayes, "Roman Pottery from the South Stoa at Corinth," *Hesperia* 42 (1973), pp. 416-70, "it has been amply demonstrated that an enormous amount of Italian pottery produced in several different centers was shipped to Corinth during the early years of the Empire. . . . This, rather than Eastern wares was the chief influence on the local producers at the time" (p. 470). The general impression given in C. K. Williams and J. E. Fischer, "Corinth 1975: Forum Southwest," *Hesperia* 45 (1976), pp. 99-162, is that building activity took place in the second half of first century A.D. (pp. 136ff.). O. Borowski, "A Corinthian Lamp at Tell Halif," *BASOR* 227 (1977), pp. 63-65, tells of Corinthian hand lamps being exported all over the Mediterranean. K. S. Wright, "A Tiberian Pottery Deposit from Corinth," *Hesperia* 49 (1980), pp. 135-75, describes pottery sherds with Greek graffiti inscribed on them. C. K. Williams, "The City of Corinth and its Domestic Religion," *Hesperia* 50 (1981), pp. 408-21, focuses on family stele shrines. According to E. G. Pemberton, "The Attribution of Corinthian Bronzes," *Hesperia* 50 (1981), pp. 101-11, there is little evidence of Corinthian bronze makers during the Roman period (pp. 109f.). According to B. S. Ridgeway, "Sculpture from Corinth," *Hesperia* 50 (1981), pp. 422-48, the official language of the new city was Latin, as monuments show. There is little evidence of first-century-A.D. sculptures of women, which is surprising. The statue of Nero with headcovering is noted on pp. 433f. C. K. Williams and O. H. Zervos, "Corinth 1982: East of the Theater," *Hesperia* 52 (1983), pp. 1-47, describe how the Romans imposed a street grid on the site when they rebuilt it (p. 8). T. Rajak, "Was there a Roman Charter for the Jews," *Journal of Roman Studies,* 74 (1984), pp. 107-23, argues that even the edict of Claudius in A.D. 41-42 was not a Jewish Magna Carta that established Judaism as a *religio licita,* but rather gave the Jews the right of redress for grievances. Paganism was in fact not that tolerant of a monotheism that would not assimilate to the larger culture (p. 122). H. D. Saffrey, "Aphrodite à Corinthe," *RB* 92 (1985), pp. 359-74, argues that the temple on the Acro-Corinth was never a place of sacred prostitution. According to K. W. Slane, "Two Deposits from the Early Roman Cellar Building, Corinth," *Hesperia* 55 (1986), pp. 271-318, by the third quarter of the first century A.D., unlike earlier in the century, Corinth seems to have been the nexus of Aegean trade, consuming much local produce and providing some amenities as other Roman cities such as Ostia and the connection with Italy remained strong (pp. 317f.). Three articles by C. K. Williams and O. H. Zervos tell of the Greek theater in Corinth and its Roman restoration: "Corinth 1984: East of the Theater," *Hesperia* 54 (1985), pp. 55-96 (p. 69); "Corinth 1988: East of the Theater," *Hesperia* 58 (1989), pp. 1-50 (pp. 28-36); and "Corinth 1986: Temple E and East of the Theater," *Hesperia* 56 (1987), pp. 1-46. A lecture at the 1992 national meeting of the Society of Biblical Literature shed new light on the Demeter cult and its underworld associations: R. De-Maris, "Demeter in Roman Corinth."

On markets, food in general, and meat in particular, see N. Nabers, "A Note on Corinth VIII,2," *AJA* 73 (1969), pp. 73f.; D. W. J. Gill, "The Meat-

Market at Corinth (1 Corinthians 10:25)," *TynB* (forthcoming); P. Garnsey, *"Mass Diet and Nutrition in the City of Rome,"* in *Nourrir la plebe,* ed. A. Giovanni (Basil, 1991), pp. 67-101. According to C. K. Williams and O. H. Zervos, "Corinth 1985: East of the Theater," *Hesperia* 55 (1986), pp. 129-85, food shops with "fast food" counters discovered in Building 3 and possibly Building 1, equipped with large ovens to prepare hot meals — not *tabernae* — likely served the passing theater crowds (pp. 147f.).

On pagan cults and temples, see M. Lang, *Cure and Cult in Ancient Corinth: A Guide to the Asklepion* (Princeton: ASCSA, 1977); N. Bookides and R. S. Stroud, *Demeter and Persephone in Ancient Corinth* (Princeton: ASCSA, 1987); and S. Kasas, *Important Medical Centres in Antiquity — Epidaurus and Corinth* (Athens: Editions Kasas, 1990; I owe these references to my former ancient history and classics professor W. J. McCoy of the University of North Carolina).

Certainly one of the most important studies on the development of Christianity from household assembly to *domus ecclesiae* and finally to *domus dei,* so that there was not only a special building for Christian meetings but that building was viewed as a temple, is L. M. White, *Domus Ecclesiae — Domus Dei: Adaptation and Development in the Setting for the Christian Assembly* (Ann Arbor: University Microfilms, 1983), especially pp. 564ff. on Corinth. Part of White's dissertation appears in somewhat different form in his *Building God's House in the Roman World* (Baltimore: Johns Hopkins University, 1990).

Classical Studies

For a collection of relevant texts, see V. Ehrenberg and A. H. M. Jones, *Documents Illustrating the Reigns of Augustus and Tiberius* (Oxford: Clarendon, 1955). For the Hellenistic background to the Roman era, see C. Preaux, *Le Monde hellènistique* (Paris: Universitaires France, 1978). On the struggles among social strata, see G. E. M. de Ste. Croix, *The Class Struggle in the Ancient Greek World* (Ithaca: Cornell University, 1981). On private life in the empire, see P. Veyne, ed., *A History of Private I: Life from Pagan Rome to Byzantium* (Cambridge: Harvard University, 1987). For a helpful overview of a Roman town of the first century A.D. about which we know a great deal, see R. Etienne, *Pompeii: The Day a City Died* (London: Thames and Hudson, 1992). A very important study, though it must be used critically and carefully, is D. Engels, *Roman Corinth: An Alternative Model for the Classical City* (Chicago: University of Chicago, 1990).

On the general environment in which Paul operated, see J. P. V. D. Balsdon, *Romans and Aliens* (Chapel Hill: University of North Carolina, 1979);

S. Dill, *Roman Society from Nero to Marcus Aurelius* (London: Macmillan, 1904); E. R. Dodds, *Pagans and Christians in an Age of Anxiety* (New York: Cambridge University, 1965); R. L. Fox, *Pagans and Christians* (New York: Knopf, 1989); F. C. Grant, *Roman Hellenism and the NT* (New York: Scribners, 1962); R. MacMullen, *Paganism in the Roman Empire* (New Haven: Yale University, 1981); R. L. Wilken, *The Christians as the Romans Saw Them* (New Haven: Yale University, 1984); R. MacMullen, *Enemies of the Roman Order: Treason, Unrest, and Alienation in the Empire* (Cambridge: Harvard University, 1966), pp. 46-94 on philosophers. Two good books for beginning students and professors who wish to use artistic recreations of various aspects of first-century-A.D. life in the Roman Empire are R. Burrell's *The Romans* (Oxford: Oxford University, 1991), and J. Rutland's *See Inside a Roman Town* (London: Kingfisher, 1986). For a scholarly work on the structure of a Roman city cf. J. E. Stambaugh, *The Ancient Roman City* (Baltimore: Johns Hopkins University, 1988). On the emperor who ruled during the time of Paul's visit to Corinth and his correspondence with the Corinthians, see B. J. Levick, *Claudius* (New Haven: Yale University, 1990), especially pp. 163ff.

On the social order of the time in general, see R. MacMullen, *Roman Social Relations* (New Haven: Yale University, 1974); M. Rostovtzeff, *The Social and Economic History of the Roman Empire* I (second ed., Oxford: Clarendon, 1957). On the issue of social status, see P. Garnsey, *Social Status and Legal Privilege in the Roman Empire* (Oxford: Clarendon, 1970). On patronage, see R. P. Saller, *Personal Patronage under the Empire* (Cambridge: Cambridge University, 1982). On the upper echelons in Roman society, see M. Gelzer, *The Roman Nobility* (New York: Barnes and Noble, 1969). On Roman family life, see K. R. Bradley, *Discovering the Roman Family: Studies in Roman Social History* (Oxford: Oxford University, 1991); B. Rawson, ed., *The Family in Ancient Rome: New Perspectives* (London: Croom Helm, 1986); A. C. Bush, *Studies in Roman Social Structure* (Lanham: University Press of America, 1982); R. P. Saller, "Roman Dowry and the Devolution of Property in the Principate," *CQ* 34 (1984), pp. 195-205. According to R. P. Saller and B. D. Shaw, "Tombstones and Roman Family Relations in the Principate: Civilians, Soldiers, and Slaves," *JRS* 74 (1984), pp. 124-56, funerary inscriptions reveal that emphasis was placed on the nuclear family.

For a survey of women in Roman antiquity, see E. Cantarella, *Pandora's Daughters. The Role and Status of Women in Greek and Roman Antiquity* (Baltimore: Johns Hopkins University, 1987). On women who married only once, see M. Leitman and W. Zeisel, "*Univira:* An Example of Continuity and Change in Roman Society," *Church History* 46 (1977), pp. 19-32. A. Cameron, "Neither Male nor Female," *Greece and Rome* 27 (1980), pp. 60-68, critiques Meeks with regard to androgyny. For a sourcebook of ancient texts in translation, see R. S. Kraemer, ed., *Maenads, Martyrs, Matrons, Monastics* (Philadelphia: Fortress, 1988), and for a bibliographic survey article cf. R. S. Kraemer, "Women in the Religions of the Greco-Roman World," *Religious Studies Review* 9 (1983), pp. 127-39, especially the bibliography on pp. 133-39. A survey of inscriptional data with regard to women is provided in M. R. Lefkowitz and M. B. Fant, *Women's Life in Greece and Rome* (Baltimore: Johns Hopkins University, 1982). On why and when women's names are mentioned cf. D. Schaps, "The Women Least Mentioned: Etiquette and Women's Names," *CQ* 27 (1977), pp. 323-30. See also A. Cameron and A. Kuhrt, *Images of Women in Antiquity* (Detroit: Wayne State University, 1983), especially the articles by M. Lefkowitz, "Influential Women," pp. 49-64, and R. Van Bremen, "Women and Wealth," pp. 223-42.

On Paul's view of marriage in light of views in the Greco-Roman world see O. L. Yarbrough, *Not like the Gentiles: Marriage Rules in the Letters of Paul* (Atlanta: Scholars, 1985). On Paul's encounters with Roman authorities, including Gallio in Corinth, and his Roman citizenship, see A. N. Sherwin-White, *Roman Society and Roman Law in the NT* (Grand Rapids: Baker, reprint), pp. 99ff., and C. P. Jones, *The Roman World of Dio Chrysostom* (Cambridge: Harvard University, 1978). On the Pax Romana and its effect on Christians in the first century, see K. Wengst, *Pax Romana and the Peace of Jesus Christ* (Philadelphia: Fortress, 1987).

On pagan religion during the empire, see R. M. Oglivie, *The Romans and their Gods in the Age of Augustus* (New York: Norton, 1969). On priests and religion during the empire see the three essays by R. Gordon, "From Republic to Principate: Priesthood, Religion and Ideology," pp. 179-98, "The Veil of Power: Emperors, Sacrificers and Benefactors," pp. 201-31, and "Religion in the Roman Empire: The Civic Compromise and Its Limits," pp. 235-55, all in *Pagan Priests: Religion and Power in the Ancient World,* ed. M. Beard and J. North (Ithaca: Cornell University, 1990). On the mystery cults, see W. Burkert, *Ancient Mystery Cults* (Cambridge: Harvard University, 1987). On dining, see the essays in W. J. Slater, ed., *Dining in a Classical Context* (Ann Arbor: University of Michigan, 1991). On the use of the kiss in early Christian worship cf. S. Benko, *Pagan Rome and the Early Christians* (Bloomington: Indiana University, 1984), pp. 79-102, and W. Klassen, "The Sacred Kiss in the NT," *NTS* 39 (1993), pp. 122-35.

On the Delphic oracle and prophecy inspired by Apollo, see H. W. Parke and D. E. W. Wornell, *The Delphic Oracle* (Oxford: Blackwell, 1956), and especially J. Fontenrose, *The Delphic Oracle: Its Responses and Operations* (Berkeley: University of California, 1978), which makes abundantly clear that whatever ecstasy may have been involved, the Delphic Pythia herself delivered her oracles in intelligible speech to those consulting her. Priests or prophets may have been involved in interpretation or the handing of written responses to emissaries who came to ask questions on behalf of others. There is then no basis for the distinction between ecstasy and intelligible prophecy as the function of two distinct persons in the material from Delphi. On glossolalia, see D. B. Martin, "Tongues of Angels and Other Status Indicators," *JAAR* 59 (1992), pp. 547-89.

The collected articles and essays of A. D. Nock in *Essays on Religion and the Ancient World*, ed. Z. Stewart (2 vols., Cambridge: Harvard University, 1972), are invaluable. The first volume includes his long essay on early Gentile Christianity and its Hellenistic background. On the influence of Roman ideology on Paul cf. E. M. Lassen, "The Use of the Father Image in Imperial Propaganda and 1 Corinthians 4.14-21," *TynB* 42 (1991), pp. 127-36. Two articles by D. W. J. Gill are worth mentioning: "Corinth: A Roman Colony in Achaea" (forthcoming) and "In Search of the Social Élite in the Early Church," *TynB* 44 (1993), pp. 323-37. Also the new book by D. B. Martin, *The Corinthian Body*, from which the essay "Female Physiology and the Dangers of Desire in 1 Corinthians 7" comes, is forthcoming. On the Roman approach to death cf. K. Hopkins, *Death and Renewal* (Cambridge: Cambridge University, 1983), especially pp. 226ff.

Greco-Roman Rhetoric

One of the great problems in NT studies today is lack of knowledge of the Greek and Latin classics and failure to interact with the wealth of resources in the studies on the ancient Greco-Roman world produced by classics scholars. The place to begin any study of Greco-Roman rhetoric is with primary sources, that is, the handbooks of Roman rhetors such as Cicero and Quintilian, Aristotle's earlier work, and the samples of speeches in a variety of sources. For the beginner I would recommend consulting the relevant volumes in the Loeb Classical Library, which provide parallel translations in English. Then the surveys by G. A. Kennedy should be consulted: *The Art of Rhetoric in the Roman World 300 B.C. to A.D. 300* (Princeton: Princeton University, 1972), especially pp. 428ff., and *Classical Rhetoric and Its Christian and Secular Tradition from Ancient to Modern Times* (Chapel Hill: University of North Carolina, 1980). See also J. J. Murphy, ed., *A Synoptic History of Classical Rhetoric* (Davis: University of California, 1983), pp. 151ff. on Quintilian. For further bibliography, see D. F. Watson, "The NT and Greco-Roman Rhetoric: A Bibliography," *JETS* 31 (1988), pp. 465-72.

For an interesting study on the proximity of the Christian idea of faith to Greco-Roman notions of persuasion and rhetoric, see J. L. Kinneavy, *Greek Rhetorical Origins of Christian Faith* (Oxford: Oxford University, 1987). On the issue of Sophistic rhetoric and the rise of the second Sophistic movement as a background to understanding Paul's rhetoric in 1 and 2 Corinthians, see

B. W. Winter, *Are Philo and Paul among the Sophists? A Hellenistic Jewish and a Christian Response to a First Century Movement*, a PhD. dissertation done at MacQuarrie University in 1988 under E. A. Judge and forthcoming from Cambridge University Press, and Winter's "Paul and Rhetoric" in the *Dictionary of Paul and His Letters* (Downers Grove: InterVarsity, 1993); also G. Bowersock, *Greek Sophists in the Roman Empire* (Oxford: Clarendon, 1969). On the development of declamation during the Roman Republic and Empire, see S. F. Bonner, *Roman Declamation in the Late Republic and Early Empire* (Liverpool: University of Liverpool, 1949), especially pp. 27ff. on the period of the empire. On the use of plainstyle rhetoric during the empire, see H. F. North, "The Concept of *Sophrosyne* in Greek Literary Criticism," *Classical Philology* 43 (1948), pp. 1-17. On *insinuatio*, see E. W. Bower, "*Ephodos* and *Insinuatio* in Greek and Latin Rhetoric," *Classical Quarterly* 8 (1958), pp. 224-30. On the teaching of imitation of the rhetor, see E. Fantham, "Imitation and Evolution: The Discussion of Rhetorical Imitation in Cicero *De oratore* 2.87-97 and Some Related Problems of Ciceronian Theory," *Classical Philology* 73 (1978), pp. 1-16, and in the same issue Fantham's "Imitation and Decline: Rhetorical Theory and Practice in the First Century after Christ," pp. 102-16.

   One of the more important unresolved issues is the relationship of oral to written rhetorical sources, especially since many ancient letters were simply surrogates for oral performance, and in some cases were also texts for oral performance. Accordingly the student wishing to understand early Christian rhetoric must examine ancient epistolary theory and practice and literary criticism in general. On these matters, see C. J. Roetzel, *The Letters of Paul: Conversations in Context* (third ed., Louisville: Westminster/John Knox, 1991); W. J. Doty, *Letters in Primitive Christianity* (Philadelphia: Fortress, 1973); S. K. Stowers, *Letter Writing in Greco-Roman Antiquity* (Philadelphia: Westminster, 1986); A. J. Malherbe, *Ancient Epistolary Theorists* (Atlanta: Scholars, 1988); M. Bünker, *Briefformular und rhetorische Disposition im I Korintherbrief* (Göttingen: Vandenhoeck and Ruprecht, 1984); F. X. J. Exler, *The Form of the Ancient Greek Letter of the Epistolary Papyri (3rd c. B.C.–3rd c. A.D.* (Chicago: Ares, 1976); C-H. Kim, *Form and Structure of the Familiar Greek Letter of Recommendation* (Missoula: Scholars, 1972); C. W. Keyes, "The Greek Letter of Introduction," *American Journal of Philology*, 56 (1935), pp. 28-44. On Paul's use of secretaries, see E. R. Richards, *The Secretary in the Letters of Paul* (Tübingen: Mohr, 1991). For a short but helpful discussion of the social dimensions of letter writing see S. K. Stowers, "Social Typification and the Classification of Ancient Letters," in *The Social World of Formative Christianity and Judaism*, ed. J. Neusner, et al. (Philadelphia: Fortress, 1988), pp. 78-90.

   An introductory literary (and theological) study of 1 and 2 Corinthians is provided in C. H. Talbert, *Reading Corinthians* (New York: Crossroads, 1989). On the issue of Paul's style, see A. B. Spencer, *Paul's Literary Style: A*

Stylistic and Historical Comparison of 2 Corinthians 11.16–12.13, Romans 8.9-39, and Philippians 3.2–4.13 (Jackson: Evangelical Theological Society, 1984), and J. Zmijewski, *Der Stil der paulinischen "Narrenrede"* (Cologne: Hanstein, 1978). Both Spencer and Zmijewski take some account of rhetoric. On the specific issue of Paul's use of chiasmus, see N. W. Lund, *Chiasmus in the NT: A Study in the Form and Function of Chiastic Structures* (Peabody: Hendrickson, reprint), pp. 139-96. On the effect of Scripture citation and the larger context of citations on Paul's argument, see the very insightful study of R. B. Hays, *Echoes of Scripture in Paul* (New Haven: Yale University, 1989).

There is no better general introduction to rhetoric in the NT than B. L. Mack, *Rhetoric and the NT* (Minneapolis: Fortress, 1990). Also helpful is G. A. Kennedy, *NT Interpretation through Rhetorical Criticism* (Chapel Hill: University of North Carolina, 1984), especially pp. 86-96 on judicial rhetoric in 2 Corinthians. If one is looking for a brief introduction to rhetoric and the NT to use with students two can be recommended: C. C. Black, "Rhetorical Criticism and the NT," *Proceedings of the Eastern Great Lakes and Midwest Bible Societies* 8 (1988), pp. 77-92, and D. F. Watson's introductory chapter in his *Invention, Arrangement and Style: Rhetorical Criticism of Jude and 2 Peter* (Atlanta: Scholars, 1988), pp. 1-28. On the general issue of what forms of argumentation Paul used, see F. Siegert, *Argumentation bei Paulus* (Tübingen: J. C. B. Mohr, 1985), though his focus is on Romans 9–11. On the issue of whether and to what degree Paul used the diatribe form, see R. Bultmann, *Der Stil der paulinischen Predigt und die kynisch-stoische Diatribe* (Göttingen: Vandenhoeck und Ruprecht, 1910). Bultmann's conclusions have rightly been challenged by S. K. Stowers, *The Diatribe and Paul's Letter to the Romans* (Chico: Scholars, 1981). T. Schmeller, *Paulus und die "Diatribe"* (Münster: Aschendorf, 1987) takes into account previous discussion. On Paul's rhetorical use of antithesis, see N. Schneider, *Die rhetorische Eigenart der paulinischen Antithese* (Tübingen: Mohr, 1970).

The modern discussion of rhetoric and the Corinthian corpus is divided into two major camps. A. C. Wire, *The Corinthian Women Prophets: A Reconstruction through Paul's Rhetoric* (Minneapolis: Fortress, 1990); K. Plank, *Paul and the Irony of Affliction* (Atlanta: Scholars, 1987); and J. A. Crafton, *The Agency of the Apostle: A Dramatistic Analysis of Paul's Responses to Conflict in 2 Corinthians* (Sheffield: Sheffield Academic, 1991) seek to use modern rhetorical theory to evaluate the data, drawing on the so-called New Rhetoric discussed by C. Perelmann and L. Olbrecht, as well as other newer disciplines (e.g., Plank also draws on structuralism). Though some very helpful insights have come from such studies, unfortunately the problem of anachronism sometimes mitigates their value, and there are also epistemological problems. Some practioners of the New Rhetoric seem to reflect an antihistorical orientation. It is not true that the New Rhetoric is simply a modernization of ancient rhetoric, not least because it too often takes for granted solipsistic theories of meaning and knowledge, which unfortunately lead the practitioners to a lack of concern for proper historical judgment. M. M. Mitchell is right to stress (in *Paul and the Rhetoric of Reconciliation*, p. 7, n. 19) that

> it must be emphasized that the "New Rhetoric" . . . does not claim to be a handbook of ancient rhetoric, but rather a revision and reappropriation of it to modern philosophical problems, particularly that of epistemology. Its intention is at basic points contrary to that of these New Testament scholars — it aims at expanding the realm of argumentation rather than classifying particular texts according to genre or arrangement.

If one wishes to understand *Paul's* use of rhetoric, and not merely appropriate Paul for some modern cause or agenda, it is critical that his works be evaluated in light of ancient Greco-Roman rhetoric.

Among NT scholars who accept this premise there seem to be basically two major orientations, that of H. D. Betz and his disciples, such as Mitchell, and that of G. A. Kennedy and his students, such as D. F. Watson. My own study draws on both of these more historical approaches, but tends to agree with Kennedy's orientation more than Betz's. The major studies of the rhetoric of the Corinthian correspondence are Mitchell's *Paul and the Rhetoric of Reconciliation* (Tübingen: Mohr, 1991) and Betz's *2 Corinthians 8 and 9* (Philadelphia: Fortress, 1985). S. M. Pogoloff, *Logos and Sophia: The Rhetorical Situation of 1 Corinthians* (Atlanta: Scholars, 1992) has many helpful insights, though it equates ancient and modern rhetoric to an unwarranted degree. An early article that analyzes Paul's rhetoric, but draws on both modern and Greco-Roman rhetorical theory, is by W. Wuellner, "Greek Rhetoric and Pauline Argumentation," in the R. M. Grant Festschrift *Early Christian Literature and the Classical Intellectual Tradition*, ed. W. R. Schoedel and R. L. Wilken (Paris: Beauchesne, 1979), pp. 177-88. One of the older American theses under G. A. Kennedy dealing with this subject was that of A. Lynch, *Pauline Rhetoric: 1 Corinthians 1:10–4.21* (Chapel Hill: University of North Carolina, 1981). *Persuasive Artistry: Studies in NT Rhetoric in Honor of George A. Kennedy*, ed. D. F. Watson (Sheffield: Sheffield Academic, 1991), contains the following articles that are helpful for Corinthian studies: J. R. Levison, "Did the Spirit Inspire Rhetoric? An Exploration of George Kennedy's Definition of Early Christian Rhetoric," pp. 25-40, F. W. Hughes, "The Rhetoric of Reconciliation: 2 Corinthians 1.1–2.13 and 7.5–8.24," pp. 246-61, and F. W. Danker, "Paul's Debt to the *De Corona* of Demosthenes: A Study of Rhetorical Techniques in Second Corinthians," pp. 262-80. For a helpful essay showing how Greco-Roman rhetoric affected early Jewish teachers' patterns of argumentation, see D. Daube, "Rabbinic Methods of Interpretation and Hellenistic Rhetoric,"

Hebrew Union College Annual 22 (1949), pp. 239-64; cf. also S. Lieberman, *Greek in Jewish Palestine* (New York: Jewish Theological Seminary, 1942). Other important contributions to the discussion are A. de Oliveira, *Die Diakonie der Gerechtigkeit und der Versohnung in der Apologie des 2 Korintherbriefes. Analyse und Auslegung von 2 Kor 2.14–4.6; 5.11–6.10* (Münster: Aschendorff, 1990) and R. A. Humphries, *Paul's Rhetoric of Argumentation in 1 Corinthians 1–4* (dissertation, Graduate Theological Union, 1979).

On ancient education and the place therein of rhetoric, see H. I. Marrou, *A History of Education in Antiquity* (New York: Sheed and Ward, 1956), especially pp. 194-205, and M. L. Clarke, *Higher Education in the Ancient World* (Albuquerque: University of New Mexico, 1971), especially pp. 11-45. On the matter of Paul's education cf. W. C. Van Unnik, *Tarsus or Jerusalem: The City of Paul's Youth* (London: Epworth, 1962) and A. D. Nock, *St. Paul* (London: Lutterworth, 1938). Cf. D. Daube, "Paul a Hellenistic Schoolmaster?" in *Studies in Rationalism: Judaism and Universalism,* ed. R. Loewe (London: Routledge, 1966), pp. 67-71. On the issue of *ēthos* in Paul and Theophrastus, see W. Magass, "Theophrast und Paulus," *Kairos* 26 (1984), pp. 154-65. See also W. C. Van Unnik, "First Century A.D. Literary Culture and Early Christian Literature," *Nederlands Theologisch Tijdschrift* 25 (1971), pp. 28-43.

For general discussion of method and technique in ancient rhetoric one can consult J. Martin, *Antik Rhetorik. Technique und Methode* (Munich: Beck, 1974). On Pauline rhetoric, see J. Weiss, *Beiträge zur paulinischen Rhetorik* (Göttingen: Vandenhoeck und Ruprecht, 1897); J.-N. Aletti, "La *dispositio* rhétorique dans les épîtres pauliniens: proposition de méthode," *NTS* (1992), pp. 385-401. On the phenomenon of mixed rhetoric in speeches at the turn of the era, see R. R. Dyer, "Rhetoric and Intention in Cicero's *Pro Marcello,*" *JRS* 80 (1990), pp. 17-30. On forensic oratory in the Pauline speeches in Acts, see J. Neyrey, "The Forensic Defense Speech and Paul's Trial Speeches in Acts 22–26: Form and Function," in *Luke-Acts: New Perspectives,* ed. C. A. Talbert (New York: Crossroad, 1984), pp. 210-24; B. W. Winter, "The Importance of the *Captatio Benevolentiae* in the Speeches of Tertullus and Paul in Acts 24.1-21," *JTS* n.s 42 (1991), pp. 505-31.

From a 1992 conference on rhetoric in Heidelberg come the following essays, which will appear in print in due course: G. Holland, "Speaking like a Fool: Irony and Theology in 2 Corinthians 10–13," J. Smit, "Argument and Genre of 1 Cor 12–14," and D. F. Watson, "Paul's Rhetorical Strategy in 1 Corinthians 15." Three important articles on Paul and rhetoric have appeared in *L'apôtre Paul. Personalité, style et conception du ministère* (Leuven: Leuven University, 1986), H. D. Betz, "The Problem of Rhetoric and Theology according to Paul," pp. 16-48, W. Wuellner, "Paul as Pastor: The Function of Rhetorical Questions in First Corinthians," pp. 49-77, and B. Standaert, "La Rhetorique ancienne dans Saint Paul," pp. 78-92. Other articles on Pauline rhetoric dealing with 1 and/or 2 Corinthians in some way include D. F. Watson, "1 Corinthians 10.23–11.1 in the Light of Greco-Roman Rhetoric: The Role of Rhetorical Questions," *JBL* 108 (1989), pp. 301-18, and B. Fiore, "'Covert Allusion' in 1 Corinthians 1–4," *CBQ* 47 (1985), pp. 85-102. Fiore's article fails to note how Paul *deliberately* violates the convention by explaining his allusion as part of his anti-Sophistic use of rhetoric and his strategy to treat the Corinthians as "children." See also L. L. Belleville, "A Letter of Apologetic Self-Commendation: 2 Cor. 1.8–7.16," *NovT* 31 (1989), pp. 142-63, and J. P. Sampley, "Paul, His Opponents in 2 Corinthians 10–13, and the Rhetorical Handbooks," in *The Social World of Formative Christianity and Judaism*, ed. J. Neusner, et al. (Philadelphia: Fortress, 1988), pp. 162-77. On the triumph image in 2 Corinthians 2, see P. B. Duff, "Metaphor, Motif, and Meaning: The Rhetorical Strategy behind the Image 'Led in Triumph' in 2 Corinthians 2.14," *CBQ* 53 (1991), pp. 79-92; H. S. Versnel, *Triumphus: An Inquiry into the Origin and Meaning of the Roman Triumph* (Leiden: Brill, 1970); P. Marshall, "A Metaphor of Social Shame: *Thriambeuein* in 2 Cor. 2.14," *NovT* 4 (1983), pp. 302-17.

Other worthwhile studies include: T. S. Duncan, "The Style and Language of Saint Paul in his First Letter to the Corinthians," *Bibliotheca Sacra* 83 (1926), pp. 129-43; S. B. Heiny, "2 Corinthians 2.14–4.6: The Motive for Metaphor," *Society of Biblical Literature 1987 Seminar Papers*, ed. K. H. Richards (Atlanta: Scholars, 1987), pp. 1-22; C. Forbes, "'Unaccustomed as I Am': St. Paul the Public Speaker in Corinth," *Buried History* 19 (1983), pp. 11-16; P. Lampe, "Theological Wisdom and the 'Word about the Cross': The Rhetorical Scheme in 1 Corinthians 1–4," *Int* 44 (1990), pp. 117-31 (this entire issue of *Interpretation* is devoted to articles on 1 Corinthians); A. J. Malherbe, "Exhortation in First Corinthians," *NovT* 25 (1983), pp. 238-56; E. Schüssler Fiorenza, "Rhetorical Situation and Historical Reconstruction in 1 Corinthians," *NTS* 33 (1987), pp. 386-403; J. Smit, "The Genre of 1 Corinthians 13 in the Light of Classical Rhetoric," *NovT* 33 (1991), pp. 193-216; A. H. Snyman, "Remarks on the Stylistic Parallelisms in 1 Corinthians 13," in *A South African Perspective on the NT*, ed. J. H. Petzer and P. J. Hartin (Leiden: Brill, 1986), pp. 202-13; D. F. Watson, "1 Corinthians 10.23–11.1 in the Light of Greco-Roman Rhetoric," *JBL* 108 (1989), pp. 301-18; T. Engberg-Pedersen, "1 Corinthians 11.16 and the Character of Pauline Exhortation," *JBL* 110 (1991), pp. 679-89; C. Forbes, "Comparison, Self-Praise and Irony: Paul's Boasting and the Conventions of Hellenistic Rhetoric," *NTS* 32 (1986), pp. 1-30.

K. E. Bailey's "Paul's Theological Foundation for Human Sexuality: 1 Cor 6.9-20 in the Light of Rhetorical Criticism," *Near East School of Theology Theological Review* 3 (1980), pp. 27-41, and E. Waller's "The Rhetorical Structure of 2 Cor. 6.14–7.1," *Proceedings of the Eastern Great Lakes and Midwest Bible Societies* 10 (1990), pp. 151-65, are examples of general literary criticism, focusing on matters of parallelism and chiasmus applied to a portion of 1 Corinthians. They do not deal with Greco-Roman rhetoric per se.

Sociology and Anthropology

As with rhetoric, there have been two basic orientations to the discussion of social matters in Paul, one that engages in social description with the hope of being able to construct a social history of the situation in the Pauline communities and one that attempts to use modern social theories of M. Weber and many others to make sense of or organize the ancient data (e.g., W. A. Meeks's use of the theory of status inconsistency to explain the situation in some of Paul's churches).

Of the general introductions to sociology and the NT clearly the best introductory guide is B. Holmberg's *Sociology and the NT* (Minneapolis: Fortress, 1990). Also still useful is A. Malherbe's *Social Aspects of Early Christianity* (Philadelphia: Fortress, 1983), and see also C. Osiek, *What Are They Saying about the Social Setting of the NT?* (New York: Paulist, 1984). Perhaps the most readable of the general guides is J. E. Stambaugh and D. L. Balch's *The NT in Its Social Environment* (Philadelphia: Westminster, 1986). One of the best survey articles, though now somewhat dated, is R. Scroggs, "The Sociological Interpretation of the NT: The Present State of Research," *NTS* 26 (1980), pp. 164-79. A study that raises the issue of the integration of sociological interests and methods with the Christian faith is that of D. A. Fraser and T. Campolo, *Sociology through the Eyes of Faith* (San Francisco: Harper, 1992). For a methodological study that encourages a sociology of knowledge approach to the NT, see H. C. Kee, *Knowing the Truth: A Sociological Approach to NT Interpretation* (Minneapolis: Fortress, 1989). On social analysis of millenarian movements, see B. R. Wilson, *Magic and the Millennium* (New York: Harper and Row, 1973). On methodology and the issue of social class, see R. L. Rohrbaugh, "Methodological Considerations in the Debate over the Social Class Status of Early Christians," *JAAR* 52 (1984), pp. 519-46. It should be noted that some NT scholars who deal with the sociology of knowledge (e.g., Kee, MacDonald, and Petersen) are heavily indebted in their approach to P. L. Berger and T. Luckmann, *The Social Construction of Reality: A Treatise in the Sociology of Knowledge* (New York: Doubleday, 1966).

To my knowledge there have been no NT studies of a purely descriptive nature that are anthropological in nature. The works of B. Malina and J. Neyrey draw on modern anthropological theory, particularly the work of Mary Douglas. For a general introductory attempt to apply anthropological models to the NT, see Malina's *The NT World: Insights from Cultural Anthropology* (Atlanta: John Knox, 1981). In many ways the insights that Malina provides would seem to apply better to a less individualistic Old Testament environment. He follows some of Mary Douglas's earlier work and modifies her group-grid model. See the critique in the helpful full monograph on Pauline community by R. A. Atkins, *Egalitarian Community: Ethnography and Exegesis* (Tuscaloosa: University of Alabama, 1991), with an introduction by Douglas. A more technical study by Malina further developing the group-grid model is *Christian Origins and Cultural Anthropology: Practical Models for Biblical Interpretation* (Atlanta: John Knox, 1986).

For an examination of Paul's thought world from an anthropological perspective see Neyrey's *Paul in Other Words: A Cultural Reading of His Letters* (Louisville: Westminster/John Knox, 1990). Another of Neyrey's studies is especially important: "Body Language in 1 Corinthians: The Use of Anthropological Models for Understanding Paul and His Opponents," *Semeia* 35 (1986), pp. 129-70. That entire issue of *Semeia* is devoted to "Social-Scientific Criticism of the NT and its Social World." Of the many works by Douglas, perhaps the most accessible and useful for students of the NT is *Purity and Danger: An Analysis of the Concepts of Pollution and Taboo* (Boston: Routledge and Keegan Paul, 1966). Some caution is in order in applying Douglas's insights to the Greco-Roman world. Her analysis is based on cultures that are in various respects different from the ancient Greco-Roman world, for instance, in the definitions of honor and shame. Some of her suggestions and some of the models that have been applied are too anachronistic to be helpful. Accordingly, the works of Malina, Neyrey, and others following Douglas must be used critically and with caution.

For general essays on the issue of the role of honor and shame in the Mediterranean, see D. D. Gilmore, ed., *Honor and Shame and the Unity of the Mediterranean* (Washington: American Anthropological Society, 1985) and cf. H. Moxnes, "Honor, Shame, and the Outside World in Paul's Letter to the Romans," in *The Social World of Formative Christianity and Judaism*, ed. J. Neusner, et al. (Philadelphia: Fortress, 1988), pp. 207-18. On Corinth in particular, see S. C. Barton, "Paul's Sense of Place: An Anthropological Approach to Community Formation in Corinth," *NTS* 32 (1986), pp. 225-46.

There are now a great host of sociological studies on aspects of the Corinthian correspondence. The most seminal of these studies are the groundbreaking essays by G. Theissen collected in *The Social Setting of Pauline Christianity: Essays on Corinth* (Philadelphia: Fortress, 1982) and the influential study by W. A. Meeks, *The First Urban Christians: The Social World of the Apostle Paul* (New Haven: Yale University, 1983). J. G. Gager, *Kingdom and Community: The Social World of Early Christianity* (Englewood Cliffs: Prentice-Hall, 1975), was a preliminary effort. See also A. J. Blasi, *Early Christianity as a Social Movement* (New York: Lang, 1988); J. H. Elliott, *A Home for the Homeless: A Sociological Exegesis of 1 Peter, Its Situation and Strategy* (Philadelphia: Fortress, 1981), pp. 170ff.; R. M. Grant, *Early Christianity and Society* (New York: Harper and Row, 1977). For a helpful introductory review article, see O. C. Edwards, "Sociology as a Tool for Interpreting the NT," *Anglican Theological Review* 65 (1983), pp. 431-46. On the social implications of Paul's reflections on his symbolic universe, see N. R. Petersen, *Rediscovering Paul: Philemon and the Sociology of Paul's Narrative World* (Philadelphia: Fortress, 1985). A helpful article on the social location of Paul's teaching and preaching is S. K. Stowers, "Social Status: Public Speaking and Private Teaching: The Circumstances of Paul's Preaching Activity," *NovT* 26 (1984), pp. 59-81.

On Paul's apostolic authority and use of power, cf. A. J. Blasi, *Making Charisma: The Social Construction of Paul's Public Image* (New Brunswick: Transaction, 1991); J. H. Schütz, *Paul and the Anatomy of Apostolic Authority* (Cambridge: Cambridge University, 1975); B. Holmberg, *Paul and Power: The Structure of Authority in the Primitive Church as Reflected in the Pauline Epistles* (Philadelphia: Fortress, 1980); U. Brockhaus, *Charisma und Amt* (Wuppertal: Theologischer Verlag Rolf Brockhaus, 1972). On Paul and work in relationship to his ministry, see R. Hock, *The Social Context of Paul's Ministry: Tentmaking and Apostleship* (Philadelphia: Fortress, 1980). On the institutionalization of Paul's communities during his ministry, see M. Y. MacDonald, *The Pauline Churches: A Socio-Historical Study of Institutionalisation in the Pauline and Deutero-Pauline Writings* (Cambridge: Cambridge University, 1988), pp. 2-84. On households in the Greco-Roman world, see D. C. Verner, *The Household of God: The Social World of the Pastoral Epistles* (Chico: Scholars, 1983). On Paul's concept of the *ekklēsia*, see R. Banks, *Paul's Idea of Community: The Early House Churches in Their Historical Setting* (Grand Rapids: Eerdmans, 1980). For an imaginative recreation of what it would have been like to attend a house church meeting, see Banks's *Going to Church in the First Century: An Eyewitness Account* (Chipping Norton: Hexagon, 1980). On status and roles, see A. Funk, *Status und Rollen in den Paulusbriefen* (Innsbruck: Tyrolia, 1981), and on the part played by letters in community formation, see R. Pesch, *Paulus ringt um die Lebensform der Kirche. Vier Briefe an die Gemeinde Gottes in Korinth* (Freiberg: Herder, 1986).

On the various sorts of patronage and friendship relationships and conventions as they existed in Paul's day and communities, see the reading guide provided in J. H. Elliott, "Patronage and Clientism in Early Christian Society," *Forum* 3 (1987), pp. 39-48, and J. K. Chow, *Patronage and Power: A Study of Social Networks in Corinth* (Sheffield: JSOT, 1992); F. W. Danker, *Benefactor: An Epigraphic Study of a Graeco-Roman and NT Semantic Field* (St. Louis: Clayton, 1982); and S. C. Mott, "The Power of Giving and Receiving: Reciprocity in Hellenistic Benevolence," in *Current Issues in Biblical and Patristic Interpretation,* ed. G. F. Hawthorne (Grand Rapid: Eerdmans, 1974), pp. 60-72. See J. P. Sampley, *Pauline Partnership in Christ: Christian Community and*

Commitment in Light of Roman Law (Philadelphia: Fortress, 1980) on *societas* relationships. Especially helpful is G. W. Peterman's *Giving and Receiving in Paul's Epistles: Greco-Roman Social Conventions in Philippians and Other Pauline Writings* (thesis, King's College, University of London, 1992). On *inimicitia* (enmity) relationships, see P. Marshall, *Enmity in Corinth: Social Conventions in Paul's Relations with the Corinthians* (Tübingen: Mohr, 1987), and cf. D. M. MacDonald, "*Hybris* in Athens," *Greece and Rome* 23 (1976), pp. 14-23.

On the use and application of the theory of social networks to the NT era, see L. M. White, ed., *Social Networks in the Early Christian Environment: Issues and Methods for Social History* = *Semeia* 56 (1992), especially the essays by White, "Finding the Tie that Binds: Issues from Social Description," pp. 3-22, and "Social Networks: Theoretical Orientation and Historical Applications," pp. 23-36. In the same volume see H. Hendrix, "Benefactor/Patron Networks in the Urban Environment: Evidence from Thessalonica," pp. 39-58, and R. F. Hock, " 'By the Gods, It's My One Desire to See an Actual Stoic': Epictetus' Relations with Students and Visitors in His Personal Network," pp. 121-42. On hospitality, see J. B. Mathews, *Hospitality and the NT Church: An Historical and Exegetical Study* (Ann Arbor: University Microfilms, 1980). On the influence of Paul's Jewishness, see K.-W. Niebuhr, *Heidenapostel aus Israel* (Tübingen: Mohr, 1992). On the question of mimesis, the call for imitating the apostle, see E. A. Castelli, *Imitating Paul: A Discourse of Power* (Louisville: Westminster/John Knox, 1991). On Paul's use of common athletic imagery cf. V. C. Pfitzner, *Paul and the Agon Motif: Traditional Athletic Imagery in the Pauline Literature* (Leiden: Brill, 1967).

On the issue of rank and status and the sociological study of Paul's letters in general the essays of E. A. Judge should be studied at length: *The Social Pattern of Christian Groups in the First Century* (London: Tyndale, 1960); *Rank and Status in the World of the Caesars and St. Paul* (Christchurch: University of Canterbury, 1982); "St. Paul and Classical Society," *Jahrbuch für Antike und Christentum* 15 (1972), pp. 19-36; "St Paul as a Radical Social Critic of Society," *Interchange* 16 (1974), pp. 191-203; "St. Paul and Socrates," *Interchange* 13 (1973), pp. 106-16 (successfully critiquing Betz's work on 2 Corinthians 10– 13); "The Early Christians as a Scholastic Community: Part II," *Journal of Religious History* 1 (1960), pp. 125-37; "Cultural Conformity and Innovation in Paul: Some Clues from Contemporary Documents," *TynB* 35 (1984), pp. 3-24; "Paul's Boasting in Relation to Contemporary Professional Practice," *Australian Biblical Review* 16 (1968), pp. 37-50; "The Social Identity of the First Christians," *Journal of Religious History* 11 (1980), pp. 201-17.

On the question of participation of Pauline Christians in feasts in pagan temples, see W. L. Willis, *Idol Meat in Corinth: The Pauline Argument in 1 Corinthians 8 and 10* (Chico: Scholars, 1985), though this study has some flaws in its evaluation of dining and the temple of Demeter in Roman Corinth and on the issue of the "secular" character of dining parties in temples. The modern sacred-secular distinction is not completely applicable to a society in which religion played a part, often an important part, in *all* public life and in the home as well. On the issue of *eidōlothuta* see my article "Not So Idle Thoughts about *Eidolothuton*," *TynB* 44 (1993), pp. 237-54; G. D. Fee, "Εἰδω-λόθυτα Once Again: An Interpretation of 1 Corinthians 8–10," *Biblica* 61 (1980), pp. 172-97; and D. E. Smith, "Meals and Morality in Paul and his World," *SBL Seminar Papers 1981* (Chico, 1981), pp. 319-39.

On the question of the early Christian attitude toward property, see M. Hengel, *Property and Riches in the Early Church* (Philadelphia: Fortress, 1974). On slavery and Christianity in the Roman Empire, see H. Gülzow, *Christentum und Sklaverei in den ersten drei Jahrhunderten* (Bonn: Habelt, 1969); T. Wiedemann, *Greek and Roman Slavery* (London: Routledge, 1981); S. S. Bartchy, *First-Century Slavery and 1 Corinthians 7.21* (Missoula: Scholars, 1973); and N. Petersen's *Rediscovering Paul* (cited above). On Paul's use of slavery imagery and metaphors to discuss his roles and functions and those of others, see F. Lyall, *Slaves, Citizens, Sons: Legal Metaphors in the Epistles* (Grand Rapids: Zondervan, 1984); W. G. Rollins, "Greco-Roman Slave Ter-minology and Pauline Metaphors for Salvation," *Society of Biblical Literature 1987 Seminar Papers*, ed. K. H. Richards (Atlanta: Scholars, 1987), pp. 100-110; and especially the fine study by D. B. Martin, *Slavery as Salvation: The Meta-phor of Slavery in Pauline Christianity* (New Haven: Yale University, 1990).

Other important articles include: J. H. Neyrey, "Witchcraft Accusations in 2 Cor 10–13: Paul in Social Scientific Perspective," *Listening* 21 (1986), pp. 160-70; W. A. Meeks, "Social Functions of Apocalyptic Language in Pauline Christianity," in *Apocalypticism in the Mediterranean World*, ed. D. Hellholm (Tübingen: Mohr, 1983), pp. 687-705; R. H. Smith, "Were the Early Christians Middle Class? A Sociological Analysis of the NT," *Currents in Theology and Mission*, 7 (1980), pp. 260-76; W. Wuellner, "The Sociological Implications of 1 Corinthians 1.26-28 Reconsidered," *Studia Evangelica* 6 (1973), pp. 666-72; G. Theissen, "Vers une theorie de l'histoire sociale du Christianisme Primitif," *Études Théologiques et Religieuses* 63 (1988), pp. 199-225; G. Schöllgen, "Was wissen wir über die Sozialstruktur der paulinischen Gemeinde?" *NTS* 34 (1988), pp. 71-82; L. L. Welborn, "On the Discord in Corinth: 1 Corinthians 1–4 and Ancient Politics," *JBL* 106 (1987), pp. 85-111; T. Engberg-Pedersen, "The Gospel and Social Practice according to 1 Corinthians," *NTS* 33 (1987), pp. 557-84; B. W. Winter, "Civil Litigation in Secular Corinth and the Church: The Forensic Background to 1 Corinthians 6.1-8," *NTS* 4 (1991), pp. 559-72; M. Y. Mac-Donald, "Women Holy in Body and Spirit: The Social Setting of 1 Corinthians," *NTS* 36 (1990), pp. 161-81; and P. Duff, "The Transformation of the Spectator: Power, Perception, and the Day of Salvation," *Society of Biblical Literature 1987 Seminar Papers*, ed. K. H. Richards (Atlanta: Scholars, 1987), pp. 233-43.

Paul and Ancient Philosophy

Various studies have been undertaken to evaluate whether and to what degree Paul drew on Platonic, Stoic, Cynic, Epicurean, or other philosophical traditions. Some of the more helpful studies that deal with this subject are a collection of essays by A. J. Malherbe under the title *Paul and the Popular Philosophers* (Minneapolis: Fortress, 1989) and, on Paul's possible use of the Socratic tradition in 2 Corinthians, H. D. Betz, *Der Apostel Paulus und die sokratrische Tradition. Eine exegetische Untersuchung zu seiner "Apologie" 2 Korinther 10–13* (Tübingen: Mohr, 1972). An unconvincing study arguing that Paul presented himself as an ascetic has been offered by V. L. Wimbush, *Paul the Worldly Ascetic: Response to the World and Self Understanding according to 1 Corinthians 7* (Macon: Mercer University, 1987). Wimbush's approach is based to a significant degree on a confusion of Paul's quotations of the Corinthians views with Paul's own views and on an assumption that Paul only conceded marriage.

The festschrift for A. J. Malherbe (*Greeks, Romans, and Christians*, ed. D. L. Balch, E. Ferguson, and W. A. Meeks [Minneapolis: Fortress, 1990]) contains articles that deal with rhetoric or ancient philosophy in the Pauline epistles. See especially C. R. Holladay, "I Corinthians 13: Paul as Apostolic Paradigm," pp. 80-98; S. R. Garrett, "The God of This World and the Affliction of Paul: 2 Corinthians 4.1-12," pp. 99-117; B. Fiore, "Passion in Paul and Plutarch," pp. 135-43; J. T. Fitzgerald, "Paul, the Ancient Epistolary Theorists, and 2 Corinthians 10–13," pp. 190-200; S. K. Stowers, "Paul on the Use and Abuse of Reason," pp. 253-86; and W. A. Meeks, "The Circle of Reference in Pauline Morality," pp. 305-317. An important recent article on Paul's address on the Areopagus (Acts 17) is M. M. Adams, "Philosophy and the Bible: The Areopagus Speech," *Faith and Philosophy* 9 (1992), pp. 135-49. On marriage, see R. B. Ward, "Musonius and Paul on Marriage," *NTS* 36 (1990), pp. 281-89.

Paul the Sage and Ancient Wisdom Movements

A good number of studies have stressed that the Corinthian correspondence needs to be read in light of sapiential traditions, both Jewish and Greco-Roman. One should consult the bibliography for chapter 8, "Paul — Sage or Sophist?" in my monograph surveying biblical wisdom material, *Jesus the Sage: The Pilgrimage of Wisdom* (Minneapolis: Fortress, 1994).

On Paul's self-portrayal as a suffering (Stoic?) sage, see J. T. Fitzgerald, *Cracks in an Earthen Vessel: An Examination of the Catalogue of Hardships in the Corinthian Correspondence* (Atlanta: Scholars, 1988). See also J. Munck, *Paul and the Salvation of Mankind* (Atlanta: John Knox, 1959), pp. 135-95;

U. Wilckens, *Weisheit und Torheit. Eine exegetisch-religionsgeschichtliche Untersuchung zu 1 Kor. 1 und 2* (Tübingen: Mohr, 1959); E. J. Schnabel, *Law and Wisdom from Ben Sira to Paul* (Tübingen: Mohr, 1985).

Paul's main concern is with revealed, not discovered, wisdom, and revealed wisdom serves him as an important benchmark for determining who is in and out of touch with God. See G. W. E. Nickelsburg, "Revealed Wisdom as a Criterion for Inclusion and Exclusion: From Jewish Sectarianism to Early Christianity," in *"To See Ourselves as Others See Us": Christians, Jews, "Others" in Late Antiquity*, ed. J. Neusner and E. S. Frerichs (Chico: Scholars, 1985), pp. 73-91; H. Conzelmann, "Paulus und die Weisheit," *NTS* 12 (1965-66), pp. 231-44; U. Luck, "Weisheit und Leiden. Zum Problem Paulus und Jakobus," *Theologische Literaturzeitung* 92 (1967), pp. 253-58; T. H. Lim, "Not in Persuasive Words of Wisdom but in Demonstration of the Spirit and Power," *NovT* 2 (1987), pp. 137-49; R. Scroggs, "Paul: *Sophos* and *Pneumatikos*," *NTS* 14 (1967-68), pp. 33-55; G. Sellin, "Das 'Geheimnis' der Weisheit und das Rätsel der 'Christuspartei' (zu 1 Kor 1–4)," *ZNW* 73 (1982), pp. 69-96; A. Van Roon, "The Relation between Christ and the Wisdom of God according to Paul," *NovT* 16 (1974), pp. 207-39; J. B. Polhill, "The Wisdom of God and Factionalism: 1 Cor. 1–4," *Review and Expositor* 80 (1983), pp. 325-39; P. Stuhlmacher, "The Hermeneutical Significance of 1 Cor. 2.6-16," in *Tradition and Interpretation in the NT: Essays in Honor of E. Earle Ellis* (Grand Rapids: Eerdmans, 1987), pp. 328-43; R. A. Horsley, "Wisdom of Word and Words of Wisdom in Corinth," *CBQ* 39 (1977), pp. 224-39; R. M. Grant, "The Wisdom of the Corinthians," in *The Joy of Study*, ed. S. E. Johnson (New York: MacMillan, 1951), pp. 51-55; P. Botte, "La Sagesse et les Origines de la Christologie," *Revue des sciences philosophiques et théologiques* 21 (1932), pp. 54-67; M. D. Goulder, "*Sophia* in Corinthians," *NTS* 37 (1991), pp. 516-34. On the paternity of the sage in relation to his disciples cf. P. Guttierrez, *La Paternité Spirituelle selon St. Paul* (Paris: Gabalda, 1968), pp. 40ff.

1 CORINTHIANS

The Background and Structure of the Letter

Chronology and Composition

There is little question concerning Paul's authorship of 1 Corinthians or about its integrity or unity, though some have thought that 11:2-16 is an interpolation by a post-Pauline author, and many scholars in the past three decades have argued the same regarding 14:34b-36. We will deal with these questions of interpolation when we come to the texts in the commentary. Scholarship on 1 Corinthians usually does not present us with the partition theories that one faces when dealing with 2 Corinthians.[1]

There is more need for discussion of the date of 1 Corinthians and its place in the Corinthian correspondence. Here, perhaps more than with any other Pauline letter, we have some help from extrabiblical information. But the value of this information depends on how highly Acts is regarded as a historical source. Acts 18 tells us that Paul was in Corinth after the Jews were expelled from Rome by Claudius and while Gallio was proconsul there. Despite the qualms of Murphy-O'Connor,[2] most scholars still hold that there was such an expulsion from Rome and that it probably took place sometime in A.D. 49 or early in 50. Paul probably arrived in Corinth shortly after Aquila and Priscilla, who were among those expelled from Rome, that is, in or

---

1. There are some exceptions, particularly among European commentators. Perhaps the most prominent partitioners of 1 Corinthians are W. Schmithals, C. Senft, J. Héring, R. Jewett, and R. Pesch. For a strong nonrhetorical argument against partition of 1 Corinthians (mainly Schmithals) see H. Merklein, "Die Einheitlichkeit des ersten Korintherbriefes," *ZNW* 75 (1984), pp. 153-83.

2. Cf. above, pp. 26-27 and the notes there; J. Murphy-O'Connor, *St. Paul's Corinth: Texts and Archaeology* (Wilmington: Glazier, 1983), pp. 132ff.

The Bēma *or Seat of Judgment in the center of the Roman forum in Corinth. Here Paul appeared before Gallio in 51 or 52. The Acrocorinth is in the background.*

around A.D. 49-50. Acts tells us that he stayed for about eighteen months (Acts 18:11). On the basis of an inscription found at Delphi that mentions Gallio, along with corroborative evidence assembled by Murphy-O'Connor, it appears that Gallio served in Corinth in 50-51 or 51-52, completing only part of his two-year term.[3] It is probable that Paul's encounter with Gallio

---

3. Cf. the restored letter of Claudius mentioning Gallio in J. H. Oliver, "The Epistle of Claudius Which Mentions the Proconsul Gallio," *Hesperia* 40 (1971), pp. 239-40. Oliver argues that this letter was written in A.D. 52 while Gallio was still proconsul in Corinth.

happened between July and October of either 50 or perhaps more likely in 51.[4] 1 Corinthians must have been written sometime after that.[5]

Acts 18:18-23 may shed some further light on this matter. It suggests that when Paul left Corinth he went first to Jerusalem. Then he began another missionary tour in Asia Minor, starting from Antioch. According to 1 Cor. 16:8, Paul is in Ephesus as he writes and plans to stay there until Pentecost, after which he plans to go to Macedonia and then on to Greece. This means that he is probably writing during winter, before the Jewish festival of Pentecost. One must allow for some time to have elapsed after Paul left Corinth, went to Jerusalem, returned to Asia Minor, and rejoined Aquila and Priscilla in Ephesus. It is clear from 1 Cor. 5:9 that what we call 1 Corinthians was not the first letter that Paul wrote to Corinth after his departure from the city.[6] This, too, requires that we allow a fair amount of time after his departure. Given all this, 1 Corinthians was probably written early in 53 or 54.

Rhetorical Setting

If we are to characterize 1 Corinthians as either a problem-oriented letter or a progress-oriented letter, then it must surely be placed in the former category. Paul is still having to sort out a multitude of basics for the Corinthian Christians, whom he has not seen in some time and some of whom appear to think he is never coming back to them. As we turn to detailed analysis of the letter we pick things up in midstream. Paul is in the midst of trying to create community and dissipate conflict in the Corinthian Christian community. But

---

4. For comments on the Gallio inscription, see Murphy-O'Connor, *St. Paul's Corinth*, pp. 173, 141-52. J. K. Chow, *Patronage and Power: A Study of Social Networks in Corinth* (Sheffield: JSOT, 1992), p. 79, suggests that Jewish influence may have been weak in Corinth, which would explain why Gallio refused to hear the Jews' complaint against Paul. But Gallio, as proconsul, was presumably less susceptible to being manipulated by powerful Corinthians than the decurios, duovirs, or aediles. Acts suggests a considerable Jewish presence in Corinth. It appears that Gallio simply did not want to get involved in what seemed to be a dispute among Jews about their own religion. Pilate's initial reaction to the complaint about Jesus (Luke 23:4; John 18:29-40) was similar.

5. T. Rajak, "Was there a Roman Charter for the Jews," *JRS* 74 (1984), pp. 107-23, here p. 122: "Paganism is often said to have been tolerant and accommodating. But it was not so towards a monotheistic religion centered upon an invisible God, a religion which could not be readily assimilated in the usual fashion into the existing system."

6. The argument that a fragment of the early letter may be found in 2 Corinthians is hardly persuasive. We will say more about this suggestion in the introduction to 2 Corinthians.

it is clear from 2 Corinthians that things did not get better after 1 Corinthians arrived. Indeed, they got worse.[7]

It is a mistake to read all of the situation of 2 Corinthians back into 1 Corinthians. In particular, it is unlikely that a group of anti-Pauline agitators are already causing problems for the Corinthian *ekklēsia* at the time of 1 Corinthians.[8] The difficulties that must be overcome in 1 Corinthians are essentially internal and are resulting in divisions in the Christian community. These difficulties include:

> partisan attachments to particular Christian teachers such as Paul and Apollos and rivalries growing out of such attachments,
>
> continuing adherence to particular cultural values, especially on the part of the wealthy, which are leading to lawsuits among fellow Christians, unequal treatment at the Lord's table, and dining in pagan temples on the part of some,
>
> hubris on the part of some who are using certain spiritual gifts in ways that do not build up the community,
>
> disagreements regarding sexual conduct appropriate for Christians, both within and outside marriage, and
>
> disagreements over eschatological matters such as the resurrection and whether the present state of the believer involves reigning, glory, and the like.

Most of these problems, except perhaps the last one, were social, not theological in origin.[9]

The pedagogical milieu in the Christian community in Corinth here is

---

7. C. K. Barrett, *The First Epistle to the Corinthians* (New York: Harper and Row, 1968), p. 5.

8. This is a major flaw in an otherwise helpful study by P. Marshall, *Enmity at Corinth* (Tübingen: Mohr, 1987). Cf. the critique by S. M. Pogoloff, *Logos and Sophia: The Rhetorical Situation of 1 Corinthians* (Atlanta: Scholars, 1992), pp. 151f.; S. K. Stowers, "Paul on the Use of Reason," in *Greeks, Romans, and Christians*, ed. D. Balch, et al. (Minneapolis: Fortress, 1990), pp. 253-86, here pp. 258ff.

9. After I had nearly completed this commentary, I came across Pogoloff's assessment of the social and rhetorical situation (*Logos and Sophia*, pp. 237ff.), which is essentially the same as mine. He maintains that Paul is responding to a problem of divisions over teachers, in particular Paul and Apollos, that this division is basically related to rhetoric and matters of style (i.e., over cultural wisdom, over which group had the wisest teacher), not over theological substance. The Corinthians were, Pogoloff says, behaving like most disciples of ancient Sophists and other teachers by indulging in boasting and preening as part of their status-seeking behavior. Paul sought to deflate such attitudes and defuse such activities by offering models of concord and self-sacrifice.

illustrated by Plutarch's exhortation against just such a situation (*Prof. Virt.* 80B-C):

> Most of all we must consider whether the spirit of contention and quarreling over debatable questions has been put down, and whether we have ceased to equip ourselves with arguments, as with boxing gloves or brass knuckles, with which to contend against one another, and to take more delight in scoring a hit or knockout than in learning and imparting something. For reasonableness and mildness in such matters and the ability to join in discussions without wrangling, to close them without anger, and to avoid a sort of arrogance over success in argument and exasperation over defeat are the marks of a person who is making adequate progess.

The Corinthians were apparently taking their cues from what they knew of the educational process as modeled by the rhetors teaching in their city and taking part in debates, quarrels, boasting, arrogance, and the like.

In order to overcome these sources of discord Paul gives in his letter a lengthy discourse on concord or reconciliation using deliberative rhetoric. He is convinced that even social problems have theological roots and ethical implications.[10] He must show that it is to the Corinthians' benefit to work together, to agree with one another on essential matters, to respect differences on less than essential matters, and to allow the good or benefit of the other to guide one's actions. He must show the future good of allowing love to govern how, when, and whether one expresses one's freedom, knowledge, and gifts.

Paul structures his discourse to achieve these aims. In deliberative rhetoric one is concerned not only with what is expedient but also with what is honorable, which involves the four cardinal virtues: wisdom (cf. 1 Corinthians 1–4), justice (cf. chs. 5–6), courage (cf. chs. 7 and 15), and temperance (cf. chs. 8–14). The following is one possible way to read the rhetorical structure of the letter as a whole:[11]

---

10. I agree with Pogoloff's critique (*Logos and Sophia,* p. 90) of M. M. Mitchell, *Paul and the Rhetoric of Reconciliation* (Tübingen: Mohr, 1991), and others: To speak of political rhetoric in 1 Corinthians, because of analogies with the vocabulary of deliberative politic rhetoric (or in the case of M. Bünker, *Briefformular und rhetorische Disposition im 1 Korintherbrief* [Göttingen: Vandenhoeck & Ruprecht, 1984], analogies with judicial rhetoric) in other contexts, is to miss the transferred sense in which Paul uses such rhetoric. Paul is not appealing to a sense of civic pride or arguing about the Corinthian's duties to society at large. He is, rather, talking almost exclusively about "in house" behavior. The Christian *ekklēsia,* not the secular *ekklēsia,* is the forum for hearing and heeding his discourse.

11. Here I follow Mitchell, *Rhetoric of Reconciliation,* with some modifications.

1. The epistolary prescript (1:1-3).
2. The epistolary thanksgiving and *exordium* (1:4-9).
3. The *propositio* introducing the letter with a *parakalō* formula and making the basic thesis statement of the entire letter (1:10).
4. A brief *narratio* (1:11-17) explaining the situation or facts that have prompted the writing of the letter.[12]
5. The *probatio* (1:18–16:12), which includes arguments concerning:
   a. divisions over leaders and wisdom (1:18–4:21),
   b. sexual immorality and lawsuits (5–6),
   c. marriage and singleness (7),
   d. idol food and eating in idol temples (8–11:1, with a pertinent digression or *egressio* in ch. 9),
   e. headcoverings in worship (11:1-16),
   f. abuses of the Lord's Supper (11:17-34),
   g. spiritual gifts in Christ's body (12–14, with a pertinent digression or *egressio* in ch. 13),
   h. the future and the form of the resurrection (15), and
   i. the collection and other ministries for Corinth (16:1-12).
6. The *peroratio* (16:13-18).
7. The closing epistolary greetings and remarks (16:19-24).

The *probatio* was the heart of a rhetorical speech or letter and included the principal arguments used to persuade the audience. In a deliberative discourse these arguments could be arranged according to certain *topoi* or topics, in Greek called "heads" *(kephalia)*. Paul uses *peri de* several times in the *probatio* of 1 Corinthians to introduce his topics. In a series of arguments or "proofs" there could be one or more digressions, especially if the overall argument was long and the rhetor felt a need to bring in collateral material, which would nonetheless have some relevance for the course of the argument. In 1 Corinthians the argument has a number of subdivisions and includes two major digressions, both of which serve the larger deliberative aims of the letter (though ch. 9 has a forensic cast and defends Paul's apostolic practice with regard to support, while ch. 13 has an epideictic cast and praises love).

"The letter fictionalizes personal presence."[13] As such, a letter attempts to accomplish what would otherwise be done in person. The body of a letter

---

12. A full *narratio* is not always necessary in deliberative rhetoric, because the rhetor is basically not expected to defend *past* actions. Nevertheless, Paul offers a brief statement of the facts in 1:11-17. By contrast, we expect and receive a full *narratio* in a forensic discourse like 2 Corinthians.

13. Cf. S. K. Stowers, "Social Typification and Classification of Ancient Letters," in *The Social World of Formative Christianity and Judaism,* ed. J. Neusner (Philadelphia: Fortress, 1988), pp. 78-90, here p. 79.

"is not mere information to be communicated but rather a medium through which a person performs an action or social transaction with someone from whom he or she is physically separated."[14] The choice of what kind of rhetoric to use in a letter is, then, determined in much the same manner as the face-to-face speaker's choice of deliberative, forensic, or epideictic rhetoric. In 1 Corinthians the situation requires deliberative rhetoric. But by the time 2 Corinthians is written the situation has deteriorated further, and defense and attack, that is, forensic rhetoric, have become necessary.

While 1 and 2 Corinthians are each devoted primarily to one specific sort of rhetoric, there are elements of other species, especially in digressions, because the situation Paul addressed was complex. Sometimes advice must be combined with praise or blame and sometimes defense and attack must be coupled with advice and warnings. The situation addressed dictates to a real degree how a good rhetor will and must respond if he wishes to communicate and convince his audience. Form follows function and aims, and so Paul uses rhetoric flexibly to best achieve diverse aims and deal with complex problems.

14. Ibid., p. 85.

Epistolary Prescript: 1:1-3

1 Cor. 16:15-17 indicates that this epistle is prompted by a letter brought to Paul by Stephanas and others. The oral report brought by Chloe's people (1:11) may have made clear the gravity of the situation, which might not have been evident in the Corinthians' formal letter, which may have put the best face on things (cf. 11:2). The oral report perhaps went more behind the scenes and was thus the main stimulus for Paul's powerful response. We will discuss the main *cause* for Paul's writing of 1 Corinthians in the explanation of the *narratio* (1:11-17).

The letter Stephanus brought may have been a response to Paul's first letter to Corinth about avoiding immorality and idolatry (5:9-13). If so, 1 Corinthians may be a further expansion on that first letter, clarifying and reinforcing it. Some have thought that 2 Cor. 6:14–7:1 might be part of that earlier letter, but this is unlikely since 1 Cor. 5:9-11 refers to immorality *within* the Christian community, whereas 2 Cor. 6:14–7:1 speaks of outsiders, *even if* it is a warning about the false apostles. Furthermore, 2 Cor. 6:14–7:1 does not mention the particular incident that Paul is upset about in 1 Cor. 5:9-11.

The rhetorical situation which prompts this long and serious letter is that Paul believes it necessary to combat some serious social, ethical, ecclesiological, and theological errors in Corinth. It is no accident that he begins his arguments with a discussion of the cross and brings it to a climax with a discussion of the resurrection. A number of Corinthian Christians misunderstood the heart of the apostolic message and its implications. Paul is careful to stress that this message is not his own invention (15:3-5).

Paul assumes that his converts will both hear and heed him with some persuasion. This means that we are not yet at the stage where Paul believes that his apostolic authority is in serious question and must be defended at length. He would hardly argue for the Corinthians to imitate him and assume (ch. 9) that his apostolic example could spur them to right conduct if he believed he was dealing with a crisis of apostolic authority. The situation is markedly different when 2 Corinthians is written, which helps explain its more strident tone.

1 Corinthians begins, like most ancient letters, with a greeting and a thanksgiving. Paul always modifies the standard greeting *chairē*, a word that originally meant "joy" but came to mean simply "greetings," much as our "good day" is often perfunctory. Paul also, especially when his teaching is challenged, often puts something into the greeting to indicate by what right he calls himself an agent of Christ.[1]

Thus here in v. 1 Paul stresses that his call to be a messenger, agent, or ambassador of Christ came neither from his own inclinations or sense of vocation nor from his own will but by means of the will and call of God. This is likely an allusion to the Damascus road experience, which Paul saw as both a conversion and a call to ministry. The reference to "Sosthenes *the* brother" definitely establishes that Sosthenes is a Christian, and it could suggest that he has something to do with this letter, bearing in mind that ostensibly 1 and 2 Thessalonians also have coauthors. But in this letter Paul speaks in the first person, or when he uses "we" he refers to himself and his audience, not to any coworker.

Acts 18:17 refers to a Sosthenes who is not a Christian but is a synagogue ruler. In the same chapter (v. 8) Crispus is said to be a synagogue ruler also in Corinth. Since it is quite likely there was a significant group of Jews in prosperous Corinth, it would not be surprising if there were more than one synagogue there. We do not know that this Sosthenes and the one in 1 Corinthians are the same person, but if so it suggests that he was converted, perhaps after the episode with Gallio, and then traveled to Ephesus with Paul and was his personal secretary at this point. In 1 Cor. 16:21 Paul claims to write the *final* greeting in his own hand, which suggests that he did not actually write out the rest of the letter.

In v. 2 Paul refers to "the assembly of God that is in Corinth." *Ekklēsia* is an important word for Paul. It is the LXX term most often used for the "assembly" of Israel (in Hebrew the *qahal*). The word *ekklēsia* in itself stresses being called out, but in view of the OT background it is more likely to stress for Paul the idea of the gathering or assembly of the faithful. It may be that

---

1. Usually in this commentary I avoid the word "apostle," which is not a translation but a transliteration of Greek *apostolos* and tells us little about what the word would have connoted in the first century A.D.

Paul also used this term because of its association with the public assembly in a Greek city, where important civic matters were discussed and decided upon using Greco-Roman rhetoric. *Ekklēsia* does not refer to a building, for there is no evidence of church buildings before at least the second century A.D. Fee is right to stress that Paul refers not to "the Corinthian assembly," but "the assembly of God," indicating to whom it belongs. The Corinthians had too autonomous an attitude about what they were and did as *ekklēsia*.

The attributes that are listed apply to the whole assembly, not to isolated individuals. Together and collectively they are "sanctified in Christ Jesus" and "called to be holy" or "to be set apart." Sanctification happens not merely to individuals but is a group experience that occurs, for instance, in worship when the Spirit is moving. The stress here is probably on behavior. The Corinthians were to be different from the world in ethical character and behavior and in that sense set apart.

Paul then stresses that the congregation in Corinth is only part of the larger group of Christians *en panti topǭ*, which may mean "in every place" or possibly "in every meeting place." "Theirs and ours" modifies either "meeting place" or "Lord" (i.e., "their Lord and ours"), though the former seems more likely.

At the outset, Paul thus stresses two things about being a Christian: that it involves being set apart from the world and its dominant values and behavior patterns and that it involves being part of a group created by God that extends beyond the local congregation. Paul envisions a worldwide subculture of Christians that stands out from its environment in both belief and behavior. Perhaps Paul sees the Christian community as a different sort of colony than the *Colonia Laus Julia Corinthiensis* — the official name for Roman Corinth.

In v. 3, in what may have been a novel formulation, Paul combines the standard Greek and Jewish greetings and thus refers to both "grace" and *shalom*. "Grace," *charis,* namely, unmerited favor, and *shalom,* that is, well-being or rest, is given by both God the Father and Jesus. There can be little doubt that Paul views Jesus as in some sense divine because he gives both divine functions and divine names such as "Lord" to him. What is less clear is how he envisions the relationship between Christ and the Father. Christians are those who call upon the name of Jesus, not as though he were some departed saint but as God! This was scandalous to some Jews.

Paul's reference to the call to be holy or to be set apart from the larger culture, particularly in a spiritual and ethical sense, is part of his effort to establish moral boundaries for the community in Corinth. There is a correlation between a low sense of group identity and cohesiveness and a lack of clear boundary markers. Paul does not stress *ritual* boundary markers such as baptism or circumcision. Indeed, he repudiates the idea that his real task when he came to Corinth was to set up ritual boundary markers by baptizing (vv.

14-17). His primary concern is with ongoing behavior and the social and theological presuppositions that fuel it.

Paul also sees that there is inadequate leadership in Corinth to maintain the group's identity and boundaries, so in ch. 16 he commends Stephanas. More will be said shortly about the Corinthians' attitudes toward leadership. The problem is the Corinthians have the wrong vision of the leadership structure, of equality in Christ, and of how the two work together. They do not see how Spirit and structure are to be held together in tension without one eclipsing the other.

Epistolary Thanksgiving and *Exordium:* 1:4-9

That the majority of Paul's audience was Gentile is confirmed by such texts as 6:10-11; 8:7; and 12:2: His audience can be addressed mainly as those who have formerly been idolaters. 8:1–10:22 implies the same thing, for only Gentiles would likely want to go to temple feasts. Furthermore, Jews were prohibited from going to secular courts (6:1-11), and the right to patronize prostitutes would hardly be argued for by Jews (vv. 12-20). Thus, I must reject the suggestion of J. Davis, R. Horsley, and others that 1:1–4:21 should simply be seen as a result of a Jewish sapiential focus *on the part of the audience.* Paul says in ch. 1 that it is *Greeks* who seek *sophia* ("wisdom") while Jews are interested in "signs."

But Paul does draw heavily on Jewish sapiential traditions, as well as the kerygma, to correct whatever sort of *sophia* the Corinthians may have been interested in. He offers a revelatory wisdom that is in contrast with all merely human forms of *sophia.*[1]

This "wisdom of the world" includes "wisdom of word" (1:17), that is, eloquence. Declamation was enormously popular in Roman settings. It involved oratory on subjects abstracted from any immediate reference to persons, places, or things, oratory as mere mastery of words, not as a means of exhortation or of conveying some *content* amounting to wisdom.[2] Not surprisingly the Corinthians seem to have assumed that eloquence in speech *was* wisdom. The Sophistic movement encouraged the delusion that a person is

---

1. I have discussed Paul as a sage and 1 Corinthians 1–4 in considerable detail in *Jesus the Sage: The Pilgrimage of Wisdom* (Minneapolis: Fortress, 1994), ch. 7.
2. Cf. S. F. Bonner, *Roman Declamation in the Late Republic and Early Empire* (Liverpool: University of Liverpool, 1949), p. 3.

as he or she speaks, eloquence being impossible without a deep inner reserve of wisdom.

Besides their taste for eloquence, the Corinthians seem also to have had a pneumatic view of the source of *sophia*. Wisdom came through inspiration of the Spirit. Not only the content of what they called wisdom, but also the verbal ability to speak eloquently using rhetoric was a matter of inspiration.[3]

Along with this emphasis on rhetorical eloquence and pneumatic *sophia*, the tensions reflected in chs. 1–4 were also apparently based on immature groupie-like behavior on the part of the Corinthians in regard to certain Christian evangelist-teachers such as Paul, Apollos, and Peter. Rival groups focused on these leaders may have been initially generated by the way the Corinthians viewed the baptism of particular converts by one or another of the apostles. Apparently Apollos came to Corinth after Paul, and the tensions may have been exacerbated by the presence in Corinth of other Christian leaders such as Peter, but this is unclear. Paul is not yet combating outside agitators or people that one could really call "opponents." Even 9:12 probably alludes only to Peter and Apollos. How one assesses the situation depends in some measure on one's evaluation of the historical value of the material about Apollos in Acts 18, which I have argued correctly portrays the Alexandrian preacher.[4]

A Closer Look: The Apollos Factor and Faction[5]

According to Acts 18:24-26 Apollos was from Alexandria and was an *anēr logios*, which can mean he was eloquent, possibly implying that he used Greco-Roman rhetoric in the presentation of the gospel. It also says that he was "powerful in the Scriptures." He had been "instructed in the way of the Lord," he "taught accurately concerning Jesus," and he was "boiling over in the Spirit," an idiomatic phrase that seems to mean that he was full of the Holy Spirit, not just that he was enthusiastic (but cf. Rom. 12:11). This spiritual capacity propelled his speaking and his teaching about Jesus.

But Apollos had one deficiency: "He knew only John's baptism." Acts also says that he taught in the Ephesian synagogue and that when he was heard by Paul's coworkers he was instructed more accurately in "the way of God," which presumably included teaching on Christian baptism. Finally, Acts 18 says that Apollos wanted to go to Achaia and that the Christians in Ephesus wrote him a letter of reference or

3. J. R. Levison, "Did the Spirit Inspire Rhetoric?" in *Persuasive Artistry*, ed. D. F. Watson (Sheffield: JSOT, 1991), pp. 25-40.

4. B. Witherington, *Women in the Gospels and Acts* (Ph.D. thesis, Durham, U.K., 1981).

5. The following material draws on part of ch. 8 of my *Jesus the Sage*, with different wording.

introduction so that he would be received there. This whole episode is placed after Paul's first visit to Corinth (vv. 1-23).

There are three parallels in 1 Corinthians 1–4 with the account concerning Apollos in Acts 18 beyond the possible presence in Corinth of both Paul and Apollos:

> The issue of baptism is raised in 1 Corinthians 1 precisely in the context of divisions among the Corinthians ("I am of Apollos," "I am of Paul," vv. 12-17).
>
> Paul goes to some length to say that he eschews the use of *sophia logou* in his preaching, "lest Christ's cross be emptied of its power" (v. 17).
>
> Not only baptism but also who was a *pneumatikos* (a "spiritual" person) and what this entailed was at issue in Corinth (2:13, 15; 3:1).

So baptism, rhetorical eloquence, and pneumatic spirituality appear to have been involved in the Corinthians' factionalism.

Paul takes some pains in ch. 3 to stress that he and Apollos are working together in harmony on the same task for God, not as competitors. Only these two men are mentioned when the "I am of" slogan appears again in 3:4. The Corinthians are warned against taking pride in any mere human being, whether Paul, Apollos, or even Cephas (vv. 21f.). The crucial thing is not that they belong to one or another of these apostles but rather that they belong to Christ.

Finally, 4:6b must be taken quite seriously. Whatever 4:6a means, the second part of the verse states the nub of the problem: The Corinthians were taking sides, being inflated with pride for one apostle over against the other,[6] and in the context of what was said earlier this must surely mean Paul and Apollos. Paul must counter these divisions and does so in a variety of ways, including using himself and Apollos as an example of the unity and cooperation that the Corinthians must learn (cf. 3:5ff.; 4:6f.).[7] All this leads to a reconstruction of the situation that Paul addresses in chs. 1–4.

It is probably too much to speak of clear-cut factions or parties in Corinth since Paul is still able to address the converts in Corinth as a whole and because *schismata* (1:10) refers to cracks or fissures in a rock or tears in a garment, not to separate rocks or garments.[8] Nevertheless there seem to be serious divisions in a still somewhat unified group.[9] If one reads behind remarks like the one in 2:15 it also appears that the

---

6. G. D. Fee, *The First Epistle to the Corinthians* (Grand Rapids: Eerdmans, 1987), pp. 169f.; C. K. Barrett, *The First Epistle to the Corinthians* (New York: Harper & Row, 1968), p. 107. M. D. Goulder ("*Sophia* in 1 Corinthians," *NTS* 37 [1991], pp. 516-34, here p. 519), in order to make his view pitting Paul against Peter work, interprets 4:6b to mean that the "one" is Paul and Apollos together and the "other" is Peter standing for a Torah-centered approach. This involves reading more into "one" than is warranted.

7. J. B. Polhill, "The Wisdom of God and Factionalism: 1 Cor. 1–4," *RevEx* 80 (1993), pp. 325-39, here p. 336.

8. Cf. BAGD; Fee, *First Corinthians*, p. 31. *Schismata* is not as strong a word as English "schism."

9. One suspects in view of 4:6 that there were at most only two significant groups: those who favored Paul's teaching and those who favored Apollos's teaching. It is hard to conceive of a Christ party, for surely had there been one Paul would simply have said that

divisions involved a personal attack on Paul himself or at least a very critical judgment of him.[10] How has this happened if, as Paul says, he and Apollos are working as a team?

Paul came to Corinth first and was responsible for the initial preaching and the establishment of the congregation there. He apparently stayed a considerable period of time in order to accomplish this task (Acts 18:11: a year and a half). This would have entailed not only preaching in the synagogue and elsewhere but also instruction following up on the preaching. Paul speaks in 1 Cor. 2:1f. of a conscious decision not to use sublime words or *sophia* but rather to preach only Christ and him crucified. The focus here seems to be on avoiding Sophistic rhetoric in preaching lest the audience be swayed by the form of the message rather than by the plain unvarnished truth that Paul wishes to convey. As 2:6ff. goes on to reveal, however, Paul does speak wisdom of a sort, a wisdom "not of this age" (v. 6) but rather a "wisdom of God in a mystery" (v. 7), a wisdom that involves a revelation from God through the Holy Spirit (v. 10). For Paul, receiving the Spirit seems to be primary, and wisdom and knowledge come, then, through the Spirit.[11] While it is probably overreaching to think of Paul establishing a wisdom school at Corinth, on the order of what H. Conzelmann assumes was set up in Ephesus,[12] it does appear nevertheless that Paul made it a practice to engage in wisdom teaching, at least *en tois teleiois* ("among the mature," v. 6), and this wisdom seems to have something to do with further explication of the initial preaching about God's salvation plan operating in and through the crucified Christ.

That Paul was succeeded in Corinth by Apollos is suggested by identification of Apollos as a "waterer" (3:6) following Paul's role as a planter. If the description of Apollos in Acts 18 is anything close to accurate one may suspect that his watering entailed at least these factors:

> use of rhetoric, possibly even in a Sophistic mode, in public proclamation and presumably also in teaching (cf. Acts 18:26: he spoke boldly as well as eloquently),[13]

---

all Christians belong to it and he would have worded 3:21-23 ("you are of Christ") more carefully (cf. 2 Cor. 10:7). Cf. G. Sellin, "Das 'Geheimnis' der Weisheit und das Rätsel der 'Christuspartei' (zu 1 Kor. 1–4)," *ZNW* 73 (1982), pp. 69-96, here p. 92; Fee, *First Corinthians*, pp. 54ff.

10. Polhill, "Wisdom of God," p. 336.

11. So J. A. Davis, *Wisdom and Spirit* (New York: University Press of America, 1984), p. 108.

12. But cf. H. Conzelmann, *1 Corinthians* (Philadelphia: Fortress, 1975), pp. 14ff. I would not entirely rule out this possibility. On use of Sirach in Jewish wisdom schools see H. Stadelmann, *Ben Sira als Schriftgelehrter* (Tübingen: Mohr, 1980), pp. 27-30. On the Wisdom of Solomon as possibly a school product see D. Georgi, *Weisheit Salomos* (Gütersloh: Mohn, 1980), p. 393.

13. Cf. R. A. Horsley, "Wisdom of Word and Words of Wisdom in Corinth," *CBQ* 39 (1977), pp. 224-39, here pp. 231f. Horsley suggests that Apollos introduced a Philonic sort of wisdom to Corinth. This might explain the individualistic approach to religion in the Christian community there. "Philo's whole discussion of speech is rather single-mindedly oriented toward the relation of the individual soul and the divine wisdom"

appropriation of Alexandrian Hellenistic Jewish wisdom speculation, perhaps especially in scriptural exegesis,[14]

baptizing of some Corinthians whom Paul had not yet baptized, and

a stress on the pneumatic character of both his wisdom and of the Christian life.

It seems likely that the Corinthians have picked up hints of Hellenistic Jewish wisdom speculation in the teaching of Apollos and have gone well beyond these hints on their own. Paul was not happy with this development and insists that they must stick with what is written in Scripture (1 Cor. 4:6a).[15]

Whatever the intent of Apollos, the effect of his eloquent sapiential and pneumatic teaching was factionalism, individualism, and sapiential spiritualism. It is probably not by chance that Paul mentions that Greeks desire *sophia* (1:22). Clearly at least some in Corinth were looking for *sophia* and believed they had found it in Apollos's eloquent discourses. There is nothing in chs. 1–4 that suggests, even remotely, that Peter was the real culprit. It is not even clear that Peter had even been to Corinth, though certainly the Corinthians knew about him and his work.[16]

1 Cor. 16:12 supports this reconstruction. Whatever divisions existed between those who looked to Apollos and those who looked to Paul as their chief prophetic sage, Paul and Apollos were still working together. Paul would not have urged Apollos many times to go to Corinth (perhaps to straighten out the mess that had arisen there) if he did not think the problem ultimately lay with the Corinthians and not with Apollos and his teachings.[17] Furthermore, Apollos's unwillingness to go in the midst

---

(p. 236). To counter this Paul offers a more community-oriented sort of wisdom, drawing on a variety of other wisdom sources.

14. 1 Cor 4:6a may refer to Scripture, in which case the Corinthians are being warned not to go beyond Scripture (into Jewish halakah or perhaps more likely into esoteric wisdom speculations as in Philo). This might be supported by the reference in 1:20 to the *grammateus,* the expert in the law.

15. M. D. Hooker's handling of 1 Cor. 4:6a seems basically correct but cf. below, pp. 140-41. She has written (*From Adam to Christ: Essays on Paul* [Cambridge: Cambridge University, 1990], p. 109):

> The "wisdom" which was paraded by these teachers was something additional to Paul's own message of Christ crucified, the message which he saw as the fulfillment of God's purposes and of the "things which are written." It was a wisdom which was centered on ideas extraneous to the gospel, and which therefore was the wisdom of men, and not the wisdom of God. In following this worthless and harmful teaching the Corinthians were not simply adding to that of Paul, but were also going "beyond the things which are written," and it was this search for additional "wisdom" which had led to their divisions, and to the situation where one was "puffed up against the other."

16. But cf. C. K. Barrett, "Cephas and Corinth," in *Essays on Paul* (Philadelphia: Westminster, 1982), pp. 28-39. Polhill, "The Wisdom of God," p. 234, suggests that Paul mentions one with whom he has a harmonious relationship, namely Apollos, in order to critique indirectly those really responsible for the divisions (perhaps another apostle). This neglects the clear implications of 4:6b.

17. Cf. Sellin, "Geheimnis," p. 74. As P. Stuhlmacher points out ("The Hermeneutical

of the problems arising in Corinth may suggest that he realized that he was the unwitting catalyst of some of these difficulties. In order, then, not to cause Paul any further trouble Apollos wanted to stay with the work he was doing in Asia.

Perhaps the factions developed along house church lines if the patrons of the house churches favored different apostles. But Paul set himself at odds with *all* the factions because, unlike some other Christian leaders, he would not accept patronage in Corinth. His aim was not to foster the Paul faction, but to eliminate all such factions. It is very unlikely that there was a Christ party in Corinth, as distinguished from other Christians, or that the factions were groups with rigid boundaries.

Paul's thanksgiving prayers at the beginnings of his letters often foreshadow some of the content to be discussed later in the letters.[18] Here Paul thanks God for the very things that were causing problems in Corinth: *sophia* (including both rhetoric and its content), knowledge, and charismatic speech (v. 5). This seems inexplicable until one recognizes that this thanksgiving serves a rhetorical purpose, namely as an *exordium*. The function of an *exordium* is to use praise (in this case indirect, since it is God who is thanked for the gifts) to secure the goodwill of the listeners while encapsulating the main themes of the speech or letter.[19] "In 1 Corinthians (1:4-9), [Paul] gives thanks for the speech, knowledge, and spiritual gifts of the Corinthians. In chapters 1–4, 8, and 12–14 the reader learns that the improper use of wisdom, knowledge, charismatic speech, and spiritual gifts are, according to Paul, central problems for the Corinthian church."[20] Furthermore, an exclusive claim by some to possess certain gifts exacerbated the factionalism.[21]

If we compare 1 and 2 Corinthians we notice a parallel procedure. Paul

---

Significance of 1 Cor. 2:6-16," in *Tradition and Interpretation in the NT,* ed. G. Hawthorne and O. Betz [Grand Rapids: Eerdmans, 1987], pp. 328-43, here p. 335), Paul criticizes only the Corinthians, not Apollos, since he is rejecting *their* false estimation of their leaders. In view of Galatians, one can hardly argue that Paul would not have criticized another apostle in a public letter.

18. It is possible that we should view this thanksgiving to God in light of the newly emerging rhetorical form of the *actio gratiarum,* the speech of thanksgiving to the gods (and to the emperor) given by a consul on assuming his office. If so, then one of the rhetorical functions of this thanksgiving may be to indicate that Paul is resuming authority over the Corinthians before he addresses them in an authoritative manner. Cf. G. A. Kennedy, *The Art of Rhetoric in the Ancient World 300 B.C. to A.D. 300* (Princeton: Princeton University, 1972), p. 429.

19. D. E. Aune, *The NT in Its Literary Environment* (Philadelphia: Westminster, 1987), p. 186.

20. S. K. Stowers, *Letter Writing in Greco-Roman Antiquity* (Philadelphia: Westminster, 1986), p. 22.

21. M. M. Mitchell, *Paul and the Rhetoric of Reconciliation* (Tübingen: Mohr, 1991), p. 195, n. 47.

attempts in 1 Corinthians to deal with and even to remove the causes of factionalism, that is, to overcome the things that divide the Corinthian body. He takes on these sources of division one by one starting in 1:18ff. In 2 Corinthians Paul likewise must deal with the exigencies prompting the letter, only then he must seek to remove one by one the obstacles that divide, separate, or alienate *him* (and he believes Christ also) from his converts. Both letters contain "the rhetoric of reconciliation,"[22] but 2 Corinthians differs because in it Paul must defend his authority and ministry at length in order to be reconciled with his converts, hence the necessity for forensic rhetoric. 1 Corinthians is primarily a letter about ecclesiology, that is, about body life in Corinth, while 2 Corinthians is primarily about church *leadership,* and so about the issues of character, trust, and authenticity and the evidence for all of these things.

In 2 Corinthians Paul fully tackles what he perceives to be the worst problem only at the end of the letter, in chs. 10–13. This is a wise rhetorical strategy, but does he do a similar thing in 1 Corinthians? Paul leaves the discussion of the resurrection to near the end of the discourse (ch. 15) and the discussion of Apollos's travel plans to the very end (ch. 16). While the problems he has discussed earlier are matters of the spiritual health of the body, Paul seems to think that one's position on resurrection is a matter of spiritual life and death, not just a difficulty or problem within a body of believers. In fact it could be argued that lack of understanding of future eschatology, of the not-yet dimension of Christian faith, *engendered* at least some of the problems discussed in the earlier parts of 1 Corinthians.[23] As J. H. Roberts rightly stresses, the eschatological transition in 1:7f. has a crucial rhetorical function in that it presages important eschatological pronouncements later in the letter — not only passing remarks as in 4:5; 5:5, 13; 6:2, 14 but especially the major discussion in ch. 15.[24] This also suggests that Paul had in mind at the outset where he intended this discourse to come to a climax.

The appropriateness of the *exordium* in 1:4-9 as a means of introducing the rest of the discourse can be seen, then, in these connections:

"Every kind of speech and knowledge" (1:5) is discussed primarily in 1:18–4:21;
"the end" of being "irreproachable" (1:9) is dealt with in 5:1–11:33;

22. To borrow part of Mitchell's title.
23. This would be the negative cause of the problems (i.e., what was lacking to correct such problems). The positive cause of these problems was the Corinthians bringing their cultural values into their congregational life. There were both sociological and theological causes of the problems in Corinth.
24. J. H. Roberts, "The Eschatological Transitions to the Pauline Letter Body," *Neot* 20 (1986), pp. 29-35, here pp. 30f.

"the *charismata* (spiritual gifts)" are treated in chs. 12–14;

"awaiting the revelation of our Lord Jesus" comes up at length in ch. 15; and

"called into the sharing in common of his Son" (v. 9) may allude to the discussion of the concrete forms of *koinōnia* in ch. 16: the collection to establish *koinōnia* with the Jerusalem church (16:1-4), and the *koinōnia* between Paul, his coworkers, and the Corinthians (16:5-12).

We have therefore a masterful *exordium* that introduces all the major topics of the discourse itself. Furthermore, that this *exordium* twice points the hearer to the future as the time of accountability for actions and decisions in the present is only what one would expect in a deliberative *exordium.*

This section was traditionally just a health wish in Hellenistic letters. But Paul expands the traditional formula considerably. He emphasizes the plenitude of *charismata* that the Corinthians have received and their enrichment in every kind of speech, which surely includes rhetoric, and in knowledge. Then he attempts to temper their focus on the immediate benefits of God's grace with a stress on future eschatology: "awaiting the revelation of Jesus Christ . . . the day of our Lord. . . ." He also stresses their irreproachability, sanctification, and moral integrity, as well as what they have or share in common (i.e., their *koinōnia*), which is Jesus Christ.

It is indeed remarkable that Paul gives thanks for the Corinthians and their spiritual gifts in view of the difficulties both were causing him. He avoids saying "your" spiritual gifts, but speaks of "the grace of God given to you, which has enriched you" (vv. 4f.). He freely admits that they have many valid gifts, but use and abuse of gifts are two different things. V. 6 probably means that the gifts confirm *Paul's* "testimony to Christ," given when he was in Corinth. He adds that the Corinthian Christians are fully equipped with the gifts they need to persevere until the Lord returns (v. 7). This reference to the future, to Christ's appearing, reminds them that even with all their gifts they are not yet complete. What they have is only good enough for the interim.

In v. 8 they are told that when Christ returns he will confirm them to the end of time so that they will be seen as irreproachable on that day, the day of judgment. There are several references to the *yom Yahweh* or "day of the Lord" in this letter, since Paul must remind the audience that their conduct and character and yet to be reviewed. The world to come is not yet here in full, so they must watch themselves. God is faithful to do what he has promised, but the question is whether the Corinthians will likewise be found faithful.

Verse 9 also refers to the *koinōnia* of God's Son, into which the Corinthians have been called. Paul is speaking already here about the real spiritual bond between the believer and Christ, a form of union and communion that Christ's body shares with Christ (cf. 2 Cor. 13:13; Phil. 2:1). Christians must share this bond in common with each other if they are to share it with Christ.[25] There is hardly a more potent or appropriate message that Paul could share with a congregation threatening to come apart at the seams.

One of the major things Paul must get across to his converts in this letter is not only the character of the *ekklēsia* but also its *koinōnia*.

A Closer Look: The Character of the *Ekklēsia* ─────────────

In an important and influential book, Robert Banks has challenged us to reconsider the meaning of just this relationship, that between being the *ekklēsia of God* and "sharing in common."[26] He points out that the development of the term *ekklēsia* moved along the same lines as that of *synagōgos* before it. *Synagōgos* first referred to the gathering of God's people, then to the people who gathered, and finally to the buildings in which they gathered. Since in Paul's day there were no buildings called *ekklēsiae*, at the most we are at a stage where the first and second usages prevail in reference to the Christian community. One must bear in mind that not only was Paul a Pharisaic Jew for whom the synagogue would be the focus of everyday piety, but also that his approach to evangelism, at least for the first period of his ministry, was to go in each city first to a synagogue with the gospel message (if we may believe Luke's portrayal in Acts 13ff.). It is quite likely then that both the Septuagint use of *ekklēsia* for the gathered congregation of God (representing Hebrew *qahal*) and the synagogue setting had much to do with Paul's use of *ekklēsia*.

Banks argues that Paul almost always means by *ekklēsia* a particular local gathering of Christian people. When Paul refers to more than one such gathering he calls them *ekklēsiae*, using the plural (Gal. 1:2; 1 Cor. 16:19; 2 Cor. 8:1; Gal. 1:22). On this basis Banks concludes that "the idea of a unified provincial or national church is as foreign to Paul's thinking as the notion of a universal church."[27] On the former point he may well be right, but in regard to the latter I am not convinced. I suspect that in 1 Cor. 11:22 — "Do you despise the *ekklēsia* of God" — the issue is not just whether the Corinthians despise the local assembly of Christians. More clearly, Gal. 1:13 must refer to Paul persecuting more than one Christian assembly, though he simply says "I persecuted the *ekklēsia* [singular] of God." Thus, it is not correct to conclude with

---

25. J. Y. Campbell, "Κοινωνία and its Cognates in the NT," *JBL* 51 (1932), pp. 352-80, stresses that the normal sense of *koinōnia* is participation with others in something, and so translates here "participation in his Son. . . ." This is possible, and Campbell has also shed considerable doubt on the possibility of ever translating *koinōnia* as "fellowship."

26. R. Banks, *Paul's Idea of Community: The Early House Churches in Their Historical Setting* (Grand Rapids: Eerdmans, 1980).

27. Ibid., p. 37.

Banks that Paul has no vision of the *ekklēsia* as a single entity larger than the local assembly. The local assembly of Christians is, however, Paul's focal point.

Even more crucial for Paul is the fact that each local assembly is a full representation of *the ekklēsia,* not merely a part of it. This becomes especially clear when he uses the body image in 1 Corinthians 12–14 in reference just to the group of Christians in Corinth. They manifest locally all the members of the body of Christ. This means that Paul would deny that a local assembly is but a partial "church," though he might say that it is a part of the universal *ekklēsia.* Each local congregation is a full representation, whether small or large, of the whole body of Christ and of the whole Christ. For Paul, the Corinthian *ekklēsia* is God's whole option in Corinth.[28]

As our comments on 1 Corinthians 8–11 will show (and see also the Introduction above), there were apparently various meetings of Christians in homes in Corinth, and only occasionally did "the whole *ekklēsia*" gather, apparently for the Lord's Supper. This suggests that for all the various assemblies in a particular town to qualify as the unified "*ekklēsia* of God" there, besides some individual meetings there also had to be: (1) meetings of the whole *ekklēsia* in which the sacrament was shared, (2) a responsible, single unit that could be addressed as Paul does the Corinthians, even if they met in various homes and had divisions among them, and (3) a method of helping and supporting each other and so of building up the body of Christ in their locale. If these three criteria were not met, then it is doubtful whether the various assemblies in a given place could be called corporately "the *ekklēsia* of God" in that town. Corporate identity and interaction were needed for the phrase "*ekklēsia* in town X" to be applicable. The Christians needed, in short, to comprise an interacting community of faith, not merely competing local assemblies in the same town. Needless to say, the theology of denominationalism did not arise till well after the Reformation and has no biblical basis.[29]

We must also remember that though there are numerous problems in Corinth, social and theological, Paul still addresses and treats his audience as Christians. His approach is that they are Christians with problems that need correction, not non-Christians with aberrant lifestyles, some of whom even deny the resurrection! Only in the case of an unrepentant sinner is Paul prepared to exercise discipline in the assembly and expel one of its members (5:3-5).

Another crucial idea of Banks is his stress on the dynamic rather than static character of the *ekklēsia.* It is a living organism, not an organization that must grow or atrophy. "Churches" may *have* organizations, structures, and buildings to further their life and work, but once one identifies the *ekklēsia* with some humanly conceived

---

28. Some of this discussion is based on G. D. Fee's lectures in a course on 1 Corinthians.

29. It is in fact a peculiarly Protestant idea and was part of the process of self-legitimation. Paul is trying to lift the sights of the Corinthians to see the *ekklēsia* as something much larger than just one household group or even one set of assemblies in a particular town. To us he might say that there is no justification at all for any sort of exclusive denominationalism (i.e., saying "we are the one true *ekklesia,* and some other Christian group is not"), if not the theology of denominationalism *in toto.*

or constructed organization, structure, or building there are already serious problems in understanding the character of the *ekklēsia*.

> In these early letters of Paul the term *ekklēsia* consistently refers to actual gatherings of Christians as such, or to Christians in a local area conceived or defined as a regularly assembling community. This means that "church" has a distinctly dynamic rather than static character. It is a regular occurrence rather than an ongoing reality. The word is not used of all the Christians who live in a particular locality if they do not in fact gather or when they are not in fact gathering.[30]

Here again Banks has perhaps overstated the matter, but clearly the emphasis in Paul is that believers become *"ekklēsia"* when they assemble with one another for fellowship and worship. That is what "having" or "being" church is all about.

Paul goes even further to talk about earthly Christians as already being part of, or citizens of, a heavenly community as well (Phil. 3:19f.; Gal. 4:25-27; Col. 1:18-24). Here we have the origins of the idea of the *ekklēsia* militant and triumphant. What we do not find anywhere in Paul is the idea of an "invisible" elect *ekklēsia* in the midst of the mass of the unredeemed. The *ekklēsia* militant *is* the visible body of believers in a given locale. Indeed, they are embarrassingly too visible when they sin and fail, as was the case in Corinth.

The local *ekklēsia* is, then, the visible manifestation of an eternal and universal commonwealth. The word did not take on a supranational and supratemporal character because of some international or national organizational structure. Banks stresses that only in Paul's vision of community do we find both the idea of a voluntary association with regular gatherings of like-minded people combined with the notion of supratemporal and spatial identity with those in heaven, and also with the character of the household unit.

That the early church was thought of as a household is shown by use of kinship terms for believers — who are to treat each other as actual brothers and sisters (e.g., 1 Cor. 6:1; 9:5), by the fact that Christians met in houses, and by the fact that they lived by Christian adaptations of household codes or imperatives, adopted for the family of faith (cf. Col. 3:18–4:1).[31] The idea of a family that is family because of shared faith is a uniquely Christian development. Nowhere in the OT is Israel called God's "family," and even at Qumran we have little use of family language. The Qumran literature does use the term "household," but it always refers to the household of truth or of holiness. There is something distinctive in the household setting, family language, and family responsibilities of the early Pauline Christians toward one another. In some respects the *ekklēsia* was closer to the Greco-Roman *collegia* than to the Jewish *synagōgoi*.

The term *sōma* ("body"), when used of the whole group of Christians in a particular locale, is not simply identical in meaning to *ekklēsia*. Paul tends to use *sōma* when the unity of Christians in a particular place is at issue. "Body" language focuses

---

30. Banks, *Paul's Idea*, p. 41.

31. Can modern "megachurches" maintain the family character that is both characteristic and expected in the early church? Can one relate as family to people one does not even know? The Pauline data raises these questions for modern Christians.

more on relationships among Christians and on their responsibilities toward each other, while *ekklēsia* is more of a holistic term that focuses on Christians assembling together in God's presence. Paul speaks of "the *ekklēsia* of God," but never of "the body of God," only "the body of Christ." This is partly because there *was* an assembly *(ekklēsia, qahal)* of God's people before Christ came, but Paul believes God, by making possible faith in the dying and risen Christ, has knit believers together into a body by means of the Holy Spirit. "Body of Christ" is, then, more distinctly Christian than *ekklēsia*. The *sōma* is an entity that could exist only after the Spirit was poured out on all flesh (cf. 1 Cor. 12:12f.). Paul may have been the first to apply the term to a religious community within and smaller than the larger body politic (cf. Seneca *De Clemen.* 1.4.3-5). He uses it to stress the personal reponsibilities Christians have to each other, not to society as a whole.

1 Corinthians is partly an attempt by Paul to help the Corinthians see themselves as part of a larger entity — the people of God meeting in many different places. It was not enough in Paul's mind to give lip service to the reality of the worldwide *ekklēsia.* One must have *koinōnia.* There must be something to share and some means of sharing. At the local level Paul speaks of this entailing actual meeting together and sharing of the Lord's Supper in the context of a meal and worship. Beyond the local level, Paul envisions *koinōnia* involving monetary support of needy congregations elsewhere. In either case, much more than mere rhetoric about "one church . . . universal" is meant.[32]

32. Until the modern *ekklēsia* truly understands that the *ekklēsia* is not buildings, structures, or even organizations (though we must have all of these), but the people of God in every place, and acts on this understanding, our witness will continue to be muted at best. Or to use another metaphor, we will continue to speak with a forked tongue. When one makes the mistake of sacralizing institutions and buildings instead of meeting together and sharing together as the holy people of God, as the *ekklēsia,* it is very difficult to change to meet the needs of our time. Not denominational mergers, but deliberate celebrational union in spirit and substance is what Paul understands being and having *ekklēsia* to mean. *Ekklēsia* without *koinōnia* in both spirit and substance is neither an adequate nor an accurate representation of what we are called to be.

Propositio: 1:10

In Greco-Roman rhetoric the *propositio* is the thesis statement of the entire discourse. In a deliberative discourse it is the main advice the rhetor wants his hearers to heed and is followed by arguments to persuade the audience to follow the course of action that the rhetor recommends. Between these two elements may be a short narration of the facts that led to the rhetor speaking or writing as he does, but such a *narratio* is not required in a deliberative discourse. Nevertheless, Paul chooses to include a brief one (vv. 11-17).

Many deliberative discourses set about to produce agreement or concord in a factious body politic. Thus, it is not surprising that Paul's *propositio* has some notable parallels in the literature, for example, Demosthenes *Ep.* 1.5. The most remarkable parallel in formal terms is in P. Oxy. 3057, which is from the first or second century A.D.[1] It not only begins in almost identical fashion to 1 Cor. 1:10 with "But I exhort you, sister, no longer to have words," but also goes on to urge an alternative to divisive speech, namely concord *(homonoian)* and loving speech.

In an important monograph, C. J. Bjerkelund shows that the verb *parakalō* ("I beseech") plus a following subordinate clause in Paul's letters does not simply introduce parenesis (exhortation) but can also introduce procla-

---

1. I owe these references to M. M. Mitchell, *Paul and the Rhetoric of Reconciliation* (Tübingen: Mohr, 1991), p. 64, n. 210, p. 200, n. 81. The text of the Oxyrynchus papyrus reads in part (lines 11-18):

> *parakalō de se, adelphe, mēketi logon poiesthai, peri tēs kleidos tēs monochopou. ou gar thelō hymas tous adelphous eneka emou hē allou diaphoran tina echein. homonoian gar kai philallēlian euchomai en hymein diamenein hin ēte akatalērētoi kai me ēte homoioi hēmein.*

mation of the gospel. Paul uses the verb to introduce particularly crucial ideas
— here an exhortation to unity, in 4:16 an exhortation to imitation of himself,
and in 16:15 exhortation to acceptance of Stephanas as a local leader. These
represent three of the rhetorical strategies he uses in the letter to overcome
divisions: direct exhortation to the offending parties, modeling, and the attempt to set up effective local leadership. Bjerkelund also notes that Paul uses
parakalō because he is addressing his converts as his children.[2] This idea comes
up more explicitly in 3:1, which suggests that Paul addresses the Corinthians
in this father-children language in part because he sees them as immature in
the faith and wants them to grow up. He is trying to reinforce the thought
that *he* is their sage and father in the faith.

Paul announces at the outset that a major problem that he has heard
about orally is the *schismata* ("cracks, dissensions") within the still somewhat
unified congregation in Corinth (cf. 11:18). The group was in danger of
fragmenting into various pieces because of different kinds of social divisions
and non-unifying behaviors. I agree with Fee that there were probably not
full-blown parties in Corinth, since Paul was able to address the Corinthians
as a whole in this letter.[3] Serious divisions and tensions there were, however,
and Munck's attempt to deny *factionalism* fails to convince, especially in light
of Mitchell's recent extensive demonstration that all of 1 Corinthians is an
exhortation to "concord."[4]

Nor can we follow some exegetes in trying to place the real gravamen
with a "Christ party." Could there really have been a Christ party, since all
were claiming to be Christians? If there had been a group that said simply "we
are of Christ and are above all mere human bickering and name calling," it is
hard to see why Paul would not side with them. As it is, he is appalled by all
such views and opposes factionalism of any sort.

There also seems to be no firm evidence that the main problem for Paul
in Corinth was a Jewish "Peter party." In neither 1 nor 2 Corinthians is circumcision, sabbath observance, or table fellowship between Jewish and Gentile
Christians a real issue. The suggestion that a Peter party was the ascetic faction
in Corinth is improbable since Paul speaks of Peter traveling with a sister as

2. C. J. Bjerkelund, *PARAKALŌ. Form, Funktion und Sinn der Parakalō-Sätze in den paulinischen Briefen* (Oslo: Universitetsforlaget, 1967), pp. 141ff.

3. Cf. G. D. Fee, *The First Epistle to the Corinthians* (Grand Rapids: Eerdmans, 1987), pp. 55ff.

4. Cf. J. Munck, "The Church without Factions: Studies in 1 Corinthians 1–4," in idem, *Paul and the Salvation of Mankind* (London: SCM, 1959), pp. 135-67, and Mitchell, *Reconciliation*, p. 70, n. 30, where she rightly says that Munck's study suffers from a problem of definitions: He uses too modern and extreme a notion of what a faction is. But Munck is right in seeing *sophia* as a major issue in 1 Corinthians.

his wife in 9:5! It is not even clear that Peter had visited Corinth yet, though the same verse may suggest this.

It is clear from ch. 3 that Apollos had indeed been in Corinth and had made some real impact working with Corinthians that Paul had converted earlier. Thus, Paul says that Apollos only "watered" what Paul had "planted" (3:6). Clearly Apollos had a following among some Corinthians. He had affected some Corinthians in the matter of *sophia,* both in its rhetorical form and as esoteric content. These influences had managed to stir up the pot and cause dissensions in the Corinthian congregation.

It is unlikely that we can divide up the evident factions in Corinth simply along the lines of the dissensions mentioned in 1:10ff. I doubt, for instance, that the weak and the strong can be paired off with Peter and Paul respectively. More likely is Theissen's view that the distinction between weak and strong had a sociological basis, reflecting the differences between poorer and richer Corinthian Christians. It would have been the more well-to-do who were invited to temple feasts (ch. 10), who were more likely to be involved in litigation (ch. 6), and who might have been dining early at the Lord's Supper (11:21).[5]

It is also doubtful that we can pair up either the libertines or the ascetics with any apostle's name. All the apostles would repudiate libertine behavior. Ascetic behavior may have gotten encouragement from some of what Paul said while he was in Corinth. But it is more likely that both of these behavior patterns reflected the tensions inherent in a multi-ethnic community, the majority having various sorts of Gentile backgrounds, the minority having a Jewish background. There may be more to the suggestion that the dissensions were partly caused by Corinthians showing favoritism for the one who had baptized them, but if so who was the baptizer for the Christ faction?

Paul, in countering the dissensions, wants all of his audience to "speak the same," to "have the same mind," and to be of the same opinion and so be fit together. The problems are, therefore, intellectual in part and are a matter of diverse *viewpoints* as well as of diverse social conditions or lifestyles. In regard to "speak the same," Lightfoot rightly noted that this clause *(to auto legete)* is a classical expression connoting "to make up differences" between individuals or groups or even "to be at peace" (cf. Thucydides 4.20; Aristotle *Politics,* 2.3.3).[6] It is a major mistake to underestimate Paul's knowledge of classical culture, including Greco-Roman rhetoric.

The *propositio* raises, then, the question of the importance of agreement

---

5. Cf. G. Theissen, *The Social Setting of Pauline Christianity: Essays on Corinth* (Philadelphia: Fortress, 1982), pp. 121ff.

6. J. B. Lightfoot, *Notes on the Epistles of St. Paul* (Winona Lake: Alpha, reprint), p. 151.

on opinions within the *ekklēsia*. Paul does not *demand* here that all agree but rather urges them to do so. This comports with his commitment to use "the art of persuasion" if at all possible with his factious converts. Obviously he believes that it is important for his converts to be in agreement on matters essential to the faith, but in light of what follows in chs. 7–10 it is clear that he is able to distinguish between essential matters and matters of indifference *(adiaphora)* on which equally committed Christians might agree to differ.

What counted as an essential tenet of the faith? From 1 Corinthians one would gather that a proper faith in Christ crucified and in the resurrection was essential in Paul's mind. There was also a need to believe that to be God's assembly it was necessary for the members of the body of Christ to be at peace, to work together, to build up each other, and to put the needs of others before one's own. In the *ekklēsia*, freedom, including freedom to express gifts, must be guided by *agapē*.

The great temptation of a leader is to use raw power rather than persuasion (rhetoric). The great danger for the gifted convert is to use one's gifts as a tool for self-agrandizement and public display. This was an especially great danger in Roman Corinth, where public display, boasting, and the like were considered a necessary and indeed good part of normal life, especially if one wanted to succeed in life. Humility was seen in Greco-Roman culture not as a great virtue but as acting in a servile manner. But Paul scandalously will urge his converts to follow his and Christ's examples of self-sacrificial behavior, going against the the whole directional flow and social value system that was well established in Corinth. To justify this approach, Paul will offer the Corinthians a counter-order wisdom.

Narratio: 1:11-17

The *narratio* in a discourse has the function of stating those facts that generate the discourse, or in a forensic discourse those that constitute the charge or basis of the charge. It is necessary that the facts be stated *before* arguments are made, so the *narratio* stands before the *probatio* or proofs.

In 1 Corinthians the *narratio* serves the purpose of disarming at least some of the audience. It reveals that Paul knows more about what is going on in Corinth than what he was allowed to know in the letter written to him. Since apparently the report of factiousness has come orally to Paul (cf. 1:11 and 11:18), the main problems were reported in what he has *heard* rather than in what he has read in the Corinthians' letter, though he must take both seriously. The oral report seems to have given Paul the necessary clue as to the basic problem and the underlying cause of the various difficulties in Corinth.

There is an accusatory tone to the *narratio* here, almost like that of a forensic speech where "we make our statement of facts the opening of an incrimination of the other party" (Quintilian *Inst. Or.* 4.2.26). It is easy for this reason to see why Dahl and others have mistaken some of the material in chs. 1–4 for an *apologia* of sorts.[1] Nevertheless, these chapters are not a defense but rather an exposition of true wisdom (as offered in the gospel) meant to cause the Corinthians to decide to change their factious behavior. It is an

---

1. N. A. Dahl, *Studies in Paul* (Minneapolis: Augsburg, 1977), pp. 40-61. Dahl admits that calling this material "apologetic" may be misleading and one-sided (p. 61, n. 50). Here, as in 1 Corinthians 9, one must ask the *function* of the material, and chs. 1–4 do not function as a defense of Paul's gospel. On the contrary, the whole section is meant to persuade the Corinthians to change their behavior on the basis of a statement of the real character of godly wisdom and of the true sage.

exhortation to concord using the example of Christ and of the gospel as the standards for true wisdom and hence for true Christian behavior.

A *narratio* is supposed to be short and lucid, describing the *exigence* or problem that prompts the discourse and saying no more than is necessary and sufficient (*Inst. Or.* 4.2.45). It is important to cite briefly a credible witness to the discourse's subject, so that the initial premise (in 1 Corinthians, that there are factions that must be overcome) cannot be disputed.

Here the witnesses are "Chloe's people," members of the Corinthian congregation who have firsthand knowledge of the situation. We do not know whether these people were Chloe's slaves or members of her family, though the former is more likely.[2] In ancient society slaves had a wide variety of roles, including serving as business agents for their owners, as Chloe's people are likely to have been doing. "Slaves served in occupations ranging from personal stewards, custodians of children (*paidagogoi*) to grammarians, geometricians, musicians, managers of farms, masters of ships, estate stewards (*oikonomoi*) and money-lenders."[3] Slaves were not necessarily people of poor background and little education. Some slaves were reasonably well-to-do, well-educated people who were then captured in some Roman conquest. These conquests were the major source of slaves for the empire. Furthermore, numerous people sold themselves into slavery because of economic necessity. There was often more security and more possibility for advancement as a slave than as a free poor person. This does not mean that slavery was a good thing, but in order to perpetuate this huge pool of relatively low cost labor, the Romans had built into the system certain advantages not available to free poor people. These advantages also served as hedges against slave revolt.

Chloe herself was probably a businesswoman prominent in the Christian congregation in Corinth and perhaps one of Paul's first converts there. Her loyalty to Paul is shown by the oral report she sends him. Doubtless some of the Christians in Corinth had been converted by Apollos and others and so did not have this natural bond with Paul. Nevertheless, Paul seems to assume that he is the one father in the faith of the overwhelming majority of Corinthian Christians, and he characterizes Apollos's role as primarily that of nurturing ("watering") those who are already Christians (3:6).

2. It is possible that Chloe's people were members of her house congregation, but if so this is an odd way of putting it. Would Paul really have used a phrase suggesting "people who belong to Chloe" if he simply meant that?

3. W. G. Rollins, "Greco-Roman Slave Terminology," *SBL 1987 Seminar Papers*, ed. K. H. Richards (Atlanta: Scholars, 1987), pp. 100-110, here p. 102.

Immediately after the thesis statement in v. 10, Paul discusses in the *narratio* what he has heard in the disturbing oral report brought by Chloe's people to Paul in Ephesus, which shed new light on a letter he had already received from the Corinthians. Fee and others have suggested that in 1:10–6:20 Paul is responding to the oral report, whereas in the rest of the letter, starting with the reference to the letter in 7:1, he is responding to the letter. But this is unlikely, not only because of 11:18 ("I hear . . ."), but also because *peri de* (7:1, 25; 8:1; 12:1; 16:1, 12) can be simply a topic marker, not necessarily an indication of a subject in a letter that Paul has received.

In **1:11**, Paul speaks of *erides* — rivalries, quarrels, or dissensions — among the Corinthian Christians (cf. 11:18f.). There seem to have been attempts at one-upmanship involving boasting about one's affiliation with Paul, Apollos, or other leaders. Paul characterizes all such quarrels as nonsense and infantile, for no *apostolos* or teacher should be the focus of faith. No "called agent" of Christ died for their sins (v. **13**), and Christ is not divided.[4]

Why should there have been such rivalry and quarrels over various Christian teachers? Probably the Corinthians were caught up in the pattern of behavior that characterized those who were zealous for oratory and eloquence and became the students of the various famous Sophists and other rhetors. Dio Chrysostom records that when he visited a great city of the empire such as Corinth he was "escorted with much enthusiasm *(zēlos)* and respect *(philotimia)*, the recipients of my visits being grateful for my presence and begging me to address them and advise them and flocking around my door from early dawn, . . . all without my having incurred any expense or having made any contribution" (47:22). Corinth was a city especially known for such behavior, as is seen in Dio's description of Corinth at the time of Diogenes:

> That was the time, too, when one could hear crowds of wretched Sophists around Poseidon's temple shouting and reviling one another, their disciples,

---

4. The stress by L. L. Welborn, "On the Discord in Corinth: 1 Corinthians 1–4 and Ancient Politics," *JBL* 106 (1987), pp. 85-111 (and also M. M. Mitchell), on the use of political terms by Paul to describe the problematic situation in Corinth is correct, but it is important to ask how such language functions in Paul's discourse. It is not surprising to find such political terms as *schismata* in a Pauline deliberative discourse, since deliberative discourses were often used to resolve conflicts and produce concord in the Greek city-states. But Paul does not think of the Christian *ekklēsia* as like the secular assembly, nor is the strife in a city identical to that in a congregation. Here we are dealing with divisions over teachers, not over political figures, and abuse of spiritual gifts is part of the cause of the problems. The situation is more like a division over rhetors. For this reason I prefer to speak of social divisions, not political divisions, in the Christian *ekklēsia*. T. Engberg-Pedersen, "The Gospel and Social Practice according to 1 Corinthians," *NTS* 33 (1987), pp. 557-84, here p. 561, has the balance about right: "There is conflict with regard to theological self-understanding, to social practice, and to personal commitment."

as they were called, fighting with one another, many writers reading aloud their stupid works, many poets reciting their poems while others applauded them . . . , and peddlers not a few peddling whatever they happened to have. (8.9)

Lest his readers pass this off as the errors of a bygone age, Dio says that he has given this example because in his judgment the same sort of disgusting behavior was still going on in places like Corinth, and he wishes to steer his audience in another direction: toward *arete* (virtue).

Philostratus confirms this scenario, relating that on one occasion the pupils of a Sophist became so incensed at insults being heaped on their teacher that they ordered their slaves to beat a rival orator, who subsequently died (*Lives* 588). Loyalty to such teachers and orators could be intense, setting off violent rivalries. Dio says that the definition of a *mathetes* or disciple of such an orator or teacher was "zealot." "For whoever really follows anyone surely knows what that person was like, and by imitating his acts and words he tries as best he can to make himself like him. But that is precisely, it seems, what the pupil *(ho mathetes)* does — by imitating his teacher and paying heed to him he tries to acquire his art . . ." (55.1, 3, 5). It is no wonder that Paul takes factiousness over Christian teachers so seriously.

Paul came to Corinth with an anti-Sophistic strategy because of what he saw to be the character of the gospel and the role of Christ's called agent. The last passage quoted from Dio's oration above will help us later to understand Paul's call for the Corinthians to imitate him (11:1) — which is given only after Paul has portrayed himself as an enslaved sage. He is offering a very different model of *sophia* both in form and in content than that offered by the Sophists.[5] The Sophists sought *doxa* — glory and glorification — from the crowds. Paul, as we shall see in 2 Corinthians, sought and reflected a very different sort of *doxa*, not a glory from the crowds but a reflection of the glory of God in the face of Christ.[6]

1:14-17 has often led scholars who know of initiation rituals in Greco-Roman mystery religions to wonder if the Corinthians did not have a magical view of baptism. In view of 15:29 it seems likely that at least some of the Corinthian converts did have such a view.[7] This could explain why Paul goes

5. Here I am greatly indebted to B. W. Winter's seminal work, *Are Philo and Paul among the Sophists? A Hellenistic Jewish and a Christian Response to a First Century Movement* (dissertation, Macquarrie University, 1988, publication forthcoming).

6. J. Munck, *Paul and the Salvation of Mankind* (London: SCM, 1959), pp. 160f., rightly sees that the Corinthians are aligning themselves with various Christian wisdom teachers, and notes the connection with rhetoric (pp. 158f., n. 1).

7. Cf. the graffito on the wall of the Santa Prisca Mithraeum in Rome: "Reborn to eternity through secret baptism." This has been considered a Christian forgery, but the

on in 2:6ff. to argue that he also offers a *mystērion* to those who are mature in the faith.

Paul does not repudiate baptism in vv. 14-17, though he does reject the Corinthians' inflation of the importance of who baptized whom and of what actually happened to the convert through water baptism. In such an environment, Paul is thankful that he did not baptize many. It is impossible to believe Paul could ever have said "I thank God that I did not *convert* many of you," but he does make this sort of remark about baptism. He sees the preaching of God's word, not baptism, as the change agent, coupled no doubt with the work of the Holy Spirit. Thus, he sees his basic task as preaching the gospel, not baptizing everyone.

It may be significant that Paul mentions baptism and Christ's death in the same breath (cf. Romans 6), but he makes nothing of the connection here. He says that he baptized Crispus and Gaius. This Crispus is probably the synagogue ruler mentioned in Acts 18 as one who was converted by Paul and then baptized. Thus there are apparently some notables from the synagogue in Corinth that Paul converted.[8] It is possible but unprovable that Gaius is Titus Justus Gaius (Acts 18:7).

The baptizing of whole households, such as that of Stephanas, raises interesting questions. In 16:17 Paul identifies this household as the first converts in Achaia, the region or province in Greece that included Corinth. Without debating what it meant to baptize households, the household tables (Col. 3:18–4:1) may suggest that not only free adults but also infants, children, and slaves were involved.[9] In Roman religion it was the normal, though not universal, practice that the religion of the family was determined by the head of the household, and the other household members normally followed suit.[10]

---

word "secret" seems to rule out that possibility. Whether by pagan or Christian hand it attests to the belief that through baptism some supernatural transformation would take place. Cf. R. MacMullen, *Paganism in the Roman Empire* (New Haven: Yale University, 1981), pp. 54, 171, n. 15.

8. This reference in 1 Corinthians to Crispus may provide indirect evidence that Luke has correctly portrayed Paul's missionary strategy as going to the synagogue first in each city.

9. But would Paul have counted small children or infants among the *aparchē*, the "firstfruits," in Achaia?

10. We cannot be certain that infants, small children, and slaves were baptized. Much depends on how one views baptism. Is it in essence a response by the believer to grace already given, or is it a sign and symbol of God's gracious prevenient action in a person's life before he or she responds? That baptism is sometimes associated with faith and repentance in the NT does not settle the issue because missionary baptisms of people entering the community from the outside by choice are different from baptisms of people raised in the *ekklēsia* , children of believers, said by Paul to be *hagioi* (holy, clean, or set apart, 7:14). The NT was written before the question of the relation of children to baptism and faith was seriously raised. At first, all entered the community of faith from the outside.

It is fair to say that early Christians, including Paul, viewed baptism as a boundary marker. Its practice made the *ekklēsia* aware of who was in the fold and showed that the larger community agreed with this judgment. For Paul, ethical and theological realities were more important than the baptismal symbol of such realities in determining who was in and who was out. One could do without baptism and still be in, but not the reverse.[11]

Paul loved to use rhetorical questions, and when such a question begins with *mē*, as in v. **13b**, it expects a negative answer (cf. 12:29f.). Frequently in this letter Paul uses rhetorical questions as figures of thought. Quintilian explains them as follows: "a question involves a figure, whenever it is employed not to get information, but to emphasize our point. . . . The objective is to increase the force and cogency of proof" (*Inst. Or.* 9.2.6f.). The author of *Rhetorica ad Herrennium* reminds the reader that "not all *interrogatio* is impressive or elegant, but that interrogation is that which, when the points against the adversaries' cause have been summed up, reinforces the argument that has been delivered . . ." (4.16.22). Though we have not yet reached the full-fledged arguments, even here these questions have a way of summing up and reinforcing Paul's complaint, as those in 10:29f. also do.[12]

Paul says in v. **17** that his preaching was not in the wisdom of words, that is, not with a kind of wisdom that amounts to mere words without comparable content. Paul does not use the approach a Sophist would, where there was such an emphasis on form that *sophia* became virtually identical with eloquence rather than content. He will go on to contrast divine wisdom with mere human wisdom (vv. 20-25). The latter is skill in oratory and doubtless also in Greco-Roman *philosophia.*

Paul associates wisdom with the Greeks or Gentiles in 1:22, but it also seems that Apollos has introduced Hellenistic Jewish wisdom in a rhetorical form as part of his mediation of the gospel in Corinth. Some Corinthians much preferred this smooth presentation to Paul's simple and less polished

11. See below on ch. 5. S. C. Barton, "Paul's Sense of Place: An Anthropological Approach to Community Formation in Corinth," *NTS* 32 (1986), pp. 225-46, here pp. 226f., notes that the function of boundary markers is to separate order from chaos, dirt from non-dirt, friend from stranger, life from death, heaven from hell, and so on. For Paul belief and behavior are the primary markers, not ritual action, and thus Paul seems to take a different view from some of the Corinthians. M. Y. MacDonald, *The Pauline Churches* (Cambridge: Cambridge University, 1988), p. 76, is correct in saying that

> the impression of a team of fellow workers gained from his letters suggests a certain common understanding of how communities should be organized and who should be allowed to come in. It seems safe to assume that Paul's understanding of the unity of Gentiles and Jews was shared by at least some of the members of his communities.

12. On this subject, cf. D. F. Watson, "1 Corinthians 10:23–11:1 in the Light of Greco-Roman Rhetoric: The Role of Rhetorical Questions," *JBL* 108 (1989), pp. 301-18.

approach. Thus, it is not merely skill in rhetorical form that is at issue, but also the content of wisdom. For Paul, wisdom has to do with Christ on the cross and the Spirit in the *ekklēsia,* but for the Corinthians it seems almost exclusively pneumatic. Lightfoot in his note on the word *kenōthē* ("be emptied," v. 17) says that Paul means "dwindle to nothing, vanish under the weight of rhetorical ornament and dialectic subtlety," which is surely on the right track.[13] There is both a form and a content to Corinthian wisdom that empty the cross, and Paul must oppose both. Corinthian wisdom leads to boasting and human exaltation, not the lifting up of the crucified Christ. Some in Corinth had a taste for exaltation christology, but not for the theology of the cross.

This section of 1 Corinthians cautions against too exalted a view of baptism. For Paul what was central to his ministry and to the whole process of making converts was preaching, *not* baptizing. This counts against all magical views of baptism, whether of infants or of adults.[14] Paul sees baptism as an initiation rite, a sign of God's work in or for a person's life, to be associated with the crucifixion of Christ. It does not follow from this that he also saw it as a means of grace, and 1:14 counts against such a view. Baptism is not a means of conversion, nor is it necessary for conversion.[15] If the NT is clear about anything, it is that baptism should happen very close to the time when one is converted or enters the community of Christ, at whatever age that may be, because baptism symbolizes the transition or passage into the community of Christian faith.[16]

---

13. J. B. Lightfoot, *Notes on the Epistles of Saint Paul* (Winona Lake: Alpha Publications, reprint), p. 157.

14. The warning here against overestimating not just baptism but also the baptizer, preacher, or teacher is relevant to our own time, in which cults of personality develop around particular preachers or teachers. I suspect that this situation would have led Paul to ask the same sort of questions of us that he asks of the Corinthians: "Was John Calvin or John Wesley or Martin Luther or Billy Graham crucified for you? Or were you baptized into the name of any prominent *modern* preacher?"

One also wonders about preaching that empties the cross, that may be "full of sound and fury" but in fact is "signifying nothing." Many elegant and sophisticated sermons given in the late twentieth century have in fact neglected the heart of the gospel message about the crucified and risen Christ. The point of v. 17 is not that one should not give attention to form or detail in preaching, but that form is no substitute for content and should not detract or subtract from that content. This is why Paul approached the preaching task as he did in Roman Corinth, where there was a climate that encouraged the idea that "image — outward appearance — is everything."

15. It is also relevant to point out that the later Pauline literature stresses that baptism is *one* (Eph. 4:5), perhaps because it is an initiation rite, and by definition one can only enter the body of Christ for the first time *once.* Thereafter, if one strays one may *return* to the fold, but baptism is not a ritual of return, any more than it was intended to be a ritual of confirmation of a faith already long held firm.

16. The difficulty is in discerning when that transition actually happens for the

While Paul is very concerned in this letter to establish clearer moral and social boundaries for the Christian commuity in Corinth, he has little interest in using water baptism as the definitive boundary marker. A faith response to the preaching is what Paul sees as critical.[17]

---

children of believing parents. Some, while sincerely Christian people, nonetheless cannot pinpoint an exact moment when they made the transition from darkness to light. Even on a cursory reading of Acts, one must be impressed that not everyone had a Pauline Damascus road experience as they came to Christ. God can transform a person as quietly or as dramatically as God wills. What is most crucial is not so much *when* or even necessarily *how* one is saved, but *that* one is saved by whatever providential means, process, or persons God chooses to use. A good deal of harm has been done to some Christians, especially in Protestant churches, by insisting that unless they had some particular *kind* of conversion experience like Paul's, their Christianity is somehow suspect or of an inferior sort.

During the course of church history as the *ekklēsia* sought to regularize the practice of baptism, some began to treat it as the Christian version of circumcision, that is, as an initiation ritual, often administered prior to a faith response of the one initiated, while others treated it as a sort of Christian bar mitzvah rite, that is, as something that one participated in when one reached "the age of decision" and could freely commit oneself to the covenant community. Baptism was thus focussed on particular stages in human life when it was deemed appropriate. Well before the Middle Ages, the most prevalent practice of the Christian *ekklēsia* was infant baptism.

It is safe to say that the NT does not make perfectly clear which of these directions, if any, the church should pursue in its baptismal practice, or else we would not still be having heated debates about such matters nearly 2000 years later. It is also safe to say that both sides of the infant baptism debate have shipped some water in both their teaching and their practice of the rite down through the centuries.

17. This passage must surely challenge if not condemn denominational splits based on differing baptismal theologies and practices, much less splits based on how much water one uses in the rite of baptism — something the word *baptizō* and its cognates do not in themselves indicate with any quantifiable clarity. This passage is equally fatal to modern notions that one becomes a full member of an *ekklēsia* or is joined to the body of Christ through baptism. What is critical is preaching and the response to preaching, which is how one comes to Christian faith. But this is no attempt to denigrate water baptism, which is a beautiful and meaningful symbol of entrance, a rite of initiation commanded by Christ (Matt. 28:19). One's theology of baptism must not be allowed to take away from a proper theology of salvation coming through a faith response to the preached word.

Probatio: 1:18–16:12

Argument I, Division 1: 1:18-31

The Wisdom of the Cross, Wisdom on the Cross

In a deliberative speech or letter the "proofs" or arguments seek not to prove something true or false, as in a forensic speech, but to provide reasons for the hearers to take up the course of action that is being advised. The rhetor will usually seek to show that it is to the advantage or benefit of the listeners to take up a particular course of action in the future, though sometimes the stress is on the honorable course of action to choose.[1]

Paul's concern in this letter is with the unity of the Christian community and with the factors working against that unity. Therefore, throughout the letter he will seek to argue against factors that compromise unity while providing positive arguments in favor of that which "builds up," "benefits," or is "useful" to the body of Christ.[2] Terms like *sympheron* ("useful, benefit," cf.

---

1. M. M. Mitchell, *Paul and the Rhetoric of Reconciliation* (Tübingen: Mohr, 1991), p. 202.

2. Maximus of Tyre *Or.* 25.6 argues that of the four main virtues wisdom is most necessary for a deliberative oration. Paul's stress on wisdom in chs. 1–4 may therefore be in part an attempt to show that he has the proper knowledge and ethos to carry out a deliberative discourse. H. F. North, "The Concept of *Sophrosyne* in Greek Literary Criticism," *Classical Philology* 43 (1948), pp. 1-17, here p. 2: "Throughout the history of ancient

12:7) and *oikodomē* and its cognates (upbuilding, cf. 8:1, etc.) become critical in such an argument.

To this end, Paul will provide both "artificial" and "inartificial" arguments. The latter are arguments that the rhetor does not create but rather, as Quintilian says, come from, "decisions of previous courts, rumors, evidence extracted by torture, documents, oaths, and witnesses" (5.1.2). Some of these categories apply more readily to forensic speeches, but Paul at various crucial junctures in his argument appeals to such external authorities as Scripture (cf. 3:19-20), nature (11:14), church tradition (15:3-7), and evidence from oral reports or a letter addressed to him by the Corinthians. The primary witnesses who reveal the actual situation are apparently "Chloe's people" (1:11).

Artificial arguments are those that the rhetor generates himself, a good example of which is Paul's first argument (1:18ff.). Paul argues that "the word about the cross" is wisdom and is counter to all merely human standards or expectations about wisdom. In such circumstances he cannot appeal to previous authorities very easily, but must stress the effect of the preaching of this wisdom on the Corinthians themselves. The appeal to the audience's experience is crucial for Paul, in both 1 and 2 Corinthians, not least because the Corinthians seem to be so experientially oriented in their whole approach to Christianity. It is likely that if this sort of appeal failed, other arguments would not prevail either.

One can tell when Paul is really exercised about something by the way he argues. He will either, as in 1 Cor. 11:2ff., pull out all the stops and use many different sorts of authorities and arguments to enforce his argument, or at or near the climax of an argument he will resort to quoting Scripture or to using emotionally charged rhetorical questions that make the opponents' viewpoint look foolish (cf. 3:19-20; 14:36). These sorts of appeals provide clues as to when Paul is coming to closure in an argument. They show that Paul is an effective rhetor, for he knows how and when to use logic and witnesses and how and when to use emotion to sway the audience.

In general, arguments that depend on an appeal to *pathos* are more dependent on the style and tone of delivery than arguments appealing to logic. Since Paul uses such emotive arguments even in his letters, I suspect that he chose messengers to deliver and *perform* these letters with some consideration of their speaking abilities, so that these nuances would not be missed by the audience. Oral performance was one area in which some Corinthians thought Paul to be weak as a rhetor (2 Cor. 10:10). This may be one reason he kept sending surrogates and letters in his place.[3] Possibly the disastrous painful visit (2 Corinthians 2–3) supports this conclusion.

---

rhetoric, the Greeks and Romans tended to believe that style reflects character and that *sophrosyne* [moderation], together with the other virtues, is essential to the good orator."

3. S. M. Pogoloff, *Logos and Sophia: The Rhetorical Situation of 1 Corinthians* (Atlanta:

Isocrates reminds us that in a deliberative speech anyone "who wants to change your opinions must touch on many matters and must speak at length, reminding, then rebuking, then commending, and then advising you" (*Or.* 8.27). This is a very adequate description of 1 Corinthians, for in it there are a wide variety of arguments and subarguments, usually introduced by *peri de* (7:1, 25; 8:1; 12:1; 16:1, 12) or by phrases like "I do not want you to be ignorant" (10:1), "I would remind you" (15:1), or "I want you to under-stand" (11:3).

Paul realized that when he was dealing with a complex matter such as the eating and idol feast question (chs. 8–10) or spiritual gifts (chs. 12–14), it was a sign of a good rhetor to digress in mid-argument to relieve the tension and monotony of a long argument. Dionysius of Halicarnassus, in praising Isocrates's rhetorical skill, says that he knew when to introduce a digression in a deliberative speech "to relieve monotony by varying the treatment of the different elements of the subject and by introducing digressions from *external* sources" (*Isoc.* 4). This raises interesting questions about whether 1 Corinthians 13 or 2 Cor. 6:14–7:1 might be preexisting pieces introduced into the argument by Paul, following the rules about digressions.

W. Wuellner suggests that the rhetorical strategy of Paul in much of 1 Corinthians is not just to answer the Corinthians' questions, but more importantly to question answers they already had.[4] This is especially the case in 1:18-31: Paul is convinced that the Corinthians have a skewed vision of what amounts to wisdom, and he must correct it. The term *sophia* ("wisdom") is found seventeen times in 1 Corinthians, sixteen of those in chs. 1–3, but only eleven times elsewhere in Paul's letters. So the concept it represented is obviously of prime concern in this part of Paul's argument. *Sophia* was used not only of content, but also of form, particularly of rhetorical eloquence.[5] There is evidence from pagan inscriptions that such "wisdom" was seen as a

---

Scholars Press, 1992), p. 149, is right to point out that Paul's allowance that he might be seen as an *idiotēs* in oral performance (2 Cor. 11:6) does not distinguish him from others who had an expert knowledge of rhetoric but were teachers, not public orators. Isocrates, one of the great experts in rhetoric, was also said to be an *idiotēs* because he wrote rhetorically brilliant pieces but did not orally perform them, claiming not to be gifted in oral delivery (cf. Isocrates *Against the Sophists* 14). It is likely that what *idiotēs* means in both cases is that Paul and Isocrates do not claim to be professional orators. It does not mean that they do not know rhetoric.

4. W. Wuellner, "Paul as Pastor: The Function of Rhetorical Questions in First Corinthians," in *L'Apôtre Paul. Personalité, Style et Conception du Ministère* (Leuven: Leuven University, 1986), pp. 49-77, here p. 55.

5. Cf. C. Senft, *La première épître de Saint-Paul aux Corinthiens* (Neuchâtel: Dela-chaux, 1979), p. 36.

gift from above.[6] In view of the fact that Paul uses *sophia* only sporadically elsewhere, it may be that here Paul is picking up and redirecting the favorite vocabulary of the Corinthians concerning wisdom, knowledge, and the Spirit. Herodotus *Hist.* 4.77 reminds us that "All *Hellenes* are zealous for *pasan sophian*," that is, for all kinds of wisdom or learning.

In v. **18** Paul sets out a dramatic contrast. It is easy to see why a crucified messiah or God would be foolish to Gentiles. How can one be powerful if one suffers the ultimate penalty from Rome? It is also easy to see why a crucified messiah would be a a scandal *(skandalon)* to Jews (v. 23). They looked for a messiah who would come and triumph over their foes, not be executed by them! A crucified Messiah was an oxymoron, a contradiction in terms. It does not appear that Isaiah 53 was thought to refer to the messiah in early Judaism.[7] As for the pagan reaction to the idea of a crucified God there is the famous caricature drawing and inscription found in Rome on the Palatine that shows a slave falling down before a crucified donkey under which there are the words "Alexamenos worships [his] god."

The word *skandalon* does not focus on something that trips one up (a "stumbling block," the usual translation), but rather something that grossly offends, something scandalous. To make his point, in v. 19 Paul partially quotes Isa. 29:14 from the LXX, with his own modifications. Whereas in the original there is reference to political leaders and their counselors, Paul in v. 20 refers to the sage (whether Jewish or Gentile), the expert in the law (the Jewish scribe),[8] and the debater or Sophist (who liked to bat around concepts abstractly, declaiming on this or that subject).[9] Isocrates says in his discourse "Against Sophists" 10:

6. Cf. *New Doc. 3*, p. 48, of a Roman woman from Smyrna who was given wisdom from God.

7. We may yet find such evidence at Qumran, as there are now some hints of such a view in the materials recently made public. I have not yet been able to see and analyze those data.

8. *Grammatikoi* in Isaiah does not correspond to *grammateus* here. *Grammateus* can hardly have its non-Jewish meaning here of "secretary" as in Acts 19:35. It may be, therefore, that Paul uses terms to include all those considered wise according to two different cultural orientations.

9. On identification of the debater as the Sophist, cf. Pogoloff, *Logos and Sophia*, p. 160; E. Best, "The Power and the Wisdom of God, 1 Corinthians 1:18–2:5," in *Paolo a una chiesa divisa (1 Co. 1–4)*, ed. L. de Lorenzi (Rome: Abbazia di S Paolo fuori le mura, 1980), pp. 9-41, here p. 20. Best also speculates that the Corinthians saw Paul as the Jewish sage, Apollos as the debater, and Peter as the scribe, but would Peter really fit that category, especially if, as Galatians 2 says, he lived as a Gentile? More likely (as noted in n. 8 above), Paul is simply using terms that include all those seen as wise in antiquity, i.e., the sage or philosopher, the exegete, and the debater or rhetor.

On the supposed conventional nature of this triad, cf. W. Wuellner, "Ursprung und Verwendung der σοφός-, δυνατός-, εὐγενής-Formel in 1 Kor 1,26," in *Donum Gentilicum*,

They transmit the science of "words" as simply as they teach the letters of the alphabet, without bothering to examine the nature of each kind of knowledge, but thinking that because of the extravagance of their promises they will command admiration and that the teaching of discourse will be held in high esteem. They are thus oblivious to the fact that the arts are made great, not by those who boast about them without scruple, but by those who are able to discover all the resources that each art affords.

Paul, like Isocrates and Cicero, is concerned to oppose Sophistic rhetoric that makes oratory an end in itself, divorcing it from philosophy or true wisdom.[10]

Thus, Paul's opposition is not to rhetoric per se but to any form of speaking that emptied the gospel of its content and power and to any form of philosophy that did not comport with the counter-order wisdom Paul as a sage believed he had received through revelation and was called upon to dispense. These two things are what Paul means by merely human *sophia*.[11]

Paul speaks in v. 18 of those "being saved." He speaks of salvation in all three tenses: past (Rom. 8:24), present and ongoing (1 Cor. 15:2), and future (Rom. 10:9, 13). For Paul salvation entails a good deal more than the experience of becoming a new creature in Christ. That is but the beginning of the salvation process, which is not complete until the believer is completely redeemed and conformed to the image of Christ at the resurrection. When he uses *sōtēria* of a *present* experience or event, as do various other NT writers, he does so in a way that stands out from the usual senses of this word and its cognates in Greco-Roman literature.

Salvation in the NT is not a matter of being snatched by the gods from personal peril nor a matter of well-being or of "health of body and soul" in a strictly physical or temporal sense as in Greek understanding; nor is it

---

ed. C. K. Barrett, et al. (Oxford: Clarendon, 1978), pp. 165-84. Surely what is most notable about the phrase is how Paul alters it.

10. Cf. Isocrates *Antidosis* 260-77; Cicero *De inventione* 1.1.1ff. The discussion of these texts by H. D. Betz in "The Problem of Rhetoric and Theology according to Paul," in *L'Apôtre*, pp. 16-48, here pp. 28ff., is helpful, but his insistence on describing the milieu and *philosophia* of both the Corinthians and Paul in Roman Corinth as "Hellenistic" is somewhat misleading. One needs to speak of the Roman adaptation of such things in Corinth and of what the Romans added to earlier Hellenistic thought and rhetoric. Corinth was not Athens and should not be treated as if its character in A.D. 50 were simply "Greek" in the Hellenistic sense of the term.

11. As J. W. Beaudean, *Paul's Theology of Preaching* (Macon: Mercer University, 1988), p. 114, points out, when Paul says he did not arrive in Corinth preaching with a *hyperochē* of word or wisdom (2:1), he means he did not overwhelm the Corinthians with an abundance or superiority of words. He abstained from ornamental rhetoric that tries to overpower the audience with its impressive verbosity. The term reflects a conscious choice or strategy on Paul's part.

simply the guarantee of life after death mediated by a "magical sacramental act" as with the Mysteries; nor is it a matter of liberation of the people of God from their enemies, as in late Judaism. Salvation in the NT in general, but in Paul specifically is the liberating not of the soul, but the whole person, from sin and its effects, including the divine wrath. As such, *sōtēria* in Paul is both a present (realized) and future (yet to be realized) reality, including not only the self but all creation.[12]

When Paul speaks of salvation in the present tense there is a personal and apolitical character to the term. It entails the transformation of an individual spiritually, morally, and intellectually so that the person has a new worldview and a new capacity to be faithful to that worldview enabled by the Holy Spirit. Present salvation does not necessarily transform a person physically, for Paul sees that happening at the resurrection. Thus the *sōtēria* Paul offered meant something rather different from what was offered at the Asklepion where physical health and wellness were the very *raison d'être* for the religion.

This is not to say that Paul did not believe in miracles of healing, but that he, like Jesus, does not see that as the essence of what *sōtēria* is all about. Healings are acts of compassion performed on request. If asked, Paul might have stressed that such healing can only have temporary benefits and thus cannot be identified with what he means when he speaks of an *eternal* state of affairs that begins in this life and continues into the next. Only resurrection can finally remedy the problem of disease, decay, and death that affects all people. It is surprising how seldom the subject of miracles comes up in the Pauline corpus.

A Closer Look: Pagan Views of Salvation ─────────────────

To the modern person it comes as somewhat of a surprise how seldom ancient pagans express any hope for or interest in eternal life or personal resurrection. What they generally sought from religion was blessings in the present such as health, wealth, rescue from peril, or the promise of a good harvest or of a child. This is especially clear when one reads through the numerous personal questions asked of the oracle at Delphi: "How may I become a parent?" "What can I say or do to please the gods?" "Shall I succeed?" "What is the truth about X?" "Where shall I go or settle?"[13] All the questions are about affairs in this lifetime and about how things will turn out. They

12. W. G. Rollins, "Greco-Roman Slave Terminology and Pauline Metaphors for Salvation," *SBL 1987 Seminar Papers*, ed. K. H. Richards (Atlanta: Scholars, 1987), pp. 100-110, here pp. 100f.

13. J. Fontenrose, *The Delphic Oracle: Its Responses and Operations* (Berkeley: University of California, 1978), p. 39.

are prompted by disease, death, plague, famine, war, problems of rulership, career opportunities, desire for marriage, infertility, portents in the heavens, and the like. In short, the oracle was looked to for answers about mundane matters, even if they were quite important mundane matters. We will say more about pagan prophecy when we discuss 1 Corinthians 14.

MacMullen points out that even in some of the Oriental cults that were growing in power and popularity during the Roman Empire, though there may be talk of a god rising from the dead, the evidence is lacking that the worshipper asked for the same experience for himself or herself. Even in a cult in which the initiate undergoes ritual cleansing by the blood of a bull, it appears reasonably certain that what the initiate hoped to gain was new virility and extension of earthly life in a state of ritual purity, not life after death.[14] Though some few hoped to reach the Elysian Fields, in general salvation to a pagan meant a material benefit sought in and for this life. MacMullen, having reviewed the inscriptional evidence, writes:

> "Savior" in them, or "salvation," had to do with health or other matters of this earth, not of the soul for eternal life. Or in epitaphs, people so often joke about annihilation that the jokes at last congeal into commonplaces or abbreviations: "I was not, I am not, I care not," boiled down to six letters [n(on) f(ui), n(on) s(um), n(on) c(uro)].[15]

It is hardly surprising that some of the converts at Corinth had this worldly view of the benefits of faith in Christ, or were able to think that there was no future bodily resurrection of the dead. It is easy to see why from Paul's point of view pagans before they convert to Christ are "without hope and without God in this world" (Eph. 2:12).

It was not God's plan that the world should be able to know God on the basis of its own wisdom; rather, God was to be revealed through the foolishness of preaching. Paul is not suggesting that a person can have no knowledge through human endeavor, but specifically that one cannot know *God* through human wisdom.[16] God is known through God's self-revelation. Paul expounds a wisdom from above that counters human expectations about the character of wisdom. This wisdom has to do with the salvation made possible through Christ's apparent weakness in allowing himself to be crucified.

Paul speaks in v. 18 of being saved — an ongoing process — and in v. 21 of believing — again an ongoing process. The Corinthians apparently tended to think that they already had it all. Paul keeps stressing by various means that this is not the case.

Verse 22 characterizes Jews as those who seek miraculous signs. This

14. Cf. R. MacMullen, *Paganism in the Roman Empire* (New Haven: Yale University, 1981), p. 55.

15. Ibid., p. 57 and p. 173, n. 30.

16. P. Lampe, "Theological Wisdom and the 'Word about the Cross,'" *Int* 44 (1990), pp. 117-31.

should be compared to the requests made of Jesus (cf. Mark 8:11ff.; Luke 21:7). The reference is to an *'ōt* or validating sign, not just a miracle, but a miracle meant to demonstrate or prove one's power. The term *hellēnes* ("Greeks") in v. 22 probably includes not only Greeks but also hellenophiles such as most Romans, so "Gentile" or "pagan" is an appropriate rendering.[17] They are said to seek wisdom.

In contrast to both Jews and Gentiles, Paul preaches the paradoxical notion of a crucified God. This apparently powerless and foolish deity allowed himself to be killed by Romans — a scandal to Jews and foolishness to pagans. Yet this crucified messiah is both the wisdom and power of God for salvation for believers, so that salvation would not be the result of human effort or wisdom. Thus the foolishness of God outstrips human wisdom and the weakness of God exceeds human strength.

In an apt phrase Lucian (*De morte Peregr.* 13) speaks of Jesus as "the crucified Sophist" *(ton aneskolopismenon ekeinon sophistēn).* Paul is concerned to portray Christ as God's wisdom in this passage. Christ became the believer's wisdom by dying on the cross.[18] Had he not died, salvation would not have been possible, and thus he could not have been God's wisdom and power for believers.

In order to bring the Corinthians down to earth, Paul reminds them of their station in life. Here "calling" (v. **26**) refers not to religious calling but to socioeconomic position or social status. This reminder is certainly an attempt to deflate at least some of the Corinthians who have accepted the larger culture's valuation of high social status.

Not many of the Corinthian Christians were "wise"[19] by human standards, nor powerful, nor of noble birth. This triad has been endlessly scrutinized and has been used to argue both for and against the idea that Christians were of low social status in the Greco-Roman world. Probably it means that there were some Corinthian Christians who were in one or more of these high status categories. I disagree with those commentators who think this phrase as used here is merely conventional. Paul is addressing a socially diverse congregation, though he focuses especially on the socially pretentious and privileged at several points in the letter, as they especially seem to have

---

17. Best, "The Power and the Wisdom of God," p. 27, points out that on various occasions Paul uses "Greek" when we might have expected "Gentile" (here and in 1 Cor. 10:32; 12:13; Gal. 3:28; Rom. 1:16; 2:9f.; 3:9; 10:12). "Gentile" is a broader term that would have included barbarians. Perhaps the reason Paul uses "Greek" is that his focus is not ethnic but on those who are the cultural heirs of Greek and Hellenistic religion, namely Greeks and Romans.

18. I discuss this matter at some length in *Jesus the Sage: The Pilgrimage of Wisdom* (Minneapolis: Fortress, 1994), ch. 7.

19. This could mean "educated."

been causing problems. This statement in 1:26 should be taken for what it is worth, while what Paul says in 4:10 is to a certain degree ironical.[20]

Nevertheless, it is likely that the more well-off had an inordinate degree of influence in the *ekklēsia*, out of proportion to their actual numbers.[21] We can name several of these people — Erastus, Stephanas, Gaius, Titius Justus, Chloe, Phoebe from nearby Cenchreae, and Paul's coworkers Aquila and Priscilla, apparently in Ephesus as Paul writes (16:19). There were probably more since Paul generally leaves those whom he is currently opposing anonymous. We know from 1 Corinthians 8–10 that some in Corinth, called the "strong," were arguing for the right to attend feasts in pagan temples. There was also one or more going to court against fellow believers, which in view of the Roman system of justice only a well-to-do person or a person with a powerful patron was likely to do. This surely must mean that there were more relatively well-to-do Christians in Corinth than those whom Paul names. It is only his allies or neutral persons that he mentions by name.[22]

In 11:18 Paul seems to envision the whole Christian community in Corinth coming together in one house to celebrate the Lord's Supper in the context of a meal. In even notable Roman villas the dining room, where people reclined on couches for meals, normally accommodated only nine to twelve people (see the illustration on the opposite page), and, even making allowances for dining in the atrium, kitchen, and elsewhere in the house, a dining party in a home would at most allow for a crowd of fifty or perhaps sixty people.[23] Unless this meal was held in a pavilion or tent, which was in fact done in Roman antiquity, frequently on the grounds of a temple,[24] we may conjecture that there were about sixty Christians in Corinth.

If we are correct about this number, then at least ten percent and perhaps more of the congregation would fall into one or more of the classifications of "wise," "wealthy" (which is probably what *dynatoi* means in this context), and "wellborn." They would still be a minority, but in view of the household structure of Christianity, since the natural leadership might fall to the head of

20. I agree with U. Wilckens, *Weisheit und Torheit* (Tübingen: Mohr, 1959), p. 41: In view of the contrast between the foolish and the wise in this passage, a sapiential perspective, and not just a sociologically correct analysis, is being conveyed.

21. Cf. G. Theissen, *The Social Setting of Pauline Christianity: Essays on Corinth* (Philadelphia: Fortress, 1982), pp. 69ff.; F. Lang, *Die Briefe an die Korinther* (Göttingen: Vandenhoeck, 1986), p. 33.

22. This also means that the problems in Corinth were not perceived by Paul to be just a matter of the more well-off causing problems for the less well-off.

23. Cf. J. Murphy-O'Connor, *St. Paul's Corinth: Texts and Archaeology* (Wilmington: Glazier, 1983), pp. 156f.

24. Is Paul in 1 Cor. 11:22a suggesting that they have homes to eat in, *as opposed to the place where they are meeting as an ekklēsia?* This might suggest a Christian community with more members than could be guests in one villa.

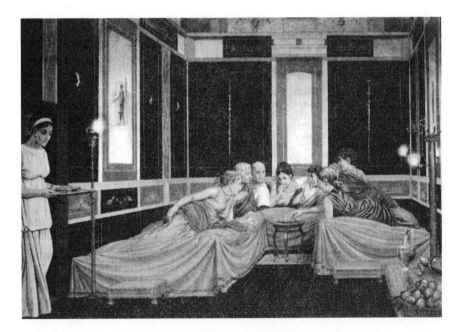

Dining in a triclinium

Illustration by P. Connolly, from R. Burrell, *The Romans*
(Oxford University Press, 1991), used by permission.

the household, their influence probably far exceeded their numbers. E. A.
Judge has struck the balance when he says that the Corinthian Christians "were
dominated by a socially pretentious section of the population."[25] This was
possible not only because of patronage relationships, but also because it is
likely that slaves and other dependents of these well-to-do Christians who
were already under their authority joined the Christian community with them.
Betz is probably right in saying that the Corinthian congregation was in a
different class than some of Paul's other congregations (e.g., Philippi).[26]

Asymmetrical household and patronage relationships did not suddenly
cease when a family joined the Christian *ekklēsia*. I suspect that Paul takes
some of his audience down a peg in 1:26 precisely because the well-to-do and
wellborn, or perhaps more likely the *nouveau riche*, were threatening to dom-

25. E. A. Judge, *The Social Pattern of Early Christian Groups in the First Century*
(London: Tyndale House, 1960), p. 60.

26. Betz, "Problem of Rhetoric and Theology," p. 24, suggests plausibly: "In Corinth
the Pauline mission had succeeded — for the first time, it seems — in winning converts
from the better educated and cultured circles of a prosperous and cosmopolitan city."

inate the congregation in Corinth in a fashion that was deleterious to the familial yet multi-status character of the group.

If Paul is referring to the Corinthian Christians' social origins when he speaks of their "calling," he might be reminding them, many of whom had as freedmen and freedwomen done well for themselves in Corinth, that they had not been born into noble, rich, or well-educated families. If this is the intent of his remark, then Paul wished to humble both the social-climbing freedmen and freedwomen and some of the *nouveau riche* in the Corinthian *ekklēsia*. If one combines these two groups one could come up with considerably more than ten percent of the congregation being reasonably well-off and status conscious. But against this conjecture are the way in which Paul uses the idea of "calling" in 7:20 and the fact that in the classical sources the word "calling" seems to refer to what one has taken on in one's life, that is, a vocation, position, or station.[27]

God chose those who were modest in means, pedigree, and intellect to "shame" those who are high and mighty (v. 27). *Kataischynō* can mean to take pride in or boast, but it can also mean to put one's full confidence or trust in. It can have a pejorative sense or a positive sense, and Paul uses it both ways in this passage. God chose the ignoble and despised of the world, the nonentities, to "shame" or "bring to nothing" the wise and wealthy. Thus, no one has anything to boast of in the presence of God since no one has what they have in Christ on the basis of accomplishment or pedigree.

God made the crucified Christ "our" wisdom.[28] Calling Jesus "Wisdom" was one of the most important developments in early christological thinking, since it enabled early Jewish Christians like Paul to think of a preexistent as well as postexistent Christ. It allowed them to see in Christ the fulfillment of all that was said about personified Wisdom in such OT passages as Proverbs 8 and 24 or, from closer to Paul's time, Wisdom of Solomon 7–9. Paul's use of Scripture in 1 Corinthians 1–4 also reflects an indebtedness to late sapiential handling of such texts, particularly in the Wisdom of Solomon.[29] Paul is consciously trying to present his message in sapiential form, and to present himself as a sage who reveals counter-order wisdom, as a response to whatever sort of wisdom with which the Corinthian Christians were enamored. At the end of our discussion of 1 Corinthians 1–4, we will see how Paul the sage reveals how his lifestyle and life experiences reflect the same pattern as Jesus who was both sage and Wisdom.

27. Cf. BAGD, p. 436. That there are no verbs with the threefold "not many" leaves the question somewhat open. One can translate it as "not many are" or "not many were." But one would expect a verb like "remember" rather than "see" if Paul were referring to the past.

28. Note the stress on the action of God the Father throughout this passage.

29. Witherington, *Jesus the Sage*, ch. 7.

The terms righteousness, sanctification, and redemption in v. 30 are probably not predicated of Christ, though there is a sense in which such a predication would be appropriate. Paul does not elsewhere use *sophia* as a synonym for salvation though he is willing to talk about wisdom coming to the person who is saved. While in the mystery cults, salvation came on the basis of some special inside wisdom or knowledge, and some Corinthians apparently thought this was the way it worked in Christianity as well, Paul believes that salvation comes from accepting the "foolishness" of what he preaches.

Is Paul saying that Christ *is* righteousness, sanctification, and redemption for believers, since they are not wise, or that they have these things through God in Christ? While this passage does suggest that Christ has been made the new definition of *wisdom* — that is, true wisdom is to be understood in terms of Christ — the sentence should be read as it is structured: "But *you are* — from God in Christ, who was made wisdom for us by God — righteousness, and sanctification, and redemption."[30] The Corinthian Christians themselves are "righteousness, sanctification, and redemption." "Wisdom" is separated from the other three predicate nouns because it is applied to one subject and the other three to another. Salvation (as expressed in these three metaphors) comes to believers through a crucified Christ, and thus there is a sense in which believers *are* these things, just as they are frequently called *hagioi* ("saints, holy") by Paul.

This understanding of the sentence is supported by the following observations made by W. Bender: (1) *En Christō* is probably used here in an instrumental sense ("through Christ") as it so often is elsewhere in Paul's letters, (2) 1:23f. encourages us to see Christ being identified with Wisdom and power but not with these other terms, and, most pertinently, (3) in 2 Cor. 5:21 one finds instrumental *en Christō* together with the believer being called the *dikaiosunē theou* (righteousness of God). Furthermore, it is believers, not Christ, who are said in 2 Cor. 6:11b to be washed, consecrated, and justified. Paul wishes in 1 Cor. 1:30 to tell his audience not only what Christ is but also what they are through Christ.

The three metaphors — a juridical metaphor (right standing), a religious metaphor (holiness, set apartness) and a slavery metaphor (redemption, the freeing of those in bondage, or ransoming by payment)[31] — are three different ways to speak of salvation. This whole section is basically about the means by which one is saved.

---

30. Cf. Senft, *La première Épître*, p. 44.

31. As G. D. Fee, *The First Epistle to the Corinthians* (Grand Rapids: Eerdmans, 1987), pp. 86ff., rightly notes, Paul usually focuses on the idea of liberation of those in bondage rather than on the ransom payment.

To close off this subsection of his argument, Paul offers in v. 31 his adaptation of Jer. 9:24. In view of the discussion that follows about boasting, this quotation is not just an afterthought but sets down a crucial principle that Paul wants the Corinthians to heed. They must come to understand that what they are and what they know in Christ they have by grace. Therefore boasting in anyone or anything but God and God's work is totally inappropriate. Salvation did not come to them because of their social status, wealth, or heredity. Indeed, it came to most of them in spite of their lack of such status indicators.[32]

An adequate theology of grace undercuts any thought of earning salvation. Salvation in Christ is not a human self-help or self-improvement scheme, but a radical rescue from a form of slavery out of which one cannot earn or buy one's way. Paul must establish this theology of grace at the very outset of his arguments because it is on the basis of that theology that he will undercut all factors that promote factionalism. Grace is not only the great unifier but also the great leveler in the Christian community, which if taken seriously nullifies the importance of all cultural devices used to create social stratification. It can also stifle rivalries about and between Christian teachers, since it makes possible the rejoinder: "Was Paul (or Apollos, or whoever) crucified for you?" (v. 13).

> The cross always remains scandal and foolishness for Jew and Gentile, inasmuch as it exposes man's illusion that he can transcend himself and effect his own salvation, that he can all by himself maintain his own strength, his own wisdom, his own piety and his own self-praise even towards God. In the light of the cross God shows all this, and ourselves as well, to be foolish, vain and godless. For everyone is foolish, vain and godless who wants to do, without God and contrary to God, what only God . . . can do. . . . Only the creator can be the creature's salvation, not his own works.[33]

The problem in Corinth was partly that many if not most of the Corinthian Christians were not fully socialized into the *ekklēsia*. They had not fully understood what it meant to be saved by and to live by grace, but rather

32. W. A. Meeks, *The First Urban Christians: The Social World of the Apostle Paul* (New Haven: Yale University, 1983), pp. 271ff., has suggested that Christianity may have been attractive to people whose social status was ambiguous since the symbol of the exaltation of the crucified messiah may have lent a strong sense of personal power and prominence to them. I doubt that this could be so. First, Paul is quite right in stressing that this is a scandalous message, and second, it appears that the Corinthians had not grasped its positive significance, namely that salvation was by grace.

33. E. Käsemann, "The Saving Significance of the Death of Jesus in Paul," in idem, *Perspectives on Paul* (Philadelphia: Fortress, 1971), pp. 32-59, here pp. 40f. (with apologies for the non-inclusive language in this quotation).

continued to dance to the piper that played the favorite cultural tune about social advancement through hard work, wealth, rhetoric, and the like. In an honor-shame culture *public* recognition and standing is more important than the actual facts about one's life and accomplishments. In such an environment Paul's gospel must have come as a shock to many.[34]

Probably E. P. Sanders is right in saying that Paul is not trying to speak of a "third race" of humanity when he speaks of Christians, even though he clearly distinguishes them from non-Christian Jews and pagans.[35] Paul's vision is for a whole new humanity, both Jew and Gentile, male and female, poor and rich, and indeed a new cosmos, all united in Christ. He sees Christ as the eschatological Adam starting the *whole* human race over again. Paul's status-conscious converts can be part of a new world order, or they can continue to be part of their provincial culture.

Some opponents of early Christianity understood quite well the radical character and implications of this vision. It threatened to level a carefully built-up system of social stratification, not only by creating a new diverse community but also by refusing to participate in the old social system in various crucial ways (e.g., in pagan worship and in the military). R. Wilken, commenting on the frequent complaint by pagans that Christianity was a *superstitio*, aptly remarks:

> To say then that Christianity is a superstition is not a matter of simple bias or the result of ignorance; it expresses a distinct religious sensibility. When Tacitus wrote that Christianity was "the enemy of humankind," he did not simply mean he did not like Christians and found them a nuisance (though this was surely true) but that they were an affront to his social and religious

---

34. 1 Corinthians 1 raises deep and abiding questions for our own culture, which is in many ways very much like the culture of Roman Corinth. For instance, this chapter requires that we ask how much of our sense of self-worth and identity is grounded in our culture's evaluation of us in terms of wealth, education, and the like, and how much it is grounded in our identity as sinners saved by grace. It also requires us to ask how much our values in life, what we really long for, are dictated by culture and how much by the gospel. Christian attitudes about wealth, family, country, and other things held dear are often more grounded in certain cultural assumptions than in any Christian teaching. Demographic studies of Christian congregations show that race, class, occupation, and numerous other factors often *determine* where one goes to worship. Whatever else one may say about Corinthian Christianity, it was not ethnically, racially, sexually, or socially monochrome.

35. E. P. Sanders, *Paul, the Law, and the Jewish People* (Philadelphia: Fortress, 1983), pp. 171-79. I would add that Paul sees Jew and Gentile united in Christ as the true Israel of the present and thus the *ekklēsia* as the true development of Israel, with non-Christian Jews temporarily broken off from the covenant community. See my *Jesus, Paul and the End of the World: A Comparative Study in NT Eschatology* (Downers Grove: InterVarsity, 1992), pp. 99-128.

world. When later critics faulted Christians for not participating in civic affairs or in the military, the point of such criticism was as religious as it was social, though the specific acts mentioned do not appear to us to be religious. "You do not go to our shows, you do not take part in our processions, you are not present at our public banquets, and you shrink in horror from our sacred games" (Minucius Felix *Octavius* 12). Roman games were religious events, as were shows for gladiators and gymnastic contests. As one early Christian put it, thus reflecting the world in which he lived, "What is a stage show without a god, a game without a sacrifice?" (pseudo-Cyprian *De spectaculis* 4).[36]

There was a strong countercultural element to early Christianity, along with support for aspects of the culture that did not specifically conflict with Christian life and belief. Christians were called to live still in the world without being of the world.[37]

---

36. R. L. Wilken, *The Christians as the Romans Saw Them* (New Haven: Yale University, 1984), p. 66.

37. Does the *ekklēsia* offer the same sort of critique of an increasingly pagan Western culture today? By and large, I suspect that it does not. Apart from exclusive groups that withdraw from the dominant society such as the Amish, Christians seem much more interested in fitting into the dominant cultural worldview than in standing out, perhaps because of the universal human desire to be liked by one's peers and elders.

Argument I, Division 2: 2:1-16

Wisdom for the Mature

Here Paul states plainly the rhetorical strategy he resolved on when he came to Corinth, which was to eschew "sublime words or wisdom," that is, to avoid Sophistic or ornamental rhetoric, and perhaps also to avoid drawing on the various Greco-Roman philosophies of the day in his initial preaching in Corinth.[1] The Corinthians associated "wisdom" in the form of rhetorical eloquence with their goals in life: "If wisdom is present as the moderator of all things, then those who have attained it gain glory, honor, and prestige from it and also the most certain and safe defense of their friends" (Cicero *De Inventione* 1.5). It is no accident that mysteries and their different grades are mentioned in the Sophists' writings (cf. Clement of Alexandria *Strom.* I.15.3)[2] and that Paul claims that he can convey mysteries (2:7). But he stresses that only the mature are ready for such things (2:6), and the Corinthians are not yet mature (3:1f.).

Paul took this approach knowing the great love for rhetoric and debate in a Roman colony like Corinth.[3] We should not argue that Paul uses or avoids one or another sort of rhetoric by accident. His choice of words and message is intentional.[4]

E. Best has provided the following reasons why we should conclude that

1. Stoics called the sage "rich, handsome, well-born, and a king" (Plutarch *Mor.* 58E, cf. 472A). This suggests that in 1 Cor. 3:18 and especially 4:8 Paul is mocking some Corinthians' pretensions to be sages or wise. On Paul avoiding the Sophistic approach to rhetoric, see M. Bünker, *Briefformular und rhetorische Disposition im I Korintherbrief* (Göttingen: Vandenhoeck and Ruprecht, 1984), p. 49: "The tradition that he thus has rejected is then primarily the Sophistically influenced theory of forensic speech as intentional and systematic persuasion." Bünker's attempt to view 1 Corinthians 1–4 as a discrete piece of rhetoric having to do with factions, in distinction to what follows, is shown to be incorrect by M. M. Mitchell, *Paul and the Rhetoric of Reconciliation* (Tübingen: Mohr, 1991), pp. 65ff.

2. Cf. the discussion of this in J. Munck, *Paul and the Salvation of Mankind* (London: SCM, 1959), p. 159, n. 2; Philostratus *Lives* 586.

3. I doubt that Paul resolved to follow this strategy because of his experience in Athens shortly before coming to Corinth. He did draw on Greco-Roman *philosophia* in Athens, at least as Luke records the occasion in Acts 17:16-34. Perhaps Paul did feel that he had indulged in too much accommodation, since he does not mention Christ crucified in the Acts account.

4. For the view that Paul chose to avoid rhetoric *in toto* in his *preaching*, see A. D. Litfin, *St. Paul's Theology of Proclamation: An Investigation of 1 Cor. 1–4 in Light of Greco-Roman Rhetoric* (dissertation, Oxford, 1983), pp. 296ff.

in 1:18–2:5 form rather than content is uppermost in the discussion: (1) while mentioning the content of the gospel, Paul does not really discuss it here; (2) in 2:4 Paul distinguishes his preaching from good rhetoric;[5] and (3) in 1:17 Paul emphasizes the activity of preaching, not a theory of preaching.[6]

There are, as Mitchell admits, epideictic elements of praise and blame in 1 Corinthians 1–4, since Paul must censure the Corinthians for their boasting, among other things. This mixing of rhetorical types is not unusual, but the lesser serves the greater, the epideictic elements serving the larger deliberative purpose of arguing for concord.[7]

The connection between what precedes 2:1 and what follows is shown not merely by *kai egō*, contracted to *kagō* ("and I also"),[8] but also by the content.

> "And this divine rule was illustrated in my case also. Just as God has ordained the weakness of the cross as the means of salvation (i.22-25), just as He has chosen the weak of this world as the objects of salvation (i.26-31), so I too observed the same rule among you. . . ." "Humility characterised my preaching (ii.1, 2). Humility was stamped upon my person and penetrated my feelings (ii.3)."[9]

Chapter 2 is crucial for understanding what some of the difficulties in Corinth were. It has also been wrongly used to insist that there are several different kinds of Christians (some carnal and some spiritual). Paul accepts the idea that there are more and less mature Christians and that there is teaching appropriate to each level of Christian maturity,[10] but this is very

5. I would say from rhetoric that is Sophistic and ornamental.

6. E. Best, "The Power and the Wisdom of God, 1 Corinthians 1:18–2:5," in *Paolo a Una Chiesa Divisa (1 Cor. 1–4)*, ed. L. de Lorenzi (Rome: St. Paul Abbey, 1980), pp. 9-41, here p. 14.

7. Cf. Mitchell, *Rhetoric of Reconciliation*, pp. 213ff.

8. At various points in this section Paul introduces an idea with *kagō* (2:1, 3; 3:1).

9. J. B. Lightfoot, *Notes on the Epistles of Saint Paul* (Winona Lake: Alpha Publications, reprint), p. 170.

10. As Litfin, *St. Paul's Theology*, p. 317, puts it, not a wisdom reserved for an elite, but a gospel explained in more or less depth according to the audience. S. K. Stowers, "Paul on the Use and Abuse of Reason," *Greeks, Romans, and Christians: Essays in Honor of Abraham J. Malherbe*, ed. D. L. Balch, E. Ferguson, and W. A. Meeks (Minneapolis: Fortress, 1990), pp. 253-86, here p. 261, suggests that the advanced teaching based on revelation is "entirely different from the basic teachings Paul brought to the Corinthians and is apparently unessential to their Christian life." But the *mystērion* spoken of in 1 Cor. 15:51 *is* essential and has to do with belief in the resurrection, and from chs. 2 and 3 it is clear that Paul wants the Corinthians to grow up and believes that they need to do so, as there is more essential truth for them to comprehend, more wisdom from God.

different from suggesting that some Christians are "spiritual" or have the Spirit while some do not. For Paul, part of the very definition of what it means to be a Christian is having the Holy Spirit in one's life.[11]

Paul will continue to use "wisdom" here to refer to the divine truth of Christ crucified and its ramifications. But he suggests that more mature Christians can delve further into what this eschatological "mystery" entails.[12] He uses *sophia* ("wisdom") of the *form* in which wisdom is expressed as well, that is, usually, words that have rhetorical polish. In 2:1 *logos* would seem to refer to the form of the message and *sophia* to its content. Paul is repudiating using either the form or substance of a wisdom that might be called "worldly" in his preaching of the gospel. This might mean that he used rhetoric not in his preaching but in his letters, but more likely it means that he did not use ornamental or Sophistic rhetoric lest he distract the audience from the real power of the gospel message. Paul's rhetorical strategy in his letters may have varied somewhat from the strategy he folowed in missionary preaching in new locations.[13] Paul uses rhetoric in 1 and 2 Corinthians even to the point that there are passages that reflect real rhetorical skill and polish. Accordingly, the Corinthians noted the power of his letters and that the same power was not seen in his personal presence (2 Cor. 10:10).

Paul freely admits that he came to the Corinthians in fear and trembling (v. 3). Some have suggested that this may have been related to his ongoing illness or "thorn in the flesh" (2 Cor. 12:7; Gal. 4:13), or it may be a frank admission that Paul came as one who was nervous and somewhat intimidated by the task set before him in Corinth. I suggest that it means that, for whatever reasons, whether physical appearance, a weak voice, lack of training in declamation, or inadequate rhetorical delivery, Paul in his oral performance did not come across as rhetorically adept. He freely admits that he comes across in humble fashion in person in 2 Cor. 10:1, so much so that some saw him as an *idiotēs* (cf. 2 Cor. 11:6), a rank amateur in public rhetorical performance. The real complaint against Paul may have been that he was not arrogant in

11. Cf. the helpful study by B. A. Pearson, *The Pneumatikos-Psychikos Terminology in 1 Corinthians* (Missoula: Society of Biblical Literature, 1973), pp. 28ff., in which he rightly points out that Paul uses *teleioi* here to refer not to those specially initiated but to the mature and that *teleioi* was in any case not the usual term for initiates in the mystery religions.

12. Irenaeus *Against Heresies* 5.6.1. Paul could mean "perfect" by *teleioi*, but this is unlikely in view of his usage elsewhere and in view of 3:1ff.

13. J. W. Beaudean, *Paul's Theology of Preaching* (Macon: Mercer University, 1988), pp. 103ff., rightly notes that *kērygma* was used of the essential task of a herald, one who declares publicly an event, such as games or terms of a peace settlement, on the authority of someone else. The herald is commissioned. There seems then to be some sort of integral connection between Paul's understanding of himself as an *apostolos*, a commissioned agent of Christ acting on Christ's authority, and his form of initial communication with people.

his presentation or did not engage in boasting, unlike the Sophists.[14] In view of the character of 2 Corinthians 10–13, this last suggestion ranks as a real possibility.

Numerous commentators have realized that 1 Cor. 2:1-5 has something to do with Paul's use of rhetoric, whether it is "the commencement of Paul's theme of shame in socio-cultural terms" (P. Marshall), the use of a Socratic-Cynic *topos* to establish a methodological consistency with his theology of a crucified Christ, or a renunciation of rhetoric (C. M. Horne), of "the grand style" of rhetoric (E. A. Judge), of epideictic oratory (J. Weiss), of the rhetorical practices of other Christian preachers in Corinth (T. H. Lim), or of all technical rhetorical devices (L. Hartman).[15]

I view the scenario as follows: Paul was the first to evangelize Corinth, he had a good deal of success there, and then he stayed there long enough to get a viable Christian community established. Problems arose, however, after he left and had been gone for some time, in particular, when Apollos went to Corinth and used an Alexandrian rhetorical style of preaching and teaching that Paul had avoided. This led to a comparison of Paul's rhetoric with that of Apollos, and with Sophistic rhetoric in general. The audience was *expected* to evaluate a rhetorical speech and compare it to others. Rhetors expected the audience to judge their oral performance. The Corinthians were not acting differently from others who had been raised in a culture that had certain expectations about rhetorical performances. It was believed that a person is as he or she speaks, that there is a correspondence between words and life, and that one who is eloquent is also wise. Paul's personal presence seems to have been weak, and by rhetorical standards this reflected on his *ēthos*, his ability to establish his good character and credibility. He seeks to counter this complaint in v. 5, but he admits the principle that the message and the messenger should comport with one another. God chose a weak agent to proclaim the message of God's weakness on the cross.

In v. 4 Paul contrasts the use of persuasive wisdom, "words of wisdom," with the demonstration of "the powerful Spirit" ("Spirit and power" is probably a hendiadys with that meaning). The latter might refer to miracles that happened while Paul was in Corinth or more likely to the powerful transformation of the Corinthians under Paul's preaching, in spite of the fragility of the preacher and the lack of polish in his preaching. Paul deliberately chose to present the gospel in this unpolished manner so that the Corinthians' faith would be in God's power, not in the power of human words or rhetorical skill.

14. Cf. Philostratus *Lives* 535.
15. B. W. Winter, *Are Philo and Paul among the Sophists? A Hellenistic Jewish and a Christian Response to a First Century Movement* (dissertation, MacQuarrie University, 1988, publication forthcoming), p. 152, q.v. for references.

Despite this, the Corinthians continued to be enamored of rhetorical skill, and this made many of them more favorably disposed toward Apollos and some other preachers.[16]

This brings us to the crucial word *apodeixis* in v. 4, a technical rhetorical term that Quintilian says refers to "a clear proof," "a means of proving what is not certain by means of what is certain" (*Inst. Or.* 5.10.7). Cicero defines it as a "logical proof" (*Academia* 2.8).[17] If we bear in mind that the standard definition of rhetoric in Quintilian's day was the *dynamis* ("power") of persuasion (*Inst. Or.* 2.15.2-4) and that Dio Chrysostom refers to the gift of eloquence simply as *dynamis* (33.3), this passage becomes clearer. Paul says that the "proof" he offered of the truth of the gospel about Christ crucified was not in the form of formal rhetorical proofs, but came from the experiential proof that the powerful Spirit had changed the Corinthians' lives when he preached. Because of this their faith would not be in the power of human rhetoric or wisdom but in the power of God (2 Cor. 12:12).[18] This spiritual "proof" also showed that Paul was a genuine agent of Christ.

Paul deliberately decided to take up an anti-Sophistic strategy. His *ēthos* was weak, he eschewed the usual proofs (the *logos* or argumentation), and his *pathos* was not all it should be, since he wanted all to rest on the message about the crucified Christ. In 2 Corinthians 10–13 we will see Paul parody the love for histrionics and *pathos,* the emotional appeal, and thus caricature the Sophistic approach to speech-making.[19]

> The message Paul brought did not require a *dialexis* on himself or an *encomium* on the greatness of Corinth. He did not need a topic to be nominated by a critical audience on which he could then rise up and declaim, thereby giving himself the opportunity to establish his credentials on the say-so of the Corinthians in order to function as a recognized public speaker. His "topic" had been determined before he arrived in Corinth, for

16. L. L. Welborn, "On the Discord in Corinth: 1 Corinthians 1–4 and Ancient Politics," *JBL* 106 (1987), pp. 85-111, here p. 106, argues that in 2:6–3:3 Paul is mainly addressing the leaders of the rival factions. I would argue that Paul is taking issue with the primary troublemakers throughout the letter, though the address is meant for all to hear. Perhaps, as Welborn argues (pp. 110f.), some had associated themselves with the *ekklēsia* in hopes of increasing their own scope of power, list of clients, and opportunities for self-expression.

17. Here and elsewhere in this section I am indebted to Winter's fine work on the subject (see n. 15 above).

18. When Paul speaks of the "mystery" of God in v. 1 he refers to the content of the revelation about Christ crucified and its implications. For the mature this "mystery" can be further expounded (cf. below).

19. It is possible but not probable that *pistis* in 1 Cor. 2:5 has its rhetorical sense of "logical proof" since Paul refers to *"their pistis."*

he had long ago resolved the content of his message, and there was nothing else for him to speak on as he faced an audience.[20]

Verses **6-16** must be read very carefully with the following points in mind:

First, Paul continues to address all the Corinthians as Christians who have the Spirit. The section ends with the statement that "we" — that is, both Paul and the Corinthians — "have the mind of Christ," and in v. 12 Paul writes: "We have the Spirit of God."

Second, Paul is not trying to give either an ontology lesson about God's nature (that is, that God is a being with a spirit, much like humans), nor is he trying, by and large, to teach spiritual anthropology.

Third, Paul uses eschatological and apocalyptic language to describe the revelation of God in Christ crucified. What he says should be judged according to the kind of language he is using.

The link between God and Christians is the Spirit. The believer may know God because the believer has the Spirit, not because she or he has received some advanced course in esoteric human rhetoric or wisdom. One knows God only in God's self-revelation by the Spirit. Humans cannot reason their way up to God. Thus, despite the arguments of E. E. Ellis and others,[21] Paul does not use *pneumatikos* ("spiritual person," v. **16**) of a particular class of elite or leader Christians who have been given advanced knowledge about God in Christ. It is simply a term for believers, that is, people with the Spirit in their lives. To the believer, all of what God might reveal is potentially available through the Spirit.[22]

When Paul says in v. **6** that he *does* speak a wisdom to the mature, while going on to contrast only human and Christian wisdom, he means that the wisdom he dispenses, while potentially available for any Christian, can only be fully received and understood by the mature believer, not the immature believer. Lightfoot is right in saying that this distinction is confirmed in the first few verses of ch. 3, where Paul speaks of babies and adults in Christ. This

20. Winter, *Are Philo and Paul,* p. 163.

21. E. E. Ellis, *Prophecy and Hermeneutic in Early Christianity* (Grand Rapids: Eerdmans, 1978), pp. 23ff. Due attention must be paid to the difference between *-inos* and *-ikos* endings with such words. The latter ending can denote an ethical relation; the former implies material continuity. Cf. R. Jewett, *Paul's Anthropological Terms* (Leiden: Brill, 1971), p. 122. But does Paul really maintain such distinctions in 1 Corinthians 3 with the *sarkinos/sarkikos* ("fleshly") terminology?

22. It is not clear that Paul is taking up the Corinthians' own terminology, though that is possible since he does not usually speak of "the spiritual ones."

is not unlike the distinction in 1 John 2:13f. between "fathers" and "children" in the faith.[23] Perhaps Heb. 5:11–6:8 provides us with an exegesis from within the Pauline circle of some of the discussion in 1 Corinthians 2–3.[24] Paul admits that he has some advanced sapiential teaching, but the Corinthians were by and large not mature enough to receive it.

The *archontes* (rulers) "of this age" (vv. **6, 8**) are probably not supernatural forces but earthly rulers who live according to the conventional wisdom of the world.[25] Rulers were thought to have access, through God and their many counselors, to the greatest amount of wisdom (cf. Wisdom of Solomon 6). Therefore, Paul's words here are to be understood as ironic. Possibly he was thinking of emperors who had a great love for rhetoric and philosophy. Paul's point is that they totally missed out on the greatest "mystery" or revealed secret of all human history. Otherwise they would never have crucified Christ (v. **8**).

The rulers of this age and their wisdom are all in the process of passing away, because the life, death, and resurrection of Christ have transformed the time line. The things of the end time have already broken into human history and have relativized all purely human values, wisdom, and structures. Paul says he speaks "a secret wisdom," meaning one that is only known because God has revealed it to him. It is not a wisdom that God dreamed up as an afterthought. Christ crucified was what God planned before the foundation of the world. The rulers of the world, particularly those who crucified Christ, knew nothing of this wisdom. Otherwise they would not have acted as they did.

Paul does not believe that so-called "natural revelation" ever leads to a saving knowledge of God or an understanding of his saving plan. In v. **9** he quotes in part Isa. 64:4 and 65:16 from the LXX, though neither text is exactly like Paul's words.[26] He was happy to exegete and give dynamic equivalents when he quoted rather than separating commentary from quotation. V. **9** speaks of the human heart, but Paul could have easily referred to the mind: These terms are basically interchangeable for him since the heart in Hebrew thinking is the center of reflection and thought as well as of will and feelings.[27]

Verse **11** is a simple analogy that should not be pressed too much. Its meaning is simply that like knows like. What is in a person's mind only that

23. Lightfoot, *Notes*, p. 173. Pythagoras also distinguished between the *teleioi* and the *nēpioi* among his disciples.

24. I would suggest that Apollos may have penned Hebrews.

25. Cf. my *Jesus the Sage: The Pilgrimage of Wisdom* (Minneapolis: Fortress, 1994), ch. 7.

26. On the translation of this difficult verse, see B. Frid, "The Enigmatic *ALLA* in 1 Corinthians 2:9," *NTS* 31 (1985), pp. 603-11.

27. Jewett, *Paul's Anthropological Terms*, pp. 286f.

person knows. Here the human spirit is referred to, not the Holy Spirit, but the human spirit is made an analogy for the Holy Spirit.

Paul's anthropology seems to involve for the Christian at least

the natural faculties, that is, the "mind" or "heart" and the five senses,
the natural life principle, what one might call physical life, and
the "spirit": When Paul wants to talk about the spiritual side of humankind
he speaks of both the human spirit and the Holy Spirit.

Paul calls the principle of natural life the *psychē*, recalling the Hebrew *nepeš* — the life-breath that God breathed into us all. Therefore, *psychē* should not be translated "soul" in most instances in the Pauline corpus, if by that translation one means the spiritual side of the human being. For instance, in 1 Cor. 15:44-46 it is quite clear that "spirit" is set over against *psychē*.[28] In 1 Thess. 5:23 Paul wishes health for the whole person, spirit *(pneuma)*, natural life force or principle and natural faculties (*psychē* — not "soul"), and body *(sōma)*. The *psychē* is what naturally animates the body.

When Paul speaks in v. 14 of the *psychikos* person, he means the "natural person," the human being with a normal physical life and natural human faculties, but without the Holy Spirit. He is not speaking of a "soulish" person, much less a "carnal" Christian. In v. 12 Paul is not speaking of a supernatural *Zeitgeist* when he refers to "the spirit of the world"; he means simply that Christians are not to live by conventional worldly wisdom and have not received that sort of wisdom through the gospel. *Charisthenta*, "bestowed," makes it clear that what Christians have from God by the Spirit is a free gift, not a knowledge of God that one might deduce or develop. Paul did not use conventional rhetoric or wisdom, either in form or content, when he spoke to the Corinthians. He spoke, rather, in spiritual terms.

The last portion of v. 13 has spawned numerous translations. The verb *synkriontes* and the term *pneumatikos* are under debate. While the verb can mean "combine," in the LXX it normally means "interpret" or "explain," and it probably has the same meaning here (cf. Gen. 40:8, 22; 41:12; Dan. 5:12). In view of the clear use of *pneumatikos* in vv. 15f. of spiritual persons, not spiritual things or words, that rendering is more likely here: "We . . . interpret spiritual matters to spiritual people."

But the non-Christian, using his or her natural faculties, is not able to understand or judge spiritual matters (v. 14). They appear to be foolishness. This is a general principle, and probably Paul would say that the only way the nonbeliever understands enough to accept the gospel in the first place before receiving the Spirit is that the Spirit has already been working unnoticed.

28. Ibid., pp. 352f.

The problem, then, in Corinth is not that some Christians are not spiritual or do not have the Spirit or mind of Christ. It is, rather, that though all the Corinthian Christians have the Spirit they are not living as spiritual persons ought to live. They are acting like non-Christians, and Paul's basic response is "STOP!" Their practice has not caught up with what they have accepted in principle. Their cultural assumptions have not been critically evaluated in light of their Christian faith and of the presence of God in their lives.

Paul quotes Isa. 40:13 in v. **16**. The Hebrew has "*Spirit* of the Lord" but the Septuagint has "*mind.*" Obviously these terms were interchangeable to the Septuagint translator. Here we have a structural indicator that enables us to understand Paul's compositional technique. He ends the section of an argument with a paraphrase of Scripture, as he did in 1:30. He uses this technique with some frequency in 1 and 2 Corinthians because he is attempting to ground the experientially oriented Corinthians more completely in the Word. As Quintilian says, documentary evidence is frequently in conflict with oral evidence (*Inst. Or.* 5.7.32), and in antiquity there was often a preference for oral witness. But Paul himself came from a culture that invested sanctity in a specific collection of written words, the testimony about God's dealings with humankind called the Torah. Because many of the first converts to Christianity were Jews, the Torah was recognized as a special authority for all Christians, alongside whatever new revelations or "mysteries" God was offering through his Christian prophets and preachers. Even with a congregation in which the majority were Gentiles, Paul assumes that his audience will accept the authority of Scripture. Hence on more than one occasion he allows *the Word* to have the last word.

Argument I, Division 3: 3:1-23

THE WISE MASTER BUILDER AND HIS COWORKERS

In this section of the argument, several important points become clear. When Paul is discussing divisions in Corinth, he has in mind divisions caused by the response of the Corinthians to Paul and to the chief coworker who followed him in Corinth, Apollos. The so-called "Christ faction" (cf. 1:12) is nowhere to be found here, and Cephas (also mentioned in 1:12) is only named in passing in 3:22. I see no evidence that Paul is trying to tiptoe around a problem really caused by Peter, that is, Cephas, in Corinth. It is the relationship between himself and Apollos that he must explain. He refers to Peter in ch. 1 and in 3:22 because some Corinthians, perhaps especially Jewish Christians, admired Peter, not because there was a "Peter party" created by Peter's visit to Corinth. The argument in 3:4ff. also makes it very likely that the reference to the "Christ" group in ch. 1 was simply a *reductio ad absurdum* of the whole foolish divisive behavior, functioning rather like the question "Was Paul crucified for you?" in 1:13.

A phrase used to characterize Apollos in Acts 18:24, *anēr logios*, literally "a man of words," is used by Philo to refer to a person well-trained in rhetoric (*Post.* 53, 162; *De Leg. Alleg.* 142, 310; *Mut.* 220; *Cher.* 116). If this is an accurate representation of Apollos, then it provides a clue to what happened in Corinth after Paul left. Apollos came and "watered" Paul's mission field. Unfortunately, the method of watering he used amounted to pouring fuel on an already existing fire. In view of the evidence of 1 Corinthians 3–4 and 16 there is nothing to suggest strongly that the relationship between Paul and Apollos was strained. Apollos likely did not know about Paul's anti-Sophistic strategy when he went to Corinth, and thus he unwittingly became one of the causes of factiousness. When a "real" rhetor came to Corinth, the congregation began to engage in *synkrisis*, comparison and judgment of the relative merits of their teachers. This led to rivalries for one teacher over against another. That Apollos had no intention of creating this mess is confirmed by the report in 16:12 that "he was not at all willing to come now" while things were in such a state, even though some Corinthians were apparently clamoring for him.[1]

Paul sets up a "covert allusion" to himself and Apollos in ch. 3, which he then explains in ch. 4. This defies the standard rhetorical conventions, since

---

1. I say "apparently" because it is likely but not certain that *peri de* in 16:12 refers to a topic the Corinthians raised with Paul, perhaps in their letter.

it was bad form to explain such allusions. Paul does so because, despite the great enthusiasm of the Corinthians for Sophistic rhetoric, they are spiritually still children and still acting and judging things according to worldly standards. So Paul treats them as novices, even in rhetoric. This put-down is followed by real *pathos* in 4:8ff., where Paul parodies the Corinthians' overinflated view of themselves, followed by his self-portrayal as a suffering sage.

Paul's response to factionalism in Corinth is to offer

> a counter-order wisdom, one that goes against natural human predilections and even against common sense wisdom. It is a wisdom that lifts up the humble and humbles the proud, a wisdom that builds up the congregation rather than puffing up the individual. He will present the Gospel in a sapiential way so as to offer a different sort of wisdom to his audience. Paul offers a revelatory wisdom, a wisdom that must be called a *musterion* for unless it is revealed it could never be known, for it is not the sort of wisdom one could deduce from close scrutiny of the world or human behavior. He offers a wisdom that squashes individualism, elitism, and human pride and counters factionalism in the congregation. What is interesting about this is while Paul in this letter does not engage in a sort of rhetoric that might be called eloquence or ornamentation for its own sake, he does engage in rhetoric, the content of which is counter-order wisdom, particularly in 1 Cor. 1–4.[2]

As Paul says later in 2 Cor. 10:1-6, he has a rhetorical strategy that destroys Sophistic arguments. He will use rhetoric against its own tendencies toward self-exaltation in order to exalt the Christ and hold up both Christ and his agents in their cruciform life-pattern as a model for the Corinthians.[3]

One of the slight variations that makes a difference in Paul's argument in ch. 3 is between *sarkinos* and *sarkikos*. They both ostensibly mean "fleshly," but the former emphasizes the physical side of human makeup as opposed to the spiritual side. *Sarkikos* (twice in v. 3) means "manifesting fleshly characteristics" and has a definite ethical quality.[4] *Sarkinos* (v. 1) points to the Corinthi-

---

2. B. Witherington, *Jesus the Sage: The Pilgrimage of Wisdom* (Minneapolis: Fortress, 1994), ch. 7. R. L. Fox, *Pagans and Christians* (San Francisco: Harper and Row, 1986), pp. 293-312, probably misreads the diversity of social levels in early Christianity, underestimating, for instance, the significance of Erastus (p. 293). Fox's comment that Paul totally lacked rhetoric having "no grasp of . . . literary style and content" (p. 305), also badly misreads the evidence. Paul's polemic against ornamental rhetoric does not mean that Paul knew and used no rhetoric at all.

3. J. J. Wetstein, in commenting on 1 Cor. 2:4 (1751-52), wrote that "Corinthia verba" was a proverbial expression for elaborate language.

4. Cf. J. B. Lightfoot, *Notes on the Epistles of St. Paul* (Winona Lake: Alpha, reprint), p. 184.

ans' fallen human nature when Paul first preached to them, while *sarkikos* expresses their present moral tendency to act according the assumptions and value system that they were supposed to have left behind.

Verse 2 suggests that even after four to five years the Corinthians have still not made noticeable progress toward leaving behind their old social orientation and internalizing a Christian orientation. Fee stresses that *sarkinos* is not a synonym for *psychikos* since the Corinthians are *sarkinos* but only act *psychikos,* since to actually be *psychikos* ("natural," 2:14) would be to lack the Spirit.[5] Paul is arguing in 3:1 that they are acting childishly, not as they could and ought to act. He is not addressing just a particular class of Christians with these comments, but in principle all of them, and especially the notable offenders. His proof that they are acting like mere ordinary mortals is their jealousy and quarrels. They are acting like the dueling disciples of the Sophists.[6] This all too human behavior reveals their actual spiritual condition. Verse 4 suggests that only some of them are appealing to one or another human leader. Paul's point is that all such leaders are only servants of God through whom the Corinthian Christians came to believe.

"To each" at the end of v. 5 probably means that these servants act as they were gifted by God. Paul claims to be the planter of the congregation; Apollos only watered. This means that Paul came first, laid the foundation, and converted the Corinthians, that Apollos nurtured them, and that a certain distinction of labor exists between Paul and Apollos. Though both are servants, Paul is the church planter. He argues that it is God who causes conversions and church growth regardless of what human instruments God uses. Both conversion and spiritual growth are *of God* though they are *through* human beings.

Verse 8 stresses the unity of Paul and Apollos. They are one in purpose and one in being only servants. They work together to the same end, and so should not be pitted against one another, which would amount to a nullifying of the work of both men.

Paul believes that Christians are rewarded for the good work that they do in the Lord, but he does not say what the reward is (v. 8b). The future tense of "receive" suggests that it will be an eschatological reward at the day of judgment (see below).

Paul and Apollos are coworkers *of God* (v. 9).[7] While the idea of possession is implied here (Paul and Apollos belong to God), this is not the whole

---

5. G. D. Fee, *The First Epistle to the Corinthians* (Grand Rapids: Eerdmans, 1987), pp. 121-23.

6. Cf. pp. 40-43 above.

7. See V. P. Furnish, "Fellow Workers in God's Service," *JBL* 80 (1961), pp. 364-70, for the translation suggested by his title. The metaphorical language about *apostoloi* planting and watering while God gives the growth supports the translation we have suggested.

point since the metaphor makes evident that they work *with* God as well (cf. 2 Cor. 6:1). They are his servants *(diakonoi)* just as the Corinthians are God's field or building.

Paul is calling the whole Corinthian congregation "God's building." Collectively they are God's temple, in which God's Spirit dwells, though Paul is also willing to say that an individual Christian's body is God's temple as well (6:19). One of the great challenges to understanding Paul's thought is the relationship between the one and the many: Paul affirms both, holding them in tension. To be a Christian is to be a member of the body of Christ, not an isolated saved individual. At the same time, Paul holds individuals responsible for their behavior, expecting the community to discipline them.

Paul says that he acted according to the grace given him, and like an engineer and architect together in one — since that is what a "master builder" was[8] — he laid a foundation in Corinth for the church there (v. 10). That foundation was Christ crucified. While for most rhetors the subject matter of their discourse could and would vary depending on the audience, for Paul the content of his oral performance is to a significant degree fixed, while the form may vary.[9] Others have built on this foundation, and here Paul is probably thinking of the Corinthians mainly, though Apollos must also be included, and there is a remote chance that Cephas is also meant (cf. v. 22).[10] In view of the stern warning in vv. 16f., which is directed toward the Corinthians and which presupposes what is said in v. 12, we must assume that some in Corinth, presumably some who are taking the lead in the Corinthian congregation, are building on Paul's foundation.[11] Once again he consigns such people to oblivion by not naming them, but clearly this whole passage cannot be directed just against Apollos or Peter, neither of whom is in Corinth *when Paul writes*.

Paul's work could be harmed either by the Corinthians tinkering with

8. J. Shanor, "Paul as Master Builder: Construction Terms in First Corinthians," *NTS* 34 (1988), pp. 461-71, shows that the key term *(architektōn)* refers to the person in charge of the day-to-day work of building, here the building of a temple.

9. A. D. Litfin, *St. Paul's Theology of Proclamation: An Investigation of 1 Cor. 1–4 in Light of Greco-Roman Rhetoric* (dissertation, Oxford, 1983), p. 353. I take this to mean not that Paul preached exactly the same message everywhere, but that there were certain elements of the basic preaching, such as Christ crucified, that Paul felt were so fundamental to the faith that they were invariably included in his preaching.

10. Lightfoot, *Notes,* pp. 189f., puts it this way: "St. Paul feared that Apollos might not be quite free from blame: that he might have conceded too much to the cravings of the ears and intellect of the Corinthians."

11. On Paul's use of the building and building-up language as part of his rhetorical strategy to create unity in a fractured community, see I. Kitzberger, *Bau der Gemeinde* (Würzburg: Echter, 1986), pp. 64ff. Building up is seen as an essential task of the Christian in and for the community. It is perhaps the paramount expression of Christian love for one's brothers and sisters (cf. Kitzberger, pp. 304f.).

the foundation and changing it or by the Corinthians building the wrong sort of superstructure on the right foundation.[12] Paul develops the latter possibility here. In v. 12 he speaks of various possible superstructure materials in descending order of their value or worth in antiquity. The main distinction here is between a perishable and an imperishable superstructure. One will stand the test of fire and one will not.

Verse 13 again introduces an eschatological note. The testing by fire on judgment day will show whether the superstructure is perishable or imperishable.[13] Paul may be implying here that the character of each Christian's work is not perfectly evident *now*. The purpose of the eschatological fire will be to test or prove the strength and endurance of the superstructure. Those who have built well will be rewarded, and those who have not will not be rewarded. The reward is not heaven or salvation. The reward is, rather, the sort of heavenly rewards that Jesus talks about (e.g., Matt. 5:12). Paul might call them rewards on earth at the eschaton.

Paul believes that the works of the Christian will indeed be judged and that there will be rewards, or suffering of loss, perhaps diminution of one's place in heaven or in the eschaton according to one's work. One whose work is burned up by this final exam will also be saved "but as through fire." This cannot be a reference to purgatory since Paul is referring to what happens on judgment day on the earth after the return of Christ and the resurrection of believers (cf. 2 Cor. 5:10). He is not referring to what happens to a person after death and before the final judgment. Furthermore "escape as through fire" is actually a *metaphor* for escaping, as we might say it, by the skin of one's teeth, that is, with nothing beyond one's eternal life, barely escaping destruction and bringing no credits into the kingdom, though the metaphor might suggest that such a person goes through an agonizing trial when seeing a life's work destroyed by God's testing.[14]

In v. 16 Paul calls the Corinthian Christians God's *naos* in Corinth. The *naos* was that part of an ancient temple where the god was thought to dwell — the sanctuary proper.[15] Paul does not use *hieron*, which was a broader term that would include the temple precincts. Remarkably, Paul believes that even these badly mixed-up Christians are still God's temple where God still dwells.

Verse 17 may be called an oath curse: Anyone destroying God's temple — in this case harming the Corinthian Christians spiritually, emotionally, mentally, or physically — God will destroy (on judgment day). God will take

12. J. Héring, *The First Epistle of Saint Paul to the Corinthians* (London: Epworth, 1962), pp. 30ff.

13. So rightly, Lightfoot, *Notes*, p. 193.

14. It can only be a metaphor since deeds are not material things that can experience real fire and Paul is not talking about burning up church buildings on earth.

15. The noun comes from the verb *naiein*, which means "to dwell."

this action because God's people are God's sacred dwelling place. Those who mistreat God's people are mistreating God and therefore face this punitive action. The term *hagios* ("holy") surely has an ethical color to it here.

In vv. **18ff.** Paul returns to the language of inversion and paradox. The kingdom's coming has turned things upside-down: Human wisdom is foolishness, what seems foolish to common sense is God's wisdom, leaders are servants, the poor are exalted. Vv. **19** and **20** simply stress that the so-called wisdom of the world is not wisdom in God's eyes and that God will catch a person who is found living by his or her own cunning.

As the Psalmist says, the thoughts of the worldly wise are futile or pointless. The quotations here are from Job 5:13 (the only quotation from Job in the NT) and Ps. 94:11. The Job text is closer to the Hebrew than to the Septuagint while the latter part of the Psalm quotation is closer to the Septuagint. Paul uses whichever Scripture version best suits his meaning. This was a common hermeneutical move among Jewish exegetes in early Judaism.[16]

In v. **21** Paul makes the most striking inversion or reversal of expectations of all: The leaders all belong to the Corinthians! "We are yours," says Paul, even Peter. But this is so only in Christ, and Paul hastily adds that the Corinthians are Christ's. Only in him do they have all that is listed in v. **22**.[17] It is fruitful to compare this doxologically prompted list to the one at the end of Romans 8. Since all things are now Christ's, in him they belong to believers as well, though at present this is so mainly in principle, and only in part is it a present experience.[18]

Verses **22** and **23** speak of possession. The leaders belong to the body of Christ, the body belongs to Christ, and Christ belongs to God. Christ is functionally subordinate to God, just as the leaders serve the followers and are functionally subordinate to them, though they are also ontologically equal with them. This is not a discourse on the nature of Christ, but it does show that Christ is ranked under God (cf. ch. 15). Christ is *God's* Messiah: He belongs to the heavenly Father.

---

16. Cf. the Qumran community's application of Isaiah and other prophets to itself. On Paul's use of Scripture, see R. B. Hays, *Echoes of Scripture in Paul* (New Haven: Yale University, 1989).

17. It has often been noted that there is a certain similarity between Paul's way of speaking here and elsewhere and the Stoic way of putting such matters. But the differences are perhaps more signficant. For instance, as Lightfoot, *Notes,* p. 195, points out, the phrase "everything is yours" is spoken not to the wise of the world, to whom all virtues belong, but to those who are in Christ, namely to the fools that Paul has mentioned in ch. 1. Furthermore, for Paul this dominion over everything comes not by isolation and concentration on self, but by the negation of self. "All things are the believer's; but they are only his, in so far as he is Christ's, and because Christ is God's" (Lightfoot, p. 195).

18. Believers do have the Spirit of life and some gifts, but not yet the resurrection body.

Argument I, Division 4: 4:1-21

This section brings to a climax the first major argument of Paul in 1 Corinthians. From the standpoint of rhetoric the first six verses are especially important. In them Paul explains the covert allusion(s) to himself and Apollos that he has introduced in ch. 3. 4:6 suggests that the major function of ch. 3 was "that you may learn from our example." Paul is seeking to do for the Corinthians what Plutarch advises in another context: "It is your duty to reduce this man's swollen pride and restore him to conformity with his best interests" (*eis to sympheriton, Lives, Cato Minor* 65.5). It is the task of any deliberative speech to show what is to the audience's advantage, benefit, or profit.[1] So Paul's point is to change the climate of overinflated rhetoric and self-congratulation in Corinth by holding up the example of a suffering sage and his coworker so that the Corinthians will come to their senses and see what is truly to their benefit.[2]

Paul accomplishes this deflation by giving an explanation of a covert allusion, an explanation that only rank novices in rhetoric would need, and by giving a catalog of the hardships of the sage. First, Paul says in v. 6 that he has "applied" *(metaschēmatisa)* to himself and Apollos the metaphors of ch. 3 about building and planting. This is surely an allusion to the *logos eschēmatismenos* or covert allusion much favored by rhetors (cf. Martial 3.68.7; Quintilian *Inst. Or.* 9.1.4ff.).[3] This form of "figured speech" was used not just

---

1. The main function of this section is not that of an *apologia* defending Paul's apostleship. Paul could hardly hold himself up as an example to the Corinthians if he thought his status as God's agent was seriously in question.

2. Paul's references to boasting and arrogance in ch. 4 may themselves be a clue to the social location of the real culprits in Corinth. So J. V. P. D. Balsdon, *Romans and Aliens* (London: Duckworth, 1979), pp. 170f.: "The higher a Roman's rank, the worse he suffered from the disease which the Greeks called *hyperēphania*, bossiness, arrogance, the sense of innate superiority."

3. This was quickly recognized by the older commentators who knew rhetoric. Cf. J. B. Lightfoot, *Notes on the Epistles of St. Paul* (Winona Lake: Alpha, reprint), p. 199. It is only recently that this sort of understanding of this passage has been revived; cf. B. Fiore, "'Covert Allusion' in 1 Corinthians 1-4," *CBQ* 47 (1985), pp. 85-102. Unfortunately, Fiore misses Paul's reason, in defiance of good Sophistic or ornamental rhetoric, for explaining his "figure." Paul wishes to wean the audience away from their love for ornamentation and to make clear to them that they are immature.

because a rhetor wanted to speak in an indirect manner but often because he wanted to use irony. In fact, this whole section of Paul's letter is loaded with irony, as the detailed studies of J. Fitzgerald and K. Plank have shown.[4] Dionysius of Halicarnassus says that there are three sorts of "figured speech," and Paul is using in 4:6 the sort where one simply expresses oneself indirectly, while in v. 8 we have an example of pure irony — of saying one thing and meaning another.[5] Quintilian warns in *Inst. Or.* 9.2.69 that if a figure is perfectly obvious, it ceases to be a figure. More importantly, covert allusion is successful "because the listener takes pleasure in detecting the speaker's concealed meaning, applauds his own penetration, and regards the other's eloquence as a compliment to himself" (*Inst. Or.* 9.2.78). He concludes that the use of such a figure is a sign of weakness or perhaps jesting. But Paul here is interested not in boosting the Corinthians' image of themselves as clever connoisseurs of rhetoric but in portraying himself as a suffering sage. To make it clear that he regards his audience as immature, he explains his meaning as one would with a small child. This comports with what he said in 3:3: They were still not ready for solid food.

All of this is prepared for by 4:1-5, where Paul speaks of being judged by the Corinthians. This surely refers to judgment of his speech and example as a rhetor. In their minds it was their right to judge Paul, since that is what audiences did with rhetoricians and their oratory. The reference to judgment has to do not so much with whether Paul was a legitimate agent of God as with the *form* of his ministry — both his words and his personal presence. In short, he was rhetorically uncouth. But he was not interested in conforming to their expectations for a rhetor. Indeed, his anti-Sophistic strategy amounted to using rhetoric to burst the bubble of their rhetorical chauvinism. Vv. 1-5 are not so much a defense of Paul's ministry as Paul's preparation for setting himself up as an example for the audience, as v. 16 makes abundantly clear.

Chapter 4 makes it plain that the problems in Corinth were not primarily due to outsiders, but to "some among you" in Corinth (v. 18) that had affected and infected many others. Because of this Paul had to address the whole Corinthian church as though all were involved in these problems. The "some" had become arrogant, apparently because they had concluded that Paul would not return to Corinth. It is probably these "some" whom Paul had in mind in his description in v. 8.

4. J. T. Fitzgerald, *Cracks in an Earthen Vessel* (Atlanta: Scholars, 1988); K. Plank, *Paul and the Irony of Affliction* (Atlanta: Scholars, 1987). The ancient rhetorical handbooks say that one may use such an allusion out of respect or possibly out of fear of condemnation for what is being said. But if using the "figure" is a way of honoring the rhetorical acumen of the audience, then explaining it is a way of taking them down a peg or two.

5. Compare Dionysius *Technē rhetorikē* 9 *peri eschēmatismenon* 2.1.323; 7.341; and 8.2.281f. to Quintilian *Inst. Or.* 9.2.66.

One is immediately struck by the sarcasm, irony, and biting tone of much of this chapter. It is obvious that Chloe's people have reported matters that have struck Paul, the father of the Corinthian *ekklēsia,* to the heart. It is on the basis of his "fatherhood" (vv. 14f.) that Paul especially believes he has the right to exhort and if necessary command the Corinthians, though he prefers to use persuasion and sweet reason.[6] As E. M. Lassen has pointed out, there was a "predominance of the father-figure among family metaphors employed in the public sphere, including politics and religion."[7] In Roman sources the image indicates a hierarchical relationship. What is intriguing about Paul's use of the image is his redefinition of it in terms of servanthood and the image of the suffering sage. To be a father in the faith means to serve, to save, and to persuade one's children, even if one must resort at times to irony and sarcasm. Only as a last resort will a Christian "father" make use of his vast power, unlike the Roman *paterfamilias* who could and sometimes did discard an infant daughter with impunity if he desired (cf. 4:21; 2 Cor. 13:10).

The Corinthians seem to have thrived on displays of power, both in word and deed.[8] They had imbibed the Roman imperial ideology, which used father-figure imagery to support social stratification and to legitimate a steeply inclined hierarchy of power. Lassen notes: "It was the official ideal to subordinate oneself to a hierarchical structure. We can therefore conclude that Roman Corinth was *not* dominated by old Greek democratic ideals. In contrast the father image seems to have been a powerful tool in asserting imperial authority in this important colony."[9] In such an environment, the sort of rhetoric that flourished was ornamental, since power relationships controlled everything, even the vaunted system of justice (cf. ch. 5).

Paul begins here by describing the form and character of his ministerial role. He says he is Christ's assistant (cf. 3:9) and a steward of the mysteries of God (4:1). The latter metaphor is a telling one. "Steward" *(oikonomos)* was used of an estate manager, usually a slave who ran the house for the master, who was sometimes even an absentee landlord. According to Paul's use of the metaphor, then, even leaders are servants and have their orders. Stewards must take care how they handle their owners' property. Paul, then, was not free to proclaim the gospel in whatever form or fashion he pleased

---

6. The metaphor of fatherhood was used in varied ways, including, of course, the teacher as father, especially in the portrayal of sages. See P. Guttierez, *La Paternité Spirituelle selon Saint Paul* (Paris: Gabalda, 1968), pp. 40ff.

7. E. M. Lassen, "The Use of the Father Image in Imperial Propaganda and 1 Corinthians 4:14-21," *TynB* 42 (1991), pp. 127-36, here p. 129.

8. This may in part explain why Paul's now lost severe letter referred to in the opening chapters of 2 Corinthians seems to have worked better than the more mildly worded 1 Corinthians.

9. Lassen, "Father Image," p. 134.

A Roman teacher and his students depicted in a second-century relief
(Rhineland Museum, Trier, Germany; photo by E. Ferguson)

or that might please the Corinthians. The "mysteries of God" are probably not the sacrament but the apocalyptic secret that Paul has spoken of — that salvation is to be had by faith in Christ crucified. The main thing one is looking for in a steward is faithfulness (v. 2). A good steward is one who does what the master expects.

Paul has now used three metaphors to describe the sort of ministry he and Apollos do: planting (3:5-8), building (3:10ff.), and household management (4:1f.). He says that he is not bothered that the Corinthians are scrutinizing him (v. 3). The verb *anakrinō* has the sense of critically examining or looking to find fault. The reference to a "human tribunal" might conjure up Paul's episode with Gallio in Corinth for the audience. Paul has to answer to only one person, his Master the Christ.

Paul also says that he does not prejudge himself. While he is not conscious of having failed in his ministerial duties, this does not acquit him. One's self-estimate and the estimate of one's fellow Christians do not matter ultimately. Only Christ's judgment counts. No one should be judged before judgment day, and then only the Lord will assume the role of judge.

Here as repeatedly before, Paul introduces future eschatology to correct the over-realized or over-spiritualized eschatology of the Corinthian Christians.[10] One thing that may have fostered their attitudes regarding eschatology was the imperial eschatology, which flourished in Roman colonies and which suggested that the emperor was already the dispenser of the blessings of the gods in this life, as was proved by his having brought the *pax Romana*, peace throughout most of the empire.[11] This could easily have nurtured the idea that "already we reign" (cf. v. 8).[12]

Paul reminds the audience that on judgment day all will be revealed, even one's inner thoughts and motives of the heart (v. 5). Only then will approbation be offered. One will be praised *by God*, the ultimate bestower of true status.

We have already discussed v. 6 and the use there of the verb *metaschēmatizō*, which normally means to change the form of something, though many have thought it should be translated "apply" here, though there is little basis for this conclusion. Barrett urges the translation "appear to apply," but still the stress in the verb is on changing *schēmata*, that is, forms.[13] Paul has been changing the form of his description of the ministry that he and Apollos are engaged in: First it was planting, then building, then household management. All along, he has been developing a covert allusion. V. 6b is clearly connected to v. 6a by *hina* ("in order that"): Paul has used a covert allusion "so that" the Corinthians might learn the meaning of something.

Verse 6b appears to refer to some text or rule, or perhaps the whole OT. M. D. Hooker is to some degree on the right track in saying that Paul is countering what others had taught or modeled in Corinth.

> The wisdom which was paraded by these teachers was something additional to Paul's own message of Christ crucified, the message which he saw as the fulfillment of God's purposes and of "the things which are written." It was a wisdom which was centered on ideas extraneous to the gospel, and which was therefore the wisdom of men, not the wisdom of God. In following this worthless and harmful teaching the Corinthians were not simply adding to that of Paul, but were also going "beyond the things which are written," and it was this search for additional "wisdom" which has led to their divisions, and to the situation where one was "puffed up for the one and against the other."[14]

10. Cf. A. C. Thiselton, "Realized Eschatology at Corinth," *NTS* 24 (1978), pp. 510-26.

11. See the comments below on ch. 15 and the discussion there of J. R. Lanci's unpublished paper, "Roman Eschatology in First-Century Corinth," given at the 1992 national meeting of the Society of Biblical Literature.

12. It is possible that this attitude was exacerbated by the numerous spiritual gifts in Corinth as well.

13. Cf. C. K. Barrett, *The First Epistle to the Corinthians* (New York: Harper and Row, 1968), pp. 105f.

14. M. D. Hooker, *From Adam to Christ* (Cambridge: Cambridge University, 1990), p. 109.

There are two problems with Hooker's assessment of the situation. First, Paul has been offering models of how the Corinthians' *apostoloi* have been acting, models of leadership. This is what the "covert allusion" is all about. It is not specifically about a rival wisdom teaching. It is thus much more likely that Paul is suggesting that the way the Corinthians should evaluate their teachers is by following the OT model. Leaders, like Moses, are "servants of God," indeed often servants with certain human drawbacks like Moses' speech problem.[15] Presumably Paul is suggesting that the Corinthians should not in their estimation of their leaders go beyond a biblical view of leadership or of what a *sophos* ("sage") should be.

Verse 6c should probably be taken to mean that the Corinthian Christians should not get puffed up ("inflated with air") about Apollos over Paul, simply because he uses a certain kind of Greek rhetorical skills or Hellenistic wisdom ideas in his gospel presentation. The phrase "for the one . . . and against the other" should not be underestimated. Paul is countering factiousness that included rivalry, quarrels, boasting, and other sorts of bad behavior all too common during the empire among students of rival Sophistic rhetors.[16]

Verse 7 is also a deflation device. Paul is asking "What makes you think that you are so special that you should be judging God's agents?" Paul reminds the Corinthians that whatever they know, they know it because it has been given to them through the gospel preaching. When all is of grace and is a gift, there is no room or reason for boasting, even about being a follower of one's favorite Christian leaders. It was a commonplace in antiquity that hubris and arrogance led to excessive behavior, so I suspect that Paul is laying the groundwork for the critique of excessive behavior that begins in ch. 5 by dealing with the root cause here. The Corinthians are a perfect example of how abundance, not just material abundance but even abundance of spiritual gifts, leads to loss of restraint and perspective (cf. Philo, *Abr.* 134f.).[17]

One could view the four short sentences in v. 8 as either exclamations or questions since there was no punctuation in the original Greek text, though the second of these sentences makes it more likely that they are all sarcastic exclamations or statements. Already the Corinthian Christians have become gorged, already they are rich, already they have begun to reign even without

---

15. This reconstruction is strongly supported by the analogy Paul draws in 2 Corinthians 3–4 between the ministry of Moses and his own ministry. I would not rule out J. T. Fitzgerald's novel suggestion in *Cracks in an Earthen Vessel*, pp. 123-27, that the phrase in question means "stay within the lines," the advice of a teacher to a young pupil learning how to write. The point then would be in this case to follow the lines of the example set by Paul and Apollos and not go beyond them.

16. Cf. A. Strobel, *Der erste Brief an die Korinther* (Zurich: Theologischer Verlag, 1989), pp. 38f.

17. Cf. Fitzgerald, *Cracks*, p. 132.

the help of their "father"! Should these exclamations be taken literally or figuratively? Is Paul talking about their social status or about something else?

First of all, the irony is such in this section that it is quite impossible to take these statements as straightforward social commentary. Paul is not revoking the "not many" of 1:26 by suggesting that all or most of the Corinthian Christians are of high social status. Furthermore, as "already" suggests, Paul is saying that the Corinthians have gotten something in advance of and without the help of their "father." This surely must refer to some status, ability, or teaching that they have gotten *since* they became Christians. Probably this has something to do with their view of wisdom both in form (eloquence, rhetoric) and in content. Their pneumatic eschatology perhaps led them to think that already through the Spirit they were sages, had achieved kingdom status, and were full of *sophia* (wisdom). The connection here with sages seems clear in light of what Philo says about the Sophists' claims to reign and to be full of *sophia* (*Det.* 33f.).

This "pneumatic sapiential" mentality had been exacerbated by the coming of Apollos and perhaps even more by teachings offered by some local Christians in the absence of Paul and Apollos. If it was possible for one like Apollos to combine *sophia* of form so ably with the *sophia* of Christian content, then surely the Corinthians inspired by the Spirit could do no less!

The phrases "in Christ" and "through Christ" in v. 10 make it clear that the comparison made there is metaphorical.[18] Seneca, like others influenced by Stoicism, said that true kingship is equivalent to wisdom: It is the *sophos* who really rules in this world (*Ep.* 85.2). In Corinth a little wisdom proved to be a dangerous thing, leading to arrogance, elitism, rivalries, and factiousness.

Paul says somewhat forlornly, "I only wish it was so, so we could reign with you" (v. 8). But instead the *apostoloi* have partaken of the character of the cross in their ministry. Fitzgerald points out that Paul's hardship or tribulation catalog in vv. 9-13 stresses in various ways that the *apostoloi* are *last*.[19] By means of a *synkrisis*, a standard rhetorical device (a comparison, used in this case to point out a contrast), Paul will offer both example and admonition.[20] The "status opportunities Paul declined remain the measure of his

---

18. So, rightly, ibid., p. 138, n. 68. This is not to deny the deprivations of Paul, but one suspects that there is ironic hyperbole on both sides of the comparison. Had Paul really already been led around in Roman triumph as a slave? Plank, *Irony of Affliction*, p. 48, is right in saying that Paul overstates the Corinthians' strengths (cf. 4:8 and 1:7), but Paul also likely overstates his own weakness (cf. 4:13 and 2:3). The Corinthians' giftedness is real but overestimated by them (cf. the *exordium*, 1:4-9). Does this suggest that one or more people in Corinth were striving for power and wishing to be head sage in the absence of the *apostoloi*?

19. Fitzgerald, *Cracks*, p. 136.

20. As M. M. Mitchell, *Paul and the Rhetoric of Reconciliation* (Tübingen: Mohr, 1991), p. 220, n. 181, says, a *synkrisis* presupposes that an illustrious person is being held

potential professional standing, and of the expectation of his supporters for him. The extent of his renunciation helps to explain Paul's intense conscious-ness of debasement. He was stepping firmly down in the world."[21]

Perhaps Paul is thinking of the image of those last in the line of a Roman chain of prisoners, the ones who were to die in a spectacle in the arena.[22] Paul may be alluding to his brushes with the law and his treatment by civil and religious officials. The *apostoloi* have looked like fools in public, being ill-treated and, indeed, brutalized.[23] Paul elaborates on this more in 2 Corinthians 10–13. The word translated "wise" in v. 10 is *phronimoi*, not *sophoi*. It has the nuance of the "sensible person." Paul seems to know various sapiential tradi-tions about sages in the Greco-Roman world, and here he sets himself up in contrast to them. For example, Cicero says that the "weak" person is one who has not yet become wise (*Fin.* 4.28.77; cf. Plutarch *Mor.* 1057B), while the Stoic sage was said to be a person worthy of one's gaze and of public admiration (Seneca *Prov.* 29; Epictetus *Diss.* 3.22.58-59) — unlike Paul, who has become a "spectacle." By contrast, Philo says that the true lover of virtue, unlike the Sophist, is very likely to go through these sorts of trials (*Det.* 34). Paul's catalog thus shows how God exhibits the ideal sage, making a spectacle of him.[24] In an upside-down world the truly first or wise are treated like the last or like fools. The dilemma for the Corinthians is that they associate *dynamis* (power) with authority, not weakness, and so for Paul to affirm his weakness is to deny his authority.[25]

Paul paints no glamorous picture of ministry. It involves hunger, thirst, dishonor, weakness, and being ill-clad and always on the move. In addition to all that, Paul adds that he works with his own hands. This is important, because the well-to-do usually considered manual labor too demeaning for any real

---

up as an example. The irony here is that Paul is notable for being a leading example of being *last* or of being a servant.

21. E. A. Judge, "The Social Identity of the First Christians," *Journal of Religious History* 11 (1980), pp. 201-17, here p. 214.

22. We will discuss the Roman triumph and Paul's repeated use of this imagery in the comments below on 2 Corinthians 3–4.

23. The contrast between fool and wise man is basic to Cynic and Stoic thought; cf. Dio Chrysostom 69.4; Diogenes Laertius 7.92. Paul seems to be well aware of these traditions and is distinguishing his view from theirs. For him, the wise man is a fool, or at least appears to be so to the viewing world.

24. Fitzgerald, *Cracks,* p. 147.

25. So rightly, Plank, *Irony of Affliction,* pp. 17f. Paul may well have further exacer-bated the problems by this comparison, for when we get to 2 Corinthians 10–13, where Paul's authority is really at issue, one of the main complaints is about Paul's various weaknesses, which, his opponents point out, he freely admits. Authority cannot be exercised without both power and recognition by those under one's charge. 2 Corinthians faces a crisis of *recognition* of authority: Paul has not lost his *dynamis.*

teacher or philosopher (cf. Epictetus *Diss.* 3.22.45-47). This reference to manual labor clearly distinguishes Paul from both the begging Cynic preachers who wandered the Greco-Roman world and the rhetors, especially the Sophists who took pay for their teaching. The Jewish view of manual work by teachers was different, but this is another little clue that Paul is writing mostly to Gentiles. His polemics seem directed against the well-to-do who looked down on manual labor. He will have to go on and defend his refusal to receive patronage from the Corinthians later in his correspondence.

In vv. **12b** and **13** Paul seems to be drawing on not only the example of Christ but also a portion of the Sermon on the Mount (Luke 6:28). In regard to Paul's use of the Jesus tradition, one must remember that he is writing to those who are already Christians, so his various allusions to words of Jesus (e.g., Romans 14) and his few quotations of Jesus (e.g., 1 Cor. 7:10) reflect his approach with those who are already converted. Indeed, most of Paul's letters are written to those who had been converted for some time, not merely a few days or weeks. Therefore, they probably do not give a clear picture of how he may have used the Jesus tradition in his preaching or in his initial teaching with new converts. If we are to guess from 1 Corinthians 1 and 15, it seems probable that Paul's preaching focused in the main on the soteriologically crucial events in Jesus' life, that is, on Jesus' death and resurrection. This is hardly surprising since Paul was basically a missionary, preaching with hopes to convert many.

In 1 Thessalonians 4–5 we have a few clues suggesting that Paul drew on the Jesus tradition, in this case some eschatologically focused traditions, in his *early* teaching in Thessalonica. In addition, Paul says that the Corinthians are to follow his example as he follows that of Christ (1 Cor. 4:16; 11:1). This presupposes that both Paul and his converts know and care about such traditions. Fee puts it well by saying: "Thus Paul's actual ethical instruction as it appears in his Epistles rarely uses the *language* of Jesus as it is recorded in the Gospels; but on every page it reflects his example and his teaching. . . ."[26] A more detailed comment on imitation of Christ is in order.

A Closer Look: Rhetors, Teachers, and Imitation ──────────

Isocrates, in his important treatise *Against the Sophists* 17, points out that

> the teacher, for his part, must so expound the principles of the art with the utmost possible exactness as to leave out nothing that can be taught and must set such an example of oratory that the students who have taken form under

26. G. D. Fee, *The First Epistle to the Corinthians* (Grand Rapids: Eerdmans, 1987), p. 187.

his instruction and are able to pattern themselves after him will, from the start, show in their speaking a degree of grace and charm that is not found in others.

As E. A. Castelli has pointed out, the teaching methods of the Sophists were based specifically on imitation.[27] This makes Paul's special stress on mimesis in 1 and 2 Corinthians especially telling. He is countering the sort of example a Sophist would set and does so with his example of the sage who is the servant of God and God's people and by using anti-Sophistic rhetoric. It is a failure to recognize this that leads Castelli to the incorrect conclusion that Paul is using mimetic language to make a coercive move and to establish himself at the top of the ecclesiastical hierarchy.

Much closer to the mark is B. Sanders, who urges that the goal of Paul's call for imitation is for the Corinthians to manifest unitive behavior as Paul and his coworkers have set the example in doing. Sanders rightly points to 10:23–11:1 as filling out Paul's meaning. Imitation is not to seek one's own advantage but that of the many. This is the sort of rhetorical move one would expect in a deliberative piece concerned with the issues of future benefit or advantage to the group.[28]

Paul believes that his role and status are established by God. 1 Corinthians 1–4 is not an *apologia* or an attempt to reestablish a lost authority. Paul distinguishes himself both from the sort of father figure the emperor might be and from the sort other teachers, especially Sophists, might be, especially by means of his hardship catalog (vv. 9-13). Unless one wants to argue that all fathers are bad parents and inherently oppressive and that therefore all father-figure imagery is necessarily the imagery of coercion and manipulation, Castelli's argument will not stand.

Second, it is quite untrue to say that Paul is imposing himself between his converts and Christ by calling for them to imitate him as he does Christ. Paul is not interested in keeping the Corinthians in a state of perpetual infancy. He wants them to grow up. He would like nothing better than if they truly imitated Christ and did not cause him so much work and heartache. He is not threatened by the presence of other mature Christians, such as his coworkers, both male and female, or by other *apostoloi*. Whatever sort of hierarchy Paul presupposes, it entails an inverted pyramid where leaders are enslaved, belong to the community, and must serve it from below.

---

27. E. A. Castelli, *Imitating Paul: A Discourse of Power* (Louisville: Westminster/John Knox, 1991), p. 83; cf. also G. A. Kennedy, *Classical Rhetoric and Its Christian and Secular Tradition from Ancient to Modern Times* (Chapel Hill: University of North Carolina, 1980), pp. 116-19. Roman oratory most often took its cues in regard to imitation from Greek rhetor-teachers or ambassadors. This may explain in part why Paul presents himself as an ambassador of Christ to the Corinthians in 2 Cor. 5:20, where he comes clean about being a rhetor, trying to persuade and making appeals on Christ's behalf. Cf. pp. 396-97 below. Imitation was widely stressed by rhetoricians in general, and everything was thought to be dependent on the character and model of one's teacher. See E. Fantham, "Imitation and Evolution: The Discussion of Rhetorical Imitation in Cicero *De Oratore* 2:87-97 and Some Related Problems of Ciceronian Theory" and idem, "Imitation and Decline: Rhetorical Theory and Practice in the First Century after Christ," *Classical Philology* 73 (1978), pp. 1-16, 102-16.

28. B. Sanders, "Imitating Paul: 1 Cor. 4:16," *HTR* 74 (1981), pp. 353-63.

This is hardly modeled on the hierarchical pyramid of the larger patriarchal Roman society, where being a slave was the most despised status.

On the positive side, when Paul speaks of imitating Christ, he means that he models himself on the narrative pattern of Christ's whole career of self-sacrificial giving, as the Christ hymn in Philippians 2 shows. There he calls his converts to have the same mind as Christ, just as in 1 Cor. 2:16 the "we" who have the mind of Christ refers to "we" Christians, not just the *apostoloi*. At times, imitating Christ means being conformed to the pattern of Christ's death in one's life events while one tries to serve Christ (cf. 2 Corinthians 10–13). At other times imitation is Paul's conscious effort to act and live humbly, deliberately stepping down the ladder of social status so that he might relate to and help all, even slaves. Imitation for Paul is both an event and a choice, both being conformed to Christ's image and choosing to conform to it. 1 Corinthians 4 stresses acting in a way that promotes the unity of the congregation and not its disintegration.

Some have thought Paul audacious, especially when he speaks of bearing the sufferings of Christ in his body (2 Cor. 4:10). But it would be wrong to read Paul as a deluded individual with a messiah complex. Texts like 1 Cor. 15:8-10 rule that out. Paul believes that by God's grace one can live life *like* Christ. This is so because Paul also believes, as the hymn in Philippians 2 attests, that Christ lived and died as a human being who set aside his divine prerogatives and during his time on earth acted by the power and guidance of the Holy Spirit and of God's Word, the same resources available to every believer.[29] Mimesis for Paul means what the word suggests: imitation without total identification. The glorious conclusion of mimesis comes, in Paul's view, at the resurrection of believers, when they are truly conformed to the image of the Son, even in their bodies, though even then Christ remains the only Christ and Christians only become perfect likenesses.

There has been considerable debate about the final two terms Paul applies to himself and the apostles in v. 13 — both terms denoting something that is a castoff. The first word literally means "sweepings" or "scrapings," things that are thrown out. The term also came to mean scapegoat, one who is thrown to the gods to appease them. The word may have that meaning here, but probably Paul is simply using two words to say the same thing: The *apostoloi* are being treated like the scum of the earth. In v. 12 Paul may be thinking of how some Corinthians are treating him behind his back — slandering him, swearing at him, and the like.

In v. 14 Paul says that he does not intend to put his audience to shame

---

29. I am not suggesting Paul believes in a kenotic christology, according to which Christ emptied himself of his divine nature. The hymn in Philippians 2 does suggest that Paul believes that Christ chose to give up the right to draw on his divine prerogatives and power in order to experience the true character of human limitations. This meant that Christ accepted limitations of time, space, power, and knowledge. He lived and died in the strength of those powers of word and Spirit available to all believers.

in what he writes them. This denial is a rhetorical move since he is, in fact, trying to shame them into reevaluating their views and lifestyle. Paul chooses to use the father-children metaphor to describe his relationship with them. He is exhorting them as beloved children and has a right to do so because he begat them by means of the gospel and in Christ.

The term *paidagogos* (v. 15) refers not so much to a "teacher" as to a "guardian" (cf. Gal. 3:24), the servant who walked a rich child to school and back home and helped him with his recitations at home and so was also a tutor to some degree. Paul's use of this word may be a reference to the many local "sages" of the *ekklēsia* in Corinth, rather than Apollos, whom Paul classes with himself.

Paul's exhortation to the audience in v. 16 to imitate him, as he imitates Christ, must not be taken out of context. It refers to his moral way of life and his ministerial lifestyle, which he has just described. According to v. 17 Paul has sent along his number one son in the faith.[30] Timothy is being sent to remind the audience to imitate Paul and Christ, taking a servant approach to leadership and seeing wisdom in light of the cross.[31] It is not merely Paul's way but his *ways* in Christ of which they need to be reminded.

Paul says that he teaches in the same manner everywhere he teaches, in all the *ekklēsiae,* presumably meaning in all the congregations that he has established. So he is not asking anything special of the Corinthians. There is no evidence that Timothy ever got to Corinth. He seems to have gotten no further than Macedonia.

In v. 18 Paul reveals that it is just "some" in Corinth that have become puffed up or conceited, and his comments are especially directed to them. One suspects that unfortunately it is some of the leaders in Corinth, the guardians he has referred to in v. 15, who in their leadership role have been setting a bad example for other Corinthians. Paul hopes to come to them soon, but it is always as the Lord wills, and when we get to 16:5-9 it may appear that he has changed his plans. It is not impossible that this lengthy letter was composed over some period of time and that Paul's plans had to change during that time. He says that when he comes he will get to the bottom of things and find out not merely about the bombast of the conceited but what their real power is

---

30. It is not completely clear whether Timothy was converted by Paul, but 1 and 2 Timothy suggest that he received the laying on of hands from Paul and so might be thought of as a sort of adopted son of Paul.

31. There are numerous imponderables here. It does not appear that we have an epistolary aorist in 4:17, though I am tempted to take it that way. But if Timothy was sent with the letter rather than before it, 16:10 makes little sense, and it is strange that Paul did not mention Timothy in the initial greeting if he was still present with him. Acts 19:22 is not decisive either. Perhaps Sosthenes was the bearer and oral performer of this letter; otherwise the sole mention of him in 1:1 is strange.

(v. 19). God's dominion is not just rhetoric or eloquent talk, but is in the end a matter of the transforming power of the Spirit. This verse strongly suggests that Paul assumes that the "some" are using Sophistic rhetoric to bewitch the Corinthians into a false view of what *sophia* really is and that he thinks that God's kingdom is partly present already, but unlike at least "some" of the Corinthians he also thinks it is partly future. He gives them an alternative. He can come like a father with a rod of discipline or he can come in a spirit of gentleness, in love.[32] Obviously he would rather do the latter and is hoping that this letter will change them before he arrives.[33] This proved to be a vain hope.

This concludes the first major argument of the letter, which has been concerned with the character of true wisdom, true leadership, and true self-evaluation. As Plank says, for Paul God's scandalous activity on the cross sets up a pervasive paradox that not only reverses the destiny of humankind but also transvalues the very categories by which one evaluates people. God vindicates human powerlessness and humiliates merely human power.[34] This is what Paul's counter-order wisdom of the cross is all about, and it is radical enough that, if taken seriously, it will require the Corinthians to give up many of the dominant values and presuppositions of their culture about power and wisdom. One expects both consistency and clarity in one's world and worldview, and Paul's message here profoundly disturbs the social equilibrium that the Corinthians appear to take for granted. To see Paul here as just another oppressive patriarchal power broker totally misunderstands the character of this material.

Paul has portrayed the Corinthians in two irreconcilable ways, in regard to their calling (1:26) and in regard to their self-perception (4:10).[35] He questions their answers and assumptions about themselves and in chs. 5–15 will go on to provide example after example that he is right. Their excessive behavior represents a misunderstanding and misuse of their gifts, calling, and status in Christ. This whole argument, especially the powerful and evocative language in 4:9-13, which is full of rhetorical polish and meant to be ear

32. D. Daube, "Paul a Hellenistic Schoolmaster?" in *Studies in Rationalism, Judaism, and Universalism*, ed. R. Loewe (London: Routledge, 1966), pp. 67-71, points out that the metaphor of the rod could point to either a Jewish or a Greco-Roman schoolmaster. Paul is rather like Quintilian here in preferring not to use the rod, an exceptional attitude among ancient educators.

33. It is clear that Paul is drawing to a close the first major argument of the letter, and one cannot help but note the similarities to what he says in 2 Cor. 13:1ff. He would rather use the art of persuasion, but he is not afraid to use discipline on his unruly and immature children if needed.

34. Plank, *Irony of Affliction*, p. 55.

35. Ibid., p. 61.

catching,[36] is an attempt to break down the Corinthians' perceptions of social status, power, and wisdom and their self-perceptions based on those misunderstandings. The function of this argument is to leave the audience open to change, to adopting a more Pauline view of self and world.

It has been said that figurative speech is speech with the volume turned up.[37] It is also speech that requires pondering and that prevents the immediate pigeonholing of the speaker's words into one's preexisting worldview. Paul has made it the central issue that both Jesus and he are enslaved sages whose power is made evident in weakness. This is meant to force the Corinthians to rethink what really amounts to status, power, and wisdom.

> That ironic vision sets the afflicted free, not from the existence of suffering, but from the fear of its assumed meaning; the expectation that human plight drives away the presence of God and the communion of human beings; the dread that in our dying we are alone, cut off from life. . . . That elemental fact of suffering nails theology to a world where life and death commingle. . . . The world which hosts the intimacy of life and death demands theology to speak through paradox and allows it to do so in good faith. Aware of the irony of affliction, theological discourse must respect the existence of suffering, but neither condemn nor glorify its circumstance.[38]

Paul's goal in 1 Corinthians is unity, not uniformity, as his use of body imagery shows (12:14ff.). For him, equality is based on all being created in God's image and thus all being of equal and sacred worth, not all having the same roles and functions. 1 Corinthians suggests that roles and functions should be determined by what God has gifted and called people to do, not by race, gender, or ethnic extraction. These gifts can be so-called natural abilities or resources, or they can be supernatural endowments such as a gift of prophecy or tongues.

It is true that social position, because the rich had more time and resources, did lead quite naturally to positions of leadership in the early *ekklēsia.* What prevented this from being simply a baptism of the status quo is Paul's theology of Christ-shaped leadership, which is not gender-specific in character and thus not a mere endorsement of the patriarchal hierarchy of the Roman household or society. A Phoebe as well as a Stephanas could be a leader of a household congregation, but as leaders they were *diakonoi* and were to function as *diakonoi* — servants of God and of God's people. All leaders were

---

36. E.g., the response in vv. 12b-13, which includes both syntactic and phonic repetition: *loidoroumenoi eulogoumen, diōkomenoi anechometha, dysphēmoumenoi parakaloumen.* Cf. Plank, *Irony of Affliction,* p. 83.

37. Cf. Plank, *Irony of Affliction,* p. 73, following R. Tannehill.

38. Ibid., pp. 94, 93.

servants of the community, even the *apostoloi,* and so to those to whom more resources were given of them more was required.

It is sobering to compare Paul's resumé in 4:9-13 with what is usually presented to a modern congregation. One wonders how many congregations would hire someone like Paul, who touts his weakness in personal presence, his penchant to find or stir up trouble, his run-ins with the law, and his lack of the skills so often most valued today in a preacher, namely, good oral form, verbal eloquence, powerful delivery, and meaningful gestures.

I suspect that all too often we evaluate our ministers using Corinthian, not Pauline, criteria. In doing so, we, too, have bought into the world's dominant vision of what it means to be wise, powerful, and of great worth, and have, like the Corinthians, made void the preaching of the cross. The wisdom of the cross is a message not about strength *instead* of weakness, but in fact about power *through* weakness, *through* self-sacrificial behavior, *through* reliance on God's power to work through us. It is not about our human power to manipulate a situation. Until we learn the meaning of the words "when I was weak, then I was strong," until we learn what it means to be empty of self and full of Christ, we will continue to misread Paul's theology of leadership, status, power, and wisdom. Until then, the *ekklēsia* will continue to play the game of power politics with the ministry, an all too human and too Corinthian game indeed.

Argument II, Division 1: 5:1-13

Beyond All Bounds

Beginning in ch. 5, Paul moves on to other concerns that have been raised by the oral reports he has received. Should we treat chs. 5 and 6 as a unit or as dealing with different and unrelated concerns? One plausible proposal is that the court case referred to in ch. 6 concerned the sexual scandal mentioned in ch. 5. But it is more likely that discussion of the forensic process *within* the community in ch. 5 leads Paul to discuss the forensic process *outside* the community in ch. 6.

Paul wants the Corinthian Christians to be involved in the internal judicial process, but not to take their disputes to outside courts, which is precisely the opposite of what is happening. This reveals Paul's view of Christian community. He sees the Christian community as having reasonably well-defined boundaries and thus as a subculture that even has its own judicial procedures.[1] This is how Paul wants the community to be, not how it was actually functioning.

The difficulty in applying modern sociological concepts such as group-grid analysis (a means of plotting the degree of stratification and cohesiveness of a group on a four quadrant grid map) to the Christian community in Corinth is that we have no report of what the community was like apart from Paul's assessment.[2] While the community may have been functioning with a limited amount of organization, it is not clear that Paul thought that this was a good thing. 1 Corinthians is surely a letter about achieving the right balance between Spirit and structure. Since it was structure that was lacking in Corinth, Paul tries to inject some order without quenching the Spirit.

---

1. Paul emphasizes the community's responsibility for judging the case of the incestuous person. Only one verse deals with the person and twelve with the congregation's culpability in the matter. Cf. B. Rosner, "Corporate Responsibility in 1 Corinthians 5," *NTS* 38 (1992), pp. 470-73, here p. 471.

2. Cf. R. A. Atkins, *Egalitarian Community: Ethnography and Exegesis* (Tuscaloosa: University of Alabama, 1991), especially pp. 128ff. There are several other problems as well with Atkins's stimulating work. Paul's body metaphor in 1 Corinthians 12 is not an anti-hierarchical argument but an argument for unity amid a diversity of gifts, some of which he in fact affirms as being of greater benefit to the body. Furthermore, it is very difficult to argue that the actual state of the Corinthian community was a "high group" situation, though I would agree it was "low grid" in terms of a stratified structure of leadership. It appears more likely that the Corinthians were in a low group situation where factiousness was always a threat and ego-oriented goals took precedence over group unity.

I would argue that Atkins's description of a quadrant A environment likely fits the Corinthian community as it actually functioned:

> The social environment of quadrant A is dominated by strongly competitive conditions between individuals. Individuals contract with each other freely. This means the social scale within the cultural unit is open to anyone to move, up or down. Each person is responsible for him or herself. This is the entrepreneurial culture where rules for making contracts and specialists in each field of human endeavor abound. This is a stable social environment of competition and achievement.[3]

This is a very adequate description of the environment of the Corinthian boomtown, where patronage relationships and the social mobility of freedmen and freedwomen dominated the scene.

Two other clues show that the Corinthian community was in a quadrant A mode: It was they, not Paul, who made much of baptism and baptizers, which indicates that they had an elaborated symbolic system. And many of the dominant members of the community obviously believed that society and nature were separate realms, as indicated by their attitudes toward incest and the body in general as manifested in chs. 5–6. They thought that what they did with the body did not affect their honor or status either in society or in the *ekklēsia*. It even appears that the community *as a whole* was arrogant about the incestuous relationship.

The sexual problems discussed in chs. 5 and 6 were created by the male members of the community. There was in Greco-Roman society a very clear double standard with a shame code in regard to the behavior of married women. 6:12ff. is not, any more than 5:1-5, about the behavior or arguments of Christian women trying to justify their behavior.

In regard to *Paul's* vision of community, he is trying to establish a high group consciousness with what I would call a mid-grid in terms of both stratification of roles and individuation. Paul believes that human identity must be established by the right dialectic between the one and the many, between identity as an individual and identity as a group member. He knows that "in order for the group to work or have substance there must be a collection of individuals who give over some of their identity and independence explicitly and/or implicitly to the group."[4]

Paul knows that he is dealing with a voluntaristic community, much like a guild or club in Roman society. In accord with this similarity, he wishes to affirm some asymmetrical roles, such as his own and that of his coworkers toward the Corinthian *ekklēsia* and some roles at the purely local level as well,

---

3. Atkins, *Egalitarian Community,* p. 70.
4. Ibid., p. 61.

as seen in 16:15f., though Stephanas may be an example of achieved status. Paul's own status as Christ's agent is in his view not an acheived status but a designated status verified through Paul's actual work.

In Paul's thought there is a dialectic between factors that lead to ordering in the community and factors that tend, conversely, toward leveling in the community. One might expect that possession by all of the Holy Spirit and of the Spirit's gifts would be a totally leveling factor. Paul makes it clear, however, that there is a ranking of roles — listed in chs. 12 and 14 — based on what is most beneficial to the group as a whole. Paradoxically, Paul's view of leadership as obligatory service to the group prevents a more stratified approach to leadership.

For Paul the Christian society stands over against nature because nature and human nature are fallen. Therefore, clear boundaries must be established between what may seem natural and what is appropriate behavior. "A concern for purity is not a concern for a hierarchy among the participants, but a concern about the boundaries of the group. Purity and the perception of danger in taboos are markers for group separation from the rest of the world, which is perceived as impure."[5]

In the Greco-Roman world, extramarital sex, indeed a wide variety of forms of nonmarital sex that Jews and Christians would find aberrant, including various forms of incest, was not considered shameful. Jews and Christians were in a notable minority in their attitudes about fornication, prostitution, adultery, incest, and the like. But what Paul faces here, a man having incestuous relations with his father's wife, was considered inappropriate by most pagans in the Greco-Roman world. As MacDonald points out, it is not in this case the impurity of the outside world that is in danger of polluting the community but the immorality that has been allowed to penetrate the sacred community itself.[6]

---

5. Ibid., p. 90. It is the failure to recognize this that leads A. C. Wire (*Corinthian Women Prophets* [Minneapolis: Fortress, 1990]) and others to misread what Paul is doing in texts like 1 Corinthians 11. Paul is not trying to put women in their place but to regulate both male and female behavior so that group boundaries can be clear. The men, more than the women, would have most felt the restrictive character of Paul's advice, and it appears from 6:16ff. and chs. 8–10 that it is primarily if not exclusively the men who are arguing for certain sexual and social freedoms that violate the boundaries of the Christian community. Wire's attempt to argue that there was a radical feminist pneumatic group in Corinth that Paul was countering at every turn in 1 Corinthians involves a tremendous amount of mirror reading and question begging.

6. M. Y. MacDonald, *The Pauline Churches: A Socio-Historical Study of Institutionalisation in the Pauline and Deutero-Pauline Writings* (Cambridge: Cambridge University, 1988), p. 68. In ch. 7 Paul does not see the unbeliever as a pollutant of the believing spouse. In ch. 14 he regards the presence of an unbeliever in Christian worship as acceptable. "Paul forbids the community members to eat with the believer who is guilty of immorality (1 Cor. 5.11), while apparently legitimating eating with unbelievers, irrespective of their life-styles (1 Cor. 10.27)" (MacDonald, p. 68).

A Closer Look: Honor and Shame in the Roman World ————————

In the Roman world honor was bound up with male ideology and was a male value. It was only educated males who could aspire to most public offices (except some specifically religious roles such as that of priestess) or be lawyers, rhetors, or masters of the games *(agōnothetes)*. Honor was basically bound up with the public order and was a matter of establishing one's public reputation by public works, like those Erastus undertook in order to become aedile in Corinth (see pp. 32-34 above). Honor was very closely linked to *exousia* (power), and thus also to authority. The reward for honorable behavior that bolstered the values of the society was public acclaim in the form of inscriptions, proclamations, and celebrations.[7] In such a culture one looks for, and many live for, the acclaim of others. The common quest for honor and praise was one of the main forces that bound society together.[8]

It was difficult to shame a person who already had high status or considerable power or authority, since in a stratified society shaming is normally what superiors do to inferiors or equals to equals. It is a way of putting someone in his or her place. Since honor in a Roman city like Corinth had a *public* and male face, it had little to do with a man's sexual involvements, with certain clearly defined exceptions.

What Paul actually says about male sexual behavior would have seemed to the target audience an unnecessary, if not irrelevant, restriction of male privileges. In their minds, what Paul was talking about had little to do with shame or honor. But "apparently it is within the area of 'lifestyle' that Paul wants to establish the distinctive characterizations of a specific Christian identity."[9] Paul was redefining the whole zone of honor and shame for his converts.

If honor was primarily a male matter in the patriarchal Greco-Roman society, shame was primarily a female matter, or, more broadly, a matter of the behavior of the so-called inferior members of society: women, slaves, and minors. Wives were expected to uphold the honor of their husbands by avoiding shame, that is, by avoiding illicit sexual unions or infidelity of any sort. Successfully avoiding such shame led to public recognition for wives, as is seen from the numerous grave inscriptions praising one woman or another for having been an *univira* — married to just one man and faithful to him throughout life.[10] For women, the negative task of avoiding shame predominated because their primary domain was still the family. But there is evidence that during the empire women were rising in status and so were beginning to be able to gain honor during their lifetime by, for example, being patronesses of clubs or societies or obtaining considerable wealth in business ventures.

The first-century culture that Paul is writing to is an *agonistic* culture.

7. What a society gives homage to is a sure clue to what it most values.
8. On all this see H. Moxnes, "Honor, Shame, and the Outside World in Paul's Letter to the Romans," in *The Social World of Formative Christianity and Judaism,* ed. J. Neusner, et al. (Philadelphia: Fortress, 1988), pp. 207-18.
9. Ibid., p. 213.
10. W. Zeisel, "*Univira:* An Example of Continuity and Change in Roman Society," *Church History* 46 (1977), pp. 19-32.

[Almost] every social interaction that takes place outside one's family or outside one's circle of friends is perceived as a challenge to honor, a mutual attempt to acquire honor from one's social equals. Thus gift-giving, invitations to dinner, debates over issues of law, buying and selling, arranging marriages — all these sorts of interaction take place according to patterns of honor called challenge-response.[11]

In a sense almost every public activity was a competition for praise and honor.[12] In such an environment it is easy to see why there were rivalries among Corinthian Christians over their teachers. Sophistic debates and competitions where audiences were urged to make a *synkrisis* or comparison and decide in favor of one or the other are but one manifestation of this dominant cultural orientation. In such a society a fool is one who gives honor to that which should not be honored or to a person who should not be honored.[13]

This is of special relevance to 1 Corinthians 5 and 6, because legal proceedings were part of this larger cultural game and were seen as a means of shaming people.[14] Paul's strategy in this cultural situation is to redraw the lines of honor and shame, so that male sexual behavior can produce shame and works by women that benefit the community, including remaining single to serve the Lord, can lead to public honor. Paul is not in the business of simply baptizing the cultural values of Roman society. To the contrary, he undermines many of the most cherished values and redefines what real status amounts to, namely being in Christ or being sons and daughters of God. For Paul it is God, not society, that can bestow real honor and dispense lasting shame. It is God, including God in Christ, that is at the apex of Paul's pyramid of values, and as such only God is immune to Paul's telling criticisms of his world. Paul was attempting to set up a *counter*culture with a set of values often at odds with that of the larger society.

11. B. Malina, *The NT World: Insights from Cultural Anthropology* (Atlanta: John Knox, 1981), p. 32. Malina draws on the work of Mary Douglas, which is based on modern anthropological research and some of which does not apply to the kind of honor-shame culture that existed in Roman Corinth in Paul's day.

12. This may be in part because honor was seen as a "limited good." There was not an infinite amount of it to go around, and thus as in an athletic contest there had to be both winners and losers. All could not succeed in the competition for status, honor, and power.

13. This may be of special relevance in regard to why Paul calls the word about the cross foolishness and himself a fool for Christ's and the community's sake (see below on 2 Corinthians 10–13). What Paul esteems as of highest value — the crucified Jesus and living a life that is cruciform in pattern — is considered shameful by the larger culture. Humility was not seen as a virtue in the Roman world, but was despised as characteristic of the behavior of slaves. Paul goes against the grain of many of the cultural indicators of status by proclaiming himself an enslaved sage who follows an enslaved and crucified Messiah.

14. It is also true that refusing to honor someone was to shame that person, and this too created quarrels, factions and rivalries.

In ch. 5 Paul must deal with a notorious case of incest. Apparently he tried to deal with this and other matters of sexual immorality in a previous letter (v. 9), to which the Corinthians replied, perhaps with some protests and demurs. Paul is now responding to their response. His vehemence is in part because he has covered this ground before, but the Corinthians ignored or misinterpreted him.

The term *porneia* (v. 1), which by derivation relates to the frequenting of prostitutes, had in Paul's era become a term for all sorts of sexual aberrations, including incest.[15] He is dealing with a man having sex not with his own mother but apparently with his stepmother. Paul's ruling comes out of the levitical code, specifically Lev. 18:8 (cf. 18:7), and he closes off his response in v. 13 with another ruling from the Torah, Deut. 17:7, as before concluding a section with an OT quotation to reinforce the authority and validity of his teaching. This suggests not only that Paul believed that some of the holiness code still applied to Christians, but also that there must have been a large enough number of Jewish Christians in Corinth who would take Paul's side in this matter to interpret his ruling if there was any doubt about its implications.

It is not clear from v. 2 whether the smugness of the Corinthians is maintained *in spite of* this immorality or whether it has to do specifically with being broad-minded enough simply to accept it. J. K. Chow argues that the issue here involves a wealthy family that stood to lose considerable money if the mother was allowed to remarry into another family and take her assets with her (cf. Juvenal *Sat.* 6.135-41).[16] One of the more common forms of marriage during the empire was free marriage *(sine manu),* where the woman retained control over her inherited property.[17] To a large extent, ancient arranged marriages of the more well-to-do were property transactions in any case. A possible clue that this is the issue here is that Paul twice names the greedy *(pleonektēs)* after referring to men who are sexually immoral (vv. 10f.).[18]

Chow then suggests that the man (or the woman) may have been a

15. It is not, however, a technical term for either fornication or adultery. The latter would be *moicheia.*

16. J. K. Chow, *Patronage and Power: A Study of Social Networks in Corinth* (Sheffield: JSOT, 1992), pp. 137ff.; A. D. Clarke, *Secular and Christian Leadership in Corinth* (dissertation, Cambridge, 1991), pp. 82ff.

17. It is unlikely that Paul is dealing here with a stepmother married because of the size of her dowry, since during the empire dowries were generally not that large. Cf. R. P. Saller, "Roman Dowry and Property Devolution," *Classical Quarterly* 34 (1984), pp. 195-205, especially pp. 204f.

18. Chow, *Patronage and Power,* pp. 137f. It is also relevant that men normally married in their twenties, while women were often as much as ten or more years younger. Fathers often did not live long enough to see their sons married. There may have been little age difference between the stepmother and the son.

patron of the Corinthian *ekklēsia* with whom the congregation had cordial relations and whom it was therefore reluctant to offend.[19] This is possible but the text does not say that this was the case.[20] Clients were expected to support their patrons in whatever major decisions they made, since they knew which side their bread was buttered on. At the very least they would be afraid to challenge the patron.

Paul says that the Corinthians ought to have been in mourning, as though there had been a death in the family. In a spiritual sense there had been a death, and Paul was about to tell them to remove the unclean corpse from their midst (v. 2) and would quickly reinforce this with a graphic leaven metaphor (vv. 6-8). It has often been thought that the Corinthians were operating with a *theologia gloria,* believing that what they did with their bodies was of little or no consequence or that they were above petty morality, being too spiritual to bother with such matters. But ch. 7 makes it clear that many of them *were* concerned about what was done with the body. So it is more likely that they had bought into the pagan patriarchal ideology, according to which there was normally no shame involved in men having sexual relationships outside marriage. An honor and shame culture often does not measure right and wrong against some absolute law code given by God, as did Jews and Christians, especially when "internal" family matters are involved. What was right was whatever brought honor or was not shameful — so long as one did not fall afoul of the Roman law. And when doing what some Roman law did forbid was not thought dishonorable, the law would sometimes be ignored, if not openly broken.

Verses 3 and 4 are difficult in two regards: First, what does Paul mean by being "present in spirit"? Is he present spiritually by means of this letter, or will he be spiritually present in some way when the Corinthian congregation deals with this matter? Or is this just a figure of speech, something like "with you in my thoughts"? Second, with what is the phrase "in the name of the Lord Jesus" connected?

Paul is basically not a trichotomist in his understanding of human nature. There are the outer bodily physical parts and the inner nonphysical dimension, which includes everything else and is called the "spirit."[21] It seems from v. 4 that Paul does envision himself as in some sense actually present

19. Chow, *Patronage and Power,* p. 139. Cf. below, pp. 162-65.

20. Chow also advances the more controversial thesis that Paul is basically countering the same sort of people in all of chs. 1–16, namely rich, powerful members of the congregation who were loath to give up their social status and the privileges that went with it in the larger society (p. 139). While I doubt that all the problems can be pinned on this group, Chow is probably right in saying that they were the main troublemakers. They obviously had the most to lose by following Paul's program of deinculturation.

21. See below on 2 Corinthians 4–5, pp. 389-91.

with the Corinthians. Perhaps "with you in spirit" in that verse refers to the Holy Spirit, with Paul's letter also conveying a sort of apostolic presence. This letter, as others, would be read and acted on while the congregation was gathered. Paul has already passed sentence but the Corinthians will not know or act on that until the letter is read in worship, and so it will be as if the decision were just being made when the letter is read.

But Paul does not try to act unilaterally here. V. 5 should be understood as saying "*we* should deliver him" and suggests that the congregation in Corinth is expected to participate in the expulsion of the immoral brother and to assume the authority with Paul to carry out the expulsion. The power of the Lord by the Spirit will be with them when they assemble to make this decision possible and effective.

In the light of Matt. 18:20, the phrase "in the name of the Lord" (v. **4a**) probably goes with "when you are assembled." The expulsion is to be carried out not by the Corinthian leaders but by the believers as a body. The offender is to be cast out into the realm where Satan is still the ruler "for the destruction of the flesh" (v. 5). The ultimate aim of the expulsion is not punitive but rather "that the spirit may be saved" on the eschatological day of judgment.[22]

How are we to understand "the destruction of the flesh"? This could mean physical abuse or even death, but how would death save an unrepentant person? More likely Paul refers in this way to the destruction of the sinful inclinations of this brother. *Sarx,* "flesh," often refers in Paul's letters to human sinful inclinations. It can be asked how Satan would accomplish this or whether Satan would not *strengthen* the man's sinful inclinations. But delivering the man into Satan's *realm* is not quite the same as delivering him to Satan. There was neither social compulsion nor probably any social advantage for most people to be Christians in Corinth. This brother was a Christian by free choice. It is likely that his stepmother was not a believer since Paul does not try to deal with her as well. One must not confuse this text with 11:30-32, and it is unheard of for Paul to talk about salvation being purely a matter of saving the spirit.

Probably Paul envisions two things. First, he hopes that this shock therapy, expulsion of this man, might douse his sinful inclinations and shame him, which in the Greco-Roman culture was often thought of as a fate worse than death. There were no other *ekklēsiae* in Corinth, so this action would be

---

22. A. Y. Collins, "The Function of 'Excommunication' in Paul," *HTR* 73 (1980), pp. 251-63, adduces some interesting parallels from Qumran (CD 2:5f., 15-17; 8:21-24) that lead her to suggest that "the spirit" here refers to the Holy Spirit in the community, not the spirit of the man in question. This is possible, since the larger concern is with the moral integrity and holiness of the Corinthian congregation. The problem with this view is that "the flesh" is that of the individual, and so one would expect "spirit" to refer to the individual as well (cf. v. 13).

effective if the man wanted to remain a Christian. If he was a person of wealth and status this would be a very daring move, for it was "not done" in such a culture to shame one's superior. If he was a patron it would be a complete *faux pas* to do what Paul recommends. Second, Paul hopes that this action will lead to repentance and restoration and ultimately to final salvation of both body and spirit. Hubristic behavior often leaves one out of touch with how things are and really ought to be.

Paul illustrates the principle with a leaven metaphor (vv. **6-8**). Leaven was not the same as yeast. It was fermented dough left over to be used as a rising agent with the next batch of bread. The point of the illustration is that tolerating this immorality could tempt others to see how far they could push things. The bad apple will spoil the barrel if it is not thrown out.

Paul uses the metaphor flexibly. Cleansing out the old leaven (immorality) comes after the sacrifice of the lamb, who is Jesus,[23] though in the celebration of the Jewish Feast of Weeks casting out the old leaven comes before the Passover meal. Paul's basic exhortation, here as elsewhere, is "Be what you already are" or "Live out what Christ has worked in you." So he says "You are already unleavened; therefore cast out the old bad habits and existing bad examples and get on with being the new batch." This also meant casting out malice, greed, and immorality and cultivating sincerity and truth. Paul is not urging his audience to be or do something they do not have the internal resources from the Holy Spirit to be or do. Always his exhortations are based on a transformation that his audience has already experienced, which has made them a new creation. He is trying to help them get on with living out of what they are.[24]

Paul can only say "be what you are" because he really believes that they are changed and are capable by the power of God of being what they ought to be. Paul was no utopian ethicist. The imperative is always built on the indicative of what Christ has already done on the cross and what the Spirit has done in the *ekklēsia* and in the individual believer.

Verses **9-11** give us a clue as to what Paul wrote to the Corinthians in the letter that has been called Corinthians A (see below, pp. 329-30), which preceded 1 Corinthians. This letter apparently included some comments about idolatry as well as immorality (cf. 1 Corinthians 8–10). Though the verb

---

23. He is simply called the Passover, not the Passover lamb.

24. In Paul's view, the horror of sin in the Christian is not that the old nature creates an irresistible impulse but that one sins against the new creation when one has the spiritual resources to resist doing so. He believes that God's grace is more powerful in the believer than the effect of the remaining *sarx* or sinful inclinations. But the resources of grace within must be drawn on. They do not work automatically, since God gives these gifts to persons. Therefore, believers must work out their salvation with fear and trembling as God works in them (Phil. 2:12f.).

egrapsa (written) is the same in v. 11 as in v. 9, probably v. 11 refers to what Paul has just now written them, not to what he wrote in the earlier letter.

Paul stresses that it is not his or any Christian's job to judge the world (vv. **12f.**). Christians must bear a prophetic word, but should they try to enact a Christian worldview in a pagan world without voluntary compliance and conversion? Paul does affirm a judicial process inside the *ekklēsia*. This disciplinary process is a judgment, not a personal vendetta, against a particular action. It does not involve a human judgment about a person's eternal salvation, which is for God to judge. Paul continues to call this errant brother a brother, and the disciplinary action is meant to be remedial.

Paul's position here is not one of withdrawing from the world and living in a community physically set apart. It is rather one of being the *ekklēsia* in the midst of the world. Not the world but the unrepentant brother is to be shunned. Christians are not to associate with him, and this includes not allowing him to partake of the Lord's Supper or the Christian love feast while he is still in sin. It may also mean total dissociation — not even sharing a meal in his home with him, but this is not certain.[25] What Paul says is addressed to the congregation as a whole and therefore speaks for the most part of the behavior of the gathered congregation.

In v. 11 Paul gives a short vice list of traits unacceptable in a Christian. There are numerous other such lists in Paul's letters and elsewhere in Hellenistic Jewish and non-Jewish literature. While these lists overlap (cf. Gal. 5:19-21; 1 Cor. 6:10f.), it does not follow that they are merely conventional.[26] It is not acceptable for a Christian to be a drunkard or greedy or to use abusive language. In v. 13 *krinei* (judge) is probably future tense in view of v. 5b and because elsewhere Paul indicates that the world's judgment comes on judgment day.

Paul's basic rule is free association outside the community[27] and strict discipline within the community. Discipline was one of the key tools for making clear the limits of acceptable behavior and so establishing the com-

---

25. Dio Chrysostom 34.40 gives similar advice to the people of Tarsus (Paul's home!): "When you decide that you are going to remove someone and it is thought that he is guilty of such wrongdoing that it is not beneficial to ignore it, make yourself ready to convict him and immediately behave toward him as you would toward a personal enemy and one who is plotting against you."

26. On Paul's use of vice catalogs here and in ch. 6, see P. Zaas, "Catalogs and Contexts: 1 Corinthians 5 and 6," *NTS* 34 (1988), pp. 622-29. Zaas is right that Paul is not merely repeating traditional material in vice lists, since no two of his lists are the same. Those in chs. 5 and 6 "extend the apostle's prior prohibition of *pornoi* to include these other vicious types" (p. 626). So Paul is trying to be concrete about what it means to be a holy community.

27. With exceptions in regard to immoral or idolatrous activities.

munity's moral boundaries[28] and for unifying a community. As Mitchell puts
it,

> factionalism is a division of persons within the confines of community
> ranks. One way to eliminate a cause of division is to remove some persons
> from membership. . . . The man who commited the act of *porneia* in ch. 5
> has contributed to community divisiveness (5:2, 6). Paul advises expelling
> this offender. He is to become an outsider (5:5, 11-13), and is therefore not
> included in the unity to which Paul calls the Corinthian church.[29]

28. Paul is dealing with an extreme situation here, and so it is reasonable to assume
that the congregation would only exercise such discipline in extreme situations. Obviously
if all sinners of any sort were expelled from the *ekklēsia* there would soon be no one left.
    29. M. M. Mitchell, *Paul and the Rhetoric of Reconciliation* (Tübingen: Mohr, 1991),
p. 112.

Argument II, Division 2: 6:1-20

COURTING TROUBLE

To understand 1 Corinthians 6 it is necessary to understand some basic characteristics of the judicial process in a Roman colony. It appears that by the mid-first century A.D. trial by jury was reserved mainly for criminal proceedings, and even then there might be exceptions.[1] Trials would be handled by some sort of judge, perhaps one of the colony's *duoviri*, but it is possible that an aedile like Erastus might handle a case that arose out of some conflict or problem in the *macellum* (the meat market) or the marketplace.[2] The earliest and most famous of Roman courts was the "extortion" court, "the need for which became acute as Roman governors . . . discovered the possibilities of enriching themselves at the expense of the provincials. . . . Many of the great cases of the late republic and early empire were heard before this court."[3]

There was a three-stage judicial process for civil cases. First, the plaintiff would appear before one of the city's magistrates requesting a suit. If the magistrate agreed that there were grounds for a suit the defendant would be summoned *by the plaintiff* to court. The factual details of the case would be discussed and debated and a *formula* (statement of the factual details that both parties agreed on) arrived at. The trial would be based on what was in the *formula*. Second, the magistrate would then asssign a judge, agreeable to both parties, to the case and pass along to him the *formula*. Finally, the case would be heard by the judge and the sentence passed, but it was the plaintiff's responsibility to see that the judgment was carried out by the defendant. This process could drag on for some time and could be aborted at various points, for example if the defendant refused to come to court in the first place and the magistrate was not inclined to use force. Going to court could be a very expensive proposition. Tacitus tells us that a lawyer in A.D. 47 could command a fee of as much as 10,000 sesterces (*Ann.* 11.5-7). The annual salary for a *duovir*'s clerk in a Roman colony in Spain was only 1200 sesterces.[4]

---

1. Jesus' case might have been such an exception since Pilate, not the Sanhedrin, was in the end the one who decided it.

2. Cf. J. K. Chow, *Patronage and Power: A Study of Social Networks in Corinth* (Sheffield: JSOT, 1992), p. 80.

3. G. A. Kennedy, *The Art of Rhetoric in the Roman World 300 B.C. to A.D. 300* (Princeton: Princeton University, 1972), pp. 11f.

4. Cf. Chow, *Patronage and Power*, p. 76.

A number of forces in Roman society affected the adminstration of justice.[5] Social status and rank vis-à-vis one's opponent were major determining factors. While "the situation of the weaker plaintiff improved with the end of the Republic and the coming of the Empire," the system remained heavily weighted in favor of people of higher status.[6] From at least the time of Augustus certain people — fathers, patrons, magistrates, and men of standing — were basically immune from prosecution for fraud by some kinds of other people — children, freedmen, private citizens, and men of low rank. Only if a lower status person had a powerful patron was there a likelihood that he or she could bring a successful suit against someone higher up the social ladder.[7]

Another factor in civil cases was the lawyer. If he was a good rhetorician, highly skilled in forensic rhetoric, one had a chance, even if social standing stacked the odds otherwise. In courts the art of persuasion became much more than a mere exercise in public oratory. People packed many trials to hear the great orators of the day.

Nevertheless, the Roman judicial system was pervaded by "improper influences" and this "made equality before the law unattainable" or virtually so.[8] Citizens were less likely to be arrested, beaten, and imprisoned than foreigners. "The principal criterion of legal privilege in the eyes of the Romans was *dignitas* or *honor derived from power, style of life, and wealth.*"[9] To the wealthy, well-born, and well-connected went the chief rewards of the legal system, along with many of the other benefits available in society. There was a strongly aristocratic bias to the whole culture. Justice during the empire was far from blind and was often looking over its shoulder.

The importance of this for 1 Corinthians 6 is that at the very least one or both of the Christians going to court were probably well-to-do and hoping

5. See P. Garnsey, *Social Status and Legal Privilege in the Roman Empire* (Oxford: Clarendon, 1970), pp. 183ff.

6. Ibid., p. 192, cf. p. 217: "The possibility of suits brought by men of comparatively humble origin and position against men of rank cannot be ruled out; but they are unlikely to have been a frequent occurrence."

7. It is better to speak of social status or level and not social class, since the modern notion of class does not really suit the situation in the Roman Empire. There was nothing quite equivalent to our middle class. The three basic distinctions were between citizen and foreigner, *honestiores* and *humiliores,* and freeborn and slave. Depending on which distinction was being used, one could be higher or lower. For example, a freeborn person could be poor, whereas a freedman or freedwoman could be rich, and this was of great importance in a city in which one bought one's way into society, public office, and sometimes even justice. Furthermore, some *honestiores* did not have citizenship while some *humiliores* did. See A. Clarke, *Secular and Christian Leadership in Corinth* (dissertation, Cambridge, 1991), pp. 26ff.

8. Garnsey, *Social Status,* p. 207.

9. Ibid., p. 279.

to exploit the judicial system to their advantage.[10] As in ch. 5 we find further hints here that Paul's chief troubles in Corinth were caused by well-to-do members of the *ekklēsia*.

Chapter 6 has been traditionally divided into two parts, the first on a case in a pagan court involving differences between two Christians (vv. 1-11) and the second on another case of sexual immorality (after the one in ch. 5), in this instance a man going to prostitutes (vv. 12-20). It is often doubted that the case in 6:1-11 is directly connected to the incest case addressed in ch. 5, since it has to do with fraud (v. 7) and thus is likely a property matter. But since marriage often *was* a property matter, there may be a close connection.

There are close links between 6:12-20 and what follows in ch. 7. Paul is trying to establish both a Christian view of the importance of the human body in the order of redemption and the practical implications of an eschatological worldview for present sexual conduct. He continues to address his audience's view of human sexuality and their aberrant theology of salvation in ch. 7.[11]

Both cases discussed in ch. 6 deal with a serious breach of community and an ensuing bad witness to the world. Paul argues that by taking disputes to a pagan court and by fulfilling one's sexual drives outside the body of Christ one is violating Christian community and Christian witness. He uses several sarcastic rhetorical questions, not detailed arguments, to express himself here. Especially sarcastic is the question whether there is not one *sophos* (wise person) among the Corinthian Christians who could judge the matter (v. 5), in view of their claims about being wise. All these rhetorical questions are meant to shame the Corinthians into seeing their real moral condition and to deflate their unwarranted pride. This letter would be read before the whole congregation and would be a humiliating public shaming.

The point in v. 1 could be that Gentile courts are inherently unrighteous. Dio Chrysostom, commenting on Roman Corinth about A.D. 100, says that there were "lawyers innumerable perverting justice" there, and refers to young men declaiming forensic pieces in the courtyard next to the Temple of Poseidon during the Isthmian games, hoping to drum up business (8.9).[12]

10. Cicero (*Pro Caecina* 73) complains that three things hinder justice from being done in the provinces east of Rome: *gratia, potentia,* and *pecunia,* that is, "excessive favor," power or great resources, and money, that is, bribery.

11. Many Corinthian Christians apparently thought that salvation did not involve the body.

12. If one also considers the analogy with Jesus' parable in Luke 18, it is believable that Paul may have been referring to judges in Corinth. Unlike B. W. Winter, "Civil Litigation in Secular Corinth and the Church," *NTS* 37 (1991), pp. 559-72, I doubt that Paul's reference is to juries, since small civil claims did not usually call for a jury. The plural "the unrighteous ones" does not require a reference to a jury, since Paul is generalizing here.

K. Wengst has stressed that in view of the experiences listed in his tribulation catalogs (1 Cor. 4:9ff.; 2 Cor. 11:23ff.), Paul had little reason to trust Roman justice and that this passage should be read in that light.[13]

But Paul's sweeping dismissal of the practice of law does not amount to an attack on the law as such, and his statement that it would be better to suffer wrong (v. 7) "presupposes the recognition of law." "Going to law here is itself regarded as doing injustice and robbing one's adversary. That injustice and robbery thus appear in the garb of law . . . makes it clear why Paul can describe the judges as unjust."[14] Paul believes that Christians, like Jews before them, should settle all disputes among themselves on their own. He does not deal here with the case of a Christian and a non-Christian entangled in legal matters.

In both this and the next case, Paul provides the wider Christian perspective by bringing in eschatological matters. In the first case, he brings in the fact that on judgment day believers will judge the outside world and even angels (vv. 2f.); in the second case, he refers to the future resurrection, which shows the value that God has placed on human bodies (v. 14). The Corinthians' problems arose not just from bad ethics or bad social values but from bad theology, which affected all worldly affairs and matters including sexual and legal matters. They had an inadequate if not non-existent future eschatology, or at least future eschatology was not shaping their values and decision making. Paul's point in vv. 2f. is that if they are going to go on and judge the world, then surely they can handle an ordinary mundane matter now on their own.

Some have identified "the despised" (or "the least esteemed") in v. 4 as Christians,[15] in which case Paul is showing his contempt for the litigators, or possibly he wants to invert the secular pyramid by putting the least esteemed of the congregation on top as judges. But if the word in question really means "despised," then this view seems unlikely. It is more likely that the *ekklēsia* in this verse is the secular assembly, not the Christian congregation.[16] *Men oun* ("no, rather," "therefore") in the first clause must be given its due weight, so that v. 4 answers to v. 3.[17] In v. 4, then, Paul asks rhetorically whether resorting

13. K. Wengst, *Pax Romana and the Peace of Jesus Christ* (Philadelphia: Fortress, 1987), pp. 76f.

14. Ibid. This assessment does not conflict with what Paul says in Romans 13 since there he speaks of the divinely ordained and intended function of government, not of some particular practice of it, and he is not referring to Christians making use of the judicial system but of actions initiated by the authorities.

15. Winter, "Civil Litigation," p. 570.

16. It is possible that *en tȩ ekklēsia̧* means "*of* the assembly" so that Paul's complaint is about making pagans judges of the Christian *ekklēsia*. In any case, if Paul could call secular judges "unrighteous" (v. 1), he could equally well call them "despised."

17. J. B. Lightfoot, *Notes on the Epistles of Saint Paul* (Winona Lake: Alpha, reprint), p. 213.

to a pagan court does not amount to appointing outsiders ill-suited to the task to judge among Christians.

Paul is clear in v. 7 that going to pagan court already amounts to moral failure. He asks the plaintiff, in words probably drawing on the Jesus tradition, would it not be better to be defrauded? In v. 8 he addresses the one who did the defrauding and reminds him that people who behave in this manner will not inherit God's dominion when it finally comes.

In the vice list in vv. 9f. we have the heavily debated terms *malakoi* and *arsenokoitai*. These two terms are probably intentionally paired together, and their meaning should stand or fall together. *Malakoi* in its root meaning means "smooth" or "effeminate." Dionysius of Halicarnassus (7.2.4) uses this term to refer to a young male prostitute. Pederasty, molestation of minors by adult males, was the most common form of homosexuality in antiquity (cf. Philo *De Spec. Leg.* 3.37-39). The two terms refer respectively, then, to the leading and following partners in a homosexual pederastic tryst.[18]

Some have urged that only pederasty is condemned in the NT, not homosexuality in general. If this were the only passage where Paul addressed the issue, one could argue in that way. But Rom. 1:26f. clearly shows Paul's view of homosexual relationships in general. The reference there to lesbian relationships shows that Paul's condemnation of same-sex relationships is not limited to pederasty.[19]

As with the other sins in this list,[20] Paul is talking about behavior, not inclinations, orientations, or natures. He may have believed that some people experience, as part of their inherent fallenness, desire for sexual relationships with people of the same sex. Whether or not this is so, he goes on to say "such *were* some of you" (v. 11), which means that he believes in the power of God to transform human lives, desires, and inclinations. At the least, Paul believes that God can give Christians enough power to resist sinful desires, even if they continue to have them. "Such *were*" implies that they do not have to act that way anymore, whatever their internal struggles. Paul believes that Christ frees believers from sin addiction so that they have a choice about their actions (10:13).[21]

When Christians come to Christ they are "washed" of the guilt of pre-

18. Though *arsenokoitai,* when it stands alone, refers to any participant in male homosexual activity. It is never used of heterosexual intercourse.

19. Cf. R. B. Hays, "Relations Natural and Unnatural: A Response to John Boswell's Exegesis of Romans 1," *Journal of Religious Ethics* 4 (1986), pp. 184-215.

20. Homosexual activity is not singled out here as more heinous than the other items in the list.

21. And this would include the sin of homophobia. The *ekklēsia* should relate to homosexuals in the same way as it relates to other sinners, that is, to all people.

vious sins, "set apart" ("sanctified") for God and God's ways,[22] and given right standing with God ("justified"), a new relationship with God that entails no more condemnation for their past sins (v. 11). The past tenses of all three verbs indicates that Paul is referring to a definite event in the past, namely the conversion of the Christians he is addressing.

The implicit trinitarianism here and elsewhere in this letter is note-worthy.[23] Only God saves, and it is God as Father, Spirit, and Lord Jesus who assumes various roles to accomplish this. There is no elaborate doctrine of the Trinity in the NT, unlike the creeds created at Nicea and Chalcedon, but the implicit stuff of later developments is here.

Beginning in v. 12 Paul quotes some of the Corinthians' slogans and then qualifies or rejects them. These slogans include:

"Everything is permitted to me" (6:12; 10:23),
"It is good for a man not to 'touch' a woman" (7:1),
"All of us possess knowledge" (8:1),
"No idol in the world really exists" (8:4),
"Food will not bring us close to God" (8:8), and
"There is no resurrection of the dead" (15:12).[24]

It is possible to argue that Paul begins his *refutatio* in 6:12. Before this point he has simply questioned the Corinthian Christians' assumptions and actions, but now he begins to question and refute their answers in the form of these slogans. This will continue on in the following chapters. Quintilian lists docu-ments among things that one may find it necessary to speak against, indeed rebut (*Inst. Or.* 5.5.1ff.), and it seems likely that these slogans were some of the evidence cited in the letter by those who wrote to Paul to justify their behavior. Possibly the ultimate origin of one or more of these slogans is Paul himself, though if that is the case Paul clearly believes that the Corinthians have misunderstood the implications of what he said. Here and in what follows Paul basically takes a "yes that is so, but . . ." approach to these slogans. This in itself may suggest that they originated in some form with him.

Paul does not seem to reject the slogan "Everything is permitted to me."

22. Here the reference is probably not to internal sanctification in view of the word order.

23. On the carefully crafted structure of 6:9-20, see K. E. Bailey, "Paul's Theological Foundation for Human Sexuality: I Cor. 6:9-20 in the Light of Rhetorical Criticism," *Near East School of Theology Theological Review* 3 (1980), pp. 27-41.

24. The general impression given by these slogans, especially when they are examined in context, is that they come from two groups, one libertine, the other ascetic. The same group cannot be arguing for the right to visit prostitutes and also arguing that "It is good for a man not to 'touch' a woman."

There is a sense in which it is true: There really is freedom in Christ. But because that freedom is "in Christ" there are some qualifications on it. Not all forms of behavior are beneficial to the body of Christ, much less to oneself. Paul might well have said to the Corinthians about adiaphora "all things are permitted," so long as they build up the body of Christ.

Paul was not an antinomian, however, and on most matters he had rather definite principles that Christians were to follow. Some Corinthians did not see how bodily behavior defiled the spirit or one's spiritual condition. Paul's approach to ethics with its soteriological and eschatological foundation was different from anything the Corinthians had encountered, and no doubt they had trouble grasping it.

With a twist of irony, Paul says in v. 12b that one must not be enslaved by an attempt to live by an "everything is permitted to me" kind of approach. A person who feels that he or she can and should try everything is in fact enslaved by the drive for the ever new and different.

It is hard to say whether the Corinthian slogan quoted in v. 13 consists of only the first sentence or also includes "and God will destroy it all." The latter seems most likely, in which case they reasoned "The body for food and vice versa. What does it matter, since God will destroy it all?"[25] On this view Paul agrees with their premise, but then in the rest of the verse makes it clear that this principle does not apply to the body and *all* its activities. But if Paul adds "and God will destroy it all," his meaning is that "one who lives by and for his or her belly will ultimately be destroyed by God."[26] In any event, Paul stresses that the body belongs to the Lord because God's Spirit dwells in the Christian so that God has rights over the Christian and because the Christian's body has been bought by God by the sacrifice of Christ. Thus the bodies of Christians are not their own to do with as they please, but God's to do with as God pleases.

Verse 14 establishes a principle to be elaborated in ch. 15 at great length. Just as God raised Christ, so also will God raise Christians. Salvation in the Christian worldview entails the body, and therefore what one does with one's body has moral consequences. The Greek idea of the immortality of the soul is not Paul's idea of eternal life.

Paul proceeds in v. 15 to say that each Christian's body is in a sense

---

25. In view of this slogan and the Epicurean-sounding quotation in 15:32, one wonders if the "strong" in Corinth had been influenced by Epicurean philosophy. Cf. B. Fiore, "Passion in Paul and Plutarch," in *Greeks, Romans, and Christians: Essays in Honor of Abraham J. Malherbe*, ed. D. L. Balch, E. Ferguson, and W. A. Meeks (Minneapolis: Fortress, 1990), pp. 135-43. Plutarch argues against locating all of the good in the belly and other pleasure centers of the body (*Suav. Viv.* 1086C-1107C).

26. Hedonism is no Christian virtue and gluttony is positively a sin, a form of greed applied to food.

attached to Christ as a limb or member of him. It is a contradiction in terms to take one of Christ's limbs and attach it to a prostitute. Paul believes that more than a physical coupling happens when one has sexual intercourse with a prostitute. There is also a spiritual bonding, which is diametrically opposed to the union in one spirit that believers have with Christ (v. 16). The union with the Lord is not physical, of course. It is characterized in v. 17 as *en pneuma* ("in spirit"), as opposed to the union with the prostitute, which is *en sōma* ("in body"), though it also entails a spiritual bond. Then Paul states a rule: "Flee immorality!"

Verse **18** is not to be pressed too hard, since other sins are also against one's own body, for example, drug abuse.[27] Paul's point is that sexual sin, unlike other sins, involves one's very body in a union with others and is a sin against self as well as others. It involves the whole self and thus is dangerous and deadly to one's spiritual well-being, for it puts one into the hands and mastery of someone other than the Lord.

In v. **19** Paul returns to the idea, which we saw in 3:16f., of Christians as the temple of God in Corinth. But here he speaks of individuals as the temple of the Holy Spirit, while in ch. 3 the collective entity, the congregation, is God's temple.[28] Paul thus reminds the Corinthians that they do not have the Spirit because of something they inherently are, or because of something they have accomplished. It is a gift from God. They are not their own persons. They belong to God and therefore should glorify the one who is over them, in them, and by them in all things, even in their bodily behavior (v. **20**).

---

27. Bailey, "Paul's Theological Foundation," pp. 37f.

28. The distinction between God's temple and the Holy Spirit's temple may be inconsequential, since in Paul's view the Spirit is the form and means by which God is present and active in the world.

Argument III: 7:1-40

Holy Wedlock and Unholy Deadlock[1]

Often the study of passages like 1 Corinthians 7 has been attempted without consideration of the character and conduct of Roman marriage and family life. Such background study might help to explain why the Corinthians were acting as they were and why they were making statements like "It is good for a man not to 'touch' a woman."

Roman marriages were for the most part arranged and involved little personal choice on the part of the participants, at least among the prosperous.[2] The disposition of property was all-important, and marriage became a means of enhancing one's property and status. Hence, one often reads that a cardinal characteristic of good Roman marriages was *concordia,* a state of peace or harmony between husband and wife, rather than great love or affection.[3]

Though life was better for women during the empire than during the earlier period of the Roman Republic, marriage was still basically an asymmetrical relationship with the husband wielding greater power and authority. The *patria potesta* had by no means disappeared. The phrase "buying a wife" was still common during the empire (Gaius *Inst.* 1.113). The relationship between husband and wife was often much like that between father and daughter or uncle and niece, because a man was often considerably older than his wife.[4] When Quintilian writes that a notable trait of a good husband is *moderatio* (restraint) in his relationship with his wife and that this is a sign of his *caritas* (affection), he is voicing common assumptions about the dominant position of the husband.[5]

---

1. For a more detailed treatment of 1 Corinthians 7, see B. Witherington, *Women in the Earliest Churches* (Cambridge: Cambridge University, 1988), pp. 26-42.

2. For a useful summary of Roman laws bearing on marriage and divorce, see M. R. Lefkowitz and M. B. Fant, ed., *Women's Life in Greece and Rome* (Baltimore: Johns Hopkins University, 1982), pp. 180-203.

3. Cf. K. Bradley, *Discovering the Roman Family* (Oxford: Oxford University, 1991), pp. 6f.

4. On the age of women at marriage in this era, see *New Doc.* IV, pp. 222f. A man was sometimes twice his wife's age.

5. *Inst. Or.* 6.2.14. E. Cantarella, *Pandora's Daughters* (Baltimore: Johns Hopkins University, 1987), pp. 142ff., stresses that during the empire "women who enjoyed new privileges and fought for others all belonged to a single social class — the aristocracy." She is also right that working outside the home was certainly not necessarily a sign of a woman's

Because most marriages were arranged

there could never at the outset be any assurance of harmony between husband and wife, and in the likely absence of any strong affective tie chracteristic of modern marriage, the potential for discord was always as great as that for concord. Affective expectations in Roman marriage had to be low, and it is for this reason that spousal commemorations of deceased partners often draw on phraseology of a highly dispassionate tone, even as the "success" of the union is being signaled.[6]

Tacitus intimates that for various men he knew, including Agricola, what was really critical was the public image of the marriage, not its inner life, since in the Roman hierarchy of values what made a marriage good was that it was "a source of social distinction and an aid to advancement" (*Agricola* 6.1). This was a male-centered point of view, and it comports with what we have noted earlier about public honor being part of the male ideology of the culture.

Unlike modern Christian practice, the basis of a Roman marriage was the intent to live together in a marital state. It did not require a formal ceremony, though many preferred to have one. Equally, there was no public legal act required to dissolve a Roman marriage. Normally divorce occurred when the husband declared the formula *tuas res tibi habeto* ("take your things [and go]"). Women had the same rights to divorce as men, at least officially.[7]

There are various other ways in which Roman family life differed from the modern family. First, while moderns tend to view a home as a haven or refuge from public life, the demarcation between public and private life was by no means as strong in antiquity. Not only did some families have shops in the fronts of their homes (see the illustration of a Roman villa on p. 194), but if one was a patron, one's clients would show up at the doorstep most mornings to consummate deals or at least to collect a *sportula*, a basket of food or other necessities (cf. Cicero *De Orat.* 3.133).[8] Education most often took place in the home as well, except when a well-to-do family sent a son off to school to learn rhetoric and other subjects. A lower value was placed on privacy in

---

liberation. In some cases it was a necessity and supported the Roman male ideology that it was beneath the dignity of a free Roman male to work, especially with his hands, for money.

6. Bradley, *Discovering*, p. 8.

7. Cantarella, *Pandora's Daughters*, pp. 136f.

8. There is some debate in the literature as to whether there was an emphasis on the nuclear family during the empire. In either case, it is clear that *oikos*, used of a "household," often included more than just the nuclear family. Household slaves would be included, perhaps some extended family, and possibly some clients and friends. Cf. L. M. White, *The Christian Domus Ecclesiae and Its Environment* II (Ann Arbor: University Microfilms, 1990), p. 569; J. H. Elliott, *A Home for the Homeless* (Philadelphia: Fortress, 1981), pp. 170ff.

Roman homes than in modern homes. Most expected the home to be a place of social relations and business.

Not only the wealthy had slaves. Many of medium income, including freed slaves, owned five or six slaves, and some rich slaves themselves even owned slaves. Even Martial, who was a rather poor man, had a slave or two. The Roman family became virtually identical with the Roman household, which included slaves and often members of the extended family as well.[9] The modern practice of the nuclear family living in a single-family dwelling is notably different from the way many ancient Romans lived. It is not an accident that the Pauline household codes include advice for and about slaves (Col. 3:18–4:1; Eph. 5:21-33).[10] Thus, "Roman parents were not linked in egalitarian marriage, and their offspring did not rely exclusively on them for all their household and material needs."[11]

Urban families of modest means lived in cramped apartments.

> Even in the little alleys a vibrant sense of community joined the inhabitants, leaning on their window-sills to see the sights and talk with each other from apartment to apartment, while, lacking room at home, the flayer below stripped the hide off a carcass on the sidewalk, the teacher taught his circle of pupils their ABCs, the notary or scribe drew up a rental contract at his table, the barber shaved his customers, the clothes-cleaner hung garments out to dry, the butcher cut up the meat. Rarely they asked official permission. After all, was it not *their* city?[12]

While the more well-to-do women of Roman Corinth might not have to work outside the home, many women did.

> Graffiti from Pompeii, tomb carvings from Ostia, and occasional references in the literature show us women at work as weavers, dressmakers, copyists, midwives, physicians, grocers, innkeepers, barmaids, entertainers and barbers. Such women would have been free of some constraints of traditional rectitude: their economic contribution to the family was too important, and their background, whether in the slums or the dormitories of a house where

---

9. Unlike American slaves before the Civil War, Roman slaves normally lived in the master's house, not in separate quarters.

10. Witherington, *Women in the Earliest Churches,* pp. 42-61.

11. Bradley, *Discovering,* p. 10. Urban Roman families frequently had nurses to look to the needs of children so that the parents could tend to the management of the estate or business. Frequently children must have become more attached to their nurses than to their parents (Seneca *Controversiae* 4.6: the wealthy send their children to the country to be nursed; cf. 1 Thess. 1:7).

12. R. MacMullen, *Roman Social Relations* (New Haven: Yale University, 1974), pp. 63f.

they had been slaves, would not have socialized them to the niceties of aristocratic femininity.[13]

Whether because of work or because of arranged marriages, Romans frequently looked outside the home for pleasure and for much else that we would associate with home and family. The "imported religions which won so many followers at this time must also have provided their members with many of the things traditionally associated with the family — togetherness, a feeling of belonging, a spiritual comfort, the opportunity to 'be one's self.' "[14] This was surely the case with Christian groups, which met in homes and would have appeared to the outsider as *collegia* of some sort, like the clubs and associations that were formed to foster social relationships.

A good deal of this background information comes into play in 1 Corinthians 7 because of the household setting of the *ekklēsia,* which meant that "sexuality and sex roles . . . represented an area Christians themselves could influence and control, whereas the public world was outside their control."[15]

The structure of the chapter may be broken down as follows:

general discussion of marriage and conjugal rights (vv. 1-7),
advice to widowers and widows (vv. 8f.),
advice to Christian married couples about separation and divorce (vv. 10f.),
advice to those married to non-Christians (vv. 12-16),
an illustration of how the principle "remain as you are" applies not only to marital status but also to social status — therefore, to all people (vv. 17-24),
advice to those considering engagement and to those already engaged (vv. 25-38) and,
reiteration of advice and commandments given to women in vv. 8-11 with an additional comment on a widow's right to remarry (vv. 39f.).

Here again Paul is using a deliberative form of argumentation and urging behavior that leads to peace. He urges the Corinthian Christians to do what is for their benefit (v. 35), that is, what allows couples to be united and

13. J. Stambaugh, *The Ancient Roman City* (Baltimore: Johns Hopkins University, 1988), pp. 99f.; cf. Witherington, *Women in the Earliest Churches,* pp. 16ff.

14. B. Rawson, "The Roman Family," in *The Family in Ancient Rome* (London: C. Helm, 1986), p. 38.

15. H. Moxnes, "Honor, Shame, and the Outside World in Paul's Letter to the Romans," in *The Social World of Formative Christianity and Judaism,* ed. J. Neusner, et al. (Philadelphia: Fortress, 1988), p. 215.

individuals to be sure of what their marital status ought to be.[16] As Mitchell says, this argument is clever, since Paul does not address the ascetic or libertine factions in the Corinthian *ekklēsia* directly, though he quotes the view of the ascetics at the outset. He discusses each possible marital status in turn. But Mitchell is wrong to conclude that Paul is merely being socially conservative in the interest of the *ekklēsia*'s survival.[17] To the contrary, a good deal of his advice is closer on these issues to that of more radical thinkers such as some of the Stoics and Cynics.

In Roman Corinth, one who advocated singleness as a better state than marriage would hardly be seen as one who was baptizing the status quo. Some emperors, especially Augustus, had done all they could to encourage Romans to marry and have many children. Augustus even put into law penalties on women who remained unmarried too long after being widowed.[18]

Some scholars have asked recently whether Paul was an early example of Christian asceticism.[19] If by "ascetic" one means a person who believes that being single is preferable to marriage because a single person can give his or her undivided attention to serving the Lord, then the term is accurate. But if one means that Paul saw human sexual relations as somehow base or as less than a good thing, indeed bordering on sin, one has badly misunderstood Paul, not only in this passage but elsewhere as well (1 Thess. 4:3-8).[20] To the contrary, verses like 1 Cor. 7:14 show that Paul saw marital love as a cleansing or sanctifying force on the unbelieving partner (cf. 1 Thess. 4:3f.).

The ascetic interpretation of Paul rests on several misunderstandings of

---

16. Cf. S. K. Stowers, "Paul on the Use and Abuse of Reason," in *Greeks, Romans, and Christians*, ed. D. L. Balch, E. Ferguson, and W. A. Meeks (Minneapolis: Fortress, 1990), pp. 253-86, here p. 266: *sympherein*, "be of benefit," e.g., 6:12 — cf. *symphoros*, "benefit," 7:35 —

> is important in both Hellenistic philosophical ethics and in rhetoric, where it is the kind of term that characterizes the symbouleutic rhetoric of advice. "Your own benefit" points to the fact that Paul's arguments are often nontheological and consequentialist (for example 7:9, 14-16, 35, 36). To justify his advice, Paul often uses not divine authority but the desirability of consequences. By *to symphoros* Paul means that the Corinthians as individuals and as a community ought to make decisions with a view to their own advantage.

This is the sort of argument one would expect in deliberative rhetoric. It is not Paul's only strategy, for when he must use forensic rhetoric he does not appeal to advantage at all.

17. M. M. Mitchell, *Paul and the Rhetoric of Reconciliation* (Tübingen: Mohr, 1991), p. 235.

18. Witherington, *Women in the Earliest Churches*, pp. 16-23.

19. E.g., V. Wimbush, *Paul the Worldly Ascetic: Response to the World and Self-Understanding according to 1 Corinthians 7* (Macon: Mercer University, 1987).

20. Witherington, *Women in the Earliest Churches*, pp. 64-68.

1 Corinthians 7.[21] First, while Paul would agree that there are contexts in which it is good for a man not to "touch"[22] a woman (cf. 6:16-20), he strongly qualifies this slogan in vv. 2ff.[23] Second, his egalitarian treatment of the rights of each partner is remarkable and would have amounted to a serious qualification of the status quo. Few Romans could have conceived of arguing that the husband's body *belonged* to the wife.[24] Against the ascetic view, Paul says that sex should be abstained from only in a time of prayer. Third, those who argue for the ascetic view have misread what Paul is conceding in v. 6. He is not conceding sexual relationships. The nearest and proper antecedent of *touto* ("this") at the beginning of v. 6 is the concession of abstinence during a time of prayer.[25] This is why he has just said that marital partners should only abstain for a specific limited period of time.

Finally, the ascetic view of ch. 7 fails to see that Paul's preference for singleness is motivated by ideas that set him decidedly apart from some of his contemporaries who did have ascetic tendencies:[26] First, his eschatology stands

---

21. M. Y. MacDonald, "Women Holy in Body and Soul," *NTS* 36 (1990), pp. 161-81, like A. C. Wire, wishes to argue that there was a group of ascetic women in Corinth and that their asceticism was related to their ecstatic experiences in worship. There are several problems with this thesis. There is no evidence in chs. 7 or 11–14 that asceticism is associated with ecstatic speech. Second, there are several hints in ch. 7 that women were *seeking* to marry or stay married. In particular, v. 16 (cf. v. 39) probably alludes to this. If the text suggests that some women were seeking to get out of marriage, it also suggests that some men were, for Paul addresses each group in the same manner. In ch. 7 Paul assumes that a variety of views or positions were manifest in Corinth. It is more likely that the slogan in v. 1 is being touted by some men, perhaps those who had qualms about marrying their fiancées (cf. vv. 25-38, especially vv. 36-38).

22. "Touch" is a euphemism for "have sexual relations with," as is shown by Plutarch *Pompey* II.3; Aristotle *Pol.* 7.14.12; Josephus *Ant.* 1.163. Cf. G. D. Fee, *The First Epistle to the Corinthians* (Grand Rapids: Eerdmans, 1987), p. 275 and n. 31.

23. If one compares 7:2 to 1 Thess. 4:3b-4, the theory that Paul had previously advocated some sort of ascetic viewpoint, such as is found in 7:1, becomes untenable. Cf. O. L. Yarbrough, *Not like the Gentiles* (Atlanta: Scholars, 1985), pp. 93ff., who rightly argues that the pattern of response to a slogan in 7:2 is like what one finds in 6:12f.; 8:1f.; and 10:23f. As Yarbrough says (p. 94), Paul's emphasis throughout is on remaining as one is, *not* on sexual abstinence.

24. R. B. Ward, "Musonius and Paul on Marriage," *NTS* 36 (1990), pp. 281-89, rightly points out that Musonius is in various ways more ascetic than Paul about marriage, since he does not regard desire as appropriate, even in marriage. The two also differ in regard to abstinence, which for Paul is not to be expected of a married couple except for limited times for prayer.

25. So rightly Yarbrough, *Not like the Gentiles,* p. 100.

26. See D. B. Martin's helpful discussion of ancient physicians' views of sex in his chapter on 1 Corinthians 7 in his forthcoming study *The Corinthian Body.* I am indebted to him for allowing me to see a portion of this work at the 1992 meeting of the Society of Biblical Literature.

behind a good deal of what he says here (cf. vv. 29, 31).[27] There is also the matter of the *present,* not future, distress, which is not further defined.[28] Second, Paul's theology of giftedness *(charisma)* is crucial. Paul sees both being single for the Lord and being married in the Lord as gifts from God. Third, his pragmatic reason for preferring singleness is that a single person can give more time, and undivided time, to the Lord's work. This hardly reflects an allergic reaction to sex. Had Paul truly been ascetic, he would hardly have argued that it is fine if a widow remarries "in the Lord."

I will quote here the summary of this lengthy passage I wrote elsewhere:

> That women are addressed first in vv 4, 10, 11, 16 and 39 may indicate that they in particular were considering divorce or separation. That the man is addressed in vv 25-38 likely indicates the customs of the day whereby the man took the initiative in seeking engagment or, being already engaged, took the responsibility in deciding about the marriage. Paul's use of different verbs of the man and the woman in regard to divorce (vv 10-11) may indicate something about his source and its view that only a man can divorce, for Paul himself goes on to speak of a woman divorcing (v 13), a custom known in Corinth at that time. The repeated theme of sexual passion or misconduct and, in response, Paul's stress on self-control (cf. vv 2, 5, 9, 36, 37) probably tells us more about the problems in Corinth than about Paul's view of the purposes of marriage. Paul shows no bitterness toward those married or contemplating marriage, but he does show concern about their having to face troubles, anxieties, distractions, etc. that might make difficult full devotion to the things of the Lord. Nevertheless, even if one does not accept Ephesians as Pauline, we have here enough evidence to show that Paul, far from being an ascetic, saw marriage as good, something that once undertaken should be fully consummated. As with all things, however, marriage for Paul must be seen within the perspective of the priorities of faith. The Christ-event conditions how one should live, whatever one's marital or social status. It calls for both a transformed attitude toward such worldly institutions as marriage, and an unqualified allegiance to Christ. This is why Paul can say on the one hand "the one marrying his own virgin does well," and on the other hand, "the one not marrying will do better."[29]

---

27. Cf. my full-length treatment of Paul's eschatology in *Jesus, Paul, and the End of the World* (Downers Grove: InterVarsity, 1992), pp. 1ff.

28. B. W. Winter, "Secular and Christian Responses to Corinthian Famines," *TynB* 40 (1989), pp. 86-106, thinks Paul is referring to economic distress caused by a famine. Perhaps, but do we have any concrete evidence of such a condition affecting Corinth when Paul *wrote* 1 Corinthians in the mid-50s, not merely in A.D. 51?

29. Witherington, *Women in the Earliest Churches,* p. 42; cf. Cantarella's judgment that Christianity introduced new degrees of equality into the Christian marriage relationship and provided more security for women in that relationship (*Pandora's Daughters,* pp. 157ff.).

Despite what classics scholars sometimes tell us about Roman marriages, it is obvious from 1 Corinthians 7 that emotions and passion were sometimes involved for those who were planning on marriage. Paul's strong advocacy of singleness, however, would have allowed some women the opportunity to establish their own lives and work "in the Lord" in a way that went against the grain of the patriarchal culture, which liked to keep family property, including female family members, in the hands of one or another male of the family.

I would agree with Wire that the evidence of chs. 5–7 strongly suggests that the libertine behavior in the Corinthian Christian community was basically, if not almost exclusively, male. She is equally right in saying: "Women in the Christian community were not immune from the radical systemic disadvantages of women in that society as a whole — inferiority by age and possible slave heritage in marriage, dependency on men in all civil and judicial matters and special vulnerability to death at birth and again at giving birth."[30] But she goes awry in failing to see that Paul's advice, both about preferring singleness and about following the Lord's command of no divorce, works to restrict male privileges, to give women more security in marriage, and to give them freedom to abstain from marriage.[31] Paul is not treating women as a mere remedy for male lust and sexual immorality.

It is not necessary to envision a radical group of Corinthian women at odds with Paul's teaching on sexual matters. To the contrary, most women surely would have welcomed Paul's attempt to reform the patriarchal approach to marriage and singleness. Paul permits marriage for women such as widows in a way that suggests that some were seeking to remarry and encourages separated women to return to their husbands if they wish to be married, which also suggests that they may have been contemplating other unions. More strikingly, he encourages women who desire to remain single to do so for the Lord's sake. If there *was* a movement of Corinthian women in the community

---

30. A. C. Wire, *The Corinthian Women Prophets: A Reconstruction through Paul's Rhetoric* (Minneapolis: Fortress, 1990), p. 75. A. Rouselle, "Body Politics in Ancient Rome," in *A History of Women*, ed. P. S. Pantel (Cambridge: Belknap, 1992), pp. 296-336, here p. 317, argues that Jewish women who became Roman citizens and lived under both Jewish and Roman law were not free to leave their husbands. This may suggest that those raising the questions in Corinth were Gentile women. Wire may be right in arguing that there were *some* ascetic women prophetesses in Corinth because of the traditional association of prophecy, sexual purity, and women in Greece, particularly at Delphi. Cf. L. B. Zaidman, "Pandora's Daughters," in *A History of Women*, pp. 338-76, here pp. 374f.; Rouselle, p. 330. Did the example of the priestesses at the Temple of Demeter and Kore at Corinth affect any of these Christian women's behavior?

31. It is probable that the ascetics are some of the more well-to-do members of the congregation, not least because poorer people could not afford the luxury of not having children to support them in their old age.

away from marriage, Paul's original teaching there may have fostered it.[32] On balance, the evidence of ch. 7 suggests that Paul here and in chs. 8–10 is mainly taking the part of those of lower status, though in various ways it would have been more natural for him to identify with those of higher status and power. His egalitarian rhetoric in this chapter does not have some nefarious purpose of putting women in their place.[33] Rather, his advice throughout chs. 5–7 would have served to severely restrict male privilege in Roman Corinth.

The advice about married people living "as if not" married, along with the other "as if not" clauses, have attracted much attention. Various scholars have chronicled the rise of an ascetic trend during the empire, though E. R. Dodds went much too far in claiming that the entire Greco-Roman culture was caught up in the disease of renunciation of the world, "in contempt for the human condition and hatred of the body."[34] In Christian Corinth there were both renouncers and over-indulgers.

Is Paul's advice to "remain as you are" and then live "as if not" a baptizing of a fragile status quo in the wake of a larger ascetic trend? One key to understanding Paul's somewhat puzzling advice is to realize that he is reacting against men and women who are trying to "depart," that is, abandon their pagan families. To them, Paul wishes to make clear that they are not defiled by such a relationship. Indeed, they have an opportunity to be a sanctifying influence in the situation, and this is one reason for his advice to "remain." He believes that it is possible to have worldly relationships without being stained by the world. It is also correct to say, with Wimbush, that

> "remain" was not intended to support the status quo; it was designed only *to relativize the importance of all worldly conditions and relationships.* Yet more important, even the "remaining" is relativized: those who are afforded the opportunity (for example, slaves, vs. 21) or those who experience the pressure of temptation (for example, engaged parties, vss. 36-38) can change their social condition or status without having their status with God affected.[35]

---

32. Though it is also true that Paul encourages married women to stay married, unless a pagan partner wishes to depart.

33. Nevertheless, one of the more surprising elements of Paul's teaching here, at least to Christian women of a more well-to-do and Roman background, would be the advice about *not* abstaining from sex except during times of prayer. Roman matrons had been brought up to expect that once one had one's two to three children, one might expect to forego sexual relations thereafter. In the Roman view, sex in marriage was for procreation, not recreation. Cf. Rouselle, "Body Politics," pp. 323f.

34. E. R. Dodds, *Pagans and Christians in an Age of Anxiety* (Cambridge: Cambridge University, 1965), p. 35.

35. Wimbush, *Paul the Worldly Ascetic,* p. 16, emphasis added.

The reason for this relativization is not some ascetic streak in Paul, but his eschatology. He believes that the form or pattern *(schēma)* of the world is passing away, and this includes the institution of marriage, which is a this-worldly phenomenon.[36]

Throughout this letter Paul tries to inculcate in the Corinthians a sense of what it means to live in the eschatological age.[37] Paul believes Christians are already living in that age begun by Christ's death and resurrection, and so are living on borrowed time. The past eschatological events are the dominant force creating the relativizing "as if not" advice.[38] The nearness of the end is only a possibility in Paul's mind, and it is not the sole driving force behind his counsel. The tandem of the *certainty* of the already of Christ's death and resurrection and the *possibility* of the nearness of the not-yet is the reason for this advice.

For Paul, the one thing of eternal significance that humans can do in this world is serve the Lord, proclaiming the good news of eternal salvation available through the crucified Messiah Jesus. Paul is not so narrow-minded that he thinks all must become full-time missionaries like himself, but he does believe that all must bear witness in whatever social situation they find themselves with their lives and their words. This is one reason that he encourages Christians to remain in their current state.

And there is another reason. The Corinthians were very status-conscious people. As part of his argument against divisions and factions created by status stratification, Paul injects a dose of eschatology, which relativizes the importance of *all* social status. What is really important is not one's social position but one's soteriological condition.[39] Even a slave can be the Lord's freedman.

---

36. Wimbush, *Paul*, p. 34, is right that this phrase refers not to the end of the world *in toto*, but to the end of its institutions, morals, and ideals and, I would add, its present physical form.

37. Against Wimbush, *Paul*, p. 26. Paul does not say that the time is short, but rather that it is *shortened* (by the Christ-event, which has already happened). He does not speak of a future crisis but rather of a present necessity. He does not say that the world will pass away, but that it is already doing so.

38. Pace Wimbush, *Paul*, p. 33, who fails to see the connection between the two. Paul's advice is created not primarily by what Christ will yet do but by the reality of what he has already done. This is quite different from what one finds in 4 Ezra 16:40-44, which, though it is a similar passage, says that all has been relativized because the end is definitely imminent. While Paul believes that the end is *possibly* imminent, what is definite is the effect on the present of Christ's past eschatological work, which has set in motion the dissolution of the world's form.

39. Wimbush, *Paul*, p. 47, says that Paul advises "the Corinthians against equating Christian existence with worldly status, or more accurately the loss of worldly status." But did the Corinthian Christians think they were losing status by becoming Christians? If so, why would this status-conscious group become Christians at all?

Thus, what is crucial is whether or not one is a Christian. Everything else is of relative worth in a world that is winding down.[40]

Thus, finally, the relativization Paul speaks about is not a matter of a *degree* of interaction with the world as if Paul were counseling a bit less interaction or a gradual tapering off. It is, rather a matter of the *quality* of that interaction — one interacts knowing what is of lasting importance in the eternal scheme of things.[41] This is not a model of asceticism but of putting all earthly goods into a heavenly perspective so as to understand their real and lasting significance or lack thereof.[42]

40. Paul not only believes that being single is a legitimate gift of the Lord, he believes it is preferable in many ways to marriage. I am convinced that one of the main reasons the church is facing so many fracturing families today is that it has encouraged and sometimes even goaded people into marriage, people to whom God has given no such gift. There are two gifts from God, and one of them is singleness for the sake of the kingdom, as Jesus himself makes clear in Matt. 19:12.

It does not follow from this that Paul gives any warrant for an entirely celibate "clergy," any more than for an all-male clergy. Indeed, he says in 1 Cor. 9:5 that he has the right to be married and travel with his wife, as Peter apparently did. Paul does not think married people are somehow less "holy" or "pure" than single people. 1 Cor. 7:14 positively rules out such ideas — sanctification can happen to anyone regardless of status or relations in life. Paul was not an ascetic. What Paul does believe is that, all things being equal, a single person has fewer distractions and thus can concentrate more fully on the things of the Lord. He recognizes two gifted states, however, and frequently commends the ministerial labors of some of his married coworkers such as Priscilla and Aquila.

What is desperately needed and seldom found in the church is an adequate theology of the family of faith. Paul believes that being brothers and sisters in Christ and sons and daughters of God transcends all other loyalties and should transform all other social relationships. Blood should not be thicker than the baptismal waters in the church. Rather Paul calls for a "relativized" view of all this-worldly institutions, including marriage. His idea of a family "church" is actualized where God's people treat each other as their *primary* family, not just as some *secondary* social gathering that happens once a week and that promotes the agenda of the nuclear family. This is not to say that Paul is against the physical family. He does, however, believe that in the eternal scheme of things one's loyalty to Christ comes above and before one's loyalty to any other group or entity and that therefore one's loyalty to the body of Christ should likewise be at the top of one's priorities. If the physical family will serve the family of faith, that is fine, and it can exist within the *ekklēsia*. Paul also says that in a religiously mixed marriage the believing partner is not "bound" to that relationship, if the unbeliever wishes to depart. Separation or even divorce in such cases does not bother Paul a bit because, for Paul, "marriage" is not the be-all and end-all of Christian life. As he would not denigrate marriage, so also he would not deify it either.

41. Pace Wimbush, *Paul,* p. 43. For example, Paul does not counsel Christian husbands and wives to limit or gradually taper off their sexual relations. Rather, he counsels abstinence only for short periods of time, even though marriage is relativized.

42. Pace Wimbush, *Paul,* p. 53. N. R. Petersen, *Rediscovering Paul: Philemon and the Sociology of Paul's Narrative World* (Philadelphia: Fortress, 1985), p. 135, is right in saying that

Paul integrates his social instructions within a symbolic universe rather than a social one, for the consequences of compliance or non-compliance are not determined

It is a model of Christian devotion regardless of one's status, marital or other-wise.[43]

A Closer Look: Slavery in Roman Corinth and Paul's Advice in 7:21[44]

The Roman Empire was dependent on slave labor. Slavery was a burgeoning enterprise. The more territory the Romans captured, the more prisoners they sold as slaves. Corinth, due to its location and its status as a colony, was a significant center for the buying and selling of slaves. There were also slaves who were allowed to have children within a family and to pass down part of an inheritance. Then, too, some people sold themselves and their own family members into slavery. Most of the slaves in Paul's day came from the eastern part of the empire, though in Palestine very few Jews had slaves, but some had become slaves.[45]

The slave in antiquity was by Aristotle's definition a piece of "living property." As such, slaves had no legal rights and so were subject to the will of their owners. In the early empire there were some efforts to mitigate the absolute power of the owners. There is considerable evidence not only for large numbers of slaves buying themselves out of slavery, but also of slaves whose owners allowed them to develop their own businesses and so earn large sums of money.[46] The legal device making it possible for

---

socially, that is by social actors, but eschatologically by the Lord. In this respect, therefore, the force of Paul's instructions is derived from a symbolic universe which makes them non-negotiable and gives them the status of commands.

43. Paul's rhetorical strategy to change the social world of his converts is complex. Into inequality created by social culture in Corinth Paul injects leveling agents — eschatology, body imagery, and reciprocal advice to marital partners. Into equality created by all having the endowment of the Spirit and one or more spiritual gifts, Paul injects a ranking and ordering system so the body of Christ will be most benefited and not continue to fracture.

44. For a survey of slavery in the first three centuries of the Christian era and the relationship of Christians to slaves, see H. Güzlow, *Christentum und Sklaverei in den ersten drei Jahrhunderten* (Bonn: Habelt, 1969), with pp. 29-56 on Paul. The best survey in English of the primary sources is T. Wiedemann, *Greek and Roman Slavery* (Baltimore: Johns Hopkins University, 1981).

45. Cf. pp. 25-26 above.

46. An interesting inscription from Corinth, found in J. H. Kent, ed., *The Inscriptions, 1926-1950* VII/3 (Princeton: ASCSA, 1966), no. 321, tells of a slave freed by a prestigious family, one Quintus Maecius Cleogenes, who rose high enough to marry his master's granddaughter. Seneca *Apocolocyntosis* 3, 12 satirizes Claudius's era as a heyday for slaves, a great Saturnalia when slaves could not only become free but also rise high in society as freedmen or freedwomen, sometimes even while they were still slaves (cf. *On Benefits* 28.5f., where Seneca complains about a free man dashing off to pay an obligatory social call on a wealthy slave). Cf. D. B. Martin, *Slavery as Salvation: The Metaphor of Slavery in Pauline Christianity* (New Haven: Yale University, 1990), p. 43.

*A slave depicted in
the captive's façade*

slaves to own property was called the *peculium*. It had originally been for sons and was extended to slaves as well.[47] Some slaves had, of course, been well-to-do and well-educated before being captured and sold into bondage.

Westerners are used to thinking of slavery purely in terms of the agricultural slavery that existed in the United States or of indentured servants in Europe. But in antiquity a slave might perform almost any task. The government had numerous slaves who served as civil servants throughout the empire, some in rather prestigious roles and capacities. The imperial slaves had considerable power and respect. At the other end of the scale were slaves who worked in the mines in intolerable conditions. Between the two extremes were temple slaves, agricultural slaves on great estates, pedagogues, domestic servants, artisans, and business agents.

Though many slaves were able to save enough money to buy themselves out of slavery, many chose not to do so because of the security they had in a home, especially if they had a good master. In some cases it was worse, at least economically, to be free and poor, than to have security — food, clothing, shelter, and good employment. On this basis we can understand inscriptions like one a freed slave had carved on his own

47. On all of this see Martin, *Slavery as Salvation*, pp. 1-49.

tombstone: "Slavery was never unkind to me."[48] Furthermore, the patron-client system provided enough benefits and opportunities that it considerably dampened any thoughts of revolutionary behavior.[49] It seems that the main function of the patron-client system in the empire was to mitigate the harsher effects of a highly stratified society while at the same time keeping that stratified, aristocratic, and patriarchally biased structure essentially intact.

Slaves could be manumitted by several means, for instance sacral manumission, where the slave or someone else purchased his or her freedom in a temple in the name of a deity. The deity was thought to be the mediator in this transaction. More commonly an owner would specify in his will that a slave was to be freed, or manumission might be done formally before a magistrate or informally before friends.

It is likely that most of the slaves Paul knew were those one would meet in a urban context like Corinth — mercantile slaves such as traders, artisans, and business men and women, pedagogues (whom Paul mentions in a metaphor about the law in Galatians 3–4), and household servants, such as those in the home of Lydia in Philippi (Acts 16) and probably those mentioned in 1 Cor. 7:21-24. Since Corinth was a Roman colony and the governing seat of the province of Achaia it is quite likely that there were some slaves of the goverment — civil servants of various rank.

Paul knew that slavery was basically unquestioned in the West and that slaves were basically unprotected by the law, while in Jewish society there were laws to protect slaves. At least in ordinary Jewish families it seems to have been less common to have slaves.[50] If Paul did convert several households first in Achaia (e.g., Stephanas's household), probably some domestic slaves were among the first converts in Corinth. In 1 Corinthians 7, however, he is likely discussing the case of a Christian slave with a non-Christian owner.

Conservative estimates of the growing Roman economy in Roman Corinth strongly suggest that at least one-third of the population there in Paul's day were slaves. Apparently Corinth was the clearinghouse and major slave market town for slaves being shipped westward from the East. In Corinth more and more *nouveau riche* freedmen and freedwomen would want to have villas, live as the well-to-do Romans, and be waited on hand and foot.

What were ancient attitudes to slavery? Consider the following:

No ancient government, even a Jewish government, ever sought to abolish slavery,
no former slaves who became writers ever attacked the institution of slavery as such,
slave revolts did not seek to abolish the institution but to protest abuses (this may even be true of the Spartacus revolt),[51]

---

48. *CIL* 13.7119.

49. Cf. Martin, *Slavery as Salvation,* p. 29.

50. See for example Jesus' parable about the day laborers in Matt. 20:1-16. One did not need to hire large numbers of day laborers if one had a considerable number of slaves.

51. S. S. Bartchy, *First-Century Slavery and the Interpretation of 1 Cor. 7:21* (Missoula: Scholars, 1973), p. 63.

Epictetus, a former slave, says that true freedom has nothing to do with one's legal
status, but with submitting one's freedom of choice to God (4.1.89), and
more often than not it was free workers, not slaves, who were abused by foremen
and bosses, since an owner stood to have an ongoing loss if he abused a slave.

In the American South, unlike Rome, there was no prospect and in many places
no legal possibility of manumission. In the first century A.D., manumission was so
common and occurred so often that Augustus set up laws restricting it. Because of
increasing flexibility slaves were building up some savings and saw prospects as freedmen and freedwomen to make an economic go of it. There were more requests for
manumission in the first century A.D. than ever before. Finally, there is evidence that
some early Christian congregations purchased the freedom of some of their slave
members (cf. 1 Clement 55.2, Ignatius to Polycarp 4.3, Hermas Mandate 8.10, Simil-
itude 10.8). There is, however, much debate as to whether slaves could ever do more
than ask to be set free. Apparently, they could not legally choose freedom, since they
were not considered legal persons with rights under Roman law.

Therefore, it seems unlikely that Paul means in 1 Cor. 7:21 that if one has a
chance to *choose* freedom one should take it. By working hard or by earning money a
slave might make a strong case for freedom, but could not force the issue with his or
her owner. It was not the slave's choice, unless the owner agreed. Furthermore, Bartchy
argues that the slave was not free to reject manumission either, if the owner was
determined to be rid of the slave. The slave could only plead against it. This means
that 1 Cor. 7:21 certainly cannot mean "if you have the option to become free, do not
avail yourself of it." The slave had no such options.

There seems to have been a marked difference in the treatment of domestic
slaves as opposed to agricultural slaves in regard to manumission.

When a Roman manumitted his slave, [the slave] would (if the correct formali-
ties had been observed) attain restricted citizenship status, extending even to
the right to inherit his patron's estate. There is evidence that the feeling that a
loyal domestic servant ought automatically to be granted freedom and civic
rights after a number of years was so widespread that the "model" of slavery as
a process of integration may be useful here. . . . Roman jurists recognised a
slave's right to use his *peculium* to buy himself free from his owner. On the other
hand the *familia rustica,* those slaves working on agricultural estates, received
very different treatment and had virtually no opportunities to benefit from this
ideal.[52]

So with regard to slaves Paul gives an exception to the rule "stay as you are," that
is, in the station you found yourself when you became a Christian: *"If indeed you are
to become free by all means make use of it."* But Paul's basic word to slaves is "If you
find yourself a slave when you convert, *don't let that worry you."* In his view, one's
social status or position is of no major importance and certainly of no eternal significance in Christ. All persons are equally brothers and sisters in Christ regardless of
their social station. Paul's advice is not to evaluate oneself by the larger society's values.

---

52. Wiedemann, *Greek and Roman Slavery,* p. 3.

He is even able to say that there is a sense in which a Christian slave is already the Lord's freedman in terms of freedom from sin, and for that matter the freedman or freedwoman in Christ is actually Christ's slave. Thus values and status are turned upside down in Christ.

It is clear from v. 23 that Paul is opposed to the trend of people, especially Christians, selling themselves into slavery to support their family or to pay off debts. There is no point in changing one's status in that way. One of the themes of the chapter is that one should not try to change one's status just *because* one is in Christ. This sort of approach amounts to saying that no social status of whatever kind prevents one from becoming or being a Christian, and therefore it is not necessary to change one's social status to become or be a Christian. Even a slave as a slave in Roman Corinth can be a Christian, and thus how much more anyone else.

But Paul does see slavery as making things more difficult for the Christian who has a pagan owner. Therefore, he encourages the slave to take advantage of the opportunity if freedom is offered. Paul minimizes present social status and its weight, but he recognizes that in the case of slavery things could become difficult for the Christian, so he makes an exception to his rule "stay as you are."

Paul's feelings about slavery are made a little clearer in Philemon, where he pleads for Onesimus's manumission. It will be noted that Paul is no revolutionary here. He is not arguing for a slave revolt, only that one slave be freed. Paul's principle that all Christians, of whatever background or status, are brothers and sisters in Christ, led eventually to a situation in which it was clear that slavery and Christianity, with its views of human dignity, freedom, and complete availability to only one Master, are basically incompatible.[53]

Paul's approach is to put the leaven of the gospel into the structure of the Christian community, not into the larger society directly, and let it do its work over the course of time. As with the matter of women, Paul believes in living a true Christian life and letting the natural implications of that bring transformation to the patriarchal and slave society. He meant for the Christian community to live out its new freedom, thus bearing witness to the larger community about their values. Apparently, no early Christian, by litigation or by appeal to governing authorities or by revolt, ever tried to change the social fabric of ancient society. It was by means of witness and change *within* the Christian community that a new worldview was promulgated.

53. C. F. D. Moule, *The Epistles of Paul the Apostle to the Colossians and to Philemon* (Cambridge: Cambridge University, 1957), pp. 11f. Contrast Wiedemann, *Greek and Roman Slavery,* pp. 229ff. As Petersen, *Rediscovering Paul,* p. 175, notes, Paul does not address the role of masters or the relationship between slaves and masters in 1 Cor. 7:21-24, so this text reveals rather less than Philemon.

Argument IV, Division 1: 8:1-13

The Party of the First Part

The next major subsection of this letter, 8:1–11:1, continues to deal with issues the Corinthians raised in their letter to Paul and in fact with positions that they strenuously argued for in that letter.[1] The issues involved are complex and understanding of them requires an understanding of the social situation in Corinth. It also requires an understanding of the technical vocabulary used in Paul's combative response to the Corinthians.

The situation seems to have three components. First, some of the Corinthians who claim to have "knowledge" are rejecting Paul's earlier prohibition of going to pagan temples, even in the case of dinner parties being held there.[2] Second, in their letter to Paul they are defending their right to go to a temple for a meal with the words "there are no such things as idols, and food is irrelevant so far as our standing with God is concerned." Their argument is based on their Christian *gnōsis* (knowledge) that only God is God and food is morally neutral. Therefore, eating in temples dedicated to so-called gods is harmless. Their position entails a rejection of Paul's advice since he already ruled on this matter.[3] Third, bad as their rejection of Paul's earlier dictum is, this group of Corinthians is going a step further in the wrong direction by encouraging, perhaps even causing, some Christians ("the weak") to join with

---

1. On this whole subsection, cf. P. Gardner, *The Gifts of God and the Authentication of a Christian* (dissertation, Cambridge, 1981).

2. It is instructive to ask where the more well-to-do or *nouveau riche* members of the Corinthian congregation got their money. Here we are helped by M. Rostovtzeff, *The Social and Economic History of the Roman Empire* I (Oxford: Clarendon, 1957), p. 172: "Our survey of the evolution of the commerce in the Roman Empire in the first two centuries A.D. establishes the fact that commerce, and especially foreign and inter-provincial maritime commerce, provided the main sources of wealth in the Roman Empire. Most of the *nouveau riches* owed their money to it." Corinth was ideally situated to have many such people. It was necessary for such people to maintain their social contacts, e.g., in the temples, in order to keep their businesses growing. In turn, the growth of new cities in the empire came to depend on "the wealth of the *bourgeoisie* . . . in the first two centuries A.D." (Rostovtzeff, p. 187).

3. For the view that Paul had earlier tried to impose the Apostolic Decree of Acts 15 in Corinth, cf. J. C. Hurd, *The Origin of 1 Corinthians* (New York: Seabury, 1965), pp. 115-49. I would not rule this out, but more likely 1 Corinthians 8–10 shows how he would apply such a decree in a situation like Corinth.

them in meals at temples, with the result that their Christian character and lives are being destroyed and their moral consciousness is being defiled.

In response, Paul, in a diatribe-like form used in schools, quotes "those in the know" and then qualifies their dictums in a running dialogue.[4] In Paul's view the issue is not what kind of meat one eats. It is, rather, the social and moral effects of eating in certain contexts. Thus, this discussion is primarily about interpersonal behavior in certain contexts, not about cuisine.[5] One must be careful in comparing this text to Romans 14: The differences are more crucial than the similarities. In Romans Paul seems to be refereeing a debate between the strong and weak in Rome about eating meat, not about dining in a pagan temple. Here there is no reference to "the strong," as there is in Rom. 15:1; rather it is "we who have knowledge" vs. "the weak," and the debate is essentially between the *"gnostic"* Corinthians[6] and Paul. It is not over meat that has been sacrificed to idols in itself, but the setting in which one partakes of such meat. Those "in the know"[7] may have modeled themselves on the Stoic or Cynic ideal wise man who possessed an *exousia* or power that allowed him to claim that everything is permitted him because he is truly free. This attitude failed to reckon with the Christian attitude toward the human body and the body of Christ.[8]

The position of those writing to Paul is that "all have knowledge" that the idols are not gods. Paul must counter this and say that not all in practice

4. The diatribe form is perhaps even more evident in 6:12-20; cf. S. K. Stowers, "Paul on the Use and Abuse of Reason," *Greeks, Romans, and Christians,* ed. D. L. Balch, E. Ferguson, and W. A. Meeks (Minneapolis: Fortress, 1990), pp. 253-86, here p. 263. Stowers is right in saying that the diatribe style is pedagogical in origin, not a form of mass propaganda used by Cynic preachers. See also A. D. Litfin, *St. Paul's Theology of Proclamation: An Investigation of 1 Cor. 1–4 in Light of Greco-Roman Rhetoric* (dissertation, Oxford, 1983), p. 361. The important point is that the use of this form shows that Paul is operating as a teacher with students and treating these Corinthians as immature students.

5. Cf. J. C. Brunt, "Love, Freedom, and Moral Responsibility," *SBL 1981 Seminar Papers,* ed. K. H. Richards (Chico: Scholars, 1981), pp. 19-33, here pp. 24f. Brunt, following H. Conzelmann, *1 Corinthians* (Philadelphia: Fortress, 1975), p. 177, is wrong to reject Fee's point that place is an important concern, though type of meat is not (G. D. Fee, *The First Epistle to the Corinthians* [Grand Rapids: Eerdmans, 1987], pp. 359f.). In Paul's view, the character of the meal is partly determined by where one eats, if it is in a pagan temple, not just how or with whom one eats.

6. I use the term here in its generic sense of those "in the know," not to refer to the second-century heresy.

7. It is sometimes argued that these people were not elitist. This is forgetting that it is they who are bandying about the slogan "all have knowledge," not the weak, and they do so as a justification for their own behavior. This was apparently not the view of either Paul or the weak.

8. Accordingly, J. Murphy-O'Connor, "Freedom or the Ghetto," in *Freedom and Love* (Rome: St. Paul's Abbey, 1981), pp. 7-38, here p. 13, argues that the "gnosis" people have a Hellenistic Jewish approach to wisdom. Perhaps, but since they are Gentiles, one would have to posit that they had previously been synagogue adherents.

have that knowledge and furthermore that it is not correct to say that there are no other supernatural beings besides the true God involved in the world.[9]

It is clear that Paul quotes the Corinthians' letter but not as certain which of his phrases and clauses are included in these quotations. I offer the following analysis: "We all possess knowledge" (v. 1) and "An idol is nothing and there is no God but one" (v. 4) are Corinthian slogans that Paul is quoting and qualifying, following his usual "yes . . . but" procedure. Willis has argued that vv. 5f., except for the parenthetical remark in v. 5b, are also quoted, and this may be so. We will examine this possibility below.[10] At any rate, despite v. 1, it is not Paul's view that *all* have the sort of knowledge in question.

Several temples in Corinth had dining rooms where feasts were held on many occasions, including birthdays. Temples were the restaurants of antiquity.[11] There is archaeological evidence at the Asklepion in Corinth of a dining room with couches along the four walls and a table and brazier in the center.[12]

Paul distinguishes between eating at home and eating in temples and strictly forbids the latter (10:14-23). His view is that though the "gods" are not gods, there are demons present, using pagan feasts in temples to prey on unsuspecting people. In fact, the sacrifices are offered unwittingly to demons (10:20f.). Thus in a limited sense Paul allows that there are "many gods and lords" (8:5). Supernatural evil powers use pagan religion to lead people away from the true God. The idols themselves are dumb and nothing, but they are used by the powers of darkness to enslave human minds and hearts. "Gods"

9. It may be that those "in the know" had been influenced by Epicurean ideas. Cf. Stowers, "Paul on the Use," p. 277:

> When new converts entered the Epicurean community they were first instructed to give up the traditional false beliefs and superstitions about the gods, and then taught true knowledge based on reason. Epicureans were allowed, and indeed even encouraged, to worship the traditional Greek gods as long as they did not involve themselves in this world and [recognized] that rituals had no effect. Some of the Corinthians were very proud of their true beliefs about the divine and the powers of those beliefs to desacralize the world.

Perhaps some Corinthians had read Paul's monotheistic teaching (cf. 8:6) through Epicurean glasses.

10. W. Willis, *Idol Meat at Corinth* (Chico: Scholars, 1985), pp. 65ff.

11. Cf. in *New Doc. 1*, p. 5, the three invitations to dine at the banquet of the god; in two cases it is clearly Sarapis (e.g., "Herais asks you to dine in the room of the Sarapeion at a banquet of the Lord Sarapis *[en tō oikō tou Sarapeiou eis kleinēn tou kuriou Sarapidos]* tomorrow . . . at the ninth hour"). The meals were clearly seen as having a religious character and not just a religious component.

12. Cf. the picture in *The Interpreter's Dictionary of the Bible, Supplementary Volume*, ed. K. Crim, et al. (Nashville: Abingdon, 1976), p. 180. For the various papyri inscriptions of invitations to "dine at the couch of Lord Sarapis," cf. A. Deissmann, *Light from the Ancient East* (Grand Rapids: Baker, 1978 reprint), p. 351, n. 2, and pp. 114-15 above and pp. 191-95 below.

(8:5) refers to the traditional pagan deities, and *kyrioi* ("lords") probably refers to the gods imported into Greece and Italy from the eastern part of the empire, including those associated with the mystery religions, such as Isis and Sarapis.

Eidōlothuton ("idol food," 8:1, 4, 7, 10; 10:19) is not a pagan term, since pagans would hardly call their gods "idols." It is rather a polemical term that arose in early Christianity for the sacred food eaten in pagan temple precincts after a sacrifice.[13] It is not to be confused with *hierothuton* ("temple food" or "sacred food"), which Paul uses of food that comes from the temple but is bought in the market and eaten at home (10:28).[14]

Some, if not most, of the meat available in the market had a history of being a temple sacrifice. But one could buy many other things in the market — fish, sheep butchered there in the *macellum,* and various grains, vegetables, and fruits.[15] The poor person did not often eat meat. Garnsey rightly stresses that "meat was relatively expensive, and could only have been available on a regular basis to those with money to buy." And apparently during religious feasts "sacrificial meat was monopolized by senators and others of high status."[16] If the poor got meat, it was likely at such a feast as part of a celebration

13. I have given detailed evidence for this conclusion in "Not So Idle Thoughts about *Eidolothuton,*" *TynB* 44 (1993), pp. 237-54. Cf. Gardner, *Gifts of God,* p. 15, who says that the term originated at the Apostolic Council, which is summarized in Acts 15. With the possible exception of the occurrence of the word in 4 Macc. 5:2, there is no hard evidence that it originated in Hellenistic Judaism; even if that text is not part of a Christian interpolation, it probably post-dates the writing of 1 Corinthians. The reference in *Sibylline Oracles* 2.96 seems to be a Christian interpolation.

14. We have yet to identify with certainty where the market that sold meat was in Corinth, though J. B. Ward-Perkins, "From Republic to Empire: Reflections on the Early Provincial Architecture of the Roman West," *Journal of Roman Studies* 60 (1970), pp. 1-19, seems to think it is a known and identifiable entity. Latin *macellum* is a general term for a market and among other things can refer to a meat market. D. W. J. Gill has recently laid out the inscriptional evidence that there was such a market in Roman Corinth ("The Meat-Market at Corinth [1 Corinthians 10:25]," *TynB,* forthcoming). I take it that the Latin phrase *macellum cum* means "market with," after which the Latin word for meat or fish was mentioned. Gill seems to think *macellum* is a technical term for the meat market, but P. Garnsey of Cambridge denies this suggestion (personal conversation).

15. N. Nabers, "A Note on Corinth VIII,2,125," *AJA* 73 (1969), pp. 73f.

16. P. Garnsey, "Mass Diet and Nutrition in the City of Rome," *Nourir la plebe,* ed. A. Giovanni (Basel: Herder, 1991), pp. 67-101, here p. 100. A. J. Blasi, *Early Christianity as a Social Movement* (New York: Lang, 1988), p. 61, notes that meat was given to the poor on special holidays in honor of one god or another. This is yet another reason why the poorer Corinthian Christians might necessarily associate eating meat with idols. For the view that Paul is talking about funerary meals see C. A. Kennedy, "The Cult of the Dead in Corinth," in *Love and Death in the Ancient Near East: Essays in Honor of Marvin H. Pope,* ed. J. H. Marks and R. M. Good (Guilford: Four Quarter, 1987), pp. 227-36. The three major problems with this view are: (1) the mention of immorality, (2) the mention of the context of the temple (8:10), and (3) the frequency with which Paul assumes that this occurs.

involving eating in temple precincts or as a bequest given by the more well-to-do in honor of a god.

The ancients were not the meat-eaters we are today, except at special banquets *(convivia)* and sacrifices. The normal diet consisted of different types of porridge, or barley meal (from which bread and porridge were made), olives, a little wine, perhaps some fish as a relish, and meat on holidays or special occasions.[17] Thus, a middle or lower-status person buying in the market would seldom purchase anything that came from the temple. Probably, as Theissen suggests, "the weak" in Corinth are poorer Corinthians for whom *eidōlothuta* was especially likely to have religious associations, because they had eaten it before only at some public temple feast or on a holiday in the temple. This would explain their strong scruples.[18]

1 Corinthians 8–10 provides further evidence that there were some well-to-do members of Paul's congregation in Corinth, as is shown by their meat-eating in home and temple, and that they were causing Paul no end of trouble. It is surely this elite group that was bandying about the slogans Paul repeats in ch. 8. The Corinthian congregation was socially diverse, and "the weak" were being scandalized by the behavior of the well-to-do.

"Weak in moral consciousness" in 1 Corinthians 8 means the opposite of what it might mean today. It refers to those who have *more* scruples than some, not less. It is often argued that Paul's own position is that of those "in the know" in Corinth, not that of the weak, but that is far from obvious. Paul, like the weak, has scruples about going to a pagan temple, and it is unlikely that he ever had or would do so. Unlike the weak, however, he had no scruples about eating meat from the *macellum* in a private home. Thus, he gives only a qualified endorsement to either of the views in Corinth.

Paul's reason for associating idol food, temples, and *porneia* (sexual immorality, primarily prostitution, 6:13) is that on some occasions in the temple precincts part of the entertainment was likely sexual. I would suggest that this is also what the Apostolic Decree of Acts 15 is concerned with, and as such Paul is happy to implement the decree in Corinth and elsewhere. Gentiles are to avoid going to temples, where they would get idol food, improperly sacrificed meat with the blood in it, and *porneia*. This also explains the association of prohibitions against idol food and *porneia* in texts like Rev. 2:14 (cf. especially Rev. 9:30ff.). In due course, this prohibition was extended

17. Garnsey, "Mass Diet," pp. 79-85; C. K. Barrett, *Essays on Paul* (Philadelphia: Westminster, 1982), p. 48.

18. G. Theissen, *The Social Setting of Pauline Christianity: Essays on Corinth* (Philadelphia: Fortress, 1982), pp. 121ff. The other possibility is that they were people of Jewish background. On Alexandrian Jews abstaining from dining at guild meals in pagan temples even though they were members of the guild, cf. B. W. Winter, "Theological and Ethical Responses to Religious Pluralism," *TynB* 41 (1990), pp. 209-44, here p. 218.

to eating improperly sacrificed meat of all kinds, perhaps in deference to Jewish Christians.[19] It is doubtful that this is what the Apostolic Decree intended, and certainly Paul does not interpret it this way.[20] Paul's view on this matter did not prevail after his death, however, and his ability to make nice distinctions between eating food from the temple at home and eating in the temple was misunderstood soon after the NT era.

Paul's rhetorical strategy in chs. 8–10, since he is presenting a long argument, is to include a partial digression in ch. 9, though it is related to the subject at hand. This A-B-A structure is not uncommon in Paul's letters.[21] Rhetorically speaking, Paul uses the *egressio* (digression) at an appropriate moment, for if one's argument has a very strong tone, then one needs to provide some relief from that tone, lest the audience be put off (cf. *Inst. Or.* 4.3.2, 10). Paul shifts the focus from the Corinthians' conduct to his own in ch. 9, giving them an opportunity to reflect. It was a rule that digressions have some bearing on the case at hand (*Inst. Or.* 4.3.14). Quintilian notes that digressions are especially likely to be inserted when the goal is to admonish (cf. 4.3.16), as is the case in this part of 1 Corinthians. Part of Paul's strategy is to show "those in the know" the logical consequences of their un-Christian attitudes and actions, rather than just condemning them.[22]

A Closer Look: Dining in Roman Corinth ──────────────────

Dining took place in a variety of venues in Roman cities. The poorer residents in a city had two choices — they could eat in the cramped quarters they lived in, or if they had a small amount of money they might seek out friends and companions at a *caupona*, a *popina,* or a *taberna.* A *caupona* provided full service and offered meals and drinks as well as rooms. It might have a stand-up snack bar,[23] a room with tables and chairs, and possibly a garden with private dining areas with couches. A *popina* was a simpler affair serving wine and some hot food and was the equivalent of a modern fast food restaurant. In either a *popina* or a *taberna* one was likely to find all kinds of

19. Barrett, *Essays on Paul,* pp. 43f., on Justin Martyr, the Didache, and later authors.

20. Witherington, "Not So Idle Thoughts," pp. 237-51.

21. See below on chs. 12–14 and the literature cited there. It is strange that N. W. Lund, *Chiasmus in the NT* (Peabody: Hendrickson, 1992), fails to deal with 1 Corinthians 8–10.

22. Murphy-O'Connor, "Freedom or the Ghetto," p. 21.

23. These have been found at Pompeii and at Roman Corinth; cf. O. H. Zervos, "Corinth 1985: East of the Theater," *Hesperia* 55 (1986), pp. 129-85, here pp. 147f., on fast food counters in buildings 1 and 3 at Corinth equipped with large ovens to prepare hot meals, but not called *taberna.* Williams is likely right that they served the passing theater and games crowds.

people. Juvenal (8.146-78) mentions a man who was born poor and then rose to be a consul but still frequented the *popinae*, where he drank with muggers, sailors, thieves, butchers, coffin makers, and eunuch priests. The *taberna*, from which we get the word tavern, was what its name suggests. Early in the empire, Tiberius, Claudius, and Nero all placed restrictions on such places, seeing them as breeding grounds for trouble of all sorts, including political chaos (cf. Suetonius *Tiberius* 34; *Nero* 16; Dio Cassius, *Roman History* 60.6.6f.; 62.14.2). Both Claudius and Nero even banned selling of meat in such establishments.[24] Paul is not talking about dining at such places or in the homes of the poor in 1 Corinthians 8–10.

Well before the time of the empire the distinction between the "feast" *(deipna)* and the symposium (from *symposion*, a group sharing a meal) as a ritual carried out in a closed club, had become somewhat blurred. The latter had started in classical Greece as a sort of drinking party where a close-knit group enjoyed company, conversation, and wine mixed with water. A second important change from classical times is that the feast with extensive meat courses that followed a communal sacrifice, which in earlier times had been held in a private home, was moved to the temple precincts. This happened even before the time of Augustus. The result was that the *deipna* in a private home became increasingly more like a symposium, mainly confined to drinking.[25]

It was not uncommon for *deipna* and *symposion* to form two stages of one evening's entertainment, a feast followed by a drinking party. This is of some importance for understanding 1 Cor. 11:17-22. The Romans called such a feast *cena* and drinking parties *convivia*. As even a cursory perusal of Plutarch's *Lives* will show, disorderly conduct, displays of excess and extravagance, treachery and plotting, sexual dalliance, and immorality were not uncommon, especially at drinking parties. Drinking parties were generally all-male affairs, as the classical club meetings had earlier been, though with entertainment including dancing and flute-playing girls, and *hetairai*, as well as prostitutes at less refined meals, such as those held by some freedmen.

At the symposium, besides drinking, the chief entertainment was, at least officially, conversation about all sort of things including politics, philosophy, religion, and economics. Sophists were regularly the guests of honor at such feasts, because they could entertain the guests with a simple *encomium* or some other form of epideictic rhetoric and get the conversation going (cf. Athenaeus *The Deipnosophists;* Philostratus *Lives* 20). Tacitus (*Agr.* 21) tells us that the chief enticements to Romanization among non-Romans were the cultivation of rhetorical oratory, elegant banquets, and use of the promenade and the toga.

Plutarch (*Lyc.* 13.607; cf. *Mor.* 227C) describes the meals of the wealthy like those held in Roman Corinth, telling the tale of a Spartan named Leotychidas who when dining at Corinth gazed up at the expensive coffered ceiling and asked his host if trees grew square in Corinth (because he was used to simple feasts held outside in a grove). Plutarch also polemicizes against the vulgarity of silver-footed couches, purple

24. On the above, cf. J. E. Stambaugh, *The Ancient Roman City* (Baltimore: Johns Hopkins University, 1988), pp. 208f.

25. W. Burkett, "Oriental Symposia: Contrasts and Parallels," in W. J. Slater, ed., *Dining in a Classical Context* (Ann Arbor: University of Michigan, 1991), pp. 7-24, here p. 18.

coverlets, gold cups, and the like in simple homes or the homes of *nouveau riche* freedmen on the basis of the assumption, made also by other writers of the period, that behavior at the *convivia* was a microcosm of the character of society.[26]

A *convivium* was usually a smaller private dinner party. Formal banquets, such as official city banquets, were called *epulae*. Guests at *convivia* were usually served by male slaves called *ministri*, who also served as gatekeepers to keep out potential party crashers and as bouncers to handle unruly guests. While there was some concern for equality at a banquet, it was common for the choicest foods and wines to be reserved for the master and the higher-status guests, just as it was the usual practice to observe a pecking order in assignment of couches. The closer one was to the host and to the head of the table, the more important one was thought to be.[27]

In many ways the most important slave at a *convivium* was the wineserver. He was expected to be young and sexually attractive, catering to pederastic lust.

> The wineserver has to dress like a woman and wrestle with his advancing years. He is not permitted to escape from his boyhood, but is continually dragged back to it. His body hair is plucked off and he is kept beardless. He is kept awake all night, dividing his time between his master's drunkenness and his lust. (Seneca *Ep.* 47.7)

The Roman *convivium* was legendary for fostering a degree of decadence "associated not only with the pleasures of the palate but also of the pillow."[28]

Convivia were basically restricted to men. Roman men began to attend in their late teens, when they had begun to wear the *toga virilis*.[29] Wives and daughters, while they might attend the beginning of a feast held in their home, would retire when it was time for the heavy drinking to begin. Public banquets were also largely restricted to men.[30] In an important essay, K. E. Corley summarizes the evidence as follows:

26. G. Paul, "Symposia and Deipna in Plutarch's Lives and Other Historical Writings," in *Dining in a Classical Context,* pp. 157-69.

27. Cf. Juvenal *Sat.* 125-27.

28. A. Booth, "The Age for Reclining and Its Attendant Perils," in *Dining in a Classical Context,* pp. 105-20, here p. 106.

29. The practice of emperors, such as Claudius, of bringing their children to such *convivia* to show them off, allowing them to sit at the end of the table quietly, should not be taken as characteristic of all such occasions (cf. Suetonius *Claudius* 32). That it did happen on occasion at a different sort of meal in private homes when an employed rhetor would share a meal with his charges is shown by Quintilian's lament: "I do not approve of boys sitting with young men. For even if the teacher be such a one as we would desire to see in charge of the morals and studies of the young . . . it is nonetheless desirable to keep the weaker members separate from the more mature" (*Inst. Or.* 2.2.14f.). He is concerned about homosexual advances, because he is aware of the sorts of activities that often went on at banquets and drinking parties.

30. The suggestion of A. C. Wire, *The Corinthian Women Prophets: A Reconstruction through Paul's Rhetoric* (Minneapolis: Fortress, 1990), p. 103, that women other than entertainers, prostitutes, or *hetairai* regularly attended such dinner parties in temples is both unlikely and without basis in the sources. Her argument is strange since she also wishes to argue that the Corinthian women prophets were *ascetics!* It is true that a family might well

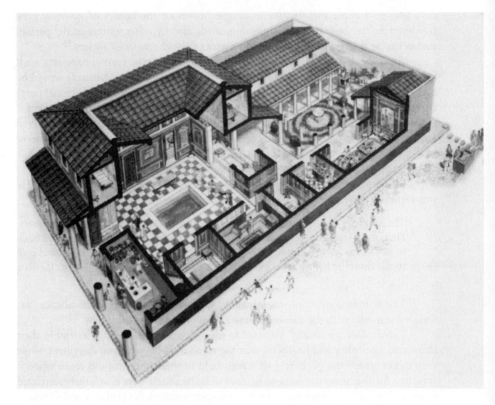

A typical wealthy home in a Roman town;
note the triclinium at the upper right

Used by permission from *See inside a Roman Town,* ed. R. J. Unstead
(published by Kingfisher Books, copyright © Grisewood & Dempsey, Ltd. 1977)

It is clear that women who were associated with banquet settings were seen in the popular imagination as prostitutes. Certain Greco-Roman women did in fact attend dinners with their husbands, but the practice may not have been all that common, even in the associations, and its pervasiveness outside the upper classes is difficult to determine. Areas still influenced by Greek ideals and practices would also still adhere to a certain extent to the exclusion of women from some meals, and certainly from those meals characterized as *sumposia*. Women who did attend such parties would have engendered a great deal of social

---

attend at least the meal portion of a public cultic feast or family sacrifice, but it is doubtful that Paul has the former in view, and probably not the latter either. He is discussing dinner parties, perhaps in particular those put on by *collegia* in temple precincts. In ch. 10 he turns briefly to meals in private homes.

criticism, particularly after the time of Augustus, when the interest in the maintenance of the nuclear family as a means to insure the political stability of the empire caused a shift in the social consciousness which reemphasized ideal women's roles. Absence from public banquets became part of that complex of ideas which eventually determined a woman's social classification, and eventually limited her ability to participate in the public sphere in the centuries to follow.[31]

Study of *triclinia* in places like the Asklepion in Corinth and of dining couches and spaces in private homes shows that Romans liked the *triclinium* pattern of three couches arranged in a ⊏, each couch holding up to three diners in comfort. A large dining room in a home might accommodate twelve to fourteen guests, while in the dining facilities at a temple about twenty-two was the maximum.[32] Vitruvius describes a Corinthian-style dining room as having rows of columns along three sides, separating the dining area from a surrounding gallery where slaves would linger to wait on the guests (6.3.8). Garden *triclinia* could be hired, both at *tabernae* and at temples for outdoor dinner parties, but *tabernae* catered to private affairs, while temples catered to public dinner parties.

The *gnōsis* group in Corinth seems to have been the origin of the letter addressed to Paul (7:1). Their letter apparently defended their behavior and gave reasons for rejecting Paul's counsel.[33] It is likely, as Theissen suggests, that the members of this group were more well-to-do and socially enlightened male members of the *ekklēsia*, those who regularly had occasion to eat at the temple dinner parties. This same group may also have been the cause of the troubles mentioned in 11:17ff.: Some were treating the agape meal like a dinner in a temple by eating with their elite friends ahead of the poor and slaves, who came later, when the food was gone and the meal had come to the *symposion* stage, that is, had become a drinking fest.

Paul follows his standard procedure of first dealing with the error's theological root, the point at which it touches at the heart of the gospel, and then dealing with the fruit of the bad theology. The root of the problem is

---

31. K. E. Corley, "Were the Women around Jesus Really Prostitutes? Women in the Context of Greco-Roman Meals," *SBL 1989 Seminar Papers*, ed. D. J. Lull (Atlanta: Scholars, 1989), pp. 487-521, here p. 513.

32. Cf. K. M. D. Dunbabin, "*Triclinium* and *Stibadium*," in *Dining in a Classical Context*, pp. 121-48, here pp. 122f.

33. The *gnōsis* that they were arguing for does not appear to have been received through a new revelation. It represents, rather, their understanding of what Paul had taught, pace Gardner, *Gifts of God*, p. 28. I do not find Gardner's attempt to connect chs. 8–10 with the gift list in ch. 12 very plausible. I do agree that the problem was not that some had knowledge, but rather the way in which they were allowing this knowledge to function.

that the members of the *gnōsis* group,[34] while having some of the right Pauline ideas, have drawn the wrong social consequences, perhaps in an attempt to justify their continued participation in society. Their approach is either very individualistic, as was true of Greeks seeking wisdom or *gnōsis* in many cases, or very status conscious. They are trying to keep up with others of their social station despite the effect of such behavior on other Christians, especially those who might have been their social inferiors or of different ethnic extractions.[35]

For Paul the essence of Christian theology is love, not knowledge (**8:1b**). Knowledge leads to an elitist approach to the faith. Those "in the know" see themselves as superior. Paul will have none of this. He ardently defends the weak, and indeed his theology comes to "in weakness there is strength," weakness being defined as Christ on the cross (ch. 1). Self-sacrificial love, unlike *gnōsis*, builds up the community and is egalitarian in its effects. Paul's chief concern is the building up and knitting together of the factious Corinthian congregation.

There are close parallels between chs. 8 and 13, which says "though I have all knowledge, if I do not have love I am nothing" (13:2). One of the major problems in Corinth reveals itself in the treatment of the weak. Love as a basis for Christian living and behavior deflates elitism, since it entails self-sacrificial service even to the weak, not self-aggrandizement. The Corinthian *gnōsis* group, in an egocentric move, were trying to claim their right or *exousia* to do as they had been doing. Paul is insisting that just because one knows something does not give one license to act. Before action one must ask: "Is this loving? Does it build up the body of Christ?" Salvation is fleshed out not in self-helping actions, but in self-sacrificial actions.

This Corinthian group's view might be summed up as "knowledge is power and power gives freedom and rights." Paul counters with his own slogan: "Love builds up the *ekklēsia* and gives opportunity and power for service to others." As Willis points out, for Paul freedom is not the first and fundamental cry, which then is crimped or limited by love. Rather, love is the fundamental thing, and it indicates how one's power ought to be used. A Christian's power and authority are to be expressed in and by love. Paul does not see freedom as liberation from obligations or from the restraints of interpersonal relationships, which was the common view in some parts of Greco-Roman society and still is today. For Paul, freedom is freedom *from* sin, *from* fear of death,

---

34. Chapters 8–10 are further confirmation of the factious and divided state of Corinthian Christianity, but also evidence that those "in the know" and the "weak" were still eating and fraternizing together. These chapters also show that the divisions were not just theologically engendered. Social factors must be considered.

35. It is possible that the "weak" are Jewish Christians, not just those of lower social status. Perhaps this explains Paul's use of the example from the Hebrew Scriptures in ch. 10.

from the law, and *for* service to Christ and his people. This is what Christians have been saved and empowered for — freedom to do what pleases God, not what pleases self.

For Paul, community is primary and what is good for community should guide conduct. For the Corinthians that Paul is addressing, the individual or one's social clique is primary, and personal fulfillment is primary. These Corinthians' idea of helping the weak amounts to making them like themselves — participants in pagan feasts!

Those "in the know" were right to a point. There is only one God, and there is no such thing as an idol, if by that one means another god (v. 4).[36] They had failed, however, to reckon with the demonic. This is somewhat strange, since pagans certainly did believe in hostile or malevolent spirits as well as benign spirits.[37] These gods the Corinthians were calling "so-called gods" (v. 5).[38] The profession in v. 4, "There is no God but One," is reminiscent of the Shema (the Jewish confession of one God, drawn from Deut. 6:4) and came into Christianity from Judaism. There was also some Greek speculation about there being only one God (cf. Plutarch *On the Delphic Ei*).

Willis has argued that we should see the parenthesis in v. 5b as Paul's qualification of the Corinthian remark. Paul is not just arguing for the subjective reality of "many gods and lords,"[39] but is in fact in the odd position of arguing against former pagans that the "so-called gods" do have some objective reality.[40] As he will explain in ch. 10, there are demonic forces behind idols,

---

36. *Ouden*, "no" or "none," could be seen as either subject or predicate, but probably is the former so that the statement means not "an idol is nothing," but rather "there is no [real] idol in the world." Cf. Deut. 6:4; Isa. 14:8; 15:5.

37. *Daimonion* in pagan usage normally referred to something somewhat less than gods, but still a supernatural being or power. The term was not pejorative in the pagan sources. It referred to those spirits or beings that were assigned certain specific spheres of activity such as the oversight of animals, delivery of human prayers to the god, and control over human events or natural processes, including over specific cities and tribes. They were viewed in some ways by the pagans as the equivalent of what Jewish and Christians called guardian angels or angelic mediators. Julian the apostate Roman emperor summed up earlier pagan views by saying in his "Oration against the Galileans," i.e., against Christians, that "over each nation is a national god, with an angel acting as his agent, and a demon [i.e. spirit], and a hero and a peculiar type of servant-powers and subordinates" (143A-B). For the pagan, familiar spirits could be found everywhere. One particular type was the *genius* or spirit of a departed ancestor who was reverenced in a Roman home in religious ceremonies held there. On all this, see R. MacMullen, *Paganism in the Roman Empire* (New Haven: Yale University, 1981), pp. 79-83.

38. Verse 5a is an anacoluthon.

39. So Fee, *First Corinthians*, pp. 372f.

40. Here Murphy-O'Connor's argument in "Freedom or the Ghetto," pp. 25ff., fails to convince. Paul really believes in demons and does not accept the Corinthian slogan without a qualification of significant proportions. The problem of the "weak" is not just a

using the idols to enslave human beings.[41] But then he adds in v. 6, "but of course for us (for whom such demons have no power) there is one God the Father and one Lord Jesus."

Verse 6 is probably a Pauline adaptation of the Shema, one that reflects a reading of it through a sapiential lens.[42] The gist of it is that God is the source and Jesus the mediator of all things, but it also says that "we are *for* God" *(eis auton)*. The stress in this creedal fragment is on the uniqueness of both the Christian God and the Lord Jesus.[43] Jesus is seen as the divine mediator of both creation and redemption. The argument that this passage is just soteriological, not also cosmological, creates a false dichotomy, especially because Jesus is being portrayed as Wisdom, who in the Wisdom of Solomon has a role in both creation and salvation.[44] Jesus is assigned the role that divine personified Wisdom has in the OT (cf. Proverbs 3). N. T. Wright is correct in saying that this new Christian Shema is exactly what Paul needed at this juncture of his argument to reassert a proper "Christian" monotheism, the primacy of love, *and* to counter any under-estimation of Christ that may have existed in Corinth.[45]

Monotheism does not rule out the reality of lesser spiritual beings, some of them malevolent. The *gnōsis* group had not reckoned with that; therefore their practice was also wrong. The weak were wrong in continuing to associate idol meat (apparently in whatever context it is eaten) with idol worship: From custom they still eat idol food as though the idols were real gods. The consequence is that their *syneidēsis*, their "conscience," is defiled (v. 7).

Syneidēsis is an important term for Paul. His usage of it is probably derived from the pagan world, not from his Jewish background. The noun appears eight times in 8:7-12 and 10:25-29, three times in Romans, three in

---

gap between theoretical knowledge and emotion. The problem is that they rightly have qualms about eating in an environment where there are hostile forces present, and yet are doing it, going along with the *gnōsis* group. The problem was not between the head and the heart of the weak but with what the *gnōsis* group understood the implications of monotheism to be and the way in which the weak were violating their own moral awareness.

41. On the OT background to Paul's thinking, cf. the LXX of Isa. 65:11: What is referred to in Hebrew as a table set for the god of fortune becomes in the Greek translation the *daimoni trapeza*, i.e., the table of demons. This text bears clear witness to the close association of the idea of pagan gods with *daimonia* in Jewish thinking. Cf. Deut. 32:17, 21, 39.

42. B. Witherington, *Jesus the Sage: The Pilgrimage of Wisdom* (Minneapolis: Fortress, 1994), ch. 7.

43. Not on their unity. This is not a statement about relationships within the Trinity, i.e., about the unity of Father and Son.

44. For a critique of Murphy-O'Connor's and Dunn's views on this passage, see Witherington, *Jesus the Sage,* ch. 7.

45. N. T. Wright, *The Climax of the Covenant: Christ and Law in Pauline Theology* (Minneapolis: Fortress, 1991), pp. 120-31.

2 Corinthians, six in the Pastorals, and in only a few other places in the rest of the NT. The related verb appears in 1 Cor. 4:4. Sometimes, as in Rom. 2:15 and 13:5, it does seem to mean something like "conscience," the moral faculty that guides human action. But its root meaning is "awareness" or "reflective consciousness." It has been argued that for Paul the "conscience" only reviews past actions, not warning about future actions. The scholarly debate suggests that while the term primarily has to do with past actions, for Paul it may also have to do with future actions.[46]

Here the idea is that though the weak have moral qualms about eating in a temple, they do it anyway, with the result that their moral sensitivity or awareness is defiled. Paul, unlike the Corinthians, says nothing about how to *strengthen* a weak consciousness.[47] Those "in the know" thought it could be "built up" by participation in the idol feasts, by getting used to the idea and seeing that fears are unwarranted. They assumed that what the weak needed was to have their awareness or consciousness *raised* in regard to what really is true about idols and idol meat.[48]

The slogans in v. **8** are probably from the Corinthians' letter. Their point is that food is morally neutral, that there is no moral or religious advantage or disadvantage to eating such food. Paul would agree with this if it were simply a matter of eating at home and if one were not observed by other less bold Christians. But in v. **9** Paul invokes the "stumbling block" principle, which guides one's actions in cases with no clear right and wrong, that is, in *adiaphora*. Paul does not dispute that the Corinthians have a right to eat such food, so far as the food is concerned. Chs. 8–10 make clear how far from Judaism Paul had moved on the matter of food. He no longer believed that food commended one to God or offended God. He had come to the view that food was morally and religiously neutral.

Proskomma (v. 9; cf. Rom. 14:13, 20) is best translated "stumbling block" and is basically a synonym with *skandalon*, though the latter stresses the idea of scandal a bit more.[49] The sense of *proskomma* is not of something that

46. Cf. C. A. Pierce, *Conscience in the NT* (London: SCM, 1955), for a survey of the relevant data; R. Jewett, *Paul's Anthropological Terms* (Leiden: Brill, 1971), pp. 421ff. Jewett accepts Pierce's argument that *syneidēsis* can connote the painful awareness of transgression. Perhaps, but Paul also seems to think of *suneidēsis* as a positive moral awareness (cf. Rom. 9:1).

47. I suspect that P. W. Gooch, "Conscience in 1 Cor. 8 and 10," *NTS* 33 (1987), pp. 244-54, is right in concluding that in some places *syneidēsis* has its minimal sense of self-awareness, in this case self-awareness of one's guilt or innocence.

48. Gardner, *Gifts of God*, p. 50, suggests on the basis of Wis. Sol. 9:5 that the weak are those who are insecure and weak in self-confidence about their faith and its implications, not weak in moral decision-making. This may be right, especially if they were Christian Jews.

49. They could be virtually synonymous, as is shown by Paul using the one to translate the other (cf. Isa. 8:14 LXX; Rom. 9:33).

merely offends but of something that causes someone to stumble morally. In v. **10** we finally learn the location of the offense: *en eidōleiǭ*, that is, in the temple precincts dining room. Here is the heart of the problem. Paul uses "build up" ironically in v. 10. "A fine building up of the weak you're doing!" says Paul to his interlocutors. The weak are, in fact, being destroyed (v. 11).[50]

Verse **11** makes clear that "those in the know" should not shrug off this matter. They are causing the gradual spiritual destruction of a brother for whom Christ died![51] By encouraging a weak believer to eat, they themselves are sinning against that fellow believer and in fact against the body of Christ in Corinth. Paul believes that Christ so identifies with his people and especially with the "least of these" that a sin against them is a sin against Christ.

Verse **13** leads Paul into the lengthy explanation in ch. 9 of his own conduct. He says here that he would rather be a vegetarian forever than cause a believer to stumble. In ch. 9 he will provide "those in the know" a personal example of what "knowing" really means. It means being sensitive to the moral sensibilities of others. What really counts is loving God and God's people and being known by God (8:3). In summary (as Fee, Willis, and Gardner maintain) the issue is not eating meat, but eating meat in an idol temple.[52]

It is not clear when Paul came to this conclusion, but as 9:20 shows, Paul believed that Christianity could not be an ethnically specific religion. If it was to be for everyone, accepting all as they were in their cultural orientations, it could not in its essence be about food, clothing, or other ethnic and culture-specific customs (such as circumcision). Paul did not accept the alternative advocated by proselytizing Jews, that of turning Gentiles into Jews, culturally speaking.[53] Christianity had to be based on more universal ideas such as "one God for all," "freedom in Christ," and universal love as a principle to guide behavior and direct the exercise of this new freedom. It is no accident that it is precisely in those areas of action that would ethnically mark off a group from others that Paul says a Christian is free either to act in that way or not.[54]

---

50. Present continual tense of *apollyomai*.

51. I use the term "brother" deliberately, since the problem arose in all-male social settings.

52. On the latter misunderstanding of Paul's ruling on this matter, cf. J. C. Brunt, "Rejected, Ignored, Misunderstood?" *NTS* 31 (1985), pp. 113-24.

53. Rom. 14:5f. even suggests that Paul did not require the honoring of a specific day as "unto the Lord."

54. This chapter helps us realize that a large part of the Christian life is not regulated by specific NT rules. For instance, most choices of apparel, food, cars, and the like are not dictated by some pre-existing regulation. That Paul, a former Pharisaic Jew, thinks this is true of food shows just how much of the Levitical code he thinks is not applicable to Christian believers. The only safe assumption in dealing with how much of the OT is still binding on Christians is that if a given rule is reaffirmed for the Christian community, it still applies; otherwise it probably does not.

Why does Paul take this approach? Surely one main reason is that he knows that food, clothing, shelter, ethnic customs, and even language are the means of creating a specific ethnic identity.[55] It was the goal of many Corinthians, and probably many in the Christian *ekklēsia* in Corinth, to be truly *Roman,* to fit into their society as best they could. Roman Corinth was a freedman and freedwoman's town in many ways and the opportunities for upward mobility were considerable. In such an environment there was tremendous incentive to want to fit in. For Paul, the boundaries of the Christian community should be defined theologically (one God and one Lord with no participation in worship of false gods) and ethically (no sexual immorality), but *not* socially or ethnically. All social levels, all races, all ethnic groups, and both genders can be Christians as they are.

Gal. 3:28 is more than just an idealistic statement. It makes clear that the Christian community would have neither socioeconomic nor gender nor culture requirements for entry or continuation in the body of Christ. This is part of the reason that Paul has argued in 1 Corinthians 7 that people can "remain" as they are and still be Christians and still bear Christian witness. Christians were called to be neither Jews nor Gentiles but "a new creation" (2 Cor. 5:17) inclusive of both groups. Neither making Gentiles Jews nor, as 1 Corinthians 8 suggests, paganizing former Jews was a Christian way to show that one was "in the know" and known by God in Christ.

Many Corinthian Christians seem to have been stuck in a state of spiritual infancy. The faith they held to had not yet caused a sufficient revolution in their thinking about culture. They had not worked out some of the faith's most crucial implications. Perhaps 1 Corinthians should be called Paul's guide to dealing with the half-converted.[56]

> Paul's rhetoric functions like nuclear fission: the controlling and cultivating of once-released energy. At Corinth, as in all other places, where as church

---

55. Doubtless many Christians who have grown up in denominations with rules about dress, entertainment, drink, food (in the case of Seventh Day Adventists), or Sabbath or Sunday observance might find the implications of what Paul says disturbing. They might even argue that the Corinthian Christians are perfect examples that too much freedom is harmful to one's faith. This in the end is not Paul's view. He wrote "You were called to freedom, but do not use your freedom as an opportunity for self-indulgence, but through love become slaves to one another" (Gal. 5:13) at the climax of a discussion in which he urges Gentile converts not to submit to circumcision, to observance of special days, and to other Jewish rules. Even with the Corinthians "in the know" he will grant freedom about such matters, so long as it is not abused but tempered by other-regarding love.

56. Paul does not doubt that his audience has been converted, but conversion is only the beginning of the Christian life, not its be-all and end-all. The renewal of the mind must be an ongoing part of the sanctification process and an active Christian discipline. It is this that Paul urges in Rom. 12:2.

of God believers call on the name of the Lord, the social, cultural energy released called for continuing pastoral concerns in the need for harnessing for stabilizing, for [upbuilding]. After first revolutionizing traditional controls, as the effect of the initial missionary preaching at Corinth, there emerged and remained then the need for controlling the revolution — the need for upbuilding "till the perfect comes."[57]

---

57. W. Wuellner, "Paul as Pastor: The Function of Rhetorical Questions in First Corinthians," in *L'Apôtre Paul. Personalité, Style et Conception du Ministère* (Leuven: Leuven University, 1986), pp. 49-77, here p. 64.

Argument IV, Division 2: 9:1-27

FOR EXAMPLE

This chapter has often, and wrongly, been seen as *in toto* a defense by Paul of his apostleship. Though it does have a certain forensic tone and though v. 3 makes it clear that Paul is in part offering an *apologia* to those who have given or would give him negative reviews, it is important to see that this forensic material is made to serve a larger deliberative purpose, that of providing an example of self-sacrificial behavior to the audience. Mitchell rightly calls it a "mock" self-defense speech.[1] If this chapter were a serious and substantive attempt to defend Paul's apostleship, it would look more like what we find in 2 Corinthians. But Paul is not defending his apostleship or apostleship in general. If he is defending anything it is his right as an agent of Christ to receive or refuse support.

There is no hint here that Paul thinks that his apostolic office is seriously doubted by any significant number of people. The real proof of this is that in this very chapter he holds himself up as an example of self-sacrificial behavior, using the very matter on which he is supposedly being questioned as proof, maintaining that he practices self-denial in regard to his rights for the greater good and calls for his audience to imitate him.[2] Thus, Paul is not seeking here to establish his rights but to reassert them.[3] The rhetorical questions in vv. 1-5 assume that the audience will answer yes.

1. M. M. Mitchell, *Paul and the Rhetoric of Reconciliation* (Tübingen: Mohr, 1991), p. 130.

2. P. Gardner, *The Gifts of God and the Authentication of a Christian* (dissertation, Cambridge, 1981), puts it this way: If Paul is to establish an analogy with how *exousia* ("power, right, authority") should function by how it functions with him he must first either establish or assume the premise that he is indeed an *apostolos* with legal rights. Only then will the *synkrisis* (comparison) work. It must not be forgotten that the whole segment ends in 11:1 with the command "imitate me." Paul's rights must be established or else he cannot make so much of renouncing them. Indeed, some of the Corinthians were upset that he did renounce them, as 2 Corinthians will show. Cf. W. Willis, "An Apostolic Apologia? The Form and Function of 1 Cor. 9," *JSNT* 24 (1985), pp. 33-48.

3. One can argue that when Paul wrote this letter he had badly misread the situation in Corinth, underestimating the forces undercutting his authority there. I doubt that this is so, not least because there is little or no evidence of *outside* agitators causing problems in Corinth yet, unless one counts Apollos or Peter, and also because when Paul writes 2 Corinthians, he does not feel the need to reemphasize what he has stressed in 1 Corinthians. Surely this implies that he thinks the first letter had some positive effect, though by no means did it heal all the wounds.

Furthermore, had Paul believed he was being seriously charged with inconsistency, he would not have put things the way he does in vv. 19-23. Being "all things to all people" so far as is ethically possible reflects not only Paul's missionary strategy, but also how he acted in relation to fellow Christians.[4] "All things to all people" thus defines Paul's role as a conciliator of the Corinthian factions.[5]

A Closer Look: Paul's Self-Presentation ─────────────────────

Similar Pauline autobiographical remarks crop up in very different Pauline contexts, for example, 2 Cor. 11:22 and Phil. 3:4-7. In an illuminating study, G. Lyons has argued that the major function of these autobiographical remarks is to establish Paul's *ēthos*, customary moral character not apostolic authority. Lyons criticizes Betz's important commentary on Galatians for the view that Paul only rarely and reticently speaks about himself, and then only by way of defense.[6] Lyons's basic theory is that "Paul's rhetorical approach, not his opponents' reproaches, is responsible for the form in which he presents his 'autobiography.'"[7] While this thesis can stand for autobiographical remarks such as those found in 1 Corinthians 9, I do not think it can be applied everywhere. In particular it does not work well with the material in 2 Corinthians 10–12.[8] But even there the opponents' reproaches are only one factor, one bit of fuel for the fire, acting as a catalyst for Paul's masterful rhetorical response.

What is rightly noted by Lyons but missed by many commentators is that Paul never presents autobiographical information simply for its own sake. He is, like a good rhetor, trying to be persuasive. The crucial point that Lyons misses is that autobiographical remarks function differently in different types of rhetoric. All of Paul's biographical statements have a part in tendentious arguments of various sorts, for such is the very nature of rhetoric. In a deliberative piece Paul must establish his *ēthos* if he wishes to present himself as an example. In a forensic piece, he must establish *ēthos* in order to defend himself. In forensic rhetoric autobiography is one among other

4. "All things to all people" is not, as P. Marshall, *Enmity in Corinth: Social Conventions in Paul's Relations with the Corinthians* (Tübingen: Mohr, 1987), pp. 309-17 argues, a charge already leveled against Paul. But Paul's words did come back to haunt him: It seems clear that by the time 2 Corinthians was written some were pointing to this material in 1 Corinthians 9 as clear proof that Paul was both inconsistent and in fact no apostle. This probably shows what could happen when Pauline ideas or a Pauline letter fell into the hands of an opponent. On "by all means win some" not being limited to Paul's missionary strategy, cf. 10:32 and Gardner, *Gifts of God*, p. 105.

5. Mitchell, *Rhetoric of Reconciliation*, p. 134.

6. G. Lyons, *Pauline Autobiography: Toward a New Understanding* (Atlanta: Scholars, 1985), p. 3.

7. Ibid., p. 8.

8. Lyons does not really deal with 2 Corinthians 10–13, which he would need to do to make his case effectively.

defensive weapons; in deliberative rhetoric it is part of the effort to urge a specific course of action by presenting oneself as a model (in 1 Corinthians, a model of non-factious, self-sacrificial behavior). In epideictic rhetoric, biographical remarks were common in *encomia* lauding the deceased, but the Sophists were not above praising themselves, though trying not to appear obnoxious or offensive when doing so. It is interesting how Paul uses various forms of "inoffensive self-praise" in his defense of himself in 2 Corinthians 10–12, thus finding a place for epideictic material in an argument that is largely forensic in character.[9]

Another flaw in Lyons's treatment of Greco-Roman rhetoric is his failure to notice the considerable difference between Sophistic rhetoric and the more responsible and ethically motivated kind of rhetoric discussed by Isocrates and Quintilian. Litfin, among others, has shown that truth was not always sublimated to the larger goal of persuasion in such a way that the facts were necessarily distorted, ignored, or even replaced by fiction masquerading as facts.[10] There were responsible and irresponsible ways to persuade, and there is no reason to think that Paul is intending to distort the truth in his autobiographical remarks, even when he uses irony and sarcasm. Paul both praises and mocks his own history, but the facts remain the same. This explains the very similarities that Lyons notes in the different autobiographical portions of Paul's letters. Paul's rhetoric is used in service of the truth he believes in, not the other way around. In this regard it is much closer to plainstyle Roman rhetoric than to Sophistic rhetoric. As Cicero reminds us in *De Orat.* 2.15.62-64, Roman style, as opposed to Greek style, seeks both plain truth and a pleasant but not overly ornamental presentation.

Here in a paradoxical argument full of rhetorical questions, both positive and negative, Paul asserts both his right to support or patronage from the Corinthians and his right to do without such support if he wishes.[11]

Rhetorical questions could be used in different ways:

to increase the force and cogency of an argument (Quintilian *Inst. Or.* 9.2.6),

to make an assumption of that which in a dialogue would take the form of a question (5.11.5), or

---

9. It is clear that the material in 2 Corinthians 10–12 is not simply epideictic, not least because its function is not to entertain but to deal with the real division between Paul and his converts. Paul is trying to show that he is honorable in his behavior, but he is using such aims to serve the larger purpose of defense. See below, pp. 429-32.

10. A. D. Litfin, *St. Paul's Theology of Proclamation: An Investigation of 1 Cor. 1–4 in Light of Greco-Roman Rhetoric* (dissertation, Oxford, 1983), pp. 107ff.

11. Preaching free of charge and refusing hospitality would not necessarily be linked. It should be clear from Rom. 16:23 that Paul is happy to accept hospitality, even in Corinth, so long as it does not entail the establishment of a certain sort of patronage relationship. J. W. Beaudean, *Paul's Theology of Preaching* (Macon: Mercer University, 1988), p. 119, overlooks this point.

to anticipate objections that could be raised against one's argument and to dismiss them in summary fashion (cf. 9.2.16; *Rhetorica ad Alexandrum* 34.1440a.25).[12]

In 1 Corinthians 9 Paul assumes the answers to the questions he poses and indeed assumes that his audience will know the answers as well: He does not actually attempt to defend the truth of what is represented in the questions. The answer to the questions in vv. 1-5 is Yes. They thus serve to anticipate possible arguments, not to answer actual arguments. It becomes clear in what follows that the issue Paul wishes to highlight is not the legitimacy of his ministry, but his right as a legitimate minister to accept or refuse support.

In this chapter we learn a good deal about Paul's real view of where he stands vis-à-vis Jewish and Gentile Christians. It becomes clear that in various ways, while still manifesting various aspects of his Jewish heritage, Paul has distanced himself from some of its most fundamental aspects, such as the necessity to keep food laws.

> Paul does not accept the different *standpoints . . .* of Jews and Gentiles, but he does recognize their respective positions as the *historical places . . .* where the "calling" of each [person] occurs through the gospel. From this perspective religious tradition and social position are relativized. . . . They are no longer religious qualities in themselves, i.e., conditions for the way to salvation.[13]

The chapter opens with Paul making clear that he is as free as his audience in regard to adiaphora. This freedom has little or nothing to do with financial independence, despite Hock's arguments.[14] We learn indirectly that Paul sees as an essential criterion for being an *apostolos* both having seen the risen Lord and having been a church planter with converts to attest to the reality of one's *exousia* as an apostle (vv. 1f.), though Paul does not defend these criteria here. Paul believes that he has seen the Lord, to the same degree or perhaps even in the same way that the post-Easter Christians did. Of course as Acts tells the story (cf. Galatians 1–2) Paul saw the ascended Jesus long after the forty-day period between Jesus' resurrection and ascension.

12. On the various functions of rhetorical questions in rhetoric, cf. D. F. Watson, "1 Corinthians 10.23–11.1 in the Light of Greco-Roman Rhetoric: The Role of Rhetorical Questions," *JBL* 108 (1989), pp. 301-18, here pp. 312-14.

13. G. Bornkamm, "The Missionary Stance of Paul in 1 Corinthians 9 and in Acts," *Studies in Luke-Acts*, ed. L. E. Keck and J. L. Martyn (Nashville: Abingdon, 1966), pp. 194-207, here p. 196.

14. R. F. Hock, *The Social Context of Paul's Ministry: Tentmaking and Apostleship* (Philadelphia: Fortress, 1980), pp. 50ff.

Since the Corinthians were converted by Paul, he points out that they surely had to see him as a legitimate agent of Christ. In fact, he calls them the "seal" of his apostleship, meaning that they authenticate the reality of that apostleship. They are its living proof. To call Paul's apostleship into question would be for the Corinthians to call their own Christian existence into question. This is in fact what they later did, and in 2 Corinthians Paul would have to respond accordingly. It appears likely that some of his arguments here in 1 Corinthians provided grist for opponents, who would argue that Paul was not an authorized agent of Christ, partly on the basis of his refusal of support.

It remains unclear who and how many people Paul would include among the *apostoloi*. V. 5 recognizes that there are other *apostoloi*, and v. 6 implies that Barnabas is one. The reference in the same verse to the Lord's brothers and Cephas may suggest that they also are *apostoloi*, or it may simply suggest that Paul feels that he has the same rights as these luminaries. What is interesting about the reference to Jesus' brothers is that we would not know from Acts of the activity of any of Jesus' brothers other than James as missionaries or perhaps *apostoloi*, and we do not learn from Acts of James carrying on an itinerant ministry. Acts always has him in Jerusalem, but Paul's brief reference here need not contradict that.

Using the language of the courtroom, Paul makes a mock *apologia* in vv. **3ff.**, though he does not deem it necessary to actually engage in a full defense. V. **4** enunciates the key issue: The Corinthians should recognize that he has the right to receive support, that is, room and board, as an authorized agent of Christ. He also claims the right to take a wife with him on his journeys, as do Peter, other *apostoloi*, and the Lord's brothers. Early Christian leadership, in Paul's view, was not exclusively celibate. V. **5a** may also suggest that the wife of an apostle might expect support or patronage while traveling with her husband.

Verse **6** suggests that Paul's apostleship was different from that of other apostles in that he was no longer married and in that he and Barnabas practiced a trade while serving as apostles. *Exousia* here and elsewhere in this passage should be translated "right" (not "power" and probably not "authority").

The purpose of the three diverse metaphors in v. **7** is to make clear that a person should expect to get his living from his or her work. Paul proceeds from these human analogies to enunciate the same basic principle on the basis of an OT law (Deut. 25:4, cited in vv. **8f.**).[15] Paul is not suggesting in v. **9b** that God cares nothing about oxen, but that these laws were primarily written for human benefit. In particular, Paul is following his eschatological principle that all of the Law was written ultimately for those living in the eschatological

---

15. Cf. the similar quotation in 1 Tim. 5:18, but with a different verb for "muzzle." The LXX is reproduced more exactly in 1 Timothy.

age.[16] In v. 11 Paul suggests that he, like a sower, has sown spiritual things in the Corinthians, and it is asking little to expect a certain material harvest from such work. V. 12 seems to suggest that others, perhaps Apollos, were, in fact, receiving such support or patronage from the Corinthians. Paul's point is that if those others have a right to share in such a harvest, and he does not dispute it, he, who humanly speaking founded the Corinthian *ekklēsia*, should all the more have the right.

If the argument proceeded on this course one would expect the next line to be a request by Paul for his rights to material support to be honored. But in fact in v. 12b Paul turns around and says that he also has the right not to make use of such support, sustenance, or patronage. Paul sees the receiving of ongoing support or patronage as a possible hindrance to the preaching of the gospel.

A Closer Look: Why Paul Made Tents ——————————————

It would be wrong simply to say that Paul refused support in Corinth but accepted it elsewhere. 1 Thess. 2:5-9 suggests that he also worked in Thessalonica and did not accept support there and therefore that his basic strategy had been in place long before 1 Corinthians (cf. 1 Thess. 2:9-10; 2 Thess. 3:8).[17] Furthermore, the support he received from the Macedonians was for work done elsewhere (2 Cor. 11:8f.; Phil. 4:14-16). A number of factors may have been behind Paul's policy.

There were itinerant teachers throughout the Mediterranean region, some of whom accepted fees or patronage or like the Cynics begged for a living. Apparently Paul did not want to be identified with such people even in the least, especially where some might suspect that he was in the preaching business in order to bilk people. The Sophists were particularly noted for bilking patrons; the Cynics turned to work and begging as a protest against such greed.[18] Paul may have worked at his trade for similar reasons.

Though Paul had accepted hospitality or even periodic gifts from the Philippians,

16. D. I. Brewer, "1 Corinthians 9:9-11: A Literal Interpretation of 'Do Not Muzzle the Ox,'" *NTS* 38 (1992), pp. 554-65, argues that Paul is using a literal, but Pharisaic, interpretation of this quotation, in which "ox" is understood to mean all laboring species, including human beings. That is, Paul is offering halakah here, not allegory. This may be correct, but it raises the question whether most of Paul's audience would have recognized this hermeneutical move as something other than allegory.

17. 1 Thess. 2:5-9 amounts to a claim that Paul did not come like a Sophist and engage in ornamental rhetoric as a pretext to be supported and receive adulation. Cf. B. W. Winter, "'If a Man Does Not Wish to Work . . .': A Cultural and Historical Setting for 2 Thessalonians," *TynB* 40 (1989), pp. 303-15.

18. Cf. Hock, *Social Context*, pp. 54-56. Sophists liked to boast that they knew nothing of manual labor; cf. Philo *Det.* 33.

there is no evidence that he was on any sort of regular salary or patronage from them (cf. Acts 16:15). It may well be that some in Corinth wanted to be Paul's ongoing patrons and have him as their in-house teacher. This Paul would clearly refuse as it went beyond temporary hospitality and would have hindered him from fulfilling his calling as an itinerant church planter.

The later practice of Jewish rabbis having a trade may or may not be relevant in regard to Paul's practice. It may be that Paul's working at his trade is one way in which he sought to be the Jew to the Jew, since he was still preaching to at least some Jews and Jewish Christians.

It was the upper echelon of Greco-Roman society that looked down on manual labor, including leather-working (cf. Plutarch *Pericles* 2.1). Artisans and merchants themselves did not share this view, as their funerary inscriptions show. They were proud of their work. It is possible that Paul worked not only to avoid appearing to be a Sophist and to avoid entangling alliances of a cumbersome sort, but also because he was thus deliberately placing himself in a lower status category so that he could identify with the lower strata of society. Paul's self-identification as "slave of all" (9:19) supports this conjecture. Furthermore, a preacher receiving patronage would probably be an "obstacle" in the way of the gospel only for those of the lower strata of society, those who could not support Paul in such a fashion.[19]

Finally, Paul was probably in Corinth during the Isthmian games in Spring, 51, and the numerous visitors usually stayed in tents. He may have worked at his trade deliberately in order to make more contacts and thus to win more converts (though this would not explain his use of the same strategy in Thessalonica).[20]

Verse **13** is a rhetorical question that expects a positive response. Certainly the Corinthians should have known that even workers in pagan temples ate from the sacrifices they performed for others. Presumably "those sitting at the altar" also refers to temple workers.[21] V. **14** clinches the argument. The Lord commanded that those proclaiming the gospel should get their living from the gospel. Paul alludes here to a saying of Jesus that is something like the one in Luke 10:7.[22]

On the face of it, it might seem that Paul is violating a specific command

19. Alternately, one could argue that receiving patronage might be an "obstacle" in that it could create factions, as the well-to-do might be in competition for teachers to support.

20. Cf. B. W. Winter, *Are Philo and Paul among the Sophists? A Hellenistic Jewish and a Christian Response to a First Century Movement* (dissertation, MacQuarrie University, 1988), pp. 173ff. O. Broneer, "The Apostle Paul and the Isthmian Games," *BA* 25 (1962), pp. 2-31, here pp. 16-20, suggests that Erastus may have helped Paul get established selling tents at the games.

21. On the translation "attending *(paredreuontes)* at the altar" in a cultic context, see *New Doc. 4*, p. 34, and the inscription cited there.

22. Note the citation also in 1 Tim. 5:18.

of Christ. But what Jesus says is that the worker is *worthy* of his wages. He does not command that one *must* be supported by the proclamation of the gospel. Matt. 10:10 is a bit sharper. The disciples were to depend on the system of local hospitality in Israel as they traveled. It may be that Paul did not think that such a rule was binding because it was given for his benefit, not as something he had to do to be a true missionary. Fee urges that Jesus' words are actually more of a command to his audience than to the missionaries: The people should support them because their work is worthy of such support.[23] Thus, strictly speaking Paul probably did not violate Jesus' teaching.

In any event Paul cites this word of Jesus[24] to show that he has the *right* to such support and then goes on to say (v. 15) that he makes no use of this right. That one has a right is different from saying that one has an obligation to be dependent on the system of standing hospitality in a particular place.[25] Paul adds in v. 15b that he is not mentioning this as an implicit plea for Corinthian support now.

Verse 15c is an incomplete sentence. The gist of what Paul seems to be saying is that he wants to go above and beyond the call of duty and thus not make empty his boast for preaching the gospel free of charge, especially to Gentiles. It may be that he sees this as the consistent way to operate since he is preaching free grace in Christ.[26]

Paul's point in vv. **16ff.** is as follows: For Paul it is part of his call and thus a necessity that he preach the gospel. He is under obligation to do this as an *apostolos,* and so he does not do it voluntarily. It is a moral urgency or necessity. He is entrusted with a commission and therefore like a soldier does not work voluntarily, in the strict sense, for it is his obligation. As a result, there can be no eschatological reward for this work. Paul preaches free of charge, not using his full rights as an agent of Christ, in order to do something truly gracious, meritorious, and deserving of the sort of reward discussed in ch. 3.

One should also note the parallels between 9:16-18 and 4:1-2, where Paul refers to himself as a specific sort of slave, the *oikonomos* or household

---

23. G. D. Fee, *The First Epistle to the Corinthians* (Grand Rapids, Eerdmans, 1987), p. 413.

24. This shows that Paul and his audience know the Jesus tradition, though to what extent we cannot be sure. On Paul's possible knowledge of the Matthean missionary discourse, cf. D. C. Allison, "Paul and the Missionary Discourse," *Ephemerides Theologicae Lovanienses* 61 (1985), pp. 369-75.

25. It appears that by the time 2 Corinthians was written some Corinthian Christians were upset at Paul for not accepting support while he was in Corinth, as did some itinerant teachers and especially other Christian *apostoloi.* They questioned whether this was not a telltale sign that Paul was no *apostolos* or true teacher.

26. On the various translations of this fragmented verse, cf. R. L. Omanson, "Some Comments about Style and Meaning: 1 Corinthians 9.15 and 7.10," *Bible Translator* 34 (1983), 135-39, here p. 139.

steward who has been found faithful *(pistos).*[27] Here he calls himself a slave entrusted with the stewardship of the gospel. In both cases Paul is disavowing the idea of the minister as a patriarchal overlord or master. Paul believes that there is only one Lord over the *ekklēsia* — Jesus Christ. *Apostoloi* are only called and chosen servants under Christ's authority.[28]

In vv. **19-23** Paul indicates his *modus operandi.* He sees himself as free of obligations from all persons, yet he has made himself a slave to all in order to win over more of them. He accommodates his style of living, not his theological or ethical principles,[29] to whomever he is with so as better to win that person to Christ.[30] He is, in short, flexible in his general lifestyle — food, clothing, and the like.

An important study by D. B. Martin helps us understand the significance of this passage. As Martin points out, taking a lower station or place in society was not seen as a virtue. It was seen as slavish and servile behavior, not the sort of thing to which the upper crust would ever aspire. Paul is saying that he deliberately moved from high status to low status, not least because he wants to produce an attitude adjustment among some of his converts who have an all too worldly vision of Christian leadership.

> In 1 Cor. 9:16-18, by depicting his leadership as slavery to Christ, Paul takes one step away from their position. They think of Christian leadership as modeled on the benevolent, free, high-status *sophos.* Paul, however, depicts his leadership as the derived authority by association with his master Christ.

27. Cf. S. M. Pogoloff, *Logos and Sophia: The Rhetorical Situation of 1 Corinthians* (Atlanta: Scholars, 1992), p. 217.

28. Paul does not affirm the idea that the minister's power or authority comes from the people. Rather his is a more charismatic vision of ministry. The minister is called by God and endowed by the Spirit with words and power. Ministry is confirmed or verified in the positive effect it has on people. This means that Paul has a hierarchical vision of source and empowerment for ministry, but also believes that it must be confirmed by the actual evidence of converts or the growth of converts in Christ.

29. Which concerns Paul does not regard as involving fundamental theological or ethical issues is at least as significant as what he does so regard. Here keeping kosher, among other Mosaic regulations, is not seen as essential. Bornkamm, "Missionary Stance," pp. 202f. is right in saying that "Paul intends the statements to characterize a practical stance of solidarity with various groups, rather than to describe several ways of adjusting his preaching in terms of content and language to various environments. . . . It is a matter of solidarity in practical conduct."

30. P. Richardson, "Pauline Inconsistency," *NTS* 26 (1980), pp. 347-62, equates what Peter did in Antioch (Galatians 2) with what Paul is talking about here. But Peter, it appears, was not acting on principle but reacting to pressure. Furthermore, those involved in Antioch were all Christians, and Jews and Gentiles were being divided within the church, while Paul's concern is a missionary principle, one meant to bring Jew and Gentile together. For a full and proper critique of Richardson, see D. A. Carson, "Pauline Inconsistency: Reflections on 1 Cor. 9.19-23," *Churchman* 100 (1986), pp. 6-45.

This does constitute a claim to authority but one different from that of the strong. Then in verses 19-23, Paul takes a further, more radical step away from the position of the strong. By using the demagogic model of the leader as slave of all, Paul more specifically rejects the status-maintaining leadership of benevolent patriarchialism. Again, he still claims leadership, but it is a leadership from below. It is an exercise of authority, but a more subtle, ambiguous authority that is not based on normal social position and normal status hierarchy. In both sections, slavery depicts leadership. The purpose of neither is to depict humility. They are different ways of picturing abnormal structures of authority — abnormal, that is, from the point of view of the *sophos* leader.[31]

From the Christ hymn in Phil. 2 we may conclude that Paul deduced this model of leadership from the trajectory and character of the career of Christ. It is important to bear in mind that Paul was not simply supporting the patriarchal status quo in his vision of leadership in the *ekklēsia*. Nor was he simply baptizing the structure of the household and applying it in the Christian community. By his own example, by holding up the example of Christ and the cross in word and deed, and by reforming the family structure in the community (evident in 1 Corinthians 7), Paul sought to revise existing notions about status, leadership, and the source of authority and power.[32]

That Paul says he becomes a Jew to the Jew might seem odd for one who is, in fact, a Jew! But it might only mean that he resumes freely some of his Jewishness when the occasion warrants, because he no longer feels under obligation to be under the yoke of the Law. Here is the clearest evidence that Paul feels no compulsion to be Jewish in the sense that he did before he became a Christian. He does so only as an evangelistic strategy, not even out of habit. It may be that the second group named here, "those under the Law," is also Jews, or this may refer to God-fearers and prosleytes. But Paul says in v. **20b** that he is "not under the Law" as a matter of principle or as an ongoing manner of life.

Verse **21** could refer to lawless people, but it probably refers to those outside the scope of the Mosaic Law, that is, Gentiles. And it may be that Paul

31. D. B. Martin, *Slavery as Salvation: The Metaphor of Slavery in Pauline Christianity* (New Haven: Yale University, 1990), p. 135. A "demagogue" in antiquity was one who at least appeared to be a populist, leading from below on the basis of service and congruence with popular notions, rather than imposing his will from above.

32. Paul's vision of the Christian family is not egalitarian in the modern sense of the word, i.e., one that makes no differentiation on the basis of gender. He does, however, set in motion a reform of the existing patriarchal structure. In regard to the family of faith, the structure seems even less traditional. Paul apparently sees matters of rank or "order," such as gender, and the authority of government, as givens but regards matters of social status or position, which is what the Corinthians were most concerned about, as alterable in Christ and of no eternal importance in Christ. See above on ch. 7, pp. 176-77.

is making a play on these two possible meanings of *anomos,* namely, without Law, or lawless, that is, wicked. He says to those without Law, "I acted as without law, even though I am not lawless under God but in the law *(ennomos)* of Christ," which presumably means subject to the law of Christ.[33]

What is this law of Christ (cf. Gal. 6:2)? I take it to be those ethical imperatives imposed on Christians by Christ or by his example. It is not law, if one means by "law" a way of gaining right standing with God, but it is no less obligatory than the OT law, from which Paul distinguishes it, though without specifying the nature of the distinction. The law of Christ is a requirement of Christian living in order to work out one's salvation. In short, it is not optional, and Paul has already warned that those Christians who violate fundamental Christian ethics will not inherit the kingdom (6:9f.). Good behavior cannot get a person in, but bad behavior can apparently get a person out of the community of Christ.

Paul becomes weak to the weak (v. 22), and since he does so "in order to win the weak" it is unlikely that he is talking here about weak Christians. That the object of "win" is non-Christians has been made clear in its occurrences in the three preceding verses, and here "save" is used along with it. It is unlikely, though possible, then, that this verse means that Paul made himself like the "weak" Christians in order to improve and strengthen the faith they have already. Paul will go on to say that the stumbling block principle applies when one is around overly scrupulous Christians, but here he is commenting on his basic way of evangelizing and presenting the gospel to the lost. He becomes all things to all in order by every means possible to save some. He does all of this so that he too might be a participant in the gospel and its benefits (v. 23).

But Paul does not say he becomes strong to the strong, probably because it is "strong" Christians to whom he is directing many of his corrective remarks in this letter. Furthermore, his accommodating behavior has clear limits. He does not say that he became an idolator to idolators or an adulterer to adulterers. But in matters that he did not see as ethically or theologically essential or implied by the gospel, Paul believed in flexibility. This shows that the phrase

---

33. Carson, "Pauline Inconsistency," p. 12, is right in stating that becoming a Gentile to a Gentile equally requires accomodation on Paul's part. This is because, despite the views of Georgi and others, Paul sees being a Christian as a third sort of thing, being neither simply Jewish nor simply Gentile. It is a matter of being in-lawed *(ennomos)* to Christ. I agree with E. P. Sanders, M. Y. MacDonald, and others that Paul is referring here not to a third race of people called Christians, but to a new humanity composed of Jew and Gentile in Christ. Cf. Sanders, *Paul, the Law, and the Jewish People* (Philadelphia: Fortress, 1983), pp. 171-79; M. Y. MacDonald, *The Pauline Churches: A Socio-Historical Study of Institutionalisation in the Pauline and Deutero-Pauline Writings* (Cambridge: Cambridge University, 1988), pp. 32f.

"all things to all people" is part of Paul's demagogic rhetoric and is not to be taken literally.[34]

Finally, in vv. 24-27 Paul returns to straight metaphor. He speaks of the Isthmian games and points out that all the runners run but only one wins the prize.[35] Paul's emphasis here is not on running or on there being only one winner. His stress in this metaphor is on self-control exercised so as not to be disqualified. His objective will be to get the Corinthians, in particular the Gentiles who were attending idol feasts, to exercise self-control so as neither to cause others to stumble nor to disqualify themselves from final salvation.

Paul does all that he does with a purpose. He does not waste motion or engage in activities that prevent him from achieving the goal. So he does not run falteringly.[36] And he does not, like some boxers or Sophists, throw punches that only hit the air.[37] He says what he says and lives as he lives not for the sake of the words and life practices themselves; they work toward a purpose (v. 26). He gives himself a black eye and enslaves his body so as to be an example of self-control (v. 27). Thus, what he asks of others he does first, so that he himself will not miss out on the eternal crown. It is quite clear that Paul considers it possible for him and his audience to lose the crown if they do not follow the law of Christ. Paul cuts a peculiar figure. His life has a cruciform shape; its rejection of status is what he wishes his converts to exemplify.

This passage has sometimes been thought to warrant the idea that ministers should not be paid for their work. But Paul says that he, and by extension other ministers of the gospel, have both the right to expect such support and also the right to refuse it. With the increasing stress in many denominations on the professionalization of the ministry has also come the expectation on

34. Cf. Carson, "Pauline Inconsistency," pp. 14ff.

35. The crown at Isthmia in Paul's day was made of celery. In the second century it was made of olive branches. The celery crown was already withered when bestowed and thus could well be called a "perishable crown."

36. This suggests that his lifestyle is consistent with his principles, unlike that of some of the Corinthians.

37. This may well be an allusion to the Sophists, whom Philo calls shadow boxers, those who box with the air, i.e., with imaginary opponents. Cf. *Det.* 1.41f.; Winter, *Are Paul and Philo*, p. 177: "The discipline and self-control which Paul exercises over his own appetites in vv. 23-27 contrast starkly with the self-indulgence of the sophists with their lifestyle which they clearly defended on philosophical grounds." Cf. *Det.* 33: The Sophists are those "who take care of themselves . . . and are fat, smooth, and robust, who live luxuriously, are proud, know nothing of labor, and are conversant with pleasures." V. C. Pfitzner, *Paul and the Agon Motif: Traditional Athletic Imagery in the Pauline Literature* (Leiden: Brill, 1967), pp. 82ff., is right to note the overlap in Paul of athletic and military imagery in his description of his endeavors for Christ, but he overlooks the further possible allusion to rhetors and their struggles.

the part of some ministers that they should be paid handsomely for their work, especially because it is so "essential" to the well-being of the "church." There are several problems here.

In the first place, ministers should always be professional in their work. By this I mean that they should do their job effectively and efficiently, having first sought out the proper education and practical training to prepare them for such tasks. But while they must be professional, they must understand that what they do is first and foremost a "calling" and not simply a profession.

In the second place, ministers should not endorse, much less follow, the status-seeking behavior of their peers in other professions. Paul's model for ministry is one of self-sacrificial, status-rejecting behavior. This means among other things that ministers should not measure themselves or the worth of their work by their salaries or their lack thereof. Some ministers, notably certain televangelists, have bought into the American success-syndrome or have been infected by the disease of the health-and-wealth gospel, so that their lifestyles belie something essential about the gospel they preach. It would be salutary if those who have contracted such maladies would reread not only 1 Corinthians 9 but also Paul's tribulation catalogs in 1 Corinthians 4 and elsewhere. Self-control, self-denial, and self-discipline are essential attributes of a minister of Christ, since ministers are called to be servants of Christ and of all for whom Christ died. Not only so, they are to model Christ crucified, not Christ glorified. This becomes even clearer in 2 Corinthians, where Paul speaks of strength and power that only come to the minister through self-emptying.

Here and elsewhere in 1 Corinthians, Paul contrasts himself with the Sophists on a number of points. In their proclamation they focused on form, pleasing the crowd, and gaining applause, fame, and wealth. Paul concentrates on Christ and him crucified, on pleasing God and helping the people (which often meant stepping on their toes), on gaining an eternal crown, and on working so as not to burden others. He did not for a minute think that anyone was converted simply by dint of his rhetoric or his own personal attributes. Indeed, he believed that many were converted in spite of his noticeable handicaps, by the power of the Spirit and the truth of the Word. Pulpit committees would do well to keep such things in mind, for too often they look for a silver-tongued orator when what they really need is a minister who is a faithful servant like Paul.

This is not to say that Paul had an inferiority complex. To the contrary, he could boast "in Christ" of his extraordinary labors, though somewhat tongue-in-cheek. It was simply that Paul knew that he was a person under authority and that his power and abilities came from a higher power. What mattered was for him to give his all for Christ and then leave the results in God's hands. While Paul is daring enough to speak of being a coworker with

God in the ministry (2 Cor. 6:1; cf. 1 Corinthians 3), he does not allow himself to believe that it is *his* ministry in any sort of exclusive or possessive sense. He knows quite well that God can accomplish the same results without him. Therefore, he sees ministry as a great honor and privilege, of which he feels unworthy (cf. 1 Corinthians 15); it is not a *right* owed to him or to anyone.

Recently, a district superintendent told me that he had had occasion to play golf with two "high-steeple preachers." He said he became sick at heart because all these ministers could talk about was how they could not wait to be appointed by the bishop to a bigger and better congregation so that they could make more money and live more comfortably. It is a story that could be repeated many times. Many denominations have so emphasized the professional side of ministry that they have ordained some people with numerous talents but little or no understanding or sense of call in the Pauline sense of the word. The result is that some flocks get fleeced instead of fed.

Neither I nor Paul would condone any sort of blanket condemnation of ministers and ministry. Thousands have labored through the centuries faithfully, frequently in obscurity, and often at great cost. But I do think it is time to reemphasize the necessity of an understanding that ministry is essentially a calling and that it calls a person to great personal sacrifices. The following words from John Wesley's covenanting service should help us avoid the pitfall of having our expectations about ministry shaped largely by our larger cultural agenda:

> This taking of His yoke upon us means that we are heartily content that He appoint us our place and work, and that He alone be our reward. Christ has many services to be done: some are easy, others are difficult; some bring honour, others bring reproach; some are suitable to our natural inclinations and temporal interests, others are contrary to both. In some we may please Christ and please ourselves, in others we cannot please Christ except by denying ourselves. Yet the power to do all these things is assuredly given us in Christ, who strengtheneth us.

To which the covenanter responds:

> I am no longer my own, but Thine. Put me to what Thou wilt, rank me with whom Thou wilt; put me to doing, put me to suffering; let me be employed for Thee or laid aside for Thee, exalted for Thee, or brought low for Thee; let me be full; let me be empty; let me have all things; let me have nothing; I freely and heartily yield all things to Thy pleasure and disposal.

Argument IV, Division 3: 10:1–11:1

JUST THE TYPE

10:1–11:1 concludes Paul's discussion of questions raised by the Corinthians about partaking of *eidōlothuta*. In ch. 10 we have an example of typology, and in fact Paul uses the word *typos* (type, example) to describe what he is doing. The idea behind typology is that since God's character never changes God acts in similar ways in different ages of history and, perhaps more importantly, provides persons and events that foreshadow other later persons and events in salvation history. Combined with this is the idea that all previous ages of salvation history prepare the way for and point toward the final eschatological age, which Paul believes has already begun. For Paul everything that happened to the OT people happened as examples for the benefit of the last age of believers. The OT is seen as the *ekklēsia*'s book, meant to teach Christians by analogy and example how they ought and ought not to live, with Israel providing both negative and positive examples.

Strictly speaking, what we have in 1 Corinthians 10 is not a full typology like one finds in Hebrews in the comparison of Christ and Melchizedek. The correspondence is incomplete because the Corinthians have not yet perished in the "desert" (v. 5). In fact, Paul uses the Israelite example so that the Corinthians will repent and *not* perish. He sees an analogy between the wicked behavior of the Israelites and that of at least some of the Corinthian Christians. Since God still judges such behavior, Paul warns them that their fate could be the same as that of those Israelites. Paul thus reckons with the possibility that some Corinthians might actually willfully wrench themselves free from the grasp of God and so be judged by God.

Quintilian tells us that of the various sorts of *paradeigma* (paradigms) "the most important proofs of this class is what is most properly called 'example' *(exemplum)*, that is to say the adducing of some past action real or assumed that may serve to persuade the audience of the truth of the point we are trying to make" (*Inst. Or.* 5.11.6). The term *paradeigma* was especially reserved by the Greeks for historical parallels (5.11.1).[1]

---

1. Although there are certain similarities between a midrash and the way Paul handles the OT text here, it is better to call what he does an example of typology or analogy. Paul is not contemporizing or allegorizing the OT text here (unlike Galatians 4). He is, rather, drawing parallels between OT history and the present. But cf. E. E. Ellis, *Prophecy and*

Mitchell has demonstrated that Paul is offering examples of factious behavior from the OT here. As she points out, Josephus says that the episode recorded in Numbers 11 (cf. 1 Cor. 10:5) is an example of factionalism (*Ant.* 3.295), and Philo refers to the Baal Peor incident, which Paul mentions in v. 8, as an instance of factiousness (*Post.* 184). Both Josephus and Philo refer to the Korah episode in Numbers 16 as an instance of *stasis* (sedition).[2]

Most striking of all, in Num. 11:4, 13 we are told that what the murmuring Israelites desired was *meat.*[3] These examples are especially apt, then, in Paul's effort to promote the idea of concord in a group of factious Corinthians willing to sacrifice the concord of the body of Christ for the sake of eating meat, whether in a temple or at home. It matters little if the Israelites were baptized into Moses in the Red Sea and partook of the OT "sacrament" of manna. They still ended up being judged by God as rebellious people unworthy of the Promised Land. Underlying both the OT texts and the discussion in 1 Corinthians 8–10 is the charge of idolatry and thus of apostasy.[4]

Paul begins ch. 10 with a reference to the experience of "our ancestors." This reference could imply that most of his audience was Jewish, but that is flatly contradicted by the subject matter of the passage, namely, eating in idol temples. More likely Paul sees salvation history as a continuum and thus sees the *ekklēsia* of Jews and Gentiles as the true development of the people of God.[5] This idea is further reinforced in v. 18 where Paul reminds the audience of "Israel according to the flesh," which surely means OT Israel and implies a distinction from an Israel according to the Spirit, that is, the *ekklēsia* — both Jew and Gentile in Christ.

In fact, Paul will work in two directions. He will interpret the OT christologically, in part because he believes that Christ was preexistent in OT times helping God's OT people along. This is the most natural way to interpret the difficult "the rock *was* Christ" (v. 4). "Was" indicates that the divine Christ was really a part of Israel's history, providing them life-giving water.[6] What

Hermeneutic in Early Christianity (Tübingen: Mohr, 1978), pp. 151-62. On the use of typology in rhetorical arguments, see F. Siegert, *Argumentation bei Paulus* (Tübingen: Mohr, 1985), pp. 218-24.

2. Cf. 1 Cor. 10:10 to *Ant.* 4.12f.; *Vit. Mos.* 2.174, 283; see M. M. Mitchell, *Paul and the Rhetoric of Reconciliation* (Tübingen: Mohr, 1991), pp. 138-40.

3. Cf. Mitchell, *Rhetoric of Reconciliation,* p. 139, n. 439.

4. Cf. P. Gardner, *The Gifts of God and the Authentication of a Christian* (dissertation, Cambridge, 1981), p. 120.

5. Cf. my discussion of Romans 9–11 in *Jesus, Paul, and the End of the World* (Downers Grove: InterVarsity, 1992), pp. 99-128.

6. Here the role given to Wisdom in Wis. Sol. 11:4 is predicated of Christ. I have discussed at length the importance of the sapiential material for Paul's reflections on Christ in *Jesus the Sage: The Pilgrimage of Wisdom* (Minneapolis: Fortress, 1994), ch. 7.

happened then is relevant for the instruction of the Corinthians now because their situation is analogous and because the benefits from Christ are comparable. The argument cuts both ways.

Paul begins by stressing that the Israelites received the benefits of the Exodus-Sinai experiences and the manna and water in the wilderness. It is crucial for him to point out that *all* the Israelites had these spiritual experiences (vv. **1-4a**). He is not arguing that the Red Sea crossing was a sacrament (v. 2), since actually the Israelites went across on dry ground and did not get wet. Nor is he suggesting that the manna was in some sense a sacramental food just like the Lord's Supper. His point is the Israelites had the same sort of benefits as Christians do, even benefits from Christ himself, and even this did not secure them against perishing in the desert and losing out on God's final and greatest blessing.[7]

Paul draws on a series of OT texts and Jewish tradition about them. He first alludes to Exod. 14:19-22. He then moves on to Exod. 16:4-30 and Exod. 17:1-7/Num. 20:2-13, the latter being the story about water from the rock. Paul's interpretation of that story is indebted to the sapiential treatment of it in Wisdom of Solomon 11, where personified Wisdom provides the water to the Israelites. There was also a rabbinic tradition, probably from as early as Paul's day, about Miriam's well, shaped like a rock, which followed the Israelites in the desert and provided water whenever they needed it (cf. Num. 21:16-18).[8] Paul probably did not take such rabbinic traditions as literal history. His historical point is that Christ provided the miraculous water then just as he provides benefits to the Christian now, as the Lord's Supper makes clear.

In v. 3 Paul calls the manna "spiritual" food, by which he probably means food miraculously provided by the Spirit of God, not food with a heavenly taste or texture. Nor indeed was the water spiritual in character. It was, rather, spiritually provided, just as the rock was spiritually enabled to give water. Despite all these spiritual benefits to all Israelites, God judged most of them. They died with their bodies strewn around in the wilderness.[9]

---

7. Gardner, *Gifts of God,* p. 126, rightly points out that what is uppermost in Paul's mind is not the sacraments and their abuse, but the community to which all the Israelites belonged. All the Israelites were truly part of that community, "baptized" into Moses no less, and yet they were judged in the desert. The focus of the passage is on immoral behavior, though a magical view of the sacraments may also be confronted.

8. The clearest but latest form of this tradition is in the Babylonian Talmud, *Sukka* 3a-b; cf. 11d-b.

9. Gardner, *Gifts of God,* p. 137, helpfully surveys the development of all the wilderness wandering traditions in the Hebrew Scriptures and beyond and concludes that these traditions are markedly similar in function: They all show that the people sinned in forgetting God's gifts to them, in always craving more, *and* in turning to other gods, which inevitably led to divine judgment. The function of the traditions was to make sure a later generation did not make the same mistake and to recall God's ongoing faithfulness.

Here as before Paul is largely arguing against those who wrote to him, who were claiming the right to eat in pagan temples. He warns them in particular of possible serious spiritual consequences. Possibly the Corinthians had a magical view of the Christian sacraments and thought that since they had partaken of the Christian initiation rite (baptism) and the Christian communion rite (the Lord's Supper) they were immune to spiritual danger at pagan feasts. They seem to have held to some form of an "eternal security by means of sacraments" view. Paul is trying to dissuade them from this false sense of security.

That they might have held such an understanding of the sacraments is understandable in view of the mystery rites in Greece and elsewhere in the Greco-Roman world, by which one was thought to be put on a higher spiritual plane.[10] The Corinthians viewed the Christian rites as being like such pagan rites in their efficacy and benefits[11] and so may have assumed that they were immune to harm now or later, whatever they did ("everything is permitted"!). This may also explain why Paul responds as he does in regard to temptations and their danger.

Paul then disabuses them of this false view by drawing an analogy between the so-called Jewish sacraments and the Christian sacraments. This he sets in place of the analogy the "in the know" Corinthians have apparently assumed between Christian sacraments and pagan rites. Paul says that the OT story has become an example so that the Corinthians will not likewise suffer destruction (v. 5). He accuses them of being covetous of evil things (v. 6), meaning by the latter whatever they might gain at a feast in a pagan temple.

One key to understanding Paul's point here is his use of the term *pneumatikon* ("spiritual"). In what sense was the rock or the food and drink the

10. R. MacMullen, *Paganism in the Roman Empire* (New Haven: Yale University, 1981), pp. 52ff., points out quite rightly that most pagans sought not eternal life but present benefits from religion. There is evidence that they believed that certain rites of passage conveyed certain spiritual benefits here and now. For example, cleansing in the blood of a bull was thought to convey an extension of one's earthly life in a state of ritual purity (cf. *CIL* 6.510, 13.511, 13.520). Theon of Smyrna, during the reign of Hadrian, speaks of initiation rites (which ones is uncertain) that bestow "a blessed state of divine grace and companionship with the gods" (cf. MacMullen, p. 172, n. 20). Perhaps most telling is Plutarch *Mor.* 1105B, which asserts that many people feel no fear of death, believing that initiation rites will assure them a happy afterlife.

11. This may also explain the *gnōsis* cry in Corinth since esoteric knowledge is what some of these pagan cults offered to the initiated, knowledge being thought of as the key to "salvation." E. Ferguson, *Backgrounds of Early Christianity* (second edition, Grand Rapids: Eerdmans, 1993), pp. 249-59, stresses that the deliverance the mysteries offered was from fate and the terrors of the afterlife. The initiate was brought into favor with the deity, promised his protection in the present, and sometimes promised a blessed afterlife.

Israelites had "spiritual"? I would suggest that the term is chosen by Paul to stress the *source* of this sustenance, that is, that it came from God, who is spirit. Another suggestion draws on an assumed analogy with cult meals in the mystery religions, in which case Paul would be referring to food that conveys *pneuma* or life. This seems unlikely since Paul will go on to argue that these gifts did not prevent the Israelites from perishing. Still others have thought that the term means "allegorical" on analogy with the use of the adverbial form *pneumatikōs* in Rev. 11:8. The problem with this view is that Paul is not saying that the manna is a figure of or for something else.[12]

Gardner is likely right to point to the parallel in 2:13ff. Spiritual people should be wise enough to discern the deeper spiritual significance or meaning of such phenomena. More to the point, the giving of bread and drink to the Israelites is called "spiritual" because they come from God, and thus need interpretation, aided by the power of discernment given by the Holy Spirit. The food was not figurative or allegorical but real. But its real significance had to be seen.[13] Paul's addition to the wilderness traditions is the idea that such gifts actually came from Christ, since he was present and helping God's people back then. This is a strategic rhetorical move. Without it some might have objected that the Israelites had sacraments inferior to those of the Corinthians.[14]

Paul exhorts the Corinthians not to be idolators and then quotes directly from Exod. 32:6, the story of the golden calf (v. 7). He uses this text for its special relevance, in particular its allusion to sexual play or amusement after the idol feast.[15] This is why the warning against sexual sin immediately follows in v. **8**. Paul believes that more is going on in the pagan temple than just feasting. It is true that there is no clear evidence of sacred prostitution in Roman Corinth, but there certainly were numerous stories of sexual immorality in pagan temples. Josephus *Ant.* 18.65-80, for example, tells of the lady Paulina engaging in sex all night long after dinner in the temple precincts with Mundus, assuming he was the god Anubis. This common association in the larger culture would explain why sexual immorality and idol food are also *always* linked in the NT (cf. Acts 15:29; Rev. 2:14, 20). It is worth adding that

12. Rightly, Gardner, *Gifts of God*, p. 147.

13. Ibid., pp. 153ff.

14. The very force of Paul's argument is impaired if one follows J. D. G. Dunn, *Christology in the Making* (Philadelphia: Westminster, 1980), pp. 183f., who maintains that Paul is saying that Christ is now the equivalent of what the rock was then. This defeats the very force of the analogy, which depends on arguing that God's activity in Christ was the same then as now. Paul does not say that the "rock *is* Christ" or that "the rock represents Christ" but that the rock *was* Christ. The tense of the verb is crucial.

15. Rightly, G. D. Fee, *The First Epistle to the Corinthians* (Grand Rapids: Eerdmans, 1987), pp. 449ff.

the rabbis certainly interpreted "play" in Exod. 32:6 to refer to sexual play (cf. Babylonian Talmud *Soṭa* 6b).[16]

It is also wrong to underestimate the religious character of meals held in temple precincts. Plutarch says, "It is not the abundance of wine or the roasting of meat that makes the joy of festivals, but the good hope and belief that the god is present in his kindness and graciously accepts what is offered" (*Mor.* 1102A). Nor was this only true at public festivals, for, as MacMullen stresses, one must

> place religion at the heart of social life as surely as it must be placed at the heart of cultural activities of every sort. For most people, to have a good time with their friends involved some contact with a god who served as guest of honor, as master of ceremonies, or as host in the porticoes or flowering, shaded grounds of his own dwelling. For most people, meat was a thing never eaten and wine to surfeit never drunk save as some religious setting permitted. There existed — it is no exaggeration to say it of all but the fairly rich — no formal social life . . . that was entirely secular. Small wonder, then, that Jews and Christians [held] themselves aloof from anything the gods touched. . . .[17]

This suggests again that it was the more well-to-do Gentile male converts in Corinth who were arguing for the right to go to idol feasts in their letter to Paul.[18] Paul says that the Corinthians, by participating in these idol parties, are trying to provoke Christ just as the Israelites did.[19]

The reference to serpents causing death (v. 9) alludes to Num. 21:5f., and the grumbling (v. 10) comes in Num. 14:2, 36; 16:41-49 (cf. Ps. 106:25-27).

16. In v. 8b we have a notable problem. Paul says 23,000 fell in the desert; the OT clearly says 24,000 fell (cf. Num. 25:9). In fact all known Jewish sources have 24,000, and there is really no textual evidence to suggest that 1 Cor. 10:8 ever read anything other than 23,000. One may say Paul is dealing in round numbers just as the OT is, which is true, but his is not the correct round number.

17. MacMullen, *Paganism*, p. 40.

18. On Christians refusing to participate in or partake of sacrifices in temples, see R. Gordon, "Religion in the Roman Empire," in *Pagan Priests: Religion and Power in the Ancient World*, ed. M. Beard and J. North (Ithaca: Cornell University, 1988), pp. 235-55. Gordon rightly notes that this refusal separated Christianity from all other religions, including Judaism, which at least offered sacrifices *for* the emperor in its own temple. The ideological implications of this difference were considerable, especially since, as Gordon shows, during the empire the emperor tied himself closely to sacrifice, having numerous statues of himself sacrificing placed in locations all over the empire, including Roman Corinth. This was part of the larger propaganda agenda of portraying the emperor as the great benefactor of the empire (cf. Gordon, "The Veil of Power," pp. 201-31 in the same volume). The rejection of idol meat, especially at a festival in honor of Caesar, would carry the larger message of the rejection of imperial patronage.

19. Again an allusion to Christ's preexistence.

Is the latter also an allusion to current Corinthian conduct? Are they also covetors, idolators, fornicators, provokers of Christ, and grumblers?[20] If so, then the analogies would be especially apt. The "Destroyer" (v. 10) is apparently the destroying angel (cf. Exod. 12:23 LXX), which is not directly referred to in the OT incident in question.

These OT events, says Paul in v. 11, happened as a warning to himself and his audience, "on whom the ends of the ages have come." The word *telos*, "end," here in the plural and coupled with "ages" in the plural, has baffled many. Does "ends of the ages" mean "end of the world," or is Paul using *telos* to mean "*goals* of the ages"? Did he think he and his converts were living in the eschatological time when one would see the completion of divine designs for God's people? Was it the time when God's purpose would become apparent, as one looked back on it? Paul is likely *not* referring to the overlap of the old and new ages.[21] Probably Paul believed that the goals to which history has been pressing had in his day begun to be realized since Christ had died and risen.

Verse 12 is a clear warning that the Corinthians need to watch lest they fall as the Israelites did. Gardner points out the repeated references to rocks and stumbling in this whole argument in 1 Corinthians 8–10:

> Paul does not want "those in the know" to be stumbling blocks and so cause the weak to stumble (8:9),
> he does not want to put any obstacle in the path of his proclamation of the gospel (9:12),
> Christ is the rock (10:4), and
> the Corinthians are warned about falling (10:12), which surely in light of the OT parallel means losing their salvation.[22]

---

20. Cf. Juvenal *Sat.* 6.314-41. Though this is satirical exaggeration, it shows that such practices in temples were familiar.

21. If so, "ends" would refer to the ages touching each other.

22. Gardner, *Gifts of God*, p. 167. Actually the term "losing" is not very apt. When Paul talks about apostasy he refers to a willful act of rebellion, of wrenching oneself free from the firm grasp of God and wasting the benefits already provided by God. Apostasy is not something that happens by accident or without concentrated intent and persistent action. Paul obviously does not believe apostasy results from one particular sinful act, however heinous. Therefore, he appeals to the Corinthians as sinning Christians to repent. His view seems to be that one is eternally secure only when one is securely in eternity. This is why his exhortations to stand apply to all the audience and are meant in deadly earnest. Paul does believe, as Rom. 8:38f. shows, that one cannot be *forced* by powers either celestial or terrestrial to apostatize. No temptation is so great that God's grace is not ample to deal with it (1 Cor. 10:13). The only force, power, or person that can separate the believer from fellowship with Christ is that believer, and only then after a protracted struggle. Paul does not believe that God desires anyone to perish.

Paul says that the Corinthians have undergone only human temptations, and for these God can provide a way out (v. 13). Fee makes an elaborate distinction between ordinary temptations and deliberately putting God to the test, which the Corinthians are doing and which may cause them to fall. He contends that Paul is saying that for the ordinary trials that one does not seek but that come on the believer, God's normal provisions are more than sufficient to enable one to stand, but there is no such provision for deliberate, willful putting of God to the test. In favor of this view is the verb "seized," which suggests not something one seeks out but something that leaps out and grabs a person.[23]

Paul is not saying that the supposedly "strong" Corinthians had not yet faced an extraordinary temptation. What they were doing in the pagan temple was just that. Thus, Paul's point is that even in such cases God can provide a way out of their present situation. It is a human, if not the ultimate human, temptation to put God to the test. There is by God's grace even a way out of this, or Paul would be wasting his breath warning them.

The Corinthians then are to endure and prevail over the temptation to go to idol feasts. God will provide them with an out so that they can escape their present malaise. Paul believes that God never allows a Christian to be tempted to such a degree that by God's grace one cannot resist or find a way of escape. This does not mean one *will* necessarily resist.

In v. 14 Paul gives the directive that all of chs. 8–10 has been arguing for: Flee from idolatry. V. 15a should likely be seen as rhetorical irony.[24] Paul calls the audience "wise," though their behavior indicates otherwise. Paul knows, like any good rhetorician, that he must rely on the power of persuasion. He can only exhort; they must consider and respond.

A further argument for avoiding idolatry is presented in vv. 16ff., which is not a discourse on the Lord's Supper. Paul mentions only those elements of the sacrament that are relevant to the present discussion and that will help in persuading the audience to avoid idolatry. In v. 16 he refers to the "cup of blessing," a technical term for the cup of wine drunk at the end of a Jewish meal and over which the thanksgiving or grace is said: "Blessed are you, O Lord, who gives us the fruit of the vine." In the Passover meal this was the third cup of the four to be drunk. This was probably the cup Jesus identified as the cup of the new covenant in his blood at the Last Supper. The point is that this new covenant was enacted by Christ's death.

The term koinōnia has as its fundamental meaning to have or to share in common in something with someone.[25] The question then becomes

---

23. Fee, *First Corinthians*, pp. 460ff.

24. It could be countered that Paul assumes that they have some wisdom since he does count on them to use their better Christian judgment in these matters.

25. Cf. H. Seesemann, *Der Begriff Koinonia im Neuen Testament* (Giessen: Töpelmann, 1933), pp. 99f., who argues for the sense "participation" in most Pauline contexts, and that it

whether this term is referring to a sharing between God and the worshipper, among worshippers, or perhaps both. I would suggest that some of both is entailed. Barrett's translation "common participation" is a good one.[26] It is something worshippers do together and share as an act of the Body. What the believers are sharing or participating in is not just each other, nor is it just a matter of an individual's private communion with God.

What then does it mean to share or participate in the blood of Christ, especially since for Jews drinking blood was considered something horrible? Apparently Paul believes that there is more than mere symbols involved in the Lord's Supper. There seems to be some sort of real spiritual communion with Christ, or one might say an appropriation of the benefits of his death — forgiveness, cleansing, and the like.

Fee makes the intriguing suggestion that the sharing in the cup is vertical (with Christ), but the sharing in the bread represents and facilitates believers sharing in one another as the body of Christ.[27] This requires that the reference to the body of Christ in v. 16b refer to the body of believers, *not* either the physical body or the transcendent body of Christ in heaven or some sort of spiritual participation in the ascended Christ's body. Paul would not have been so upset with the Corinthians participating in idol feasts if he did not believe that it entailed some sort of real spiritual communion with demons. He thought one was giving, at least tacitly, one's allegiance and self over to that demon by participating in the feast.

In v. 17 Paul is talking about the bread as that which binds believers together into one body, not merely the common sharing in bread, but the more profound spiritual uniting that it signifies. All the believers share from the common loaf. Another clue to the meaning of *koinōnia* here must be the use of the verb "partake/share" *(metechō)*. Paul stresses *all* sharing because of the analogy in v. 18 with OT Israel.

The eating of the sacrifice in the Jewish temple entails a common participation in the altar (v. 18). According to Philo (*De Spec. Leg.* 1.221), "he to whom sacrifice has been offered makes the group *(koinōnon)* of worshippers partners in the altar and of one table." This could suggest that Paul sees the Lord's Supper as a sacrificial meal. But what does it mean to be participants in the altar? Is it merely to share in the meat and the benefits of the sacrifice, or does it mean participation in the god as well? It would seem that Paul has

---

is a religious concept for Paul. The exception to both these dictums, Seesemann says, is 2 Cor. 6:14, which may point to a non-Pauline origin for that text. He follows J. Y. Campbell, "Κοινωνία and its Cognates in the NT," *JBL* 51 (1932), pp. 352-80, here pp. 375-77.

26. C. K. Barrett, *The First Epistle to the Corinthians* (New York: Harper and Row, 1968), p. 232.

27. Fee, *First Corinthians*, pp. 469ff.

Deut. 14:22-27 in mind here, and thus it is unlikely that he envisions the participants actually consuming the deity. In Judaism the sacrificial food was never thought to convey God in that sense.[28] Thus sharing in the altar would mean sharing in the material and spiritual benefits of the sacrifice, just as in the Lord's Supper believers share in the material and spiritual benefits of Christ's sacrifice. Paul does not refer here to a direct sharing in Christ's metaphysical being, much less in his physical or glorified flesh.

Though idols are not anything, nor idol food, nonetheless Paul believes that the demons who use them are something, and in his mind one cannot offer allegiance to demons and share in the dubious benefits that they have to offer while also sharing in God's meal and the benefits that God offers. Paul says bluntly that he does not want the Corinthian Christians to become sharers in or common participants with demons by partaking of idol food in the temple (vv. 19-21). There is a fundamental incompatibility between eating and drinking at the table of the demons, sharing activities and benefits with them, and doing so with the Lord. These are mutually exclusive fellowships. Paul concludes this subsection in v. 22 by asking: "Are you trying to make the Lord angry, or do you think yourself stronger than even he, by binding yourself to and receiving 'benefits' from two supernatural sources at once?"

Paul once again reports the Corinthians' inevitable response to his argument: "Everything is permitted" (v. 23). But not everything is useful or profitable or builds up the body of Christ, and in a deliberative argument it is critical to stress what is beneficial or advantageous. The Christian is one who does not seek his or her own advantage but rather that of others.[29]

One should, Paul says, buy and eat whatever is sold in the market without inquiring because of conscience (v. 25).[30] Inquiring because of conscience is

---

28. Such an understanding of sacrifice was not unknown in the Greek sources. In a paper given at the 1992 Society of Biblical Literature meeting in San Francisco entitled "The Warmth and Breath of Life," L. J. Ciraolo has shown that in the Greek magical papyri from Egypt, animals (e.g., birds) would be strangled and then held up to the deity's statue to provide breath and animate the statue. The point is to endow the statue with magical potency, not to make the animal sacred to the god. These references are interesting because they may provide a further clue to understanding the reference to "things strangled" in the decree in Acts 15. Strangling was not a Roman practice. In Roman sacrifices the animal's throat was slit. Nevertheless, these papyri show that such practices were known in the pagan Greco-Roman world.

29. Notice that Paul does not say "not *only* his own."

30. Since this whole argument has been directed to those "in the know," it is hardly believable that for one verse and without any indication Paul suddenly addresses the "weak," who probably did not write to Paul anyway. Paul is not saying to the weak "Don't ask!" As Gardner, *Gifts of God*, pp. 190ff., notes, the "strong" have been at issue since 8:1, and it is only they who would likely take offense or be worried about the limitation of their freedom; pace C. Hill, *Hebrews and Hellenists* (Minneapolis: Fortress, 1992), p. 110, n. 23.

precisely what a Jew would do, and this shows how far Paul had come from his days as a zealous Pharisee.[31] He no longer felt it necessary to keep kosher since all creatures and thus all meat are the Lord's and thus one may freely share in it. There may be some irony in Paul's use of Ps. 24:1 here since this passage was used by the rabbis to argue that one must say the blessing over each meal, a blessing that they would say only over kosher food. Even in v. 25 Paul is not addressing the "weak" but the strong, as he has done throughout the whole argument in chs. 8–10. The strong are those who would be inquiring — so that they might demonstrate the extent of their freedom and their moral awareness that food is food and idols are nothing.

In v. 27 Paul deals with a real situation, as *ei* ("if") with the indicative verb indicates. When an unbeliever invites Christians to dinner in his home and they decide to go, they are simply to eat what is set before them. By contrast in v. 28 we have *ean* ("if perhaps") with a subjunctive verb: "But if perhaps anyone may say. . . ." Here Paul is dealing with a hypothetical possibility, one that his audience has not asked about.[32]

Probably the "anyone" who would say "this is sacred food" is a pagan, perhaps the host, since the pagan term *hierothuta* is used here, and not the pejorative term *eidōlothuta*.[33] In that case one is not to eat because of the conscience of the one who has spoken. In short, it would be a poor witness, because the host was trying to be sensitive to the Christian's religious persuasion and perhaps had assumed that Christians, adherents of some sort of derivative form of Judaism, would like Jews not partake of such food. In such a circumstance, if one would go ahead and eat, then the host would see that as a violation of one's own religion. It would be a bad witness to that person.

---

31. This is why the text has suggested to some that the weak, i.e., Jewish Christians, are in view, those for whom not only idol feasts but even idol meat had strongly negative moral associations. If one supposes that strong and weak together have gone to a dinner party, the weak not knowing in advance that "sacred food" would be served, it is perfectly plausible to think v. 25 is directed to the "strong" who would ask questions in order to demonstrate *their* moral awareness and freedom, especially to the weak.

32. These two verses also show how dangerous it is to assume that because Paul argues about something his converts must already be saying or doing the opposite of what he commends. The argument in vv. 28f. is purely hypothetical, though possible. In rhetoric it was common to forestall possible future problems in this fashion. Such artificial proofs were common in deliberative rhetoric, since that sort of rhetoric seeks to advise concerning future behavior and future possible consequences. On the use of examples in artificial proofs, see Quintilian *Inst. Or.* 5.9.1ff.

33. Witherington, "Not So Idle Thoughts about *Eidolothuton*," *TynB* 44 (1993), 237-54. There is clear evidence that sacrifices were sold to the general public; cf. Thorikos Test. no. 50 line 23 — 'sacrifice for Athena, a sheep which may be sold' in *New Doc. 2*, p. 36, though they wrongly refer to vol. 27 instead of vol. 25 in the *Zeitschrift für Papyrologie und Epigraphik*, where it was published by G. Dunst.

So Paul says to abstain for the pagan's sake so as to uphold a good image of moral consistency in the pagan's eyes.[34]

Verses **29b-30** are difficult to explain, but perhaps the least objectionable view is that the rhetorical question, "Why should my freedom be determined by another's conscience?" is again the objection of the Corinthians, as in v. 23a, and does not represent Paul's own view. In v. 28 Paul offered a hypothetical example, and here he offers a hypothetical objection or retort to his own argument.[35] Paul himself has just argued that he *does* limit his freedom, and the Corinthians ought to limit theirs precisely because of someone else's conscience. Thus v. 30 would also be a further hypothetical rhetorical question from the Corinthians to Paul: "Why should someone curse me if I partake of food having given thanks to God and partaking with gratitude?" Paul's answer is: because it is not just a matter of one's relationship with God; it is not purely a vertical matter. There are also the horizontal relationships, that is, the effect one's eating has on others. V. **31** then states the basic Pauline principle: "Whether I eat or drink or whatever I do, I do it for God's glory," and thus for the building up of Christ's body.

Paul's missionary or evangelistic approach then is repeated in v. **32**: In adiaphora one should strive to give no offense to Jews or Greeks or to the church of God.[36] This includes everyone outside or inside the congregation. The rule is "consider others first." V. **33** explains further that Paul strives to fit in with everyone in all such matters, not for his own benefit so that things will go smoothly for himself, but in order to save many for Christ. He is not trying to be a people-pleaser in a way that would amount to compromising

---

34. The problem with arguing that it is the strong's self-awareness that Paul alludes to in v. 25 comes in v. 29, where he makes it clear that he has been talking about the *other* person's moral self-awareness.

35. S. K. Stowers, *The Diatribe and Paul's Letter to the Romans* (Chico: Scholars, 1985), has demonstrated that the so-called Stoic-Cynic diatribe style was the style of dialogue and debate in Greco-Roman schooling.

> The model exponent of the diatribe is not the wandering Cynic street preacher. Moreover, the dialogical element of the diatribe is not an expression of polemic or an attack on the enemies and opponents of [one's] philosophy. The diatribe is a type of discourse employed in the philosophical school. Its style, however, may be imitated literarily. The form of the diatribe and the way it functions presupposes a student-teacher relationship. (p. 175)

One of the more important points to be gained here is that use of this dialogical style in his letters does not necessarily reflect Paul's preaching style, but rather his style of instructing those already in the school of Christ. It was used by rhetoricians and philosophers alike.

36. As Fee, *First Corinthians,* p. 489, says, to cause "offense" is not to hurt someone's feelings, but either to cause a believer to stumble or to put a stumbling block in front of a potential convert.

the gospel, but in indifferent matters such as food he is more than happy to be socially easy to get along with.[37]

This section closes with the exhortation "Imitate me as I do Christ" (**11:1**). All along Paul has been holding up himself as an example, but only because he follows Christ's example. This may suggest that he is alluding to Jesus' practice of eating with anyone, even notorious sinners, and to his ruling about no food being unclean. It is also possible that he alludes here to Christ's servanthood example of giving up all for the sake of others, even to the point of death on the cross.

To sum up, in chs. 8–10 Paul is exhorting certain "in the know" Gentile Christians who have been arguing for their freedom, including the right to attend feasts in pagan temple precincts. To set an example for them to imitate, so that the factions between this group and "the weak" will be healed, Paul identifies with the weak in three ways: by manual labor, by defending the weak to those "in the know," and by using the language of slavery and casting himself as a servant. Paul deliberately defies the social expectations and concerns especially of the upwardly mobile and those who had already arrived.

Paul's manual labor was partly a way for him to avoid a certain kind of patronage, but this move was destined to cause him major trouble. One who refused patronage was likely to incur enmity, since one thus shamed publicly a sponsor.[38] Paul's strategy was to dismantle such patronage systems within the community of Christ, *insofar as* they created a status hierarchy.[39] Paul was not a maintainer of some patriarchal and patronal status quo. Instead, he turns the tables on the strong by calling for them to imitate him in his slavish behavior, which turns conventional roles and expectations upside down.[40]

---

37. *Areskō* can mean "give pleasure to."

38. Cf. E. A. Judge, "Cultural Conformity and Innovation," *TynB* 35 (1984), pp. 3-24, here p. 15: "If you refused an offer of friendship by not taking someone's money you openly declared yourself his enemy. Enmity also entails a painful and exhausting ritual of confrontation."

39. This is not to say that Paul always refused all support or patronage. In the Corinthian situation, however, when it came with the cultural strings and baggage that went with it — such as the patron's assertion of moral superiority and of power over Paul and his itinerary and the recipient's removal from the poor in order to be either an in-house teacher for the better-off or a Sophist — Paul had to turn it down. I will argue in a forthcoming commentary on Philippians that Paul accepted support from those who were willing to relate to him on an equal partnership or friendship basis. This may or may not have something to do with the *societas* conventions discussed by J. P. Sampley in *Pauline Partnership in Christ* (Philadelphia: Fortress, 1980).

40. Judge, "Cultural Conformity," p. 23:

The Corinthian letters show him in a head-on confrontation with the mechanisms by which [the patron-client system] imposed social power defined as moral superi-

In his discussion of the importance of a rhetor providing an example for his students to imitate and how imitation is only a *first step* in becoming a good orator,[41] Quintilian writes that imitation implies the superiority of the person one is imitating. It also implies that the one called on to imitate another is at an elementary level of learning. It is not enough to imitate in words only (*Inst. Or.* 10.2.1-28). The strong, who were enamored with words and slogans, in part taken from Paul their teacher, were immature (cf. 1 Cor. 3:1ff). Therefore Paul must tell them to use the elementary pedagogical device of imitation. They must follow his foolish and slavish example, learning not to go beyond "the things that are written." Only in this fashion could factions become fictions in Corinth.[42]

> [Paul] picks up many established terms and notions that as words belong to the language of the philosophical schools, or other elements of Greek cultural tradition. Similarly in his social practice he takes up and uses, examines, and exploits social institutions such as slavery or the system of patronage or the conventions that surrounded the well-to-do . . . who supported his enterprise. In such cases he takes up existing social institutions and subjects them on the one hand to a radical critique and on the other hand to careful cultivation because of the advantages they have to bring to what he has to do.[43]

---

ority. His positive response to this collision was to build a remarkable new construction of social realities that both lay within the fabric of the old ranking system and yet transformed it by a revolution in social values.

41. One must eventually find one's own arguments and style.

42. To say Paul was unconventional is putting it mildly, though the church has ever after tried to domesticate him and has even tried to make him the great defender of the status quo. He was a man who fit no such formula. He was willing to go to extremes, even to appear extremely foolish and servile, in order to let the gospel speak for itself and do its own work. He was not interested in being unconventional for the sake of unconventionality or for the sort of reasons that Cynics were unconventional, but only in order to win all sorts of people to Christ and to try to form a more perfect union called the body of Christ made up of Jew and pagan, male and female, slave and free, and all social strata. For Paul, social status and worldly fame were unimportant, but resources for ministry mattered a great deal, and so he was happy to work even with those who were relatively more well-off, so long as they would work with him on his terms, not the terms of the usual patron-client relationship.

43. E. A. Judge, "St. Paul and Socrates," *Interchange* 13 (1973), pp. 106-16, here p. 109.

Argument V: 11:2-16

Heads Up[1]

Arguments that this section is a later interpolation into Paul's letter should be seen as examples of special pleading.[2] We will continue to treat this text as Pauline, as do the vast majority of scholars. That many find the arguments in this text difficult and unappealing is no sound basis for assuming that they are not Paul's.

A. C. Wire conjures up the old image of the chauvinistic, repressive Paul as a foil for arguing for a radical feminist group of mostly well-to-do celibate Corinthian women prophetesses, which Paul is trying to bring back in line by most of his arguments throughout 1 Corinthians. Her arguments are flawed by overuse of mirror-reading, that is, taking certain Pauline statements and assuming that Paul is opposing an equal and opposite opinion held by certain nebulous opponents in Corinth.[3] Furthermore, in chs. 11 and 14 Paul is clearly

1. For a fuller treatment of this section see B. Witherington, *Women in the Earliest Churches* (Cambridge: Cambridge University, 1988), especially pp. 78-90. I am not persuaded by the argument of A. Cameron, "Neither Male nor Female," *Greece and Rome* 27 (1980), pp. 60-68, that Judge is wrong about there being a cultivated social elite, both men and women, among the Corinthian Christians. In Corinth one did not need to be an aristocrat to be among the elite, especially as the cult of the emperor, served by freedmen and freedwomen, grew in importance in the first century A.D.

2. See further Witherington, *Women in the Earliest Churches,* pp. 78f. W. O. Walker's attempt to shift the burden of proof in order to justify the idea that this text and some others in the Pauline letters are interpolations ("The Burden of Proof in Identifying Interpolations in the Pauline Letters," *NTS* 33 [1987], pp. 610-18) is hardly convincing. It is not satisfactory to argue that "it is to be assumed simply on *a priori* grounds that the Pauline letters, as we now have them, do, in fact, contain interpolations" (p. 611). This is based on unverifiable assumptions about the early stages of the editing of Paul's letters. Walker concedes that "we have no way of knowing the history of Paul's letters between the time of their writing and the time of their final editing" (p. 612), in which case we also have no substantive basis for arguing for interpolations on the basis of supposed early creative editing. We also do not know that earlier copies of Paul's letters were suppressed or destroyed during the second century because of their content (p. 614). All of Walker's arguments for interpolation are arguments from silence or from unverifiable hypotheses. Cf. J. Murphy-O'Connor's compelling arguments against seeing 1 Cor. 11:2-16 as an interpolation in "The Non-Pauline Character of 1 Cor. 11:2-16?" *JBL* 95 (1976), pp. 615-22, and "I Corinthians 11.2-16 Once Again," *CBQ* 50 (1988), pp. 265-74.

3. Mirror-reading is especially dangerous when one is dealing with a rhetorical piece such as 1 Corinthians, where some of the arguments are meant to forestall future possible views, not presently held ones.

giving instructions to men as well as women about praying, prophesying, and head-coverings.[4] Wire is correct in saying that Paul thinks he is dealing with a serious breach of community, hence his extensive and varied arguments.[5] He uses both inartificial and artificial proofs, appealing to Scripture, nature, conventions of honor and shame, Pauline custom, and custom in other Christian assemblies in order to make his rhetoric persuasive.[6]

A Closer Look: On Headcoverings and Religion in Roman Cities ———

Though we will discuss prophecy in antiquity when we reach 1 Corinthians 14, here is the place to say several important things about headcoverings, specifically head-coverings worn by one who was performing a religious act such as praying or prophesying. Paul's discussion of hair (vv. 14f.) is brought in toward the end as a supporting argument, as one example of a kind of headcovering. This means that the discussions by Murphy-O' Connor, Hurley, Padgett, and others of hair and hairstyles are quite beside the point.[7] The issue is headcoverings.

4. Paul does not usually name his opponents. If women were among his antagonists in Corinth this would be especially interesting in view of the practice of ancient Greek orators to mention women by name only when they were connected with one's opponent, when they were women of ill repute, or when they were dead and might be mentioned by name on an inscription. Cf. D. Schaps, "The Women Least Mentioned: Etiquette and Women's Names," *Classical Quarterly* 27 (1977), pp. 323-30. Probably Paul's primary antagonists in Corinth are not women but well-to-do Gentile men; cf. pp. 151ff. above.

The analysis by A. Funk, *Status und Rollen in den Paulusbriefen* (Innsbruck: Tyrolia, 1981), pp. 110ff., also would not support the idea that women are the major group that Paul is targeting for criticism. Funk points out that only two Christian women are mentioned by name in 1 Corinthians, Chloe and Prisca, with only one of the two still in Corinth, while none are mentioned or even alluded to in 2 Corinthians. Furthermore, the word "sister" comes up only twice in 1 Corinthians and not at all in 2 Corinthians. One could argue that Paul does not name specific women because he is treating them as enemies, but this does not explain the absence of references to anonymous Christian women. Furthermore, 1 Corinthians 5–6 and 8–10 certainly point to men as the source of trouble, and in chs. 11 and 14 both men and women are criticized. Even ch. 7, when studied closely, does not support the reconstruction of an ascetical pneumatic group of women in Corinth that Paul is particularly targeting.

5. Cf. E. Schüssler Fiorenza, "Women in the Pre-Pauline and Pauline Churches," *Union Seminary Quarterly Review* 33 (1978), pp. 153-66, which rightly points out that Paul had several women coworkers, which makes all the more unbelievable Fiorenza's interpretation of 1 Corinthians 11 as an attempt to repress women and limit the expression of their gifts.

6. Cf. A. C. Wire, *The Corinthian Women Prophets: A Reconstruction through Paul's Rhetoric* (Minneapolis: Fortress, 1990), pp. 116-34, on headcoverings, pp. 220-23.

7. J. Murphy-O'Connor, "Sex and Logic in 1 Corinthians 11.2-16," *CBQ* 42 (1980), pp. 482-500; J. B. Hurley, *Man and Woman in Biblical Perspective* (Downers Grove: InterVarsity, 1981); A. Padgett, "Paul on Women in the Church: The Contradictions of Coiffure in 1 Corinthians 11:2-16," *JSNT* 20 (1984), pp. 69-86.

*The Cn. Ahenobarbus altar piece: A woman bringing a sacrifice
for the god Mars. She alone has her head covered.*

(Louvre; photo courtesy RMN)

We know a good deal about such headcoverings in Roman settings, for example, what was worn when one was offering a sacrifice. Besides the statue found in Corinth of the Emperor Augustus about to offer sacrifice with his head covered,[8] we may also point to the important altar of Cn. Domitius Ahenobarus found in the Louvre (see the photograph above), which clearly shows a woman with her head covered about to offer a sacrifice. None of the others in the sacrificial procession have their heads covered, not even the man who holds the tablet with the votive inscription — just the one person about to offer a sacrifice.[9] There is also the clear evidence of a stone relief in the Museo Archeologico in Milan depicting the sacrifice of a steer, where only the one offering the sacrifice has the head covered.[10]

The literary evidence also supports the contention that we are dealing with headcoverings rather than hair. Plutarch uses the same phrase that Paul does, *kata kephalēs,* to refer to something resting on the head, not hair and much less long, flowing hair (*Regum* 200F; *Aetia Romana* 267C; *Vitae Decem Oratorae* 842B; *Pyrrhus* 399B; *Pompeius* 640C; *Caesar* 739D).[11] An incidental remark by Livy (10.7.10) shows that

8. D. W. J. Gill, "The Importance of Roman Portraiture for Head-Coverings in 1 Corinthians 11.2-16," *TynB* 41 (1990), pp. 245-60, is right that this statue, found in the Julian basilica, from its posture, even though the right hand is missing, "would almost certainly have held a *patera,* or shallow dish, for pouring libations" (p. 246).

9. I doubt that it is significant that all the others in this procession are Roman males, since we know that Roman males also covered their heads when offering sacrifice.

10. Cf. R. M. Oglivie, *The Romans and their Gods* (New York: Norton, 1969), p. 41.

11. One of the few roles reserved exclusively for women in Greco-Roman cults was that of carrying, on the head, baskets in the Isis procession or the *kistē* in the Eleusinian cult; cf. *New Doc. 3,* p. 44 and see the picture on page 11.

the head was covered not only when offering a sacrifice but also during the prophetic reading of the entrails. That such liturgical covering of the head applied equally to women is mentioned by Varro (*De Lingua Latina* 5.29.130) and confirmed by Juvenal (*Sat.* 6.390-92).

Such covering of the head was "not a general form of dress adopted by people attending a sacrifice" but was done only by those "taking an active part."[12] This is crucial because Paul in 1 Cor. 11:2ff. is only addressing those actively involved in praying and prophesying in Christian worship. Plutarch (*Quaest. Rom.* 266D-267A) indicates that Romans uncovered their heads in the presence of other people, particularly social superiors, to acknowledge them as worthy of honor.

R. E. Oster has advanced the discussion of this material, not only by stressing the proper Roman rather than Greek context for understanding 1 Cor. 11:2ff. but also by showing the differences between the way Romans and Greeks distinguished themselves, especially in liturgical settings.

> The Greeks' self-identity arose most from their speech and education, while a Roman often distinguished himself by what he wore. It was not that Greeks eschewed head apparel. Rather it was clear to them and Romans that the habitual propensity of Romans to wear head apparel in liturgical settings stood in sharp contrast to the practice of others.[13]

Romans were more dominated by status and rules in their choice of garb when praying or sacrificing. Sometimes these rules were rigidly maintained; for example, the flamen dialis, a Roman sacerdotal official, was not allowed out of his house without a tight-fitting cap with a spike at the top (cf. Aulius Gellius *Attic Nights* 10.15.16f.). It appears that such headcoverings were worn in Roman contexts to demonstrate respect and subservience to the gods.[14] Oster is correct to stress that Paul is correcting both men and women in this passage in regard to headcoverings, not just women.

Existing public portraits of women (presumably well-to-do women) from Roman Corinth often show them bareheaded.[15] This is not to be confused with a woman having a shaved head or hair closely cropped, either of which was a sign of

---

12. Gill, "Roman Portraiture," p. 248. Cf. the inscription from a temple which indicates what sort of dress and activities are permitted in the temple, *IG* V,2, conveniently cited in *New Doc. 4*, pp. 108f., particularly lines 10f.: "nor [let it be permissible] for women [to enter] with their hair braided, nor for men with their heads covered." This inscription reflects Greek practice in third-century-B.C. worship of Despoina in Arcadia and is not directly relevant in regard to Roman women's attire.

13. R. E. Oster, "When Men Wore Veils to Worship: The Historical Context of 1 Corinthians 11.4," *NTS* 34 (1988), pp. 481-505, here p. 494.

14. C. L. Thompson, "Hairstyles, Headcoverings and St. Paul: Portraits from Roman Corinth," *BA* (1988), pp. 99-115.

15. Another plausible suggestion is that of A. Rouselle, "Body Politics in Ancient Rome," in *A History of Women*, ed. P. S. Pantel (Cambridge: Belknap, 1992), pp. 296-336, here p. 315: The headcovering was meant to warn men (and angels?) that the wearer was a respectable woman and thus untouchable. If so, then the headcovering would serve as a sign of respectability, not subordination.

public shaming and humiliation (Dio Chrysostom 64.2f.) or of misfortune or mourning (Plutarch *Quaest. Rom.* 267B).

This text raises a number of questions for us. First, why does Paul want to maintain for women, but not for men, the Roman practice of covering the head when engaging in a religious act? The bulk of his argument is taken up with providing a theological rationale for this (vv. 2-12). The theological rationale is not brought in as an afterthought to prop up an argument primarily grounded in custom, or in "nature itself," but rather the reverse. Paul appeals to nature and custom because he is pulling out all the stops in his closing arguments (vv. 13f.) to forestall objections on any other possible grounds. Apparently, as v. 16 suggests, he anticipates that some will seek to be contentious about this matter.

Is Paul imposing some sort of Jewish practice on a largely Gentile audience? The Jew-Gentile issue does not come up here at all, as it did in chs. 8–10. Considering what Paul says in 9:20ff., it is difficult to believe that he would impose a specifically Jewish custom on Christians, either men or women, in Roman Corinth, some of whom were certainly not Jewish. Furthermore, both Roman and Corinthian evidence make it unlikely that Paul would impose any foreign or specifically Jewish custom on the ethnically mixed *ekklēsia* in Corinth.[16]

Is Paul talking about behavior of husbands and wives, or of men and women in general? In some parts of the text it is clearly impossible to argue that *anēr* means "husband" and *gynē* "wife,"[17] and elsewhere these translations are implausible, especially because Paul keeps saying things like "every man" or "any woman." The argument is not about family relations but about praying and prophesying in Christian worship.

Finally, does Paul take back in vv. 11ff. what he argues for at some length in vv. 2-10? We have seen Paul's rhetorical adeptness earlier in this letter, so it is difficult to believe that this is the case. Such a move would be rhetorically ineffective and inept. It is more plausible to see two stages of one argument: first an argument from the order of creation and then an argument from that order as it has been transformed and to some extent reaffirmed in the order of salvation manifested in the Christian community.

Returning to the first of these questions, Paul is not simply endorsing standard Roman or even Greco-Roman customs in Corinth. Paul was about the business of reforming his converts' social assumptions and conventions in the context of the Christian community. They were to model new Christian

16. Witherington, *Women in the Earliest Churches*, p. 82.
17. For example, in v. 8 Paul is not arguing that wives are made from their husbands!

customs, common in the assemblies of God but uncommon in the culture, thus staking out their own sense of a unique identity.[18] The whole flow of the argument leading up to 11:2ff. leads one to suspect that Paul is opposing factious or divisive behavior here as well.[19]

Perhaps some were urging the following of Roman practices in regard to headcoverings in worship while others were urging Jewish customs or possibly even the customs in some pagan mysteries, where women might worship without headcoverings and with their hair unbound.[20] One thing is clear: In a Roman city like Corinth it would not have seemed strange for women to have their heads covered during religious acts.[21] But that Paul uses a lengthy theological argument is no sure sign that he is opposing one. All we can say from the point of view of rhetorical analysis is that it is obvious that Paul regards this as a very important matter.

I would suggest that Paul places little stock in social or cultural conventions or social status and a great deal of stock in the way God has made human beings and is remaking them in Christ. For Paul, human duality, maleness and femaleness, is good and is to be celebrated, just as the interdependence of male and female is to be appreciated. Maleness and femaleness are part of the order of creation and are also reaffirmed in certain ways in the new creation. In Paul's view, people are redeemed as men and women of God and are to continue to be men and women, not some neutered or neutral third sort of creature. It is possible and likely, in light of ch. 7, that some in Corinth thought that through knowledge or other spiritual gifts and experiences they transcended distinctions of gender in Christian worship.

Paul's view is that the creation order should be properly manifested, not obliterated, in Christian worship, especially because even angels, as guardians of the creation order, are present, observing such worship and perhaps even participating in it.[22] Worship is the act of praising and glori-

---

18. E. A. Judge, "The Social Identity of the First Christians," *Journal of Religious History* 11 (1980), pp. 201-17, here p. 215:

> By setting powerful new ideas to work within and upon the most familiar relationships of life, Paul created in the church a social force of a unique kind. The domestic framework was soon outstripped, as the movement of thought and belief generated institutions that were to become an alternative society to the civil order as a whole.

19. C. S. Keener, *Paul, Women, and Wives* (Peabody: Hendrickson, 1992), pp. 22ff.

20. Witherington, *Women in the Earliest Churches*, pp. 80ff. On women's roles as priestesses in the Demeter cult in Corinth and statues of them in the temple precincts, cf. Pausanias *Descriptions* Corinth 35.6-8 (second century A.D.).

21. Pace Wire, *Corinthian Women Prophets*, p. 122.

22. That the *angeloi* mentioned in v. 10 are human emissaries of the *ekklēsia* is possible in the abstract, but this understanding makes little sense of the *dia touto* that apparently connects v. 10 to what precedes. Cf. J. Winandy, "Un curieux *casus pendens*,"

fying God for who God is, which at the same time entails that human beings recognize who *they* are as beings under God and in Christ. The proper human response to redemption is that both women and men not only bear witness to who they are but also to *whose* they are. As Paul will argue in ch. 15, redemption involves the body. Therefore male-female differentiation is part of what God intends to redeem, not transcend or supersede. It seems clear from ch. 15 (and chs. 11–14) that the Corinthians had not reckoned with the role of the body, and therefore of human sexual differentiation, in the order of salvation.

There are, therefore, five major issues for Paul here: First, he affirms that both men and women may pray and prophesy so long as both reflect the glory of God. Since woman is the glory of man and her hair is her own glory (vv. 8, 15), she must cover her head so that only God's glory is reflected in Christian worship. Especially in view of the reference to the *peribolaion* in v. 15, Paul must be thinking of a woman pulling her cloak or *himation* over her head. He is probably not thinking of veils or any other sort of headcovering, including hair.[23] The headcovering also serves to indicate that the woman has authority to pray and prophesy. Paul's concern is with a Christian practice, not with a Jewish or pagan practice.[24]

Second, *kephalē* can certainly mean "head' in the metaphorical sense of "leader," of a person or group who is over others or over nations (cf. 1 Kgs. 20:12; Isa. 7:8f.; 2 Sam. 22:44 LXX), as has been demonstrated clearly by J. A. Fitzmyer.[25] The real issue here is whether or not the meaning "source," which is also attested for *kephalē*, is likely here in 1 Cor. 11:2-16. V. 8 may suggest such a translation, but then the question becomes: Is Paul really also arguing that Christ's source is God? This is possible, but since the context has to do

NTS 38 (1992), pp. 621-29, here p. 628, for a critique of the suggestion of A. Padgett, "Paul on Women in the Church," p. 81; and J. Murphy-O'Connor, "I Corinthians 11.2-16 Once Again," pp. 271f.

23. Cf. rightly G. Theissen, *Psychological Aspects of Pauline Theology* (Edinburgh: Clark, 1987), pp. 159f. That it is shameful for men to have long hair (v. 14) probably has nothing to do with countering homosexual affectations in the Corinthian community, which, in light of 6:9, Paul would simply have prohibited rather than arguing about the honor and shame potential of long hair. It may, however, have to do with some in Corinth affecting the dress and hairstyles of their favorite rhetors! Showy clothes and elaborate hairdos were part of the Sophist's regular public demeanor, a sort of badge of identity. Cf. Philostratus *Lives* 2.10.587; Epictetus *Diss.* 3.1.1ff.; Dio Chrysostom 72.16; S. K. Stowers, "Social Status: Public Speaking and Private Teaching: The Circumstances of Paul's Preaching Activity," *NovT* 26 (1984), pp. 59-81, here p. 75.

24. In Apuleius *Met.* 11.10 we read of a woman in the Isis cult in Corinth who has anointed hair and her head covered with light linen. The Christian practice Paul insists on would not seem completely novel in Corinth.

25. "Another Look at ΚΕΦΑΛΗ in 1 Corinthians 11.3," *NTS* 35 (1989), pp. 503-11.

with authority, authorization, and order in worship it would seem more probable that *kephalē* has the metaphorical sense demonstrated by Fitzmyer.[26]

Third, whatever may be true in the order of creation, vv. 11ff. makes
clear that men and women are mutually interdependent, not independent, "in
the Lord," and that they all ultimately come from God. Men and women share
a horizontal dependence on each other and a vertical dependence on God.
Paul clearly believes in a hierarchy of God and Christ over human beings.
Whether he also affirms a male human hierarchy in Christ, that is, in the
Christian community, seems doubtful in view of vv. 11ff. and in view of the
fact that he is quite comfortable talking about women as his coworkers, as
fellow servants of God, and possibly even as *apostoloi* (Rom. 16:7).[27]

Fourth, the argument about nature and hair is meant to bolster Paul's
contention that the distinctiveness of male and female should be outwardly
manifested, especially in Christian worship.

And fifth, in view of the argument about *both* men and women and
headcoverings, it is likely that both, not just women, were creating the
disorder in Christian worship.[28] In light of Roman practice, it is very believable that some Christian Roman males were covering their heads when they
were about to pray or prophesy. Paul is not interested in baptizing the status
quo or normal Roman practice. He is setting up new customs for a new
community, and these customs are deeply grounded in his theological understanding of creation, redemption, their interrelation, and how they should
be manifested in worship.

Finally, T. Engberg-Pedersen has argued that v. 16 refers to the habit of

---

26. Another point against interpreting *kephalē* as "source" here is Paul's rationale in
v. 7: Man is the image and glory of God, and woman is the glory of man. For discussion
of the view that *kephalē* often means "person of higher authority," see W. Grudem, "Does
kephalē ('Head') mean 'Source' or 'Authority Over' in Greek Literature?" *TrinJ* n.s. 6 (1985),
pp. 38-59; R. S. Cervin, "Does *kephalē* mean 'Source' or 'Authority Over' in Greek Literature?
A Rebuttal," *TrinJ* n.s. 10 (1989), pp. 85-112; Grudem, "The Meaning of *kephalē* ('Head').
A Response to Recent Studies," *TrinJ* n.s. 11 (1990), pp. 3-72; J. Delobel, "1 Cor. 11,2-16,"
in *L'Apôtre Paul. Personalité, Style et Conception du Ministère* (Leuven: Leuven University,
1986), pp. 369-89, here pp. 378f.

27. Paul does not simply equate the family structure, which in the household codes
is somewhat patriarchal, with the structure of the family of faith, especially because he
believes that the Holy Spirit's dispensing of gifts determines many if not most functions in
the body of Christ. There is no gender-specific dispensing of those gifts. Fiorenza reads a
strongly patriarchal structure *into* the *ekklēsia* in her handling of 1 Corinthians 11. Cf. her
"Rhetorical Situation and Historical Reconstruction in 1 Corinthians," *NTS* 33 (1987), pp.
386-403, here p. 397.

28. If both were taking their cues from pagan ritual contexts, perhaps the men were
following the normal Roman practices, and the women practices they had learned in the
rites of Dionysius or some mystery cult where they were not expected to wear headcoverings
or to have bound hair.

Statue of a man bringing a sacrifice (note the head covering)

being contentious rather than to the habit of going without a headcovering. This is not impossible in view of v. 18.[29]

In this chapter, then, Paul is trying to reform both men and women in the Corinthian congregation who continue to take their cues for religious behavior from analogous practices in other religious settings in Corinth. He celebrates the mutual interdependence of male and female and the dependence of all on God as the source of everything and everyone. For Paul, equality in Christ has more to do with *whose* one is than with who one is. All are equally

29. T. Engberg-Pedersen, "1 Cor. 11.16 and the Character of Pauline Exhortation," *JBL* 110 (1991), pp. 679-89, here p. 684.

creatures of God and people for whom Christ died and thus of sacred worth. All are not gifted in the same way and all do not share the same function or task. But Paul's conception of equality is not just a nebulous theological idea. It has social implications. Social ranking is the world's way of valuing or evaluating people, and in Paul's view the form of this world is passing away. Therefore, he is happy to dismantle such ways of measuring people.

But gender distinction is not something human beings created. Paul sees it as a good gift of God, and he wishes it manifested and so celebrated in Christian worship. He does not believe that there is some neutral core of personhood that has nothing to do with sexual identity. Nor does he believe that sexual distinctions are or will be obliterated in the order of redemption. His theology of the redemption of the body points to belief that Christians are both initially and finally redeemed as men and women of God. One must not confuse the social structures of fallen human patriarchy with Paul's arguments about the structure of the *ekklēsia*, which involve the importance and value of affirming gender differences. Furthermore, Paul's vision of headship or leadership involves the leader in being the head servant — the *oikonomos* or household steward in the house of God. In Christ, Paul thus inverts the world's order of who must serve and who will be served.[30]

---

30. It is difficult to come to grips with a Paul who is neither a radical feminist nor an ardent patriarchalist. It is too easy to claim him for one or the other extreme. But Paul, like Jesus, was a man who was not and is not easily pigeonholed.

Argument VI: 11:17-34

MAKING A MEAL OF IT

This section continues the discussion of abuses in worship that began in 11:2 and continues through ch. 14. Since Paul is correcting abuses he does not provide a full positive exposition of his views of the Lord's Supper here. Nonetheless, we learn a great deal here about how the Lord's Supper was being practiced in Corinth and about Paul's views of the Supper.

To this point in Paul's discourse we have seen a variety of factors at work in the divisions among the Corinthian Christians. There were divisions over teachers centered on the matter of wisdom both in the sense of rhetoric and the sense of sapiential content, over legal matters, over marriage, divorce, and singleness, and over whether to attend idol feasts. Here we hear of divisions coming out in an act of Christian worship, that is, in an agape meal that was the context for sharing in the Lord's Supper. These divisions seem to have been created by some more well-to-do members of the congregation treating the agape meal like a private dinner party, perhaps a banquet followed by a drinking party *(convivium)*. The result of this was that the social stratification of the congregation was overemphasized and exacerbated. A serious division between haves and have-nots was thus threatening the fragile unity of the Corinthian Christian community.[1]

Paul is concerned with at least two social facets of the problem, namely, the disorderliness and inequality of the proceedings.[2] Neither of these characteristics was at all unusual at Greco-Roman banquets followed by drinking parties. Even the larger dining rooms in homes were equipped to hold only nine to twenty people, and there were certainly more Corinthian Christians than that. It was the normal practice to rank one's guests in terms of social status, with those of higher status eating with the host in the dining room and others eating elsewhere and getting poorer food. The only exception to this rule was during the Saturnalia, when normal social values were turned upside down for a day and slaves and

---

1. E. A. Judge, "The Social Identity of the First Christians," *Journal of Religious History* 11 (1980), pp. 201-17, here p. 212, describes early Christian meetings as "talkative, passionate, and sometimes quarrelsome circles that met to read Paul's letters over their evening meal in private houses. . . ."

2. Cf. S. M. Pogoloff, *Logos and Sophia: The Rhetorical Situation of 1 Corinthians* (Atlanta: Scholars, 1992), p. 239.

poor people were treated well. Lucian describes the Saturnalia, contrasting it with the normal practice of a Greco-Roman banquet (*Sat.* 21f.):

> Tell them to invite the poor to dinner, take in four or five at a time, not as they do nowadays, though, but in a more democratic fashion, all having an equal share, no one stuffing himself with dainties with the servant standing waiting for him to eat himself to exhaustion . . . only letting us glimpse the platter or the remnants of the cake. And tell him not to give a whole half of the pig and its head to his master when it is brought in, leaving for the others just the bones. And tell the wine servers not to wait for each of us to ask seven times for a drink but on one request to pour it out and hand us at once a big cup, like they do for their master. And let all the guests have the same wine. Where is it laid down that he should get drunk on wine with a fine bouquet while I must burst my belly on new stuff?[3]

Paul expects the meal that Christians share to be more democratic, more like a Saturnalia. He is attempting to construct a practice for the Christian community that is at variance with the customs of ordinary meals and is upset that some Corinthians are treating the agape like an ordinary banquet.[4] Paul's strategy, as S. C. Barton argues, is to make a distinction between private meals in one's own home and a meal shared in and by the *ekklēsia*, no matter whose home it may be held in.[5] This is a matter not of sacred space but of sacred time and occasion.[6] Paul does not talk about sacred buildings, but he does

---

3. Lucian is not exaggerating the differences. Cf. Martial *Epigrams* 3.60:

Since I am asked to dinner . . . , why is not the same dinner served to me as to you? You eat oysters fattened in the Lucrine Lake while I suck a mussel through a hole in the shell. You get mushrooms while I get hog funguses. You tackle turbot, but I brill. Golden with fat, a turtledove gorges you with its bloated rump, but a magpie that has died in its cage is set before me. Why do I dine without you, Ponticus, even though I am dining with you?

4. It may be significant that at Roman banquets, the religious ceremonies were regularly reserved to the end of the dinner proper (or even after the *symposium,* if it was to follow). If the Christian meal was in any way analogous, the Lord's Supper may have come at the end of the agape meal. Cf. D. E. Smith, "Meals and Morality in Paul and His World," *Society of Biblical Literature 1981 Seminar Papers,* ed. K. H. Richards (Chico: Scholars, 1981), pp. 319-39.

5. S. C. Barton, "Paul's Sense of Place: An Anthropological Approach to Community Formation in Corinth," *NTS* 32 (1986), pp. 225-46. Here again we have evidence that Paul does not simply apply the structure of the household and its conventions to the community of faith. When the community meets in a house, Paul insists that they meet in a way that comports with the equality that exists in the body of Christ, and thus without regard to social status and social distinctions.

6. On homes as places where *collegia* would meet for dinner, cf. *CIL* 9148: "collegium quod est domo Sergiae Paullinae." Normally *collegia* met in temples or in their own club houses. As J. D. G. Dunn points out ("The Responsible Congregation," in *Charisma und*

talk about holy persons and holy occasions when such people gather for worship and fellowship. These occasions are to be regulated by sacred traditions, in this case the narrative of the Last Supper. The Lord's Supper was meant as a sacrament of both horizontal and vertical communion, not as a rite of incorporation.[7]

A Closer Look: Association Rules and Teaching at Meals ————————

Probably some people saw Christian gatherings as meetings of some sort of association or *collegium*, especially in view of the fact that early Christianity had no temples, no priests, and no sacrifices. Furthermore, just like a Christian meeting, an association meeting could involve a variety of people from up and down the social strata. It could involve a wealthy patron, male or female, a group of artisans both freeborn and freed, and even some slaves, who perhaps had taken up a trade or started a business using their *peculium*, money of their own.

There was a trade association of leatherworkers.[8] Since Paul practiced his trade in Corinth and stayed, according to Acts 18, with Priscilla and Aquila, who also practiced this trade, we can assume that he was involved in setting up or participating in some sort of trade association, which, to avoid suspicion or banning by the authorities, had a variety of religious functions and activities.

One of the main functions of these associations was to provide for those who were not among the very wealthy or the aristocrats but who had social aspirations a venue in which they could feel appreciated and gain honor and acclaim from their peers.

> No one smiled at their pretensions when their banners paraded through the streets in homage to a god or emperor; no one found their honorific decrees or their emphatically advertised votes of thanks, even to people [such as patrons] miles above them socially, in the least ridiculous. . . . The arrogation of fancy titles raised no laugh against the Sacred Craft of Linen-Workers, the Most August Work-Center of Wool-Washers, the Most August Union of Fishers. . . . It followed that their internal organization should ape the high-sounding terminology of larger municipal bodies, the nomenclature of officialdom, and honors like . . . the award of gold crowns in their meetings.[9]

Agape, ed. L. De Lorenzi [Rome: Abbazia di S Paolo fuori le mura, 1983], pp. 201-38, here p. 204, n. 12), a meeting of clients with their patron in his house in the morning is not a parallel to what we find in 1 Corinthians 11.

7. Pace Barton, "Paul's Sense of Place," p. 242. For Paul, if there is a rite of passage or incorporation it is baptism.

8. Cf. R. MacMullen, *Roman Social Relations 50 B.C. to A.D. 284* (New Haven: Yale University, 1974), p. 73.

9. Ibid., p. 76. In addition, a craft association could have as many as a hundred members in a particular place, and so in regard to size as well the Christians may have appeared to outsiders as some sort of guild (cf. ibid., p. 82).

We have clear evidence of what club or association rules for banquet meetings were like in this era. D. E. Smith summarizes the more common rules as follows:

1) injunctions against quarreling and fighting; 2) injunctions against taking the assigned place of another; 3) injunctions against speaking out of turn or without permission; 4) injunctions against fomenting factions; 5) injunctions against accusing a fellow member before a public court; 6) specifications for trials within the club for inter-club disputes; 7) specifications for worship activities.[10]

Paul addresses nearly all of these concerns in this letter.

Smith goes on to argue that 1 Corinthians 11 should be connected with chs. 12–14 and that what Paul is discussing is a worship event that involves a meal, a *symposion,* followed by the religious acts described in chs. 12–14, this being the normal order of events in Greco-Roman ceremonial meals, including club meals.[11] A formal transition was marked between the meal and the drinking party by a wine ceremony, in which wine was poured out to the god. Smith suggests that the Christians substituted for this the cup of blessing of the Lord's Supper to mark this formal transition. After the transition (cf. Plato *Symposium* 176A), a hymn or chant would be sung to the god, and perhaps the god would be invoked as savior (cf. Athenaeus *Deipnosophists* 15.675b-c). The drinking party could then continue with entertainment or, for the more sober-minded, conversation, which was considered an essential feature of *symposia.* Plutarch, writing shortly after Paul's time, notes that proper conversation at such an occasion could focus on history, current events, lessons in philosophy or piety, or exhortations to charitable or brave deeds (cf. *Quaest. Conviv.* 697E). The conversation often was prompted by a guest teacher or Sophist.[12]

In many ways such a meal was an occasion for gaining or showing social status. And it might be in many regards a microcosm of the aspirations and aims of the culture as a whole. Paul's attempt to deconstruct the social stratification that was happening in the Lord's Supper goes directly against the tendency of such meals.[13] The *ekklēsia,* of course, was not exactly identical with an association.

The Christian groups were exclusive and totalistic in a way that no club nor even any pagan cultic association was. . . . [Baptism] signaled for Pauline converts an extraordinarily thoroughgoing resocialization, in which the sect was intended to become virtually the primary group for its members, supplanting all other loyalties. The only convincing parallel in antiquity was conversion to

10. Smith, "Meals and Morality in Paul," p. 323. Very striking are the rules of the guild of Zeus Hypsistos, a first-century-B.C. religious association in Egypt, which include prohibitions of factions *(schismata),* of "chattering" (cf. 1 Cor. 14:33ff.), and of taking fellow members to court (cf. 1 Corinthians 6).

11. If this is correct, then it would explain some of the chaos described in ch. 14: Some participants were inebriated.

12. Nero's usual practice was to call in the teachers of *sophia* after dinner to amuse the guests, who might include philosophers and rhetors. Cf. R. MacMullen, *Enemies of the Roman Order* (Cambridge: Harvard University, 1966), p. 59.

13. The association meals, though somewhat more democratic, still involved a pecking order in terms of seating and food.

Judaism. . . . Students of private associations generally agree that their primary goals were fellowship and conviviality. . . . The goals of Christians were less segmented; they had to do with "salvation" in a comprehensive sense.

On the other hand, the Christian groups were much more inclusive in terms of social stratification and other social categories than were the voluntary associations.[14]

The point is not that the *ekklēsia* was identical with such an association, but rather that the similarities were great enough that some Corinthian Christians could well have viewed the Christian assembly as some sort of association, perhaps even a cultic association, and might have behaved accordingly at Christian fellowship meals.[15] Furthermore, in the topics he advises the Corinthians on, Paul seems to be cognizant of the sort of rules set up in such associations. In his view, the sacred tradition concerning the Last Supper is recited specifically to encourage social leveling, to overcome factionalism created by stratification and its expression at meals, and to create unity and harmony in the congregation.

Paul's letters and Acts give little evidence that he preached and taught outdoors in some forum, agora, or theater and much evidence that he preached and taught indoors, whether in a synagogue, a private home, possibly in his own shop if he worked outside a home, or occasionally but rarely in a rented hall (Acts 19:9). Both Acts and the letters (cf. 2 Cor. 11:24) suggest that he started his ministry in a new city at the synagogue. This is hardly surprising since he was a former Pharisee and had excelled in Judaism. The synagogue was the one social location in a town without Christian assemblies where he could claim to have the social standing to speak and would have an audience ready to listen to a pupil of the famous Jerusalem teacher Gamaliel. That Paul was subjected to the lash five times by synagogue leaders for teaching things contrary to the Jewish faith (2 Cor. 11:24) tells us that he was allowed initially to teach freely in synagogues and that he persistently went back to Jewish worship meetings to teach.[16]

---

14. W. A. Meeks, *The First Urban Christians: The Social World of the Apostle Paul* (New Haven: Yale University, 1983), pp. 78f. Meeks also points out the similarity of the *ekklēsia* groups to the voluntary associations: Both were small and involved intense face-to-face interaction, with membership decided by free decision rather than birth, though trade associations had the prerequisite of involvement in a particular trade.

15. Cf. E. A. Judge, *The Social Pattern of Christian Groups in the First Century* (London: Tyndale House, 1960), pp. 44f.:

There need be no doubt that . . . they were not distinguished in the public's mind from the general run of official associations. Like many others they could be labelled conveniently from the god whose patronage they claimed. "Christites" is certainly not the sort of name they would have chosen for themselves. . . . The term *ecclesia* (sc. meeting) itself, and the names for the various officials may have developed special connotations within the Christian community, but to non-Christians, and to Christians themselves in the early stages, they need have suggested nothing out of the ordinary.

Cf. Pogoloff, *Logos and Sophia*, pp. 248ff.

16. This makes it clear that whatever one makes of Paul being "the *apostolos* to the Gentiles," to him it did not mean that he was not called to preach to Jews as well. Indeed,

Apart from Acts 14:8ff. and Acts 17, there is little evidence of Paul standing on street corners hawking the Word of God. Instead, the evidence suggests that he began in synagogues and then progressed to private homes for his speaking venues.

It required a certain amount of public recognition and social standing to be asked to speak in a public venue such as a theater or gymnasium or at the games or in a court of law. In the Greco-Roman world

> the private home was a center of intellectual activity and the customary place for many types of speakers and teachers to do their work. Occasional lectures, declamations and readings of various sorts of philosophical, rhetorical and literary works often took place in homes. Such sessions might be continued for two or three days.[17]

Only Cynic preachers normally stood on street corners and accosted people, often also begging. The evidence does not suggest that Paul followed this practice. The Sophists were normally visiting lecturers, ambassadors, and dinner conversationalists, but until a Sophist gained a notable public reputation, he would not be asked to speak in a public forum. Young rhetors could be heard declaiming in some public locations, hoping to get someone to hire them as their advocate in court, but Paul was not seeking that kind of attention or employment.

The one other place besides the synagogue where Paul might be granted the social status to speak to a ready audience would be the private home of a reasonably well-off person. That Stephanas and his household were the first converts in Achaia and were baptized by Paul (1 Cor. 16:15; 1:16), that Gaius hosted Paul and the whole *ekklēsia* in Corinth, and that the public official Erastus sent greetings through Paul (Rom. 16:23) strongly suggest that Paul not only stayed with reasonably well-to-do converts but also preached and taught in their homes. This is one probable reason that his insistence on working at a trade and his refusal of some kinds of patronage galled some Christians in Corinth.

Stowers concludes from all this that

> the earliest Christian teachers did not organize themselves into academies as did the Rabbis and reach a consensus, but usually followed the pattern of the Greek philosophical or rhetorical teachers.

> It is no accident that patrons, households, and house churches are so prominent in the letters of Paul the missionary. As a . . . social context for preaching the Gospel, the private house offered certain advantages over preaching in syn-

---

the evidence suggests that he preached to Jews *first* in each new location (cf. the various visits to the synagogue first in Acts to what Paul says in Rom. 1:16). Paul understood his commission to mean that he was to go to the Gentile nations and be a church planter there, and in his mind this meant preaching to all and sundry in such places, being the Jew to the Jew, and the Gentile to the Gentile. What was new was his concentrated effort to recruit many Gentiles to the faith.

17. S. K. Stowers, "Social Status: Public Speaking and Private Teaching: The Circumstances of Paul's Preaching Activity," *NovT* 26 (1984), pp. 59-81, here p. 65; cf. Epictetus *Diss.* 3.23.33; Seneca *Ep.* 76.4; Pliny *Ep.* 3.18; Dio Chrysostom 77-78.34.

agogues and public places. . . . Speaking in public places often required things which Paul did not possess or would find difficult to obtain, such as an invitation, a sponsor, an audience and credentials as a certain type of speaker corresponding to a specific genre of speaking event. Above all, speakers needed some type of social status or recognized role. An invitation to teach in someone's house would provide Paul with all of these things and give his preaching activity a kind of stability and security which the explosive situation of the synagogue or the competition of public speaking could not offer.

In light of the contemporary practices of sophists and philosophers, this use of the house is not unusual, but rather an accepted and recognized way of doing such things.[18]

Paul begins by expressing mock disbelief that factiousness could be happening when the Lord's Supper is shared (v. **18**). It is not that he does not believe it, only that such division is a monstrous violation of Christian unity, however common the behavior may have been in pagan contexts. It was not an uncommon rhetorical move to express incredulity in this fashion, knowing very well the particular charge was true. For example, Demosthenes says, "I am at a loss to know whether I should believe or disbelieve the news Menecrates brings me" (*Ep.* 4.1), using almost the exact same Greek formulation as Paul. The function of such a statement is to shame the audience, since it implies that the behavior in question is so inappropriate that the report of its occurrence should not be true and that a charitable person would hardly credit such a report.[19]

Mention of an oral report ("I hear") this far into Paul's series of arguments shows that he is not simply arranging his arguments according to a schema of response to first oral and then, beginning in ch. 7, written reports. Perhaps his rhetorical strategy is to deal first with the presuppositions that are creating division (chs. 1–4), then with the ethical and social problems created by — and creating — division, and finally in ch. 15 with the theological problem fostering division. But a better way to view Paul's strategy is to say that after treating the foundational issue of wisdom in chs. 1–4, he then deals with boundary issues, where the *ekklēsia* meets the world, through ch. 10, turning then to "in-house" matters, matters affecting the community when it gathers for worship and fellowship.[20]

18. Stowers, "Social Status," pp. 73, 68, 70.

19. Cf. Dio Chrysostom 24.3; 48.5 for incredulity as a shaming device. Quintilian says a rhetor should not be quick to believe a rumor or common report because it may be based on "vague talk based on no sure authority, to which malignity has given birth and credulity increase, an ill to which even the most innocent of persons may be exposed" (*Inst. Or.* 5.3.1).

20. So M. M. Mitchell, *Paul and the Rhetoric of Reconciliation* (Tübingen: Mohr, 1991), p. 152.

In v. **19** Paul seems to be alluding to a tradition, perhaps a traditional saying of Jesus, according to which there must be divisions so that the real Christians can be discerned in the end. J. Jeremias points to both Matt. 10:34-37 (or 24:9-13) and an extracanonical saying of Jesus found in Justin, the *Didascalia,* and elsewhere: "There will be divisions (*schismata,* see above on ch. 1) and dissensions *(haireseis).*"[21] Paul uses both words, *schismata and haireseis,* to describe what was happening among the Corinthian Christians (vv. **18f.**). Paul believes his listeners are living in the eschatological age when such divisions will arise so that true believers may be discerned.

The divisions manifested among the Corinthians when they gather for worship are probably those that Paul has mentioned in ch. 1. Theissen is probably right in saying that these divisions are between the relatively well-to-do and the poor.[22] Some are going hungry at the communal meal, while others are gorging themselves and getting drunk (v. **21**). Here is more evidence that the main troublemakers for Paul in Corinth are the more well-to-do Gentiles who continue to follow the social conventions of the larger pagan culture, here in regard to dining and drinking. *Hairesis,* from which we get our word "heresy," did not have that later technical sense. It referred, rather, to sociological divisions. The Corinthians were assuming that, as at a pagan feast, it was proper in celebrating the Lord's Supper to separate or distinguish between wealthier and poorer Christians.

Paul takes the side of the poor or weak and argues against the strong or rich. They, the hosts for these Christians meals, would be responsible for the protocol followed at the meals. V. **20** mentions times when the Christians come together in one place, which suggests that they do not always meet in this way and that an occasion for doing so was the Lord's Supper. The Supper was celebrated after a normal meal, in the midst of such a meal, or even in two parts before and after the meal. That some were drunk when it was celebrated (v. **21**) suggests that it came after the meal, and perhaps also after the drinking party as well.

It may be that the wealthy are going on ahead with the meal without the poor, who arrive late after work and therefore go without. This understanding depends on a translation of *ekdechesthe* in v. **33** as "wait for," which is perfectly possible.[23] But more likely is the suggestion that the wealthy are eating in the *klinē* (dining room) while the poor are eating in the atrium and that two sorts

---

21. J. Jeremias, *Unknown Sayings of Jesus* (London: SCM, 1957), pp. 59-61.

22. G. Theissen, *The Social Setting of Pauline Christianity: Essays on Corinth* (Philadelphia: Fortress, 1982), pp. 145-74.

23. It also depends on stressing *prolambanei* ("take before") in v. **21**; cf. S. Scott Bartchy, "Table Fellowship with Jesus and the 'Lord's Meal' at Corinth," in *Increase in Learning: Essays in Honor of J. G. Van Buren,* ed. R. J. Owens and B. E. Hamm (Manhattan: Manhattan Christian College, 1979), pp. 45-61.

of food are being served, as was customary at ancient pagan banquets. *Ek-dechomai* often has the sense of "welcome" or "entertain" when it is used in the context of an act of hospitality (cf. 3 Macc. 5:26; Josephus *Ant.* 7.351). At any rate, whether the problem is timing or location, the result is a split in the congregation between haves and have-nots.

Paul does not mean in v. **21** that literally "everyone" has his or her own meal, since some of the have-nots are, in fact, going without. He probably means that those whom he is particularly addressing, the hosts and the wealthy in Corinth, have their own dinners. Much depends on how we take the verb *prolambanei.* Does it mean "go before" or "anticipate," in which case the wealthy were eating before others, or does it mean simply "take," that is, "eat"? Lexical evidence favors the former, but even so the point may not be that some poor people are arriving late, but that while all are already present the wealthy are being served first and are receiving the better portions, and then the poor in the atrium get what is left over.[24] The result is that one gets gorged and drunk while another goes hungry. This hardly amounts to a shared and common meal. Paul's main concern here as elsewhere in the letter is to remove obstacles to unity among the members of the Corinthian congregation.

Verse **22a** shows plainly that the problem is with the well-to-do, who have houses large enough to have their own feasts. Paul does not try to rule out such sumptuous banquets; his point is that pagan rules of protocol do not apply when one meets at the Lord's table. The better-off Christians are showing no respect for the have-nots and humiliating them and thus showing no respect for the *ekklēsia* of God, which is supposed to be a united body.

Part of Paul's way of correcting the abuses is to remind the Corinthians of traditions concerning the Lord's Supper that they and he share. In v. **17** he uses the technical language of Judaism for the passing on of sacred traditions. This suggests there was a systematic transmission of at least some of the Jesus material. This is only what we would expect since the earliest Christians were all Jews. When Paul says that he received these traditions "from the Lord" (v. **23**), he is referring to the origin of these words and not implying that they

---

24. Cf. the remarks of J. Murphy-O'Connor, *St. Paul's Corinth: Texts and Archaeology* (Wilmington: Glazier, 1983), pp. 158f.:

> The mere fact that all could not be accommodated in the triclinium meant that there had to be an overflow into the atrium. It became imperative for the host to divide his guests into two categories: the first class believers were invited into the triclinium while the rest stayed outside. Even a slight knowledge of human nature indicates the criterion used. The host must have been a wealthy member of the community and so he invited into the triclinium his closest friends among the believers, who would have been of the same social class. The rest could take their places in the atrium, where conditions were greatly inferior.

came in a direct revelation to him,[25] which is ruled out by the similarity of the Lord's Supper tradition found here to that found in Luke.[26]

Two forms of the Lord's Supper tradition are found in Mark and Matthew, on the one hand, and in Luke and Paul, on the other hand.[27] Luke preferred over the version he saw in Mark either Paul's or one deriving from a common, perhaps Antiochian, tradition. Only Paul and Luke indicate that the bread is to be taken "in remembrance" of Jesus, and Paul alone has the same clause in reference to the cup (vv. 24f.). "Given for you" is also found only in the Pauline/Lukan version. This clause probably alludes to Isa. 53:12 and indicates that Christ gave his body on the believer's behalf or in the believer's place. Only Paul says that Christians are to celebrate the Lord's Supper as often as they drink of the wine cup. Not all meals involved wine, and for many it was only for special occasions. Paul's version is the earliest record we have of the Lord's Supper tradition, but Paul only selectively quotes the tradition to make his point about the abuses in Corinth.

Verse 23 makes it clear that the tradition of the Lord's Supper involved a historical memory, which immediately distinguishes the Lord's Supper from all pagan memorial meals. It was not uncommon for those who could afford it to leave in their will a stipend and stipulation for an annual memorial feast in their honor. Diogenes Laertius records (10.16-22) that Epicurus left provision for an annual celebration "in memory of us." The Corinthians may have seen the Lord's Supper as such a funerary meal. But the tradition as Paul records it shows that what Jesus did at the Last Supper was not to institute a funerary rite. The word "new" is fatal to the view that Jesus' words recorded here in vv. 24f. were intended to be his last will and testament. *Diathēkē* is, rather, a reference to the founding of a new covenant relationship, probably by Christ's death. Thus the remembering that occurs in the Lord's Supper is not merely an occasional, perhaps annual, memorial service for Jesus. Something more positive is involved, namely, the proclamation of the dying but risen Lord, of what he has done for believers through his death and resurrection, and of his death "until he comes" (v. 26).

That Jesus was betrayed or handed over (*paredideto*, v. 23, can mean either) marks off the Lord's Supper from all pagan celebrations focused on some myth. Reference to this fact also recalls that one of Jesus' own disciples handed him over — in the context of a meal meant at least in part to stress loyalty to Christ and the forgiveness received from him.[28]

25. *Apo* here indicates source.
26. Cf. C. Senft's attempt to compare Paul's version to Mark's in *La Premiere Épître de Saint-Paul aux Corinthiens* (Neuchâtel: Delachaux and Niestle, 1979), p. 151.
27. Cf. the chart in G. D. Fee, *The First Epistle to the Corinthians* (Grand Rapids: Eerdmans, 1987), p. 546.
28. Ibid., p. 549.

The Lord's Supper stands out from Passover in that it celebrates a human person and his final deeds on earth, while the Passover celebrates divine actions — the Exodus-Sinai events. Jesus broke the bread after giving thanks, but this does not prove that he was celebrating a Passover meal, since thanksgiving over bread was a part of every Jewish meal.[29] Jesus probably modified the Passover traditions, though the Passover also had elements with symbolic significance, such as the bread of haste and the bitter herbs.

The tradition as cited by Paul does not associate the breaking of the bread with the breaking of Jesus' body (despite the later textual variants). The Supper is not a reenactment of the Passion.[30] Similarly, Paul does not specifically link the cup to Jesus' blood, but calls it "the cup of the new covenant." The covenant was "in [Jesus'] blood," that is, it was instituted by Christ's death. Jesus did not ask the disciples to drink blood, and this would have been, at any rate, something against which a Jew would react with horror. Accordingly, Paul says nothing about the wine representing Christ's blood.[31]

Paul stresses that the celebration of the Supper entails not only eating and drinking but also the proclamation of Christ's death until he returns (v. 26). It looks to the past, the present, and the future.[32] It may well be that *marana tha*, which probably means "Our Lord, come," was an integral part of the Lord's Supper for early Jewish Christians.[33] The Lord's Supper is then part of the Christian witness to the crucified, risen, and returning Lord. The mention of the Lord's coming prepares the way for the discussion of judgment in vv. 27ff. It is part of Paul's plan to persuade the Corinthians to add a "not-yet" to their eschatological "already."

The reference in v. 27 is to Christ's actual crucified body, as the reference to blood makes clear. With "unworthy" Paul refers to those who are partaking in an unworthy manner, not to persons who are themselves unworthy.[34] The examination called for in v. 28 is to be one's consideration of how properly to partake of the Supper, not an introspective assessment of one's worthiness to partake. Those who partake in an unworthy fashion, abusing the meal, are liable or guilty in some sense of the body and blood of the Lord. They are partaking without discerning or distinguishing "the body" (v. 29). While here

29. Cf J. Jeremias, *The Eucharistic Words of Jesus* (London: SCM, 1966), pp. 15ff.

30. The breaking of bread would not do this anyway, since none of Jesus' bones were broken.

31. This is found in the Markan version of the Lord's Supper.

32. The present aspect is the present proclamation and perhaps also the presence of the risen Christ with the community.

33. See below on 16:22. That the letter concludes with this phrase may suggest that it was to be read when the whole congregation was assembled for the Lord's Supper.

34. Which would, of course, include everyone. One does not share in the Lord's Supper because one is personally worthy of doing so; it is a gift of God's grace.

"body" might refer to Christ's death, forgotten when one eats, it more likely refers to believers as the body of Christ.[35] Some of the Corinthian Christians are eating without taking cognizance of their brothers and sisters. They are, Paul might mean, thus guilty of standing on the side of those who abused and killed Christ — an atrocious sacrilege. Instead, they are to partake with their brothers and sisters as one body in Christ, rather than following pagan protocol.

Juridical language dominates and sets the tone for this entire section.[36] The Corinthians were bringing judgment on themselves, both temporal and eternal. Paul even says that because of their failure with regard to the Supper some have died (v. 30). He must have believed that he had some prophetic insight into the situation which we do not have. It was not the food that made them ill, but the judgment that came on them for partaking in the Supper in an unworthy manner. This disaster could be avoided, Paul believed, if they would simply examine themselves and their behavior before partaking. Perhaps Paul saw the judgment of illness as a temporal judgment meant to prevent the worse disaster of condemnation with the world of non-believers at the last judgment (vv. 31f.). Paul may view this temporal judgment as not final, but remedial or disciplinary in character.[37]

Verse 33 provides a final word of remedial advice — *ekdechesthe* may mean "wait for one another" here, a common meaning of the word, or more likely it means "welcome one another," that is, that all should partake together, with no distinctions in rank or food. The point of the Lord's Supper is not to satisfy hunger, and so it must not be treated as just another banquet (v. 34a).

Verse 34b lets us know that Paul had more to say on these matters, and demonstrates the very occasional or ad hoc character of his letters: They are not preconceived divine treatises, but occasional rhetorical arguments given in the heat of battle.

35. The least probable option is that the clause refers to one forgetting the sacramental presence in the elements and thus committing a sacrilege against the sacrament.

36. Even so, this is forensic language used deliberately, which simply shows once again that evaluation of the rhetorical thrust of a discourse must be directed to its function, not simply to the usual provenance of the language used in it.

37. Cf. 2 Cor. 6:9 and 1 Tim. 1:20 for *paideuomai* with the meaning "discipline."

Argument VII, Division 1: 12:1-31a

BODY LANGUAGE

Chapters 12–14 constitute a single rhetorical unit with a three-part argument. W. Wuellner takes 11:2–14:40 as one argumentative unit, which is possible,[1] but *peri de* in 12:1 would seem to mark a new topic within Paul's dealing with problems in Christian worship.[2] It is not clear whether this marker indicates another subject in the Corinthian letter to Paul or something that he has heard about orally. If 11:18 is any clue, it may be the latter.

It was characteristic of deliberative rhetoric to use examples or paradigms *(paradeigmata)*, and in 1 Corinthians 12 we have an often-used example, though Paul uses it in an unusual way. The image or metaphor of the body has a considerable history. One important instance is from M. Agrippa, who draws an analogy between the state and the human body in which the body's members or parts represent the quarreling parties or factions in the

---

1. W. Wuellner, "Greek Rhetoric and Pauline Argumentation," *Early Christian Literature and the Classical Intellectual Tradition*, ed. W. R. Schoedel, et al. (Paris: Beauchesne, 1979), pp. 177-88, here p. 187. Wuellner rightly argues that ch. 13 must be seen as a rhetorical digression that serves the purpose of amplification.

2. It is possible, as J. Smit has argued ("Argument and Genre of 1 Cor. 12–14," a paper given at a 1992 conference on rhetoric in Heidelberg), to see chs. 12–14 as an example of what we can call micro-rhetoric, i.e., an instance where a particular argument functions as a speech in itself and so has all the necessary rhetorical parts from *exordium* to *peroratio*. But while chs. 12–14 do constitute an argument, this argument is not a self-contained unit but is closely related to the material in the first half of ch. 11. Paul is not dealing with a new topic when he discusses prophesying in the congregation in ch. 14. And ch. 14 is not simply a different form of the same argument in ch. 12. Ch. 12 is primarily concerned with the unity of the body in the midst of diverse persons and gifts. Ch. 14 deals with how two of those gifts should function in such a way as to promote order, peace, and unity. To say that ch. 12 is really about prophecy and tongues is straining credulity, and calling 14:37-40 a *peroratio* for the whole section is not completely convincing.

Another analysis that tries to find the elements of a rhetorical piece in chs. 12–14 is that of B. Standaert, "Analyse rhetorique des chapitres 12 à 14 de 1 Cor.," in *Charisma und Agape,* ed. L. de Lorenzi (Rome: Abbey of St. Paul, 1983), pp. 23-34. His argument is somewhat more convincing. He maintains that ch. 12 should be seen as a *narratio* of the facts, ch. 13 as a *digressio,* and ch. 14 as an *argumentatio.* If this is correct, then the real argument does not come till ch. 14. But it appears better to say that ch. 12 is the general argument about gifts and their function in the body while ch. 14 amplifies the argument with regard to two particular gifts.

state. With this analogy he exhorts the revolting plebeians to cease their strife and be united with the patricians, submitting to their authority (cf. Plutarch *Cor.* 6; Dionysius of Halicarnassus *Ant. Rom.* 6.86; Livy 2.32). This deliberative argument against sedition speaks of a revolt of the hands, mouth, and feet against the stomach, which weakens the whole body.[3]

Strikingly, Paul's use of the argument moves in precisely the opposite direction. He urges the strong (probably the well-to-do) to give more honor and respect to the weak, and so cease *their* factious behavior.[4] It is the "more respectable members" (v. 24) to whom this argument is directed, since it is they who might be tempted to say to the weak "I have no need of you."[5] It was apparently the "respectable" who were enamored with the gifts of prophecy and tongues and were using them in self-serving ways in worship services.[6]

There is much debate as to whether the analogy with the human body is meant to stress the unity of the body to a fractured congregation or the diversity of gifts to a group enamored of one gift in particular, namely, speaking in tongues. As the text progresses it appears that Paul is concerned about both issues — both diversity in unity and unity in diversity. He thus uses the body analogy to resolve the difficult question of the relation of the one and the

---

3. For a helpful, full-length discussion of the use and development of this metaphor, cf. M. M. Mitchell, *Paul and the Rhetoric of Reconciliation* (Tübingen: Mohr, 1991), pp. 157-64. She is right in saying that the crucial point is that this metaphor or example had a history of use against factions, and that is precisely how Paul uses it as well.

4. Here I would strongly disagree with Smit, "Argument and Genre": Paul is not alluding to himself or to the *apostoloi* in general in this metaphor, but rather to the various members of the Corinthian Christian community, which includes no *apostoloi* but does include the weak. Vv. 22f. are a defense of the weak *in Corinth.* Paul identifies with them and defends them against the "more respectable members," a clear reference to those of higher status and income in the community, who were tempted to think that they, with their *gnosis* and gifts, could do without the "weak."

5. The language of honor and shame here surely has the social strata of Corinthian society in mind. Paul is talking about the *honestiores* and the *humiliores* in Corinth. See further below.

6. It is also useful to compare Epictetus *Diss.* 2.5.25f.:

What are you? A human being. If you see yourself as something else, it is natural for you to want to live to old age, to be rich, and to enjoy health. But if you regard yourself as human and as part of a whole, for the sake of the whole you may have to suffer illness, make a voyage and run risks, be in want, and even die before your time. Why then are you vexed? Do you not know that as the foot, if detached, will no longer be a foot, so you too, if detached, will no longer be part of humanity? For what is a human being? Part of a city: first that of the gods and humans, and then, that city that is very close to it, the city that is a miniature of the universal city.

For Paul it is the Christian *ekklēsia,* not the city, that is the subject of the analogy. This passage from Epictetus can be compared to what Paul says about himself in the tribulation catalogs in 1 Corinthians 4 and 2 Corinthians 11.

many. But it is not merely an analogy, since he believes that it describes a real supernatural entity: Christ's people bound to him and to each other by God's Spirit.

J. Neyrey has stressed the obvious connection between the social body of Christ and the individual bodies of the Corinthians in this letter.[7] This connection is clearest in 6:15, where Paul speaks of an act of sexual immorality committed by a Corinthian Christian as the uniting of the "members of Christ" with a prostitute. This connection between the corporate body and the individual's body is important because in order to unify the former Paul must restrict the behavior of the latter. That is, "control of the physical body is an expression of social control"[8] and is in particular a way of preserving the unity of the corporate body. Certain kinds of deviant behavior threaten the health, if not the existence, of the body of Christ, not just the moral health or well-being of the individual Christian.

Therefore, Paul's attempts to direct and regulate the head, mouth, hands, feet, and genitals of the Christians in Corinth arise not simply from concern for personal morality. He also seeks to protect the body of Christ from acts and attitudes that can harm it. In such a context, it is no accident that the climax of all the arguments in the letter has to do with the resurrection body (ch. 15). Paul is so concerned about bodily behavior not just because it affects the body of Christ now but also because the bodies of Christians will play a role in the new creation. The human body, as well as the human spirit or personality, is destined for redemption. What one does with one's body now has ecclesiological and soteriological implications.

Pneumatika and *charismata* are important terms in this passage, and both are used of "spiritual gifts." *Pneumatika* (12:1; 14:1) stresses the spiritual nature or source of a particular ability or gift, while *charismata* (12:4, 9, 28, 30, 31) stresses their nature as gift, that is, the unmerited character of these functions or activities. *Pneumatika* was apparently a favorite term for many of those Paul has been concerned about in Corinth, while *charismata* is Paul's own term, meant to bring these people back down to earth. He wants them to realize that the functions they have are unmerited gifts of God's grace. There is thus no room for egotism or boasting.

---

7. J. Neyrey, "Body Language in 1 Corinthians," *Semeia* 35 (1986), pp. 129-70. Like Malina and others, Neyrey is too dependent on the work of Mary Douglas, who has not really explored the contours of honor and shame in the world of Greco-Roman antiquity. Some of what she says is applicable to a Roman culture where there were indeed honor and shame conventions (e.g., the *cursus honorum* or the distinction of *honestiores* and *humiliores*). But some of what she says would be better applied to some OT texts, not to Paul's letters, and some does not apply at all.

8. Neyrey, "Body Language," p. 131.

Verse 1 reads like a slap in the face. Paul does not want his audience to be ignorant about the very things that the Corinthians thought they were most well-versed in — spiritual gifts.

Verses 2-3 have been seen by some as an intrusion into the argument. This is unfortunate because these verses are important. Though there are various possible interpretations of them, it is clear that Paul believes he is addressing mainly Gentile Christians who were in their past irresistibly drawn to pagan idols. What v. 2a suggests is an irresistible leading or draw-ing that contrasts with the leading and drawing of the Holy Spirit. Perhaps Paul is pointing to the inspired or ecstatic speech that took place in various forms of pagan worship. Though the idols were speechless, that does not mean there was no speech in pagan worship. Paul may be referring to the idea that demonic powers were the source of inspired speech in pagan temples and indicating that this sort of ecstatic speech leads one to curse Jesus. But the problem with this view is that *anathema* ("a curse upon!") as Paul uses it is basically a Jewish term. Bassler has, therefore, suggested, quite plausibly, that Paul is remembering what he himself said about Jesus before his conversion.[9] In the second century Pliny mentions pursuing a Roman policy of causing Christians to curse Christ, but it seems doubtful that this practice would be alluded to this early in the first century (but cf. Pliny 10.96.1-10).[10]

In pagan settings *anathema* usually referred to a votive offering, but among Jews it was used to translate Hebrew *ḥērem*, "ban" (e.g., Deut. 7:26 in the Septuagint). It seems unlikely that anyone was saying "cursed be Jesus" or "Jesus is cursed" in the Christian assembly, but one could imagine an ecstatic doing so in a pagan setting.[11] Apparently some of Paul's audience thought

---

9. J. M. Bassler, "1 Cor. 12:3 — Curse and Confession in Context," *JBL* 101 (1982), pp. 415-18; cf. Gal. 3:13f. Another possibility is that *anathema* here has its Greek meaning and that Paul is talking about a practice that took place in Corinth at a later period. The offering of votive lamps was a pagan practice, and such lamps with Jewish or possibly Jewish-Christian inscriptions have been found in Roman Corinth. The inscription on one of these lamps includes a reference to deceased humans as angels. Cf. J. A. Wiseman, "The Gymnasium Area at Corinth," *Hesperia* 41 (1972), pp. 1-42. This bears witness to the fact of syncretism in Roman Corinth. Could some Corinthian Christians have been offering votive lamps with Jesus' name on them, as a prayer, but in a pagan location? Less probable is a link between this verse and the curse tablets found at the Demeter temple, which all direct curses against particular people who lived in Corinth.

10. This passage from Pliny also mentions a distinction between sacrificial and non-sacrificial meat offered for sale in the *macellum*. The latter is called "innocent food," apparently because it does not entail eating blood and because it is distinguished from sacrificial animals, which are called *victimas*.

11. Cf. A. Strobel, *Der erste Brief an die Korinther* (Zurich: Theologischer, 1989), p. 185, who suggests that it might have been uttered in a mystery cult.

ecstatic speech was proof of inspiration by the Holy Spirit.[12] The point then of v. 3b is not that one cannot possibly say "Jesus is Lord" without the Holy Spirit, but that one cannot *confess* Jesus as Lord without the prompting of the Holy Spirit in the human heart. Throughout this section Paul stresses the agency of the Spirit and of God over against the agency of the individual human who does the speaking. Thus he speaks of the "manifestation" (*phanerōsis*, v. 7) of the Spirit, what is to be attributed ultimately to the Spirit, not to the human speaker. He does this to deflate the self-estimate of certain members of his audience.

Verses **4-6** are important because of their implicit trinitarianism. God is the source of grace gifts, ministries, and activities. The stress here is also on the variety of such gifts and activities. This is Paul's way of countering an overemphasis on one gift (tongues), or possibly two (tongues and prophecy). *Diakonion* does not have its later technical sense but means "service" or "ministry" here (v. 5). God is the one who is ultimately working all things in all believers. The believers are not the source of such gifts or actions. V. 7 further stresses that the gifts have been given to each, not primarily for each person's own edification but for the common good.

The three lists of gifts and functions in vv. **8-10**, 28, and 29f. (cf. 14:26) are representative, not exhaustive. Paul's point is simply to show that there are varieties of gifts. He does not explain or comment at any length on the gifts, except those that were causing problems in Corinth. We are not at all sure what some of these gifts were (e.g., the "word [or message] of wisdom/knowledge," v. 8). There are as many guesses as there are commentaries. In the first list Paul groups together gifts of instruction (wisdom and knowledge), then gifts of supernatural power (miracles, healings) and of inspired utterance (prophecy, tongues), but the other lists follow other orders, so a ranking of gifts is not the main issue here.[13] Tongues and interpretation of tongues are placed last in all three lists to deemphasize what the Corinthians were overemphasizing, not because it was not a valid or valuable gift. Paul does not call it the least of the gifts.

In v. **9** "faith" probably refers to a special sort of faith, perhaps miracle-working faith, such as that mentioned in 13:2. Otherwise it could not be predicated of only some. If there is a difference between "healings" and "miracles" (vv. 9f.), perhaps the latter refers to exorcism.[14] "Distinguishing of

12. The gift of speaking in tongues seems to be the real focus of the problem in Corinth in this regard.

13. It may be a subsidiary concern, at least in regard to the authority of the *apostoloi* (vv. 28f.) over all other sorts of gift bearers or functionaries in the *ekklēsia*. Ch. 14 may also suggest that Paul saw prophecy as the second most important gift to the body.

14. On Paul as a healer, see pp. 466-67 below. Jas. 5:12-14 hints that there was a regular healing ministry in the early *ekklēsia*. Cf. *New Doc. 4*, p. 246.

spirits" (v. **10**) is probably an ability to discern whether an utterance comes from the Holy Spirit or from some other spirit. The reference to it may allude back to vv. 2f.

Paul's phrase "a kind of tongues" is important. As Héring points out, *glossai* ("tongues") was used of ancient or esoteric languages.[15] Plutarch uses it of the obscure but intelligible speech of the Pythia (*De Pythiae* 24.406). It is a term that in Corinth would likely connote something other than ordinary, contemporary, comprehensible speech or language, namely, speech in an unknown or forgotten language. It is nonetheless a sort of speech (cf. 13:2; 14:9, 14). I agree with Fee that Paul is talking about what he mentions in 13:2, namely angelic tongues.[16] This is why he calls it a *sort* of tongue, and such a tongue clearly requires interpretation to be intelligible.[17] *Intelligibility* is the reason that Paul prefers other gifts to speaking in tongues in public worship.

V. **11** reminds us that it is the Spirit, not the believer, who decides who gets what gift.

In vv. **12ff.** Paul embarks on his body analogy. Its function is to affirm the variety of gifts and the oneness of the body, neither at the expense of the other, and to defend the weak and redirect the misbehavior of the "more presentable" ones. "Christ" in v. 12c is a synonym for the *ekklēsia*, the *body* of Christ, and v. **14** stresses the multitude of body parts.

In v. **13** Paul is probably referring to conversion, not to what happens at water baptism (cf. Acts 8). The past tense shows that he is referring to what happens *once* to an individual, and "all" shows that it has happened to every Christian. There are no Christians without the Spirit. At conversion the Christian is united to the body by the Spirit and is given the Spirit to drink.[18] This drinking is in the past for the Corinthians, and in view of the verb tenses it is unlikely Paul sees it as occurring after baptism.

Verses **15ff.** contain Paul's modification of a popular fable. In one form of it the body's parts speak to one another (cf. Livy 2.32). The fable as we have it here indicates that no bodily part is without value or importance, so that the lack of any particular gift makes no one less a member of the body. The body does not consist of just one organ. It is, rather, made of a variety of interdependent parts, all of them necessary. Paul's stress here is on unity but also on the necessity of variety and diversity. It takes all kinds of parts to make

15. J. Héring, *The First Epistle of Saint Paul to the Corinthians* (London: Epworth, 1962), pp. 124ff.
16. G. D. Fee, *The First Epistle to the Corinthians* (Grand Rapids: Eerdmans, 1987), pp. 598f.
17. Interpretation of tongues is not to be confused with weighing or sifting of prophecy, which is mentioned in 14:29.
18. The image is both external and internal: The Spirit works on believers to unite them to the body and works in them as an ongoing source of life and spiritual sustenance.

up a body. To think otherwise is to criticize God, because, as v. 18 indicates, it is God who has placed the various members in the body. It is believers who are enabled and used by God; God is not used by them.

Verses 21ff. stress that no particular body member can devalue another or declare it to be of no worth. This then applies to people with gifts differing from one's own. In vv. 22-24 Paul speaks of the weaker, less honorable, and even indecent body parts, referring at least in the latter case to the genitals, while the weaker organs may be the tender inner organs. His point in v. 23 is that these seemingly less honorable parts get more attention, being protected with more clothing. The "presentable" parts by contrast would be those that are not clothed. God composed the body by giving the parts that were lacking in appearance even more honor, bestowing on them the most crucial of functions, that is, reproduction. With this Paul is alluding to weaker and perhaps less apparently gifted Christians. His point in any case in v. 25 is that differences or divisions (*schisma* again) in the body are avoided by making the body of multiple interdependent parts.

D. B. Martin rightly concludes that Paul's use of body imagery is at variance with usual use of such imagery. Instead of using it to support an existing social hierarchy where the lesser members of society serve the greater, Paul uses it to relativize the sense of self-importance of those of higher status, making them see the importance and necessity of the weaker, lower-status, Corinthian Christians. Paul questions the usual linking of high social status and honor by saying that God gives more honor to the "less presentable" members.[19]

A Closer Look: The *Honor* Roll in a Roman Colony ──────────

In order to understand the force of Paul's language in vv. 22-24 one needs to understand something about the *cursus honorum,* the pecking order of power and dignity in a Roman colony.[20] Broadly speaking the Romans divided society into two groups with regard to honor: the *honestiores,* or privileged and "honorable" strata of society, and

---

19. D. B. Martin, "Tongues of Angels and Other Status Indicators," *JAAR* 59 (1991), pp. 563-69. Martin rightly concludes that Paul's primary rhetorical strategy in this letter is to identify in part with the high-status members of the congregation in order to get them to change their behavior and attitudes toward the lower-status Christians in the community.

20. Properly speaking the *cursus honorum* was a hierarchical list of local officials, whereas the *honestiores* would include both such officials and other people. Cf. A. D. Clarke, *Secular and Christian Leadership in Corinth* (dissertation, Cambridge University, 1991), pp. 14ff. On all the matters treated in this section, see P. Garnsey, *Social Status and Legal Privilege in the Roman Empire* (Oxford: Clarendon, 1970), pp. 221ff.

the *humiliores*, who did not qualify for reasons of birth, lack of wealth, or possibly education to be among the elite.

Senators and equestrians were in general at the top of the hierarchy of Roman honor, dignity, and power, but in a Roman colony such as Corinth a senator or equestrian was rarely to be found. Next in line were officials called *decuriones* who were members of city councils. They held the office of the duumvirate, and in Corinth the *duoviri* were basically the top officials. Roman Corinth was a city first populated primarily by veterans and freed former slaves (cf. Strabo *Geo.* 8.6.23C). Veterans could be said to have the same honor as *decuriones*, and in the colonies they not infrequently held the top adminstrative posts. They were also given at least partial immunity from taxation as well as gifts of land in lieu of money when they mustered out. "Veterans were socially and politically prominent in the main in smaller cities of recent foundation. . . ."[21]

Below the veterans, if a city had veterans, would have been a variety of officials such as aediles, who in Rome were minor magistrates, but in a colony could play a larger role. Not only did one have to pay a good deal of money to serve in public office in a Roman city, but one was also expected to perform various "liturgies" or services to the city. "To the Romans the source of legal privilege was *dignitas* (honor, prestige). *Dignitas* was derived from political position or influence, style of life (character, moral values, education, etc.) and wealth. Each of the privileged groups . . . possessed these attributes in some measure."[22] Among other benefits, being among the *honestiores* exempted one from the death penalty, with rare exceptions (revolt against the government, for example). Roman citizenship did not automatically put one in the upper echelon of society, among the *honestiores*, though citizens had more "honor" and therefore more privileges than noncitizens. Noncitizens could be arrested, beaten, and imprisoned, but "it was potentially dangerous to give citizens the same treatment."[23] The *honestiores* and the *humiliores* were not large homogeneous groups. Furthermore, in a new and mercantile city like Roman Corinth, money talked, and the *nouveau riche* could buy their way into public office, at least the lower offices like that of aedile. There were therefore various sorts of status indicators in Corinth, and money was a very important one.

When Paul speaks of the "more presentable ones" who do not need extra honor (v. 24), he is likely referring to the socially more elite Christians, who would include the likes of Erastus and perhaps Gaius (Rom. 16:23). They may have been freedmen or veterans or the sons of such who had prospered in a situation where considerable upward mobility was possible. At least some of these people were by their behavior not only belittling but humiliating some of the *humiliores*. Paul seeks to correct this in various ways, here by using the "body politic" example in a surprising new way.

Some Corinthians no doubt saw themselves in a very individualistic light as sufficient to themselves, especially in spiritual matters. Paul is disputing such

---

21. Garnsey, *Social Status,* p. 249.
22. Ibid., p. 258.
23. Ibid., p. 268.

notions. God has deliberately made the members of Christ's body interdependent so that all would have concern for the others (v. 25). The suffering, or otherwise, of one member affecting all is an obvious illustration (v. 26). That this is an analogy is evident, since it is not always true that one believer rejoices at another's good fortune. That is how the body ought to react, however.

Paul, unlike the Stoics or Seneca, uses the body imagery to speak not of a natural unity of all humans or of the republic, but of a community that is a supernaturally created unity with diversity, the product of God's creative Spirit. As Theissen points out, one can tell where Paul's points of emphasis lie by the way he modifies this traditional image. For example, "schism" in the body (v. 25) is alien to the traditional body metaphor and pinpoints Paul's problem, which is divisions and factionalism.[24] The allusion to the threefold character and unity of God in vv. 4-6 is another model for unity with diversity in the community of God.

Verse 27 makes the point directly: "You are the body of Christ, and individually members of it." Paul does not mean that believers are actually Christ's physical body, which Paul believes is in a glorified state in heaven. He also does not dissolve the individual into the whole. One remains an individual though one is part of the whole Body of Christ.

In vv. 28ff. there is a twice-repeated ranking of three church roles — *apostoloi*, prophets, and teachers. It is not clear whether they are ranked in order of authority or of responsibility in founding or maintaining churches. The functions of all three roles are carried out by proclamation of the Word. The rest of both lists (v. 28 and vv. 29f.) is not of persons but of functions, and there is no indication that the ranking continues (from most to least important or in any other way) with these functions. They are given as simply a representative listing to show the diversity of the body. There is also no hint of the idea that the first three roles are itinerant and the rest local. Probably only the "agents" or *apostoloi* as church planters were seen as itinerant, and perhaps some of the prophets and teachers on occasion. The important word *kybernēseis* is often unfortunately translated "administration." It really refers to those who give guidance or wise counsel.

The second of these two lists (vv. 29f.) is given in the form of rhetorical questions, each beginning with *mē* and so expecting a negative answer. Not all have the same gifts. Paul urges the Corinthians in v. 31 to seek earnestly or be eager for the greater gifts, the intelligible ones that build up the body. They are greater only because they more easily function to strengthen the body. V. 31b does not refer to love as another gift. It is, rather, an "incomparable way," the proper way and context in which all gifts should be exercised. The

24. G. Theissen, *Psychological Aspects of Pauline Theology* (Philadelphia: Fortress, 1987), p. 271.

verb *deiknymi* could mean "reveal" because the truth about love had not dawned on some Corinthians, but it more likely means "show" and would be a cue to the rhetorically adept that Paul was about to shift rhetorical gears.

Paul's use of the body metaphor to speak of the Christian community in Corinth implies that he believes that God the Holy Spirit bequeaths to each Christian community all the gifts and graces it needs to be what it ought to be. In addition, the lists of gifts in this chapter strongly suggest that God gives not only abilities but also persons as gifts to the community, whether *apostoloi,* prophets, teachers, or others.

But does God still do all these things for the *ekklēsia* today? We can certainly affirm that God provides amply for the modern Christian community, but in some ways the provision is different. For one thing, if we are to follow Paul's ideas on this matter, *apostoloi* were gifts given to the *ekklēsia* in its first two generations, but not since then. Paul assumes in 9:1 that an essential criterion for apostleship is to have seen the risen Lord during the period of his resurrection appearances at the beginning of the church age. Furthermore, Paul tells us that he was the last to see the risen Christ (15:8). While we can certainly talk about the passing down of the apostolic teaching through the ages of the *ekklēsia,* we cannot talk about the passing down of the apostolic office. "Apostolic succession," in the sense of a continued apostolic presence through a church office, is a myth, since no one after the initial witnesses can meet the essential criterion. *Apostoloi* were God's temporary gift to found the community of Christ, and this was probably already recognized by the end of the NT period, as Rev. 21:14 suggests (cf. also Acts 1:22). Neither "the twelve" nor "the apostles" (1 Cor. 15:5, 7) were a continual presence even in the first century.

But nothing in the NT suggests that any of the other persons as gifts or gifts to persons ceased with the early *ekklēsia.* Indeed, there is considerable evidence throughout the course of church history to the contrary. How might this conclusion be applied today?

Paul is apparently referring to all the Corinthian house congregations *collectively* as the body of Christ. This might well suggest that one particular local house church would not have all the gifts needed in that city to serve the purposes of Christ's body. Perhaps there is a lesson here for us. As many churches as we have in every city, none of them has all the gifts, graces, and human resources necessary to be the *ekklēsia* of God fully and adequately in that place. There is a warning here to every singular assembly that the "church" does not cease at its doorstep. Every local assembly needs every other local assembly to be complete. Just as gifted individuals cannot say to other Christians that they are unneeded, since no Christian has all God's gifts, so, too, this is apparently true with congregations as well. It is not accidental that different Christian faith traditions have specialized in manifesting different gifts. For example, not all truly Christian congregations have prophets or tongues speakers in them, but some do. Or again, some churches have especially nurtured the role of elder or deacon(ess).

My plea here is not just for tolerance or ecumenical cooperation and appreciation but also for recognizing that we all need each other. Paul is correcting abuses of various gifts in chs. 12–14, but to correct abuse of a gift is not to rule out its proper use. I suspect that Paul would tell us that just as "charismania," an overemphasis on prophecy or tongues, is not healthy, neither is "charisphobia," the anathematizing of all such gifts. We are not called to act in the chaotic and selfish fashion the Corinthians did, but we are also not called on to quench the Spirit and arrange Christian worship so that there is no room for the spontaneous Word from above to be shared. There is a balance between Spirit and structure, order and spontaneity, that should be maintained in any local congregation.

Finally, Paul's word about giving more honor to the weaker members of the body of Christ, the less "presentable" ones, needs to be heeded. He believes that even these folk have essential gifts and functions to exercise. It is a mistake to bring the world's evaluative system into the *ekklēsia* and to set up an honor roll that favors the more presentable and dignified, or those with the more outwardly showy or dramatic gifts. Paul believes that the body of Christ is only truly strong when it gives special honor and attention to its weakest members. The more presentable members do not need such attention.

Argument VII, Division 2: 12:31b–13:13

DISPLAYING LOVE'S WAY

1 Corinthians 13 has long been recognized as an epideictic showpiece,[1] and recent studies have also noted "its highly rhetorical . . . form."[2] It is characteristic of epideictic rhetoric to give more concentrated attention to elements of style. Commentators have long noticed the more elevated and almost poetic style of this chapter, but being unfamiliar with rhetoric have had no solid explanation for the change of style.

Chapter 13 is a digression.[3] Though it is an epideictic piece exalting love, it is used in a deliberative argument to exhort the Corinthians to let love be their guiding principle in all that they say and do and, more specifically, to stress the manner in which all gifts, such as those discussed in ch. 12, should be used.[4] It was not uncommon for a rhetor to insert in the midst of a forensic argument an epideictic excursus or digression focusing on presentation, not argumentation (cf. *Rhetorica Ad Herennium* 3.8.15; Quintilian *Inst. Or.* 3.7.1-4; 4.3.12-15). Quintilian tells us that a digression could be used for an emotional appeal (*Inst. Or.* 4.3.15-17), and there is something of that quality in this chapter. Strikingly, Paul signals that he will move into a demonstrative or

---

1. Cf. A. von Harnack, "Das hohe Lied des Apostels Paulus von der Liebe (1 Kor. 13) und seine religionsgeschichtliche Bedeutung," *Sitzungsberichte der preußischen Akademie der Wissenschaften* 1 (1911), pp. 132-63. For another older treatment of this passage as rhetoric, see J. Weiss, "Beiträge zur paulinischen Rhetorik," in *Theologische Studien*, ed. C. R. Gregory, et al. (Göttingen: Vandenhoeck und Ruprecht, 1897), pp. 165-247, here pp. 196-200.

2. C. A. Holladay, "1 Corinthians 13: Paul as Apostolic Paradigm," in *Greeks, Romans, and Christians*, ed. D. L. Balch, E. Ferguson, and W. A. Meeks (Minneapolis: Fortress, 1990), pp. 80-98, here p. 80. Unfortunately Holladay does not recognize that the differences between ch. 13 and the surrounding chapters is not between what is rhetorical and what is non-rhetorical, but between showpiece epideictic rhetoric and plainstyle deliberative rhetoric.

3. W. Wuellner, "Greek Rhetoric and Pauline Argumentation," *Early Christian Literature and the Classical Intellectual Tradition*, ed. W. R. Schoedel, et al. (Paris: Beauchesne, 1979), pp. 177-88, here p. 187. According to Wuellner this digression "amplifies by intensifying the point Paul leads up to with a series of seven rhetorical questions (12:29-30). . . . The three 'tokens of contrast' with which the digression opens (13:1-3) can be taken as three aversions from excesses generated by eagerness for manifestations of the Spirit (14:12)."

4. The chapter is, then, not about a gift of love as one gift among many, but about love as the modus operandi of all gifts.

epideictic mode in ch. 13 by using *deiknymi* ("show," "demonstrate") in 12:31, his only use of the verb in this letter.[5]

We have a clue already in 8:1 of how Paul intends "love" to serve as part of his larger deliberative argument for concord and unity in Corinth: "Love builds up." Building up is the opposite of divisive or factious behavior or, as Mitchell puts it, "love in 1 Corinthians is indeed Paul's positive counterpart to Corinthian factionalism."[6] Perhaps the whole argument in chs. 8–14 is aimed at making clear the truth stated in 8:1f. Chs. 8–10 then would demonstrate how (partial) knowledge puffs up, while chs. 12–14 show that love builds up.

The concept of love was often used in arguments for social concord and against factiousness (Polybius 23.11.3; Plato *Symposium* 197C-D; and especially Aristotle *Eth. Nic.* 8.1.4). John Chrysostom saw each clause of 1 Cor. 13:4-7 as an antidote for the sickness of Corinthian factionalism (*Hom.* 34.1, *NPNF* 1 XII, 201f.).[7] There is a sense in which this is clearly true. In vv. 1-3 tongues and prophecy are shown to be potentially divisive while love unites.[8] Then love is said to be *not* the very things that Paul has already said that the Corinthians are: jealous (cf. 3:3), self-promoting, puffed up (cf. 4:6), shameful (cf. 5:2; 11:4), each one a seeker of his or her own advantage (cf. chs. 8–10), easily provoked, and reckoners of wrongdoing (cf. ch. 6).[9]

But there is another element to this chapter. It not only targets specific Corinthian maladies but also presents Paul as an example of proper behavior, as did ch. 9.[10] This has been demonstrated by C. R. Holladay in a brilliant article that should lay to rest once and for all the idea that Paul intended ch. 13 as a paean of praise to an abstract ideal called "love."[11] This chapter is as much a "word on target" as the rest of the letter and an indirect means of chiding the Corinthians for their childish behavior (cf. 13:11 and 3:1).

Paul is not calling love the supreme gift, but rather the way of life for

---

5. Rightly, J. Smit, "Argument and Genre of 1 Cor. 12–14," a paper given at a 1992 conference on rhetoric in Heidelberg (p. 17 in the distributed manuscript). He also points to *Rhetorica ad Herennium* 2.30.47, which shows that each separate part of a speech may end with a *peroratio*. But I doubt that 1 Cor. 14:37-40 functions as such.

6. M. M. Mitchell, *Paul and the Rhetoric of Reconciliation* (Tübingen: Mohr, 1991), p. 165.

7. I am indebted to Mitchell, p. 169 and n. 631, for pointing out this reference.

8. This also prepares for the argument in 14:2-5, 29-32.

9. Rightly Mitchell, *Rhetoric of Reconciliation*, pp. 169f. I agree with Mitchell that factionalism is perhaps the main thing Paul is combating throughout this letter. "Enthusiasm" is most definitely one cause of this divisive behavior, so it is not an either-or matter.

10. In fact it was not unusual for epideictic rhetoric to involve self-presentation, but unlike the Sophists Paul is doing this not for the sake of self-promotion but in order to curb the Corinthians' factious and loveless behavior.

11. Holladay, "1 Corinthians 13," pp. 80ff.

Christ's agent. It is meant also to be the way of life for any Christian, the norm and guide for the exercise of all gifts. Only the first three verses might be called a love poem. Most of the chapter is exalted Greek prose, perhaps Paul's best.[12]

Many have noted what seems to be an abrupt shift in the middle of **12:31** from the second person plural to the first person singular, which continues in 13:1-3. The function of this shift is to prepare the audience for Paul's self-presentation as a personal example to illustrate his teaching.[13] His rhetorical method is basically the same in chs. 12–14 as in chs. 8–10: An example passage is placed in the middle of the argument and is signaled by the change of person and number. Ch. 13 is even more clearly marked off than ch. 9, since in 14:1 Paul suddenly shifts back to the second person plural.

This rhetorical strategy is commended by Quintilian as the way a rhetor should deal with his pupils:

> For however many models for imitation he may give them from the authors they are reading, it will still be found that fuller nourishment is provided by the living voice, as we call it, especially when it proceeds from the teacher himself. If his pupils are rightly instructed, he should be the object of their affection and respect. And it is scarcely possible to say how much more readily we imitate those whom we like (*Inst. Or.* 2.2.8; cf. Seneca *Ep.* 6.3-5; 71.7).

Ch. 13 is thus further confirmation that the major struggle in this letter is not between Paul and some opponents in Corinth. Nor is Paul seeking to establish his apostolic authority by this missive. Rhetorically it would be a very poor strategy for him to hold himself up as an example if he believed that he was not admired or was actually opposed by his audience. But Paul assumes that his authority is accepted and that he can present himself as a model.

His self-presentation as an enslaved leader in ch. 9 involved hyperbole, and 12:31b might mean "I will display a way, by means of hyperbole," if we take *hyperbolē* there in its technical rhetorical sense of a figure of speech that uses exaggeration to make its point (cf. Isocrates *Ep.* 4.88; Aristotle *Rhet.* 1413a29). There is an element of exaggeration in ch. 13: Paul is not really claiming to know all languages or all things.[14] I am inclined to accept this interpretation of 12:31b, but elsewhere Paul uses *kath 'hyperbolēn* adverbially to mean "superlative" or

---

12. The chapter may have existed before Paul put it to use here, but in view of its specific targeting of the Corinthian vices and its use of Paul as an example, this seems most unlikely.

13. Cf. Holladay, "1 Cor. 13," pp. 82f.

14. On this possibility, cf. ibid., p. 88.

"more excellent" (2 Cor. 1:8; Rom. 7:13; Gal. 1:13). If the rhetorical sense is granted in 1 Cor. 12:31, then Paul is saying that he will present himself as an example of self-sacrificial love in hyperbolic fashion.[15]

Chapter 13 naturally falls into three parts: vv. 1-3, 4-6, and 8-13. Fee's division of it into sections concerning the necessity, character, and permanence of love seems apt.[16] From the outset of this chapter, Paul strikes his listeners right in the heart. He begins by referring to their favorite gift, speaking in tongues (v. 1). It is difficult to be certain whether he envisions glossolalia as involving both human languages that one does not know and so is supernaturally endowed with and languages of angels, or just the latter. *Testament of Job* 48–50 provides extracanonical evidence of Jewish belief in an ecstatic gift of speaking in angelic languages. This was apparently also Paul's view.

This gift is unintelligible, and thus an analogy to sounding brass[17] or a clanging cymbal is appropriate.[18] Strikingly, Sophists were often caricatured in such language.[19] Holladay even suggests that when Paul speaks of the tongues of humans and angels he may be referring to the eloquence manifested by some rhetors.[20] This raises the question whether the Corinthians may have thought that human eloquence, as well as glossolalia and prophecy, was inspired by the Spirit. Paul, it will be remembered, while using rhetoric does so in an anti-Sophistic fashion. J. R. Levison suggests that

> Paul appears to disclaim rhetorical eloquence while at the same time writing with considerable rhetorical skill. This communicates that, although he appears to reject rhetoric, he is a masterful proponent of rhetoric. The true rhetoric to which Paul adheres is the studied rhetoric of the sage who pores

15. Cf. Paul's use of hyperbole, irony, and sarcasm in 2 Corinthians 10–13, where he engages in mocking self-commendation.

16. G. D. Fee, *The First Epistle to the Corinthians* (Grand Rapids: Eerdmans, 1987), p. 628.

17. Many have thought that this is an allusion to the Corinthian trade in brass vases, and possibly in brass acoustic jars used in theaters; cf. W. W. Klein, "Noisy Gong or Acoustic Vase?" *NTS* 32 (1986), pp. 286-89, but cf. Murphy-O'Connor, "Corinthian Bronze," *RB* 90 (1983), pp. 71-91. The word *chalkos* is never used in any ancient text for a musical instrument.

18. This is likely an allusion to the use of such instruments in pagan worship, particularly the cult of Cybele, which also was known for ecstatic speech. Paul then would be alluding to pagan practices the Corinthians knew and had possibly even participated in before. The point is that their current use of tongues was no more valuable or viable than that sort of pagan practice, *unless* the gift is exercised in love, i.e., not in public worship unless a known interpreter is present. Otherwise it is an act of self-indulgence and public display. See below on ch. 14.

19. Cf. Plato *Prt.* 329A; Pliny *Nat. Hist.* pref. 25 (a particular rhetorician is called a *cymbalum mundi*); Tertullian *De Pallio* 4.

20. Holladay, "1 Cor. 13," p. 92.

over ancient wisdom and turns of phrases, and who is renowned for instructive and persuasive speech.[21]

In v. 2 as well, Paul attacks the Corinthians who prophesied in abundance and who claimed to have inside knowledge of the mysteries of the Christian faith.[22] Paul says that if one has either of these gifts, or even the gift of miracle-working faith so as to move mountains,[23] without love one is still nothing. In v. 3[24] he says if he gives up all his possessions and then continues by giving his body to abuse so that eventually he will have something to brag about,[25] without love he is not helped or profited. Paul is combating here the false view of Christian spirituality present in Corinth and its consequences, which entailed a fractured community. For Paul the essence of true spirituality is self-sacrificial love, not gifts, knowledge, or miraculous power. At least some Corinthians were focused on power and ego and had a different view of the real heart of Christianity. Paul's point is that such egocentric behavior hurts not only others but also self. One has no profit without love. The argument here about "profit" or "benefit" points to a deliberative function of this otherwise epideictic chapter.

How does all this relate to Paul as an example? First, Paul later claims explicitly that he speaks in tongues (14:18). Second, Paul's prophetic status is apparent at various points (1 Cor. 2:2-16; 7:40; 14:37). Third, he claims both to know and to teach mysteries (cf. 2:1, 10; 4:1, 15:51; 2 Cor. 12:1-7) and to have special revelatory knowledge (1 Cor. 2:16). Fourth, Paul claims and Acts confirms that he was a miracle-worker (2 Cor. 12:12; Rom. 15:19; Acts 14:3; 16:16-24; 19:11; 28:3-6). In regard to a self-chosen poorer state, one must bear in mind what Paul says in ch. 9 about refusing patronage and working with his hands as an enslaved leader, as well as the tribulation catalog in 4:11f. (cf. also 2 Cor. 6:3-10). In regard to Paul boasting, besides what he says in chs. 4 and 9, one will think of the mocking self-commendation in 2 Corinthians 10–13.[26]

To some extent, Paul's hyperbole, especially in vv. 1-3, is a mocking of

21. J. R. Levison, "Did the Spirit Inspire Rhetoric?" in *Persuasive Artistry*, ed. D. F. Watson (Sheffield: JSOT, 1991), pp. 25-40, here p. 40. While affirming the Jewish sapiential component of Paul's rhetoric, I would suggest that its specifically Christian content is to a large extent revelatory in character, not the wisdom of long hours of study of the ancients.

22. Or *mystēria* might refer to secret rites. Is this an allusion to baptism for the dead (cf. 15:29)?

23. Surely an allusion to the Jesus tradition (Mark 11:25 par.).

24. Again alluding to Jesus' teaching (cf. Matt. 19:21 par.).

25. For the abuses Paul suffered for the gospel, see 2 Cor. 11:23-29; 12:10. On the positive use of boasting, see 2 Cor. 1:14; Rom. 5:2f.

26. Cf. also 2 Cor. 8:24; Phil. 2:16; 1 Thess. 2:19; 2 Thess. 1:4. On all the above, see Holladay, "1 Cor. 13," pp. 88-91.

the Sophistic boasting going on among the inspired and eloquent ones in Corinth.

> The hyperbole recasts the self-portrait so that each item is stretched to the limit of incredibility because it is recast with the assumptions of the Corinthian enthusiasts. That is, even if he were to allow his apostolic work to be shaped by the assumptions of those Corinthians who are not content with speaking, but insist the apostle must speak with eloquence surpassing human capabilities . . . , yet . . . unmotivated by ἀγάπη it would be for nought.[27]

Paul ultimately believes that love, not freedom or knowledge, is the final watchword for Christians, both as a key to understanding the mysteries of the faith and as a guide to behavior.

The second paragraph (vv. 4-7) has often been taken as a description of Christ's character, which is true enough, but Paul intends it as a description of how a Christian ought to behave and of the way in which Paul has been attempting to behave. He contrasts blameworthy behavior, which seems to characterize the Corinthians, and the behavior that he is trying to model for his converts. It is clear from 10:24 that Paul expects all believers, not just leaders, to seek the good of others (cf. 10:33) rather than their own benefit. He operates with the philosophy that the leader's behavior should be exemplary in every sense of the word.[28]

For the NT writers love is a matter of behavior, not feeling. In particular it is other-directed behavior, not self-directed action. This is the character of Christian *agapē*. The word *agapē* is not uniquely Christian. Christians likely derived it from the Septuagint, where it is often used of God's love, not ordinary human love. It is a unique privilege to be a bearer, by means of the Spirit, of God's love. This love differs from both natural human affection (*philia*, so-called brotherly love) and *erōs* (desiring love, usually related to physical attraction).[29]

Paul calls this love "patient," or as the KJV has it, "long suffering." It is also "kind." These are the passive and active faces of Christian love: It puts up with a lot, but it also gives generously without thought of return. It is not the sort of love associated with jealousy or envy or Sophistic rivalries over teachers, where the love of one means enmity toward other teachers and their followers.

---

27. Holladay, "1 Cor. 13," p. 94.

28. In other words, he would have agreed with the thought behind Chaucer's query: "If gold rusts, what then will iron do?"

29. On this whole subject one should see the classic studies by C. Spicq, *Agape dans le nouveau testament* (Paris: Gabalda, 1958-59), and A. Nygren, *Agape and Eros* (London, 1932 and 1939). There is some obvious overlap between *agapē* and *philia;* cf. John 21:15-19.

It rejoices when someone else has a victory or triumph; it is not envious of that. It neither shows off nor is puffed up. Those who express Christian love are not self-inflated windbags.[30] Love does not behave indecently or in a way that is shameful. It does not seek its own ends, nor is it hot or quick-tempered.[31] It does not take account of or reckon evil: It keeps no record of wrongdoing. It does not delight in wrongdoing even against one's enemies. Rather it rejoices with the truth. It bears all. The specific thrust of the rest of v. 7 is difficult to determine. It probably means that if one has Christian love, then one's faith, hope, and endurance always keep going. It clearly does not mean that one is gullible, trusting all when there is no good reason to do so.

What Paul says in this paragraph goes directly against the enmity conventions that existed in the Greco-Roman world, which set up tremendous rivalries between Sophists, patrons, and officials, all of whom were striving for public recognition and honor. If one believes that honor is in limited supply and that one must have it above all else to amount to anything in one's city and culture, then one must be very possessive and particular in one's allegiances and must oppose others who are striving for the same goal of recognition.[32]

J. Weiss rightly saw that there is a sort of A-B-A structure to ch. 13: In vv. **8ff.** we return to language reminiscent of vv. 1-3.[33] The key to understanding how Paul addresses the problem in Corinth is that the Corinthians, or at least some of them, think that they are truly and perhaps fully "in the know" already. This comports with and is part of their realized eschatology. They have failed to realize that the knowledge and even the prophecy they have now are only partial, and that full knowledge only comes at the eschaton.

> The Corinthians have erred because they have reversed this fundamental eschatological truth. For them, essentially partial gifts possess finality, and these gifts are worth making ultimate claims about, when in fact ἀγάπη alone can be seen to possess such finality. . . . It is the only such reality to have invaded the now in any absolute sense.[34]

Verse **8** says literally that love never "falls to the ground," which likely means that it is never defeated or that it never fails. Other good gifts that are

---

30. *Physioutai,* as earlier in the letter (the verb in 4:6, 18f.; 5:2; 8:1), is clearly a jab at the Corinthians and probably at Sophistic rhetors.

31. Neither quick to take offense, nor slow to forgive when wronged.

32. See pp. 259-60 above on the "honor roll" in Corinthian society and P. Marshall, *Enmity in Corinth: Social Conventions in Paul's Relations with the Corinthians* (Tübingen: Mohr, 1987), pp. 10ff.

33. J. Weiss, *Der erste Korintherbrief* (Göttingen: Vandenhoeck & Ruprecht, 1925), p. 311.

34. Holladay, "1 Cor. 13," p. 97.

quite valuable, such as prophecy or knowledge, are specifically meant to equip the believer to endure in this age. In due course they will be brought to nothing. Tongues will cease when the Lord returns and completes his plan for Christians. Partial knowledge such as the Corinthian Christians now have will be brought to nought. Paul stresses "we know now but in part, but one day the completion of our knowledge of and relationship with God will happen." Then believers will know as they are known by God. Then they will see face to face.

The Corinthians are childish because, unlike Paul, they have mistaken the part for the whole and the partial for the final and in particular have overlooked the fact that while *love* already has finality here and now, knowledge is only in part. These verses are part of the larger rhetorical strategy to demonstrate the childish nature of the Corinthians' behavior and thinking throughout this letter (cf. 3:1ff.; 14:20).[35]

Verses 11f. should probably *not* be understood as saying that it is childish to speak in tongues or to prophesy, since Paul himself still does such things. He is saying that there is an age appropriate to such things and that now is that age. When the completion of the age finally comes, then it will be time to set aside what was appropriate and needful in that age. Only later will one know as one is known by God.

For now, Christians, even the most mature,[36] see through a glass or mirror *en ainigmati*, which can be transliterated as "enigmatically." The phrase may mean "obscurely," but its literal meaning is "in a riddle." Paul's point is not to castigate mirror-making, which was a trade practiced in Corinth. Nor were ancient bronze mirrors necessarily all that bad. His point is, rather, that as a mere image of the truth a mirror only partially tells the tale of what we look like. What we know of Christ, self, others, or salvation through the Spirit is not necessarily inaccurate, just incomplete. Some scholars have suggested plausibly that vv. 12a and 9b should be coordinated, in which case Paul would be referring in this image to the partial or fragmentary nature of prophecy. One may see a vision, but it is enigmatic and incomplete. This makes sense in light of what follows in ch. 14.[37]

The present tense of *menei* ("continue") in v. 13 could be interpreted in several ways. It could mean that faith, hope, and love will continue and remain into the age to come. But this is unlikely since elsewhere Paul speaks of faith and hope as being completed in the next age or life (cf. 2 Cor. 5:7 or Rom. 8:24). Rather we should take seriously the adversative *de* ("but") and the use

35. Ibid.
36. Notice the emphasis on "we" in this final section of ch. 13, where Paul places himself in the same eschatological situation as his converts.
37. Cf. below and R. E. Heine, "The Structure and Meaning of 1 Corinthians 13:8-13," in *Increase of Learning*, ed. R. J. Owens, et al. (Manhattan: Manhattan Christian College, 1979), pp. 63-72.

of the temporal *nyni* ("now") here. It is now, in this age, that faith, hope, and love are the three great qualities or attributes for the Christian. But love is the greatest because it alone never fails and will in fact carry on into the next life. Faith will become sight and hope will be fulfilled, but love will simply carry on, presumably amplified and purified into a perfect condition. It is the one attribute that is to bridge this age and the eschatological reality.[38]

A few words about the ethical implications of this passage are in order. An ethic motivated by Christian *agapē* is an ethic that defies calculation. T. Engberg-Pedersen puts it this way:

> One may in fact doubt whether the idea of equality as the result of a radical practice of ἀγάπη can in the end be made fully clear. What is a "material good"? How may goods be "compared"? Will supposed "needs" play any role in determining what makes shares equal? And there is the general point . . . that ἀγάπη can never be equated with an attitude that is directed toward creating equality. Ἀγάπη is an attitude of radical and completely selfless concern for others, which cannot be readily combined with concepts like rights or fairness, both of which imply that the person has certain legitimate claims *for* himself. Ἀγάπη, by contrast, requires that in his relation with others a person goes the whole way in their direction.[39]

The setting of ch. 13 makes evident that Paul is not talking about "natural" human love, but of a sort of love that a human being can only express and share when he or she has been touched by God's grace and enabled by God's Spirit. It goes quite against natural human inclinations to love the unlovely or those who do not love in return. *Agapē* love, as V. P. Furnish has aptly said, is not the sort of love that is dispatched like a heat-seeking missile due to something inherently attractive in the "target."[40]

---

38. Note the profoundly social character of the love that Paul is speaking about. In all these verses Paul is talking about love in action, not mere feelings. Real Christian love does not amount to mere pious platitudes about love, but doing love. Nor is Paul exhorting his audience to have warm feelings about others, since he believes that one can love someone that one does not feel attracted to or even like. The Corinthians wanted to exalt what they *knew,* but Paul lifts up what they should be *doing* for each other. This included, among other things, not keeping any personal record of wrongdoing, and on the other hand taking on the role of a servant and helping others, even those of lower social strata. Paul is asking the Corinthians to go against the grain of the social attitudes of Corinthian culture, which encouraged striving for personal status and seeking to get oneself out of any position where one would have to serve others. Were a person really to follow Paul's teaching here, one would find it to involve a humbling and in some ways even humiliating experience, as 4:9ff. shows Paul himself had found it to be.

39. T. Engberg-Pedersen, "The Gospel and Social Practice," *NTS* 33 (1987), pp. 557-84, here p. 574.

40. On this whole subject, cf. V. P. Furnish, *The Love Command in the NT* (Nashville: Abingdon, 1972).

Because Paul believes that this love is something that only God can give and does give in Christ, he also believes that Christians like himself can manifest such love. His call to imitate himself and Christ (11:1) is based on the assumption that both he and Christ act on the basis of the grace of God, which is in Christ. This love is neither conditional nor generated by circumstances, but is often best seen when the circumstances are not favorable or likely for its expression.[41]

41. It has been said that we become like those we admire. The early Christian writers who saw in this passage a portrait of Christ were not far wrong — here is a description of how Christians may imitate Christ. It is important to bear in mind that Paul expects that all that Christians say and do they will say and do with one eye on the eschaton. This means always realizing that perfection is not to be had in this life. Christians know, believe, and hope only in part, but when they love they comes closest to approximating the eschatological state and the character of Christ.

Argument VII, Division 3: 14:1-40

The Agony of the Ecstasy

To this point in Paul's discourse, he has used a variety of rhetorical techniques and arguments to overcome the divisions and factionalism that existed in Corinth. As W. Wuellner reminds us, this was not just a matter of transformation of various individuals into a unity.[1] "Paul works also for the transformation of the multiplicity of different social and ethnic/cultural value systems into a unity," that is, "a new social order."[2] We have seen how much certain cultural assumptions affected the Corinthian Christians' practice of worship (e.g., the Lord's Supper). We should ask, therefore, whether they may have viewed prophecy and tongues as they were viewed in the larger pagan culture, particularly since in 12:1f. Paul has drawn an analogy between pagan and Christian ecstasy, or between the ways in which people are led by the spiritual forces behind pagan and Christian religion.[3]

In ch. 14 Paul returns to a fully deliberative form of argumentation, and in vv. 6-19 he continues to make a personal appeal, setting himself up as an example, as in ch. 13.[4] The flow of the argument in chs. 12–14 is from the

---

1. Pace W. A. Meeks, *The First Urban Christians: The Social World of the Apostle Paul* (New Haven: Yale University, 1983), p. 159.

2. W. Wuellner, "Paul as Pastor: The Function of Rhetorical Questions in First Corinthians," in *L'Apôtre Paul. Personalité, Style et Conception du Ministère* (Leuven: Leuven University, 1986), pp. 49-77, here p. 73.

3. G. Theissen, *Psychological Aspects of Pauline Theology* (Philadelphia: Fortress, 1987), p. 276. This analogy suggests that Paul knows the Corinthians are viewing their Christian gifts in the light of pagan views of such gifts. Cf. C. S. Keener, *Paul, Women, and Wives: Marriage and Women's Ministry in the Letters of Paul* (Peabody: Hendrickson, 1992), p. 78:

> In fact, 1 Cor. 12:2-3 suggests that many of the Corinthians from pagan backgrounds had learned inappropriate forms of worship, forms which had carried over into their excesses in chapter 14. Paul in no way limits this background or its present consequences to the women, but assumes that this has affected many of his readers' ecstatic activity, whether they were women or men.

I quite agree. Keener's discussion of chs. 11 and 14 is much nearer the mark than that of A. C. Wire, *The Corinthian Women Prophets: A Reconstruction through Paul's Rhetoric* (Minneapolis: Fortress, 1990).

4. Cf. J. Smit, "Argument and Genre of 1 Cor 12–14," a paper given at a 1992 conference on rhetoric in Heidelberg, p. 16 in the distributed manuscript.

general to the more specific. Ch. 14 now focuses on two spiritual gifts in particular: prophecy and tongues. We learn how disorder and division was created not by the gifts themselves, but by the way in which they were used. Not wishing to quench the Corinthians' zeal for spiritual gifts and expression, Paul tries to concentrate their focus on the speech gift that, because it uses intelligible language, has the greater potential to unify the congregation: prophecy.

Dio Chrysostom pursued a similar rhetorical strategy when he suggested that in the assembly it was important for a common language to be spoken, so that unity, singleness of purpose, and harmony would result in the community (39.3; cf. 38.46). Similar also is Aristides's praise of the Rhodians: "When we visited you, we saw you even in the assembly using not only a single voice, but . . . for the most part even a single word. For often it was enough for you to exclaim, 'Well said!' and 'Crown him!' and such like, with the name of the speaker" (*Or.* 24.56).[5]

Unfortunately what was happening in the Corinthian Christian assembly was more like what Dio disgustedly says of his fellow Prusans: Their gathering was characterized by "shouts of the partisans, . . . outbursts that characterize not reasonable people or temperate cities but rather those who . . . 'go in rage to the assembly and quarrel with one another . . .'" (40.28f.). Though Christian worship at Corinth does not seem to have involved open quarrels, it certainly involved rivalries and competition for "air time" as "each one has his or her own kind of speech" (14:26). All were speaking simultaneously and few apparently were polite enough to listen to the other. Theissen is right in saying that "with his position on tongues, Paul is intervening in a struggle for influence and prestige within the community."[6] The same applies to the way Paul handles prophecy in this passage. It is wrong to see just one or the other of these two speech gifts as the single cause of the problems Paul is dealing with here.

Paul tries to bring order out of this chaos, and peace where there has been discord. As Aristides remarked, "factiousness destroys peace" (*Or.* 23.55), and Paul, too, must counter factiousness. His concern is with social behavior within a minority group, not specifically political behavior,[7] but his strategy for dealing with the problem of discord in the assembly is similar to that of the orators just cited. If Paul's argument succeeds, he will have won concessions and submission that produce unity and harmony in the body.[8]

---

5. On this, cf. L. L. Welborn, "On the Discord in Corinth: 1 Corinthians 1–4 and Ancient Politics," *JBL* 106 (1987), pp. 85-111, here p. 93.

6. Theissen, *Psychological Aspects*, p. 275.

7. I.e., behavior that directly affects or manifests the mood of the city writ large.

8. Cf. M. M. Mitchell, *Paul and the Rhetoric of Reconciliation* (Tübingen: Mohr, 1991), p. 281.

The argument is not gender specific. Paul requires respect, submission, and silence of any listener when any prophet is speaking (vv. 28-32), and his dealing with some women who are asking questions (vv. 34f.) is a specific implementation of principles already applied in general to everyone. One must assume that he singles these women out for comment because he had heard that some of them were notable violaters of these principles.[9] Throughout the chapter Paul is correcting abuses, and his words must be read in that context.

The material in 1 Cor. 14 completes Paul's discussion of "spiritual things" (*pneumatika*, v. 1). In particular, he has two major concerns in this discussion: that Corinthian worship should manifest *intelligibility* (vv. 1-25) and that it should manifest *order* (vv. 26-40) so that all believers are built up and the unbeliever present in the assembly is challenged by the gospel, convicted, and converted (vv. 21-25).[10] It becomes clear in this chapter that Christian worship in Corinth was fairly chaotic, that Paul saw even the most "charismatic" of the gifts, tongues and prophecy, as controllable by the one speaking, and that Paul was himself a "pneumatic," a person who had such spiritual gifts. To understand Paul's argument, we need some familiarity with views of prophecy and ecstatic speech that were likely to exist in Roman Corinth.

A Closer Look: Prophecy and Glossolalia in Corinth

There are two important issues to be addressed: How did the Corinthians view prophecy and tongues and how did Paul view them? It is easier to get at the latter than the former, but both are crucial to understanding this passage because Paul is definitely correcting abuses of these gifts, and this involves him in trying to persuade the Corinthians to view these gifts in a different manner than they have viewed them. This passage is not only about the use of the gifts but also about the *reasons* that they should be evaluated and used in certain ways. We need a clear understanding of the nature of the phenomena in question.

One problem in some works by NT scholars on prophecy is that certain assumptions are made about the relationship between ecstasy and prophecy in the Greco-Roman world, in particular at Delphi, and these assumptions are then predicated of at least the Corinthians, if not of Paul as well. For example, Wire assumes

---

9. Keener, *Paul, Women, and Wives,* pp. 80ff., argues that the women were asking irrelevant questions because they had not yet fully learned what they needed to know about various matters. This is possible, but I offer another suggestion below.

10. L. Hartman, "1 Co 14,1-25," in *Charisma und Agape (1 Ko. 12–14),* ed. L. de Lorenzi (Rome: Abbey of St. Paul, 1983), pp. 149-69, here p. 161, argues that vv. 26-40 represent practical advice while vv. 1-25 argue for the corrected practice. He sees two passages that stress the preferability of prophecy over tongues — vv. 1-4 arguing from an insider's viewpoint, vv. 20-25 with outsiders in view.

that the Corinthians experienced prophecy and tongues as an integrated phenomenon and suggests that "this movement into tongues could occur as the climax of prophecy when it reveals 'unspeakable speech' (2 Cor. 12:4) or as a final sign confirming to believers that the prophecy is divine."[11] Apparently this is based on the assumption that ecstasy was the basis if not the very essence of pagan prophecy, particularly at Delphi.

J. Fontenrose, however, has stressed that these sorts of assumptions need to be checked against what we actually know about practices at Delphi and other similar Greek oracle sites.[12] He argues that a "close study of all reliable evidence for Delphic mantic procedures reveals no chasm or vapors, no frenzy of the Pythia, no incoherent cries interpreted by priests. The Pythia spoke clearly, coherently, and directly to the consultant in response to his question."[13]

The messages given at Delphi had three basic forms: commands, sanctions, or instructions to do something; predictions; and statements of past or present fact. The most common form was the sanctions, and one particular form of sanction that is especially interesting for our purposes began with "It is better and more good to do X (than Y)." For example, the oracle told the Heraclids on one occasion: "It is better to bury Alkemene in Megara."[14] This should be compared to the "slogan" in 1 Cor. 7:1: "It is good for a man not to 'touch' a woman." I would suggest that at least some of the Corinthian Christians' slogans may have begun life as prophetic words or sanctions, cast in one of the traditional forms used at Delphi. Delphi was

---

11. Wire, *Corinthian Women Prophets*, p. 140. Cf. B. A. Pearson, *The Pneumatikos-Psychikos Terminology in 1 Corinthians* (Missoula: Society of Biblical Literature, 1973), p. 44; J. D. G. Dunn, "The Responsible Congregation," in *Charisma und Agape*, ed. L. De Lorenzi (Rome: Abbazia di S Paolo fuori le mura, 1983), pp. 201-38, here p. 208. Wire also seems to assume that all or nearly all of the Corinthian Christian women were ecstatic prophetesses and by an unfortunate bit of mirror-reading argues (p. 143):

> It is possible that some of Paul's negative images for speaking in tongues are direct reversals of positive images used in Corinth: tongues seen as cultivated speech, as signs of maturity, as fruitful for the community, as special intelligence, as a music particularly appropriate to the revealing of God in Christ.

This is part of Wire's larger argument in support of a Corinthian theology supported by the prophetesses, which she finds more palatable than Paul's alternative.

But Paul is not trying to correct just women in this passage. Furthermore, he is not trying to stifle either prophecy or tongues in Corinth, but to order their expression so that *everyone* benefits from them, not just the individual speaker. At the close of his argument he makes certain that no one will misunderstand him to have been forbidding such expressions (14:39). He is concerned only about prioritizing them according to what best edifies and witnesses to those present.

12. For an example of an oracular answer promising guidance and prosperity to the inquirer, cf. *New Doc. 2*, pp. 37-44.

13. J. Fontenrose, *The Delphic Oracle* (Berkeley: University of California, 1978), p. 10.

14. Fontenrose, *Delphic Oracle*, pp. 14f., rightly takes a critical approach to the oracles at Delphi, dividing them into clearly historical responses and legendary ones. The modes of command or sanction have a strong historical basis, whereas "obscure" or barely intelligible commands and instructions seem to have none.

a shrine to Apollo, the god of prophecy, and the ancient temple in Corinth was likely his shrine also. It is not surprising that the Corinthians might view prophecy in a Delphic light.

It is possible, too, that some of the other pronouncements in 1 Corinthians such as "There is no resurrection of the dead" (15:12) or "Everything is permitted" (10:23) were prophetic in character and thus because of their supposed sacred origin Paul had to counter them at length. This raises the question whether he would have seen his own teaching, say in ch. 7 or ch. 14, as prophetic in character, as he responded to the Corinthians' queries. 14:37 suggests that an emphatic Yes is the proper answer to this question.[15]

The predictions supposedly given at Delphi are in the form of commonplaces or proverbs, but Fontenrose thinks the evidence is weak that the Pythia ever historically used such proverbs as part of a response.[16] But during the Roman Empire Delphi was past its glory days, and certain tendencies manifested in this late period, such as responses in poetic form, were not characteristic of the oracle's words in classical or Hellenistic times. Still, it is not clear that the priests or prophets of Delphi transformed the oracles of the Pythia into poetic form (hexameter).[17]

The oracular statements at Delphi were given in response to questions. This may provide a clue to the meaning of 1 Cor. 14:35: *Eperōtaō* normally means "ask a question." The evidence suggests that the oracle responded in intelligible speech directly to the questioner, or if an ambassador had been sent to ask on someone else's behalf a response would be given and perhaps written down by one of the priests.[18]

Plutarch was a Delphic priest for a time and witnessed consultations and heard responses (*Mor.* 792-93; 700e; *SIG* 829A). But he "says nothing about vapors, toxic or otherwise, nothing about a frenzy or trance of the Pythia, nothing about wild or incoherent speech from the Pythia's mouth except in one passage — a report of an *exceptional* consultation. . . ."[19] Plutarch does speak of *pneumata* that affected the oracle (*Mor.* 402B; cf. 437c). It is a mistake to draw conclusions on the basis of late Latin writers who never visited Delphi, because the Greek word *mania* means "transport, rapture, ecstasy, inspiration," *not* frenzy, delirium, hysteria, or insanity. But the word was translated into Latin as *insania* or *vecordia* with the result that Lucan and others described a

15. On Paul as a prophet and the prophetic claims he makes in ch. 14, see H. Merklein, "Der Theologe als Prophet," *NTS* 38 (1992), pp. 402-29, here p. 427. G. Dautzenberg, "Botschaft und Bedeutung der Urchristlichen Prophetie nach dem Ersten Korintherbrief (2:6-16; 12–14)," in *Prophetic Vocation in the NT and Today,* ed. J. Panagopoulos (Leiden: Brill, 1977), pp. 131-61, is hardly convincing in arguing that Christian prophecy barely outlived the time of Paul in the Pauline communities. This conclusion comes from too narrow a definition of prophecy.

16. Fontenrose, *Delphic Oracle,* p. 87.

17. Strabo 9.3.5 speaks of poets who put the oracles into verse and worked at the sanctuary. On oracles in metric verse, cf. Plutarch *Mor.* 623a.

18. Fontenrose, *Delphic Oracle,* p. 217.

19. Fontenrose, *Delphic Oracle,* p. 197. The one exceptional incident is recorded in *Mor.* 438b, and Plutarch stresses there that the Pythia was not at all herself on this occasion. She entered the *manteion* unwillingly, became hysterical, cried out, and rushed for the door. Plutarch says nothing about ecstatic speech.

mad or raving Pythia, which is not historically accurate.[20] There is no historically credible evidence of the Pythia taking leave of her senses when prophesying. "The Pythia's inspiration is not Dionysiac, but thoroughly Apolline in nature, i.e., mantic."[21]

While inspiration or ecstasy led to speech at Delphi, the historical evidence for "ecstatic speech" interpreted by a priest is lacking. The Pythia gave her answer clearly and directly to the one who had come for a consultation. If the Corinthians were taking their cues from their larger culture in regard to ecstatic *speech*, what we call glossolalia, they would likely have thought of it in light of what they knew about the Dionysiac rites and would have distinguished it from prophecy, which they would have associated with Apollo and Delphi. There is no hard evidence that the Corinthian Christians confused or fused prophecy and tongues. Paul's responses suggest that they had simply been practicing both in worship without regulation and order and that the tongues spoken in Corinth had been left uninterpreted.

At Delphi not only was the Pythia often called a *prophētis* (Euripides *Ion* 42, 321), but the priest was called a *prophētēs,* though

> in most instances a προφήτης is not himself a mantis; he is a god's representative, a man who oversees and administers an oracular session. The priest-prophet who attended the Pythia presided over the mantic session at Delphi, answering all questions except the question put to the Pythia as the god's mouthpiece.[22]

This likely means that along with the female Pythia the male priests were also viewed as holding the prophetic office and answering some questions. What the priest did not do was answer *for* the Pythia when the oracle was being consulted directly.

Finally, it will be worthwhile to note some of the questions most frequently asked of the Pythia. There are basically three types:

> questions about religious matters such as whether a sacrifice should be offered, a temple built, or a certain rite followed,
> questions about public matters such as whether a city or colony should be founded or a war undertaken and about how rulers should conduct themselves, and
> questions about domestic matters such as one's birth or origin, career, or profession, whether one should buy some land, and about death and burial.

One of the most frequent sorts of questions in the legendary sources is those about marriage and childbearing, and the papyri from Egypt show that questions and answers about marriage, separation, and the death of a spouse were not uncommon at other locations.[23] It is this third category of domestic questions that most likely would have been asked of prophets in the Corinthian congregation.

20. On the intelligibility of the Pythia's responses see Plutarch *Mor.* 407bc.
21. Fontenrose, *Delphic Oracle,* p. 207. It is a mistake to associate too closely the Dionysiac rites and what went on at Delphi.
22. Fontenrose, *Delphic Oracle,* pp. 218f.
23. Cf. *New Doc. 2,* pp. 42f. The similarity of the questions here to those asked of the Pythia at Delphi in the legendary sources suggests that marriage and family questions *were* asked of her, since such questions seem to have been commonly asked of oracles in the Greco-Roman world, though we lack hard evidence for this at Delphi.

What Paul meant by prophecy and who might prophesy has been the subject of enormous debate.[24] We will now sum up what ch. 14 and other texts tell us about Paul's view of prophecy:

Prophecy is an intelligible phenomenon that does not require the sort of interpretation that tongues requires, but it does require weighing or sifting.[25]

The function of prophecy is building up, exhortation, and consolation (v. 3). This suggests that it is some sort of instruction.

V. 25 suggests that prophecy might also involve divine insight into a present problem or the present condition of someone's heart.

A prophecy was certainly not a sermon by twentieth-century standards. It was a spontaneous utterance prompted by the Spirit (cf. vv. 29ff.) and based on a sudden and uncontrived revelation from God (v. 30). It was controllable by the speaker, however, and thus was unlike pagan ecstatic utterances of the Dionysiac sort. In Christian prophecy both the mind and the spirit are edified.

Prophecy is a gift that all Christians should seek from God (v. 1) and thus not a gift reserved for a particular group of Christians.[26]

Paul does not regard prophecy as completely identical with teaching, since he distinguishes the two in 12:29 and elsewhere. Nonetheless, Paul does see prophecy as having a didactic function (14:19).

Paul may not see Christian prophecy as having the same authority as Scripture, including OT prophecy, since he speaks of judging or weighing the prophecies and thus sifting the wheat from the chaff. As W. Grudem has pointed out, Rom. 12:6 suggests that one prophesies according to the measure of one's faith. If enthusiasm exceeds inspiration then true prophecy may be mixed with the residue of an overheated imagination. Thus, it must be carefully weighed or sifted.[27]

Prophecy was obviously a very important function in the early *ekklēsia* or Paul would not urge it so strongly on the Corinthians. It probably had

---

24. Three studies are of particular help in sorting out these matters: D. Hill, *NT Prophecy* (Atlanta: John Knox, 1979); W. Grudem, *The Gift of Prophecy in 1 Corinthians* (Washington: University, 1982); and D. Aune, *Prophecy in Early Christianity and the Ancient Mediterranean World* (Grand Rapids: Eerdmans, 1983).

25. C. Forbes, "Early Christian Inspired Speech and Hellenistic Popular Religion," *NovT* 28 (1986), pp. 257-70, here p. 259, is right in saying that for Paul the prophet is inspired and needs no spokesperson beyond himself or herself.

26. Pace E. E. Ellis, *Prophecy and Hermeneutic in Early Christianity* (Tübingen: Mohr, 1978), pp. 22ff., who sees this whole discussion as directed to a particular class of Christians, prophets, despite the plural address to all the audience.

27. Grudem, *Gift of Prophecy,* pp. 58ff.

a measure of similarity to OT prophecy in content, often consisting of parenetic forthtelling, telling the truth about the believer's condition or about God's plans or promises, but sometimes also foretelling if that was of relevance to the immediate audience.

The authority was in the word and the Spirit inspiring it, not in the vessel or instrument, that is, in the person speaking the prophecy. In fact, if one added anything purely human to a prophecy, then that was to be discerned and not attributed to a divine source. At most, we may talk about authoritative functions, not authoritative offices, here.

Prophecy was a gift that both men or women could and did exercise, as ch. 11 makes clear.

It is not clear that tongues with interpretation is thought of by Paul as equivalent to prophecy. Both build up the *ekklēsia* and are intelligible. Since tongues seems to be a prayer language, a way of praising God beyond the rational level, the equation should probably not be made.

Paul's criterion for exercise of spiritual gifts is intelligibility and edification of others. That the argument is driven by a concern for what profits or benefits the group in the future shows clearly the deliberative character of this discourse. If one is exercising one's gifts in love, then one will think of the benefit to others first. Corinthian worship was at times an exercise not of a body but rather of a collection of isolated individuals all displaying their gifts, rather like merchants at a fair. Paul, for the sake of intelligibility, stresses one gift in particular, prophecy, and urges the Corinthian Christians to seek it (v. 1). This implies that in theory any member of the congregation could exercise this gift.

Verse 2 says that the person who speaks in tongues is speaking to God, a clear indication that glossolalia was seen as a prayer language or as a way to talk to God, not as a human language. Paul calls it the Spirit speaking mysteries. Here *mystēria* surely means "unknown or secret things," probably, that is, what is unintelligible.

It is not clear whether by *pneumati*, the dative case of "spirit," which appears in v. 2 and three times in vv. 15f., Paul means just the human spirit, the Holy Spirit, or perhaps the former prompted and guided by the latter. Sometimes it seems to be both, though the emphasis in a given occurrence may focus on one or the other. The human being has control over his or her human spirit and thus over whether or not to speak. This distinguishes Christian ecstasy from the sort one would find in the cult of Cybele. Perhaps Corinthian Christians' worship was so chaotic because, being of Roman extraction, they associated *mania* with the Roman idea of *insania* and thus thought that ecstasy meant being out of control.

Paul indicates that the function of prophecy is edification, exhortation and consolation (v. 3). It thus has a mainly parenetic quality, as was true of OT prophecy, though some theology would also be involved if it spoke of God's comfort, actions, or promises.[28] V. 4 indicates that speaking in a tongue builds up the individual. Paul does not see this as bad, but it is not the primary function of corporate worship. Worship is mainly meant to be a group experience where one gives worship to God and *koinōnia* to others, so that all benefit. As v. 4b says, prophecy is more useful because it edifies the assembly.

Verse 5 reveals that prophecy is not inherently a greater gift than tongues, for if the gift of tongues is interpreted, it, too, can build up others. The "greater-lesser" language is based on the criterion of intelligibility and edification, not on the inherent worth of some gifts as functions. This verse also suggests that the individual speaking in tongues might also interpret. This is not automatically so, since Paul says that one must pray that someone will interpret the tongues. If it is known that there is no interpreter present, then the tongues speaker should remain silent and speak internally, only to self and God.

In v. 6 Paul reveals he, too, is a tongues speaker, something his audience may not have known since he likely did not exercise the gift in their presence. There is no solid evidence that the ancients viewed glossolalia as a sign of irrationality or of lack of education or social standing. To the contrary, D. B. Martin has shown that quite the opposite seems to have been the case.[29] If this is correct, Paul may again be trying to bring those of higher social status into line in these chapters, by providing himself as an example.[30] Thus, Paul says he would rather come with a revelation, some knowledge, or some teaching. By "revelation" he might mean an apocalyptic revelation such as we find in the Book of Revelation, or perhaps just a spontaneous word of insight or exhortation.

28. Paul is trying to supplant any pagan notions about prophecy among his converts with Christian ones, but the latter are grounded in the OT. I agree with Forbes, "Early Christian Inspired Speech," p. 268, that the attempt to parallel Christian inspired speech with Hellenistic oracles and cultic procedures ought to be abandoned, if one is referring to the actual Christian phenomena, but I would disagree if Forbes means that it is unlikely the Corinthians viewed Christian prophecy and tongues in light of their pagan background.

29. D. B. Martin, "Tongues of Angels and Other Status Indicators," *JAAR* 59 (1992), pp. 547-89.

30. Ibid., 580:

It seems likely that glossolalia, as was the case with other theological issues at Corinth, divided the church along social status lines. Paul therefore uses the same rhetorical strategy here as elsewhere in the letter: to appropriate the position of the strong to himself, and then to use himself as the example of one of high status, in this case a tongue speaker, who has given up his own interests for those of lower status. He argues that the status of angelic tongues must be reevaluated in order to meet the needs of the entire church. . . .

In the series of analogies in vv. 7-9 Paul may be drawing on a well-known tradition in the pagan world, that of a description of inspiration in musical metaphors (cf. Plutarch *Mor.* 418d; 436f; 437d). The harp and flute make inanimate sounds. If the player does not change pitches, then how will the instrument convey a coherent melody and thus a coherent message to the listener? It cannot. If the trumpeter does not play the call to battle, how will anyone know that the message is to prepare for war? In each case, the instrument should convey some intelligible *message.* Tongues speaking without interpretation conveys no clearly defined meaning.

In vv. **10f.** Paul uses an analogy with foreign languages. It does not follow from this that he thought of tongues as simply another foreign language. He is thinking of the analogous *effect* of listening to a completely unknown foreign language: One receives no intelligible communication. *Barbaros,* from which comes our word "barbaric," was the common term for a foreigner who did not speak Greek, a stranger to the Mediterranean lands.

Verse 12 has a peculiar expression: "Be eager for spirits" or "You *are* eager for spirits." Many have assumed that "spirits" means spiritual gifts, though Paul could have said that more easily if it were what he meant. He may be urging eagerness to have both the human spirit and the Holy Spirit, but how can one be eager for a human spirit that one already has? Alternatively, the plural could be collective: "Each of you is eager about your own spirit speaking in tongues by the moving of the Holy Spirit." If one is going to use glossolalia one must pray for the gift of interpretation.

In vv. **14f.** Paul distinguishes between "my spirit" (which is nonrational) and "my mind" (the center of thought and judgment). Only the human spirit is active if one prays or sings in tongues without interpretation. Paul prays both ways (with spirit and mind) and urges others to follow his example. There is no denigration of the gift of tongues here, just a recognition of its proper function and limitations in terms of the group experience. *Psallō* means "sing," and Paul also envisions singing in tongues.[31]

In v. **16** a new party is introduced into the discussion, namely the *idiōtēs.* This term technically represents the "uninitiated" or "unlearned" person. Here it means one who understands neither the phenomenon of tongues nor its message without interpretation. Perhaps there was a special place in the Corinthian assembly for the *idiōtēs.*[32] There is considerable debate as to whether this person is a believer (as v. 16 might be construed), a nonbeliever, or something in between, such as a catchecumen. It is probably wrong to see

31. If it was anything like the modern charismatic phenomenon that goes by that name, it was a very beautiful and haunting gift.

32. If chs. 12–14 is an extension of the discussion in ch. 11, then perhaps the *idiōtēs* was a guest of the one hosting the household assembly in the *agapē* meal and the worship that ensued.

later church practices here, and the term does not refer to Christians with no spiritual gifts. In view of vv. 23f. it seems that this person is an nonbeliever, or at least associated with such. Yet this person might say the "Amen" if someone speaks intelligibly. Probably the *idiōtēs* is an outsider visiting the congregation, perhaps a guest of the one hosting the Christian assembly or the nonbelieving spouse of a Christian.

Despite the usual translations of v. 23, Paul does not say there that the outsider will consider tongues speakers insane. Rather they will see them as ecstatic, carried away by some external powerful force, as a devotee of Dionysius might be.[33] Glossolalia at Corinth made it appear that supernatural expression among Christians was like that sort of phenomenon: uncontrolled and uncontrollable. V. 16 indicates that early Christians followed the Jewish practice of the responsive Amen ("so be it") to a word of the Lord, a thanksgiving, or a word of praise spoken in the *ekklēsia*.

Verse 17 seems to be an affirmation by Paul. The Corinthians know how to give thanks, but how they do it makes it not a group-building experience. V. 19 has the expression *en ekklēsia,* which is roughly equivalent to our term "in church," that is, in the gathered assembly. It does not mean "in the church building" since there were no such buildings. Five words with the mind is better than ten thousand in a tongue (unless interpreted), because it edifies.

In v. 20 Paul makes a contrast by using two different words for children (*paidia* and a verb related to *nēpioi*). The Corinthians are exhorted not to be like children, but to be mature. But in regard to evil deeds[34] they are to be like infants.

V. 21 quotes Isa. 28:11f., which Paul says is in the Law, though *nomos,* "law," had become a term for all the OT, including the prophets. The form of the quotation has notable similarities to Aquila's Greek OT translation and differs from the Hebrew and the Septuagint in some ways.[35] One crucial difference is that Paul has changed the word "hear" in the last line to "obey."

The larger context in Isaiah 28 indicates that the Lord can only teach those weaned from the breast (v. 9), those who are not spiritually children. In v. 10 there may actually be a sort of Hebraic imitation of glossolalia: ṣaw lāṣāw, ṣaw lāṣāw, qaw lāqāw, qaw lāqāw, zeʿêr šām, zeʿêr šām. The next line describes this as stammering in a foreign tongue, and refers to the impression made on the Judahites by Isaiah's preaching. As a judgment against hardhearted Judah, God spoke to them in a foreign tongue that they could not understand, because they would not hear the truth in their own tongue.

---

33. Here is another clue that the Corinthians viewed their speech gifts in light of the pagan parallels.

34. *Kakia* refers to deeds, not thoughts.

35. Cf. G. D. Fee, *The First Epistle to the Corinthians* (Grand Rapids: Eerdmans, 1987), pp. 679ff.

This larger context becomes very interesting when we look at what follows the quotation in 1 Corinthians 14: In v. 22 Paul says that glossolalia is a sign for nonbelievers, those who do not hear and obey. Here the word "sign," in view of the Isaiah quotation, surely means an 'ōt, a sign of judgment that they are out of touch with God. This is the effect of uninterpreted tongues on the nonbelievers in Corinth. They cannot respond positively but only say that tongues speakers are ecstatics.

By contrast prophecy is a sign for believers. Here Paul means presumably that what is given in prophecy is a word of judgment or exhortation for all believers.[36] It is also a word that convicts and convinces nonbelievers, even if it is neither directed to them nor a sign *for* them. Vv. **24f.** describe how such prophecy can affect the nonbeliever, and we should probably see here a description of a conversion. It convicts them, challenges them, and reveals the secrets of their hearts with the result that they fall down prostrate and worship the true God, saying "God is really with you!" Therefore, even though prophecy is directed toward the congregation, being a sign for Christians, it can have a powerful effect on nonbelievers because it is both supernatural and intelligible.

In v. 25 Paul turns from the concern for intelligibility to the concern for order. V. 26 gives us a clue about one form of early Christian worship. There is no mention of worship leaders or of reading the Torah.[37] Rather each brings a song (perhaps sung in the Spirit), a teaching, or a revelation. The impression is of a real act of the body, not merely the performance of a noted few. Paul restates his rule: "Let all be done to edify," and adds "in order." In v. **27** he limits the number of people speaking in tongues to two or three, each in turn, and then says that someone should interpret.[38] This may mean only two or three in the whole service or only two or three before the interpretation must be given.

If there is no interpreter, then, Paul says, the tongues speakers should be silent during the assembly (v. **28**). This injunction should be compared in form and content to the one given to some women in vv. 33b-35. Here as there Paul is correcting abuses. It was conventional in the Greco-Roman world to

36. In 14:23 and in Rom. 16:23 "assembly" refers to the whole *ekklēsia*. As Dunn, "Responsible Congregation," p. 212, notes, this implies that there were meetings that did not involve every Christian. He envisions a meal with the Lord's Supper as one sort of meeting, while ch. 14 describes another sort of service. This may be incorrect; cf. pp. 241-52 above. But *CIL* XIV, 2, 112 does gives evidence that the business meetings of societies were separate from banquets on feast days.

37. Dunn, "Responsible Congregation," p. 210: "No Jew could read 1 Cor 14,26 without being struck, even shocked, by the absence of any explicit mention particularly of . . . the reading of the Torah."

38. Dunn, "Responsible Congregation," p. 219, thinks Paul is being more restrictive of tongues because he says two or *at most* three in regard to tongues, but only "two or three" in regard to prophecy. Since he is regulating both, I doubt this distinction.

command silence when a religious act was about to be performed. At state sacrifices the command was given: *favete linguis* ("check your tongues").[39] The major purpose of ch. 14, indeed of the whole letter, is correction, not just instruction. This chapter should not be seen as a "how to" manual. V. 28b may allow speaking in tongues silently or under one's breath even in the assembly.

Likewise with prophecy, two or three should speak and then others[40] are to weigh the prophecy carefully because it may be part inspiration and part imagination (v. 29). It is not like OT prophecy, which was to be applied, not sifted, and had a "Thus saith the Lord" sort of authority. Christian prophecy has an authority of *general* content, for "we prophesy in part" (13:9).[41] And the judging here should not be confused with OT rules about judging false prophets. Here it is the prophecies, not the prophets, that are being weighed.

Verse **30** suggests that the prophet stood while prophesying, and others sat. If a revelation suddenly came to one sitting, the one standing was to stop speaking, the implication being that it was more crucial to get this fresh word from God while it was being transmitted to the one sitting.[42] This, too, suggests that Christian prophecy, which involved words of comfort, exhortation, challenge, and edification, was not of such a crucial nature that one would not dare interrupt or judge it. Prophets should prophesy one at a time for the sake of good order. Worship should reflect the character of the God being worshipped, and in Paul's view the biblical God, unlike pagan deities, was a God of both order (not chaos) and peace (not competition for air time).

Verse **31** indicates that learning and being exhorted or encouraged are

---

39. The similarity here to how we do things today is striking. R. M. Ogilvie, *The Romans and Their Gods* (New York: Norton, 1969), p. 48, describes the scene as follows:

> Silence is now commanded (in state sacrifices a herald uttered an age-old cry, *favete linguis*, "check your tongues" [cf. 1 Cor. 14:30]) except for the steady music of the flute-player [cf. 14:7] who is employed, as at times of solemn prayer, to drown extraneous noises [cf. 14:23]. The priests cover their heads [cf. 11:4] with the folds of their togas and take up a square platter heaped with the sacred flour mixed with salt. . . .

40. Not the ones who have just spoken, thus perhaps distinguishing this from the procedure for tongues and interpretation. Dunn, "Responsible Congregation," p. 226, suggests that this means "the other prophets." This is possible but uncertain. Cf. C. Senft, *La Premiere Épître de Saint-Paul aux Corinthiens* (Neuchâtel: Delachaux and Niestle, 1979), p. 182.

41. B. Witherington, *Women in the Earliest Churches* (Cambridge: Cambridge University, 1988), pp. 92ff.

42. Dunn, "Responsible Congregation," p. 219, suggests plausibly that the first prophet was to take it as a sign that his or her speaking was outrunning its inspiration if another prophet stood up or began speaking or both. Contrast 1QS 6:10: "Let no one interrupt the words of another before he has finished speaking." This practice of allowing interruption strongly suggests that Paul did not see this prophecy as of the same caliber as OT prophecy.

the result of prophecy done properly. V. **32** has been much controverted. What it likely means is that the human spirits of the prophets are controllable and thus that they can stop speaking whenever that is required. There is an element of urgency to speak, but it is not an uncontrollable urgency. *Hypotassō* means "be subject to" or "be subordinate to."

It is debated whether v. **33b** goes with what precedes or what follows. If it goes with what precedes, the point is that worship should be undertaken with the same orderliness in Corinth as elsewhere, since God is the same everywhere. More likely it goes with what follows: In vv. **34ff.** Paul is repeating what was a general rule in his congregations or in all early Christian congregations.

During the time of the weighing of the prophecies some women, probably married women,[43] who themselves may have been prophetesses and thus entitled to weigh what was said, were asking questions, perhaps inappropriate questions, and the worship service was being disrupted. Paul urges in vv. **34f.** that Christian worship not be turned into a question-and-answer session.[44] In light of the discussion of pagan prophecy above, it is very believable that these women assumed that Christian prophets or prophetesses functioned much like the oracle at Delphi, who only prophesied in response to questions, including questions about purely personal matters. Paul argues that Christian prophecy is different: Prophets and prophetesses speak in response to the prompting of the Holy Spirit, without any human priming of the pump.[45] Paul then limits such questions to another location, namely home. He may imply that the husband or man who was to be asked was either a prophet or at least able to answer such questions at a more appropriate time.

Keener may be right in saying that a pedagogical problem is involved here. Those asking questions were not yet educated enough in the school of Christ to know what was and was not appropriate in Christian worship.[46] Paul affirms their right to learn, but suggests another context. In any case, Paul is correcting an abuse of a privilege, not taking back a woman's right to speak in the assembly, which he has already granted in ch. 11. The adversative particle *ē* ("or") in v. **36** does not imply that Paul is rejecting a statement that he has quoted in vv. 34f. — it is his own statement. He is, rather, anticipating opposition to his ruling and forestalling it in v. 36. Fiorenza may be right that vv.

---

43. I am less sure now than before that these verses refer to married women. The phrase "their own men" (v. 35) need not refer to husbands. It could also refer to whoever was the male head of a particular woman's household. But probably "husband" is what is meant.

44. See further Witherington, *Women in the Earliest Churches,* p. 103.

45. Dunn, "Responsible Congregation," p. 227, rightly sees the problem as women disturbing the process of evaluation with questions, and thinks vv. 34f. are authentic.

46. Keener, *Paul, Women, and Wives,* pp. 81ff.

33b-36 are intended, with 11:1-16, to frame the whole discussion in chs. 11–14.[47] Vv. 34f. are, in any case, definitely not a digression.

The theory that vv. 34f. are, in fact, a post-Pauline interpolation should be rejected for several reasons.[48] The two verses are found after v. 40 in a few manuscripts and other textual authorities, but displacement is no argument for interpolation. Probably these verses were displaced by scribes who assumed that they were about household order, not order in worship, scribes working at a time when there were church buildings separate from private homes. Wire has argued convincingly that the displacement may be traced to one particular Western text.[49] Furthermore, the text is not sufficiently close to 1 Tim. 2:11f. to warrant the argument that they were based on a scribe's editing of that text. In 1 Timothy the issue is teaching and authority, not asking questions and learning as here. Recent detailed studies by two capable women NT scholars have both concluded that these verses are Pauline and belong where they are.[50]

It was a common rhetorical technique to end a discussion with rhetorical questions, and we have already seen Paul do so in 12:29f. The rhetorical questions in v. 36 serve to anticipate future protests (cf. Quintilian *Inst. Or.* 9.2.16). Rhetorical questions in an argument did not need to receive a reply, according to the rules of rhetoric, but could do so.

V. 37 should be seen as Paul's rebuttal of an insinuation suggested by the rhetorical questions. He, too, has the Spirit (cf. 2:16; 7:40) and may speak as a prophet, so it is not true either that the Word of God originated only in Corinth or that it came only to the Corinthians.[51] Only here and in Col. 4:10 does Paul use the word *entolē,* "command," of his own words. Elsewhere, as pointed out by Dunn, he is hesitant about any assertion of his authority (1 Cor. 7:6, 25; 9:4-18; 2 Cor. 8:8; 13:10 [cf. 10:8]; 2 Thess. 3:9), though he could be

---

47. E. Schüssler Fiorenza, *In Memory of Her* (New York: Crossroad, 1983), p. 230.

48. Cf. Wire, *Corinthian Women Prophets,* p. 152; F. Lang, *Die Briefe an die Korinther* (Göttingen: Vandenhoeck & Ruprecht, 1986), p. 200, on the problems and possibilities of arguing for an interpolation.

49. Wire, *Corinthian Women Prophets,* p. 151.

50. From different points of view, Mitchell, *Rhetoric of Reconciliation,* pp. 281f., n. 536, who thinks the "question" hypothesis in regard to the character of the speech is most likely; Wire, *Corinthian Women Prophets,* pp. 153f., who is right about the authenticity but fails to note the rhetorical function of these verses as a correction of abuses in worship — as is most of the rest of chs. 11–14. 14:34f. is not a programmatic silencing of women in the *ekklēsia.* One must weigh not only what Paul says but also the function of his words in context to discover his rhetorical intent. Cf. Keener, *Paul, Women, and Wives,* pp. 86ff.

51. On rhetorical questions see D. F. Watson, "1 Corinthians 10.23–11.1 in the Light of Greco-Roman Rhetoric: The Role of Rhetorical Questions," *JBL* 108 (1989), pp. 301-18, here pp. 312ff. If this reading is correct, then it rules out the view that vv. 34f. are a quotation and that the questions respond to the quotation. And where is there evidence that any Corinthians were arguing for what vv. 34f. urge?

direct in his exhortation (e.g., 1 Cor. 11:17; 1 Thess. 4:11; 2 Thess. 3:4, 6, 10, 12).[52] Dunn suggests no explanation for this remarkable reticence, but when one recognizes the rhetorical character of Paul's letters an explanation is ready to hand: A rhetor's task is to *persuade*, using arguments, emotion, and personal charisma. Commanding can only be a last resort when one uses rhetoric.

Paul's argument ends on an extraordinary note. He urges zeal for prophesying, despite the problems such activities were causing him in Corinth, and refuses to ban tongues or to allow any Corinthians to ban them (v. **39**). The discussion concludes with a repetition of the concern for decorum and order in the congregation (v. **40**). This is desirable, first, because the congregational assembly is an open forum in which nonbelievers can participate and any bad witness should be avoided, and secondly because Christian worship should bear witness to the character of God, who embodies both peace and order. God is the ultimate model of *concordia*, something Paul has been arguing for throughout the letter.

The overall impression of Christian worship given in this chapter is noteworthy. As C. K. Barrett once remarked, Corinthian worship could scarcely have suffered from being dull. E. A. Judge summarizes worship in the early Christian meetings as follows:

> In that scene of lively social intercourse there was neither solitude nor mystery, no shrine, no statue, no cult, no ceremony, no offering to ensure that all was well betweeen gods and [human beings]. Instead there was talk and argument, disturbing questions about belief and behaviour (two matters of little or no concern to religion in antiquity) conscious changes to accepted ways, and the expectation of a more drastic transformation soon to come. The purpose of classical religion was to secure what was already there against just such an upheaval.[53]

Christian worship was also distinctive because Christians had no special buildings for worship. The point of Christian worship was

> the sharing of the shared grace *(charis)* of God in its particular expressions *(charismata)*. It was not characterized by an established pattern or liturgy or depend[ent] on an official leadership to give it direction; rather it was to be expected that the Spirit would exercise sufficient control through the interplay of gifts and ministries ordered by him. Its aim was to bring about

52. Dunn, "Responsible Congregation," pp. 233f.
53. E. A. Judge, "Cultural Conformity and Innovation in Paul," *TynB* 35 (1984), pp. 3-24, here p. 6.

the mutual edification of all through a being together and through a doing
for one another in word and action as the body of Christ in mutual interdependence on the Spirit.[54]

This worship, at least in Corinth, involved the participation of most, if
not all, of those present. It was not a performance of a few superstars for the
benefit of the many, who were reduced to an audience. Worship and fellowship
were acts that required giving by all the participants. Paul says nothing about
a sermon being part of early Christian worship. This may be because he
expected the reading of his letter to serve as the revelatory content for the
worship in Corinth. He definitely does not assume or support the notion of
a preacher or a service dominated by preaching, unless one concludes that
prophecy was the equivalent of preaching. Paul, however, expects *several*
prophets, not just one, to speak in a given act of worship.

Paul also knows nothing about a special class of Christians with "ministerial" gifts, a special class of Christian priests or clergy. The clergy-laity
distinction does not come from the NT.[55] Women along with men were not
only allowed but expected to exercise their gifts in early Christian worship.
Paul does believe in a sort of hierarchy of leadership, but this leadership was
to be determined primarily by who was called and gifted by the Spirit, and
not at all by gender or cultural background.[56] Furthermore, leaders were to
be models of how *all* should exercise their gifts in worship.

54. Dunn, "Responsible Congregation," p. 235.
55. I would add that a Christian *priesthood*-laity distinction arises from an inappropriate application of OT institutions to a NT situation.
56. We have already mentioned how certain social factors affected the structure of
the *ekklēsia;* see pp. 241-63.

Argument VIII: 15:1-58

RISING TO THE OCCASION

The function of Paul's rhetoric in ch. 15, as previously in this letter, is not to do apologetics but to correct Christians gone significantly astray. His major tactic is to show "some" of the Corinthians the logical implications of their position, cited in v. 12, that "there is no resurrection of the dead." Since the implications of this position are unacceptable, then *a fortiori* there must be something wrong with it. To show this Paul uses both artificial and inartificial proofs or warrants, appealing to witnesses, written documents, both Scripture and popular Greek writings (Menander in v. 33), and syllogistic logic to achieve his ends. B. Mack may be right in saying that the various arguments in ch. 15 are being used to support the thesis that "in fact Christ has been raised, the firstfruits of the dead," particularly in the second half of the chapter, because the Corinthians seem to lack any significant grasp of future eschatology.[1]

There have been several important attempts to analyze the rhetoric of ch. 15, notably by Mack, M. Bünker, M. Mitchell, J. N. Aletti, and D. Watson.[2] Bünker's argument is the least convincing because he identifies ch. 15 as forensic rather than deliberative.[3] Mack, Watson, and Bünker all agree against Mitchell that this chapter should be seen as an example of micro-rhetoric, in which a particular argument manifests all the rhetorical parts of a speech in itself, while still being part of a larger whole.[4] Mitchell's failure to see this has also led her to wrongly identify v. 58 as the conclusion or *peroratio* of the

---

1. B. Mack, *Rhetoric and the NT* (Minneapolis: Fortress, 1990), p. 58.

2. Mack, *Rhetoric*, pp. 56-59; M.. M. Mitchell, *Paul and the Rhetoric of Reconciliation* (Tübingen: Mohr, 1991), pp. 283ff.; M. Bünker, *Briefformular und rhetorische Disposition im 1 Korinthierbrief* (Göttingen: Vandenhoeck & Ruprecht, 1984), pp. 59-72; J.-N. Aletti, "La *dispositio* rhetorique dans les épîtres pauliniens. Proposition de methode," *NTS* 38 (1992), pp. 385-401, here p. 396; D. F. Watson, "Paul's Rhetorical Strategy in 1 Corinthians 15" (unpublished). Aletti and Watson agree on the arrangement of the speech, arguing for a double *probatio* and a double *peroratio*.

3. As Mitchell, *Paul and the Rhetoric of Reconciliation*, p. 285, n. 557, points out, Bünker's argument requires too many qualifications, i.e., that large portions of the chapter be seen as digressions or excursuses.

4. R. Pesch, *Paulus ringt um die Lebensform der Kirche* (Freiburg: Herder, 1986), pp. 13ff., mistakes the organization of several of Paul's arguments in 1 Corinthians that have all the rhetorical parts of a speech as indications of separate letters or sources.

whole series of proofs in 1 Corinthians, when it is at most a *peroratio* for the argument in ch. 15 alone. The proper *peroratio* for the letter does not appear until 16:13ff.

It is possible, therefore, to see this whole chapter as a speech in minature, with these different parts:[5]

> the *exordium* in vv. 1f.,
> the *narratio* in vv. 3-11,
> the *propositio* in vv. 12-19,
> the thesis, stated in short form in v. 20,
> a series of arguments in the *probatio* in vv. 21-50, using paradigms, examples, analogies, and closing with a scriptural analogy, that is an appeal to a recognized authority, and
> the conclusion in vv. 51-58, with a recapitulation, a citation of Scripture for a final appeal (vv. 54f.), and a *peroratio* in the form of an exhortation to act on the basis of all that has just been said (v. 58).

Ch. 15 provides an example of Paul at his argumentative best, ably using the tools of deliberative rhetoric including examples, analogies, logical consequences, rhetorical questions, and the like.

Verses 32f. should be seen as Paul's penetrating social analysis of why some of the more well-to-do Corinthian Christians were arguing as Paul suggests they did in chs. 8–10. They were not counting on a future reckoning or resurrection, so they could eat, drink, and be merry, since only death was on the horizon. Their ethics were negatively affected by this lack of future eschatology.[6] Paul responds that they will be held accountable, and in the meantime "bad company," that is, pagan friends at dinner parties in the temple and elsewhere, "ruins good morals." The rhetorical force of Paul's use of this proverb is powerful: These Gentile Corinthians are condemned out of the mouth of their own cultural heritage even apart from Scripture and apostolic tradition.

Scholars have frequently noted the realized eschatology of at least some of the Corinthians,[7] but have not provided a convincing explanation of this

---

5. Here I follow Mack, *Rhetoric,* pp. 56f., with small modifications.

6. For the suggestion that Paul's eschatological views changed before he wrote 1 Corinthians from a belief that resurrection happened through baptism, see C. L. Mearns, "Early Eschatological Development in Paul: The Evidence of 1 Corinthians," *JSNT* 22 (1984), pp. 19-35. For a proper and convincing critique of this suggestion, see A. Lindemann, "Paulus und die korinthische Eschatologie zur These von einer 'Entwicklung' im paulinische Denken," *NTS* 37 (1991), pp. 373-99, here pp. 376-80. Lindemann is correct in saying that different situations, not different theologies, explain the form of Paul's expression in the Thessalonian correspondence as opposed to 1 Corinthians.

7. E.g., A. C. Thiselton, "Realized Eschatology at Corinth," *NTS* 24 (1978), pp. 510-26.

eschatology from a sociological standpoint. We are now in a better position to provide that explanation. Greco-Roman paganism did not place much stress on a blessed afterlife. Religion was to be practiced for its present benefits, such as health and safety.[8] In this very chapter, in v. 29, there is evidence that pagan beliefs continued to shape the Corinthian Christians' view of these matters.

Justin, the second-century Christian apologist, refers to the practice of pagan "magic" at tombs, the calling forth of departed spirits (*Apology I* 18).[9] From a Roman point of view, the spirits of one's ancestors, in particular the *genius* of the *paterfamilias,* were especially important and even a part of daily family religion in the home and sometimes at tombs.[10] S. Dill stresses:

> No small part of old Roman piety consisted in a scrupulous reverence for the dead, and a care to prolong their memory by solid memorial and solemn ritual, it might be to maintain some faint tie of sympathy with the shade which had passed into a dim and rather cheerless world. The conception of that other state was always vague, often purely negative. It is not often that a spirit is sped on its way to join a loved one in the Elysian fields, and we may fear that such phrases, when they do occur, are rather literary and conventional.[11]

Among other practices there were sacrifices offered on behalf of the dead[12] and the famous *taurobolium,* baptism in bull's blood for the welfare of the

---

8. See R. MacMullen, *Paganism in the Roman Empire* (New Haven: Yale University, 1981), pp. 53ff., for a penetrating analysis, and pp. 211-12 above. On Roman pessimism about the future of civilization, see G. A. Kennedy, *The Art of Rhetoric in the Roman World 300 B.C. to A.D. 300* (Princeton: Princeton University, 1972), pp. 447-49.

9. Cf. A. Strobel, *Der erste Brief an die Korinther* (Göttingen: Vandenhoeck & Ruprecht, 1986), pp. 254f., on later practices of this sort.

10. The *genius* could also be thought of as the ancestral spirit playing the role of a guardian angel or attendant spirit, which in Greek would be rendered *idios daimon* (cf. Horace *Ep.* 2.2.188). Members of burial societies would gather at a tomb or temple to celebrate the life of the departed one, especially on the anniversary of the day of death. If some of the Corinthians viewed the Christian community as a burial society, they may have been drawn to proxy baptism (cf. v. 29). One can see how the Lord's Supper, since it was partaken of in the context of a meal and included the words "proclaiming the Lord's death until he comes," might fuel such a practice on the part of former pagans. If one could celebrate the Lord's death, why not the deaths of other dear departed ones? The problem with this view is that it does not explain why the rite of proxy *baptism* was being performed. Baptisms were not, so far as we know, a part of such celebrations on the part of burial societies.

11. S. Dill, *Roman Society from Nero to Marcus Aurelius* (London: Macmillan, 1904), pp. 256f.

12. For example, cf. *ILS* 116: "To the genius of Augustus and Tiberius Caesar, to Juno Livia [this has been dedicated] by Mystes, a freedman." Cf. R. K. Sherk, ed., *The Roman Empire: Augustus to Hadrian* (Cambridge: Cambridge University, 1988), p. 13.

emperor.[13] There were also meals eaten in dining areas adjacent to tombs (cf. *CIL* 6.26554).[14]

The baptismal rite on behalf of the dead suggested by v. 29[15] might be considered an expression of the strong Greco-Roman belief in the power of ritual. Ritual was considered likely to be effective if it was performed correctly in every detail. Some of the Corinthian Christians apparently made much of water baptism (cf. ch. 1),[16] and perhaps some believed that if they performed proxy baptism on behalf of the dead correctly, the dead would then receive salvation as the benefit conveyed by this Christian water ritual.[17] Ch. 10 at least suggests that some Corinthians had a very high view of the spiritual benefits that participation in the sacraments could convey, apparently including some form of eternal security.

Another factor that may have fueled the practice of proxy baptism among Corinthian Christians is cremation, which in some places was the predominant means of disposing of human remains during the first century A.D.[18] Those who could not afford land or expensive tombstones may have been practicing cremation in Corinth.[19] Perhaps Paul's preaching about resurrection led to concern that the departed who had been cremated would not get such a benefit, hence the practice of proxy baptism.

At any rate, those who were being baptized for the dead were not among those who said "there is no resurrection of the dead" (v. 12), since Paul uses

13. Cf. MacMullen, *Paganism,* p. 105; J. K. Chow, *Patronage and Power: A Study of Social Networks in Corinth* (Sheffield: JSOT, 1992), pp. 160ff.

14. On all this, see K. Hopkins, *Death and Renewal* (Sociological Studies in Roman History 2; Cambridge: Cambridge University, 1983), pp. 201-55. Hopkins refers to the remarkable fact that some tombs have been found not only with adjacent dining benches, but with tubes so that one could pour drink and perhaps even food down to the deceased (p. 234). Certainly the Romans were preoccupied with death, honored the dead, and worried about their fate. Hopkins conjectures that this made them susceptible to the Christian idea of eternal life (p. 232).

15. Cf. Chow, *Patronage,* p. 162.

16. See the discussion above, pp. 83-87.

17. On the spirits of the dead remaining in a state of semi-existence near the tomb or the body's ashes, cf. R. M. Ogilvie, *The Romans and Their Gods in the Age of Augustus* (London: Chatto and Windus, 1969), p. 75. On rites for the dead, cf. Horace *Odes* 1.28.34.

18. Cf. *CIL* 6.35887, 9.1837; A. D. Nock, *Essays on Religion* I (Cambridge: Harvard University, 1972), pp. 276-93. Later when the implications of the concept of resurrection were clearly understood, Christians objected to cremation. Cf. Minucius Felix *Octavius* 2.4f.; 34.10. Nock's final word on the matter is apt in respect to the Roman adaptation of Greek and Near Eastern practices: "The educated Roman ... took freely [from Eastern practices], but he was not dominated by that which he took" (p. 307). This is why it is a mistake to speak of Roman colonies like Corinth as "Hellenistic" in character.

19. On burial clubs that helped those of modest means to avoid burial in mass graves, and on their rules, see Hopkins, *Death and Renewal,* pp. 211-17.

them as an illustration in support of his argument for resurrection. More likely it was the more wealthy members of the congregation, those who had considerable social status and continuing strong ties to pagan society, that denied the resurrection.[20]

The more well-to-do may have held on to some form of Roman realized eschatology.[21] This imperial eschatology promulgated special blessings for those of social standing, and for those who supported the hierarchial status quo of the empire, with a "trickle down" view of how those of lesser status benefited from the *pax Romana*. H. Koester and J. R. Lanci argue that some Corinthians, particularly wealthier former pagan men, were likely to endorse this Roman eschatology, because it comported with their former endorsement of, and perhaps participation in, venues where Roman imperial eschatology was important.[22]

A Closer Look: Roman Imperial Eschatology ————————

Roman imperial eschatology was part of the larger enterprise of imperial propaganda meant to aid in binding the empire together.[23] It involved both a political agenda and a religious agenda, as the two were always intertwined in the Greco-Roman world.[24]

20. 1 Corinthians 15 manifests clear evidence of factionalism: Only *some* were saying "There is no resurrection of the dead." Others, whom Paul uses as an illustration against this first group, were practicing proxy baptism. Paul's rhetorical strategy throughout this chapter is to unify the Corinthians in a proper belief in resurrection by critiquing the view of the more prominent "some," not the views of the less prominent, even if he thought that the latter involved some aberration.

21. Cf. Mitchell, *Paul and the Rhetoric of Reconciliation*, p. 177: "Throughout 1 Cor. 15 Paul stresses that *all* shall share in the resurrection, not a select few (15:22, 51), thus combatting the factionalists' claims."

22. Koester, "Jesus the Victim," *JBL* 3 (1992), pp. 3-15, especially pp. 10-13; J. R. Lanci, "Roman Eschatology in First-Century Corinth," a paper delivered at the 1992 meeting of the Society of Biblical Literature in San Francisco. Apparently Lanci intends to include this information in the dissertation he is finishing at Harvard. My thanks go to him for giving me a copy of his paper and allowing me to learn from it.

23. D. Engels, *Roman Corinth: An Alternative Model for the Classical City* (Chicago: University of Chicago, 1990), p. 92, rightly points to the changing religious climate as the empire grew and needs changed. One of the changes this brought in religion was "increasing loyalty to the new imperial cults of . . . the emperors and Roma." One can see this reflected in the building priorities in Roman Corinth.

24. D. Warden's lecture at the 1992 Society of Biblical Literature meeting entitled "The Emperor Cult: Political and Religious Dimensions" rightly stressed this fact, and he also rightly argued that the purely religious content of the imperial cult was minimal. Almost all of it had some social function or aim. On the prophecy of Vulcanius when the comet appeared after Caesar's death in 44 B.C. and Augustus's attempt to inculcate a Golden Age eschatology in 17 B.C., see Ogilvie, *Romans and Their Gods*, pp. 118f.

It also included some astounding statements, such as the following, written in 9 B.C. in Priene (its similarities to the birth announcements in Luke 1–2 have often been noted):

> Because providence has ordered our life in a divine way . . . and since the emperor through his epiphany has exceeded the hopes of all former good news *(euangelia)*, surpassing not only the benefactors who came before him, but also leaving no hope that anyone in the future will surpass him, and since the birthday of the god was for the world the beginning of his good news [may it therefore be decreed that]. . . .[25]

As Koester stresses, this inscription as a whole bears witness to several key features of Roman imperial eschatology:

> The new age inaugurated by Augustus is the fulfillment of a divine plan and of prophecy;[26]
> the new age involves earth as well as heaven and is universal, including all nations;
> there is a celebration of the new age wherever and whenever imperial games are held; and
> the new age has a savior figure, the victorious Augustus, who is called either a god or "son of the god."[27]

The evidence for the existence of the imperial cult in Roman Corinth is clear:

> Cult personnel such as the *flamen, pontifex,* and *augstali* are mentioned in Corinthian inscriptions.[28]
> By A.D. 50 two additional sets of imperial games had been instituted in Corinth and apparently elsewhere as well: the Caesarea to honor the deified Augustus and the imperial contests to honor the current emperor.[29]

---

25. W. Dittenberger, *Orientis graeci inscriptiones selectae* (Hildesheim: Olms, 1960) II, no. 458, pp. 48-60, here lines 40-42. On the *res gestae,* see pp. 451-53 below.

26. Roman emperors often saw prophecy as potentially subversive and so destroyed books of prophecy. It was the past and the present, not the future, on which they wanted the residents of the empire to focus. Cf. J. V. P. D. Balsdon, *Romans and Aliens* (London: Duckworth, 1979), pp. 188f.

27. The latter term appears in an inscription found at Cosa: "[To Imperator Caesar], son of the deified, Augustus, pontifex maximus, [this altar was dedicated] by Quintus Lucretius Eros Murdianus [and] Lucius Voluminius Eros, masters and priests of the deified Augustus" (Sherk, ed., *Roman Empire,* p. 13). Cf. *IGR* 4.975: "The people [dedicate this temple?] to the goddess Roma and to Imperator Caesar, son of a god, god Augustus" (cf. Sherk, p. 14).

28. A. B. West, *Corinth: Latin Inscriptions 1898-1927* VIII/2 (Cambridge: ASCSA, 1931), nos. 67f., 77, and 132. These priesthoods were much more common in the West than in the East. Their presence in Corinth is therefore another indicator that the Romanness of Corinth in Paul's day should be stressed. Chow, *Patronage and Power,* pp. 148f.

29. It is another sign of the Romanness of Roman Corinth that it was the first and for some time the only city in Greece to have gladiatorial contests at such games. Cf. Dill, *Roman Society,* p. 240, and the account in Apuleius *Met.* 10.18; 4.13.

A statue of Augustus about to offer sacrifice was found in the Julian basilica in Corinth.

Coins portraying emperors and images of Roman peace and plenty were minted in Corinth and replaced earlier coins with images of local deities as Corinth's Romanness was increasingly stressed in the first century A.D.

A statue has been found with an inscription on its base honoring a priestess of the Providence of Augustus (that is, Tiberius).

The remains of a Roman style temple, Temple F, apparently dedicated to Venus, the patronness of Julius Caesar's family, have been found.[30]

The archaeological evidence suggests that in the first century of the common era, the whole of downtown Corinth was gradually realigned architecturally to form a huge, composite, splendid monument to the imperial family, with an altar to Julius Caesar in the center, numerous imperial statues, and a huge temple dedicated to the *genus*, or family, of the Julians. Anyone who visited Corinth in the mid to late first century would have confronted a breathtaking panorama in the center of town testifying to the Victory of the Roman imperial rulers and the glorious arrival of salvation for the Roman people (among whom Corinthian citizens counted themselves, since Corinth was a Roman colony).[31]

This salvation amounted to the present blessings of safety, health, and wealth for Corinth, and it was the more well-to-do families who got the lion's share of the benefit and who would have supplied from their numbers the priests and priestesses for the imperial cult. Virgil's famous Fourth Eclogue celebrated the edenic conditions supposedly created by Augustus and the *pax Romana*. In view of the economic prosperity of Roman Corinth, there was special reason to believe in the Roman imperial eschatology there, especially on the part of those who had benefited most from Roman rule.

Paul, by contrast, associates salvation not with the coming of Caesar, but with the coming and the return of Christ. Theissen notes that the language and to some degree the structure of the relationship between emperor and subjects parallel the way in which Paul discusses the relationship of the glorified Christ to *his* people.[32]

It is not accidental that when Paul addresses Christians in the Roman cities of Corinth and Philippi, he most stresses that it is from Christ that one receives and will receive the benefits of real salvation. He refers to the *parousia* of Christ in 15:23, as opposed to the appearing of Caesar, and to Christ subjugating all kings and kingdoms when he comes in 15:24, as opposed to the boast of Caesar to have already done so in imposing his *pax Romana*. The only reference to Christ as "Savior" in the undisputed

30. The evidence for the statues, the coins, and the temple are conveniently summarized in Lanci, "Roman Eschatology."

31. Ibid., pp. 21f.

32. G. Theissen, "Vers une theorie de l'histoire sociale du christianisme primitif," *ETR* 63 (1988), pp. 199-215, here p. 211. "Primitive Christianity had an opportunity wherever supra-regional loyalty was lacking and where the imperial government lacked sufficient social and religious force. The new faith offered an alternative integration, one that was different from that which dominated the empire" (p. 213).

Pauline letters comes in a very similar passage, Phil. 3:10-21.[33] Probably the reason for these parallels to the imperial eschatological propaganda in both passages is that Paul is countering that propaganda with his own brand of Christian "already . . . not yet" eschatology. For Paul the *tagma* or proper ordering (cf. 15:23) that really matters is Christ first and then those who are in Christ. This is the only sort of social order that ought to be truly important to Christians, not society's ranking systems. The Corinthians should be concerned about being "found in Christ" when he returns, not about being found among the social elite in Corinthian society.

Paul's words did not amount to a program of revolution against the empire, since he stresses that it is only the returning Christ who will accomplish this reversal and transformation. In other words, Paul seeks to replace the present imperial eschatology of some Corinthians with his own "already . . . not yet" Christ-centered eschatology. Surely some if not all in Corinth would have heard the political overtones of vv. 23ff. If one lives in the light of such future eschatology, all loyalties to any sort of human realized eschatology have become pointless, for as ch. 7 makes clear, all purely human things and institutions have been relativized by the eschatological first coming and promised return of Christ.

There is thus a social component to Paul's thought here in that eschatology is being used to unify the community by critiquing Roman imperial eschatology.[34] This critique is intended to have a leveling effect because participation in the imperial cult or in sponsorship of the games would have been a status indicator in Corinth. If the "some" who denied the resurrection gave up their secular eschatology, they also would be giving up the basis for certain claims to superior status.

The chapter may be divided as follows:

1. a discussion of the resurrection of Christ and his resurrection appearances (vv. 1-11),
2. a discussion of the future resurrection of the dead as linked to and logically implied by Christ's resurrection (vv. 12-34), and
3. a discussion of the nature of the resurrection body (vv. 35-58).[35]

---

33. K. Wengst, *Pax Romana and the Peace of Jesus Christ* (Philadelphia: Fortress, 1987), pp. 78f. In similar fashion to 1 Cor. 15:32, Paul refers to "those whose god is their belly" in Phil. 3:19.

34. The social relativization takes place *en ekklēsia*, not in society at large.

35. There are numerous useful studies on the Christian and Pauline concept of resurrection. The reader wanting more resources should consult B. Witherington, *Jesus, Paul, and the End of the World: A Comparative Study in NT Eschatology* (Downers Grove: InterVarsity, 1992), pp. 184-215 and the notes there; M. Harris, *Raised Immortal: Resurrection and Immortality in the NT* (Grand Rapids: Eerdmans, 1985). For a brief survey article showing the bearing of the empty tomb traditions on the idea of resurrection, see W. L. Craig, "The Historicity of the Empty Tomb," *NTS* 31 (1985), pp. 39-67.

At the argument's outset, Paul chooses to draw on the common gospel tradition about the death, resurrection, and appearances of Jesus in order to affirm the reality of Jesus' resurrection. He reminds the "some" (v. 12) who are in error about the resurrection of what he has preached and they have believed. Jesus' resurrection is a truth that they have already received as part of the very core of Christian faith and by which they are being saved (vv. 1f.). For Paul there is no salvation without the bodily resurrection of Jesus. It is nonnegotiable, a tradition to which they must hold firmly. Otherwise they have believed in vain.

In v. **3a** Paul again uses the Jewish language for the passing on of traditions, as he did in ch. 11. He thus makes clear that what he proclaimed was not something that he has dreamed up. It is what all true Christians hold in common.[36] The phrase *en protois* could mean "in the first place," but more likely it means "of first importance."

Paul then in vv. **3b-4** quotes this early Church tradition, the heart of the creed. Twice he uses the phrase "according to the Scriptures," and while there are some Scriptures that may be said to relate to these matters (Isaiah 53 and Hosea 6) it is likely that Paul is using the phrase in a general sense to indicate that these events were something planned by God in accord with and as a fulfillment of his Word in the OT.

Paul affirms that Christ died for believers' sins.[37] This theological understanding of Jesus' death indicates that it was for a positive purpose and to good effect. The key phrase probably means "*because of* our sins." Paul does not elaborate a theology of the atonement or explain why Christ had to die for sins. He is probably alluding to Isaiah 53 and thus thinking of Jesus dying as a substitute. Christ died in our place, not just on our behalf.

The second item in the creed, "he was buried," makes quite plain that Paul is talking about Jesus having died a real death. "Buried," when combined

---

36. E. E. Ellis, "Traditions in 1 Corinthians," *NTS* 32 (1986), pp. 481-502, here pp. 495f.:

> As an apostle Paul defines himself as a bearer of the word and works of another, Jesus the Messiah. By that designation he represents himself not as an innovator *de novo* but as one who stands within the context of a tradition. . . . Paul's insertion into a letter of pre-formulated traditions composed by [his] colleagues is instructive in many ways. It reveals the extent to which his mission was a corporate enterprise involving many participants.

37. Paul is focusing here on the Christians whom he is addressing in this letter, hence the use of "our." He does not mention the fate of nonbelievers in this chapter, mentioning only the resurrection of those who are "in Christ." It is thus not possible to conclude from this verse that Paul believes that it is God's intent that Christ die only for the elect. He certainly does believe, however, that only believers get the benefit of that atoning death (e.g., Phil. 1:28).

with the third element in the creed — "he was raised" — implies belief in an empty tomb. Considering Paul's Pharisaic background, to speak of resurrection surely implies belief that Jesus had a material body.

Jesus "has been raised," and this is not something he did himself, but something God did to or for him. Furthermore, it is something that has an ongoing or permanent effect. Paul's theology of resurrection includes the idea that resurrection was God's way of vindicating Jesus and his claims (cf. Rom. 1:1-4).

Paul then begins to list people to whom Jesus appeared (vv. 5-8), mentioning along the way that some of these witnesses are still alive as he writes the letter (v. 6). They can be consulted if anyone will not take Paul's word for it. Notable by its absence is any reference to appearances to women. This may be because Paul is quoting an early official witness list, possibly from a Jerusalem source, and the women are omitted due to the general attitude to testimony from women throughout the Mediterranean, including among Jews in Palestine.[38]

It is not clear where Paul begins adding to the list, but it seems in view of *eita . . . epeita . . . epeita . . . eita* ("then, afterward, afterward, then") in vv. 5-7 that he refers to the appearances in chronological order. The appearance to Cephas, that is, Peter, is not recorded in the Gospels other than a passing reference in Luke 24. The appearance to the Twelve (which by then were the Eleven) is probably another of the Jerusalem appearances. The appearnces to the five hundred, to James, and to "all the apostles" may have occurred in Galilee (cf. Matt. 28:16ff.). James is apparently Jesus' brother (cf. 9:5); if another James, such as Zebedee's son, were meant, there would be no reason to single him out from the Twelve. It is unclear what Paul means by "all the *apostoloi,*" but they are distinguished from the Twelve, and in Paul's mind would likely include Barnabas, Andronicus, Junia, and others (cf. Rom. 16:7).

Finally, Paul distinguishes himself from all the others he has listed, adding at least v. 8 to the tradition. He calls himself "the abortion" or "miscarriage." Perhaps this was a term of scorn some used behind his back. It might suggest that he was disfigured or odd in appearance. It has often been taken to mean that he was rushed into the apostleship, in an untimely haste, which might be the nuance here. One day he was persecuting the *ekklēsia* of God, and seemingly in no time had done a complete about-face and was an *apostolos.*

Paul is engaging in the sort of self-deprecation that was not uncommon

---

38. Cf. Luke 24:11; B. Witherington, *Women and the Genesis of Christianity* (Cambridge: Cambridge University, 1990), pp. 3ff. Paul may not know about the appearances to female disciples.

among rhetors when he says that he is the least of the *apostoloi* (v. 9).[39] Had he believed that he had opponents in Corinth, not just that there were factions among the believers in Corinth, it is unlikely that he would have given them the sort of ammunition that this text and ch. 9 provide. It is even possible that he is playing on his own name, since *Paulus* meant "little one,"[40] and for the same reason he may have been called the prematurely born one.[41]

Paul, again in self-deprecation, says he is unworthy to be an *apostolos*,[42] but quickly adds, "I am what I am by God's gracious choice and activity." The Corinthians could not gainsay his status unless they wanted to quibble with God. He may have gotten a late start, but by God's grace he has worked harder than all the others. He reminds the Corinthians that they themselves have believed what he preached about Christ and his death and resurrection.

The creedal fragment that Paul has been citing is surely one that he taught them when he was in Corinth in 51-52 and one that he received at least as early as 35. The term *ōphthē* speaks to the objectivity of the appearances: Jesus "appeared," not "they claimed to see him." There is no hint that Paul sees the appearance to him as any different from the others except that it was the last. He does not call it a vision. According to Luke's reckoning Paul's appearance certainly seems to have come after Christ's Ascension. This raises the question whether some early Christians believed that all of Jesus' appearances, even on Easter morning, were appearances from heaven.

Having established the common ground of the tradition about Jesus' resurrection, in vv. 12ff. Paul develops the implications of the tradition. He does not oppose his view of past (Jesus') and future resurrection to a Corinthian assumption of "present" resurrection, perhaps through baptism. The group he is countering believes that "there is *no* resurrection" (v. 12), not "there is *no longer* any resurrection."[43] His appeal to those who were baptizing

---

39. See below, the comments on 2 Corinthians 10–13, on inoffensive self-praise, pp. 432-37.

40. See above, p. 5 n. 12.

41. Another possible suggestion is that of J. W. Beaudean, *Paul's Theology of Preaching* (Macon: Mercer University, 1988), p. 130: The meaning of *ektrōma* is focused on the result, not the manner, of birth and therefore indicates one that is incapable of sustaining life on his or her own. Cf. J. Schütz, *Paul and the Anatomy of Apostolic Authority* (Cambridge: Cambridge University, 1975), pp. 104f.

42. Note the universal use of *ekklēsia* in v. 9. Paul does not confine the term to just the local assembly.

43. That some Corinthians believed new spiritual life was to be had in Christ here and now does not mean that they believed that that life amounted to "resurrection from the dead." I am less sure now than when I wrote *Jesus, Paul, and the End of the World* that the "some" in v. 12 meant that the resurrection was entirely past. The sticking point may have been with the idea of resurrection involving a body, and the "some" may not have thought through what that might imply about the Easter event. They may have thought

for the dead (v. 29) is an appeal to another group of "some" in the community, those who do affirm the resurrection, probably including future resurrection, *against* the influential people who simply deny any resurrection.[44]

To most Greeks or Romans resurrection would probably have been understood as the resuscitation of a corpse, a return to the bodily condition the person had before death (cf. Acts 17:31f.).[45] This would not have sounded like eternal life to a Greek or Roman, especially if he or she had believed in the immortality of the soul as the only form of eternal life. So it may have been resurrection, so understood, that the "some" in Corinth were denying.

The phrase as it stands in v. 12 refers to resurrection "out of" *(ek)* the dead. "If the dead" in v. 16 makes it clear that Paul does not merely mean resurrection from the grave or from death, though both are entailed. Perhaps some Corinthians had understood Jesus' coming to new life to be like their own, as a spiritual transformation. There was a sense in which Paul would agree that such a transformation was a sort of resurrection (cf. Rom. 6:4). Probably some Corinthians had spiritualized Christ's resurrection, much like many have today, and therefore when confronted with the phrase "resurrection out of the dead," denied that they believed in such a thing.

Paul stresses that resurrection is "out of" the dead; it is not merely a

---

that Jesus' appearances were like the mythological appearances of gods in the guise of human beings and so that faith in Christ's resurrection amounted to belief in such appearances. Cf. B. A. Pearson, *The Pneumatikos-Psychikos Terminology in 1 Corinthians* (Missoula: Society of Biblical Literature, 1973), pp. 15ff.

44. Pace A. C. Wire, *The Corinthian Women Prophets: A Reconstruction through Paul's Rhetoric* (Minneapolis: Fortress, 1990), pp. 159ff. Wire's discussion of resurrection, like the rest of her book, tries to read a nefarious attempt by Paul to silence or disenfranchise women into the text. But that Paul deliberately omits a discussion of dying and rising in baptism to avoid affirming the Corinthian viewpoint is an argument from silence. It is not at all clear that Paul believes or ever preached that such a thing happens *through* water baptism, as ch. 1 suggests. His view is that new life in Christ comes through receiving and believing the preached word, not through the sacrament of baptism. He does use baptismal imagery to describe this event of transferal, but to argue that he or other early Jewish Christians believed that the rite effected the change is to go too far (so rightly A. J. M. Wedderburn, *Baptism and Resurrection: Studies in Pauline Theology against its Greco-Roman Background* [Tübingen: Mohr, 1987], pp. 90-163; J. D. G. Dunn, *Baptism in the Holy Spirit* [London: SCM, 1970]). Furthermore, Wire's argument that there was no official witness list because Paul adds to the list forgets that Paul sees himself as a prophetic figure who can also offer an inspired word or inspired interpretation and expansion of an earlier tradition. Finally, her argument that Paul is trying to stifle the Corinthians' present life in Christ by pushing off the gift of true life into the future fails to take the measure of the "already . . . not yet" character of Paul's eschatology and especially his affirmation of present spiritual gifts when properly used (chs. 12–14).

45. Witherington, *Jesus, Paul, and the End of the World*, pp. 189ff.; A. J. M. Wedderburn, "The Problem of the Denial of the Resurrection in 1 Corinthians XV," *NovT* 19 (1977), pp. 229-41, here p. 236.

spiritual matter but also a bodily matter. Thus he must correct *both* the Corinthians' "already" about resurrection and their "not yet." If they deny resurrection from the dead totally, then they deny that Christ was raised. It was a regular practice for a rhetor to try to refute an argument by showing that its logical consequences were unacceptable and thus that the logic must be flawed. Paul offers a kind of syllogism to correct their view:[46] If Christ was not raised, then it follows (vv. **14-19, 29-32**) that:

> Paul's preaching and the Corinthians' faith are empty, worthless, and futile,
> Paul is guilty of bearing false witness about what God did,
> Christians are all still in their sins (i.e., sins are not atoned for or forgiven),
> those who have died as Christians have already perished,
> believers are not the most enviable but rather the most pitiable persons
>   since faith in Christ only has temporal and temporary benefits,[47]
> those who are baptizing by proxy are engaging in a pointless activity,[48]
> all effort at moral uprightness is pointless,[49] and
> all Paul's work and the risking of his life are pointless.[50]

This is one of the most rhetorically powerful and detailed arguments in the letter. The deliberative form of this argument is clear since Paul shows what the necessary future consequences are of the erroneous view of resurrection, with a goal of changing the Corinthians' view, lest they believe in vain (vv. **2, 10, 14, 17, 58**).[51]

Paul argues for Christ's and the believer's resurrection in vv. **20-22** using the idea of firstfruits and an Adam-Christ analogy, with Adam and Christ each

---

46. This syllogism does not work unless Paul really assumes that "some" were totally denying resurrection *from the dead*.

47. There is some question as to what *monon* ("only") in v. 19 modifies, probably "this life."

48. On this practice, see above, pp. 101-3 and below, pp. 307-9.

49. "Why not eat, drink, and be merry?" is an allusion to Isa. 22:13, but also recalls anti-Epicurean polemic. The Epicurean view may have been cherished by "some" Corinthians.

50. The reference to fighting with beasts in Ephesus is probably a "not uncommon description of the sage's struggle" (A. Malherbe, *Paul and the Popular Philosophers* [Minneapolis: Fortress, 1989], p. 88), a metaphor for an endangered life (cf. Ignatius *Romans* 5:1). As a Roman citizen Paul would never have been put in the ring, or if he was it is doubtful that he would have survived, especially if he had physical problems. Cf. the reference to adversaries in Ephesus in 16:8f. and the tribulation catalog in 4:9ff.: It is part of Paul's rhetorical agenda to portray himself as the enslaved leader or beleaguered sage in conflict with the dominant orientation of the world.

51. On "in vain" as a deliberative *topos*, cf. Aristotle *Rhet.* 1.3. 1358b.5; Quintilian *Inst. Or.* 3.4.16; 3.8.1-6, 22-35.

understood as founders of a new humanity.[52] With "firstfruits" Paul might be alluding to OT practices in regard to the wheat sheaf after Passover, but he more likely uses the idea to stress the connection between Jesus' resurrection and the believer's future resurrection. Christ's resurrection is the first part of the harvest of those who have "fallen asleep" and also that which assures the Corinthians that the rest of the harvest will eventually come in.

In vv. 21f. Paul treats Adam as an historical person who was responsible for death entering the human world (cf. Rom. 5:12-21). But another Adam brought the resurrection of the dead. Just as all were affected by the action of the first, so also all those who are "in Christ" will be brought to life, being affected by the action of the second.

Paul does not discuss the fate of those outside Christ here. It is possible to read various ideas into his silence. It could be that he saw the nonbeliever's resurrection as separate from the Christian resurrection, but we cannot be sure. His point is to focus on what will happen to Christians, so the analogy is not perfect. There is a corporate solidarity in death and in new life in each case, but not all will be in Christ, and so not all will be affected by him in the way that all are affected by Adam.

In vv. **23-24a** Paul gives a thumbnail sketch of the order (or rank: *tagma*) of the eschatological events:

> Christ the firstfruits has been raised, inaugurating the eschatological age;
> at Christ's *parousia* those who are in Christ will be raised;[53]
> then the end or goal (the *telos*) will have been reached.

This is followed in vv. **24b** and **28** by three *hotan* ("when, after") clauses referring to future events of unknown timing, all saying what will happen before the absolute "end" (v. 24a) of human history can come: Christ must deliver the kingdom to the Father, but first he must "bring to nothing all rule, power, and authority," subjecting all powers to himself (v. 24). Then, having done that, he must subject himself to the Father (v. 28).

Paul is probably countering Roman imperial eschatology in this section, which may also explain his stress on the fatherhood of God, because in the

52. Not a new race or kind of humans. Paul believes in a whole new creation in Christ; see below, pp. 395-96.
53. The term *parousia* is used here by Paul for the last time in his letters (cf. 1 Thess. 2:19; 3:13; 4:15; 5:23; 2 Thess. 2:1, 8, 9). The word means "coming" and was used of the arrival of a king at a town. This is the image Paul seems to use in 1 Thess. 4:15ff., which makes unlikely the idea of a rapture of the *ekklēsia* into heaven. Those who go out to meet the king when the trumpet sounds return to the city together once they have met outside the gates. *Parousia* was also used of the epiphany of a deity, as here. See Witherington, *Jesus, Paul, and the End of the World*, pp. 152ff.

imperial propaganda the emperor was portrayed as not only divine but also as "father of the fatherland" *(pater patriae)*. "The *Pater-Patriae* image had more appeal to Roman citizens and subjects with a Roman background, wherefore it was primarily in the city of Rome and in Italy and probably in Roman *coloniae* that this aspect of the Roman propaganda was the strongest."[54] An inscription dedicated to the emperor dating from A.D. 47-50 has been found in Corinth which calls him both *pontifex maximus* and *p(ater) p(atriae)*.[55] Paul is trying to supplant the imperial eschatology, which was clearly extant in Corinth and which looked to the emperor as the father and benefactor providing the current blessings, with an eschatology that involves Christ and a truly divine Father. He says that all merely human rulers will be subjected to Christ (v. 24), so Christ is superior and these lesser rulers are not to be worshipped. The often overlooked social implications of this passage are that Paul is indirectly arguing for some in Corinth to disengage from previous commitments to imperial eschatology. The evidence just cited shows that Roman Corinth was not dominated by the old Greek democratic ideals but by the more hierarchical ideals propagated by the emperor and his officials in the colonies.[56]

Paul associates Ps. 8:6 with Christ in v. **27**. The forces being subjugated are being put under Christ's feet by God the Father.[57] The last enemy is death (v. **26**), which is subjected by means of the final resurrection of believers. Resurrection loosens death's grip on human life.

Verse **29** probably refers to Corinthian Christians who are being baptized for other Christian loved ones who have died without baptism.[58] While Paul does not endorse this magical view of baptism's efficacy, he also does not see

54. E. M. Lassen, "The Use of the Father Image in Imperial Propaganda and 1 Corinthians 4.14-21," *TynB* 42 (1991), pp. 127-36, here p. 133.

55. J. H. Kent, ed., *The Inscriptions, 1926-1950* VIII/3 (Princeton: ASCSA, 1966), no. 77. One can also point to a Corinthian coin minted in this same period that reads TI CLAVD CAESAR AVG PP, the last part being the normal abbreviation for *pater patriae*. Cf. the discussion in Lassen, "Father Image," p. 134.

56. Paul offers two sorts of hierarchical arguments here. One is based on the authority of the eyewitnesses to the resurrection, whose testimony the Corinthians should submit to, but more important is the hierarchy created by Christ's coming and subjugating human and demonic forces, then submitting to the true divine Father, who supplants all merely human fathers. Paul does not see the kingdom of God, which Christians only inherit or enter at the eschaton, as a democracy; cf. Witherington, *Jesus, Paul, and the End of the World*, pp. 51ff.

57. On Paul's christological use of the Psalms and Genesis in vv. 20-28, see J. Lambrecht, "Paul's Christological Use of Scripture in 1 Cor. 15:20-28," *NTS* 28 (1982), pp. 502-27.

58. Cf. above, p. 294. Are "the dead" to be identified as Christians who have died without being baptized or as ancestors who never heard the gospel? The text is not clear on this point. That there was concern in Paul's communities about Christians who died before Christ's return is shown by 1 Thess. 4:13ff.

this as a serious enough aberration to debate the point; he simply uses it as part of his *ad hominem* argument.

Verse **31** is somewhat convoluted. Paul says that he swears by the Corinthians' boasting, which apparently means that their faith is his boast, since he converted them. As Fee points out, Paul ends a major section of theological discussion here, as before, by bringing out the ethical consequences of the discussion.[59] An incorrect and inadequate understanding of resurrection has led to defective living. "Bad company destroys good ways" (v. **33**) is a quotation from a now lost play of Menander entitled *Thais.* This verse and v. 32b suggest that Paul is alluding to where the "some" who were denying the resurrection may have gotten their alternate eschatology: by dining in temples with those who espoused the imperial viewpoint. If so, then ch. 15 must be read in light of the whole discussion in chs. 8–10, which in turn suggests that the "some" here are the same "some" who are criticized there, namely certain reasonably well-to-do Gentiles (likely males) who were arguing for the right to dine in temples.

Appropriately, then, Paul tells them to come out of their drunken stupor and stop sinning (the present continual tense indicating the cessation of ongoing action). They should know God better. There will be eschatological consequences to their actions, a judgment of deeds, as ch. 3 makes clear. They will be held accountable when they rise from the dead. Paul publicly shames them, asking, in effect, "How could you be so ignorant of God that you do not know about the future resurrection and future judgment?"[60] The mention of "knowledge" of eschatological mysteries (v. 51) suggests that Paul is criticizing the same group whose claims of "knowledge" of the faith's mysteries and of Christian freedom to dine in temples he mentions in chs. 8–10.

D. Watson has urged that we have a second argument from v. 35 to the end of the chapter with all the parts of a rhetorical piece, as in vv. 1-34. He may be correct, but it appears to me that vv. **35ff.** are but a further development of the one deliberative argument for resurrection that is the content of the whole chapter. Here Paul is using the sort of proofs that will rule out objections to resurrection based on its means and character.[61]

Apparently a major stumbling block — if not *the* major stumbling block — for the Corinthians in accepting the notion of resurrection was that having a body seemed synonymous with mortality and corruptibility so that the

59. G. D. Fee, *The First Epistle to the Corinthians* (Grand Rapids: Eerdmans, 1987), pp. 762ff.

60. On Paul's use of the same rhetorically potent shaming tactic in chs. 8–11, see above, pp. 226-30.

61. But cf. Watson, "Paul's Rhetorical Strategy," especially pp. 4ff.

combination of *body* and *immortality* did not make sense. This, along with the Greek idea that immortality involved the soul and was inherent to having a soul, as opposed to the Christian idea that eternal life or salvation is a gift that will affect both body and spirit, makes the confusion understandable. Having discussed the *fact* of resurrection in vv. 1-34, Paul turns in v. 35 to analogies aimed at making the *how* and *what* of resurrection plausible to such a mentality. He is particularly concerned to get across the idea of eternality or immortality involving a body.

Perhaps J. Jeremias is right in saying that the two questions in v. 35 are not two forms of one question but the two related issues to be discussed in this section: First, "how are the dead raised?" To this the answer is: by God's power. Second, "with what sort of bodies do they come?" Here the answer is: a body with elements of both continuity and discontinuity with the present body.[62]

Resurrection was inconceivable for the Corinthians, so Paul argues by way of a common analogy, the ancient idea that a seed put into the ground dies and is brought to life again miraculously as the plant. This is botanically untrue, but Paul simply uses the widely believed idea to make a point about resurrection, not to teach agriculture.

In v. 36 the Corinthians in question are likened to the fool in the Psalms — the one who fails to take into account God's actions. Paul has spoken of himself as a beleaguered sage, to whom his converts should have been listening. Now he portrays his charges as immature learners, as is shown by his use of shaming language earlier in the letter.

There are two major points in vv. 35-41: First, resurrection is a miraculous event brought about as God wills it, just as God causes the crops to grow. Second, what is put into the earth is a naked seed that has to be clothed with a new and different body, just as human beings must. It is difficult to keep the balance of continuity and discontinuity between the body of this life and the next body. If there is a stronger emphasis here, it is on discontinuity between the present physically animated body and the resurrection body animated by the Spirit.[63]

In v. 38 Paul argues that God gives each seed its *own* plant body. Resurrection occurs to each believer: Each person receives his or her own distinct body. There is no corporate body of Christ being raised. To emphasize that

62. J. Jeremias, "Flesh and Blood Cannot Inherit the Kingdom of God," *NTS* 2 (1955-56), pp. 151-59.

63. This passage incidentally makes quite clear that R. Bultmann's dictum that for Paul a human being *is* a *sōma* ("body") and does not *have* a *sōma* will not work for certain crucial Pauline passages. Indeed, I would suggest that R. H. Gundry has shown that it is basically an incorrect notion. Gundry, *SOMA in Biblical Theology (with Emphasis on Pauline Anthropology)* (Cambridge: Cambridge University, 1976).

there are different sorts of bodies, Paul stresses in v. **39** that even in present physical existence there are different sorts of flesh. Human flesh is not the same as fish flesh or bird flesh. So also *mutatis mutandis* there are different sorts of bodies, both earthly and heavenly. V. **40** makes the further point that these different bodies also have different sorts of splendor or brightness, just as star differs from star in brightness (v. **41**). In v. **42**, moving away from the analogy, Paul says that the same is true of the resurrection of the dead.

Paul *does* speak of a resurrection body and of resurrection of dead persons, but he does *not* speak of resurrection of *the* body or resurrection in the *same* body.[64] This is not a minor point, for Paul is surely aware that bodies decay into dust. He is prepared to insist that there will be a resurrection body for each believer, not the same body necessarily, though in the case of at least those who live to the *parousia* Paul affirms that there will be a transformation of the present flesh into the other sort. In the latter case, Paul seems to envision a process that is more a matter of metamorphosis than of replacement.

Paul also affirms that it will be the same person or personality in the new body. The two major elements of continuity between this life and the next are the presence of *a* body and of the same person. The analogy points to continuity because it is the planted seed that comes up, but in a very different condition.

In vv. **42-44** the elements of discontinuity are discussed. The present body, which will be buried, is in decay, dishonor, and weakness and is animated by a mere physical life principle. But the resurrection body will not be subject to decay or death and will have a splendor that contrasts with the believer's present state of humiliation. It will be a body constituted in and by power, in contrast to the present vulnerability and weakness. Finally, it will be a body animated by God's Spirit, which Christ gives the believer.

It is crucial to say something about the words *psychikon* and *pneumatikon*. As has been pointed out by M. Harris, adjectives or qualifiers ending in -*ikon* normally carry an ethical or functional meaning.[65] It is thus unlikely that Paul means by *sōma pneumatikon* (v. 44) a "body made up of spirit." That would be a non sequitur, since Paul elsewhere assumes that spirit is immaterial. He means, rather, that the resurrection body will be animated and empowered by the Spirit, just as the present physical body (the *sōma psychikon*) is animated and empowered by a physical life principle or force, which the creation story says God breathed into human beings. So the *psychē* that Adam was animated

---

64. Cf. J. Héring, *The First Epistle of Paul to the Corinthians* (London: Epworth, 1962), pp. 170ff.; J. Gillman, "Transformation in 1 Cor 15,50-53," *ETL* 58 (1982), pp. 309-33, here p. 329. R. J. Sider, "The Pauline Conception of the Resurrection Body in 1 Cor. 15:35-54," *NTS* 21 (1974-75), pp. 428-39, presses the seed analogy too far.

65. Harris, *Raised Immortal*, pp. 112ff.

by (v. 45) is the physical life principle, not a "soul," as the word is so often translated. *Psychē* is decidedly this-worldly, of the earth. It is not an immaterial soul or spirit.[66]

It would have been a jolt to the Corinthians for Paul to make clear that ultimately being *pneumatikos* had something to do with bodily existence, not merely with spiritual life as the believer now experiences it. In Paul's view, the truly "spiritual" person is ultimately one who has the resurrection body. Perhaps the Corinthian problem was that some had a one-step soteriology, according to which the spiritual life is purely a present immaterial condition followed by another immaterial condition later. What one did or did not do with one's body had little or nothing to do with spirituality on this view.

Paul emphasizes the "already . . . not yet," the "not yet" being that believers are still in their physical bodies. Paul's soteriology has at least two stages. Full salvation comes only in the future because the body remains to be changed. It is doubtful that the "some" (v. 12) would have agreed to the proposal in v. 44b that if there is a body animated by physical life, then there will also be one animated by spiritual life.[67]

In v. 45 Paul returns to his Adam-Christ analogy, not for the sake of making particular christological points, but rather to make eschatological and soteriological points. The contrast between the first Adam and the last Adam is that the former received only physical life as a gift, whereas the latter bestows spiritual life. The physically animated life precedes the spiritually animated life.

It is difficult to assess the precise force of v. 47 since it is elliptical. It is unlikely that Paul is saying that Christ was made of heavenly stuff since he does not say that Adam was made out of the dust of earth. Does *ek* ("out of") here indicate source, or perhaps more likely character? The first Adam was characterized by having an earthly life principle and body, but not so the second representative of the human race.[68]

Verse 48 indicates that Christians are and shall be indebted to both founders of humankind, having bodies and principles of animation like both, but now believers only bear the bodily likeness of the first Adam (v. 49). If they persevere in the faith, then they will bear the likeness of Christ as well. Perhaps Paul is thinking in two stages: Now believers manifest in part the moral likeness of Christ and have the taste of the Spirit as an *arrabōn*;[69] after the resurrection they will manifest both the outer and inner likeness of Christ.

66. Witherington, *Jesus, Paul and the End of the World*, pp. 192f.

67. Therefore, we must take v. 44b as a bare statement of fact or principle, not as an argument in itself.

68. It seems that Paul has Christ's exalted resurrection body in view.

69. A "first installment" or "down payment" toward eternal life (cf. 2 Cor. 1:22; 5:5; Eph. 1:13f.).

J. D. G. Dunn shows that conformity to Christ's bodily image is part of the larger Pauline schema in which the believer imitates or is modeled on Christ.[70]

Jeremias has made an impressive case that "flesh and blood" in v. **50** refers to the living while "the perishable" refers to the dead,[71] in which case the verse would mean that neither the living nor the dead can inherit the kingdom in their present condition. But this verse is probably just another case of synonymous parallelism, since in v. 42 "the perishable" seems to refer to those who are alive and decaying, not to the dead.[72] A drastic change in one's life, life principle, and body must happen if one is to inherit the kingdom. Indeed, Paul's stress throughout the rest of the chapter is on the necessity of transformation: One must not be so satisfied with one's present spiritual life as to mistake the part for the whole of Christian existence.

This mystery or eschatological truth now revealed by Paul probably surprised some Corinthian Christians: "We will not all sleep, but we will be changed" (v. **51**). This "mystery" must be kept in mind when one arrives at v. **52**, because initially it would seem there that "change" is what happens to living Christians ("we") while resurrection happens to dead Christians. But I would suggest that Paul means that *all* believers will undergo some kind of change with the same results for all: believers in resurrection bodies. So "changed" refers to both sorts of changes — transformation and resurrection.

Paul believes that there will be some Christians left alive when Christ returns. He uses the common Jewish and Christian metaphor of sleep for death (cf. 1 Thess. 4:13; Mark 5:39; John 11:11) since in Christ death is no more harmful or permanent than sleep. This does not mean that he subscribes to the idea of soul sleep. This transformation/resurrection will occur "in the blink of an eye," when the last trumpet sounds. One should compare this passage to 1 Thess. 4:13–5:11, where Paul is also describing the last events, including resurrection. Believers must "put on" (using the metaphor of donning clothes) an imperishable and nondecaying life form.

Verses **54f.** are the only place in his letters where Paul cites an OT text as a prophecy yet to be fulfilled. He interprets and gives a contemporizing application of the Septuagint text of Isa. 25:8 combined apparently with Hos. 13:14. He changes "penalty" (*dikē* in the LXX) to "victory" (*nikē*) in v. 55 to conform the Hosea text to the Isaiah text and substitutes "death" for "grave" in the second quotation to make both lines a mocking of death. The Septuagint has "Where is your *penalty*, O death?" Paul speaks of death's "sting." *Kentron* could mean "goad," but the meaning would be the same.

---

70. "1 Cor. 15:45 — Last Adam Life-Giving Spirit," in *Christ and the Spirit in the NT*, ed. B. Lindars, et al. (Cambridge: Cambridge University, 1973), pp. 127-41, here p. 137.

71. Jeremias, "Flesh and Blood."

72. For another analysis, see A. C. Perriman, "Paul and the Parousia: 1 Cor. 15:50-57," *NTS* 35 (1989), pp. 512-21.

In v. 56 Paul connects sin, death, and Law. Jesus, through his death and resurrection, forgives sin, overcomes death, and annuls the condemning power of the Law. Paul does not develop here the relationship of sin and Law, but in Romans 5–7 he makes it clear that the Law's effect on a fallen creature is condemnation or even goading into sin and rebellion, though this was not the Law's intention or purpose.[73]

Paul does not see death as a natural conclusion to human life, but rather as an enemy, indeed the last enemy of human life to be overcome (v. 26). He sees it as punishment for sin, so that sin is only finally overcome when death is overcome at the resurrection.

Typically, in v. 58 Paul ends this section, as he did in v. 34, with an exhortation to stand firm and to get on with Christian work, perhaps meaning ministry in particular. No such labor is in vain. Thus Paul ends the chapter where he began, speaking of what is and is not in vain for a Christian, that is, for one who believes in resurrection. V. 58 may be seen as the *peroratio* of the chapter, summing up the ethical implications and import of the argument and making an emotional appeal, after the equally emotive rhetorical questioning of death personified in v. 55.

For Paul resurrection, both Christ's and the Christian's, is the basis for a new moral order.[74] This new moral order affects the Christian not only in that he or she has meaningful work to do in this lifetime, but also, if I am right about Paul's critique of Roman imperial eschatology, socially as well: He is calling for detachment from certain pagan ways of viewing the historical process, which would in turn affect how one views the social structures of this world, including political institutions and social ranking systems. His rhetorical strategy is to show how the importance of such institutions and systems has been relativized in light of the truth of the eschatological gospel.

Were the "some" of v. 12 to accept Paul's eschatological teaching, they would have to change their behavior and social habits in several ways. The resurrection of Christ did not immediately lead to Eden regained, but there is one place where the new life and God's agenda should be manifest on earth: in the behavior of Christians, in particular in the Christian community as it gathers for worship and fellowship.[75] Paul expects his converts to manifest and

73. The Mosaic Law is likely in view, and Paul believes its purpose is to reveal and warn against sin.

74. Cf. O. O'Donovan, *Resurrection and Moral Order* (Grand Rapids: Eerdmans, 1986).

75. F. B. Craddock has remarked on how little distance there sometimes seems to be between early and modern Christianity when one compares the modern *ekklēsia* to the Christian congregation in Corinth. He maintains that we, too, are often preaching to

bear witness to the new creation already begun in the midst of the old, all the while keeping their gaze firmly fixed on the future, when the process of salvation, sanctification, and glorification will be completed.[76]

At the same time, Paul was under no delusion that if the Corinthians just got their theology right, all would be well. As F. B. Craddock says,

> It is naïve to think one can function with the simple formula: People have problems and the gospel resolves them. The fact is, the gospel generates in individual lives and in society a new set of problems. One has only to love impartially and hatred is threatened and stirred to violence. One has only to speak the truth and falsehood takes the stand with pleasing lies. Invite persons of different social and economic backgrounds around the same table and the fellowship is strained, often breaking apart. . . . Plant the cross in a room and the upwardly mobile convert it into a ladder. Evil, by whatever name it is called, will not sit idly by and allow the gospel to transform a community. . . . Let the preacher, therefore, be encouraged . . . when having to deal with those problems which clearly have their origins in the fact that the gospel has been released in the community. A difference is being made, and that is seldom without pain.[77]

"Corinthians" today. Without trying to "modernize the past" or "archaize the present," to use Craddock's phrases, I submit that it seems all too familiar and relevant when Paul complains, "How can some of you say there is no resurrection?" Cf. Craddock, "Preaching to Corinthians," *Int* 44 (1990), pp. 158-68.

76. Pace Wire, *Corinthian Women Prophets*, p. 176, who comes to the amazing conclusion that Paul is arguing *against* the new life one already has in Christ, in order to affirm the "not yet." This badly misjudges the "*already* . . . not yet" character of Paul's argument. Here he must emphasize the "not yet" because that is what the "some" have denied, not because he minimizes the present new life in Christ.

77. Craddock, "Preaching to Corinthians," pp. 167f.

Argument IX: 16:1-12

COLLECTIONS AND PROJECTIONS

Chapter 16 is a potpourri of various items. There appear to be three final issues with which Paul wishes to deal. Possibly two, the collection for the Jerusalem church and the return of Apollos to Corinth, were brought up in the letter that some of the Corinthians wrote to Paul (cf. 7:1), as *may* be indicated by the occurrences of *peri de* in 16:1 and 12.

I have suggested that the main, though not the only, source of problems for Paul in Corinth was a group of relatively well-to-do (possibly some *nouveau riche*) Gentile male converts. Possibly they were the main drafters of the letter sent to Paul defending their right to attend temple functions and to participate in Greco-Roman society as they had done before. It was likely from within this group that the problems of rhetoric, wisdom, and knowledge originated, that the problem of incest confronted in ch. 5 arose, that the problem of civil litigation addressed in ch. 6 came about, that the various dining problems were instigated (chs. 8–11), that the denial of the resurrection began (ch. 15), and probably that some of the chief abuses of spiritual gifts (chs. 12–14) got started.[1]

These people were enamored with the rhetoric of Apollos and wanted him back. But they seem not to have expected Paul to return. It may also have been that they were looking for opportunities to be benefactors in and to the Christian cause and had asked about the collection for the saints in Jerusalem. It is plausible then that the majority of the troubles in Corinth were instigated by one particular group.

But not all higher-status Christians in Corinth were at fault. Paul urges the Corinthians to aid Stephanas after his return from visiting Paul (vv. 15-18), and he mentions Gaius (1:14), who was a major supporter of Paul and the *ekklēsia* in Corinth (Rom. 16:23). It appears that Gaius was a leading well-to-do Christian figure throughout the whole period of the Corinthian correspondence and beyond it, and one must not overlook Chloe and her people (1:11),

---

1. Some of the problems in Christian worship were caused by the behavior of women, as chs. 11 and 14 make clear, but in both of those chapters the behavior of some men is also criticized. In ch. 7 the problems seem to involve a larger number of the Corinthian congregation, both men and women.

who also seem to have been prominent members of the Corinthian *ekklēsia* who were among those causing no problems for Paul.[2]

Because of Paul's general practice of not naming those he is criticizing, a closer identification of the major troublemakers is not possible, except to say that Erastus and his circle (Quartus?) may have been some of those at fault. If so, then Paul apparently corrected the error because he mentions Erastus (and Quartus) later in a positive context (Rom. 16:23). As sorely as Paul was tried by these troublemakers, he still treats them as erring Christians who are and should be part of the Christian *ekklēsia* in Corinth. He is not fighting against "opponents" in 1 Corinthians or defending himself against attacks. What he criticizes is errant social behavior and theological beliefs, not Corinthian views on apostolicity or the legitimacy of his own ministry.

Paul's rhetorical strategy in 1 Corinthians has been to concentrate on correcting the main source of the problems in Corinth, while also addressing others and their complaints, problems, and queries to a lesser degree. Since the basic problem is factiousness, caused especially by the group we have described, his strategy is to address the *ekklēsia* as a whole, emphasizing the importance of unity. By doing so he also accomplishes another goal, that of shaming the offending parties by criticizing them before their fellow Corinthian Christians, since his letter would have been read when the assembly was gathered. These tactics must be kept in mind as we examine 16:1-12.

Verses 1-4 deal with the collection for the poor Christians in Jerusalem. Paul also refers to this collection in Gal. 2:9f.; 2 Cor. 8:13; 9:9, 12; and Rom. 15:26.[3] Here he does not make explicit that the collection is for the poor, but it appears that the Corinthians already knew this, perhaps by hearing of the Galatians' efforts (v. 1). Apparently this collection was something Paul agreed to with the Jerusalem "pillars" (Gal. 2:9) early on, perhaps to cement the Jewish and Gentile parts of the *ekklēsia* and perhaps also to show that he and his congregations were and wanted to remain part of the same Christian fellowship with the Jerusalem *ekklēsia*. We do not have general remarks on tithing here; Paul is talking about a special collection.[4]

2. So L. M. White, *Domus Ecclesiae — Domus Dei: Adaptation and Development in the Setting for the Christian Assembly* (Ann Arbor: University Microfilms, 1983), p. 564, n. 185. It is unclear whether we should count Phoebe as well. She was a church leader, but in the household congregation in Cenchreae. It is unclear how closely that group was linked to the Christians in nearby Corinth.

3. I will reserve most of my comments on this subject until the discussion of 2 Corinthians 8–9; cf. pp. 411-28.

4. Cf. D. Georgi, *Remembering the Poor* (Nashville: Abingdon, 1992), pp. 52ff. Georgi is right that the use of the term *charis* rules out the idea that this was some kind of tax,

According to v. 2 the money was to be set aside by each individual Corinthian and then collected at each home[5] on the first day of the week, that is, Sunday. We have evidence here that the day of religious duty and worship for the Christian, even in Paul's time, was Sunday, not the Jewish sabbath. Acts 20:7 is clearer on this point (cf. Rev. 1:10).[6] Collecting the money repeatedly every week would result in a larger sum than if Paul simply took up a collection when he arrived. The weekly collection was to consist of whatever of one's treasure, profit, or savings one could afford to give.

Paul is very cautious about how he handles this matter. In order to unify his audience, he asks *everyone* to give what they can afford. He does not simply appeal to the wealthy to be patrons of this project.[7] He is not interested in fostering certain kinds of patronal hierarchical relationships in Corinth and so does not allow a few patrons to give large sums, gain all the honor, and so further divide the haves from the have-nots in Corinth.[8] His policy is to build up the group by strengthening certain horizontal, not vertical, relationships, not to add to the social status of the better-off.

The Corinthians' own chosen emissaries will take the money to Jerusalem. This, too, is a unifying strategy, since it will mean that the congregation as a whole must make a decision, and it wards off any hint that Paul might be indirectly trying to get funds for himself from the Corinthians. He may accompany the emissaries to Jerusalem, and he will certainly write letters of recommendation for them (vv. 3f.). These letters will authenticate the mission and indicate to the Jerusalem church who the givers are.

Paul's plan as he wrote was to come to the Corinthians the long way around, passing through Macedonia, undoubtedly to visit the churches there first (v. 5). But as it turned out he was forced, when he received new infor-

---

much less a repeated collection like the tithe. He is also right that nothing is said about these funds being collected each Sunday *during the worship service*. The text simply speaks of funds being laid aside on that day, presumably to be collected when Paul or his coworker arrived.

5. As opposed to the congregational collection mentioned in Justin *Dialogue I* 67.

6. There is no NT evidence that Christians in the biblical period ever treated Sunday as if it were the sabbath. Indeed, many Jewish Christians still observed the Jewish sabbath (Friday sundown to Saturday sundown) in addition to the Lord's Day. It was a later practice to merge sabbath with Sunday. Cf. G. D. Fee, *The First Epistle to the Corinthians* (Grand Rapids: Eerdmans, 1987), p. 813 and n. 25. and the literature cited there.

7. The way the verse is worded suggests giving out of one's surplus, not out of one's basic budget. Fee, *First Corinthians*, p. 814, suggests that this means giving in accord with whatever success or prosperity may have come one's way in the past week.

8. So J. K. Chow, *Patronage and Power: A Study of Social Networks in Corinth* (Sheffield: JSOT, 1992), pp. 185f. Issues of patronage and of church leadership are to be distinguished. Paul will speak in favor of Stephanas's leadership (vv. 15f.), but not because Stephanas is male or a patron, but because of his role as a leader.

mation, to make a sudden sea journey to remedy problems in Corinth. And that was to no good effect, as we see from 2 Corinthians. That his travel plans when he wrote 1 Corinthians had to be altered shows how ad hoc his letters were. He planned to stay in Corinth, perhaps through the winter (v. 6), since it was the season to avoid traveling, especially by sea. He knew that there was still much to correct in Corinth (v. 7).

The second part of v. 6 may be seen as an attempt to meet the Corinthian desire to give Paul some financial support. He will not accept support for preaching there or an offer of patronage that would make him someone's in-house teacher or rhetor, but he will accept provisions and aid so that he can get to his next destination, thus not violating his plan to offer the gospel free of charge.

Verse 6 also indicates that Paul is not sure where he will go after Corinth. He is in Ephesus as he writes and plans to stay until Pentecost (v. 8), presumably, that is, until the day of Pentecost, not just the fifty-day season of Pentecost, which preceded the day of Pentecost. This suggests that he is writing in the spring. Paul will stay where he is because of the great opportunities and opposition there (v. 9). This was typical of Paul's experience in many places.

Paul has sent Timothy along in his stead, though he is unsure when Timothy will arrive in Corinth.[9] Vv. 10f. suggest that Paul fears that Timothy will be treated with disrespect, since he is Paul's envoy and there are ongoing tensions in the Corinthian community, with one group championing Apollos, another Paul, and perhaps other *apostoloi* are being lionized as well.[10] The Corinthians are to protect Timothy from any untoward behavior and to enable him financially to return to Paul when the time comes. They are to recognize him as one of Paul's coworkers, a legitimate Christian leader to be respected and heeded.

Verse 12 suggests that some Corinthians asked Paul to send Apollos to them again.[11] This means that Apollos must have been working with or near Paul in Ephesus at the time, after having made an initial visit to Corinth (cf.

9. The wording suggests that Timothy is not the bearer of this letter, and thus M. M. Mitchell's argument (*Paul and the Rhetoric of Reconciliation* [Tübingen: Mohr, 1991], p. 293) is only partly correct. Paul will take the treatment of Timothy as a barometer of how his cause fares in Corinth, but since Timothy is probably not the bearer of this letter, Paul will not be able to tell from Timothy's treatment how the letter has been received. Cf. above, p. 147, on 4:17. It appears that Timothy never got to Corinth (2 Cor. 1:1).

10. This is why both Apollos and Paul are likely staying away from Corinth at present until this letter has had its effect. Cf. C. K. Barrett, *The First Epistle to the Corinthians* (New York: Harper and Row, 1968), p. 392. As Mitchell (*Paul and the Rhetoric of Reconciliation,* p. 293) notes, they are still objects of controversy in Corinth.

11. Whether by letter or orally is not clear, but I suspect it is the former, since the negative reports seem to have come orally through Chloe, while the positive requests, the questions, and the arguments seem to have been in a letter.

Acts 18:24-28). It is not clear who did not want Apollos to go back. The statement is impersonal: "it was not the will," and the most natural antecedent would be Apollos, though this could refer to God's will. If Apollos's will is in view, as seems likely, this suggests that Apollos did not want to add fuel to the fire of Corinthian party spirit and to their playing of favorites. But Paul makes it clear that he himself did not impede Apollos from returning. Indeed, he strongly urged it. In Paul's view, he and Apollos are not at odds but are coworkers in the same cause.

The diplomacy with which Paul handles this delicate matter suggests that, as with the issue of the collection, this was very much a concern of those who wrote to Paul, that is, those whose concerns he is giving attention to in order to heal the divisions in the congregation. It was good rhetorical strategy to leave Apollos's travel plans till the end of the letter, unlike the earlier references to Paul's own plans (cf. 4:17f.), since this meant that Apollos's advocates would have to hear the whole of the letter's argument before they got their answer about their champion rhetor's plans. By then, Paul must have hoped that some of what he had said against factions based on Christian rhetors would have been accepted. In any case, he has done the best that he could do without actually being present to heal the rifts in the Corinthian congregation, and he intends to build on whatever success the letter might have with a personal visit, despite what "some" (4:18) may be thinking.

The *Peroratio:* 16:13-18

A Word to the Wise

As W. Wuellner rightly argues, in 16:13f. we have the beginning of the *peroratio* in the form of an emotive recapitulation of the basic thesis *(propositio)* of the whole letter, which was stated in 1:10.[1] This in turn is followed by a final *parakaleō* period that sets off 16:15-18 as a final exhortation, a final attempt to end factiousness in the Corinthian congregation, and amplifies some key points that Paul wishes to reiterate.[2] In 1:10 Paul urged the Corinthians not to be divided but to be of one mind, and 16:14 has the same focus, arguing that everything should be done in love, that is, with consideration for others. This is how the factious congregation will be built up and unified.

Quintilian tells us that the *peroratio* of a speech ought to be brief and can either deal with the facts previously presented or give an emotional appeal *(Inst. Or.* 6.1.1). He adds that it is effective, in the *peroratio,* to deal with that which one's adversaries have dealt with poorly or have failed to consider in their speech (6.1.4). It is possible that we should see 16:15-18 in this light, since Paul is apparently offering a new view of Stephanas here that the Corinthians have not considered. Had they thought of Stephanas in this way, they might not have written to Paul (in the letter referred to in 7:1) in the manner, or with all the issues, that they did. In *Rhetorica ad Alexandrum* 33.1439b.12ff. we are told that a deliberative recapitulation can take five dif-

---

1. W. Wuellner, "Greek Rhetoric and Pauline Argumentation," in *Early Christian Literature and the Classical Intellectual Tradition,* ed. W. R. Schoedel and R. L. Wilken (Paris: Beauchesne, 1979), pp. 177-88, here p. 183.

2. The three main functions of the closing *peroratio* were recapitulation, emotional appeal, and amplification. Cf. Aristotle *Rhet.* 3.19.1; *Rhetorica ad Herennium* 2.30.

ferent forms: argument, enumeration, proposal of policy *(proairesis)*, interrogation, or irony. I would suggest that 16:15-18 should be seen as a proposal of policy after the appeal to emotions and recapitulation of the major theme in vv. 13f.

Verse **13** provides some general exhortation to stand fast, be brave (literally "play the man"), and stand firm in the faith.[3] V. **14** indicates that everything should be "done in love," that nothing should be done that cannot be done in love toward fellow believers. This would rule out much of the behavior that Paul has criticized in the letter.

Paul also pleads for the Corinthians to recognize Stephanas and his household as Christian leaders in Corinth (vv. **15ff.**). They were the first converts in Achaia, or at least in that part of Achaia, which is doubtless also why they were among those that Paul baptized (1:16). The mention of Stephanas's household suggests that he was a man of considerable means. Paul is not correcting in this letter all the wealthy members of the Corinthian congregation — some were on his side. Stephanas devoted himself to service to the Corinthians. He was probably not anointed or appointed by Paul, though Paul clearly approves his leadership.[4]

Verse **16** indicates that the Corinthians are to recognize *all* such laborers and coworkers in the Lord's work, which would include people like Priscilla and Aquila, Phoebe from the congregation in Cenchreae (Rom. 16:1), and perhaps Chloe as well (1 Cor. 1:11), if not also her people.[5] This suggests that some in Corinth may not have been recognizing the work and leadership of Stephanas.[6]

3. This is a clear indication that Paul does use *pistis* with the article to refer to the content of the gospel, as we find in the Pastorals as well.

4. Stephanas's leadership was an achieved status, not something that simply went along with his social status. Paul simply affirms a leadership role that Stephanas had already assumed. Cf. J. K. Chow, *Patronage and Power: A Study of Social Networks in Corinth* (Sheffield: JSOT, 1992), p. 190, and his critique of the view espoused by E. Schüssler Fiorenza, "Rhetorical Situation and Historical Reconstruction in 1 Corinthians," *NTS* 33 (1987), pp. 386-403, here p. 397.

5. The reference to "all the coworkers" makes abundantly clear that Paul is not foisting some gender-specific leadership agenda on the congregation in Corinth.

6. J. D. G. Dunn, "The Responsible Congregation," in *Charisma und Agape,* ed. L. de Lorenzi (Rome: Abbazia di S Paolo fuori le mura, 1983), pp. 201-38, here p. 229, may well be right that Paul has a particular kind of service in view as Stephanas's field of ministry, and not simply a general leadership role. He is not mentioned in ch. 14 as a worship leader or in ch. 6 when someone wise is needed to settle legal disputes. One conjecture is that he was a patron of the Christian poor during the famine in 51. Cf. B. W. Winter, "Secular and Christian Responses to Corinthian Famines," *TynB* 40 (1989), pp. 86-106.

These verses would serve as a sort of letter of recommendation for Stephanas and his household, who are with Paul as he writes. Presumably Stephanas has told Paul of some of the problems in Corinth and was preparing to return to the city. Perhaps he was the bearer and intended presenter of this letter, though that Sosthenes (1:1) had that role cannot be ruled out.[7]

The visits of Stephanas and two other men have made up for Paul's absence from Corinth and have been an encouragement by representing the devoted Christians of Corinth (vv. 17f.). Fortunatus and Achaicus may have been two of Stephanas's freedmen or hired hands, for both of their names suggest that they were former slaves.[8] The Corinthians are urged to "recognize" these men, which likely means to obey them and accept their leadership and work. Paul would only recommend that others be "recognized" if he was convinced that they basically accepted his authority and thus would accept his advice. Much of the force of the deliberative argument of this whole letter depends on the assumption that the speaker has the authority to propose or modify policy.

In terms of the leadership structure of the Pauline communities, these verses, coupled with hints elsewhere in the letter, rightly lead M. Y. MacDonald to this conclusion:

> The picture of the organization of the Pauline communities as being purely pneumatic, which represents the starting point for much writing on the development of the church, is deficient because it does not fully take into account the relationship between beliefs, social structures, and social setting. The leadership structures of Paul's communities are not shaped in a straight-forward manner by his theology;[9] the relationship between the structures and ideas is dialectical. . . . A purely charismatic ministry and concept of authority based exclusively on Spirit endowment presents an unrealistic picture of the human society of the Apostle.[10]

Paul seems to identify easily with people of higher social status like Stephanas and Gaius and perhaps Chloe and Phoebe, and it is revealing that

---

7. Cf. A. C. Wire, *The Corinthian Women Prophets: A Reconstruction through Paul's Rhetoric* (Minneapolis: Fortress, 1990), here p. 178.

8. G. D. Fee, *The First Epistle to the Corinthians* (Grand Rapids: Eerdmans, 1987), p. 831. Fortunatus is a Latin name meaning "lucky." Achaicus means "from Achaia." Such nicknames or impersonal labels were common for slaves.

9. Or, I would add, by the Corinthians' theologies.

10. M. Y. MacDonald, *The Pauline Churches: A Socio-Historical Study of Institution-alisation in the Pauline and Deutero-Pauline Writings* (Cambridge: Cambridge University, 1988), p. 60.

the members of the household of such a person, including the head of the household, were the first of his converts in Achaia. But Paul also rejected social status as a fundamental basis for determining one's standing in Christ and in Christ's community.[11] This must have made for interesting conversations between Paul and Stephanas, especially since Paul regularly defends and tries to protect the weaker and socially less advantaged members of the congregation, as chs. 8–10 have made evident.

It is a mistake to assume that early Christianity only appealed to and converted the poor, slaves, and other oppressed minorities in the Greco-Roman world, especially if one is talking about Roman Corinth. As E. A. Judge says, "The Corinthians . . . were dominated by a socially pretentious section of the population. . . . Beyond that they seem to have drawn on a broad constituency, probably representing the household dependents of the leading members."[12]

The Good News that Paul preached was for all people, but it often required the greatest sacrifices of the socially better-off, since they had more to give and the most to lose in honor, power, and social position by converting to a new minority religion. While Paul drew on the benefits of the social structures of his day, he would not allow those structures to dictate the structure of relationships in the *ekklēsia*. He made use of a person like Stephanas, but also made clear that he endorsed Stephanas because Stephanas, like Paul himself, had voluntarily set aside his social status in order to serve other Christians in Corinth.

11. Cf. E. A. Judge, "Cultural Conformity and Innovation in Paul: Some Clues from Contemporary Documents," *TynB* 35 (1984), pp. 3-24, here p. 12: "While accepting rank he repudiates the status conventions which permitted people to exploit the system to private advantage."

12. Judge, *The Social Pattern of Christian Groups in the First Century* (London: Tyndale, 1960), p. 58. It is also likely that Paul made converts among those he contacted through his work as an artisan. These would include fellow artisans and people from a variety of social strata.

Closing Epistolary Greetings and Remarks: 16:19-24

The conclusions of Paul's letters follow in a broad sense the usual epistolary conventions of closing greetings and final remarks, which for Paul might include exhortations, an indication that he is writing the closing remarks, a description of his travel plans, a benediction, and an eschatological note.[1] His letter closings usually show us that he had a considerable support network and that many early Christians were highly mobile, for instance, Priscilla and Aquila. This blurs the distinction between local congregational officials and traveling leaders, because some seem to fit both categories. There are also elements in Paul's closing remarks that reflect the final part of a Christian worship service, which suggests that the reading of his letter was normally the last thing done in corporate worship.

The greetings in vv. **19f.** are typical. Aquila and Priscilla, who is called Prisca here, went to Corinth from Rome (Acts 18:1f.), but now have a house congregation in Ephesus, where they straightened out Apollos on Christian baptism (Acts 18:24-26). Later we will find these mobile merchant missionaries in Rome (Rom. 16:3).

The holy kiss (v. **20**) is also mentioned in 1 Thess. 5:26; 2 Cor. 13:12; Rom. 16:16; and 1 Pet. 5:14. Obviously this form of greeting was a regular part of early Christianity. It was probably derived from the family practice of a kiss of greeting at the door, for not only did Christians meet in homes like family, called themselves family, and adapted family codes of behavior, they were also expected to love and treat each other as family. "It is interesting that after the

---

1. Cf. Gal. 6:11-18; Rom. 16:1-27; Phil. 4:15-23. On the form of Pauline letter closings, cf. G. D. Fee, *The First Epistle to the Corinthians* (Grand Rapids: Eerdmans, 1987), p. 826, and literature cited there.

New Testament writings the liturgical kiss is not mentioned in the early church for almost a hundred years. Justin Martyr is the first Christian to refer to it again in the middle of the second century."[2]

In v. 21 Paul indicates that he is writing these closing remarks in his own hand. It was normal practice in ancient letter writing when one used an amanuensis to authenticate the letter and to add a personal touch at the end. Paul also alludes to this practice in Gal. 6:11.

Verse 22a indicates in strong language that not loving Christ is the ultimate sin in Paul's eyes. The "anathema" statement found here is very similar in form to the one in Gal. 1:8. It is not clear whether *anathema* and *maran atha* go together here. If so, then the curse formula would be followed in the worship service by the plea for the Lord to come as judge and act on the curse. It is also not clear what connection there is, if any, of this curse statement with the anathema against Jesus in 12:3.

The Aramaic clause *maran atha* (v. 22b) obviously comes to us from the Aramaic-speaking Christian community, probably in Jerusalem. If we read it as *maran atha,* which is possible, it would mean "our Lord has come." Read as *marana tha,* which seems more likely, it is a prayer: "Come, Lord." This latter interpretation is supported by what is probably a Greek translation of the clause in Rev. 22:20: "Come, Lord Jesus." Didache 10.6 also supports the view that this was an early eschatological prayer for the Lord to return. There is no evidence for the view that it was used as an invocation of Christ over the Eucharist during the NT era. In the Didache it is found among the prayers at the close of the Eucharist.

Paul concludes by wishing the Corinthians God's grace and his own love. Despite all the problems he has had and will have with them, he loves them. He still treats them like his brothers and sisters. He still rejoices in them when he can and especially when he is able to be with some of them, as he was when he wrote (vv. 17f.). This bespeaks a man with a very large heart. The sternness of much of the letter is that of a father who cares too much to let his spiritual progeny go astray, so he both loves and disciplines them. Paul believes that in the Christian family of faith discipline should be exercised at times, but in love, just as one would hope it would be in the physical family. In Paul's eyes some of the Corinthians, while highly gifted, were also notably immature in the way they practiced their faith. This explains the pedagogical and paternal character of much of this deliberative discourse. It is an attempt to help these converts grow up, not a patriarchal power play to stifle their growth and force

---

2. S. Benko, *Pagan Rome and the Early Christians* (Bloomington: Illinois University, 1984), pp. 79-102, quoting p. 81. Benko's attempt to trace the kiss back to John 20, where Jesus breathes on the disciples, cannot be right, but he has presented considerable evidence that this was a kiss on the lips, not on the cheek, as later abuse of the practice demonstrates.

them to remain children under the thumb of their spiritual parent. That Paul gives them all this advice about their future course of action strongly suggests that he believes that they can grow up and has hope that they will do so.

But as we will see, this hope was not soon realized. Indeed, to judge from Clement's letter to the Corinthians at the end of the first century, they were still manifesting the same sort of childish behavior. We must now turn to 2 Corinthians to evaluate the next phase in the history of this lively but troublesome group of Christians.

2 CORINTHIANS

The Background and Foreground
of the Letter

2 Corinthians is one of the most difficult of Paul's letters for the interpreter because of the critical problems in regard to the letter's integrity and because some of the issues raised in the letter are so explosive. That the letter as we have it is made up of parts of a number of separate letters has come to be almost a critical axiom. And a case can be made that Paul was nearly at war with other Jewish Christians, probably from Jerusalem, who were going around and trying to sabatoge his work in Galatia, Corinth, and perhaps elsewhere. This opposition has sometimes even been traced to Peter. Was Paul an isolated maverick in early Christianity whom most of the early *apostoloi* opposed or to whom they gave at best only guarded approval? When Paul mentions that his life has been in danger on various occasions (11:23-26), was this caused by Jewish Christians reacting to Paul's stance on the Law in general and circumcision in particular?

Setting, Literary History, and Rhetorical Structure

The Goal of the Letter

Cicero once suggested that the ability to placate or reconcile was a sign of true greatness in human character (*De Off.* I.25.88).[1] If this is so, then perhaps 2 Corinthians more than any of Paul's other letters reveals his largeness of

---

1. The translation of *placabilitate* in the Loeb edition of *De Officiis* (tr. W. Miller [Cambridge: Harvard University, 1912], pp. 88f.) is not very helpful.

soul. Here he wrestles with a variety of forces that threaten to alienate him
from his converts in Corinth. While 1 Corinthians was written to effect reconciliation among Paul's converts in Corinth, 2 Corinthians was written to
effect reconciliation between Paul and his converts there. Both letters aim at
reconciliation, but they approach that goal with different rhetorical strategies,
as the exigences calling them forth differed.

It is clear, apart from whether 2 Corinthians contains one or more letters
of Paul to the Corinthians, that his relationship with them deteriorated after
he wrote 1 Corinthians. In 2 Corinthians Paul must resort to defense and
attack in regard to his own ministry to the Corinthians. Letters exhibiting
judicial or forensic rhetoric could be either accusing or apologetic, and
2 Corinthians is both.[2] In it Paul focuses considerable attention on addressing
and trying to overcome specific obstacles in the way of full reconciliation with
his spiritual children. "The combination of . . . social and theological misgiv-
ings resulted in the shutdown of mutual affection between Paul and the
Corinthians. . . . Paul writes to restore this relationship, and to restore their
understanding and trust in him as an apostle of God."[3]

Furthermore, Paul believed that failure to achieve this reconciliation
would endanger the very Christian identity of the Corinthian *ekklēsia,* since
Paul was Christ's agent. To be alienated from the agent was to be alienated
from the one who sent him. So not only the integrity of Paul's ministry but
also the integrity of the Corinthians' faith is at stake. Paul must defend himself,
his behavior, and his ministry and he must also protect his converts from the
very real danger of apostasy. Failure to see the letter in this light has contributed
significantly to some of the partition theories.

The letter thus attempts to put into practice what Paul so eloquently
preaches in 5:17-19. If Paul is the ambassador of reconciliation between God
in Christ and the Corinthians, to discredit the ambassador is to deny the reality
of the Corinthians' reconciliation to God.

Partition Theories

There are almost as many partition theories as there are commentaries on
2 Corinthians, despite the fact that there is not a shred of textual evidence to
support the view that any part of the letter as we have it did not originally

2. S. K. Stowers, "Social Typification and Classification of Ancient Letters," in *The
Social World of Formative Christianity and Judaism,* ed. J. Neusner (Philadelphia: Fortress,
1988), pp. 78-90, here p. 84.

3. S. Kraftchick, "Death in Us, Life in You: The Apostolic Medium," *Society of Biblical
Literature 1991 Seminar Papers,* ed. E. H. Lovering (Atlanta: Scholars, 1991), pp. 618-37,
here p. 625.

belong where it now is.[4] Part of the reason for the existence of these theories is that most treatments of 2 Corinthians have not taken into account Paul's use of ancient rhetorical conventions. Recent works have begun to remedy this problem, but attention has been focused on chs. 10–13, which is something of a rhetorical masterpiece, or on chs. 8-9, not on 2 Corinthians as a whole.[5] This sort of approach fails to identify the digressions in Paul's argument in 2 Corinthians as such. But even in other letters that are not usually subject to partition theories, Paul uses substantial digressions (e.g., Romans 9–11; 1 Corinthians 9 and 13).

Before we turn to consideration of these partition theories, we must spell out what we know with some assurance about the literary history of Paul's Corinthian correspondence:

1 Cor. 5:9 mentions a letter written by Paul prior to 1 Corinthians that we will call *Corinthians A.* Some have identified it with 2 Cor. 6:14–7:1. The context of 1 Cor. 5:9 makes it clear that Paul wrote in *Corinthians A* about immoral Christians. It is possible but unlikely that 2 Cor. 6:14–7:1 speaks of immoral Christians, since it speaks of *apistoi,* probably "unbelievers" (6:14), and seems to be a discussion of the same concerns that are addressed in 1 Corinthians 8–10.

Paul wrote, probably in A.D. 53 or 54, 1 Corinthians, a piece of deliberative rhetoric using a variety of arguments to persuade the Corinthians to cease their factious behavior. We will call it *Corinthians B.*

2 Cor. 2:3, 4, 9 refers to a letter of anguish, a painful letter. Some have identified this as 2 Cor. 10–13, but the arguments for this view are generally weak, especially in view of the references to a *past* visit by Titus to Corinth in 12:18. And one would expect the subject of the painful letter, the man who offended Paul and was to be disciplined, to be mentioned in chs. 10–13, if it were part of that letter. Or if one argues that the part of the letter that mentions the man was lost or edited out, then all substantive connection of the painful letter with chs. 10–13 has

---

4. No manuscripts support any sort of partition theory for 2 Corinthians, nor do the earliest references to the letter (Marcion and the Muratorian Canon). It is puzzling that Clement, who reflects a good knowledge of 1 Corinthians in his letter to Corinth, written in the 90s, does not seem to know of 2 Corinthians. This may suggest that the Pauline corpus was not yet assembled in its present form. 2 Pet. 3:16 may suggest that there was already such a collection in the late first century, but what it included is anybody's guess.

5. Such studies include H. D. Betz, *2 Corinthians 8 and 9: A Commentary on Two Administrative Letters of the Apostle Paul* (Philadelphia: Fortress, 1985), and J. T. Fitzgerald, "Paul, the Ancient Epistolary Theorists, and 2 Corinthians 10–13: The Purpose and Literary Genre of a Pauline Letter," in *Greeks, Romans, and Christians,* ed. D. Balch, et al. (Philadelphia: Fortress, 1990), pp. 190-200.

been lost.[6] What Paul demands before his return to Corinth (12:14–
13:10) does not include punishing any Corinthian Christian.[7] Thus it
appears that the painful letter, which we will call *Corinthians C,* is, like
Corinthians A, now lost.
All of 2 Corinthians, regardless of whether we divide it or not, was written
later than *Corinthians C.*

There is a growing consensus that 2 Cor. 6:14–7:1 is a pre-Pauline or
earlier Pauline piece that Paul has adopted and used to his own ends.[8] It is
also argued that it is a later insertion into an already existing letter and that
6:13 leads smoothly to 7:2.[9] But no good reason has been offered for it being
inserted where it stands in 2 Corinthians. There is also no manuscript evidence
for an interpolation here. There are sufficient Pauline terminology and ideas
in 6:14–7:1 that even if the text is pre-Pauline, Paul has made it his own.[10]
Betz's arguments that 2 Corinthians 8–9 should be seen as a separate
document or documents have not won wide approval.[11] While Betz is right

6. Cf. A. M. G. Stephenson, "A Defence of the Integrity of 2 Corinthians," in *The
Authorship and Integrity of the NT* (London: SPCK, 1965), pp. 82-97, here p. 93. 2 Corinthians 10–13 represents an angry Paul, not a tearful Paul. Stephenson's suggestion that the
differences in tone between chs. 1–9 and 10–13 exist because Paul himself took up the pen
at ch. 10 is inadequate.

7. J. Munck, *Paul and the Salvation of Mankind* (London: SCM, 1959), p. 170. The
view that 2 Corinthians 10–13 is the painful letter is being increasingly rejected. Cf. the
discussion in R. P. Martin, *2 Corinthians* (Waco: Word, 1986), pp. xlviiff.
   It is also unconvincing to argue that 1 Corinthians is the severe letter. It is unlikely
that the matter discussed in 1 Corinthians 5 is the same as that discussed in 2 Corinthians
2, which concerns a person who personally insulted Paul during his painful visit. The only
connection between this incident and what is discussed in 1 Cor. 5 is the mention of
disciplinary action taken by the Corinthians, and disciplinary actions were probably not
rare in the Corinthian church. Furthermore, 1 Corinthians does not seem to have the tone
of one writing in distress, tears, and anguish.

8. Cf. D. Rensberger, "2 Corinthians 6:14–7:1: A Fresh Examination," *Studia Biblica
et Theologica* 8 (1978), pp. 25-49; G. D. Fee, "II Corinthians VI.14–VII.1 and Food Offered
to Idols," *NTS* 23 (1977), pp. 140-61.

9. 7:2 actually appears to be *resumptive* of the message of 6:12f., which presupposes
an interlude. Otherwise it is redundant.

10. Fee, "II Cor. 6:14," pp. 140ff. J. Murphy-O'Connor, "Relating 2 Cor. 6:14–7:1 to
its Context," *NTS* 33 (1987), pp. 272-75, has demonstrated how 6:14–7:1, though a digression, could plausibly be said to fit into its present context in light of its connections with
what precedes and what follows. Unless one is prepared to argue that a later editor has also
modified what precedes and follows 6:14–7:1 to make it fit in better, Murphy-O'Connor's
arguments must count against the passage being a later insertion.

11. Few if any of the more recent commentaries have followed Betz in this view. Cf.
especially F. W. Danker, *II Corinthians* (Minneapolis: Augsburg, 1989), pp. 19ff.; Martin,
2 Corinthians, pp. 249ff.

to note the rhetorical character of these two chapters, he fails to note that they form a deliberative argument that serves Paul's larger forensic purposes as he attempts to defend his ministry and mend fences with his converts.[12] Since some of the Corinthian Christians wished to be benefactors, Paul satisfies this desire without personally accepting patronage by urging their participation in the collection for Jerusalem. The two chapters look at the matter of the collection from slightly different angles. Danker is probably right in saying that we should see ch. 8 as dealing with details about the collection, while ch. 9 focuses on the motivation for giving to it.[13] More importantly, ch. 7 prepares for the appeals in chs. 8 and 9 and was therefore probably part of the same document from the start.

Probably most scholars still believe, despite the lack of textual evidence, that we have parts of two separate Pauline letters in 2 Corinthians 1–9 and 10–13,[14] most regarding 1–9 as the earlier of the two.[15] Certainly something is required to explain the shift in tone, and to some degree in focus, from ch. 9 to ch. 10. Only in ch. 10 does the issue of the false apostles, Paul's real opponents in Corinth, seem to arise with any vigor. Chapters 1–9 are often read as a largely conciliatory letter that stands on its own without what follows it, though this overlooks the clear evidence in those chapters of serious and still unresolved problems (1:17ff.; 2:17).

A common view has been that Paul's mood had changed and that chs.

---

12. Betz's disassembly of 2 Corinthians into several letters is summarized in his article in *The Anchor Bible Dictionary,* I, ed. D. N. Freedman (New York: Doubleday, 1992), pp. 1148-54. It reflects the problems of excessive mirror reading and too much reading between the lines. On the deliberative character of chs. 8–9, cf. G. A. Kennedy, *NT Interpretation through Rhetorical Criticism* (Chapel Hill: University of North Carolina, 1984), p. 87. One could argue that Paul's aims throughout 2 Corinthians are deliberative but that he uses mainly forensic rhetoric, except in 6:14–7:1 and chs. 8–9, to achieve his deliberative aims. When a letter has mixed rhetorical types, rhetorical form and function may be differently assessed. Different forms can serve the same ultimate aim. The crucial question concerns function.

Munck, *Paul and the Salvation of Mankind,* p. 173, points out the clear evidence (including 1:1 and 11:10) that the whole letter, not just ch. 9, was addressed not just to Corinth, but to all the churches in Achaea, including Corinth. Thus, the reference to Achaea in 9:2 does not separate ch. 9 from the rest of the document, not even from ch. 8. Paul is concerned that a whole mission field was in danger, including the *ekklēsiae* in Cenchreae, Corinth, and wherever else in Achaea there were congregations.

13. Danker, *II Corinthians,* p. 19.

14. E.g., F. Lang, *Die Briefe an die Korinther* (Göttingen: Vandenhoeck, 1986), p. 9. A general critique of this position appears in W. G. Kümmel, *Introduction to the NT* (revised edition, Nashville: Abingdon, 1975), pp. 287-93.

15. C. K. Barrett, *The Second Epistle to the Corinthians* (New York: Harper, 1973), pp. 5-21; V. P. Furnish, *II Corinthians* (New York: Doubleday, 1984), pp. 35-41; Martin, *2 Corinthians,* pp. xlii-li.

10–13 were composed perhaps just the day after chs. 1–9. Another form of the argument is that Paul wrote chs. 10–13 after he had received further information of a drastic nature that made him revise his estimate of the situation in Corinth and write a stern response. If Paul had received such earth-shattering news after he had written the letter represented in chs. 1–9 but before he had sent it, he would probably have torn up his first draft and started over, writing a whole new letter in light of the new situation.[16] Furthermore, chs. 10–13 contain no allusion to Paul learning that the situation had changed since he had last written.[17] Those who argue that chs. 10–13 were composed after chs. 1–9 was sent must explain how the ending of the letter preserved in chs. 1–9 and the beginning of the letter represented by 10–13 were lost. And why is it, if the tone of these two letters is so different, that they came to be edited together into one document?[18]

Barrett has argued that we must take the aorist tense verbs in 8:18-22 as epistolary, meaning "we send herewith," while the aorists in 12:17-18a must be taken as real past tenses, in particular *synapesteila:* "I sent the brother with Titus." That is to say, Paul sent Titus with the letter represented by chs. 1–9 and then referred to this same journey of Titus in the later letter represented by chs. 10–13.[19]

But ch. 7 indicates that Titus delivered the severe letter and brought back to Paul the news of the Corinthians' response to it. Whether the aorists in 8:6 are epistolary or not, that verse refers to Titus completing something in regard to the collection that he had already begun among the Corinthians. Furthermore, there is no reason to take the aorists in 12:17-18a as real aorists rather than epistolary aorists, even despite v. 18b, since Titus had already made a beginning in regard to the collection when he delivered the severe letter, and v. 18b is a rhetorical question expecting no for an answer.[20] Paul is pointing out that Titus's previous behavior should give the Corinthians a basis for judging his present intent when he arrives with 2 Corinthians and plans to begin again the work of the collection in earnest before Paul's third visit. 12:18

---

16. Martin, *2 Corinthians,* p. xlviii.

17. Kümmel, *Introduction,* p. 290. He also argues against identification of chs. 10–13 as the "painful" letter.

18. Not only so but one must argue that this happened at a very early date, so early that we have no manuscript evidence of either chs. 1–9 or chs. 10–13 as an independent document.

19. C. K. Barrett, "Titus," in idem, *Essays on Paul* (Philadelphia: Westminster, 1982), pp. 118-31, here p. 127.

20. The perfect tense of *apestalka* in v. 17 does not affect this point since it refers to a variety of missions in the past, including, no doubt, Titus's delivery of the severe letter and perhaps Timothy's visit as well, and need not refer back to the visit mentioned in ch. 8–9, which was still in the future when 2 Corinthians was written.

could be translated: "I am urging Titus to go and am sending the brother with him. Titus did not take advantage of you before, did he?"

What we have tried to point out in this cursory review of the partition theories is that all of them have significant drawbacks. Therefore, if there can be a theory that explains why 2 Corinthians *as a whole* has the shape it has, it would be preferable.

Forensic Rhetoric and the Structure of the Letter

Arguments for the unity of 2 Corinthians have been based on rhetorical criticism, in particular by F. Young and D. F. Ford[21] and by F. W. Danker, who draws on the wealth of benefaction literature from the first century.[22] Here we will maintain that *2 Corinthians taken as a compositional whole is an example of forensic or judicial rhetoric.*[23]

It is characteristic of forensic rhetoric that it focuses on things done or said in the past, things for which one could be taken to trial, and for which the audience will be the judge. Clues to the time frame of a letter, and thus to the type of rhetoric being used in it, come at the beginning and end of the body of the letter.[24] In 2 Corinthians, in contrast to 1 Corinthians, we find a focus on the past, not only in the first real statement of the basic proposition of the letter (2:17), but also in the *narratio* leading up to it in chs. 1–2. The narrative statement in 1:12 is particularly noteworthy: The discussion will be mainly about how Paul (and by implication the Corinthians) have behaved

---

21. F. Young and D. F. Ford, *Meaning and Truth in 2 Corinthians* (Grand Rapids: Eerdmans, 1987), pp. 27-59.

22. Danker, *II Corinthians,* pp. 18ff.

23. This does mean not that Paul might not use rhetorical techniques from other sorts of rhetoric but that 2 Corinthians as a compositional whole is an example of forensic rhetoric (so Kennedy, *NT Interpretation,* p. 87). It should not be seen as deliberative rhetoric since it has a long *narratio* and is concerned with defending past actions and words and because of the notable near-absence of the key terminology of deliberative speeches, namely the language of interest and advantage *(symphoron, sympherei,* and *symphoros).* In 1 Corinthians we find such language in 6:12; 7:35; 10:23, 33; 12:7 (cf. M. M. Mitchell, *Paul and the Rhetoric of Reconciliation* [Tübingen: Mohr, 1991], pp. 33-39). In 2 Corinthians there are only two examples of the use of such language, at 8:10 and 12:1. But Paul says in 12:1 that what he is about to recite is of no use or advantage! This leaves only 2 Cor. 8:10 where Paul talks about what is appropriate, advantageous, or useful for the audience. This appeal to the audience's best self-interest, however, comes at the beginning of a deliberative argument about the collection and in fact signals the deliberative chracter of that argument. But the rhetoric in chs. 8–9 is by no means characteristic of the letter as whole, and even chs. 8–9 function as part of Paul's defense by showing his aboveboard handling of money matters.

24. Mitchell, *Rhetoric of Reconciliation,* pp. 24f.

(anestraphēmen) in the past. So Paul defends his behavior, especially in the recent past, and makes accusations against the Corinthians. Again, in the final warning in 13:1ff., which leads up to the *peroratio* in 13:5ff., Paul focuses on what was said or done in the past. After a reference to the need for witnesses he adds "I warned those who had sinned previously. . . ." This forensic concentration on the past may help explain why 2 Corinthians focuses so much on the past saving acts of God in Christ and so little on what may be called future eschatology.

Forensic rhetoric was by far the most common form of rhetoric, providing the basis for discussion of rhetoric in the handbooks.[25] In forensic rhetoric one can expect the rhetor to pull out all the stops and use all possible proofs, both inartificial and artificial, to make his case. Inartificial proofs are those not manufactured by the rhetor. They include references to witnesses, in this case God (1:23), Timothy, Paul's other coworkers, the Corinthians themselves, and the Macedonians (cf. also 13:1-3); to promises or oaths (1:17ff.); to contracts or covenants (3:1-18); and to decisions of other courts (5:10 — though here the appeal is to a future decision).

Artificial proofs are derived from the facts of the case and include *ēthos*, *logos*, and *pathos*. *Ēthos* in forensic rhetoric has to do with the establishment of moral character by showing oneself (or one's client) in the best possible light and one's opponents in the worst. The aim here is to establish the goodwill and uprightness of the person under scrutiny. Even on a cursory reading of 2 Corinthians, it is clear that this is one of the matters that preoccupies Paul throughout the letter, but especially at the beginning. This partly explains the more conciliatory tone in the first few chapters of the letter: Paul is presenting himself as one who encourages his audience in order to build rapport with them, making them favorably disposed towards their apostle.[26]

Pathos is the effort to arouse the audience's emotions to sympathy with the case of the accused and rejection of the views of the opponents. This is accomplished at the end of 2 Corinthians, where Paul appeals to the stronger

25. S. K. Stowers, *Letter Writing in Greco-Roman Antiquity* (Philadelphia: Westminster, 1986), p. 56, points out that the social relationship between the writer or speaker and the audience was one of the major determinants of the style, structure, and *topoi* of a letter (cf. Menander 395.4-30). Paul clearly assumes authority over his converts in Corinth but stylistically prefers to treat them as equals, calling them co-workers, and fellow brothers and sisters in Christ, though he can also give advice and exhortation, assuming the posture of a superior to an inferior. Toward the end of the letter this posture becomes more evident as Paul must take charge of the situation and act as a judge over the Corinthians (cf. 13:2ff.), thus turning the tables on them.

26. D. E. Aune, *The NT in its Literary Environment* (Philadelphia: Westminster, 1987), p. 199: "The introduction and conclusion seek to influence or even manipulate the audience by initially securing their interest and goodwill and end by recapitulating the arguments and making an emotional appeal."

emotions such as anger, and thus we find more forceful techniques used, especially in the fool's discourse in chs. 11 and 12, such as invective, rhetorical questions, sarcasm, tongue-in-cheek self-praise, irony, and the like. This is typical of the way in which an effective orator would operate in a forensic situation. The best and most emotional harangue is saved for last since the audience is more apt to remember what they heard last.

Finally, *logos* involves deductive arguments and arguments based on examples from history or from some other source. 2 Cor. 9:10 contains a deductive argument, and 8:9 and ch. 3 contain arguments from examples.

The rhetorical structure of 2 Corinthians can be summarized as follows:

1. The epistolary prescript (1:1-2).
2. The epistolary thanksgiving and *exordium* (1:3-7).
3. The *narratio* (1:8–2:14), which explains some of the facts that occasioned the letter and climaxes with a further thanksgiving and transition (2:15f.).[27]
4. The *propositio* (2:17), which states the basic fact under dispute.[28]
5. The *probatio* and *refutatio* (3:1–13:4), which includes:
    a. Paul's characterization of his ministry and of his anti-Sophistic rhetorical approach (3:1–6:13),
    b. a deliberative digression (6:14–7:1), in which Paul puts his audience

---

27. Kennedy, *NT Interpretation*, p. 88, sees 2:14-17 as the *propositio*. But 2:14-16 is not just a metaphor that says the same thing as 2:17 in a different way. It is the transition to the *propositio*.

Kennedy is right, however, in saying that in 2:17 Paul divides into three parts or "heads" *(partitio)* what he will seek to prove: that he is not a peddler like so many, but rather (1) a man of sincerity, (2) commissioned by God, (3) speaking in Christ before God. Paul shows that he is not a peddler in chs. 8–9 and wherever the language of being a burden comes up. The third part of the proof is reiterated in 5:11–6:13 and 12:19 (Kennedy, p. 89). This close connection between 2:17 and 12:19 argues for the unity of the discourse. Paul deals with his *ēthos* (the first part of the proof) at length in chs. 3–7 (Kennedy notes 4:2-6 and 4:13–5:10 on sincerity) and his being commissioned by God (the second part of the proof) comes up repeatedly, especially in chs. 3–5 (Kennedy notes 3:4–4:1 and 4:7-12) and in the fool's discourse (ch. 11).

Quintilian points out that digressions may be taken from other sources and may be used as long as they are in some way germane to the discussion at hand. It is thus possible that 6:14–7:1 was an earlier Pauline broadside and that chs. 8–9, as Betz argues, involve letters originally used for the purposes suggested by Betz. This would not prevent Paul from re-using such material as part of his defense to show that there was material evidence to support his case.

28. It was not unusual in forensic rhetoric to put the *propositio* after the statement of facts or *narratio* (cf. Quintilian *Inst. Or.* 4.4.1). In forensic rhetoric the "proof" or *probatio* concerns a particular fact to be proven true or false and is a response to accusations (Mitchell, *Rhetoric of Reconciliation*, p. 202).

on the defensive, urging them to stop attending temple feasts with
pagan friends,

c. Paul's defense of the severe letter (7:2-16),

d. a largely deliberative argument concerning the collection (chs. 8 and
9), and

e. a rhetorical *synkrisis* (comparison) of Paul and his competitors in
Corinth, the false *apostoloi*, with a strong emotional appeal.[29]

6. The *peroratio* (13:5-10).

7. The closing epistolary greetings and remarks (13:11-13).

In the lengthy *probatio* Paul necessarily and rightly resorts to a major
deliberative digression in 6:14–7:1, which renews the argument in 1 Corinthians 8–10, just as 2 Corinthians 8–9 renews the discussion of the collection
from 1 Corinthians 16 and puts the audience on the defensive: They had
committed themselves to the project but had not carried through with it. These
two passages are not mere asides, since near the end of the letter Paul alludes
again to the topics raised in them (12:13-18, 21). Furthermore, the material
in chs. 8–9 flows naturally out of parts of ch. 7 and is Paul's indirect defense
of *his own* practices, both past and present, in regard to the collection. It thus
serves his larger forensic purposes of defense and attack (note especially 8:20f.
and 9:4). This defense comes in the midst of a deliberative argument exhorting
the Corinthians to complete the collection and providing them with theological and social reasons for doing so.

Young and Ford's Argument for the Rhetorical Unity of the Letter

According to Young and Ford, Paul follows rhetorical conventions in all of
2 Corinthians, and this conditions the ways in which he presents his argument.
His argument must be seen as a form of *apologia* — a defense of Paul's apostleship. The argument is, they say, really between Paul and his Corinthian
Christian audience. The opponents, the "false apostles," exacerbated the problems, but Paul does not direct his comments against them, even in chs. 10–13.

I am in general agreement with these views, but Young and Ford's more
important contribution is in pointing out hints in chs. 1–9 that the false
apostles lie behind some of Paul's comments already in those chapters and in
directing our attention to themes that bind chs. 1–9 to chs. 10–13. For example,

---

29. Munck, *Paul and the Salvation of Mankind*, p. 176, is likely correct that the
Corinthians, not the opponents, were doing the comparing in Corinth. One suspects,
however, that the opponents fed the Corinthians ideas and "facts" to encourage them to
see Paul in an unfavorable light.

in 2:17 Paul contrasts himself with his competitors, who, he says, "peddle God's word." In 4:2 Paul says that he has renounced shameful and deceptive practices and does not distort God's word.[30] In 5:12 he speaks of the Corinthians as those who will be "able to answer those who take pride in what is seen rather than what is in the heart." This may prepare the way for the argument in 11:22f. In 6:8 Paul alludes to "some" who consider him an impostor as an apostle. This prepares for the discussion of the authenticity of Paul's apostleship as it comes further into focus in chs. 10–13.

Young and Ford note that throughout both parts of the letter the issue of pride or glory comes to the fore — pride both in a good sense and in a bad sense, glorying both in the right way and in the wrong way. In both parts of the letter, again, Paul also rings the changes on the various forms and meanings of *parakaleō* and its cognates: Paul makes his appeal, beseeching, exhorting, encouraging, even comforting the Corinthians throughout the letter so that they will listen to him and be reconciled to him and thus not listen to or be swayed by the false *apostoloi*.

A clear plan of development can be seen for the letter as a whole. This plan bears some resemblance to the procedure followed in 1 Corinthians, where, after dealing with the basis or root of some of the problems (*sophia*, "wisdom"), Paul dealt with matters relating to the Christian community's boundaries with the larger world and then turned to problems in the Corinthians' worship. In 2 Corinthians Paul first introduces themes of major importance having to do with encouragement/comfort and pride/boasting and then deals with problems relating to the community's boundaries with the outside world, problems that present obstacles to their being fully reconciled to Paul and God such as the disciplinary case and associations with pagans. Both of these problems are mentioned already in 1 Corinthians. Then Paul turns to the internal matter of the collection, just as in 1 Corinthians Paul turns to internal matters at ch. 11 and concludes with the collection in ch. 16. But as in 2 Corinthians there is a new external source of problems, so in the concluding section of the letter Paul gives full attention to the false teachers.

Paul must say something about not only his own ministry but also the ministry and witness of the Corinthian Christians themselves. They are Paul's *synergoi*, his "coworkers" in ministry (1:24), and his letter to the world in Corinth (3:2f.). He is concerned about the effect on the public witness if the Corinthians are estranged from him and thus from God.

This sheds new light on the preexisting piece in 6:14–7:1. Here Paul

---

30. For a similar argument for the unity of 2 Corinthians stressing the salient hints of real trouble already in chs. 1–7, see J. L. Price, "Aspects of Paul's Theology and their Bearing on Literary Problems of Second Corinthians," in *Studies in the History and Text of the NT*, ed. B. L. Daniels and M. J. Suggs (Salt Lake: University of Utah, 1967), pp. 95-106.

speaks in several ways of partnership and cooperation. Though 6:14–7:1 is a digression, it has been prepared for as early as 6:1 (which should be compared to 6:14). There Paul is concerned with, I believe, his partnership in the gospel with God and with the Corinthians. 6:14ff. focuses on the antithesis of that partnership, namely an uneasy and unequal partnership in pagan worship and association with nonbelievers (note especially v. 16a). These two partnerships are mutually exclusive options: The latter must be rejected if the former is to be affirmed. 2 Corinthians seeks first to build on the rapport that existed in the past and more recently on the part of the majority of the Corinthian Christians, who had indicated their choice for Paul (and God) by dealing with the one who had offended Paul during the "painful visit" (ch. 2). The letter then turns to removing further obstacles to full *koinōnia* ("partnership"), the largest of which, the false apostles, Paul deals with at the end of the letter, thus following good rhetorical practice.

Young and Ford account for the shift in tone between chs. 1–9 and chs. 10–13 by arguing that in the more negative, sarcastic, ironic, and "foolish" remarks in ch. 10, Paul, following rhetorical conventions, has come to the point in the letter for a strong emotional appeal — the *peroratio*. This emotional appeal involves some recapitulation of the principal parts of the argument in terms geared to excite the emotions and involving entreaties, tears, and passion. This is to be contrasted with the the the *exordium*, where the convention was to speak gently, win favor, and influence people by eliciting goodwill, by showing oneself to be fair-minded, and by removing prejudices against oneself. Young and Ford claim that in various ways 2 Corinthians reveals a form not unlike that of Demosthenes' second epistle, which has a dramatic shift in tone with an emotional harangue at the end.[31]

The parallel with Demosthenes is important, and it reveals the crucial point that even a dramatic shift in tone is not uncommon in forensic rhetoric. But it is difficult to maintain that all of 2 Corinthians 10–13 is a *peroratio*. I would suggest that the shift in tone is there not because we have arrived at a *peroratio* but because Paul now chooses to go on the counterattack by means of a rhetorical *synkrisis,* and this will include *pathos,* an appeal to the stronger emotions.[32] J. T. Fitzgerald has concluded that chs. 10–13 are Paul's final attempt to persuade the Corinthians and thus to avoid having to go to Corinth in order to use discipline to settle the issue. He also rightly points out that these chapters are not merely an *apologia* but a counterattack against the

---

31. Young and Ford, *Meaning and Truth,* pp. 36ff.

32. Note how in Galatians 5–6 the syntax becomes more abrupt, the style becomes more violent, and *pathos* is in greater evidence than in Galatians 1–4. This parallel is especially important since Galatians is an example of forensic rhetoric. Cf. W. H. Bates, "The Integrity of II Corinthians," *NTS* 12 (1965), pp. 56-59, here p. 66.

opponents, accusing them of what they accused him: illegitimacy, ignorance, and pretensions. "The outward structure is that of an appeal, but a strong use is made of elements from a legal setting. It is within this quasi-legal setting that Paul boasts and defends himself; threatens, accuses, and reproaches the Corinthians; and launches a counterattack on the superapostles."[33]

The Need for Reconciliation

In 2 Corinthians, then, Paul seeks to reestablish positive contact and a healthy relationship with his Corinthian converts. It was important for him to do so, as we have seen, because he regarded them as his coworkers in the ministry of reconciliation (1:11, 24; 2:5ff.; 6:1). They will have received "God's grace in vain" if they are estranged from Paul, the one who first mediated that grace to them. They cannot fully be reconcilers unless they are first fully reconciled.

Obstacles were placed in the way of this reconciliation of the Corinthian Christians to Paul and thus to God by competitors opposing Paul and bidding for the hearts of his converts. In the face of this competition, Paul pulls out all the rhetorical stops in this letter. He begins by referring to *paraklēsis* as "comfort/encouragement," rather than making a direct appeal (cf. 1:3ff.). *Paraklēsis* as appeal comes to the fore later in the letter.

Paul also seeks to win favor by stressing that he is thankful that one major obstacle to reconciliation has already been removed: He is thankful that the person who caused him grief in his brief and "painful" second visit to Corinth has been adequately dealt with by the Corinthians themselves (2:6-11). Even in this matter he wishes to be a model of reconciling grace. Just as Paul has been comforted/encouraged, he now urges his converts to be comforters, to be reconcilers of the estranged.[34]

Temple Feasts

Another obstacle in the way of reconciliation was the practice of some Corinthian Christians, probably well-to-do Gentile men, who were attending banquets in pagan temples or in dining halls attached to religious buildings

33. Fitzgerald, "Paul, the Ancient Epistolary Theorists," p. 200. I would say that the appeal is made in a largely forensic piece, though there is some mixing of forensic and deliberative rhetoric in the letter.

34. This sort of modeling and appeal is characteristic of deliberative rhetoric, but Paul is using deliberative rhetoric here for forensic purposes, i.e., to build a foundation for self-defense.

such as the Asklepion. As we have seen, Paul already addressed this problem in 1 Corinthians 8–10. These dinners involved the participant in pagan worship, perhaps including the actual sacrifice of the animal that was to be eaten in the dining hall.[35] For Paul this amounted to idolatry and was to be avoided. It was an issue that concerned, quite simply, the boundaries of what it is to be Christian.

As Paul again confronts this problem in 2 Cor. 6:14–7:1, he uses a number of words that are to some degree synonyms and that all speak of people being joined together in some activity (*heterozygountes, koinōnia, symphōnēsis,* and *synkatathesis,* all in vv. 14-16). Here that activity is engaged in with the wrong kind of crowd[36] and is the wrong kind of activity. The Corinthians cannot be joined with these people in doing these things and at the same time be joined or reconciled to Christ and his apostle. Paul's statement regarding the mutually exclusive alternatives of sharing in the table of demons and the table of the Lord in 1 Cor. 10:21-22 is echoed in 2 Cor. 6:15-16, where the alternatives are sharing in a temple of idols (or in that which is associated with Belial) versus sharing in Christ (cf. also 2 Cor. 6:16 and 1 Cor. 3:16).

6:14–7:1 appears where it does in 2 Corinthians perhaps because Paul has just named all that he has done and given up in order to be a servant of God and of the Corinthians. He has spoken openly and freely with them, holding back nothing. He is asking for commensurability.[37] They, too, should be willing to give up some things and make some sacrifices in order to be in harmony with Christ and his apostle.

Paul's Travel Plans

Throughout 2 Corinthians Paul returns again and again to his travel plans. He had planned to come see the Corinthian Christians, but had not yet done so (1:15ff.). He sent his own *shalichim* or agents instead of coming in person (chs. 7 and 8). He describes his plans to come to Corinth near the end of the letter (12:14; 13:1-2, 14).

Apparently Paul's opponents were accusing him of saying one thing and

---

35. Cf. W. L. Willis, *Idol Meat in Corinth: The Pauline Argument in 1 Corinthians 8 and 10* (Chico, CA: Scholars, 1985), pp. 7-64.

36. It is remotely possible that the *apistoi* here are the false teachers, but the allusion to dining in a pagan temple makes this unlikely.

37. Danker, *II Corinthians,* pp. 78ff. has rightly drawn attention to how often Paul uses the language of commerce in this letter and not just when he is actually discussing money in chs. 8–9. This is perhaps because Paul, as the Corinthians' benefactor, wants to make clear that they are and ought to be in debt to him, not the other way around. In short, Paul's use of commercial language serves a social function.

doing another in regard to his planned visits, thus proving in their eyes that he was not a true apostle. Furthermore, because Paul wanted his next journey to be the final step in the process of being reconciled to the Corinthians, he mentions these plans more than once to undercut the charge of insincerity or hypocrisy and to make clear that he is truly concerned for the Corinthians and wants full reconciliation with them. He is delaying his visit to give them time to change so that there will not be another difficult visit. He also clarifies his plans.

The Corinthians and Patronage Relationships

The material on the collection in 2 Corinthians 8–9 is illumined by Danker's helpful discussion of benefaction in antiquity.[38] These chapters fit nicely into the flow of the argument when we consider that one of the things the Corinthians held against Paul is that he would not accept patronage from them. From 11:7ff. one may conclude that for Paul there is a certain theological fitness to not accepting patronage. The gospel of free grace should be offered free of charge. Yet from Philippi Paul was willing to accept support (11:9). How then was the situation different in Corinth? Danker rightly suggests that some Corinthians wished to be *Paul's* benefactors and thus to put Paul in the position of being in their debt.[39] Patronage was a means of putting oneself in a position of superiority and power over others. Some of the more well-to-do Corinthians were disturbed at Paul's refusal to place himself in the Corinthians' debt and so to subordinate himself to them because of their generosity.

In part, the reason for Paul's refusal was theological. He saw himself as the Corinthians' benefactor or patron. He was the one who had distributed to them the largesse of God's gift of salvation in Christ. There could be no more generous gift. Paul wanted them to understand that they were his spiritual children. Paul was *their* patron or, better put, God in Christ was their

---

38. Danker, *II Corinthians,* pp. 20ff. Equally helpful is his larger study, *Benefactor: An Epigraphic Study of a Graeco-Roman Semantic Field* (St. Louis: Clayton, 1982).

39. Some of the problems Paul is dealing with in 2 Corinthians are likely caused by the wealthier Corinthian Christians, as in 1 Corinthians. It was wealthier and more influential people who looked to be patrons in Corinthian society. The wealthy Christians were probably providing hospitality and patronage for the false apostles, they were more likely to receive invitations to dinners in the Asklepion and other pagan temples, and they were probably causing trouble at Christian meals that included the Lord's Supper (1 Cor. 11:17-34). The factions and division with regard to allegiance to Paul that are evident in 1 Corinthians are seen again when Paul speaks of having to be bold toward "some" in 2 Cor. 10:2. But he is relieved and confident in the majority (2:6) who took action against one who made Paul's previous visit painful.

patron through Paul. As such they should have been accepting his authority over them and his directions in this letter and understanding that it is the role of parents to save up for or give to their children, not the reverse (12:14). Until they understood this, they would not understand their proper relationship with him or with the one who sent him. The crisis of authority affecting the relationship between Paul and the Corinthians was in part engendered by a misunderstanding of who was the benefactor and who was the client or benefactee in this relationship.

This disagreement about the patronage relationship placed an obstacle in the way of Paul being fully reconciled with his converts. The false *apostoloi* (12:13) had seized on Paul's unwillingness to accept patronage from the Corinthians as proof that he was no true apostle and did not love them (11:1-14; 12:11-18). Paul saw these other *apostoloi* as exploiters who wanted the Corinthians' possessions.

How then was Paul to remove this obstacle? Paul's solution to the problem is to stress that the Corinthians *can* be benefactors, but not Paul's benefactors. He urges them to give generously to the collection for the relief of poor Christians in Jerusalem. Chapters 8 and 9 help the Corinthians see that Paul has already given them an opportunity to be benefactors in a very important way. He has spoken to them earlier about the collection (1 Cor. 16:1-3) and apparently they have promised a generous gift (2 Cor. 9:5). It is time, he says, to show the Christian world, and especially the generous Macedonian Christians, what they are made of (cf. 9:2-5 and 8:1-7).

There may also be a larger social agenda underlying chs. 8 and 9, one that again has to do with reconciliation. As Martin and others have suggested,[40] it appears that Paul viewed the collection as a way of healing the growing breach between Jewish Christians in Judea and the increasingly Gentile church in the Diaspora, not only in Achaea but also in Galatia and Macedonia. The collection would demonstrate both the sincerity of the Gentiles' Christian faith and their desire to have *koinōnia* with the Mother Church. This would also show at least indirectly that Paul also wanted rapprochement with James, Peter, and others who seem to have viewed the gospel and salvation history differently than Paul.

Paul wanted the Corinthians to break off their relationship with the false apostles and be reconciled to him, but he did not want in the process to sever his converts from the congregation in Jerusalem or from the "pillar apostles" (Gal. 2:9). But it appears the false apostles were making much of their connection with the Jewish roots of the *ekklēsia*. They came with letters of recommendation from some assemblies, perhaps from the Mother Church in Judea, as well as from other *ekklēsiae*. Paul tried to undercut their authority

40. Martin, *2 Corinthians*, pp. 256ff.

while being reconciled to his own spiritual children and at the same time offering an olive branch toward the Jerusalem church as well.

The Opponents

Methodological Questions

Several times we have referred to the opponents of Paul who were placing difficulties in the way of reconciliation between him and his Corinthian converts. Before we can attempt a description of these opponents, we must ask how it is we are to arrive at such a description. Very few NT scholars have even discussed their method in discerning opponents in Paul's letters, which may explain why there have been at least fourteen different proposals about Paul's opponents in 2 Corinthians. Even more problematic is the assumption that an abstract reconstruction and rearrangement of a text's various parts should govern the interpretation of the text in regard not only to things like Paul's opponents, but also to the collection.[41] To a great extent, the chronological order in which one arranges the hypothetically reconstructed text will affect, if not dictate, how one will interpret its different parts.

J. L. Sumney has revealed a variety of problems with such approaches.[42] For example, certain assumptions about the editing of Paul's letters after they were collected must be made in order to justify rearranging parts of the Pauline letters, though such assumptions seldom have any textual basis. It is also often assumed that there must have been a unified front of opposition to Paul, so that one may take parallels from all over the Pauline corpus, identified on the basis of often superficial verbal similarities, to fill out the picture of Paul's opponents in a given situation, such as in Corinth.[43] Furthermore, the character of Paul's rhetoric is seldom taken into account, which results in some passages seeming to allude to opponents when Paul is simply forestalling possible, not real, arguments or objections.

41. I am thinking here of Betz's reconstruction of 2 Corinthians in *The Anchor Bible Dictionary* (n. 12 above) and D. Georgi's *Remembering the Poor: The History of Paul's Collection for Jerusalem* (Nashville: Abingdon, 1992).

42. J. L. Sumney, *Identifying Paul's Opponents: The Question of Method in 2 Corinthians* (Sheffield: JSOT, 1990).

43. Sumney, *Identifying Paul's Opponents*, p. 85, urges that diversity in early Christianity militates against a common front against Paul. Cf. R. B. Ward, "The Opponents of Paul," *Restoration Quarterly* 10 (1967), pp. 185-95.

Sumney urges the following guidelines for the handling of texts to determine opponents and related matters:

Contemporary sources are the only legitimate sources for a reconstruction. Using later sources risks anachronism.

It is wrong to allow the identity of the opponents to be determined by a reconstruction of the text. Reconstructions should be used only to discern possibilities, not to prove or show probabilities.

Reconstructions can be used only after it has been made clear that opponents are mentioned in the text.

The identification of opponents cannot be based on the assumption that we know the historical situation Paul is addressing better than Paul himself. We should assume that Paul's assessment is accurate unless there are strong reasons to think otherwise.[44]

Context is crucial to the meaning of words, and therefore mere verbal similarity between passages in two Pauline letters is not a sufficient basis for transferring ideas about opponents from one letter to another. There must be a shared conceptual framework, which can only be determined by a full interpretation of both passages in their respective contexts.

Certainty of reference and reliability of reference should be two primary criteria applied to any statement in evaluating whether and what it tells us about Paul's opponents.

Explicit statements, allusions, and affirmations provide a descending order of reliability.

Statements in thanksgiving periods or didactic contexts are likely to be more reliable than material in apologetic or polemical contexts.

"Mirror-reading" of allusions in polemical contexts, that is, assuming that what Paul affirms is the opposite of what his opponents believed, is not very reliable and should only be used as support for explicit statements found elsewhere, for allusions in polemical contexts that do not require mirror-reading, or for allusions found in apologetic contexts.

Finally, one should begin with easier statements in explicit contexts and interpret more difficult ones in their light.[45]

Using these criteria, Sumney comes to the following cautious conclusions:

---

44. This is one of the major problems with A. C. Wire, *The Corinthian Women Prophets: A Reconstruction through Paul's Rhetoric* (Minneapolis: Fortress, 1990). See above, pp. 231-40.

45. Sumney, *Identifying Paul's Opponents,* pp. 85-125.

In 2 Corinthians 1–9 as well as chs. 10–13 Paul is combating opponents, in fact, the *same* opponents;

The opponents were not Gnostics, "divine men," or Judaizers, but pneumatics of some description;[46] and

apostolic legitimation was the central issue, and the Spirit was the major point of debate.[47]

I would add one more criterion to Sumney's list, that of cross referencing among different sorts of contexts. If the same kind of idea about opponents appears in two different kinds of texts, it probably reflects something about the opponents. In this case, while there is insufficient evidence to suggest the Corinthian opponents were Judaizers, if by that we mean those who tried to impose sabbath or food laws or circumcision on Gentile Christians, there is, nonetheless, evidence in 2 Corinthians 3 and 11:22, two very different sorts of contexts, to suggest that they were Jews. 11:13 makes it quite clear that they claimed to be Christian *apostoloi* as well. Interestingly, in the Marcionite prologue to Paul's letters we hear, "The Achaeans heard the word of truth from the apostle and were in several ways perverted by false apostles, some by verbal eloquence of philosophy, others by the sect of the Jewish law."[48]

Identifying the Opponents

It is important that we neither underestimate nor overestimate Paul's Corinthian opponents. It is difficult to assess whether they were merely exacerbating tendencies that already existed in Corinth toward pride, preening, factiousness, a critical view of Paul, and a fascination with Sophistic rhetoric and spiritual gifts and experiences, or added something new to the mix. In view of the problems already in abundant evidence in 1 Corinthians the former seems more likely, except perhaps in regard to the matter of money.

Whether or not Paul would receive support from the Corinthians had become a delicate issue. As we have seen in regard to 2 Cor. 6:14–7:1, Paul saw himself as the Corinthians' benefactor, the one through whom they received new life in Christ, but at least some Corinthians saw themselves as benefactors or patrons, and were upset that Paul did not accept money from them, as

46. So too G. Bornkamm, "Faith and Reason in Paul's Epistles," *NTS* 4 (1957-58), pp. 93-100, here pp. 98f. (in fuller form in idem, *Early Christian Experience* [New York: Harper and Row, 1969], pp. 29-46 [37f.]).

47. Sumney, *Identifying Paul's Opponents*, pp. 178-85.

48. Cf. R. P. Martin, "The Opponents of Paul in 2 Corinthians: An Old Issue Revisited," in *Tradition and Interpretation in the NT* (Grand Rapids: Eerdmans, 1987), pp. 279-89, here p. 279.

others (the false apostles) had done. This seems to have have been taken by the false apostles as grounds for criticizing Paul and for suggesting that he was not a true agent of God.

It is clear that these opponents were Jews who were proud of their Jewish heritage (ch. 11). But there is a danger in reading 2 Corinthians in the light of Galatians, where the opponents were Judaizers, that is, those who sought to impose sabbath rules, circumcision, and food laws on Gentile converts.[49] Paul makes little or nothing of these sorts of issues in 2 Corinthians.

It is also clear that the false *apostoloi* of 2 Corinthians claimed to be Christians and brought letters of commendation from various places. Paul himself brought no such letters, and therefore on this ground as well the false *apostoloi* insinuated that he was no true *apostolos*. Martin argues that after the episode recorded in Galatians 2, Paul no longer could use Antioch as a home base. He became, therefore, an itinerant preacher without letters of recommendation, unlike his opponents.[50]

Perhaps some of the opponents' recommendation letters were from Jerusalem, but this partly depends on whether Paul refers to the "pillar apostles" of Gal. 2:9 in 2 Cor. 11:5. This seems unlikely.[51] We have argued that there is no convincing evidence that Paul is already aware of opponents when he writes 1 Corinthians. This makes it exceedingly unlikely that the false *apostoloi* had any direct connection with Apollos or commission from Peter. In 2 Corinthians we hear nothing about Peter or Apollos, and this must prove fatal to the idea of a *direct* endorsement of the false apostles' agenda by them.

How long then had these other outside forces been active in Corinth? This depends on when one dates 2 Corinthians. The letter suggests in various

49. C. K. Barrett, "Paul the Controversialist" (unpublished lecture, Ashland Theological Seminary, Sept. 1990), points out that, though circumcision is not an issue in Corinth, that does not rule out the possibility that Paul's opponents are Judaizers, possibly from the Jerusalem church itself. The Judaizers' agenda need not have been the same in all of Paul's churches, and there may have been more than one such group following Paul's footsteps and engaging in what they viewed as damage control. I would maintain that the opponents were Jewish Christians, but "Judaizers" is too strong a term, since their agenda was not about circumcision, the sabbath, or apparently even food laws, none of which are mentioned in 2 Corinthians. I suggest that they are pneumatic Jewish Christians with an interest in *sophia* (wisdom).

50. R. P. Martin, "The Setting of 2 Corinthians," *TynB* 37 (1986), pp. 3-19, here p. 13. G. Theissen, *The Social Setting of Pauline Christianity: Essays on Corinth* (Philadelphia: Fortress, 1982), p. 50, makes much the same point.

51. Munck, *Paul and the Salvation of Mankind,* p. 178, argues that the false apostles could not have had letters from Jerusalem because then Paul would not have called them servants of Satan (11:14f.) after asking in the same letter for money to send to Jerusalem. Munck may be right. Other possibilities include letters from Antioch or Galatia.

ways that considerable water had gone under the bridge since the writing of 1 Corinthians and thus that there had been sufficient time for the false apostles to gain a foothold in Corinth. They may have *claimed* the support of Peter or James, who perhaps had given them some sort of general letters of reference. But once they were on their own and beyond recall or cross-examination, the false *apostoloi* may have claimed Peter's or James's support for what those early leaders had not specifically endorsed. The reference to the limits of one's mission in chs. 10–12 have suggested to many that some sort of association with Peter was being claimed by Paul's opponents in Corinth.[52]

Barrett argues that there is evidence that Paul was widely hated for destroying, so it was thought, the connection between Christianity and Judaism. His opponents went around, Barrett says, to his congregations and to one degree or another re-Judaized them in order to make fellowship with conservative Jewish Christians and even Jews possible. Paul was operating at a disadvantage since some of these false apostles may have known Jesus "according to the flesh" (2 Cor. 5:16), that is, during his earthly ministry, which Paul could not claim: He seems to be very sensitive about his lack of direct contact with Jesus in Galatians 1, 1 Corinthians 15, and 2 Corinthians.[53]

But there are some difficulties with Barrett's analysis. The material in 2 Corinthians 5 about knowing Christ "according to the flesh" refers to a worldly understanding of Christ, not to knowing him in the flesh. "Taking pride in what is seen" (v. 12) may refer to signs, wonders, and miracles (cf. 12:12) rather than to direct contact with Jesus. Furthermore, what Paul is sensitive about is his claim to have seen the *risen* Lord. Finally, the "Jewish" influence of the opponents seems to be related to matters other than the concerns of the Judaizers of Galatians, who focused on circumcision, food laws, and the sabbath. The focus of Paul's opponents in Corinth may have had to do with the Ten Commandments (cf. 3:7) and probably had something to do with pneumatic or revealed Jewish wisdom, the sort of wisdom derived from visions and dreams. It also appears that they prided themselves on their rhetorical polish (10:10-12). This may be why Paul chooses to fight fire with fire, using anti-Sophistic rhetoric to turn the opponents' arguments upside down. Apparently they were like the Sophists in accepting support for their work (2:17).

As Barrett says, this group of Paul's opponents seems to have had a ringleader, though there was certainly more than one person involved. He suggests that they may have been "those who came from James" and did more than James authorized them to do (Gal. 2:12). This is probably to read

---

52. Cf. Martin, "Opponents," p. 282, referring to Gal. 2:7-10.
53. Barrett, "Paul the Controversialist."

2 Corinthians too much in light of Galatians, but in any case, as Barrett says, who would have been able to control people at a distance?[54]

Barrett goes on to suggest that the conflict was apparently fierce and that the opponents charged that Paul was not a true apostle, that his converts still needed to be truly converted, that he was an antinomian, and that he was dishonest, that is, that he promised one thing and did another. I see no hard evidence that Paul was being accused of antinomianism in Corinth. The charges of being an illegitimate apostle, of lacking the signs of an *apostolos* in his presence and actions, and of dishonesty are, nonetheless, highly probable, and one may add the charge that Paul was no rhetor.

These charges cannot be written off as minimal. They indicate there was major conflict in the early Christian communities over matters of substance. Paul's theological and ethical expression, here as often elsewhere, was borne out of conflict and controversy in which much was at stake — in Paul's view the very salvation of the Corinthians.

Paul does not spell out his opponents' theology in 2 Corinthians, probably because practice — the character and criteria of apostolic praxis — and not theology was more at issue. I agree with Munck at this point and part company with all those who make elaborate attempts to reconstruct the theology of the opponents on the basis of such elusive allusions as "another Jesus, a different Spirit, a different gospel" (11:4) or the general discussion of the greater glory of Christ in ch. 3.[55] The real burden of Paul's attack against the opponents has to do with the practice of ministry and the criteria for evaluating both ministry and ministers.

Social and practical matters are more to the fore than theological and ethical matters at the close of 2 Corinthians. The fundamental problem is the Corinthians' image of Christian leadership. At least some of them had created in their minds an image, largely shaped by the values of their culture, of a leader who had honor, power, spiritual gifts, rhetorical skills, and good references and who would accept patronage. They looked, that is, for a Sophist, or at least for a rhetorically adept philosophical teacher.

It is plausible that the Corinthians, and probably the false apostles as well, had been strongly affected by the rising tide of the Sophistic movement. At this juncture we must provide evidence that such a movement was already influential in the latter half of the first century A.D. and in the eastern half of the Mediterranean crescent. Though G. W. Bowersock and Kennedy had sug-

---

54. I would suggest that a claimed connection with Peter is more probable. He is obviously held in esteem in Corinth, as 1 Corinthians 1–4, 9, and 15 indicate.

55. Munck, *Paul and the Salvation of Mankind,* p. 176. Cf., e.g., Martin, "Opponents," pp. 286f. Munck may be right in saying that 11:3-4 is purely rhetorical and hypothetical — forestalling a future possibility, not confronting a present reality.

gested as much,[56] B. W. Winter has now shown that this movement was a going and growing concern, not just in the second century A.D. during the period of the second Sophistic, but already in the first half and middle of the first century A.D.[57]

The following facts have a bearing on this conclusion. First, the term *sophistēs* had become almost a technical term in the first century, referring to a virtuoso rhetor with a large reputation for skill in declamation.[58] Second, there is plentiful evidence in Philo that Sophists "were winning the admiration of city after city and drawing well nigh the whole world to honor them" (*Agr.* 143).[59] Third, Dio Chrysostom's sixth and eighth oracles refer to sophistic activity in Corinth in the 80s and 90s A.D. Fourth, Corinth with its multiple games (including oratory contests) and its 14,000-seat theater was the entertainment capital of Greece, a natural mecca for orators. Fifth, Epictetus speaks of being visited by a student of rhetoric from Corinth who was "somewhat too elaborately dressed and whose attire in general was highly embellished" which included having his hair set, wearing jewelry, and having the hair plucked from his body (3.1.1ff.). This stress on outward appearance by Sophistic rhetors is commented on by others as well (cf. Philostratus *Lives* 536). Sixth, from Philo to Philostratus there is clear evidence of the quarrels between Sophists and philosophers, among the Sophists themselves, and between the students of the Sophists, each touting the merits of their teachers. This point may shed light on the "I am of Paul" material in 1 Corinthians 1

---

56. Cf. G. W. Bowersock, *Greek Sophists in the Roman Empire* (Oxford: Clarendon, 1969), p. 13; G. A. Kennedy, *The Art of Rhetoric in the Roman World 300 B.C. to A.D. 300* (Princeton: Princeton University, 1972), p. 513; idem, *Classical Rhetoric and Its Christian and Secular Tradition from Ancient to Modern Times* (Chapel Hill: University of North Carolina, 1980), p. 37.

57. Some care must be taken in how one defines "Sophist." The term was used of both speakers and thinkers, sometimes of philosophers whose teaching amounted to words without thought, sometimes of orators who offered eloquence without substance. It was characteristic of both sorts of Sophists that they took pay for their troubles, that they often failed to speak on serious subjects, and that the orators especially had very practical aims in mind. While the term could sometimes be used positively to refer to orators who brought eloquence to a new level of brilliance, normally it was a pejorative term and came to signify a charlatan or imposter. In this study I am using the term to refer to those who used rhetoric for their own ends, took pay, and specialized in ornamentation, declamation, and appeals to the emotions, and generally offered form without substance. Cf. C. P. Jones, *The Roman World of Dio Chrysostom* (Cambridge: Harvard University, 1978), p. 9 on the definition.

58. Cf. B. W. Winter, *Are Philo and Paul among the Sophists?* (dissertation, McQuarrie University, 1988), pp. 51ff. Declamation, the rhetoric of display, is called *epideiktikos*. As the word suggests, it mainly involved epideictic rhetoric. Cf. S. M. Pogoloff, *Logos and Sophia: The Rhetorical Situation of 1 Corinthians* (Atlanta: Scholars, 1992), p. 65.

59. Cf. Winter, *Are Paul and Philo*, pp. 1ff.

(cf. Philostratus *Lives* 588).[60] Seventh, the Sophist Favorinus was so well received in Corinth that his oration was recorded and a statue was erected to him in a prominent spot in the library (cf. Dio *Orationes* 37.1ff.). Eighth, when Plutarch visited Corinth (cf. *Quaest. Conviv.*) he dined with the wealthy Sophist Herodes Atticus (cf. also *Moralia* 723b). Plutarch, like others concerned with substantive discourse, is often critical of the Sophists. Ninth, P. Oxy. 2190 refers to students listening to and learning from public declamations and to one Didymus who would sell himself as a teacher who takes care of his students. Tenth, there is evidence of both students and teachers of rhetoric in Corinth during the middle and latter part of the first century A.D.[61]

Paul's Confrontation of the Problem

The false apostles apparently appealed to Moses and the Mosaic covenant. In ch. 3 Paul undermines some of this theological basis by placing the Mosaic covenant in the shadow of the greater glory of the new covenant. At first this argument might seem out of place in 2 Corinthians. But if we allow that Paul is preparing for the *apologia* in chs. 10–13 throughout chs. 1–9, then the argument concerning Moses makes very good sense indeed. His opponents, those whom he must combat in order to be reconciled to his own converts, were, as we have seen, Jewish Christians of one sort or another. The argument in ch. 3 is in part an attempt to undermine their basis for boasting or at least one source of the power that they exercised over the Corinthians.

The complex argument concerning letters of recommendation (3:1ff.) also prepares for Paul's frontal attack on the opponents later in the letter. They apparently presented letters of recommendation to the Corinthians when they came to town. But Paul says that he needs no such letters. That he did not present any earlier is no indication he is not a true apostle. Rather, the Corinthians themselves are Paul's letters of recommendation, both to the world and ultimately to God. They are, that is, the evidence that he is a true apostle and has performed his God-given tasks well.

In these ways and others chs. 1–9 prepare for chs. 10-13. This last part of the letter is not the total *volte face* that it has sometimes been portrayed as. Paul has been appealing to the Corinthians to be reconciled, and commending himself, using *parrhēsia* (free speech), and even "boasting" all along in this

---

60. Winter, *Are Philo and Paul,* pp. 127ff.

61. Such as the great Nicetes and apparently also Dio of Prusa, who can be labeled early examples of the Sophistic movement.

letter. The fool's discourse (11:1ff.) must be read in light of what Paul has already said about making an appeal (4:5; 5:11), about commending himself (3:1ff.; 5:12; 6:4), about using bold and open speech (3:12; 4:2; 6:11), and about boasting (in both good and bad senses: 1:12-14; 7:14ff.; 9:2ff.). Paul has been using words that become prominent in chs. 10–13 — *paraklēsis, parrhēsia, kauchēsis* and *synistanō* — all through chs. 1–9.[62] This is why older treatments of 2 Corinthians saw in chs. 10–13 a recapitulation of major themes from earlier in the letter. There is some justice in this assessment, but one must not overlook the new element either. Here finally in chs. 10–13 Paul takes on directly and openly what he sees as the major source of most of the troubles in Corinth: the false *apostoloi*. He has prepared for this by allusions to them in chs. 1–9, but now he must take on this major obstacle to full reconciliation with his converts.

Was Reconciliation Accomplished?

By the end of 2 Corinthians, Paul believes he has dealt with all the major obstacles to his returning to Corinth as one reconciled with his people. Thus, he speaks of a third journey to the city (13:1).

But did the letter actually accomplish the social function it was meant to accomplish? Were reconciliation and the ministry of reconciliation not only discussed but also effected? We cannot be sure. But if Rom. 15:25-26 and 16:1, 23-24 provide a clue, Paul returned to Corinth, stayed with one of the believers there, and wrote the letter to the Romans from there, sending greetings from leading Corinthian Christians. Furthermore, the collection for Jerusalem was completed throughout Achaea, which would include Corinth.

Therefore, 2 Corinthians is apparently a shining example of how message, method, and ministry may come together to accomplish a theologically grounded social aim. It reflects Paul at his most powerful and poignant. If reconciliation is a sign of greatness, then 2 Corinthians is the clearest evidence of his stature.

Composition and Chronology

It seems clear now that we must allow more than a year between 1 and 2 Corinthians. Between the writing of the two letters

---

62. This is one of the more forceful points made in Young and Ford, *Meaning and Truth*, pp. 16ff.

1 Corinthians and perhaps the ministry of Timothy or at least Stephanas
  had had their effect,
the opponents had arrived in Corinth,
Paul had made his "painful" visit to the city,
he had written his "severe" letter, which was then delivered by Titus, and
Paul and Titus had met in Macedonia to discuss the response to the severe
  letter.

Then Paul wrote 2 Corinthians there in Macedonia. With 1 Corinthians
having been written in A.D. 53 or 54, 2 Corinthians cannot have been written
earlier than very late in 55 or more probably some time in 56.[63]

---

63. Cf. Martin, *2 Corinthians,* p. xlvi; Furnish, *II Corinthians,* p. 55, though both separate chs. 1–9 and chs. 10–13 with the former written in late 55, the latter in 56. This seems to
be the most probable view, if I am wrong about the rhetorical unity of 2 Corinthians.

Epistolary Prescript: 1:1-2

When Paul set about the task of writing 2 Corinthians, he had just heard from Titus[1] about the response of the Corinthians to a "severe" letter (7:6, 8; 12:18). Paul knew that that letter, delivered by Titus, had had some success with at least some Corinthians, whereas milder forms of discourse, such as we find in 1 Corinthians, had failed to fully correct the problems at issue.[2]

To put things in rhetorical terms, Paul knows now that the Corinthians respond best to *ēthos* and *pathos*, perhaps especially the latter. It is no accident therefore that so much of the first and last parts of 2 Corinthians are devoted to *ēthos* and *pathos* respectively. Paul must take considerable time establishing his moral character or *ēthos* in the first part of the letter, appealing to the gentler emotions that induce goodwill and persuade (cf. Quintilian *Inst. Or.* 6.2.9f.). *Pathos,* by contrast, is the expression of stronger emotions such as anger, and has a more disturbing and commanding tone. If Paul cannot once again establish his good character with his converts at the beginning of the letter, then his arguments and his appeal to the stronger emotions will go for nothing. Therefore the establishment of *ēthos* begins already in the prescript.

One of the keys to understanding this letter and Paul's approach to the Corinthians is that Paul and the Corinthians seem to have different views on

---

1. We learn from Galatians 2 that Titus was an uncircumcised Gentile who had traveled with Paul and Barnabas to Jerusalem for Paul's meeting with the "pillars." This may suggest that he was seen as Exhibit A of God's work among the Gentiles through the Pauline ministry. That he was a Gentile male convert may have inspired respect even among Paul's detractors in Corinth. See below, pp. 422-26.

2. I doubt that it is an accident that Paul has Titus deliver both the severe letter and 2 Corinthians, and I mean "deliver" in both senses of the term. See pp. 422-26 and 465-73 below on chs. 8–9 and 13.

who is the client and who is the patron in their relationship. In Paul's view, God is the benefactor or patron and the apostle is God's ambassador or agent, dispensing the largess of God in the form of salvation, grace, faith, and the Spirit. The clients are the Corinthians. By contrast, at least some of the Corinthians saw themselves as patrons of various itinerant evangelists or *apostoloi* and were upset when Paul did not allow them to be such for him. On their understanding, something was wrong with him because he would not accept the financial support that they were generously extending to him. Others had come to Corinth who apparently were accepting such patronage and, on top of that, were disparaging Paul for not doing so, casting aspersions on his apostleship for that and other reasons.

Therefore, Paul is on the defensive in much of this letter. He must show how the Corinthians have misunderstood their relationship with him and how he is the emissary of the Benefactor and therefore the one dispensing patronage, not receiving it. He must also stress that he needs no letters of recommendation as he comes to them since they are his own spiritual children. Indeed, they are themselves his letters of recommendation to all who would doubt his apostleship (3:1f.). That he brought no such letters was another sticking point with his opponents, who apparently came to Corinth with such letters.

Paul's defense of his apostleship begins in the salutation, where he identifies himself as a commissioned agent through the will of God (v. 1). God's hand on him is more than enough to authorize his ministry and actions. But he will also point to the reality of the Corinthians' faith as a further validation of his apostleship.

Timothy is apparently with Paul when he writes this letter. That it is addressed not only to "the assembly of God in Corinth," but also to "all the saints in the whole of Achaia" is often overlooked. This extended address probably means that we should see 2 Corinthians as something of a circular letter. 9:2 and 11:10 point to the same conclusion.[3]

Ekklēsia is an important word for Paul. It was used in the LXX to translate Hebrew *qāhāl*, "assembly, gathering," which is an OT term for the gathering or assembly of God's people. The term as Paul uses it seems to focus sometimes on the act of assembling by God's people[4] and sometimes on the result of that act, the assembly itself. It thus refers to what the people of God both do and are. The term is never applied in the NT to any building or organization. The

---

3. Betz's attempt to separate ch. 9 from the rest of the letter, except perhaps ch. 8, because of the reference in 9:2 to the Achaians, is misguided (H. D. Betz, *2 Corinthians 8 and 9* [Philadelphia: Fortress, 1985], pp. 25ff.).

4. As in the expression "having church."

early Christian gatherings met in homes, particularly in the homes of the more well-to-do members of the congregation.

Paul says that the assembly is "of God." This strongly suggests that Paul sees the *ekklēsia,* both Jew and Gentile in Christ, as the successor to the people of God called Israel, since "*qāhāl* of God" is used in the LXX of Israel. God is the source of this gathering of his people. It is not a human creation. Since there were no denominations in Paul's day, when he speaks of "the assembly of God in Corinth" he means all the various house churches in that city. 1 Corinthians 11 makes it clear that he expects all the Christians in Corinth in these house churches to gather in assembly from time to time to share the Lord's Supper in the context of a meal.

The Christians in Achaia are called *hagioi* ("holy ones"), probably in part because *ekklēsia* literally means "the called out group," and *hagios* refers to those who are set apart. What Christians are as individuals and what they are as a group are interrelated. The character of the individual is dependent on and affected by the group, and vice versa.[5]

5. For v. 2, see pp. 79-81 above on 1 Corinthians 1:3.

Epistolary Thanksgiving and *Exordium:* 1:3-7

This first section manifests a variety of concerns and anxieties, but also reflects a good deal of thanksgiving and relief. Paul does not seem to be in an attacking mood or mode in chs. 1–9 to the same degree as he will be in chs. 10–13. In the first sections of a rhetorical piece (*exordium, narratio,* and *propositio*) it was considered important to win the audience over and thus gain a hearing. Furthermore, Paul is truly relieved by Titus's report about the Corinthians' reaction to the severe letter.

The *exordium* in forensic rhetoric was to be addressed to the judge, not the audience or jury. In 1 Cor. 4:4f. Paul said that it is the Lord who is his judge, not any human court, and he reiterates this point in 2 Cor. 12:19 (cf. 13:3-7). It is no surprise then that the *exordium* in 2 Corinthians blesses God and makes it clear that it is God, not the Corinthians, that Paul will address as the true judge of his conduct. Nevertheless, Paul must convince the "jury" as well, that is, the Corinthian Christians.

A forensic *exordium* does not need to include all the most important questions that are to be discussed in the case, just "the points that seem most likely to serve . . . our purpose" (Quintilian *Inst. Or.* 4.1.23). In a delicate case such as Paul is dealing with here, it was important to establish rapport and *ēthos* first, and not deal with contentious matters at the outset lest the audience be alienated from the start.[1] Quintilian also says, "Our case may justify an

---

1. It is possible that Paul offers in this *exordium* not merely an introduction, but also hints that he will follow a more subtle approach to his subject, signaled by an *insinuatio* (insinuation) in the *exordium* and the material leading up to the *propositio. Insinuatio* was a technique involving indirection, often used when it was felt that the audience might be hostile to one's arguments. Paul is striving to establish empathy between himself and his

appeal to compassion with regard to what we have suffered in the past or are likely to suffer" (*Inst. Or.* 4.1.27), since "the *exordium* may sometimes derive its conciliatory force from the person of the pleader. For although he may be modest and say little about himself, yet if he is believed to be a good man, this consideration will exercise the strongest influence at every point of the case" (4.1.7). This is precisely the course that Paul pursues here.

Quintilian adds that in order to win the goodwill of those to whom one is appealing, rhetorical expressions of wishing, entreaty, or anxiety are in order in an introductory statement (4.1.33). When one carefully works through Quintilian's remarks on the forensic *exordium,* one realizes that Paul is carefully following those rhetorical conventions in 1:3-7, since it is critical for him to establish as much goodwill as he can, if in the end he is to convince his converts to sever their ties with the false *apostoloi* and be fully reconciled to him.[2]

A key to understanding Paul's letters is close attention to the opening thanksgiving or blessing sections, each of which tends to foreshadow various of the issues and ideas to be treated in what follows in the letter. Here Paul uses over and over certain key terms, particularly terms relating to mercy and compassion. *Paraklēsis* and its cognates are ubiquitous. The related verb *parakaleō* has a significant range of meanings: "encourage, beseech, appeal, exhort, comfort," and the related noun has meanings like "encouragement" or "comfort." The term as used in this letter seems to have different nuances in different places. Paul often means "encourage" or "encouragement" by this word group,[3] but in this first chapter the concept of "comfort" comes to the fore. The term

---

converts by mentioning their common sufferings for the cause. Such a more subtle or indirect approach was recommended in scandalous or very difficult cases (*Inst. Or.* 4.1.42-45). In such cases one had to go to some lengths to establish one's *ēthos* and gradually undermine the opponent's case, attacking it directly only toward the end of the discourse. This is what Paul does in 2 Corinthians, and it is a measure of his skill that some have failed to take the hints in chs. 1–7 that all is not well between Paul and his converts, especially due to some "peddlers of God's word" (see below on 2:17). As E. W. Bower, "*Ephodos* and *Insinuatio* in Greek and Latin Rhetoric," *Classical Quarterly* 8 (1958), pp. 224-30, here p. 224, stresses, the "general idea, in fact, is to counter the audience's hostility by an indirect approach . . . , preferably discrediting our opponent at the same time." The issue raised in such difficult cases is often that of *doxa,* i.e, honor, integrity, or social status (p. 225). It is no accident that the issues of *doxa* and boasting come up so frequently in 2 Corinthians, especially in the comparisons of Paul's and Moses' ministries (ch. 3) and Paul's and the opponents' ministries (chs. 11-12). Paul's *doxa* and moral integrity were being severely challenged in Corinth.

2. Cf. J. Neyrey, "The Forensic Defense Speech and Paul's Trial Speeches in Acts 22–26: Form and Function," in *Luke-Acts: New Perspectives,* ed. C. H. Talbert (New York: Crossroad, 1984), pp. 210-24, here p. 211.

3. So F. Young and D. F. Ford, *Meaning and Truth in 2 Corinthians* (Grand Rapids: Eerdmans, 1987), pp. 17ff.

is apropos to Paul's situation when he writes at least chs. 1–9 because he has been comforted as well as encouraged by Titus's report that the Corinthians have responded positively to Paul's tearful but stern letter. Paul's approach in the first nine chapters is to urge or persuade, not command. Indeed, chs. 1–9 can be seen as a study in the various milder forms of the art of persuasion. Paul does not wish to control his audience in their faith. Rather, he wants them to respond voluntarily to his discourse.[4]

Paul stresses in this blessing section that he has received comfort (vv. 3-5), but he goes on to urge his listeners to be givers of comfort. He will, in particular, urge them to forgive an erring brother and to encourage him lest they lose him to Satan (2:6f.). This letter is full of evidence that Paul underwent considerable physical suffering and spiritual anxiety over his converts. Yet v. 6 suggests that the Corinthians themselves have come in for their share of suffering for their faith. Paul believes that there are some significant benefits that go with the suffering one undergoes for Christ's sake — the joy and encouragement one gets from seeing others come to or grow in Christ.

The use of *paraklēsis* language to establish rapport, the references to sufferings, and the reference to Paul and the Corinthians as *koinōnoi*, fellow participants in both suffering and comfort/encouragement (v. 7), are clues in the *exordium* as to what is to come in the letter.[5] If Paul is to be fully reconciled to his converts, then he must stress both his *koinōnia* with them and its nature. It is in some ways an exclusive bond that rules out certain kinds of relationships with both nonbelievers (6:14–7:1) and false believers (chs. 10–13). From a sociological point of view this means that Paul, as in 1 Corinthians, is trying to enhance the Corinthians' understanding of the boundaries of the community — both the boundaries of belief and, perhaps primarily, the boundaries of behavior and social praxis.

Munck has noticed how similar Paul's procedure in 1 Thessalonians 1–3 is to what we find in 2 Corinthians 1–9 in style, content, and tone. In both

4. C. J. Bjerkelund, *PARAKALÔ. Form, Funktion und Sinn der Parakalô-Sätze in den paulinischen Briefen* (Oslo: Universitetsforlaget, 1967), has argued for the unity of 2 Corinthians and sees Paul's use of the *parakaleō* word group as a key to discerning that unity. He points out that the term appears at key junctures in the letter and argues that Paul begins with a blessing *(eulogētos)* section that involves significant use of *paraklēsis* language rather than a thanksgiving section (as in most of the rest of Paul's letters) because of the apologetic character of 2 Corinthians and because Paul has less to be thankful about on this occasion than when he wrote some of his other letters (Bjerkelund, pp. 150ff.).

5. As J. Y. Campbell, "Κοινωνία and its Cognates in the NT," *JBL* 51 (1932), pp. 352-80, here p. 361, suggests, here Paul refers to an actual sharing in similar sufferings, whereas in Phil. 4:14 he refers to the Philippians' active empathy with Paul in his sufferings.

letters Paul uses digressions to prevent misunderstanding, speaks of thwarted travel plans, expresses relief at reports that all seems better than he had feared, and defends himself against accusations (cf. 1 Thess. 2:3-12).[6] Paul's work as an artisan and his refusal of patronage also arise in both texts.[7] The situation in Thessalonica seems less troubled than that in Corinth, but the parallels show that Paul is not proceeding in a totally anomalous way in 2 Corinthians, even in his use of digressions.

6. J. Munck, *Paul and the Salvation of Mankind* (Atlanta: John Knox, 1959), pp. 193ff.
7. If one includes 1 Corinthians in the comparison, then it is germane to note that both that letter and the Thessalonian correspondence reflect some significant misunderstanding of future eschatology on the part of the addressees. Later we will note the important parallels between 2 Corinthians 10–13 and Galatians 5–6, both of which are concluding sections of Pauline forensic letters.

Narratio: 1:8–2:16

In the *narratio* the rhetor was to state the facts of the case that were at issue or the main questions under debate.[1] Paul is very careful not to mention the major charge against him until just after the conclusion of the *narratio*, when he finally comes to the major *propositio* of the entire discourse in 2:17 — the proposition that must be proved true or false. Paul is following the given wisdom in this procedure; Quintilian stresses that "we must aim . . . above all in our statement of facts, at striking the happy mean in our language, and that may be defined as saying only what is necessary and sufficient" (*Inst. Or.* 4.2.45). Paul thus chooses to build up goodwill and compassion in the *narratio* by dealing with less crucial charges such as his possible dishonesty about his travel plans, his sternness in the painful letter toward the one who had offended him, and his supposed lack of love and concern for the Corinthians. These are important issues and Paul will return to them later in the "argument" section of the discourse, but it is clear from 2:17 and what follows in 3:1–6:13 that the major issue is the legitimacy of Paul's ministry. It is this above all else that is in question in Corinth and therefore also in this letter.[2]

A *narratio* was generally supposed to be brief, but as Quintilian admits,

---

1. For a different analysis of the rhetorical arrangement of chs. 1–2, see F. W. Hughes, "The Rhetoric of Reconciliation: 2. Cor. 1:1–2:13 and 7:5–8:24," in *Persuasive Artistry: Studies in NT Rhetoric in Honor of George A. Kennedy,* ed. D. F. Watson (Sheffield: Sheffield Academic, 1991), pp. 246-61. Hughes mistakes the emotions expressed in the *narratio* for *peroratio* material and overextends the *exordium* to include the epistolary prescript as well as some of the *narratio*. He also fails to see the material's forensic character.

2. On the rhetorical unity of 2:14–7:1, including the digression in 6:14–7:1, see J. I. H. MacDonald, "Paul and Preaching: A Reconsideration of 2 Cor. 2:14-17 in its Context," *JSNT* 17 (1983), pp. 35-50.

at times the case requires a rather long statement of the facts (*Inst. Or.* 4.2.47). It was perfectly legitimate to postpone some points until the *probatio*, the argument or proof section of a discourse, but one was to at least allude to them in the *narratio* or *propositio* (*Inst. Or.* 4.2.48). 2:17 serves the purpose of alluding to the major issue.[3]

A forensic *narratio*, to be convincing, had to assign some reasons and motives for what the defendant was being accused of doing. It is crucial to mention times, places, persons, and causes that give some explanation for the behavior in question (*Inst. Or.* 4.2.55f.), and this is precisely what Paul does in 1:8–2:16. He does not deny the charge that he has said one thing and done another, but rather seeks to give reasons that it was necessary for him to do this. He did it to "spare" his converts more grief (1:23). He does not deny causing his converts sadness through the severe letter, but claims that he did it for the sake of the good end of producing repentance. The rhetor was, above all, to avoid inconsistency and contradiction or the appearance thereof (*Inst. Or.* 4.2.60). Therefore Paul must spend considerable time in the *narratio* explaining why he should not be accused of contradiction. It was considered appropriate in a *narratio* to incite the gentler emotions such as compassion, and Paul seeks to do this from the first verse of his statement of the facts (cf. *Inst. Or.* 4.2.111-13).

The *narratio* indicates that Paul was writing to a fractured congregation in Corinth. Not all but only "the majority" (2:6) supported Paul's advice to discipline the brother in question. Apparently a minority had come to reject Paul's authority, probably under the influence of the false *apostoloi* (12:13). Paul seeks to overcome this and in 2:3, 5 stresses that he has confidence in *all* of them and that they all have been grieved by the offending member. In 2:3 Paul speaks charitably in an effort to build rapport. Clearly he has severe doubts, especially about the minority who did not support his ruling. Paul would not leave a promising mission field in Troas and anxiously go over to Macedonia if he had full confidence in "all of you" (2:12f.). V. 3 must be judged according to its intended rhetorical function.

There is some question as to how we should translate *apokrima* in 1:9. The word occurs nowhere else in the NT. In secular Greek it refers to a decree, verdict, or decision that settles a matter.[4] Here we are told that it was a decree or verdict of death. But Paul says that he has received this verdict *within himself*,

---

3. *Inst. Or.* 4.2.132 says that at the end of the *narratio* one ought to mention the major issue to be determined.

4. Cf. C. J. Hemer, "A Note on 2 Corinthians 1:9," *TynB* 23 (1972), pp. 103-7. The word is not used of a *sentence* of death. As Hemer shows, it is not a specifically judicial term, though in the end he favors the translation "verdict" and sees it as referring to a response to a petition by an ambassador. This is apt in Paul's case.

which leads to the suggestion that he is talking about some sort of illness. He knows that there is no cure, short of resurrection, for the terminal illness by which all, as fallen creatures, die. He believes in a God who raises the dead and so is able to talk of hope beyond and triumphing over death, not of a hope that seeks somehow to bypass death. Paul acquired this death sentence in himself (cf. the "thorn in the flesh" in 12:7) so that he would not trust in his own strength but in God who raises the dead.

But Paul has received a stay of execution. He has been rescued from imminent danger in Asia (1:8, 10), and he believes that ultimately God will rescue him, and so he fixes his hope on God. In v. 11 he speaks of the partnership he and the Corinthians have. They can both pray and give thanks for one another.

In vv. 12f. Paul launches into a major theme of this letter, namely the reasons for boasting and the different sorts of boasting. The key word here is *kauchēsis,* which can refer to either the good sort of pride one might take in someone or to the bad sort of boasting. We can translate it "reason for boasting," not "boasting," since why a person boasts is the issue. Paul says, amazingly enough, that the Corinthians are *his* reason for boasting. They are the evidence and the testimony that assures Paul's conscience that he has been doing things in the right and godly way — in sincerity and simplicity.[5] He has sought not to be a financial burden to the Corinthians in regard to his own needs. He has not followed a worldly-wise approach. I suspect that this alludes not only to Paul's simple lifestyle while in Corinth but also to his refusal to use Sophistic rhetoric in the presentation of the gospel. In both word and manner of life he would present it plainly, without ornamentation.

As v. 14 goes on to stress, Paul is the grounds for the Corinthians' boasting as well, both because of his present behavior and because they owe him their spiritual lives. What Paul envisions is that at the day of the Lord he and they will be able to stand up and testify on each other's behalf to the Lord about how good each has been to and for the other.

It seems best to translate *charis* in v. 15 as "benefit" or "kindness," as Fee has argued.[6] Paul has hoped to get a second benefit from the Corinthians, by having them send him on his way to Judea, presumably with the money collected for the poor Christians there, and then on westward on his evangelizing tour. He was willing, despite his practice of refusing support from them, to let them be supporters of his work or of a worthy cause, such as aiding starving Christians elsewhere.[7]

5. Probably not "holiness," since Paul is stressing that he took a Spartan approach.
6. G. D. Fee, "ΧΑΡΙΣ in 2 Corinthians 1:15: Apostolic Parousia and Paul-Corinth Chronology," *NTS* 24 (1978), pp. 533-38.
7. But he was not accepting missionary aid for himself from them while he was *apart* from them, as he did from the Philippians; see below, pp. 414-19, on these differences.

Here we are faced with trying to figure out Paul's itinerary (vv. **15f.**). Did he make an unannounced painful visit, going straight from Ephesus, or was his *plan* to make a double visit (to Corinth, then to Macedonia, then back to Corinth) changed when he thought better of the second visit and sent a painful letter instead? It would seem that the latter is the case, that a double visit was the initial plan and this in turn led to a charge that he was not keeping his promises.

Paul's point in vv. **17f.** is that his itinerary is not up to him but up to the Lord.[8] It was not that he simply felt it imprudent to come, despite his promise to do so, because he had been humiliated or hurt during the painful visit. There was another reason that he did not come, which was to spare the Corinthians the wrath of God's agent. 1 Corinthians 5 proves that Paul was capable of wielding the sword when necessary, but he preferred not to do so with his spiritual children. He did not want to act irresponsibly or, better translated, in a vacillating manner *(elaphria)* and denies that he would "resolve according to the flesh with the result that with me the yes is yes. . . ."[9] He is under God's authority and so must do what God leads him to do.

This would seem to deflect his apparent inconsistency back on God, so he goes on to insist that God is faithful and trustworthy. All of God's promises find fulfillment or affirmation in Christ (v. **20**). God's word to the Corinthians is a large "yes" in Christ. Paul was led not to come to the Corinthians but rather to write the letter of tears, in order to spare them something worse, because God is faithful and ultimately wants their well-being.[10] Just as all God's

8. So F. Young and D. F. Ford, *Meaning and Truth in 2 Corinthians* (Grand Rapids: Eerdmans, 1987), p. 102.

9. Cf. the New English Bible: "that it should rest with me to say yes and yes. . . ." Cf. also Young and Ford, *Meaning and Truth,* pp. 102f., following John Chrysostom.

D. Wenham, "2 Cor. 1:17, 18: Echo of a Dominical Logion," *NovT* 28 (1986), pp. 271-79 is likely correct that there is an echo in these two verses of the logion in Matt. 5:37f. and Jas. 5:12. Paul is "picking up the words that the Corinthians had used when accusing him of prevarication. In other words, Paul is not picking up Jesus' saying as such, but Jesus' saying as used by his Corinthian opponents against him" (p. 275). Perhaps 11:7f. should be considered in this way as well, which may suggest that the opponents — the Corinthians not initially but only under the prompting of the "false apostles" — had raised the issue of Paul betraying Jesus' words at various points, thus proving *him* to be a false apostle.

10. It is essential that Christian ministers take stock with some regularity and be clear in their own minds about the proper priorities in ministry, especially for those occasions when two important obligations suddenly and undeniably come into conflict with one another. This is a matter not just of being careful not to promise too much, but also of making clear to the congregation of the minister's identity as a person under authority and of being ready in any given situation to do what through God's word, circumstance, conscience, or godly counsel the Holy Spirit is leading toward. Nor is this a matter of providing for oneself an escape clause to justify any sort of action. If a minister

promises receive their "yes" in Christ, so also through Christ Paul offers the Amen — the "so be it" — to God. God is the one who establishes Paul with the Corinthians "in Christ" and "anoints" Paul.[11] Is Paul discussing baptism in vv. 21f.? He never directly mentions it, and it is doubtful that he is even alluding to it. "Anoints" is in the present tense, referring to an ongoing reality, and "sealed" and "gave" refer to the past, probably to what happens at the point of conversion (cf. 1 Cor. 12:13).

The metaphors used here are commercial and legal. "Sealed" refers to what happens to goods — they are claimed from the outset by the proper owner or claimant by being marked with a monogram.[12] The reference here is not to some sort of eschatological sealing or to an airtight guarantee of perseverance and salvation. The point is, rather, that by the Spirit, who is a foretaste and down payment of what God has promised to give believers, the Corinthian Christians have been claimed as God's property. They belong to God.

In v. 23 Paul even swears that his not coming was to spare the Corinthians worse grief.[13] He is a fellow worker of their joy. That is, he wants to cause them joy, not more grief. They "stand by faithfulness."[14] They are to encourage and gladden Paul's heart, but how can they do that if Paul saddens them further (2:2f.)? Paul trusts that he and they will share a common joy.

2:4 speaks of Paul's physical and mental state when he wrote the sorrowful letter. He was anxious in heart, undergoing suffering, and weeping while writing. Paradoxically, the letter was not intended to sadden them but was written that they might know Paul's love for them. Like God, Paul chastens those whom he loves.

Paul then refers to a particular individual (*tis*, v. 5) who has caused sadness. This man has saddened Paul, but Paul wants to stress that in part he has saddened all the Corinthian Christians as well. There is a debate as to what to make of the word *epitimia* here. The word ranges in meaning from "rebuke" or "reproof" to "punishment." How one translates it in part depends on

---

makes clear what the priorities will be in ministry in a given situation, the congregation will better understand what they can expect and ought to expect from the minister.

Sometimes a foolish consistency leads away from what God is urging in a particular situation. Paul's example suggests that one must learn when to follow a plan and when to depart from it. This wisdom comes partly through experience, partly through the Word and the Spirit's guidance, and partly from knowing ahead of time what the priorities are in one's ministry.

11. There is a wordplay here between *Christos* and the verbal form *chrisas* ("anoint"), demonstrating again that this letter, like other Pauline letters, not only manifests rhetorical features but also is meant to be ear-catching.

12. F. W. Danker, *II Corinthians* (Minneapolis: Augsburg, 1989), p. 40.

13. It was not an act of refraining from love, but an act of love.

14. *Pistis* here probably does not mean "faith," but, as in v. 18, "faithfulness."

whether one sees this person as a stranger in Corinth who caused Paul grief, matching him up with the false *apostoloi* mentioned in 11:13, or whether he is a Corinthian Christian who has insulted Paul. If the latter, then it is perfectly possible that Paul is talking about a formal disciplinary measure taken by the Corinthians against this individual.[15]

Paul says that "the majority" rightly took action against this man, but now Paul wants them to take the role of reconcilers and forgive him, as Paul has done (vv. **6f.**). This means that Paul is not referring here to the outside agitators that he speaks of in ch. 11. The congregation itself is divided about Paul, and only the majority took his side against this member. But Paul does not want this person to be overwhelmed with sorrow, so forgiveness must be extended.

In his letter of tears, Paul must have advised the Corinthians to take action against this person, and now he says that he did this to test their character — to see if they would obey. Literally the text says, "in order to know the proof *(dokima)* of you" (v. **9**). Paul has put the Corinthians to the test, and the majority passed, and so he is now in a more positive and forgiving mood. Paul sees Christ as present when the community takes action (v. **10**), as in 1 Cor. 5:4. He stresses that this forgiveness is necessary lest the Accuser take advantage of the discipline and draw this person away from Christ (v. **11**). Paul, using a wordplay, says he is *mindful* of what is in the Devil's *mind*.

In vv. **12f.** Paul reflects back on how he came to hear the good news of their obedience. It came when he, while he had an open door in Troas to preach the gospel, could not sit still to do that work but decided to go to Macedonia and find Titus as he was returning from Corinth. While Paul's concern was in part for Titus, the whole context suggests that his larger concern was for the Corinthians.[16] The situation worried Paul so much that he left a good opportunity to evangelize to find out what was happening.

In vv. **14ff.** Paul turns to thanking God for the outcome. M. E. Thrall has demonstrated that this is not the beginning of a new or separate letter but simply a fresh introductory thanksgiving section,[17] though it should be added

15. So V. P. Furnish, *II Corinthians* (Garden City: Doubleday, 1984), pp. 163ff. Possibly a temporary excommunication is involved, as in 1 Corinthians 5, though that is surely a separate case.

16. Not as C. K. Barrett, *The Second Epistle to the Corinthians* (New York: Harper and Row, 1973), p. 94, suggests, for Titus and the collection.

17. M. E. Thrall, "A Second Thanksgiving Period in 2 Corinthians," *JSNT* 16 (1982), pp. 101-24. P. T. O'Brien, *Introductory Thanksgivings in the Letters of Paul* (Leiden: Brill, 1977), pp. 239, 257, somewhat plausibly suggests that Paul uses a Jewish blessing formula first (1:3ff.) because he is speaking of his own personal experience as a Jewish Christian in the first chapter, and a thanksgiving period later because he is referring to the experience of his converts, many of whom were Gentiles. Nonetheless in both places Paul is talking about both his own experience and that of the Corinthians, stressing the interplay between the two in order to effect rapprochement.

that what came earlier (1:3ff.) was a *blessing* section while this is a true thanks-giving. Here *charis* means gratitude, a grateful response to God's grace.

There is considerable debate as to what should be made of the phrase *pantote thriambeuonti* in v. 14. This seems to refer to being led around in a Roman procession of triumph (see the picture on p. 368).[18] Paul is quite capable of putting together mixed metaphors, and here we have one. He is not saying that he is being led around in triumph, but rather that, like the captives in a triumphal process, he is being treated rudely while in the service of God. The evidence from the period strongly suggests that those being led in the triumph were being led to death. "The odor" that arises from this metaphorical procession may echo the practice of sprinkling spices in front of a triumphal Roman procession, or it may just refer to the smell of the captive himself. As God drags Paul around as his slave, the knowledge of Christ emanates from Paul wherever he goes.[19] He is the sweet aroma of Christ,[20] at least to those who are being saved (v. 15). But for those who are perishing the smell is repulsive: It is the smell of death and it leads to death (v. 16a; cf. 1 Cor. 1:18). Probably Barrett is wrong to see the idea of Christ as sacrifice here.[21] The focus is not on a sacrifice but on the odor that Paul exudes, and in light of the parallel to Sir. 24:11 Paul is probably suggesting that his life manifests the Wisdom of God, the wisdom of the Gospel, the Wisdom who is the crucified Christ himself.

18. R. B. Egan, "Lexical Evidence on Two Pauline Passages," *NovT* 19 (1977), pp. 34-62, rightly notes the lack of lexical support for a translation such as "makes us triumph" or "leads us in triumph as a general leads his victorious army." But he misses the appropriateness of Paul seeing himself as a slave of Christ, an enslaved leader put on display, being led in God's triumphal procession through the world. Paul sees himself as a former enemy of the gospel and hence of Christ and so as a captured slave (cf. Gal. 1:13, 23; 6:17; 1 Cor. 15:9). This is the presupposition behind Paul's use of the imagery here, though not the meaning or focus that he gives to it.

19. In short, Paul is both a parable and a conveyor of the life and presence of Christ. When people look at him they see the story of Jesus as well. Cf. T. B. Savage, *Power Through Weakness* (Ph.D. thesis, Cambridge, 1986), p. 123.

20. Two words are used for "odor" or "aroma": *osmēn* in v. 14 and *euōdia* in v. 15. It is possible that Paul is drawing on Sir. 38:11, which speaks of a sweet-smelling sacrifice. But Sir. 24:15, which describes the aroma (*osmēn*) that Wisdom exudes, is more likely in mind. S. Hafemann, *Suffering and Ministry in the Spirit: Paul's Defense of His Ministry in II Corinthians 2:14–3:3* (Grand Rapids: Eerdmans, 1990), p. 42, mistakenly understands Sir. 24:15 to be referring to sacrifice, whereas it refers to the incense that accompanies sacrifice and metaphorically to the presence of Wisdom in a person's life, which is "an odor pleasing to the Lord." Paul, like Christ, is the embodiment of God's Wisdom, in this case the wisdom about the cross. On Paul's use of sapiential material to describe Christ in 1 Corinthians and elsewhere, cf. B. Witherington, *Jesus the Sage: The Pilgrimage of Wisdom* (Minneapolis: Fortress, 1994), ch. 7.

21. Barrett, *Second Corinthians*, pp. 100f.

Paul asks who is equal to this task of conveying the very presence of Christ, his characteristic smell, to the world (v. **16b**). To carry out this task is to be truly Christlike, and in Paul's mind no human is fully capable of it. Ironically, it is precisely this humble view of himself, which Paul freely shares with his converts, that seems to have alienated them from him. They were looking for a leader powerful in speech, deeds, and personal presence, that is, one who exudes the self-confidence of an agent of God. Paul did not fit their profile of a Christian leader.

A Closer Look: The Roman Triumph

As S. Hafemann has demonstrated, exegetes of 2:14-16 have paid insufficient attention to the actual character of Roman triumphs.[22] Several ancient Roman, Greek, and Jewish writers mention the Roman triumph. Dionysius of Halicarnassus writes (30-32 B.C.) that in the victory procession "the trophies" were carried and that the procession was concluded with "the sacrifice that the Romans call a triumph" (2.3). The triumph was to honor a conquering general who "drove into the city," that is, Rome, "with the spoils, the prisoners, and the army that had fought under him, he himself riding in a chariot drawn by horses with golden bridles and arrayed in royal robes, as is the custom in the greater triumphs" (8.67.9f.). Plutarch uses the same term as Paul, *thriambeuein:* "To this very day, in offering a sacrifice for victory, they *lead in triumph* an old man wearing a boy's toga with a *bulla* attached to it through the Forum to the Capitol, while the herald cries: 'Sardians for sale!'" (*Romulus* 25.4). Appian says that the normal custom was to kill the prisoners who had been led in triumph (*Mithridatic Wars* 12.116f.), and Josephus *Jewish Wars* 7:153-55 confirms this. As the captive states clearly in Seneca *De Ben.* 2.11.1, "In a triumph I would have had to march only once."[23]

Hafemann rightly stresses that

> although the focus of the procession itself was on the triumphator, with its displays of the spoils of war, the recounting of the high points of the decisive battle through dramatic presentations and paintings, the army's praise for its general, and the parade of the vanquished foes, the procession *itself, as a whole* was intended to be an act of worship to the god who had granted the victory.[24]

This marriage of political and religious factors was typical, and the triumph can be seen as an expression of Roman eschatology.[25] In his definitive study H. S. Versnel writes that

22. Hafemann, *Suffering and Ministry*, pp. 19-34.
23. His complaint is that the one who "liberated" him from the triumph is constantly putting him on display as a show of his magnanimous nature.
24. Hafemann, *Suffering and Ministry*, p. 30.
25. See above, pp. 295-98, on 1 Corinthians 15.

*A Roman triumph. Note the captive being led to execution
at the left side of the picture.*

(Illustration by P. Connolly, from R. Burrell, *The Romans*
[Oxford University Press, 1991], used by permission)

the triumph characterized the greatness of Rome as being due, on the one hand, to the excellence of the victorious general, and, on the other, to the favor of the supreme god who, *optimus maximus,* ensured the continuance and the prosperity of the Roman empire. *In no other Roman ceremony do god and man approach each other as closely as they do in the triumph.* Not only is the triumph direct towards the Capitolium, where the triumphator presents a solemn offering to Iuppiter O.M., but the triumphator himself has a status which appears to raise him to the rank of the gods. . . . He is clothed in a purple *toga* and a *tunic* stitched with palm-motifs, together called *ornatus Iovis,* and in his hand he carries a scepter crowned by an eagle. His face has been red-leaded. It seems as if Iuppiter himself, incarnated in the triumphator, makes his solemn entry into Rome.[26]

Paul seems to have frequently used the imagery of the Roman triumph to describe his experience as an agent of God. For instance, Hafemann points out the notable parallels between 1 Cor. 4:9 and 2 Cor. 2:14:

26. H. S. Versnel, *Triumphus: An Inquiry into the Origin, Development and Meaning of the Roman Triumph* (Leiden: Brill, 1970), p. 1, emphasis added.

1 Cor. 4:9	2 Cor. 2:14
God	Thanks be to God
exhibited last as sentenced to death	who leads to death in the triumphal procession
us apostles;	us in Christ
we became a spectacle	and through us reveals the fragrance of knowledge of him
to the world, that is, to angels and people.	in every place.[27]

In both passages God is the author of the death verdict who leads his own agent through the empire in order to reveal his own presence, precisely through the weakness of his agent.

This imagery fits with the image of Paul as an enslaved leader in 1 Corinthians 9.[28] Delling notes the connection: In 2 Cor. 2:14 Paul describes himself as a captive, "but he regards it as a grace that in his fetters he can accompany God always and everywhere . . . in the divine triumphant march through the world, even though it be only as the δοῦλος Χριστοῦ," that is, as Christ's slave.[29]

To this one must add Hafemann's insight that the prisoner knew that the procession led to a violent death. It is not only through Paul's words but also through the very course of his life that he reveals God, because his life reveals the message and meaning of taking up one's cross to follow Jesus. Here we are at the heart of one of the great Pauline paradoxes: power in weakness, victory through death, and a victory procession that leads to death. What we will come to see in 2 Corinthians is that "it is Christ whom Paul imitates

---

27. Hafemann, *Suffering and Ministry,* 58. Cf. Col. 2:15 for a different use of the imagery of the Roman triumph.

28. See above, pp. 211-15. P. Marshall, "A Metaphor of Social Shame: *Thriambeuein* in 2 Cor. 2:14," *NovT* 25 (1984), pp. 302-17, besides providing a thorough refutation of R. B. Egan's objections to the position advanced by Hafemann and myself, also seeks to show that Paul deliberately portrays himself as a shamed individual. This is only a half-truth, however, since Paul believes that he is honored by God at the same time that he is being abased (and is abasing himself) in the eyes of human beings. In particular, Marshall overstresses the shame aspect, because he neglects the various traditions about suffering sages, who were not always thought of as shamed individuals. That Paul's *peristasis* catalogs list a few things that normal Romans or Greeks would seek to hide or omit (shortcomings, failures, faults) does show that Paul repudiates various of the social values of his day. But in the main these catalogs focus not on such things but on Paul's sufferings and tribulations, which in the sapiential tradition were not necessarily seen as shameful.

29. G. Delling, *TDNT* III, p. 160. Cf. the helpful article by L. Williamson, "Led in Triumph: Paul's Use of *Thriambeuo*," *Int* 22 (1968), pp. 317-32.

(I Cor. 11:1), the suffering of Christ which Paul shares (II Cor. 1:5), and the power of Christ which rests upon him in that weakness (II Cor. 12:9)."[30]

As S. Heiny has shown, Paul's reason for using the dramatic metaphors found in 2:14-16 to speak of his own experience is rhetorical. It is an attempt to build or reveal an *ēthos*, to appeal to the sympathies of the audience, to establish rapport with them.[31] Longinus *On the Sublime* 32:6 stresses that metaphors are to be used to move the audience and to clarify matters.[32] They serve both purposes here and are part of Paul's larger effort to persuade his audience of his good character and authentic ministry. The final question about adequacy in v. 16 seems to echo Moses' similar statement in the Septuagint of Exod. 4:10 and prepares us for the paralleling of Paul's and Moses' ministries in ch. 3.[33]

30. Hafemann, *Suffering and Ministry,* p. 48.

31. S. Heiny, "2 Cor. 2:14–4:6: The Motive for Metaphor," *Society of Biblical Literature 1987 Seminar Papers,* ed. K. H. Richards (Atlanta: Scholars, 1987), pp. 1-21, especially pp. 16ff.

32. Cf. W. C. Booth, "Metaphor as Rhetoric," in *On Metaphor,* ed. S. Sacks (Chicago: University of Chicago, 1978), pp. 54-56.

33. Cf. J. T. Fitzgerald, *Cracks in an Earthen Vessel: An Examination of the Catalogue of Hardships in the Corinthian Correspondence* (Atlanta: Scholars, 1988), p. 165. Fitzgerald makes the intriguing suggestion that Paul's confession of his inadequacy in the area of public speaking (2 Cor. 10:10) is also a parallel to Moses. This raises the further possibility that when Paul calls himself God's servant, he is modeling himself on Moses rather than on the Isaianic Suffering Servant.

The *Propositio:* 2:17

In a piece of forensic rhetoric, the *propositio* is the statement to be proved true or false by the arguments that follow in the discourse. It is thus a statement about past behavior (whether words or deeds or both) about which some sort of charge has been made. It summarizes the main bone of contention and thus gives an indication of how the defendant will handle the charge. It was not uncommon for a person to take the *propositio* of one's opponent, deny it, and seek to refute the charges in a straightforward manner (*Inst. Or.* 4.4.8). Quintilian also informs us that often the question turns on a definition of the fact (4.4.3). The defendant may admit to the actions but claim that his deeds have been misinterpreted as blameworthy.[1] Money matters were often the subject of such litigation, and this lies at the heart of the grievance some Corinthians have against Paul.

In Paul's case, it seems the basic charge is that he is no *apostolos*, as is shown by his refusal to accept patronage, all the while trying secretly to bilk the Corinthians of money through his appeal for the collection for the poor Christians of Jerusalem. Instead of being an *apostolos*, he is, as his behavior shows, a dishonest schemer unlike those who are presently in Corinth and are openly accepting support and who have legitimate letters of reference.

The charge against Paul bears some resemblance to that made against Aeschines, who was accused of misconduct as an ambassador (cf. 2 Cor. 5:20) on the basis that he lied, failed to carry out his instructions, wasted time, and accepted bribes (*Inst. Or.* 4.4.5f.). Aeschines was charged with being a bogus agent and therefore of having no right to act as an amabassador. We have seen

---

1. Thus Paul could admit that he refused patronage but deny the inference drawn from that fact.

371

in the *narratio* (1:18–2:16) that Paul is combating the charge that he failed to make good on his own promises and thus was inconsistent, if not a liar. As the letter progresses, another charge becomes clearer, which is that he is secretly taking or wanting to take money from the collection while publicly making a show of refusing support (chs. 8–9). So Paul has also been charged with misconduct as an ambassador, that is, as Christ's agent.[2] The goal of all these allegations was to prove that he was not an apostle and that his ministry had no proper basis, there being no tangible evidence to support his apostolic claims.

In 2:17 Paul denies both the fundamental charge of being a false agent or ambassador of Christ and the most crucial basis of that charge, which is his untrustworthy approach to the Corinthians' money. While it is possible that he is simply citing the opposition's charge here, more probably he has formulated this verse himself in order to go on the offensive.[3] Chs. 10–13 make the latter more likely, for what Paul alludes to here, he delivers in full there: a *synkrisis* or comparison of himself, along with his motives and actions, with those who truly are hucksters and profiteers, the false *apostoloi*.

It is no accident that from ch. 2 on the letter is peppered with commercial terminology or that money matters come up again, not only in chs. 8–9, but also as the basis of the essential charges at the end of Paul's arguments: In 13:13 he exclaims sarcastically, "How have you been worse off than the other *ekklēsiae,* except that I did not burden you? Forgive me that wrong!" Paul must completely undercut the basis of the essential charge against him in order to disprove the argument that he was no true *apostolos.* This is the essential task that he must undertake in the argument section of the letter.

Paul's basic rhetorical strategy seems to be that at the beginning of the *probatio* (3:1–6:13) he will compare his ministry with that of Moses and on that basis develop arguments to show why he should be seen as a true minister of the gospel or ambassador of Christ and thus should be reconciled to and recognized by his Corinthian converts. This is a difficult task, and so Paul goes on to engage in a digression in 6:14–7:1 and a deliberative argument in 8–9 in order to put the Corinthians on the defensive and disable their sense of

---

2. Cf. E. Richard, "Polemics, OT, and Theology," *RB* 88 (1981), pp. 340-67, here p. 364:

> In 2 Cor. 2:14-17 he prepares his audience for the main thrust of his defense. . . . At each major break Paul inserts an important element of the controversy: 3:1: letters of recommendation; 4f.: competence as minister; 12: boldness in action; and at 4:1f.: summary of his defense. The concept of ministry overshadows the entire discussion. Paul's choice and interpretation of texts are constantly influenced by his preoccupation with the role of the ministry in the new dispensation.

3. Though he does formulate his response on the basis of the charges.

self-righteousness and moral outrage. He will conclude his arguments with a comparison of his ministry with that of the false apostles in chs. 10–13.

Thus, the whole argument section of the letter is framed by two major comparisons, one with a positive example, Moses, and one with a negative example, the false apostles. The comparison with Moses is not ironic, but the comparison with the false apostles certainly is; there Paul engages in anti-Sophistic boasting to put the Corinthians and the opponents in their respective places.

Probatio and *refutatio* are thus pursued together throughout, with Paul sometimes presenting positive arguments for accepting his ministry, sometimes offering negative arguments refuting the essential charges against him or criticizing his opponents, which is especially evident in chs. 10–13, an emotional harangue where *pathos* comes to the fore. Chs. 10–13 are perhaps Paul's rhetorical tour de force. There, Paul will demolish the arguments of the opponents, but he signals already in the *propositio* that he knows well what the essential charges are and that he intends to show them to be false.

In 2:17 Paul alludes to many, some of whom are apparently already in Corinth, who are "profiteers," who preach the Word to make not only a living but also a profit. The term *kapēleuontes* is used in the Septuagint (Isa. 1:22) for wine merchants, where they are said to dilute the wine with water to make greater profits. It appears that the basic sense of the verbal form of this word as Paul and others use it is not to "dilute" or "adulterate," but to "sell" as a retailer for profit.[4]

More importantly, in secular Greek the term had been used in criticisms of itinerant Sophists who offered their *sophia* — rhetoric and sometimes philosophy — for a price.[5] This practice originated among the Sophists and led Socrates to call them "peddlers" (*kapēloi*, Plato *Prt.* 313C-D). The practice and the comparison of those who followed it to hucksters became common by the time of the empire (cf. Dio Chrysostom 8.9; Philostratus *Apollonius of Tyana* 1.13; Philo *De Gigantibus* 39; *Vit. Mos.* 2.212). But Paul refuses to take money for his teaching, not only because he has a different pedagogical model in mind, but also because he believes that there is something about the character of the gospel that requires that it be offered free of charge to the unbelieving world.[6]

4. Cf. S. J. Hafemann, *Suffering and Ministry in the Spirit: Paul's Defense of His Ministry in II Corinthians 2:14–3:3* (Grand Rapids: Eerdmans, 1990), pp. 98-125.

5. Cf. V. P. Furnish, *II Corinthians* (Garden City: Doubleday, 1984), p. 178: "Paul must be thinking here of those who teach for their own gain and, in the process, adulterate the truth."

6. The matter of support by *believers* of their spiritual parent is a different matter. See below, pp. 414-19.

He has already demonstrated his anti-Sophistic style of ministry and rhetoric in 1 Corinthians, especially chs. 1–4, but here he must remind the Corinthians again of his ways among them. While he speaks sincerely from God, before God and in Christ, he implies that the peddlers speak insincerely, away from God and apart from Christ.[7] He thus foreshadows here his later more trenchant critique of the false *apostoloi*, and classes them with the Sophists and other teachers whose profit motive renders their teaching suspect.[8] Heiny suggests that Paul could have used the term *emporoi* (wholesalers) here but chose the term that refers to retailers because this metaphor reduces his opponents not only to frauds, but petty frauds at that.[9]

Hafemann stresses that one must read 2:17 in light of the rhetorical question in v. 16. If this is correct, then there is perhaps an implied answer to that question, namely that Paul, unlike the peddlers, *is* sufficient for a ministry of apostolic suffering and witnessing, as is proved by the course of his life as it is described in vv. 14-16.[10]

Paul offers the gospel freely from a sincere heart. He must act in such a way because he believes that God watches. All that he does, he does in the presence of God and in Christ. Therefore he must act in a Christlike manner. What Paul suggests here he will state clearly at the end of his discourse, namely that God, not the Corinthians, is the real judge of his case, of the authenticity of his ministry, and thus that he is laying his case before God.[11] He is speaking "in Christ before God" (13:19). The Corinthians want proof that Christ is truly speaking in him, that is, proof that he is Christ's authentic agent and spokesperson (13:3). He gives this proof in the arguments of this letter.

7. S. Heiny, "2 Cor. 2:14–4:6: The Motive for Metaphor," *Society of Biblical Literature 1987 Seminar Papers,* ed. K. H. Richards (Atlanta: Scholars, 1987), pp. 1-21, here p. 6.

8. It would appear from chs. 10–11 that the opponents were rhetorically adept.

9. Heiny, "2 Cor. 2:14–4:6," p. 15.

10. Hafemann, *Suffering and Ministry,* pp. 98f. Notably Richard, "Polemics," pp. 340-67, recognizes that the polemical statement in v. 17 leads to Paul's self-defense in 3:1ff., without realizing the rhetorical character of Paul's discourse or the crucial rhetorical function of 2:17.

11. Paul held firmly to both salvation by grace through faith and ultimate accountability for deeds. While deeds cannot get one into the kingdom, they can certainly keep one out of it. Paul also believed that there would be both rewards to believers for work well done and punishment of some sort for shoddy work or misdeeds (1 Cor. 3:13-15). Heaven is not a reward, but there will be greater and lesser rewards in heaven, an idea that Jesus also seems to have affirmed (Matt. 5:12; Mark 10:30). For Paul, salvation by faith and accountability for works were living realities grounded in the character of God, whom Paul did not envision as an infinitely indulgent parent. He saw God as both righteous and loving, both just and forgiving, and as demanding both qualities of Christ's followers. Human moral integrity grows out of a sense of ultimate accountability.

The *Probatio:* 3:1–13:4

Argument I, Division 1: 3:1-18

A Tale of Two Ministries

Two kinds of proofs or arguments were used in forensic rhetoric: inartificial and artificial. The former were the sort that forensic cases were most preoccupied with. They involved decisions of previous or higher courts, rumors, evidence extracted by torture, documents, oaths, and witnesses (Quintilian *Inst. Or.* 5.1.2). In his defense Paul will appeal primarily to two sorts of inartificial proofs: documents, in this case the OT, and the Corinthians themselves and their faith as witnesses to the authenticity of his ministry. They are his letters of recommendation (v. 2). Later in the tribulation catalog in 4:8ff. Paul will demonstrate his authenticity by showing that while persecuted and tortured he did not give up or alter his gospel preaching. He is well aware of what sort of arguments were considered more powerful in judicial settings and does not hesitate to use them.

He begins his defense with a comparison. It was not uncommon in forensic rhetoric for a comparison "to rise from the lesser to the greater, since by raising what is below it must necessarily exalt what is above" (*Inst. Or.* 8.4.9).[1] If one was going to do a *synkrisis* one could either compare in a general

---

1. Though here Quintilian is referring to the art of amplification rather than that of giving proofs, the technique was used in both contexts. C. Forbes, "Comparison, Self-Praise

way one example with another, or one could compare two cases argument by argument (*Inst. Or.* 7.2.22). Paul seems in the main to follow the former procedure, at least until we get to the Fool's Discourse in chs. 11–12.

Self-praise by means of comparison was a delicate matter, and normally only those who took a Sophistic approach to things were shameless about it. But Plutarch says that it is warranted when "mistaken praise injures and corrupts by arousing emulation of evil" ("On Inoffensive Self-Praise," *Mor.* 545D), when one is attacked, or "when a man intermingles praise of himself with censure of another, and causes another's disgrace to secure glory for himself," which is "odious and vulgar, as one who would win applause from the humiliation of another" (547A). It appears from chs. 10–13 that Paul was in this last position when he wrote 2 Corinthians. The false ones had exalted themselves at Paul's expense, perhaps drawing on some of the enmity conventions.[2]

Paul's comparison of his ministry with that of Moses is mainly positive. His argument is in essence that one good thing is simply eclipsed by something better. But when he compares his ministry to that of the opponents and looks at the expectations of some of the Corinthians, then he resorts to parody, irony, and sarcasm, using an anti-Sophistic approach and boasting in weakness, suffering, humiliation, his inadequate rhetorical skills, and the like.

L. Belleville argues in her study of ch. 3 that this chapter, along with all of chs. 1–7, should be seen as a letter of apologetic (self)-commendation.[3] From the point of view of epistolary conventions, however, this could just as easily be said of all of 2 Corinthians. Belleville attempts to class apologetic self-commendation as a subcategory of letters of recommendation, but the latter is clearly what is written by one person on behalf of another. Therefore, while it is true that Paul is defending and commending himself in this letter and that this letter refers to letters of recommendation, it is not one itself. Rather we are dealing with an apologetic letter of the sort derived from forensic rhetoric.[4]

---

and Irony," *NTS* 32 (1986), pp. 1-30, focuses on the role of comparison in amplification vis-à-vis 2 Corinthians 10–13, and we will deal with his material in connection with that passage. Comparison was a rhetorical exercise used already in the progymnasta. One did not need to be a professional rhetor to know about it or use it. For a somewhat helpful rhetorical analysis of the material in chs. 3–5 that mistakes micro-rhetoric (evidence of all the arrangement from *exordium* to *peroratio* in this material) for signs of separate literary sources, cf. A. De Oliveira, *Die Diakonie der Gerechtigkeit und der Versöhnung in der Apologie des 2 Korintherbriefes* (Münster: Aschendorff, 1990), pp. 115ff.

2. See below, pp. 420-37.

3. L. Belleville, *Reflections of Glory* (Sheffield: JSOT, 1991), especially pp. 129ff.

4. S. K. Stowers, *Letter Writing in Greco-Roman Antiquity* (Philadelphia: Westminster, 1986), pp. 166f., especially p. 173. Stowers argues that apologetic letters are those that use the rhetorical patterns of defense or prosecution speeches and normally include a *narratio* of what actually happened.

Understanding chs. 3–4 requires a considerable amount of reading between the lines and a willingness to go with the flow of ever-developing and mixed metaphors. Paul begins by saying that while he was having to commend himself in order to defend himself, he did not need the sort of commendation that apparently his opponents had brought to town — namely letters of introduction (3:1-3).

A Closer Look: Letters of Introduction or Recommendation ————————

Letters of introduction or recommendation, for which *systatikē epistolē* was the technical term (cf. Acts 9:2; 18:27), were exceedingly common in antiquity.[5] Philemon and 3 John can be put in this category. It appears that Paul normally made it a practice of including his recommendations in letters with broader purposes, particularly at the end (1 Cor. 16:15-18; Rom. 16:1f.; 1 Thess. 5:12f.; but cf. Phil. 2:25-30; 4:2f.).

Letters of recommendation followed the same basic epistolary conventions in regard to opening, closing, and salutations as other types of ancient Greek letters. It was normal practice for the one recommended to deliver the letter, and normally the function of such a letter was of a general nature — requesting help, hospitality, employment, or instruction for the letter's bearer.[6] Sometimes, a letter of recommendation was written for someone that the recipient already knew, and thus there is not a complete overlap between the letter of recommendation and the letter of introduction. These sorts of letters reflect a social milieu in which credentialing was considered important and in which considerable weight was given to the opinion of close friends or recognized authorities.

That Paul's opponents needed such letters in order to be introduced to the Corinthian Christians surely indicates that they were not from Corinth or the region of Achaia, but rather from elsewhere in the Mediterranean crescent and elsewhere in the *ekklēsia*. It also suggests the derivative nature of their authority, charisma, or power and speaks against the idea that they had any recognized association with any of Paul's congregations. These letters must also count against the view that Paul is referring to Peter, James, or Apollos, all of whom were already known to the Corinthians, as 1 Corinthians shows, and would have needed no such letters of introduction.

Such letters were often written to obtain patronage. For instance: "Phrynichos of Larisa, a disciple of mine, wants to see horse-feeding Argos. As he is a philosopher, he will not ask much of you" (Diogenes 48).[7] I suspect it is with such letters requesting

---

5. For first-century examples see C.-H. Kim, *Form and Structure of the Familiar Greek Letter of Recomendation* (Missoula: Scholars, 1972), pp. 199-207. Cf. Stowers, *Letter Writing*, pp. 156ff.; C. W. Keyes, "The Greek Letter of Introduction," *American Journal of Philology* 56 (1935), pp. 28-44.

6. Cf. W. Baird, "Letters of Recommendation: A Study of 2 Cor. 3:1-3," *JBL* 80 (1961), pp. 166-72, here p. 168.

7. Cf. Keyes, "Greek Letter," p. 36.

support or hospitality that Paul's opponents came to Corinth. In other words, as soon as they arrived in the city they attempted to plug into the social reciprocity relationships that were common there.[8] Paul's rejection of patronage and his lack of letters of recommendation made him appear peculiar, because of the social conventions of the day.

Paul says pointedly that the Corinthians are his letter (v. 2). But on whose hearts does Paul say this letter was written? The external textual evidence strongly favors the reading "our," but many argue that the context favors "your."[9] Was there something written in Paul's heart[10] that the world saw in him, or is Paul talking about what was written on the Corinthians' hearts and could be seen in their witness to the world? Baird has shown how the reading "our" makes perfectly good sense, since it was customary for a letter of recommendation to be about the letter bearer.[11] The letter Paul refers to is about himself and the authenticity of his ministry, and he carries it in his heart. As he reiterates in 7:3, the Corinthians are in his heart, and since they are his letter of recommendation, it is not surprising that he would say that it was written in his heart. He can bring from his heart the example of the Corinthians as a basis for boasting and a testimony to his authenticity (see below on 8:24 and 9:2).

Verse 3 adds that they are shown to be a letter from Christ, though it was drawn up by Paul. The point is that Christ, through Paul, is the ultimate author of this letter. It was written not with ink but by the Spirit of the living God, not on tablets of stone but on tablets of fleshly (or perhaps "human") hearts. Perhaps the polemical background of the later comparison with the Mosaic dispensation is the basis of this last part of v. 3b.

Paul argues in vv. 4-6a that his "adequacy" comes not from himself but from God. He has confidence because the gospel and power he has come not from a human source but from Christ. Therefore, he does not seek any credit for himself (unlike others?). It is God who has made him equal to the task of being a minister of the new covenant (cf. 2:16b), a minister not of the letter but of the Spirit.

What follows in v. 6b has been subject to all sorts of hermeneutical

---

8. See pp. 414-19 below on patronage.

9. Cf. C. K. Barrett, *The Second Epistle to the Corinthians* (New York: Harper and Row, 1973), p. 96; J. Murphy-O'Connor, *The Theology of the Second Letter to the Corinthians* (Cambridge: Cambridge University, 1991), p. 32, n. 23.

10. By "we" Paul means sometimes just himself, sometimes himself with his co-workers, and sometimes all Christians. Here "we" seems to be just Paul, but cf. M. Carrez, "Le 'Nous' en 2 Corinthiens," *NTS* 26 (1980), pp. 474-86.

11. Baird, "Letters of Recommendation," pp. 169f.

gerrymandering, but Paul is certainly not talking about a spiritual reading of the OT as opposed to a literal or legalistic reading. The issue here is not the Old Testament but the Old *Covenant,* specifically the Mosaic covenant.[12] As vv. 7ff. will indicate, he is thinking especially of the Sinai revelation in stone, the Ten Commandments.

Paul is not one who administers and applies the Mosaic law, not even the Ten Commandments. He is rather a minister who both proclaims and dispenses the Holy Spirit. The ministry of the letter, that is, the Law, kills fallen people (cf. Romans 6–7), while the ministry of the Spirit gives them life. Paul's argument here concerns the effect of the two covenants on fallen humans, not on their purposes.[13] He is convinced that the OT Law was a true revelation of God and that it came attended with glory (cf. Rom. 9:4). His point is that its day has passed and its glory has been surpassed by the exceeding and super-seding glory of the New Covenant. The essential problem with the Law is that it cannot give life. Indeed, as Paul says in Romans, it has quite the opposite effect on fallen people.

In v. 7 Paul begins with a conditional statement that assumes that the administration in engraved stone was instituted in glory. Then he moves on to the effect of that administration on Moses, which was that his face shone so that the people of Israel were not able to look intently at him.[14] Paul develops the idea of the glorious face[15] by speaking of the greater glory of Jesus, which is the very mirror in which we see God and God's glory, since Jesus, unlike Moses, is the very image, the full human representation of God. Paul is surely drawing here on Wisdom traditions such as those found in Wis. Sol. 7:26, where Wisdom is said to be "a spotless mirror of the working of God."[16] For Paul, Jesus is the embodiment of all that earlier Jews had said when they extolled personified Wisdom.

As the Israelites gazed on Moses' face, so Christians look intently on Jesus' face with the effect that they, too, are transformed into the glorious likeness of Jesus (v. 18). They become what they admire. By contrast, the

---

12. Here *diathēkē* surely means "covenant," not "testament." Paul is not claiming to be a minister of the New *Testament,* which did not exist yet. For a contrary view see A. Carmignac, "2 Corinthiens 3:6, 14 et le Début de la Formation du Nouveau Testament," *NTS* 24 (1978), pp. 384-86.

13. See further B. Witherington, *Jesus, Paul, and the End of the World* (Downers Grove: InterVarsity, 1992), pp. 109-11.

14. *Atenisai* means more than just "look" or "gaze on," but rather "stare at" or "look intently at."

15. For the view that Paul thinks Moses saw the preexistent Christ, see A. T. Hanson, "The Midrash in 2 Corinthians 3: A Reconsideration," *JSNT* 9 (1980), pp. 2-28. But surely Paul is comparing two different glories, the first of which has been annulled.

16. B. Witherington, *Jesus the Sage: The Pilgrimage of Wisdom* (Minneapolis: Fortress, 1994), ch. 7.

Israelites, not having the Spirit or life, could not bear to gaze intently upon Moses. Paul says they could not bear to gaze on it because the glory on Moses' face was to be annulled (vv. 7, 13).[17] *Katargoumenos* is normally translated "transient," but in Paul's works it generally refers to that which has been invalidated or annulled or is being replaced (cf. 1 Cor. 1:28; 2:6; Rom. 3:31).[18] This also fits with the meaning of v. 11.

It is often suggested that Paul is using a traditional form of Jewish argument, the *qal wāyyomer,* that is, from the lesser to the greater. This form of argument is not from the bad to the good, but from the lesser good to the greater good. This Jewish background may be present, but as we have seen Quintilian also says that one should argue from the lesser to the greater when making a rhetorical comparison where one member of the two is to be preferred to the other.

In v. 9 Paul contrasts the administration of condemnation[19] with that of righteousness. Here again he is contrasting the effects of each covenant and its administration. The first one led to spiritual death and condemnation because fallen people could not fulfill it. The later covenant led to right standing *(dikaiosynē).* V. 11 contrasts the glory of the annulled, and so temporary, with that of the abiding *(menon).* The neuter participle *to katargoumenon,* "annulled," agrees with "that which was glorified" in v. 10 and so applies to the whole of the old covenant, symbolized by Moses. Therefore, what is spoken of as annulled through Christ in v. 14 is probably the Old Covenant rather than the veil.

It because of the character of the New Covenant that Paul is able to speak with much *parrhēsia* (v. 12), with such "free and open speech," in contrast with what is veiled or obscure (v. 13). It may be that he is contrasting his mode of speaking, which in its frankness is more like the *modus operandi* of a Cynic philosopher, with that of the Sophists, who flattered and said whatever was needed to win an audience, using elaborate and ornamental rhetoric. Paul is arguing that what one hears from him is the truth. He felt that the style of his ministry should agree with the character of the message — free and open, acting with boldness and honesty.

In v. 13 he states that Moses put a veil on his face so that the Israelites

---

17. E. Richard, "Polemics, Old Testament, and Theology," *RB* 88 (1981), pp. 340-67, here pp. 353ff., raises some convincing reasons to doubt that vv. 7-11 are a midrash on Exod. 24:28-35. He argues that vv. 7-11 and vv. 13-18 are used to further explain the Christian understanding of the new covenant. Paul's starting point is Christ, not the OT. The OT is brought in to further explicate his Christian views. This is not equivalent to a contemporizing of the OT text in Jewish fashion.

18. See the discussion in R. B. Hays, *Echoes of Scripture in the Letters of Paul* (New Haven: Yale University, 1989), pp. 133-35.

19. Which in v. 7 was called the "administration of death."

would not see the *telos* of what was being annulled. Here again "annulled" is neuter and so does not refer to the glory on Moses' face or to the Law but rather to the whole administration of the Old Covenant. It was being annulled and so replaced. *Telos* here surely means "end," as in Rom. 10:4, not "fulfillment" or "aim." The point is that the Israelites are blind to the fact that the Law has had its day, that it has been annulled. They are oblivious to the end of the annulled covenant.[20]

Then Paul adds a new thought: The Israelites were blind in this way because their minds were hardened (v. 14). This was part of the problem and part of the reason for Moses' veil. But in a clever turn of the metaphor Paul sees that the hardening amounts to a sort of veiling of the minds or hearts of the Israelites (v. 15). Paul implies that this hardening is still on them as he writes. In Romans 11 he adds that the hardening is *pro tempore*, and here he says that the veil is "even now" not lifted whenever the Old Covenant is read in the synagogue. This is the first reference to any portion of the Hebrew Scriptures as an "Old Covenant."[21] In Christ, Paul says, it is being annulled.

While some commentators think Paul is referring to a veil over the Torah in v. 14,[22] it is clear that in v. 15 he refers to a veil over the hearts of Jewish listeners, which has not been lifted.[23] Vv. 15 and 13 suggest a parallel between veiled Moses and the Israelites of Paul's day who are "veiled in heart." This agrees with what v. 14a says about their minds being hardened or made dull.[24] The metaphor does not change from v. 14 to v. 15. The veil over their hearts

20. Pace Hays, *Echoes of Scripture*, p. 137, who concludes that if one translates *katargoumenos* as "annulled" then *telos* must mean "aim." Cf. the correct assessment in V. P. Furnish, *II Corinthians* (Garden City: Doubleday, 1984), p. 207.

21. The next seems to be from Melito of Sardis late in the second century. While P. Grelot, "Note sur 2 Corinthiens 3:14," *NTS* 33 (1987), pp. 135-44, is right that we learn nothing about Paul's view of the extent of the Hebrew canon, it would be wrong to say he is simply talking about the institutions of the Old Covenant. He is referring to a written text of, at the very least, the Ten Commandments and probably the whole Mosaic covenant.

22. Hays, *Echoes of Scripture*, pp. 128-31, wants to argue that "incarnation eclipses inscription" because there is a sense in which the written code veils things. But this is to mistake where the veiling takes place. It is always on or in human beings. The reason for the contrast between letters on stone and the Spirit in the heart is not that the letter is somehow veiled but that the letter cannot in itself give life or lift the veil on the heart. In short, while the letter was clear, its recipients were not, without the Spirit.

23. The reference in v. 14 to "the same veil" has perhaps misled some. This surely cannot refer to the literal veil over Moses' face again, which is the only veil referred to in v. 13. Rather I take it that the argument is as follows: As it was with Moses, the prototypical Israelite who had a veil over his face, so also with Israelites now who have a veil over their hearts due to their hardened hearts. "The same veil" then means that the hardened Israelites of Paul's day share in a metaphorical sense the condition Moses experienced literally.

24. See further Witherington, *Jesus, Paul, and the End of the World*, p. 110.

is lifted only when they "turn to the Lord," just as Moses was unveiled when he turned to the Lord (v. **16**).[25]

Here *kyrios*, "Lord," could refer either to God, to Christ, or to the Spirit, but I suspect it is the Spirit. But Furnish thinks it refers to God and so takes *kyrios* in v. 17 as well as referring to God, not Christ. There are many ways to look at v. 17 but the simplest is to see *ho kyrios* as an epexegetical remark. Paul is saying "Now when I say 'Lord,'[26] I mean the Spirit."[27] That is, it is the Spirit of the Lord that unveils the human heart and lays it open to receive the truth and to gaze intently on the face of Christ. This is not evidence that Paul was a binitarian.[28] The Israelites must turn to the Spirit, the Spirit of the Lord, if they wish to change, for only the Spirit gives life and freedom.

It is precisely because the Spirit frees believers that Paul feels it important to speak freely. All who have that Spirit gaze with unveiled face on the face of Christ (v. 18). Here the verb *katoptrizomai* can mean either "gaze on" or "reflect in a mirror," but the point is that believers are transformed into Christ's likeness by gazing intently on him, so this is surely the meaning of the verb here. They are transformed into his image, from glory to glory, just as he bears the very image of God, being God's mirror, God's Wisdom. It may be implied then that believers are called to be the mirror of Christ to the world — an awesome task. In terms of the overall trajectory of the passage, Baird is right to urge that the

> central concern of 2 Corinthians . . . is the discussion of apostolic authority, and it is in this light that 2 Cor 3:1-3 must be viewed. When this is done, it will be evident that Paul's [main] concern in this context is not with a covenant written on the hearts of his parishioners, but with his own experience of commission in that covenant's ministry.[29]

25. G. Theissen's attempt in *Psychological Aspects of Pauline Theology* (Philadelphia: Fortress, 1987), p. 174, to parallel 1 Corinthians 11 and 2 Corinthians 3 is interesting but overdrawn. While the two passages do both mention the concepts of glory and image, the former is about headcoverings, the latter clearly about veils. There are no social conventions regarding headcoverings being abandoned in Christ in 2 Corinthians 3.

26. *Ho* being the equivalent of an English quotation mark, as may also be the case in 1 Cor. 4:6.

27. Another possibility would be that Paul means that the Spirit rules in the believer's life and thus is experientially the "lord" in the believer's life. For a discussion of all the options, see D. Greenwood, "The Lord is the Spirit: Some Considerations of 2 Cor. 3.17," *CBQ* 34 (1972), pp. 467-72. Greenwood's proposal is that Paul refers to Yahweh in Christ as "Lord" here. My view concurs with the conclusion of Richard, "Polemics," p. 357.

28. He is identifying the function of the Spirit with the function of "the Lord" in the passage cited. He is not talking about ontology, and the following phrase, "Spirit of the Lord," makes it clear that he is not simply identifying the two. Cf. J. D. G. Dunn, "2 Cor. 3.17 — The Lord is the Spirit," *JTS* 21 (1970), pp. 309-20. Cf. R. P. Martin, *2 Corinthians* (Waco: Word, 1986), pp. 70f.

29. Baird, "Letters of Recommendation," p. 172.

Since this is not a purely polemical text but in the main a positive comparison, we may expect some reliable pointers from it about Paul's adversaries. This is especially so since the crucial *propositio* in 2:17 invites us to look for clues in what follows about the "many" who are profiteers. At the least ch. 3 suggests that the opponents came to Corinth with letters of recommendation and, probably, that they had some interest in the Mosaic covenant. But it is saying too much to call them "Judaizers,"[30] or to equate them with the troublemakers in Galatia. There is no hint in the letter of any special interest in the sabbath, in circumcision, or in the food laws. The focus here, if it is on any aspect of the Mosaic covenant, is on the Ten Commandments, which were the laws written on stone.[31]

I am inclined to agree with D. Georgi, not that the opponents were portraying themselves as divine men, but that they were Jewish, perhaps Jewish Christian, itinerant preachers who arrived in Corinth after 1 Corinthians had been written and who drew on their Jewish heritage and on Hellenistic Jewish apologetics to win over the Corinthians.[32] A significant component of what they used may have been Jewish sapiential material, along with the Mosaic moral teachings.[33] This would explain why Paul goes out of his way, especially in the peristasis catalogs in ch. 4, to portray himself as a particular kind of suffering Jewish sage, unlike his opponents. We know from 1 Corinthians that there was a significant interest in *sophia* in Corinth, both in rhetoric and in other forms.

In view of the history of exegesis of ch. 3, particularly interpretations that contrast letter and spirit, it is natural enough to speak of hermeneutics on the basis of this text. But it has nothing to do with such considerations. *Gramma* ("letter") and *pneuma* ("spirit")

> are not the names of hermeneutical principles. . . . The difference between them is not a distinction between two ways of reading texts. . . . When Paul contrasts spirit to *gramma*, he is not opposing the basic intent of Scripture to its specific wording, as in our familiar distinction between "the spirit and the letter of the law." Nor is he thinking, like Philo or Origen, about a

30. Pace Murphy-O'Connor, *Theology*, pp. 32ff., and others.

31. This may be of some significance in light of the polemic against idolatry (and implicitly against immorality) in the form of dining in idol temples in 6:14–7:1.

32. P. Bowers, "Paul and Religious Propaganda in the First Century," *NovT* 4 (1980), pp. 316-23, is right to point out that there is a difference between Paul and other missionaries. Paul's plan involves a certain geographical orientation and direction — he generally attempts to go to unevangelized areas and seems to have a general east-to-west trajectory. Various Cynic preachers simply wandered around the empire, and Jewish missionaries apparently went where their business took them (cf. Josephus *Ant.* 20.34-38).

33. D. Georgi, *The Opponents of Paul in Second Corinthians* (Philadelphia: Fortress, 1986), pp. 315ff.

mystical latent sense concealed beneath the text's external form. The Spirit
that Paul is talking about is the Holy Spirit, who is palpably present in the
community as an experienced reality, manifest in spiritual gifts such as
tongues and prophecy . . . transforming lives and empowering the work of
ministry. *Spirit* is not an essence or an abstract theological concept. It is the
daily experienced mode of God's powerful presence in the community of
faith.[34]

34. Hays, *Echoes of Scripture*, p. 150. Nor, I would add, and here I part company with
Hays, is this chapter about the veiling of God's intent in mere words or written texts or
codes, the *graphē* as opposed to its revelation in the Spirit. There was nothing unclear or
veiled about the text of the Ten Commandments itself: The problem was that the text by
itself did not enable one to keep the commandments. For Paul the written Word and the
Spirit are not antagonists, but the effect of the former on fallen human beings without the
latter is death-dealing rather than life-giving.

Therefore, the believer then cannot do without either. Word without Spirit leads not
merely to legalism but to a deadening effect on hearer and reader. Spirit without Word
brings life, but no concrete criteria as to how life ought to be lived. Both are needed in the
Christian's life. In Paul's view the OT is to be interpreted not merely in the light of Christ,
but by means of the guidance of the Holy Spirit. This Spirit does indeed liberate and gives
great freedom to see all kinds of new significance in texts that goes well beyond their
historically specific and intended meanings. We must distinguish the meaning of the text
from a fruitful later significance or application it may have under the guidance of the Spirit.
We are not free to read into the text new meanings at odds with its original intent, but we
are free to read out of the text new significances in light of later developments in God's
dealing with the people of God.

Argument I, Division 2: 4:1–5:10

TREASURE IN EARTHEN VESSELS

Paul is confronted with a serious dilemma. Apparently he is opposed by a group of itinerant self-styled "apostles" engaged in Sophistic boasting. He does not approve of this self-promoting exercise, but he has been forced to commend himself, not only because he has competition but also because his integrity and ministry have been questioned and jeopardized. In short, he must engage in what Plutarch calls "inoffensive self-praise" (*Mor.* 539E-545B). According to Plutarch, self-praise was acceptable when telling the truth about oneself would serve a good end, when it was necessary to reply to those who envied one's position, when one had been reproached for one's triumphs, when self-praise could be coupled with an attribution of some of the glory to a god or with a list of one's own minor flaws or faults, in disagreement with some praise offered in favor of alternatives to one's own deeds, ideas, or methods, and when it was necessary to counter the praise and emulation of evil.

During the course of the argument section Paul will offer self-praise for one or another of these reasons, showing that he is familiar with the conventions about inoffensive self-praise. This also explains his oscillation between admitting that he is commending himself (4:2; 6:4) and saying that he is not (3:1; 5:12). This is precisely what we would expect if he is engaging in inoffensive self-praise rather than Sophistic self-promotion. Paul makes it clear that the Corinthians should have undertaken this exercise for him, and then he would not have been forced to do so (cf. 1:12-14; 2:3; 12:11).

This all comes as a reaction not only to criticism of Paul but also to the self-promotion of the false *apostoloi* (10:12-18). Paul wants his converts neither to adore nor to ignore him, so he will praise himself in a way that is consistent with his own principle that the Christian boaster should boast in the Lord (1 Cor. 1:30f.). This means that he will boast of his own weakness and sufferings in order to show that his triumphs must result from God's work through him.

Because of the mercy shown to him in all that he has spoken of in ch. 3, Paul does not lose heart about the Corinthians (**4:1**). If he can be transformed, so also can they. He has renounced hidden and shameful things and is not living in a cunning or deceptive manner since he does not want to say or do anything

385

that will falsify the word of God (v. 2). This would seem to be a counterblast against his opponents, whom Paul apparently believes were stooping to such underhanded means or methods.

Instead of some veiled or mysterious utterance, Paul speaks with an open declaration of the truth, and since he feels he has nothing to hide he commends himself to be examined by any and every human conscience, bearing in mind that those consciences are answerable to and before God. Apparently by way of concession, in v. 3 he says that even if his gospel is a bit veiled or obscure to some, it is so only to those who are perishing. Young and Ford have insisted that Paul is talking about *God* blinding the minds of the unbelievers in v. 4.[1] This is not impossible and has biblical precedent, but it seems more likely that Paul is referring to Satan, the so-called "god of this age." He had blinded unbelievers to the light of the gospel.

This gospel is about the glory of Christ. Here and elsewhere it is helpful to think of *doxa* ("glory") as referring not just to a radiance or a shining appearance but to the very manifestation on earth of the presence of God. Thus when Paul speaks of Christ's glory, he is referring to the manifestation of God's presence in Christ, just as the glory on Moses' face was the evidence of an encounter with God's presence. Christ is the very *eikōn*, the image or full and true representation of God.[2]

Paul does not preach himself but Jesus Christ as Lord, the basic early Christian confession (cf. Rom. 10:9; 1 Cor. 12:3; Phil. 2:11), and himself as the servant of Christ (v. 5). Does Paul here have in mind the image of a slave of his own time or of the Isaianic Servant, who was given a ministry, albeit one of suffering, by God? Martin has made a good case for the latter. The role of the Suffering Servant was to preach the Good News to the poor (Isa. 61:1). So Paul would in essence see himself as the suffering servant of one who himself was the Suffering Servant (cf. Philippians 2).[3] But in view of 1 Corinthians 9 an equally good case can be made that Paul portrays himself as an enslaved leader or sage, especially in view of the tribulation catalog that follows here in vv. 8ff.[4]

The contrast between darkness and light (v. 6) is appropriate in view of the preceding discussion about glory. Here light stands for knowledge of God, which in this case is gained from gazing on the glorious face of Christ. To look at him is to know what God is like. Having such knowledge is a great treasure, even though it is kept in earthenware vessels (v. 7). This may be a reference

1. F. Young and D. F. Ford, *Meaning and Truth in 2 Corinthians* (Grand Rapids: Eerdmans, 1987), pp. 115-17.

2. The word does not refer to a mere copy.

3. Cf. R. P. Martin, *2 Corinthians* (Waco: Word, 1986), p. 80.

4. On the possibility that Paul has Moses in mind, see pp. 375-80 above.

to the cheap pottery lamps made in Corinth and used for walking about at night. Precisely because of their thinness, these vessels let out more light. This frail form also makes it clear that the light comes from another source, so Paul adds that in his case his frailty ought to make obvious that the power is coming from God and not from himself.[5]

Paul then gives a catalog of trials that he has gone through that demonstrate both his frailty and his resilience and composure (vv. **8f.**). This catalog consists of eight present tense middle or passive participles in four contrasting pairs linked by *all' ouk* ("but not"). It is in set pieces like this that we see Paul's rhetorical skills most clearly. For example, the second pair, "perplexed but not totally perplexed" contains a pun of both sound and content.[6] One could be distressed without being totally desperate.[7] He has been hard pressed but not at his wits' end; at a loss but not completely lost, persecuted, abandoned, and knocked down, but not knocked out.[8] Taken as a whole this catalog suggests that Paul's vessel has plenty of cracks but is still intact, which suggests miraculous preservation.[9]

There is some question how we should translate *nekrōsis* in v. **10**. It is not the word that Paul normally uses for "death." Barrett suggests that it means "killing" or "dying," and I think this is right.[10] Paul is manifesting the spectacle of the dying or killing of Jesus in his own life and is thus being conformed to Christ's image even in this horrible way. Living believers are always being delivered over to death because of Jesus. Christianity was not a legal religion, and therefore it was subject to all sorts of abuse by all sorts of people, even governing officials. But the effect of all this is that, in spite of such sufferings, indeed through such sufferings, the life of God shines. The true sage, unlike the Sophist, was willing to take his lumps for his bold and free speech, and this took considerable courage.[11] Paul seeks to instill admiration in his audience in this catalog using conventions with which they were familiar.

---

5. Earthenware vessels were the disposable bottles of that day, being both fragile and inexpensive. There is then a great paradox in putting something so precious in something so fragile and cheap, but such things were not unknown (cf. Herodotus 3.96 and especially Babylonian Talmud *Nedarim* 50b, which refers to wisdom in an ugly vessel).

6. Cf. J. T. Fitzgerald, *Cracks in an Earthen Vessel: An Examination of the Catalogue of Hardships in the Corinthian Correspondence* (Atlanta: Scholars, 1988), pp. 173f. There is a good deal of wordplay in 2 Corinthians; cf. 1:13; 3:2; 6:10; 7:10; 10:5-12; 12:5.

7. Here again we have clear evidence that Paul was counting on the oral rhetorical performance of this document (by Titus) to produce a certain effect.

8. The paronomasia is in the Greek as well as my English paraphrase.

9. Cf. Fitzgerald, *Cracks*, pp. 176-78.

10. C. K. Barrett, *The Second Epistle to the Corinthians* (New York: Harper and Row, 1973), pp. 136ff.

11. Cf. Dio Chrysostom 32.19.

A Closer Look — The Hardship Catalogs

It is quite clear, if one looks at all of Paul's hardship catalogs in 1 and 2 Corinthians (1 Cor. 4:9-13; 2 Cor. 4:8f.; 6:4-10; 11:23-28; 12:10), that he did not compose them simply in imitation of his opponents' boasting. As J. T. Fitzgerald has shown, only ch. 11 may reflect opponents' claims, but 1 Cor 4:9-13 surely does not, as it was written before there were opponents in Corinth, and the other such lists reflect stylistic diversity and share a nonpolemical character.[12] They are used as a means of positive self-praise, and it is notable that some of what Paul says about himself in these catalogs is also seen where he praises his coworkers or congregations. Hardship catalogs are not to be confused with vice or virtue catalogs, though there is some degree of kinship with the latter.

Such catalogs were not uncommon in antiquity, and they were used most notably by Stoic and Cynic sages to demonstrate their superiority over circumstances (Epictetus *Diss.* 1.1.22, 4.24, 11.33, 18.22; Horace *Sat.* 2.7.84ff.; Seneca *Prov.* 6.1ff.; *Ep.* 82.14; outside Stoic and Cynic contexts in Plato *Rep.* 2.361E-362A). The catalogs most similar to those in the NT are found in the writings of Epictetus and Seneca. Epictetus and the NT share the conviction that *peristasis* or "tribulation" is sent by God and is an opportunity to demonstrate moral character. As Quintilian *Inst. Or.* 3.5.18 points out, a *peristasis* in a rhetorical argument is a "collection of circumstances," and this is in the main how Paul casts his hardship catalogs: They reflect what has *happened* to him. Usually he dwells on adverse circumstances in order to create empathy for his case.

It is no accident that Paul uses such catalogs so frequently in 2 Corinthians, as his character or *ēthos* was very much in doubt in Corinth. The lists are meant to show that Paul is an *apostolos*, and a heroic one at that, risking all for the gospel and for his congregations. They are also meant to show that God must be working in his life. Otherwise his survival and perseverance over so many diverse circumstances would have been impossible.

Some have argued that we have in 4:8-10 Paul's *res gestae*,[13] but only the catalog in ch. 11 really deserves this title since only there do we have the features normally found in a *res gestae:* a list of honors or offices or deeds *(leitourgiai)* undertaken in public service, the use of *pollakis,* the first person singular aorist verb, numerical data, and a short narrative at the end.[14]

These catalogs also make abundantly clear that while Paul is attempting to portray himself as a sage, he is a sage unlike the Stoic or Cynic sages, for he does not show the indifference or *ataraxia* (inner tranquility) in the face of whatever came that they did. While Seneca defined a sage as one who was fortified against all the slings and arrows of outrageous fortune (cf. *Ep.* 59.80), Paul makes no such claim. Rather he admits his weaknesses. Nor does he claim to be self-reliant or self-confident, as the Stoic or Cynic might, but rather he argues that he is God-reliant and God-confident.

12. Fitzgerald, *Cracks,* p. 26, n. 97.
13. L. Belleville, *Reflections of Glory* (Sheffield: JSOT, 1991), pp. 130ff.
14. So rightly Fitzgerald, *Cracks,* pp. 18f.; cf. A. Fridrichsen, "Peristasen Katalog und *Res Gestae,*" *Symbolae Osloenses* 8 (1929), pp. 78-82.

Paul does not pretend to be master of his universe or of all circumstances (contrast Epictetus *Diss.* 3.24.30). Furthermore, the Stoic sage was to be free of passion, indeed insensible to it (cf. Seneca *Ep.* 9.3), and this hardly describes Paul, especially as he portrays himself in 2 Corinthians 10–13. This is not to deny that he occasionally sounds like a Stoic sage, for instance when he claims to be God's friend, coworker, or imitator (cf. Seneca *Prov.* 1.5), or when he portrays himself as a great athlete in rigorous training (cf. Epictetus *Diss.* 1.18.21-23).

When one puts together the implications of Paul's use of these catalogs in regard to *sophia*, they tell us that while he is trying to portray himself as a sage, he has his own definition of what that entails. They also tell us that the rhetorical function of this material is that they are part of the attempt to establish Paul's *ēthos* or character and the credibility of his ministry in the eyes of his converts.

In v. 11 Paul uses *sōma* (body) and *sarx* (flesh) as synonyms, meaning mortal flesh. All of his suffering has the effect of revealing Jesus. In some strange way, while death is at work in Paul, life is at work in the Corinthians (v. 12). Paul probably means by this that he is absorbing some of the messianic sufferings with the result that the Corinthians do not have to endure them. He is deflecting the harm onto himself. Like the OT speaker of Ps. 116:10, Paul says exactly what he believes (v. 13). He is a free-speaking sage, not a mere Sophist or flattering philosopher. V. 14 envisions the final state of affairs, in which Paul, like Jesus, will be raised and, with his converts the Corinthians, will be presented to and before Christ. God will bring them all back together then and there, once and for all.

In v. 15 Paul again, as in 2:6, refers to "the majority." He says that he has done everything for them so that grace might increase, at least in most of them. This once again suggests a divided audience in Corinth. In v. 16 Paul reiterates the theme of v. 1: He does not lose heart even though the outer part of him is wasting away. He knows that there is a resurrection yet to come, so he has reason for hope, even in regard to his outer frame.

In 4:16–5:10 we see the sort of limited anthropological dualism Paul affirms. This entire section must be read together, as the fivefold *gar* ("for") clauses in 4:17, 18; 5:1, 2, 4 show. Paul's dualism may reflect Hellenistic influence.[15] While the outer part is being destroyed, the inner person is being renewed day by day (cf. Rom. 7:14-25). Paradoxically, it is the new person or the new creation, the spiritual part, which is constantly being renewed in the life of the Christian. Paul clearly believed in a nonmaterial part of the human personality. This does not mean that he endorsed the Greek idea of the immortal soul or of the body as the prison of the soul.

Paul calls his present suffering, which was severe, light by comparison

15. Cf. V. P. Furnish, *II Corinthians* (Garden City: Doubleday, 1984), p. 261.

to the glory[16] being worked out in him (v. 17). Therefore, unlike the Israelites, he will be keeping watch not on visible and transient things but on things that are unseen and permanent (v. 18). Like the saints in Hebrews 11, he is looking for a city whose foundations are not material or visible.

This section of Paul's argument already foreshadows what he will say in 12:10 and 13:4. He believes that resurrection life or God's power is already manifested in this life, and this is especially evident when one is afflicted, suffering, or weak. Furthermore, his labors and sufferings are not just the unfortunate cost of apostleship or occasions to demonstrate his faith, but they are at the heart of his witness. He portrays the dying of Jesus in this manner, so that his life is part of the preaching.[17]

Over and over again, Paul describes his ministry in apparent paradoxes — strength in weakness, glory through shame, life through death, riches through poverty. He creates these paradoxes partly to show that there are two opposing powers struggling in this world for control of humankind — God in Christ, and the god of this world, Satan, who has blinded unbelievers and can afflict even *apostoloi* like Paul. Yet strangely, this pattern of apostolic suffering can also be seen as a matter of being conformed to the image of Christ.

Perhaps most striking of all, Paul seems to believe that "the very existence of Christ's power in Paul depends on his humility and weakness."[18] Where there is arrogance and boasting of the wrong sort, by definition there can be no divine power. Paul believes this because he believes that the power to change the world has come through the cross and through preaching of it in the preacher's life and words. 12:10 must be taken as Paul's basic conviction: When he is weak, then he is strong. When he empties himself or is emptied of all but Christ, then indeed he becomes a true and open vessel, a true conduit of power, light, and life in Christ. The Corinthians needed a whole new conceptual framework to evaluate what did and did not amount to being a true agent of Christ.[19]

---

16. The Hebrew term *kabôd*, which in Greek is translated *doxa*, has a root meaning "weighty," "heavy," or "significant" in an extended sense.

17. Cf. S. Kraftchick, "Death in Us, Life in You: The Apostolic Medium," *Society of Biblical Literature 1991 Seminar Papers*, ed. E. H. Lovering (Atlanta: Scholars, 1991), pp. 618-37, here p. 633.

18. T. B. Savage, *Power Through Weakness* (Ph.D. thesis, Cambridge, 1986), p. 204.

19. Cf. D. Hay, "The Shaping of Theology in 2 Corinthians: Convictions, Doubts, Warrants," *Society of Biblical Literature 1990 Seminar Papers*, ed. D. J. Lull (Atlanta: Scholars, 1990), pp. 257-72. It is not just that the Corinthians are still dominated by the criteria of power and status that existed in their society in general, nor that they have relationships with nonbelievers and false apostles that mislead them about how Paul should be evaluated. Paul also believes that they are insufficiently reconciled to God, and so to him, and this too leads to their misunderstanding of the apostle.

5:1-10 shows us Paul's overall orientation. For him, home is being with the Lord, who at this point is in heaven. Earthly existence is temporal and temporary. The earthly body is a tent-like existence, a temporary shelter. Paul seems to believe that believers' resurrection bodies are already prepared in heaven, in heavenly cold storage so to speak. This is part of his overall view that what will yet be on earth is even now stored up in heaven, including the New Jerusalem.

Paul speaks of three states: the present condition in the tent-like frame, the intermediate state of nakedness, which he does not find desirable, and the future condition in which a further frame will have been put on, hopefully over the present one. For Paul fullness of life was unthinkable without a body, and thus life in heaven was for Paul not the ultimate desideratum by any means.[20] Danker thinks that Paul views the present state in the tent-like body as a state of nakedness.[21] This is surely incorrect, especially in view of Hellenistic parallels that speak of the "naked soul." Nor is Paul envisioning here the further putting on of the resurrection body at the point of death (pace Danker). His point is that he longs to bypass the intermediate condition altogether and allow this mortality to be swallowed up by real life — life in the resurrection body. In short, he would rather live on earth till the resurrection.[22]

In the meantime, Paul groans under the abuse that his body has taken for Christ. To be with the Lord, wherever the Lord is, is to be at home. Since believers do not *see* these things being realized,[23] they live by faith and courage, aiming to please God. Danker is likely right that Paul is conjuring up the image of a public assembly, where typically a person of exceptional merit *(aretē)* would be rewarded in public in the forum. Here the one seated on the *bēma* or judgment seat is Christ. He will requite believers according to their deeds — either good or worthless. At that final public hearing, Paul's ministry will be vindicated and shown to be authentic, as will the faith of the true believers in Corinth. Taken as a whole, 4:16–5:10 makes abundantly clear that Paul's eschatology has not changed after the writing of 1 Corinthians. Paul still strongly affirms and indeed longs for resurrection, not merely life in heaven.[24]

20. W. L. Craig, "Paul's Dilemma in 2 Corinthians 5:1-10: A Catch-22?" *NTS* 34 (1988), pp. 145-47, plausibly suggests that Paul found himself in a paradoxical situation. Both staying in the present body and being without a body had their liabilities and advantages. Craig concludes that the appearance of inconsistency arises out of the paradoxical situation.

21. F. W. Danker, *II Corinthians* (Minneapolis: Augsburg, 1989), pp. 70ff.

22. For a much more detailed form of this argument with discussion of the relevant literature, see B. Witherington, *Jesus, Paul, and the End of the World* (Downers Grove: InterVarsity, 1992), pp. 202-8.

23. The down payment of the Spirit does not come with physical transformation.

24. For a refutation of the idea that Paul's eschatology changed radically during the course of the writing of the main Pauline letters, see Witherington, *Jesus, Paul, and the End,* pp. 152-231.

Argument I, Division 3: 5:11–6:2

New Creatures

In this section Paul makes clear that he is relating to his audience as a particular kind of rhetor. This is evident in part because he calls himself an ambassador, one who must know all three sorts of rhetoric. An ambassador would use epideictic rhetoric to praise a ruler he was sent by or to, deliberative rhetoric to argue for a particular future course of action, perhaps of a client king, and forensic rhetoric to defend a policy of his overlord or to accuse a client king of misconduct. Like his near contemporary Plutarch, who had come as a young man with a mission to the proconsul in Corinth, Paul had come to Corinth as an ambassador prepared to persuade his audience.

Paul freely admits at the outset that his *modus operandi* is to persuade, not simply to command, and this would normally be understood to mean the use of the art of persuasion, that is, rhetoric. It is intriguing that in 5:11 Paul uses rhetoric, bearing in mind that God, not the Corinthians, is the one who is watching and will be the ultimate judge of his performance. Nevertheless, he admits that he is appealing to the Corinthians' consciences as he presents his case (5:11), for it is them, not God, that he must persuade. They are the jury even though God is the ultimate judge.

I take the references to fearing God and to God as judge to mean that there are certain sorts of rhetorical tactics and styles that Paul must avoid. For one thing he must avoid using rhetoric to deceive. It was critical to his ministry that his life and his lips both speak the same language. Second, he must avoid using pure declamation or overly ornamental rhetoric, which caused the listener to focus on the form or on mere eloquence to the neglect of content. In short, he believes that a Christian preacher or teacher might use rhetoric but not take a Sophistic approach to rhetoric. The love of Christ constrained both the content and form of his persuasion, and the sort of rhetorical moves he would make.[1] He would not be like those Sophists who boasted in appearance "and not in heart."[2]

---

1. A. D. Litfin, *St. Paul's Theology of Proclamation: An Investigation of 1 Cor. 1–4 in Light of Greco-Roman Rhetoric* (dissertation, Oxford, 1983), pp. 350ff., rightly makes this point.

2. On the Sophists' concern for appearance, dress, and form of speech, see Epictetus *Diss.* 3.1.1. Epictetus saw declamation as a fourth style, not to be classed with exhortation, refutation, or instruction. See the discussion in B. W. Winter, *Are Philo and Paul among the Sophists? A Hellenistic Jewish and a Christian Response to a First Century Movement* (dissertation, MacQuarrie University, 1988), p. 122.

While Paul will not fully undertake the task of parodying Sophistic methods until chs. 10–13, passages like this already make clear his views on such things and prepare us for when he "attacks the whole convention of self-advertisement by means of a remarkably subtle and forceful" argument.[3] They also intimate Paul's rejection of the Sophistic criteria by which he was being evaluated.[4] I would also argue that without these foreshadowings the argument in chs. 10–13 is not fully comprehensible, which is another good reason for seeing chs. 1–9 and 10–13 as parts of one document.

At the very beginning of this section Paul reemphasizes his transparency to God, and later he stresses the same in relation to his converts. His is the task of persuasion, and in this letter he uses various arts of persuasion. The most obvious rhetorical devices in chs. 5–6 are a series of rhetorical questions and an *ēthos*-affirming *peristasis*, a list of trials. Paul believes that he can stand up to scrutiny and that he should be examined closely by the consciences of his audience. A rhetor expected the audience to judge him and his art, and thus this statement would come as no surprise to the Corinthians.

While he *is* in fact commending himself, Paul says he is not (v. **12a**), by which he means that he is doing so in an inoffensive and rhetorically non-Sophistic way. The goal of this self-commendation is that the converts have a reason to be proud and to boast about his ministry and not be ashamed of it. Paul does not think this amounts to self-commendation in the crass sense of the term, but it is ultimately a boasting in God's work through him.[5]

Verse **12b** seems to provide us with a reliable aside about Paul's opponents in Corinth, especially since this is not in a particularly polemical context but rather an apologetic one. The false ones, Paul suggests, boast in matters of form or outward appearance and not matters of substance or matters of the heart that really count. This was in fact a typical complaint against the Sophists — they were all show and no substance. They paid

---

3. C. Forbes, "Comparison, Self-Praise and Irony: Paul's Boasting and the Conventions of Hellenistic Rhetoric," *NTS* 32 (1986), pp. 1-30, here p. 2.

4. On the Sophistic concern for *hypocrisis* or "presence," see Philostratus *Lives* 579f.

5. It may be important, as J. T. Fitzgerald, *Cracks in an Earthen Vessel: An Examination of the Catalogue of Hardships in the Corinthian Correspondence* (Atlanta: Scholars, 1988), p. 187, points out, that when Paul wants to say something negative about self-commendation, he puts the pronoun before the verb, i.e., *self*-commendation (cf. 3:1; 5:12; 10:12, 18; cf. 4:5), while when he wants to say something positive about his or the Corinthians' commendation the pronoun comes after the noun (4:2; 6:4; 7:1). This suggests a distinction between self-commendation and commendation of self by others or by the speaker in a nonegocentric fashion.

special attention to their clothing, appearance, and delivery and to the sound of their voices.[6]

Verse **13** seems to be a further comment in this direction. Probably the opponents were complaining either that Paul was insane or more likely that he, unlike they, did not have ecstatic visions to boast about (cf. ch. 12 and 1 Corinthians 14). He affirms that his ecstatic experiences, which would appear to an outsider as some sort of *mania*,[7] were between himself and God. To the Corinthians he had always engaged in reasonable discourse. This explains why in 1 Corinthians 14 he has to inform the Corinthians about his tongues speaking. While this verse says something about Paul's private devotional life versus his public face, it should also be read in light of that chapter in the earlier letter, where he makes it clear that in public contexts, but especially in worship, he would rather offer one word in understandable speech than engage in ecstatic speech. It is Christ's love for Paul that constrains[8] him to act in this fashion (v. **14a**), for he wants the converts to *know* Christ as well as *experience* him.

There is an irreducible cognitive content to the Christian faith, and Paul goes on to spell it out (vv. **14b-15**). It entails a christological soteriology — that the one man Jesus died for all. The word *hyper* literally means "for" or "on behalf of," and so it certainly has a representative force, but it may also have a substitutionary force meaning "in the place of." Paul goes on to add "for all died." Paul probably has in mind the idea that when Christ died, he died for, but also in place of, all. There is thus a sense in which his death was the death of all, since he was humankind's representative.

The word "all" should be taken quite seriously here. Christ died for the sins of the world, not merely the elect. Nor does Paul say "for all believers" but simply says "all." Christ died so that all those who believe in him might live for him, patterning their lives on his. Self-directed life is not legitimate in Paul's eyes. The man for others died for us so that believers might live for others, and in particular for him who died and rose.

Hōste in v. 16 shows that what follows is taken as the result of the content of the credal remarks he has just made. The result of knowing that one died for all is not only that believers must live for him, but also that believers must not regard anyone in the same way as they did when they were not in Christ. Not even Christ is to be regarded *kata sarka*. The phrase *kata sarka* ("according to the flesh") modifies "knows," not "Christ," since it is adverbial: "Knowing according to the flesh," *not* "Christ according to the flesh," is the issue. "Knowing Christ according to the flesh" might mean (1) evaluating him from a purely

---

6. Cf. pp. 348-50 above. Cynic preachers were not expected to be concerned about such things, and Stoics showed no special interest in such matters either.

7. See pp. 276-80 above on prophecy and *mania*.

8. The verb could mean "impel," but that seems less apt here.

human point of view and therefore seeing him as a failure in regard to the expectation that the messiah would be a warrior king come to throw off Roman rule, (2) knowing him according to worldly standards (this may well be nearer the mark), or (3) knowing him from an outward point of view. This would fit with the inward-outward contrast between the way Paul evaluates his apostleship and the approach of his opponents. All of these are possible renderings, but the context favors "knowing Christ according to outward appearances." Paul knows Christ better and wants to be evaluated better by his converts. The implication is that when one is converted, one ought to give up such superficial criteria for judging people. Here again is evidence that the Corinthians were inadequately socialized converts. They still evaluated things by the criteria they had imbibed from the rhetoric-infatuated culture in Roman Corinth.[9]

Verse 17 says that if a person is in Christ, not only does that person's worldview change, but he or she also realizes that the world itself has changed as a result of Christ's objective death and resurrection. There is no business as usual any longer. But what subject should we add to the sentence: "There is a new creation" or "He/she is a new creation or creature"? There are pros and cons to either view. More and more commentators are following the former and take the sentence to be referring to the whole new world that Christ's death created. On the other hand, several factors favor the latter reading:

> *Tis* in the first half of the sentence surely means "anyone," which may point to a personal referent in the second half of the sentence.
> Paul has been talking about how one's worldview changes as a result of the *subjective* change that happens in the believer at conversion.
> There is considerable precedent in early Judaism for talking about converts or proselytes as new creatures.[10]
> The reference to believers' consciences and judgment throughout this section points in this direction.
> Eph. 4:24, whether by Paul or by a Paulinist, also favors this interpretation.[11]

Thus I would give a slight edge to the latter translation. The point is that the Corinthians as Christians should no longer be evaulating Christ by worldly or external standards.[12]

9. See above, pp. 348-50.

10. See G. F. Moore, *Judaism in the First Centuries of the Christian Era* I (Cambridge: Harvard University, 1927), p. 533, on $b^e r\hat{\imath}\hat{a}$ $\d{h}\bar{a}d\bar{a}s\hat{a}$ with the meaning "new creature."

11. Cf. R. Berry, "Death and Life in Christ," *Scottish Journal of Theology* 14 (1961), pp. 60-76, here p. 69.

12. While it is true that Paul believes that Christ's death has objectively changed the state of affairs in the spiritual world, i.e., that the Spirit has come and that Christ's death has broken Satan's stranglehold on the world, the question remains whether the objective side of this question is the *primary* subject here. I think not.

All these things have happened because God has taken up the work of reconciliation (v. **18**).[13] God is the initiator of this process.[14] Had God not sent the Son to die, humans could not have been reconciled to God, regardless of human desire or goodwill. Reconcilation then is chiefly something God must accomplish, before humankind can respond to the work of Christ. This may in part explain why it is that Paul thinks the onus is on him to bring about reconciliation with his converts. He represents God in Christ in this situation. In v. 18 Christ is the agent or means of reconcilation, but God the Father initiates it.

As Danker stresses, here we find the ultimate expression of God as the great benefactor, Christ as the means of benefaction, and Paul as the human agent and ambassador of the largess of salvation.[15] This in turn makes Paul's work the "ministry (*diakonia,* service) of reconciliation." This phrase is as good a summary as any of how Paul views his task: reconciling Jew and Gentile in Christ (cf. Gal. 3:28). Therefore, one can see in both 1 and 2 Corinthians how Paul sets about his primary task, as both are letters about reconciliation. The first focuses on reconciliation among the converts, the second on reconciliation between Paul and these converts.

Verse **19** says that God was "in Christ," accomplishing all this. This has implications for christology, but the main focus is that the work of and through Christ was at the initiative of God and no one else. Christ is the divine agent. The effect of reconciliation is said to amount to what Paul elsewhere says justification accomplishes, namely a non-reckoning of sins against believers. Paul was appointed to make known all of this, not because it was his design but because it was God's purpose.

Paul then uses the formal language of envoy or ambassador (v. **20**), implicitly making clear his authority. He is not the envoy of a king, but of God, and at least in respect to "the word" and his ministry he has the endorsement and authority of God. So much is this so that Paul says it is as if God were making his appeal, exhorting (*parakaleō*) right through Paul's lips. Paul then begs the Corinthian Christians to be reconciled to God.

This exhortation is needed in Paul's view because to the degree that they

---

13. There is a fine discussion on why God must initiate the process and be reconciled to us before humankind can be reconciled to him in R. P. Martin, *2 Corinthians* (Waco: Word, 1986), pp. 154f.

14. As M. E. Thrall, "Salvation Proclaimed, V: 2 Cor. 5:18-21: Reconciliation with God," *Expository Times* 93 (1981-82), pp. 227-32, points out, there is a notable contrast between Paul's usage and Jewish usage of *katallassō,* "reconcile." When the verb is in the active voice, God or Christ is always the subject in Paul's letters; when it is in the passive voice, human beings are the subject. God reconciles and humans are reconciled. 1 Cor. 7:11 is not an exception, being a nonreligious reference.

15. F. W. Danker, *II Corinthians* (Minneapolis: Augsburg, 1989), pp. 82f.

are alienated from Paul, to that degree they are alienated from God.[16] In short, Paul fears that his converts are in danger of apostasy.[17] They should be reconciled, bearing in mind what Christ has done for them (v. 21). The sinless one has been made sin,[18] so that believers might become the righteousness of God. Paul is probably talking about condition, not just position, when he speaks of becoming God's righteousness, just as he was in speaking of the new creature (v. 17). This prepares for what he will say in ch. 6 about the need for holiness.

Thus Paul believes that there is a real danger that the believers in Corinth have received the grace of God in vain. **6:1** prepares for what follows in 6:14–7:1 by the use of *synergountes* ("coworkers"). Being a coworker with Paul and having communion and fellowship with unbelievers are mutually exclusive options.[19] God had come to them at the acceptable time, coming to their help in their hour of need (v. 2).[20] That hour and time of salvation is now and not merely in the future. The Corinthians must take this opportunity to be fully reconciled with both God in Christ *and* with Christ's ambassador.[21] It is interesting that the three key terms Paul uses to describe his role in this first argument of the letter (ambassador, servant of God, herald, cf. 4:5) are clearly interconnected and presuppose a person adept at rhetoric.[22]

16. Thrall, "Salvation Proclaimed," p. 228, is quite right in saying that Paul does not say "believe you are reconciled" but "be reconciled." This necessarily presupposes that they were to some degree alienated from God and Paul. As Thrall also notes (p. 228), the opposite of reconciliation in Paul's vocabulary is enmity. See below, pp. 418-19, on enmity conventions.

17. Apostasy is not merely backsliding, nor is it something that happens by accident. It is willful rebellion against God.

18. Perhaps this means "was made a sin offering" (cf. Isa. 53:10), or it might mean that Christ was given the position of the sinner and treated as such.

19. Cf. J-F. Collange, *Énigmes de la deuxieme épître de Paul aux Corinthiens. Étude exégétique de 2 Cor. 2:14–7:4* (Cambridge: Cambridge University, 1972), p. 282: 6:14ff. could be seen as an explication of the exhortation Paul gives in vv. 1-2. Usually in Paul's letters "coworker" refers to those who work with humans, but in 1 Cor. 3:9 and 1 Thess. 3:2 one is said to be a coworker with God. But this is probably not in view here because the purpose of the letter is to effect reconciliation between Paul (and thus also God) and the Corinthians and because 1:7 (they share in Paul's sufferings), 1:24 (Paul is a worker with them for their joy), and 2:10 (they both work together in the ministry of forgiveness) all point to Paul seeing the Corinthians as his colaborers, as may also the concept of the Corinthians as Paul's letter of recommendation (3:2).

20. Knowing the right *kairos* was especially important in Greco-Roman rhetoric; cf. Dio Chrysostom 38.

21. These last few verses make evident how serious Paul thinks the situation is in Corinth. They rule out the view that chs. 1–9 is a letter written after full reconciliation has been effected, for instance, by means of chs. 10–13. There are indications throughout chs. 1–9 that things are not well in Corinth, due to both internal and external (the false apostles) factors.

22. For example, an ambassador is said to be a messenger and a servant in Julius Pollux *Onomasticon* 8.137 (cf. also Dio Chrysostom 38.18). Cf. Fitzgerald, *Cracks,* p. 185.

Argument I, Division 4: 6:3-13

MINISTERIAL PRIVILEGES

Isocrates says that the most powerful way to be persuasive is to argue from one's own life (*Or.* 15.278). If one regards the participles in 6:3-10 as dependent on *parakaloumen* in v. 1, then this section might be seen as parenetic rather than apologetic. But such a connection seems unlikely, not least because of the tenor of the tribulation catalog that this brief passage begins with. Rather, 6:3-13 will be the last salvo in Paul's first major argument for his defense, ending in a final appeal for reconciliation before the digression in 6:14–7:1. The appeal to emotions in vv. 12f. signals the end of the argument. The Corinthians need to find a larger place in their hearts for affection toward Paul.[1]

Paul begins the last subsection of his first argument by stating flatly that no one, by which he means neither himself nor any of his coworkers, is placing any obstacles in the way of the Corinthians receiving the benefits of this reconciliation (v. 3). Indeed, the whole function of this letter is to remove such obstacles or *exigences,* saying whatever it takes within the bounds of personal integrity to produce that result. Paul is even willing to commend himself, but only as the minister or servant of God, that is, in his role as apostle, not in himself (v. **4a**). This is, then, not Paul's defense of himself, but his defense of his apostleship.[2]

Resorting once again to a rhetorical tactic to provide evidence of *ēthos* or character, Paul then lists a series of hardships (in three groups of three each) that he has undergone (vv. **4b-5**). As Fitzgerald demonstrates, this hardship catalog presupposes the earlier list in 4:8-10 and supplements or completes it.[3] Furthermore, the last three hardships named here, which could be called occupational hazards, are mentioned again in 11:27, which presupposes and

---

1. 6:12f. could be seen as the *peroratio* of the long and complicated argument about Paul's ministry that began in 3:1.

2. Cf. F. Lang, *Die Briefe an die Korinther* (Göttingen: Vandenhoeck, 1986), p. 304.

3. Both begin with *thlipsis,* "affliction" (plural in 6:4, the cognate participle in 4:8), and the reference to "God's power" in 6:6 alludes to 4:7-12. My understanding of this passage is indebted very much to J. T. Fitzgerald, *Cracks in an Earthen Vessel: An Examination of the Catalogue of Hardships in the Corinthian Correspondence* (Atlanta: Scholars, 1988), pp. 191ff.

builds on this catalog.[4] The catalog here bears a striking resemblance to one found in Achilles Tacitus 5.18.4-5, except that Paul first summarizes, then itemizes, which is the reverse of the Tacitus catalog.

This catalog of hardships is the first part of a larger list with a rhetorically powerful structure:

> the nine phrases of the peristasis catalog, all introduced by *en* ("in"), all emphasizing Paul's endurance, and introduced by "in great endurance" (vv. 4b-5).[5]
> eight phrases also introduced by *en* and listing virtues, vv. 6-7a,
> three longer phrases introduced by *dia* ("through"), vv. 7c-8a, and
> seven clauses introduced by *hōs* ("as"), vv. 9f.

The connection between the first two parts of this larger list, the hardships and the virtues, is that Paul mentions *volitional* hardships last, and this paves the way for the list of virtues in vv. **6-7a**. The point is not merely that Paul has endured, but that he has endured and has kept his integrity intact, which shows his character. His virtues show how he handled the hardships. The hardships and virtues together are meant to demonstrate that Paul has pure motives and authenticity as an *apostolos*.[6]

The phrases introduced by *dia* and *hōs* in vv. **7c-10** portray Paul as an equipped sage, armed by God against whatever vicissitudes he may face. That this is the function of this section is shown by:

> Paul's use of a military metaphor,[7]
> his scorn for fame — he is dishonored, but a sage does not care about such things,[8]
> his claim to be known by God but unknown to others,[9]
> his claim to be poor while he makes many rich, just like Christ (8:9), the ultimate sage, who is Wisdom in the flesh,
> his claim that all belongs to him even though he seems to have nothing,[10] and
> the common use of the hardships of the sage by both Stoics and Cynics to demonstrate virtue and character.[11]

---

4. Yet another point in favor of the letter's unity.
5. Cf. Fitzgerald, *Cracks*, pp. 191.
6. Cf. *ibid.*, p. 194.
7. Cf. Dio Chrysostom 16.6.
8. Cf. Diogenes Laertius 7.117.
9. Cf. Porphyry *Ad Marcellam* 13.
10. Cf. Cicero *Fin.* 3.22.75; Seneca *Ep.* 66.22.
11. Cf. Fitzgerald, *Cracks*, pp. 199-203.

What makes Paul's list stand out is its christological model and rationale. Paul has redefined what it means to be a sage in the light of Christ and his cross, but the Corinthians apparently have failed to understand the model, the motive, or the meaning of this.

The list in 6:4-10 should be compared to the one in 11:23ff. Both expose the qualities of the "servant of God," but the latter is longer and more precise and concentrates more on specific experiences of Paul.[12] One could then argue that the more general passage in ch. 6 prepares the listener for the more specific account in ch. 11, but with enough common terms that the latter builds on what was said in the former.[13]

A few more detailed exegetical comments are in order. Vv. 4f. focus on external circumstances that have impinged on Paul. In v. 6 Paul speaks of the moral character that has characterized his ministry. For this reason we should translate the phrase in v. 6c as "in a holy spirit," which prepares for Paul's insistence in vv. 14ff. on his audience's holiness. His ministry has been characterized by sincere love and purity, and this should characterize his converts as well.

In v. 7 Paul speaks of the tools or equipment of ministry that he has used: the word of truth, the power of God, and the weapons of righteousness on both the right and left hand. He is a warrior for God.[14] Then Paul contrasts the varying reactions or circumstances he has undergone during his ministry — both glory and disgrace, ill repute and good. He had been perceived as a deceiver and yet as true.[15]

Even though Paul was a person of modest means for Christ's sake, he had made many spiritually rich (v. 10). There was a sense in which he had everything in Christ, but he counted none of this as a possession because it all belonged to Christ.

Paul has "opened his mouth wide" and has shared everything concerning his feelings, attitudes, desires, exhortations, and circumstances (v. 11). What he wants is for the Corinthians not to be reserved about him, but to open their hearts fully to him again. The verb in v. 12 means "cramped." The Corinthians had not been assigned to a small corner in Paul's heart, and Paul wants reciprocity. They are to act like his children and show themselves expansive toward him (v. 13).

In light of the earlier discussion of 1 Corinthians 1–4 and 9,[16] it appears

12. J-F. Collange, *Énigmes de la deuxieme épître de Paul aux Corinthiens. Étude exégétique de 2 Cor. 2:14–7:4* (Cambridge: Cambridge University, 1972), p. 294.

13. This is yet another clue that both were likely part of the same letter originally.

14. This foreshadows and prepares for the important argument in 10:3-5; cf. Eph. 6:11.

15. It is possible that deception was a charge laid against Paul by the false *apostoloi*; cf. 12:16.

16. See above, pp. 78-150 and 203-16.

likely that Paul is once again assuming a pedagogical stance toward the Corinthians. He is their sage, and they are his children. This language was bound to conjure up images of the way their relationship was when Paul was first present — and also of his chastisement of them in 1 Corinthians, where he accused them of being immature, though they claimed to be spiritually rich (1 Cor. 3:1). In other words, Paul wants them to assume again the proper relationship to their teacher, but for the time being he must shame them and treat them like children. The proof that they are not yet ready to be treated as mature is about to be exhibited in the argument in 6:14–7:1: Some had still not given up their entangling associations with unbelievers at the idol feasts.[17]

17. Collange, *Énigmes*, p. 300, attempts to argue that 6:11-13 marks the end of a letter, but these verses can just as easily be seen as the end of an argument within a letter, a *peroratio* involving an emotional appeal.

Argument II: Digression *(egressio)*: 6:14–7:1

ENTANGLING ALLIANCES

Paul, having dealt with internal obstacles to reconciliation between himself and his converts, begins in 6:14–7:1 to mention some external factors that have caused the breach in the relationship. His rhetorical strategy in this letter is to move from lesser to greater problems. The internal problem of the one who offended Paul had already been satisfactorily resolved and the severe letter had had its proper effect. But the external problems are of a more serious and ongoing nature, and Paul chooses to address the first of these problems in 6:14–7:1.

Quintilian writes that a digression *(egressio)* may occur at any point in a rhetorical discourse *(Inst. Or.* 4.3.12) and that it may be characterized by greater vehemence and freedom of speech than the surrounding argument or arguments (4.3.9). One way a digression can function is that after a list of the services of the defendent, the opponent or in this case the audience can be denounced for ingratitude (4.3.7). This may in fact be what we find in chs. 3–7: Paul has listed some of his credentials and services for the Corinthians, concluding with a dramatic account of his trials in ministry, and now begins to make indirect accusations against the Corinthians by way of exhortation.[1] At least some of them are still maintaining some unacceptable relationships with unbelievers.

The preferred subjects for digressions were religion, duty, or historical occurrences, and they could be deliberative or epideictic in character *(Inst. Or.* 4.3.12, 15).[2] A deliberative digression would normally focus on future behavior and involve rebuke or admonition of the audience or even an expression of indignation (4.3.15f.). Two things were all important, however: A digression had to have some bearing on the case at hand (4.3.14), and it could add great distinction to the argument but "only if it fits well with the rest of the speech and follows naturally on what has preceded, not if it is thrust in like a wedge parting what should naturally come together" (4.3.5).

It is, therefore, important to show how this digression has some bearing

---

1. This depends in part on whether Paul is addressing in 6:14–7:1 a subject that he has already broached with the Corinthians. A digression may repeat what has already, at least in part, been dealt with by the rhetor *(Inst. Or.* 4.3.3).

2. A digression set in a forensic discourse would not normally be forensic in character.

on Paul's larger forensic argument and how it fits into its context.[3] This may be shown in several ways. First, we have already noted how the statements in 6:1f. foreshadow or signal the argument that comes in 6:14–7:1.[4] Second, 7:2 must be seen as resumptive of the point that preceded the digression, as Murphy-O'Connor stresses, for if 6:12f. and 7:2ff. had originally simply been adjoining verses there would be too much redundancy.[5]

Third, Fee and Thrall amply demonstrate that the style and content of 6:14–7:1 is more than sufficiently Pauline to have been composed in its present form by the Apostle, even if he was using pre-Pauline or non-Pauline material. Furthermore, Thrall has shown how every verse in the passage has a parallel not merely in Paul in general but specifically in 2 Cor. 2:14–6:13.[6] Fourth, the most brilliant part of Thrall's argument, which is amplified by Murphy-O'Connor, is that 6:11 and 6:14ff. allude to Deut. 11:16 and its context (vv. 13-16). This not only explains the references to open hearts in 6:11 and to idols in v. 16 but also connects the two.[7] The reference to eating in the Deuteronomy passage is also important since it supports the contention of Fee that Paul has in mind not merely participatation in idol worship, but rather the problem already broached in 1 Corinthians 8 and 10 — that of eating in idol temples.[8]

The studies we have been referring to also refute the suggestion of Betz that we have an anti-Pauline fragment in 2 Cor. 6:14–7:1.[9] There is nothing un-Pauline about this passage, in the light of 1 Corinthians 8–10, though it may draw on some non-Pauline material.

---

3. One point can already be stressed. In a rhetorical digression in the midst of a discourse it was expected that the rhetor would return to the point from which he digressed (*Inst. Or.* 4.3.17). I would suggest that this explains why 6:11f. and 7:2f. are so similar. The latter resumes the point introduced in the former, but enough variation is maintained that it is not simply a matter of duplication.

4. As recognized by M. E. Thrall, "The Problem of 2 Cor. 6.14–7.1 in Some Recent Discussion," *NTS* 24 (1977-78), pp. 132-48; J. Murphy-O'Connor, "Relating 2 Corinthians 6.14–7.1 to Its Context," *NTS* 33 (1987), pp. 272-75; and G. K. Beale, "The OT Background of Reconciliation in 2 Corinthians 5–7 and its Bearing on the Literary Problem of 2 Corinthians 6.14–7.1," *NTS* 35 (1987), pp. 550-81, here p. 569. I would differ from Thrall and others in that I do not see the actual argument beginning in 6:1f., with vv. 3ff. identified as a digression. Rather, vv. 1f. simply foreshadow and signal the coming new argument. If anything, it would be better to argue that a new argument begins with 6:11f., is interrupted by the digression in 6:14–7:1, and then is resumed at 7:2 (see below).

5. Murphy-O'Connor, "Relating 2 Corinthians 6.14–7.1," p. 273.

6. G. D. Fee, "2 Corinthians 6.14–7.1 and Food Offered to Idols," *NTS* 23 (1976-77), pp. 140-61, especially pp. 144ff.; Thrall, "Problem," pp. 133ff.

7. Thrall, "Problem," p. 146; Murphy-O'Connor, "Relating," pp. 273f.

8. Fee, "2 Cor. 6.14–7.1," pp. 157ff.

9. H. D. Betz, "2 Cor. 6.14–7.1: An Anti-Pauline Fragment," *JBL* 92 (1973), pp. 88-108. Few if any scholars have accepted this suggestion.

Fifth, it is now commonly argued that the reference to *apistoi* in 6:14 refers to the false apostles mentioned in chs. 10–13.[10] I do not rule out this possibility, but I think it is unlikely not only because of the allusion to pagan worship in 6:14–7:1, but also because in 4:4 the term is clearly used of pagans and, as Thrall points out, the absence of *apistoi* in chs. 10–13 is very surprising if it were a term Paul wanted to use of the false *apostoloi*.[11]

Sixth, there is an unnoticed pedagogical link between 6:13 and 6:14ff. (see further below). And seventh, Beale points out the connection of vv. 16-18 with God's promises, not only to restore Israel, but also to dwell among the Israelites in a temple if they will forsake idolatry (Ezek. 37:26-28; 20:40; Lev. 26:11; 2 Sam. 7:2-7, 11-13). He shows how 2 Cor. 6:14–7:1 supports the letter's theme of reconciliation between the Corinthians and Paul (and Christ), by ruling out other conflicting forms of *koinōnia*.[12]

Taken together, these arguments provide a compelling case for seeing 6:14–7:1 as a very appropriate deliberative digression, one that dovetails with what precedes and what follows and with the larger rhetorical purposes of the document. It thus serves to create reconciliation between Paul and his audience by defending Paul's ministry and by attacking those factors and alliances that had alienated at least some of Paul's converts from him.

It is important to ask about the function of the rhetorical questions in vv. **14-16.** It is not uncommon for Paul to begin an argument or digression with a series of rhetorical questions (cf. 1 Cor. 6:1-11; 9:1-12), which convey a certain tone of indignation meant to put the audience on the defensive.[13] It appears that such a clustering of questions is part of a dialogical or diatribal style, which was typical of a pedagogical setting.[14] As before, when Paul assumes the pedagogical mantle with the Corinthians he refers to them as babes or children (cf. 1 Cor. 3:1 and especially 4:14). Paul has, in fact, announced in 6:13 that he is about to act as teacher or sage to instruct or warn, and thus 6:14–7:1 follows quite nicely as instruction, in diatribal style.

Wuellner is right in saying that Paul often uses rhetorical questions to evoke a conventional (in this case conventional Christian) value that he expects

---

10. E.g., Beale, "Old Testament," p. 573; J-F. Collange, *Énigmes de la deuxieme épître de Paul aux Corinthiens. Étude exégétique de 2 Cor. 2:14–7:4* (Cambridge: Cambridge University, 1972), pp. 305f.

11. Thrall, "Problem," p. 143; Murphy-O'Connor, "Relating," p. 273.

12. Beale, "Old Testament," pp. 574-77.

13. See above, pp. 167-69 and 203-7.

14. See above, pp. 228 n. 35, 246-47, 376 n. 4, on Stowers's discussion and see further on this particular passage T. Schmeller, *Paulus und die "Diatribe." Eine vergleichende Stilinterpretation* (Münster: Aschendorff, 1987), pp. 408f.

his converts to uphold (cf. 1 Cor. 6:1ff.). In other words, he frequently uses such questions in a deliberative manner to advise about future or ongoing behavior. This rhetorical approach has a social function:

> Paul works also for the transformation of the multiplicity of different social and ethnic/cultural value systems into a unity. It is a new social order, an *imperium* or *Basileia* whose ideology though different from the imperial norms of Rome and of zealotic Jewish nationalism, was yet compatible with "the hope of Israel," the kingdom of God.[15]

The Corinthians, or at least some of the more well-to-do Gentile males,[16] had still not understood or accepted the full social implications of being in Christ.

Reconciliation, or giving Paul a full place in the Corinthians' hearts, means forsaking certain entangling alliances with unbelievers which have lingered on for years (cf. 1 Corinthians 10). It is doubtful that v. 14 is referring to marriages. V. 16 suggests that Paul is referring here to spiritual profligacy in the form of attendance at idol feasts in pagan temples. How can Christians attend such feasts when they are God's temple, the place where God's presence dwells? Here Paul draws on what he said in 1 Cor. 3:16 — not in 1 Cor. 6:19 — using "temple" as a term for Christ's body of believers. The word he uses represents the temple sanctuary *(naos)*, not the mere temple precincts (the *hieron*). Paul apparently believes that the Corinthians are in danger of becoming spiritually linked with the demonic forces resident in the temple.[17]

Paul uses several terms and images for partnership in this passage: the image of the yoke;[18] *koinōnia*, that is, sharing in common[19]; *metochē*, "partnership"; *symphōnēsis*, "concord"; and "agreement." This furthers the theme of partnership found already in 1:24 and 6:1. The point is that one's religious affiliation must be a single-minded commitment. Paganism and Christianity are mutually exclusive options in Paul's view. How can the true sanctuary of God parade off to a meal in a pagan sanctuary?

The catena of OT clauses in vv. **16b-18** speaks of God dwelling in the

---

15. W. Wuellner, "Paul as Pastor: The Function of Rhetorical Questions in First Corinthians," *L'Apôtre Paul. Personalité, Style et Conception du Ministère* (Leuven: Leuven University, 1986), p. 73. See Wuellner's helpful discussion of rhetorical questions on pp. 49-77.

16. See above, pp. 220-21.

17. Romans believed that the god's presence was conveyed in or through the statue of the god placed in the *naos;* see pp. 186-91 above.

18. He uses "yoke" of his coworker in Philippi in Phil. 4:3.

19. Seesemann, *Der Begriff KOINONIA im Neuen Testament* (Giessen: Töpelmann, 1933), p. 99, is incorrect that 2 Cor. 6:14 provides the one exception in the Pauline corpus to the rule that Paul always uses this term in a religious, not profane, sense. Since light and dark represent spiritual forces or conditions in this text, here, too, it has a religious sense.

midst of the Corinthian Christians and moving among them. In these brief quotations they are exhorted to sever ties with pagans and to come out of pagan associations that spiritually endanger their salvation. They are to be "separate," that is, set apart or holy. Paul's reference to his own acting in holiness of spirit in 6:6 has prepared the way for the exhortation in **7:1**. The Corinthians are called upon to follow his model.[20] This digression is about moral character and theological integrity, not about ritual purity.

The Corinthians are the sons and daughters of the true and living God (**6:18**). Paul adds "and daughters" to the quotation (cf. 2 Sam 7:14).[21] He was more egalitarian than many think, and this text shows his desire to be reconciled with both his male and female converts in Corinth.[22] The quotations lead to a final exhortation: They are to cleanse themselves from all physical and spiritual defilement, both of which they could have become involved in a pagan temple in Corinth. And they are to get on with progressive sanctification, perfecting their set apart condition from such paganism, in the fear of the one true God.

The social function of this passage was the same as its predecessors in 1 Corinthians 8 and 10, namely to create a stronger sense of what the proper moral and social boundaries were for the Christian community in Corinth.[23] There were entangling alliances from which the Corinthians needed to disengage themselves in order to be fully reconciled to Paul and the One who sent him. These alliances involved *koinōnia* with nonbelievers in pagan temples and, worse, involvement with false believers, the latter not addressed directly until chs. 10–13. Some partnerships exclude others, and the Corinthians needed to understand this because their relationship not only with Paul but also with Christ hung in the balance. This passage shows Paul going on the attack, though in a deliberative mode, and as such it serves his larger goals in this discourse of defending his own integrity and that of his work in Corinth, with hopes of a full rapprochement with his converts. He longs for full partnership in the gospel with them again.

20. On imitation as a pedagogical device and a tool of deliberative rhetoric, see pp. 203-13 above.

21. Perhaps he was also thinking of Isa. 43:6.

22. On whether or not Corinthian Christian women were participating in idol feasts, see pp. 241-52 above.

23. On this subject, see the more extended discussion on pp. 186-230.

Argument III (with *Amplificatio*): 7:2-16

HEARTS ON FIRE WITH JOY AND SORROW

It was normal practice in forensic rhetoric to place the *narratio* directly after the *exordium,* but, as Quintilian says, circumstances could force a different arrangement, as in Cicero's defense of Milo (*Inst. Or.* 4.2.5). 2 Cor. 7:5ff. again rehearses some of the material first mentioned in the *narratio* in chs. 1 and 2. Quintilian tells us that the *narratio* can indeed be a form of *probatio* or argument put forward in a continuous or sequential form (4.2.79). Thus, some have taken 7:5ff. as a *narratio* of sorts, and the similarity to material in chs. 1 and 2 has led to various letter partition theories.[1] But to go that far is a mistake, even from a rhetorical point of view.

Each argument of a defense, if there were multiple arguments, could have a brief *narratio* or rehearsal of the facts to be dealt with in that particular argument, or it could allude to and build on the original *narratio*. Pseudo-Aristotle insightfully remarks that a *narratio* within other sections of a speech does not serve the function of informing the audience of something that they do not already know, but involves a retelling in a way that would help the rhetor make as persuasive a case as possible (*Rhetorica ad Alexandrum* 1438b.15-25). This is the way the factual elements in 7:5ff. function. Therefore, there is no need to resort to partition theories to explain either the return to the discussion of Paul's travels or his painful letter. This recapitulation shows that Paul was very worried about the effect both of his apparent inconsistency in word and deed in regard to his travel plans and of his painful letter. Hence, he deals with these matters more fully here to be sure that they do not undermine the rest of his defense. This amounts to an amplification *(amplificatio)* on some things mentioned only briefly in the *narratio*[2] as a preparation

---

1. Cf. F. W. Hughes, "The Rhetoric of Reconciliation: 2 Corinthians 1.1–2.13 and 7.5–8.24," in *Persuasive Artistry: Studies in NT Rhetoric in Honor of George A. Kennedy,* ed. D. F. Watson (Sheffield: Sheffield Academic, 1991), pp. 246-61, here pp. 252-56.

2. S. B. Heiny, "2 Corinthians 2.14–4.6: The Motive for Metaphor," *Society of Biblical Literature 1987 Seminar Papers,* ed. K. H. Richards (Atlanta: Scholars, 1987), pp. 1-22, here p. 18, rightly points out that

> 2:14–6:10 prepares the way for 7:2-4 even as the latter depends on the former. A personal appeal of the sort we see in 7:2-4 would be quite out of place without the foundation laid in 2:14–6:10. The earlier passage shows by what authority the apostle may in the latter passage make such an appeal. To reverse the order of the passages

for dealing with the issue of the collection in chs. 8–9. There will be no collection if confidence in Paul and his emissary Titus are not fully restored.

In this section Paul will conclude his remarks, which began in ch. 2, about his joy over the good news from Titus about the reaction of at least the majority of the Corinthian Christians to the painful letter. In v. 2 he exhorts his audience to make room (in their hearts) for him since he has not treated them unjustly or ruined them or taken advantage of them.[3] As Danker says, "an ancient rhetorician would have termed 6:14–7:1 a digression and would have viewed 7:2 as an *epanalepsis* or resumption of the point made in 6:13."[4] The reference to ruin and being taken advantage of may be yet another implicit glance at those in Corinth whom Paul thought were ruining and taking advantage of the Christian community there.[5] The triple repetition of "no one" helps the passage build rhetorical momentum after the digression.[6]

Verse **3b** is most naturally taken as a reference *back* to 6:12 ("as I already said") and shows the resumptive character of these verses.[7] Paul stresses that he is not trying to make the Corinthians feel guilty as an end in itself, for he has them in his heart and believes or wishes the bond between them to be so close that he will share living and dying with them.[8] He has always spoken freely to them and has not played his cards close to his chest, *and* he has spoken freely about them as well, boasting about them. It is part of Paul's general rhetorical strategy to use plain speech, that is, language that is neither ornamental nor deceptive.

In general, Paul has been encouraged about them, indeed overflowing with joy (v. 4). He plays with the words *charis*, "grace," and *chara*, "joy." When God is the subject, *charis* is an undeserved benefit or grace, but when used of

would destroy the effect of the whole because it would present a personal appeal before the audience had any reason to feel disposed to entertain such an appeal.

Heiny (p. 17) also rightly sees that 2:14–7:4 has as its subject matter a defense not so much of Paul's person but of his apostleship.

3. It is interesting that in 7:2-4 the sentence length is about fifteen words, while in 2:14–4:6 it averages about twenty-six words. In other words, here the style is more staccato and clipped. Cf. Heiny, "Motive for Metaphor," p. 17.

4. F. W. Danker, *II Corinthians* (Minneapolis: Augsburg, 1989), p. 102.

5. The overall rhetorical effect of the verse suggests that the opponents were taking *financial* advantage of the Corinthians.

6. Rightly Danker, *II Corinthians*, p. 102.

7. J.-F. Collange, *Énigmes de la deuxieme épître de Paul aux Corinthiens. Étude exégétique de 2 Cor. 2:14–7:4* (Cambridge: Cambridge University, 1972), pp. 314f., tries unsuccessfully to get around this natural connection.

8. In other words, writing the painful letter was not an act of revenge.

human beings it means something like "gracious gift or benevolence" or "gracious act," the latter of which is seen in chs. 8–9.

Verse 5 is important in showing Paul's state of mind. He was very anxious, but about what? Barrett suggests that he was anxious about Titus,[9] but that does not fit the context. All that has preceded shows that Paul was concerned about the Corinthians, about their partnership with him in the gospel, and about how they would receive his painful letter. In this section *parakaleō* (vv. 6, 7, and 13) means "encourage," not "comfort," and the cognate noun *paraklēsis* (vv. 4, 7, and 13) means, correspondingly, "encouragement." God is the one who encourages the *tapeinous*, the lowly or humble (v. 6). Humility here has to do with one's condition, not with one's self-evaluation.[10]

Verse 6 speaks of the arrival *(parousia)* of Titus. *Parousia*, the term we associate with the second coming of Christ, is appropriate here since Titus was an envoy of Paul, who was an envoy of Christ. Titus's coming was in a sense a royal appearance of God's surrogate, and Paul treats it as a special coming indeed.[11] The encouragement Paul received from Titus was that he reported the longing, grieving, and zeal of the Corinthians (v. 7). We must ask, in view of what follows in chs. 10–13, whether Titus was too optimistic in his assessment. Perhaps the answer is no in regard to the majority in Corinth, but the Corinthian Christians were not united in regard to Paul.

In vv. 8ff. Paul, for almost the only time in his letters, speaks of *metanoia* (repentance).[12] He is not referring to a repentance prior to faith in Christ, but to those who are already Christians repenting of some sin they have committed. Repentance is not merely feeling sorry or being sorry. It is a turning in one's attitude and actions, not merely a change of heart but a change of life and lifestyle. Paul had some regrets about sending the painful letter and hurting his converts, but that the pain led to repentance he does not regret. This pain for a short time forestalls the Corinthians from suffering a major loss "from us." It is uncertain what this means, but perhaps Paul is thinking of the total severing of his relationship with the Corinthians.

The pain that produced repentance was "unto salvation" (v. 10), which might refer to no more than present spiritual well-being, though Paul without question does believe that one can endanger one's eternal salvation by be-

9. C. K. Barrett, "Titus," in *Essays on Paul* (Philadelphia: Westminster, 1982), pp. 118-31, here pp. 124ff.

10. This comports with Paul's portrait of himself as an enslaved leader and destitute sage (6:4ff.). Humility was not seen as a virtue in antiquity. Rather, *tapeinos* was used of the behavior of social inferiors — slavish or deferential behavior.

11. On Paul's use of *parousia* language, see B. Witherington, *Jesus, Paul, and the End of the World* (Downers Grove: InterVarsity, 1992), pp. 152ff.

12. The word appears elsewhere in the Pauline corpus only in Rom. 2:4 and 2 Tim. 2:25. The cognate verb appears in 2 Cor. 12:21.

havior. In Paul's view, the Corinthian Christians were in danger of committing apostasy, and therefore repentance "unto salvation" was necessary.[13] The pain from God works for salvation, but the pain of the world only works toward death.

The repentance of the Corinthians amounted to a rekindling of their eagerness to be in step with Paul. It also produced a defense (*apologia*, v. 11): Some of them may have felt that they were being unjustly accused. It also produced indignation, perhaps against the offender, and fear and longing.[14] The point is that they demonstrated their innocence in the matter. V. 12 seems to be a reference to Paul as the offended one. Paul says that his letter was sent as a sort of test or trial balloon to see how the Corinthians would respond. He was testing their earnestness before God.

Verses 13-16 may quite naturally be seen as the *peroratio* of this argument, where Paul will attempt to stir the emotions of the Corinthians and recapitulate some of the arguments he has made in the *narratio*.[15] He rejoices because Titus was happy about what he thought he had found in Corinth (v. 13).[16] Apparently Paul boasted earlier to Titus that the Corinthians (at least most of them) would prove true (v. 14). Their response was one of obedience, indeed of reverent fear and respect before the apostolic delegate (v. 15).

In this section then Paul builds on his earlier *narratio*, adding now more information about how his letter and Titus have been received and how Titus has perceived the state of the Corinthian Christians. On the basis of his earlier defense of his apostolic status, Paul makes a personal and emotional appeal for reconciliation. 7:2-16 also prepares the hearer for what is to be said in chs. 8–9 by mentioning Titus (7:6, 14; 8:6, 16), what happened to Paul and the churches in Macedonia (7:5; 8:1f., 24; 9:2, 4), his boasting over the Corinthians (7:4, 14; 9:2), the joy/grace (*chara/charis*) of God (7:6-8, 13; 8:1), the earnestness, zeal, and eagerness of the Corinthians (7:11; 8:8; 9:2), Titus's eagerness and concern for the Corinthians (7:13; 8:16f.), and the testing of the Corinthians (7:12; 8:8).

13. So Hay, "Shaping of Theology," p. 265.

14. Perhaps fear of God and longing to see Paul.

15. For example, Paul's confidence in the Corinthians and relief over their response to the severe letter. So Hughes, "Rhetoric of Reconciliation," p. 257.

16. The degree of Paul's real emotional investment in his converts is evident in this section, which is an example of his "free" and open-hearted speech, not merely of an ability to compose an emotionally effective rhetorical argument. It is worth pondering what this tells us about how the personal relationship between a pastor and his or her flock ought to be conducted today. What sort of level of concern and personal sacrifice are we as Christian ministers prepared to make?

Argument IV: Chapters 8–9

COLLECTIONS AND RECOLLECTIONS

In chapters 8 and 9 Paul engages in a rhetorically daring move. He concluded his previous argument by stating that he has complete confidence in the Corinthians. They have passed one test in regard to an isolated offender and he now offers them another chance to prove their genuineness and their confidence in him by following his exhortation to complete the collection for the poor Christians of Judea.[1]

In order to undertake a deliberative argument one must assume that one has established one's *ēthos* or character with the audience. Quintilian says that "what really carries greatest weight in deliberative speeches is the authority of the speaker. Whoever wants everyone to trust his judgment as to what is expedient and honorable should both possess and be regarded as possessing genuine wisdom and excellence" (*Inst. Or.* 3.8.12f.). In view of the obvious concern manifested even in chs. 8–9 about the Corinthians' readiness to accept Paul's authority,[2] this rhetorical move was risky but not inappropriate. Paul's strategy is to put the audience on the defensive about something to which they have committed themselves but have not yet fully performed. In keeping with his *propositio*, he must also show that his own behavior in regard to the collection is above reproach, lest he be labeled a peddler of God's Word.

According to Quintilian, one who intends to give advice about revenue should know the character of the audience (3.8.14). Time would tell if Paul had judged rightly that the Corinthian Christians were now prepared to accept this deliberative argument from him.[3] This was a crucial move in the discourse,

---

1. J. A. Crafton, *The Agency of the Apostle: A Dramatistic Analysis of Paul's Response to Conflict in 2 Corinthians* (Sheffield: JSOT, 1990), pp. 48ff., recognizes some of the rhetorical nuances here, but succumbs to the usual fragmentation of the text without seriously considering the alternatives. His analysis also suffers from trying to mix modern and Greco-Roman rhetorical analysis and method.

2. Otherwise he would not need to keep putting them to the test.

3. How one evaluates chs. 8–9 is in part determined by what one makes of chs. 10–13. I take the latter to be addressed *to* the Corinthian Christians, but *against* the false apostles. The Corinthians themselves are not Paul's opponents, and thus there is no reason to think that Paul was whistling in the dark when he spoke of having some confidence in them. 7:11 makes it clear that they are impressionable and that the painful letter has had its proper impact. But they are still also under the influence of the false *apostoloi*. All is not well in Corinth by any means, but the chief cause of this is external. Paul seems to think that the

meant in part to improve his credibility in the eyes of the Corinthians before he could make an argument like the one in chs. 10–13.

Paul's credibility had been dealt a severe blow because of his unwillingness to accept patronage in Corinth, all the while appealing for a collection. This led to various suspicions and, when his opponents arrived on the scene, apparently outright accusations about his handling of money matters and what it revealed about his apostolic status. Money matters were a — if not the — most serious obstacle to reconciliation between Paul and his converts, and these matters had to be addressed before he could go on the attack against the opponents. But he defends himself precisely by going on the attack.

First he implies a comparison *(synkrisis),* suggesting that the Corinthians have been recalcitrant in comparison to the Macedonians in giving to the collection (8:1-5).[4] Then he offers a deliberative argument advising them to complete their contribution (vv. 7-15, 24) and tells them that Titus and others are coming to complete the collection (vv. 6, 16-23).[5] At the close of this first division of the argument (ch. 8), Paul carefully slips in a disclaimer. He is pursuing this course of action "so that no one will blame us about this generous gift that we are administering, for we intend to do what is right both in the Lord's sight and in the sight of others" (vv. 20f.). In other words, everything he is saying and doing is part of the demonstration of his innocence and honesty. What he says about the collection is part of his defense in this letter. The deliberative argument in ch. 8 thus serves Paul's larger forensic purposes.[6]

Chapter 9, the second division of the argument, reinforces this. Paul pulls out all the stops and resorts to a threat of shaming the Corinthians by mentioning in passing that when he comes and if some Macedonians come with him (v. 4), then the Corinthians will be publicly embarrassed since the destitute Macedonians have already been generous while the wealthy Corinthians have been dragging their feet. The argument is reinforced by appeals to God, Scripture, and the benefit the Corinthians will derive from generosity.

Chapters 8 and 9 are thus both deliberative arguments, but they serve larger forensic purposes, both in Paul's defense and in his attack on the roots

---

majority, but by no means all, are largely on his side (cf. ch. 2) and will still listen to and heed his advice. It is with this hope and confidence that he writes chs. 8–9. It is difficult to get the balance right in evaluating the degree of alienation from and attachment to the apostle that the Corinthians had. It was a strange, complex, and frustrating love affair.

4. "As a rule, all deliberative speeches are based on comparison. . . . Reference to historical parallels is the quickest method of securing assent" (*Inst. Or.* 3.8.34, 36). Quintilian adds that when an audience is not entirely honorable in character it is necessary to praise them or appeal to their pride or to personal advantage (3.8.40f.), as Paul does here.

5. Titus apparently began to do so when he delivered the painful letter; cf. 8:6.

6. On the overlapping or dovetailing of forensic and deliberative themes and purposes in a speech, see *Inst. Or.* 3.8.55f.

of the alienation of some of the Corinthian Christians from him. By reminding the Corinthians about the collection, Paul gives them an opportunity to be financial coworkers with him. Since some saw themselves as patrons in their relationship with the *apostolos,* this request could help cement the reconciliation between Paul and this *ekklēsia.*[7]

Paul begins this argument by referring to the grace of God given to the *ekklēsiai* of Macedonia and to the joy they have had in spite of their circumstances (**8:1f.**). "For Paul, 'joy' is not just a happy mood; it is the saving gift from God, part of the new creation, and brought on through the Holy Spirit."[8] When Paul speaks of the Macedonian Christians to others, he speaks of their generosity, but here also of their extreme poverty. And yet they have given generously to the collection. They gave not only according to their ability but even beyond their ability, and they asked Paul to let them be benefactors in the collection (vv. **3f.**). In v. 4 "grace" means "benevolence" or "gracious action" (cf. v. 7). They wanted to share in Paul's ministry in this way, a ministry to "the saints"[9]

---

7. H. D. Betz's treatment of chs. 8–9 is helpful, especially in its sensitivity to the rhetorical dimensions of the text (*2 Corinthians 8 and 9* [Philadelphia: Fortress, 1985]). But his analysis has some serious drawbacks. That he can divide both of these chapters into the major parts of a rhetorical speech is no proof that they were originally separate documents. That his argument appears forced at several key points has been pointed out by S. K. Stowers in a review of Betz's commentary (*JBL* 106 [1987], pp. 727-30) and by F. W. Hughes, "The Rhetoric of Reconciliation: 2 Corinthians 1.1–2.13 and 7.5–8.24," in *Persuasive Artistry: Studies in NT Rhetoric in Honor of George A. Kennedy,* ed. D. F. Watson (Sheffield: Sheffield Academic, 1991), pp. 246-61, here p. 258, n. 1.

As we have seen when discussing 1 Corinthians 15, both 1 and 2 Corinthians are composed of a variety of arguments and any or all of these arguments may have any of the parts of a rhetorical discourse from an *exordium* to a *peroratio.* Micro-rhetoric should not be confused with macro-rhetoric, and letters are not completely identical with speeches. Letters include epistolary opening and closing features, which chs. 8–9 do not have. Betz's analysis also ignores how ch. 7 prepares for the discussion in chs. 8–9 (see above, pp. 407-10) and fails to account for the commercial language and the critique of Paul's rivals as peddlers of the gospel in chs. 1–7, which seems to be leading up to something crucial. Paul normally includes all kinds of things in a single letter, including what could be placed in a letter of recommendation — without writing a separate letter to accomplish this (cf. 1 Corinthians 16 and Romans 16), so why should 2 Corinthians 8–9 be any different? Since 2 Corinthians is addressed to all the congregations in Achaia (1:1), it is possible for ch. 9 to be included in the letter even though it speaks to the Christians of Achaia. Finally, 7:5 suggests that Paul is writing from Macedonia, and unless he could gather a group of Macedonians to go with him to Corinth, 9:4 would be an idle threat.

8. D. Georgi, *Remembering the Poor: The History of Paul's Collection for Jerusalem* (Nashville: Abingdon, 1992), p. 71.

9. On *koinōnia* meaning a sharing in or participation in something, see J. Y. Campbell, "Κοινωνία and its Cognates in the NT," *JBL* 51 (1932), pp. 352-80, here p. 373. The term

which may be here a technical term for the Jerusalem Jewish Christians (cf. Eph. 1:15).

Paul has asked Titus (v. 6) to carry on with what had already begun in Corinth (1 Corinthians 16) in regard to the collection. He is careful here to make clear that he is neither collecting nor administering the money, in order not to give his detractors an excuse to berate him further.

A Closer Look: Paul, Patronage, and Power

In the Greco-Roman world, there was a wide and complex variety of social relationships that required reciprocity, some between social equals and some between persons of different social status. Most of these relationships were euphemistically called "friendship" *(amicitia),* and most involved some transferal of goods, services, funds, or other material benefits in one direction and of honor, praise, votes, and influence in the other direction. Our concern here is most of all with such reciprocity relationships between people of unequal social status.[10]

In a society where banks did not loan money and in which there was not in most places an adequate social safety net, personal patronage was a practical necessity. A patronage relationship would be established by a gift or some other favor and by acceptance of the gift, which placed the recipient in the inferior role in the relationship and obligated him or her to respond with expressions of gratitude, praise, and honor. Not surprisingly, the language of commerce was sometimes used of such relationships.[11] These relationships were usually informal and supralegal, sometimes even involving actions that were not fully or strictly legal. In theory they were voluntary, but in practice social inferiors often had no choice but to engage in such relationships in order to be materially supported.

Though the terminology of friendship was often used in patronage relationships to avoid the indelicacy of calling someone a client *(cliens),* when in fact she or he was a client, social inferiors were expected to offer their verbal or inscriptional praise with such terms as *patronus.* A good example of such praise from Corinth during the time of Paul is this inscription:

> Gaius Julius, son of Laco . . . , procurator of Caesar and Augusta, awarded a
> public horse [that is, equestrian rank] by the deified Claudius, priest of the

---

does not mean "fellowship" here or even in 1 Corinthians 10. Fellowship is a result of *koinōnia,* a result of sharing or partaking or participating in common with others in something.

10. For general discussions of patronage in Corinth, see A. D. Clarke, *Secular and Christian Leadership in Corinth* (dissertation, Cambridge, 1991); J. K. Chow, *Patronage and Power: A Study of Social Networks in Corinth* (Sheffield: JSOT, 1992), pp. 19ff.

11. G. W. Peterman, *Giving and Receiving in Paul's Epistles* (D. Phil. thesis, King's College, London, 1992), p. 104.

A Roman column found at Scythopolis (Beth-Shan) honoring patrons

deified Julius, pontifex, duovir quinquennalis twice, agonothete of the Isthmian and Caesar-Augustan games,[12] high priest of the house of Augustus in perpetuity, first of the Achaians. Because of his excellence and spirited and all-encompassing munificence toward the divine house and toward our colony, the tribesmen of the tribe of Calpurnia [dedicate this monument] to their patron.[13]

12. On some of these terms, see pp. 5-7 and 33-35 above.

13. A. B. West, *Corinth: Latin Inscriptions 1898-1927* VIII/2 (Cambridge: ASCSA, 1931), no. 68. See also the patronal inscription column in the photograph above. Cf. R. K. Sherk, ed., *The Roman Empire: Augustus to Hadrian* (Cambridge: Cambridge University, 1988), p. 164. Another excellent example from Corinth is from about A.D. 43 and is addressed to a female patron:

> Whereas Junia Theodora, a Roman resident in Corinth, a woman held in highest honor . . . , who copiously supplied from her own means many of our citizens with generosity, and received them in her home and in particular never ceased acting on behalf of our citizens to any favor asked — the majority of citizens have gathered in assembly to offer testimony on her behalf. Poor people in gratitude agreed to vote to commend Junia . . . and urges her to increase her generosity to the city in the knowledge that our people . . . would do everything for the excellence and glory that she deserved.

This inscription is most easily found in the helpful book by M. R. Lefkowitz and M. B. Fant, *Women's Life in Greece and Rome* (Baltimore: Johns Hopkins University, 1982), p. 157.

This inscription was set up by a group of people, not just by an individual who had benefited from personal patronage,[14] but use of the term *patronus* was not determined by whether the clientele was one person or several people.[15]

One has only to read Seneca's *De Beneficiis* or Cicero's *De Amicitia* or *De Officiis* to see how pervasive and important reciprocity relationships, especially patronage relationships, were in the Greco-Roman world. This was increasingly the case as the vestiges of earlier, more democratic institutions disappeared and the more hierarchical structures of the empire imposed themselves on more and more aspects of Mediterranean society.[16] There were other sorts of relationships such as *societas* relationships, which were ongoing limited financial partnerships between equals working together toward common goals, but it does not appear that this sort of relationship existed between Paul and his converts in Achaia.[17]

14. Some would say it should, therefore, be called an example of a benefaction generally given to groups, rather than of patronage. But this is a fuzzy distinction. A gift from a patron to an individual could be called a benefaction in the inscriptions, and, as the inscription cited above shows, a benefaction to a group could result in someone being called a patron. Neither word is an exact technical term, since both are used of the same sort of relationship between social unequals. Cf. the helpful introductory essay by J. H. Elliott, "Patronage and Clientism in Early Christian Society," *Forum* 3 (1987), pp. 39-48.

15. In literature of the early empire *patronus* is used only of "legal advocates, patrons of communities, and ex-masters of freedmen" (R. P. Saller, *Personal Patronage under the Empire* [Cambridge: Cambridge University, 1982], p. 9; on an orator who serves as a legal advocate being called a patron, cf. G. A. Kennedy, *The Art of Rhetoric in the Roman World 300 B.C. to A.D. 300* [Princeton: Princeton University, 1972], pp. 12f.). But inscriptions show that other sorts of individuals could also be called patrons. Normally patrons would be senators or *equites,* unless an inscription was dedicated by a freedman to his former master. For a helpful definition of the patron-client relationship, see Elliott, "Patronage and Clientism," p. 42. As he notes, several factors often made patronage relationships unstable. That the relationship was entered into voluntarily did not prevent it from becoming a considerable burden and from leading to exploitation and coercion.

16. Cf. G. E. M. de Ste. Croix, *The Class Struggle in the Ancient Greek World* (Ithaca: Cornell University, 1981), p. 364. Saller, *Personal Patronage,* p. 206, mentions in this regard the "increasing integration of provincials into aristocratic networks." "When the Principate was established and the popular assemblies became unimportant, the configuration of political patronage was altered as connections with the emperor, direct or indirect, became vital for political success, and the need for the popular assemblies declined." Furthermore (p. 189), "Romanization entailed participation by the local elites in imperial culture, which in turn provided opportunities for initiating personal friendships with influential senators and equestrians." One can see in the building program of Roman Corinth, in the rise of the Augustan games, in the inscriptions, and from other evidence how Corinth tried to maximize its connections with the emperor and thus its link to imperial patronage. See pp. 295-98 above.

17. On whether it existed between Paul and his Philippian converts, see J. P. Sampley, *Pauline Partnership in Christ* (Philadelphia: Fortress, 1980). Peterman critiques this suggestion (*Giving and Receiving,* pp. 228-33). The question turns on whether or not one takes the language in Phil. 4:10-20 as technical financial language, and whether or not *koinōnia* can be a technical term, the equivalent of the Latin *societas*. Peterman is right in my judgment that Sampley has not shown that *koinōnia,* which can mean "partnership," can have the specific

A relief found at Corinth depicting a Roman official. The inscription probably places this man in the second century A.D. Citizens of this sort were often the leading patrons in Roman Corinth.

An itinerant teacher or preacher like Paul could beg, like the Cynics, or accept personal patronage and become the in-house philosopher or rhetor of a wealthy person, or support himself by working at a trade. Paul sought to avoid accepting patronage in Corinth because it would commit him to the wrong sort of reciprocity, bind him to a particular location, and place him in a socially inferior position that would make it very difficult for him to "be all things" to people of varying social status. Such a relationship would also mean that he would be perceived as taking sides with one of the factions in Corinth, which were probably led and supported by some of the wealthy and socially prominent members of the congregation. The last thing Paul

---

sense of *societas*. Paul says in 1 Corinthians 9 that he has the right to support, not due to a *societas* relationship, but because of who he is, Christ's agent, which is the case apart from what kind of relationship he has with the Corinthians. Finally, *chreia* does not mean "request" in Phil. 4:17. Here as everywhere in the Pauline letters it means "need."

wanted to do in Corinth was to promote the factious spirit that existed in the congregation by committing himself to a particular local patron.[18]

To accept a gift involved one in "an inescapable train of obligations," "but to refuse a gift was no easier, for one then incurred the burden of enmity."[19] Because Paul has refused patronage, he must respond in 2 Corinthians to all the usual themes used for ridicule when an enmity relationship had been set up: slurs on his social background, charges of immorality, attacks on his physical appearance, speech, and dress, and accusations of greed, immorality, and devious deeds.[20]

Divine reward was not normally considered in Greco-Roman reciprocity relationships,[21] but Paul tries to force the Corinthians to rethink social relationships in the light of Christ. His rejection of personal patronage in Corinth is of a piece with his rejection of other status conventions of Greco-Roman antiquity.[22] For the Corinthians to respond to what Paul says will involve them in seeing God in Christ as their ultimate patron or benefactor and Paul as the agent of that patron.[23] Another way Paul describes this relationship is by stressing that he is the Corinthians' spiritual parent (cf. 12:14f.). In either case, he wants them to see him as their benefactor, not as their client.

18. On literary patronage, see Juvenal *Sat.* 1.52, 5.12-15; Petronius *Sat.* 34, 35, 41, 48; Martial *Epigrams,* 4.49, 10.4, 10. To be involved in such a relationship would involve obligations to speak at dinners, to instruct the patron's children, and to treat the patron with deference at the morning greetings and at other times. Cf. Chow, *Patronage and Power,* p. 73.

19. E. A. Judge, "The Social Identity of the First Christians," *Journal of Religious History* 11 (1980), pp. 201-17, here p. 214. Cf. also Judge, "Cultural Conformity and Innovation in Paul: Some Clues from Contemporary Documents," *TynB* 35 (1984), pp. 3-24, here p. 15. On the character of enmity relationships, see P. Marshall, *Enmity in Corinth: Social Conventions in Paul's Relations with the Corinthians* (Tübingen: Mohr, 1987), pp. 35-69.

20. Cf. Marshall, *Enmity,* pp. 62ff. Cf. Seneca's warning in *De Amicitia* 21.78: "You must be on your guard lest friendships be changed into serious enmities *(gravis inimicitias)* which are the source of disputes, abuse, and invective." Invective came not only from Paul's opponents but also from Corinthians that they had infected. The opponents seem to have convinced some Corinthians that Paul saw them as an inferior *ekklēsia* since he took money from the Philippians but not from them. The major flaw in Marshall's otherwise illuminating study is the assumption that the opponents were already present and at work even before 1 Corinthians was written. This makes little sense of 1 Corinthians 9, where Paul uses his refusal of money as an example to the Corinthians.

21. Peterman, *Giving and Receiving,* p. 104.

22. See pp. 208-12 above. Chow, *Power and Patronage,* p. 170, n. 1, plausibly suggests, drawing on E. A. Judge's work, that Paul avoids friendship language in order to avoid the usual overtones of patronage. Judge, in "St. Paul as Radical Critic of Society," *Interchange* 16 (1974), pp. 191-203, stresses that Paul was not socially conservative as is shown by his rejection of two of the major factors in Greco-Roman society: (1) the importance of status and status indicators and (2) self-cultivation, a Greek ideal fully embraced by the Romans. Judge also stresses that Paul subverts all human patronal ideology by making all subject to one patron: God in Christ.

23. Cf. F. W. Danker, *Benefactor: An Epigraphic Study of a Graeco-Roman and NT Semantic Field* (St. Louis: Clayton, 1982), pp. 56-312, which includes numerous patron inscriptions.

So Paul refused patronage and worked at his trade, not only in Corinth but also in Thessalonica. He did so to remove hindrances to the gospel (1 Cor. 9:12, 18) and so that he could offer it free of charge, not as wisdom for hire like the Sophists and others.[24] In 1 Corinthians 9 he does argue for the *right* to be supported by his Corinthian converts while he is working among them. But he refuses this aid and later says that he will continue to do so (2 Cor. 12:4; cf. 11:9). He does not refuse to accept traveling expenses (1 Cor. 16:6; 2 Cor. 1:16),[25] nor does he always refuse *missionary* support — support of his gospel work when he is away from the group supporting him (cf. Phil. 4:16; 2 Cor. 11:19).[26] Perhaps the Philippians understood, but some Corinthians did not, that the giving and receiving between Paul and his converts had to be on a basis that did not turn him into someone's client. Paul was also not reluctant to accept Christian hospitality, even from a well-to-do Christian and even in Corinth, so long as the wrong sorts of strings were not attached (cf. Rom. 16:23).

Patronage was not just a matter of economic and social power, but also a matter of honor and shame, and it is no accident that chs. 8–9 use the language of honor and shame.[27] Paul believes he should be honored by his converts as their spiritual benefactor. He does not want to come and shame them. The discussion in these chapters is, then, about Paul's authority, but also about his right to be honored and God's right to be shown gratitude. And it is about Paul's right to give advice to the Corinthians and his right to expect them to show reciprocity — in the way he desires and determines for the benefits that they have received through him. The deliberative argument serves the overall forensic agenda of the letter. Paul knew that "benefits" or "gifts" were a vital bond in Greco-Roman society (Seneca *De Ben.* 1.4.1). So these chapters show Paul allowing his converts to bind themselves to him and other Christians, but not in the usual ways.

In 8:7 "this grace" means "this gracious gift," "this benevolence," or perhaps "this gracious act." The Corinthians were proud of their grace gifts *(charismata)*. Now Paul wants them to overflow in another sort of grace gift, the art

---

24. Cf. R. Hock, *The Social Context of Paul's Ministry: Tentmaking and Apostleship* (Philadelphia: Fortress, 1980), pp. 26ff. Marshall, *Enmity,* pp. 174ff., is right in saying, against Hock, that Paul does not use his work as an artisan as the *justification* for refusing Corinthian patronage. His work did not keep him from a giving and receiving relationship with the Macedonians.

25. The verb *propempein* frequently has the meaning of giving material help; cf. L. Michael White, "Social Authority in the House Church Setting and Ephesians 4:1-16," *Restoration Quarterly* 29 (1987), pp. 209-28.

26. Peterman, *Giving and Receiving,* pp. 181f.

27. On honor and shame conventions, cf. S. C. Mott, "The Power of Giving and Receiving: Reciprocity in Hellenistic Benevolence," in *Current Issues in Biblical and Patristic Interpretation,* ed. G. F. Hawthorne (Grand Rapids: Eerdmans, 1974), pp. 60-72. One of the few close analogies in North American culture would be to the honor, shame, and "favor"-oriented behavior of the Mafia, which has complex reciprocity conventions.

of giving.[28] Paul uses the language often used of benefactors to stimulate them to act as such. He speaks of their "eagerness" (vv. 11f.) and of Timothy's (vv. 16f.),[29] and of how the Macedonians "gave themselves" (v. 5), a description often found in the benefaction inscriptions.[30] This description of the Macedonians doing all that they could, even going beyond their means or ability, is also in language common in the inscriptions (cf. *SIG* 569.32f.). Paul says that he is not commanding the Corinthians, but he is using rhetoric to gently twist their arms, saying that this is a matter of testing *their* eagerness and love (v. 8), as the painful letter has tested their genuineness.

Verse **9** may be a creedal fragment. It reminds one of the hymn in Phil. 2:6-11.[31] Paul seems to be talking about Jesus taking on not just the humbling condition of all humanity, but the specific socioeconomic state of poverty, not unlike the Macedonians. But the riches he refers to are spiritual riches. As Furnish notes,[32] the example of Christ functions here in an intriguing way: Paul is not exhorting the Corinthians to become poor like Jesus,[33] but in light of their indebtedness to Christ's lavish gift they should give out of a concern for equity. He suggests that a relationship of giving and receiving would be set up by their gift, so that if and when the time came that the Jerusalem congregation had a surplus, then they could reciprocate by helping the Corinthians. Paul's goal is to bind two very different parts of the *ekklēsia* together, and to provide evidence to the Jerusalem assembly of the legitimacy, value, and compassion of his ministry largely to Gentiles (cf. Rom. 15:25-28).

---

28. On *charis* in v. 7 meaning "the act of giving," cf. G. D. Fee, "*CHARIS in II Corinthians 1.15: Apostolic Parousia and Paul-Corinth Chronology,*" *NTS* 24 (1978), pp. 533-38, here p. 536. In principle such a *charisma* of giving should have been understandable since the relationship between a human being and a god in Greco-Roman religion was perceived to involve reciprocity. The god gave blessings and the human being responded or petitioned with prayers, sacrifices, verbal or written praise (gratitude), and the like. With such a background, the concept of grace must itself have been quite difficult for the Gentile Corinthians to grasp, but the idea of God as a benefactor to whom one was obligated to respond would not be difficult to grasp.

29. On use of this term in benefaction inscriptions, see Danker, *Benefactor,* p. 320. Both *spoudē* and its synonym *prothymia* are frequent in the inscriptions and mean "eagerness, earnestness"; cf. the reference to "spirited" character in the inscription cited above.

30. Cf. Danker, *Benefactor,* p. 322. It is not accidental that the entire word family of which *spoudē* ("zeal, earnestness") is a part appears seven times in chs. 7–8 and only eleven times in all the rest of Paul's letters. Paul is trying hard to convince the Corinthians to complete the collection by showing them that they can thus fulfill their desire to be benefactors, only of other Christians.

31. B. Witherington, *Jesus the Sage: The Pilgrimage of Wisdom* (Minneapolis: Fortress, 1994), ch. 7.

32. V. P. Furnish, *II Corinthians* (Garden City: Doubleday, 1984), p. 417.

33. Rightly Georgi, *Remembering the Poor,* p. 83. The Corinthians are not urged to do as Christ did.

Paul reminds his audience that this good deed has already begun in Corinth; he simply wants them to complete it (vv. **10f.**). He is giving them an opportunity to be his partner in ministry and thus to be benefactors, which apparently was how some wanted to view their relationship with Paul. Paul still does not allow that, but he gives them another avenue. They are to give "from what they have." Paul is not suggesting that they go out and borrow money in order to give. Nor is it a matter of amount. If the enthusiasm is present, then the gift is acceptable.[34] They are to give in proportion to what they have, not in proportion to what they do not have (v. **12**). The aim is not for others to be eased while the Corinthians suffer, but that equity or equality be achieved (vv. **13f.**).[35]

Martin believes that v. **14b** refers to some eschatological vision of a different state of affairs,[36] but this is reading too much into the text. Perhaps Paul was thinking of the Corinthians' debt as Gentiles to their Jewish forebears in the faith (cf. Rom. 15:27). The ideal state of affairs is an equality achieved by free giving and receiving, by a sharing in common, not by all goods becoming public property, publicly administered.[37]

In v. **15** Paul quotes almost verbatim from the Septuagint of Exod. 16:18, part of the story of the manna. Those who had much had none left over; those who had little did not go short. This seems to be Paul's vision of equity — no one ever going short in the Christian community.[38]

In **8:16** Paul uses *charis* in yet another way, for "gratitude," the proper response to God, who is the ultimate benefactor. Titus is eager to come to the

---

34. His advice is remarkably similar to Aristotle's in *Eth. Nic.* 4.1.19: "Liberality should be evaluated on the basis of one's capital. It is not determined by how much is given but on the basis of the donor's disposition, which gives in proportion to capital."

35. Paul is not talking about communism here. He is appealing to the Corinthians to give, not requiring or ordering them to give. And he assumes that they have disposable income so that they will not go in debt while giving and so suffer. He is not envisioning a clearing house for all money. This is a special appeal for a special cause. He does expect that the Corinthians will be concerned about equality. No Christian should want to stand by idly while fellow Christians suffer or starve. On this occasion their surplus is to supply the lack in Jerusalem.

36. R. P. Martin, *2 Corinthians* (Waco: Word, 1986), p. 267.

37. As W. A. Meeks, "The Circle of Reference in Pauline Morality," in *Greeks, Romans, and Christians*, ed. D. L. Balch, E. Ferguson, and W. A. Meeks (Minneapolis: Fortress, 1990), pp. 305-17, here p. 312, notes, *isotēs* in Aristotle (*Eth. Nic.* 7.7.1ff.) means that the socially superior party receives more honor, affection, and goods than the inferior one. Paul has a different vision, in which all believers, being equally indebted to Christ's grace for salvation, are considered equal and not judged on the basis of social rank or ethnic extraction. This equality is to manifest itself by whatever party has a surplus giving to whatever party has a lack.

38. Paul does not urge tithing in this passage, nor is he talking about collections for the hungry in general. Paul's priorities seem to have been that one should do good to all, but especially or with priority given to the household of faith (Gal. 6:10).

Corinthians again (v. 17), perhaps even more eager than Paul. Is Paul being shrewd here, postponing going to Corinth and allowing surrogates to sort things out? Chs. 10–13 show that there are still many problems there.

Paul is sending with Titus two companions (vv. 18 and 22) — one who is praised "in the gospel" (v. 18). Does this mean that this "brother" was praised for his preaching of the gospel, or was he mentioned in the early oral kerygma? It is more likely the former.[39] He is said to be praised "in all the *ekklēsiai*," which may mean in all of Paul's "congregations," but the context suggests a wider reference.

There have been numerous guesses about the identity of these emissaries. I would suggest that one might be Timothy since v. 22 suggests a close connection with Paul ("our brother") and with the Corinthians. The other may be Apollos, in view of the mention of his eloquence in Acts 18:24.[40] Early Church writers identified the one mentioned in v. 18 as Luke, but there was no written Gospel yet in Paul's day, so this is unlikely.

The first-mentioned companion of Titus was to administer the collection (v. 19). We do not know who elected or appointed this man, but since he had been appointed Paul's traveling companion by "congregations" it seems unlikely that his appointment came from the Jerusalem church. More likely he was appointed by the congregations that had made contributions to the collection. He was appointed so that no one would find fault with Paul in the administration of this abundant gift (v. 20). Paul stresses that his own conduct has been totally honorable both in God's sight and human sight (v. 21).[41] Vv. 19-21 show that this section as a whole has as one of its main functions defending Paul's conduct and ministry. Thus while it is deliberative in form, it serves his larger forensic aims.

Titus is called Paul's partner, but for the Corinthians he is a coworker (v. 23). This again suggests that Paul saw the Corinthians as his coworkers, in this case through his surrogate Titus. He refers to the "*apostoloi* of congregations," here drawing on the broader sense of the word: envoys of assemblies, delegates appointed by churches for specific limited tasks and missions.[42] They

---

39. J. E. Morgan-Wynne, "2 Corinthians 8:18f. and the Question of a *Traditions-grundlage* for Acts," *Journal of Theological Studies* 30 (1979), pp. 172f., suggests, following J. Jervell, that the formation of *ekklēsiai* and their continuing existence were regular subjects of preaching. He argues that the early Christians wanted to hear about the progress of the gospel throughout the empire and the activities of the *apostoloi*. This might explain why this person was well known in the *ekklēsiai*.

40. See above, pp. 83-87, on Apollos.

41. Paul is applying Prov. 3:4 from the Septuagint to himself by exchanging the imperative of the Septuagint for an indicative first person plural and by adding "not only"; cf. F. W. Danker, *II Corinthians* (Minneapolis: Augsburg, 1989), p. 132.

42. This may provide a description of missionaries.

are called "the glory of Christ" and also "our brothers." Paul wants the Corinthians to show proof of their love and of his boasting before the watching assemblies of God (v. 24).

Betz and others have sought to argue that *peri men gar* ("for in the first place concerning") in **9:1** signals the beginning of a new letter.[43] He points to the use of the same phrase in Acts 28:22, but that hardly helps his case since there the phrase *concludes* the oral reply of the Jews to Paul, and the sentence in general points *back* to earlier knowledge of "this new sect." It does not introduce a new subject or a new discussion.[44] It is more natural to take *gar* ("for") as linking this verse with what precedes at the conclusion of ch. 8, while *men* anticipates *de* in 9:3.[45] 9:1 thus links what precedes with what follows, pointing in both directions. The sending of the "brothers" described in 8:16ff. is picked up again in 9:3-5.

A Closer Look: Paul and the Collection ────────────────────

Two studies have had a large impact on the discussion of what Paul says about the collection for the Jerusalem Christians, one by D. Georgi and one by K. F. Nickle.[46] The former has been more influential and we will interact primarily with it. The importance of the collection can hardly be overestimated. The subject appears repeatedly in Paul's letters (Galatians 2, 1 Corinthians 16, 2 Corinthians 8–9, and Romans 15). As with so many issues in Pauline studies, much depends on how one views the chronology of Paul's letters. My own view is that Galatians was written shortly *before,* not after, the Jerusalem Council described in Acts 15. The discussion of idol meat and immorality in 1 Corinthians 8–10 reflects the meeting as a past event.[47]

There are various points in the Corinthian letters where Paul tries to convey to the audience their indebtedness to the Jerusalem and Jewish Christians who came to faith before them. 1 Cor. 15:1-10 lays a theological foundation for the sense of indebtedness to which Paul will appeal, especially in 2 Corinthians 8–9. In 1 Corinthians 16, as we have seen,[48] Paul does not turn the collection into a taking up of money during the Christian worship service. Rather, each Christian was to lay aside funds at

---

43. Betz, *2 Corinthians 8 and 9,* p. 90.

44. It is right to distinguish this Greek phrase from *peri de,* a new topic marker. Paul is not introducing a new subject here, but pursuing the same one from a different angle.

45. Cf. A. Plummer, *II Corinthians* (Edinburgh: Clark, 1915), pp. 252f.; Furnish, *II Corinthians,* pp. 425f.; C. K. Barrett, *The Second Epistle to the Corinthians* (New York: Harper and Row, 1973), pp. 232f.

46. D. Georgi, *Remembering the Poor,* which is a translation of his earlier German work with minor updating; K. F. Nickle, *The Collection: A Study in Paul's Strategy* (Naperville: Allenson, 1966).

47. See pp. 186-230 above.

48. See pp. 313-17 above.

home as they were able on the first day of each week until Paul or one of his coworkers could come and collect it.[49] Paul also leaves to the Corinthians the task of choosing emissaries to go with the collection to Jerusalem, bearing letters of recommendation and clarification.

It appears that when Titus delivered the painful letter, he also began the task of gathering the funds, or at least preparing the Corinthians for the final collection of the money. 2 Cor. 9:2 suggests that many in Achaia were eager to contribute and prepared to give, but one cannot tell whether this included the majority in Corinth and those in Cenchreae and elsewhere. Certainly, it must have included a goodly number in Corinth. The question is, then: Did Paul's opponents cause the setting aside of funds for the collection to be interrupted, perhaps by suggesting that Paul was deceiving the Corinthians and planning to use some of the money for his own purposes?[50] When did the opponents arrive in Corinth?

It appears that they were already present by the time the painful letter (2:4, 9) was delivered, if not when it was written. They may even have been present already when Paul made his painful visit (2:1), urging the offending individual to attack Paul. We cannot be sure about this, but since chs. 1–7 and chs. 10–13 both reflect a knowledge of their presence *and their strong effect* on some Corinthians, then this suggests that they had been in Corinth for a while when 2 Corinthians was written. Perhaps when Titus arrived, either they did not make their presence known, biding their time since Titus was not the primary object of their polemics, or they may have made a point of avoiding him.[51] The result was that Titus was somewhat overly optimistic about the condition of things in Corinth. But Paul believed that there were still severe problems. These problems were mainly created by the opponents, not the Corinthians themselves. Paul still has some confidence in the majority of the Corinthians, including their willingness to contribute to the collection, but he knows that they are impressionable, easily influenced by whatever prominent teachers or rhetors are present.

Georgi hypothesizes that Paul alludes in Phil. 2:25 and 4:10-19 to a collection but not yet the Jerusalem collection, and he takes Philippians to be an early letter of Paul arising out of a supposed Ephesian imprisonment.[52] He argues that Epaphroditus

49. As Georgi, *Remembering,* p. 56, says, at least several months are envisioned before Paul will arrive to collect the funds. This was not a project undertaken or to be completed in haste.

50. Georgi, *Remembering,* p. 59 thinks that the opponents did not cause the interruption. His arguments suffer from his partition theory with regard to 2 Corinthians. For instance, he takes chs. 10–13 to be the letter of tears that preceded 2:14–7:4. But chs. 10–13 refer *back* to a visit by Titus and never mention the central concern of the tearful letter, which was the one that offended Paul during the painful visit.

51. For example, they may have gone to Cenchreae when Titus was in Corinth and vice versa.

52. W. Pratscher, "Der Verzicht des Paulus auf finanziellen Unterhalt durch seine Gemeinden. Ein Aspekt seiner Missionsweise," *NTS* 25 (1979), pp. 284-98, is correct in arguing that Paul's policy with the Corinthians in regard to receiving money differs from that with the Philippians in part because of differences between the situations in the two communities (p. 298). But the difference is not that Paul accepted patronage from the Philippians and not from the Corinthians. It is rather that Paul accepted missionary support

arranged a collection and managed to take it to Paul in Ephesus and that later the Philippians gave a small amount to the Jerusalem collection.[53] There are several problems with this analysis. First, there is no hard evidence for an Ephesian imprisonment of Paul. 1 Cor. 15:32 is certainly no evidence to the contrary, and 2 Cor. 1:8f. is weak evidence. In the latter text, Paul speaks of *affliction* in the province of Asia that brought him near death. He does not speak of imprisonment in Ephesus or of any official action by Romans or local officials amounting to a sentence of death.[54] In view of the tribulation catalog in 2 Cor. 11:22ff., even if Paul was in prison in Ephesus, there is no proof that the occasion mentioned in Philippians is the supposed Ephesian imprisonment. Second, Paul refers in Philippians to the reciprocity relationship that he has with the addressees, which provided him with relief funds, but not to the collection for Jerusalem. This silence is telling in view of how many other early Pauline letters refer to the collection and in view of the Macedonian contribution to the collection (2 Cor. 8:1-5). Since we learn nothing from Philippians about the collection, it provides no aid for a proper reading of 2 Corinthians 8–9.

Georgi's arguments that chs. 8–9 must be seen as two different letters are no more convincing than his arguments about Philippians. While he admits the strong likeness of 9:8-14 to 8:13f., he argues that 9:1 must represent a new beginning.[55] This deduction is unnecessary.[56] The phrase that Paul uses in 9:1 is nearly identical to one in 1 Thess. 5:1. In both cases Paul goes on to reiterate some of what he has said earlier. Even if chs. 8 and 9 were two separate letters, there is no reason that Titus could not have carried both of them when he returned to Corinth and no reason that Paul could not have included in the present 2 Corinthians his commendation of Titus, just as in 1 Corinthians 16 and Romans 16 he includes other commendations.[57]

It is possible that in 2 Cor. 9:10-12, as Georgi argues, Paul is alluding to Isa. 55:10 and Hos. 10:12 and to the idea of the eschatological pilgrimage of the Gentiles to Jerusalem.[58] Perhaps this is how Paul envisioned the collection from a theological standpoint. In Rom. 15:23-32 Paul seems to see the collection as an act of worship offered up to God, a religious "liturgy" that prompts thanksgiving.[59] Finally, Georgi is right that "the collection became something of a case study of Paul's overall theological position. It demonstrates that Pauline theology is deeply concerned with the historical realm and must, therefore, be placed in equal distance from Gnostic and Apocalyptic speculation."[60] Acceptance of the collection by the Jerusalem *ekklēsia* meant for Paul public acceptance of his ministry, which in turn meant acceptance of

---

from the Philippians while away from them but had taken no such funds from the Corinthians. To the latter he only gave opportunities to provide traveling expenses.

53. Georgi, *Remembering*, pp. 62-72.

54. On these texts, see pp. 345-50 above.

55. Georgi, *Remembering*, p. 77.

56. See the comments above, pp. 203-7.

57. Pace Georgi, *Remembering*, p. 196, n. 25.

58. Georgi, *Remembering*, pp. 100-102.

59. On the idea of a "liturgy" being a priestly service, cf. the sapiential material, especially Sir. 4:14; 24:10; Wis. Sol. 18:21; and Dan. 7:10.

60. Georgi, *Remembering*, p. 109.

his vision of the *ekklēsia* as Jews and Gentiles united in Christ — as Jews and Gentiles — without the conversion of the latter to Judaism.[61] When the Gentile emissaries came to Jerusalem with these funds, it must have served as a preview to many of the future of the *ekklēsia*.[62]

Paul begins ch. 9 by again using *hagious* as an almost technical term for the Jewish Christians of Jerusalem (cf. 8:4), who are starving. He reminds the Corinthians that this is no new topic for them, and they have the opportunity to play the benefactor (v. 2). He is playing both sides against the middle. He has boasted to the Macedonians of the readiness of those in Achaia, including Corinth, to give even since the year before.[63] He says that their zeal stimulated "the majority" — presumably the majority of Macedonian Christians. He is sending Titus and the two men mentioned in 8:18-22 to Corinth so that his boasting will not turn out to be in vain (v. 3). He thus makes the collection an issue of his honor and the Corinthians' honor and so forges another link between himself and his estranged converts. They will be honored or shamed together before God (cf. 7:3).

The conditional clause in v. 4 (*ean* with the aorist subjunctive) refers to what is a real possibility. Paul might, indeed, show up with a delegation of Macedonians only to find the Corinthians not ready to give, and he will be embarrassed because of what he has said to the Macedonians about the Corinthians. He is sending Titus and the two others to put everything in order before he gets there so that this embarrassment will not happen (v. 5). This passage reminds us how much stock people in the Greco-Roman world placed in honor, in having and saving face, in not being put to shame.[64]

The three brothers are to put in order the "already promised blessing."[65] The Corinthians have been blessed to be a blessing. But Paul wants this to be a matter of them freely bestowing a blessing on "the saints," not a matter of extortion *(pleonexia)*. He understands that the Corinthians are operating on

61. I take this to be also in essence James's view as it is expressed in Acts 15. Cf. B. Witherington, "Not So Idle Thoughts about *Eidolothuton*," *TynB* 44 (1993), pp. 237-54.

62. Cf. Nickle, *Collection*, p. 143. Nickle sees the collection as closely analogous to the Jewish temple tax (cf. p. 99). But Paul stresses that it is a voluntary service, hence he must exhort the Corinthians to undertake it. More plausible is Nickle's argument (p. 72) that the famine relief visit mentioned in Acts 11 served as a prototype of the collection. His suggestion that Paul's opponents in Corinth were Judaizers lacks substance.

63. Which suggests that this letter is being written at least a year after the time that they originally showed their willingness to give, though a whole year is not meant by this phrase. Probably Paul is thinking of the willingness they showed to Titus when he visited with the painful letter and made a start to gather the money.

64. See pp. 154-55 above on these concepts in the Roman world.

65. Here *eulogia* has its basic meaning.

the basis of Greco-Roman reciprocity. Therefore he develops a metaphor that speaks to such a mentality (v. **6**): One who sows sparingly will get a sparing return, but the one who sows "upon blessing" gets a blessed return. V. **7** makes it clear that Paul, though he is applying here a bit of rhetorical pressure by mentioning the Macedonians, who were the basis of comparison in ch. 8,[66] wants the Corinthians to give as they feel led in their own hearts to give, not out of guilt or compulsion. "God loves a glad giver" and has the power to make even a small gift abound to a good end.

Paul says that he hopes that they abound and have an abundance at all times so that they have "independence" or, as it is perhaps better translated here, "enough" (v. **8**). The word is *autarkeia,* an important word in Greco-Roman thinking. The Stoics and Cynics used it of self-sufficiency, a philosophy of life to which Paul did not subscribe, since he believed in the sufficiency of God. But here he refers to material sufficiency. He wants the Corinthians to be free from want, from dominance by the quest for life's necessities. He wishes them abundance, not for their own sakes, but so they may be a blessing to others.[67]

Verse **9** offers a quotation from the Septuagint of Ps. 111:9,[68] where God is the one who gives to the poor and so demonstrates divine righteousness. The Corinthians have a chance to be like God by giving lavishly to those who are in need. The connection here between material giving and righteousness is important. For both Paul and the OT, righteousness is not simply an inner quality of purity or a right heart. It also involves justice and generosity toward others. It is not righteousness unless, as with God, it is demonstrated in deeds. The evidence that one is righteous or just is in one's actions, and in this case in what one does with one's money (cf. Dan. 4:27; Matt. 6:1-4).

God has provided the Corinthians with seed, that is, money, and seed is for sowing, in this case in a poor Jerusalem field (v. **10**).[69] In part the seed was to provide bread for themselves, but God also gave it to them and multiplied it so that they could be a blessing to others and so produce a crop of righteousness. Here "righteousness" is almost synonymous with "generosity."[70] The

66. Here is yet another clear link between the two chapters. The reference to the Macedonians here brings pressure to bear on the Corinthians only if what Paul has said in ch. 8 about comparing them to the Corinthians is known by the hearers of ch. 9.

67. Note the rhetorical flair of v. 8, with alliteration based on the *p* sound, the five variations on *pas,* the double use of *perisseuein,* and use of *charis* rather than *eulogia.* Cf. Georgi, *Remembering,* p. 96.

68. Ps. 112:9 in the English translation.

69. Georgi, *Remembering,* p. 94, rightly points to the sapiential character of this argument, drawing as it does on the wisdom idea that good acts have good moral consequences and do not go unrewarded. Cf. Witherington, *Jesus the Sage,* ch. 1.

70. These chapters suggest that what is most revealing about people is what they do with surplus income, whether they spend it mostly on themselves or look for opportunities to be good stewards, helping others.

point of being made rich is "for all generosity," which creates much thanksgiving to God (v. 11).

Paul sees such giving as a *leitourgia,* that is, a public service (v. 12). While this is the word from which we get "liturgy," in antiquity it was used of civic obligations as well as of religious acts. Paul may be playing on its two senses. Generous giving to the saints is not merely a civic obligation but also an act of worship and thanksgiving to God. The term also suggests that Paul considered the collection, while a duty, not as some sort of tax but as a voluntary public service.

This giving will have two effects. It will supply the shortage of the Jerusalem Christians and will also produce from them a bumper crop of thanksgiving to God. V. 13 is more pointed: By giving the money the Corinthians glorify God and render obedience to their confession of faith in Christ, who gave self-sacrificially. Their giving is a means of Christian witness to the world. In return "the saints" will pray for the Corinthians, give thanks for them, and long for them (v. 14). The ground of all such giving is God's "inexpressible gift" in Christ, which prompts such giving in response (v. 15).

This allusion to the gift of Christ himself leads quite naturally into 10:1. As Barrett says, in ch. 9 Paul speaks of what he hopes will happen in Corinth, but in ch. 10 he responds to what is happening.[71] The shift in tenses is precisely what one would expect since Paul moves from a deliberative mode in ch. 9 to a forensic mode in ch. 10.

---

71. Barrett, *Second Corinthians,* pp. 242f.

Argument V, Division 1: 10:1-18

BRAGGING RIGHTS

The argument section of 2 Corinthians began with a masterful comparison of the ministries of Paul and Moses (ch. 3), and now Paul closes it with an even more extended *synkrisis* comparing his and his opponents' ministries. The earlier comparison prepares for and points forward to the later one, as did the essential statement in Paul's *propositio* (the key thesis to be proved) in 2:17. Paul's ministry is like, only superior to, the glorious ministry of Moses. It is unlike that of those who are "peddlers" of the Word of God. The heart of Paul's defense lies, then, in two comparisons that in the end turn out to be contrasts, especially the one in chs. 10–13.

On any showing, ch. 10 marks a new departure. If chs. 10–13 reflect a slightly later letter, as many argue, the shift in tone is not surprising. According to this argument there have been new developments since Paul wrote chs. 1–9, including the arrival or rise to prominence of the false *apostoloi*. This argument has certain strengths, and it may be correct, but the alternative I am about to offer accounts better both for hints in the text that the false *apostoloi* are already a known and active quantity when Paul wrote chs. 1–9 and for the rhetorical qualities of chs. 10–13.

Because Paul is dealing with a complex and interlocking set of problems, he must follow the procedure known as *insinuatio*,[1] the indirect approach. In this rhetorical move one only alludes to the major issue that is under dispute in the early stages of the rhetorical discourse, reserving the real discussion of the major bone of contention for the end of the discourse, where it is attacked, using much *pathos*, in a more direct fashion. Aristotle is very clear on this point. The closing stages of one's forensic argument must include both praise and defense of one's self *and* blame of one's opponent — precisely what one finds in 2 Corinthians 10–13.[2]

There have been hints along the way in chs. 1–9 of the presence and importance of the false *apostoloi*. First, in ch. 1 Paul refers to an accusation of vacillation or fickleness, of saying that he was coming and then not coming. Who raised this charge? Just the Corinthians? Perhaps not. Second, in 2:17 Paul says that he is not a peddler of God's word "like so many." He does not

---

1. On this see pp. 353ff.
2. Aristotle *Rhet.* 1419b.

429

offer the gospel for financial remuneration. This reference to the opponents is doubly important if we are right that it is the *propositio* of the whole rhetorical discourse. What Paul must prove false is the argument that he is a false *apostolos*. It is implied that he will ultimately have to do so by contrasting himself with those who are peddlers. 2:17 thus signals that eventually a *synkrisis* (comparison) with false *apostoloi* is to be expected in this discourse.

Third, in 3:1 Paul alludes to those who need letters of recommendation, and develops an extended discussion based on this. This likely has one eye on the opponents. Fourth, why is the whole matter of Moses suddenly thrown into the discussion in 3:7? Is it just because of association with the theme of letter vs. spirit or that of tablets of stone vs. human hearts? Probably the somewhat Hellenized Jewish Christian opponents are claiming Moses and the splendor of his covenant in some of their appeals to the Corinthians.[3] Paul counters this with an appeal to the greater glory of the new covenant. He even says that there is a veil over the hearts of the Jews to this day, perhaps because the false ones were urging the Christians to become more like the Jews.

Fifth, in 4:2 Paul says that he has renounced disgraceful or cunning ways and tampering with God's Word. This alludes to what he will say the false *apostoloi* are guilty of in chs. 10–13. Sixth, in 5:12 Paul says he is only commending himself so that the Corinthians will have an answer to those who pride themselves on their human position and not on what is in the heart. Those who pride themselves on appearances are *not* the Corinthians themselves, but those whom the Corinthians must answer, which implies the presence of such people already in Corinth. They are guilty of judging people *kata sarka*, not merely from a human point of view but from a fallen human position.

Seventh, in 6:3 Paul says that he will not put any obstacles in the way of the reconciliation that comes from Christ. When this is read in light of 5:21, it suggests that the Corinthians are in part estranged from Christ because someone has put roadblocks in the way of such reconciliation. Eighth, the *peristasis* list in 6:4ff. prepares for the discussion of weakness and the lists in chs. 10–13. Ch. 11 particularly builds on and to a certain degree recapitulates some of the points in that earlier list. It was considered good rhetorical practice to offer something of a *recapitulatio* near the end of a long discourse, and this Paul does not only in the catalogs but also in various other ways as major themes of chs. 1–9 (support, weakness, boasting, trials, genuineness) are revisited in 10–13.[4]

3. Their Hellenization is shown in their appeal to rhetorical standards of evaluating Paul and his communications.
4. While 6:14–7:1 *could* allude to the opponents, since Paul is willing to call them "servants of Satan" in chs. 10–13, this is not likely in view of the mention of the temple of demons in 6:16.

Finally, in 7:2 Paul stresses that he has neither corrupted nor taken advantage of anyone. Is this not an indirect broadside against those who have? Paul has some faith and confidence that the Corinthians will do the right thing, but he also knows that as long as the false ones are around the Corinthians are in danger. They have repented of being passive and have dealt with the one who hurt Paul on the short visit. They must now repent of listening to the false *apostoloi* and also deal with them.[5]

Most often scholars point to the difference in tone between chs. 10–13 and 1–9 as decisive evidence that these cannot be two parts of the same letter. This fails to take into account the rhetorical conventions that Paul is following. A sudden change in tone and atmosphere was not unusual in a document using forensic rhetoric, especially when the case was difficult and a firm appeal to the stronger emotions *(pathos)* near the end was required to win the audience. A good example of this technique can be seen in Demosthenes's oration *De Corona*. Its parallels with 2 Corinthians have been ably pointed out by Ford and Young and by Danker.[6] Demosthenes justifies his closing histrionics in this speech in rhetorical fashion by asking "But under what circumstances ought the politician and orator be vehement? Of course, when the city is in any way imperiled and when the public is faced by adversaries. Such is the obligation of a noble and patriotic citizen" (278).

It was likewise rhetorically obligatory for Paul to resort to *pathos,* irony, invective, sarcasm, parody, and the like if he really believed that his converts were endangered by adversaries. But he had to do so at the propitious moment in the discourse — at the end, when it would leave the strongest impression. There he deals directly with the opponents. He had already learned from the response to the painful letter that such a strong emotional appeal worked with the Corinthians. Thus, he uses the same technique again to solve an even larger problem.

What has been simmering on a back burner in chs. 1–9 is brought to a roaring boil in chs. 10–13. Up to this point the major focus has been on the Corinthians themselves; now Paul takes on his opponents almost head-on, which partly explains the change in tenor in the letter here.[7] Paul achieves the

5. Thus the argument that the *situation* described in chs. 1–9 differs from that in chs. 10–13 fails.

6. Cf. F. W. Danker, "Paul's Debt to the *De Corona* of Demosthenes: A Study of Rhetorical Techniques in Second Corinthians," in *Persuasive Artistry: Studies in NT Rhetoric in Honor of George A. Kennedy,* ed. D. F. Watson (Sheffield: Sheffield Academic, 1991), pp. 262-80, and the more popular treatment in F. Young and D. F. Ford, *Meaning and Truth in 2 Corinthians* (Grand Rapids: Eerdmans, 1987), pp. 27ff.

7. The goal of this rhetorical piece is to reconcile the Corinthians to Paul and thereby to Christ and God, to restore them to their proper state. The means by which this will be accomplished is by rhetoric and by removing the obstacles or exigencies along the way that prevent reconciliation or restoration: (1) The man who hurt Paul has been dealt with. (2) The problem of some still attending banquets in pagan temples is dealt with in 6:14–7:1.

willingness for his audience to listen to his whole appeal by stressing the good things at the outset of the discourse and saving the major bone of contention until the end. Thus, the somewhat abrupt shift of gears between chs. 9 and 10 simply reflects a new rhetorical stage in the argument, not a new letter.

10:1 is, in many ways, like the appeal in Rom. 12:1. Bjerkelund has pointed out that Paul's *parakaleō* periods are regularly preceded by thanksgivings or doxologies to God, as in Rom. 12:1 (cf. 11:33-36), in 1 Thess. 3:11-13 followed by the *parakaleō* period in 4:1, and here, with 9:12-15 followed by the *parakaleō* period in 10:1. Here is yet another important argument for the unity of 2 Corinthians. Ch. 10 should no more be severed from ch. 9 than Romans 12 should from Romans 11, or 1 Thessalonians 4 from 1 Thessalonians 3.[8] In fact, the tone of ch. 10 is much the same as what has preceded; it is only when Paul gets to the Fool's Discourse at 11:1 that a notable change occurs in tone. Throughout chs. 10–13, however, Paul is attacking the conventions of self-advertisement, for which the Sophists were so noted.

A Closer Look: Paul and Boasting

For many twentieth-century readers of Paul, chs. 10–13 seem not only in tone but also in substance to be antithetical to certain key Christian values such as humility and tolerance. This conclusion comes as a result of not understanding ancient conventions involving matters of honor and shame, boasting and self-promotion, and how Paul in fact *parodies* such practices in this material.

Self-admiration and self-praise were *de rigeur* in Greco-Roman society, especially for those who wanted to raise their social status and social evaluation in the eyes of others. Even more to the point, self-praise was a primary characteristic of popular teachers of the day, both rhetors and some philosophers, as a close reading of Epictetus and Dio Chrysostom makes evident. Dio himself used comparison as a means of self-praise to such an extent that he was accused of being a boaster and flatterer, to

---

(3) The problem of the Corinthians wanting to be benefactors is dealt with in chs. 8–9. (4) The problem of the false apostles is dealt with especially in chs. 10–13. (5) And there is the problem that the Corinthians want to be in ministry: Throughout the letter, Paul stresses that they are his coworkers, helping to promote the gospel. Indeed, they are his letter of recommendation to the world in Corinth (3:2).

8. Cf. the more detailed arguments in C. J. Bjerkelund, *Parakalô. Form, Funktion und Sinn der Parakalô-Sätze in der paulinischen Briefen* (Oslo: Universitetsforlaget, 1967), pp. 149-55. He also rightly notes the parallels in general between 1 Thessalonians 1–3 and 2 Corinthians 1–7, including the use of digression. Paul thus regularly concludes one argument with a thanksgiving or benediction or both and begins another with a *parakaleō* clause, especially when he has come to his final appeal or exhortation. 2 Corinthians 10 differs from some examples because it functions as part of Paul's defense of his authority.

which he replied: "My purpose in mentioning such matters was neither to elate you nor to place myself beside those who habitually sing such strains, whether orators or poets. They are clever persons, mighty Sophists, wonder-workers, but I am quite ordinary and prosaic in my utterance, though not ordinary in my theme" (32.39). This approach to the matter of self-praise is remarkably similar to Paul's at certain points, especially in its ironic tone.[9]

Cicero (cf. Plutarch's *On Inoffensive Self-Praise*)[10] provides rules on how to win the goodwill of an audience when one is under attack by an opponent who has at least in part swayed the audience (*De. inv.* 1.16.22):

> We shall win goodwill for ourselves if we refer to our own acts and services without arrogance, if we weaken the effect of charges that have been brought or of some suspicion of less honorable dealing that has been cast on us, if we dilate on the misfortunes that have come to us or the difficulties that we still face, and if we use prayers and entreaties with a humble and submissive spirit.

As J. P. Sampley has shown, Paul follows quite closely the advice given here when he engages in inoffensive self-praise in 2 Corinthians 10–13.[11]

In ch. 10 Paul is attacking those who use Sophistic rhetoric and its methods of evaluating speeches and people, and he is using rhetoric to do so. The opponents had placed Paul in a difficult position. As E. A. Judge put it, Paul "found himself a reluctant and unwelcomed competitor in the field of professional sophistry and . . . he promoted a deliberate collision with its standards of value."[12] One should not be fooled into thinking that Paul was no rhetor because he was not a professional declaimer, one highly skilled in the oral performance of rhetoric, or because he rejected a Sophistic approach to rhetoric.[13] Dio Chrysostom also had to reckon with application of the term *idiōtēs* to himself in his forty-second oration, but there as here the context is loaded with irony, saying one thing and meaning the opposite.[14] The rhetorical skill evident in the deliberately ironic *synkrisis* (comparison) Paul undertakes here between himself and his opponents shows that while he may have rated low in terms of physical presence and oral performance of rhetoric, he was highly skilled in writing rhetorical pieces, a fact even his detractors recognized (10:10).[15]

9. Dio also provides here a good example of false modesty.

10. See above, pp. 337-39.

11. J. P. Sampley, "Paul, His Opponents in 2 Corinthians 10–13, and the Rhetorical Handbooks," in *The Social World of Formative Christianity and Judaism*, ed. J. Neusner, et al. (Philadelphia: Fortress, 1988), pp. 162-77.

12. Judge, "Paul's Boasting in Relation to Contemporary Professional Practice," *Australian Biblical Review* 16 (1968), pp. 37-48, here p. 47.

13. Even Quintilian, the master teacher of rhetoric, was no declaimer.

14. Like the professional politician who begins a well-rehearsed speech with "Unaccustomed as I am to public speaking," Paul knows well how to use irony effectively. Cf. G. Holland, "Speaking Like a Fool: Irony and Theology in 2 Corinthians 10–13," a paper given at a 1992 conference on rhetoric at Heidelberg. The irony is most obvious in the *Narrenrede* in 11:1–12:10.

15. C. Forbes, "Comparison, Self-Praise and Irony: Paul's Boasting and the Conventions of Hellenistic Rhetoric," *NTS* 32 (1986), pp. 1-30, here pp. 7ff., is right in saying that

The key to grasping the real character of this argument is recognizing Paul's anti-Sophistic approach to self-praise. This has been ably demonstrated by Winter.[16] From 10:10; 11:6; and 12:14-18 we may piece together the essential criticism of Paul by the opponents and those they had swayed among the Corinthians. They claim

> that Paul is no expert in *sophia* (wisdom), as is shown by his personal appearance and his weak and uncouth delivery (his *hypokrisis*),
>
> that he is inconsistent, one way in his letters and the opposite when present in Corinth, and
>
> that he is underhanded in his financial dealings: His refusal of support is proof positive that he is no rhetor and no *apostolos*.[17]

The first and second of these criticisms can be compared with the complaint in Alcidamas *On the Sophists* 16a-b, written against rhetors who write well but who when compelled to speak *extempore* "in every respect . . . make an unfavorable impression and are no different from the voiceless."[18]

There was a heavy stress on declamation in the teaching of rhetoric in the first century A.D. Paul was being evaluated by the criteria Sophists used to judge rhetoric.

---

synkrisis was taught in the first century A.D. by the rhetorician at the upper level of Greco-Roman education, not by the grammarian who taught the beginning exercises. Not only the masterful comparison in 2 Corinthians 10–13, but also the comparison that begins the argument section of this letter in ch. 3 testifies to the correctness of Forbes's conclusion that Paul's "education reached at least beyond the level of the *grammatici*, and into the rhetorical school. This of itself bespeaks a certain social standing, as does the fact that Paul found his labor as an artisan a matter for shame and paradoxical pride."

16. B. W. Winter, *Are Philo and Paul among the Sophists? A Hellenistic Jewish and a Christian Response to a First Century Movement* (dissertation, MacQuarrie University, 1988), ch. 10.

17. Cf. the charge described in Aristides *Or.* 33.4: "They say that I do wrong because I do not declaim frequently." Paul uses the declamatory technique of *amplificatio* or an amplified tone intended to arouse anger or sympathy (cf. Quintilian *Inst. Or.* 3.13.23), but does so in a letter, not in a public declamation. Cf. S. F. Bonner, *Roman Declamation in the Late Republic and Early Empire* (Liverpool: University of Liverpool, 1949), pp. 20ff. Here is another piece of evidence that Paul must have carefully chosen as his emissary to Corinth one who could carry out the rhetorical delivery of this piece. In this case it was likely Titus, whom we learn in Gal. 2:4 was Greek. It is probably not accidental that Paul later took Titus with him to Jerusalem, probably as an example of an exemplary Gentile convert, nor that he entrusts several of his Corinthian letters to him to be delivered (in both senses of that term). I suspect that Titus was rhetorically adept, since if 2 Corinthians 10–13 was to have its proper effect, it would need to be delivered in an ironic tone. This is rhetoric that requires the volume turned up and the tone set just right.

18. This was a critique of those who used forensic rhetoric; cf. Winter, *Are Philo and Paul*, p. 215. Paul has already provided his essential answer to the third of these criticisms in chs. 8–9. Here is another good reason why chs. 8–9 and 10–13 need to be parts of one letter. The criticism of Paul's handling of money, though it is raised again in chs. 10–13, is not adequately answered there, which in view of its crucial nature means that Paul assumes that he has already answered it elsewhere in the same discourse.

Quintilian himself, who does not think declamation should be seen as the essence of rhetoric, nonetheless says that good delivery "is hampered by incurable impediments of speech. . . . Physical uncouthness may be such that no art can remedy it, while a weak voice is incompatible with first-rate excellence in delivery" (*Inst. Or.* 11.3.12f.). Could this explain why on some occasions Paul sends a coworker to Corinth for him instead of going in person? He knew his audience's taste for good extemporaneous speech-making and perhaps sent someone more adept in oral delivery in his place.[19] It is worth pondering, however, whether we should take 11:6 as ironic, as hypothetical, or as a frank admission of a liability. In view of 10:1 and other hints, I think that we should assume that Paul is admitting he is not a professional declaimer and that he has some obvious (physical?) weaknesses that count against the impression he conveys in person, if one judges by Sophistic rather than godly standards.

We have already discussed the conventions in regard to inoffensive boasting as seen in Cicero's words (see above, pp. 433-34). Paul is attempting to follow this convention so that his audience will understand that he was not boasting beyond limits, indeed that he is boasting tongue-in-cheek. He follows the basic rule that he will boast only of what God has done in and through him, and not of his own personal accomplishments. When boasting was used in the midst of a forensic comparison, it was often accompanied by invective against the opponent, since the goal was to win one's case. Hermogenes says that comparison can be a form of invective when in fact it amounts to a contrast (*Progymnasta* 11-15), and Quintilian agrees (*Inst. Or.* 2.4.21: "which of two characters is better or worse"). In such cases, comparison

> is not only the "means of amplifying misdeeds" and "good deeds" but also involves the encomiastic topics of a man's city, race, upbringing, pursuits, affairs, external relations, and the manner of death. In addition physical qualities such as beauty, stature, agility, and might were appropriate topics. . . . Actions chosen are the finest and most enduring, done freely and without compulsion. They should be rare deeds achieved by strivings, especially done beyond the normal age for active life.[20]

The relevance of this data, especially for discussion of the Fool's Discourse, should be apparent. Paul is responding there to stock themes often used in invective against an opponent, particularly when the subject of comparison focused on rhetorical matters. "The conventional themes of ridicule are . . . social background, immorality, physical appearance, religious and philosophical belief, speech, avarice, personal activities."[21] All of these come into play in chs. 10–13, and Paul responds with invective of his own.[22]

---

19. Cf. Winter, *Are Philo and Paul*, p. 224. On the crucial importance of presence, including appearance, in the evaluation of a rhetor, cf. Epictetus *Diss.* 3.1.41.

20. P. Marshall, *Enmity in Corinth: Social Conventions in Paul's Relations with the Corinthians* (Tübingen: Mohr, 1987), p. 54.

21. *Ibid.,* p. 62.

22. For this reason it becomes difficult to judge how much of Paul's criticisms of his opponents should be taken as literal fact and how much is meant for rhetorical effect. Probably the dilemma over whether Paul could call the opponents both "false apostles"

The Fool's Discourse is better evaluated as a response to these socio-rhetorical conventions than in light of the Socratic tradition, as Betz has posited.[23] Paul is responding in kind[24] to his opponents' boasting like fools, though he does so in anti-Sophistic fashion, rejecting the sort of public display seen in the Sophists and in the inscriptions to and about them. When Paul speaks as a fool, he does not parody human wisdom and follow the Socratic tradition in doing so. Rather, he parodies Sophistic eloquence and rhetorical self-praise.[25] His ethic of humility or self-humbling modeled on Christ stands at odds with the sort of classical ideas embodied in Socrates and his teaching. Also against Betz one must point out that the issue here is not just *schēma* or personal appearance, but the rhetorical issue of *hypokrisis* or presence, which entails a good deal more, including rhetorical delivery.[26] Finally, the evidence that the opponents presented themselves as *theoi andres* is weak, precisely because the evidence of their being an idea of such a figure in the first century A.D. is weak.[27]

Paul *is* at various points indebted to the Greek philosophical traditions, but he draws from them selectively and in eclectic fashion.[28] Something similar may be said of his use of rhetoric, though he is more careful in that case to follow the overarching and basic conventions. Nevertheless, Sampley is right to remind us that

> Paul is no prisoner of the rhetorical conventions and practices of his time. He uses them when he thinks they may be of advantage to him in advancing the

---

(11:13) and "super apostles" (11:5) and speak of comparing himself to them can be solved when one takes into account the invective, irony, and rhetorical character of the comparison. See below, pp. 442-45.

23. H. D. Betz, *Der Apostel Paulus und die sokratische Tradition. Eine exegetische Untersuchung zu seiner Apologie 2 Korinther 10–13* (Tübingen: Mohr, 1972). See the criticisms of Betz by E. A. Judge, "St. Paul and Socrates," *Interchange* 13 (1973), pp. 106-16; Forbes, "Comparison, Self-Praise," pp. 1ff.; J. T. Fitzgerald, "Paul, the Ancient Epistolary Theorists, and 2 Corinthians 10–13," in *Greeks, Romans, and Christians*, ed. D. L. Balch, E. Ferguson, and W. A. Meeks (Minneapolis: Fortress, 1990), pp. 190-200, here pp. 197f. Fitzgerald rightly argues that Paul is offering an *apologia,* and that Betz's attempt to match it up with a specifically Socratic *apologia* is too narrow.

24. Forbes, "Comparison," p. 1.

25. Rightly Judge, "St. Paul and Socrates," p. 114. Paul does share with Socrates an anti-Sophistic bias, rightly noted by Betz, and like him he also responds using irony, but the irony Paul uses is of a different and more rhetorical sort (it is neither Socratic nor simply Cynic or Stoic). It is also christologically shaped, which, of course, was not the case with Socrates.

26. Rightly Winter, *Are Philo and Paul,* p. 222. Betz overlooks Epictetus's *Peri kallopismou,* where the issue of a person's overall "presence" is the central issue, not just his *schēma.*

27. This counts against the arguments of both Betz and Georgi, *The Opponents of Paul in Second Corinthians* (Philadelphia: Fortress, 1986), though on other points Georgi is right, namely that the opponents are indebted to both the Jewish Wisdom tradition and the Greco-Roman rhetorical tradition.

28. So rightly Judge, "St. Paul and Socrates," p. 109: Paul "picks up many established terms and notions that as words belong to the language of the philosophical schools or other elements of Greek cultural tradition."

gospel and in seeking the Corinthians' "improvement," but he does not employ them in a rote or mechanical or simply self-serving fashion. . . . In 2 Corinthians 10–13 we encounter not gospel as an occasion for rhetoric but rhetoric in service of the gospel.[29]

Christ is categorized in v. 1 as "meek and kind." It is unclear whether Paul is thinking of the setting aside of riches in the act of incarnation (8:9) or of the character of Jesus during his ministry. Perhaps it is the latter, for Paul implies that his own meekness in the presence of the Corinthians has been modeled on the way Christ acted.[30] In antiquity "humility" was not seen as a virtue. Indeed, the word *tapeinos*, "humble," could easily be mean "abject," "abased," or "servile." It may be that Paul is taking words from his opponents and using them in different senses.[31] They were saying that Paul came to Corinth looking like a ragged Cynic, not like a professional orator or Sophist.[32] Worse still, he acted in a servile fashion while present but boldly while absent. They were saying that he was weak in personal appearance, with no rhetorical sophistication in his oral presentation, but rhetorically weighty and strong in his letters (v. 10).[33]

Throughout this whole section Paul is answering his opponents[34] but addressing the answer to the Corinthians because he cares about them and does not want them to be swayed by such slander. The rhetorical function of this material is to build up the Corinthians' estimate of themselves and of Paul's ministry.[35] He is not interested in debating for debating's sake. Therefore, in v. 2 he accuses the opponents of living in a worldly way and evaluating

29. Sampley, "Paul, His Opponents," pp. 174f.

30. But cf. Philippians 2 and Holland, "Speaking like a Fool," p. 5.

31. On this word and Paul's deliberate commitment to portray himself as an enslaved leader or sage, see pp. 204-6 above.

32. Paul was like a Cynic in his *parrēsia* or boldness of speech, but unlike them he was neither a beggar nor abusive of those in power. For a helpful analysis of the Cynics, see R. MacMullen, *Enemies of the Roman Order: Treason, Unrest, and Alienation in the Empire* (Cambridge: Harvard University, 1966), pp. 59ff.

33. On the crucial nature of "expression" and teaching regarding it, see J. Martin, *Antike Rhetorik* (Munich: Beck, 1974), p. 259; on the use of *abusio* on the audience, see pp. 262ff. G. A. Kennedy, *NT Interpretation through Rhetorical Criticism* (Chapel Hill: University of North Carolina, 1984), p. 94, stresses that the Corinthians saw an inconsistency in Paul's testifying humbly and intuitively in person, but, when his hackles were raised, attacking in letters, using all the weapons of dialectic and rhetoric.

34. Cf. F. Lang, *Die Briefe an die Korinther* (Göttingen: Vandenhoeck, 1986), p. 331, who stresses that the complaint about Paul in letter and in person must originate from someone in the group of opponents, though he wrongly dismisses the importance of the allusion to Paul's rhetoric.

35. F. W. Danker, *II Corinthians* (Minneapolis: Augsburg, 1989), pp. 148ff.

things not merely from a purely human point of view, but according to a sinful inclination. "Flesh" *(sarx)* is, then, not a neutral term here but refers to thinking that is absolutely at odds with a godly way of evaluating things.[36] This harkens back to what Paul said in 5:16ff. about the way in which he had previously evaluated Christ. Here he builds on that idea.

Paul is basically defending his ministry, but his ministry is bound up with his person. The attacks from the opponents are on his person and on his ministry, and so in chs. 10–13 he must answer both kinds of charges.[37] We shall see that Paul is willing to go to rhetorical extremes, even to the point of playing the fool, to wake up the Corinthians to the truth.

It is clear by v. 3 that he is angry and is ready to go to war, but his weapons for the campaign are not "fleshly."[38] Rather they have divine power and are able to demolish high and lofty arguments and sophistries (v. 4). It may be, as Martin suggests, that Paul is saying that the opponents have been building up a wall between himself and his converts and that he must now demolish it.[39] This fits with the idea that this letter's function is to remove obstacles to reconciliation between Paul and his people, and so between the Corinthians and the truth of God. Paul says bluntly that the rhetoric his opponents have been using against him sets itself up against knowledge of God (v. 5), and so Paul must reclaim his converts. He must recapture all their "minds" (or "thoughts"?) for Christ.

Paul has deliberately portrayed himself here as the sage described in Eccl. 9:14-16. He is the poor sage who must deliver his besieged converts from the lofty walls the opponents have built against them, and yet his wisdom is being despised. This OT passage prepares us for the tribulation catalogs in ch. 11, where Paul will portray himself as a suffering sage with a *res gestae* that even Caesar could not match.[40]

---

36. On *sarx* in Paul's letters, see above, pp. 158-59. When Paul wants to talk about something from a merely human point of view he uses *kata anthropon,* not *kata sarx.* Cf. 1 Cor. 9:8; 15:32; C. H. Cosgrove, "Arguing like a Mere Human Being: Galatians 3:15-18 in Rhetorical Perspective," *NTS* 34 (1988), pp. 536-49, here pp. 542f. Cosgrove notes that the expression *kata anthropon legō* is not found in the Greek rhetors, nor is the Latin phrase *argumentum ad hominem* documented in the first century A.D., not even in Cicero or Quintilian.

37. As D. Marguerat, "2 Corinthiens 10–13. Paul et l'expérience de Dieu," *ETR* 63 (1988), pp. 497-519, suggests, one of the goals of this entire section must be to argue that ministry is not to be evaluated purely, if at all, on the basis of the extraordinary spiritual experiences that a person claims to have had.

38. Again, "sinful," not merely "mortal."

39. R. P. Martin, *2 Corinthians* (Waco: Word, 1986), p. 306.

40. On Paul's self-presentation as a sage in the Corinthian correspondence, cf. B. Witherington, *Jesus the Sage: The Pilgrimage of Wisdom* (Minneapolis: Fortress, 1994), ch. 7; J. T. Fitzgerald, *Cracks in an Earthen Vessel: An Examination of the Catalogue of*

In v. **6** Paul says that he is ready to punish the offenders — the disobe-dient — when the obedient have fulfilled or completed their obedience. This distinguishes at least two groups in Corinth. But who are the disobedient — the false *apostoloi* or, perhaps more likely, those among the Corinthians who have been swayed by them? The obedient would then be those who have not been swayed. Paul exhorts the latter to see that right under their noses things are going wrong.[41] V. **7** strongly suggests that the opponents and probably even those Corinthians swayed by them were questioning Paul's very Christian character and faith.[42]

Paul says that he is also able to boast of the power God has given him, but it was given to build up the Corinthians, not tear them down (v. **8**).[43] The implication is that whatever the opponents were doing was having just that effect, that of tearing down the Corinthians. Paul does not want to be put to shame because of the way the Corinthians act. The purpose of the painful letter and indeed this letter was not to frighten the Corinthians out of their wits, but to sober them up and make them aware of their danger (v. **9**). In v. **11** Paul says that he is quite capable of being strong rather than meek and kind in person. Those who are criticizing him should consider their charges against him care-fully. He would rather not come to them like a destroying angel.

Beginning in v. **12** Paul speaks of comparisons and fields of service.[44] The metaphor of invading another's field clearly implies that Paul is now talking about outside offenders who have come into his Corinthian field from elsewhere and have messed things up. He accuses them of measuring them-

---

Hardships in the Corinthian Correspondence (Atlanta: Scholars, 1988), pp. 47ff. Another possibility is that Paul uses military imagery here to reflect Cynic-Stoic passages where the sage uses reason to fortify himself or demolish the sloppy reasonings of others. S. K. Stowers, "Paul on the Use and Abuse of Reason," in *Greeks, Romans, and Christians,* pp. 253-86, here pp. 266f., suggests that Paul portrays himself as the rigoristic Cynic and his opponents as Stoics here. I would suggest that the biblical sage imagery combined with the use of such imagery in rhetorical discussion better fits Paul's meaning and implications here.

41. Here is yet another piece of evidence of the factionalism in Corinth that was still extant when Paul wrote 2 Corinthians.

42. Paul never uses *Christianos* of his or other Christians' identity. His term — "of Christ" — stresses the source of this identity.

43. One of the rhetorical functions of this chapter is to prepare the audience for the attack that follows in the Fool's Discourse. It does so by establishing that Paul has bragging rights among and to the Corinthians, by warning that he is prepared to go to war, and by showing that he will take a deliberately anti-Sophistic approach.

44. Holland, "Speaking like a Fool," pp. 8-9, has misread the force of this verse. Paul is not ruling out comparison with the opponents, as chs. 11–12 will make clear. He is being sarcastic: "Naturally, I wouldn't *think* of comparing myself to them" means that there is no real comparison since they are false *apostoloi.* Therefore, his necessary *synkrisis* must be by way of contrast.

selves by themselves and not by God's divine standard. A *kanōn* was a measuring rod, rule, or authoritative standard by which something could be measured,[45] but here it seems to be a measured field, a jurisdiction.[46] Paul's criticism here then will be not just that the opponents are measuring themselves by their own standards, but that they are trespassing in someone else's measured field, namely his, since it was he who converted the Corinthians. Paul was sensitive about not trespassing on other people's turf, and he is equally sensitive when others are trespassing on his.[47]

Continuing with the metaphor of measuring in v. 13, Paul speaks of not boasting beyond measure or limits. He has been apportioned a field of service by God, and that field extends to the Corinthians. To boast about this is not to overstep bounds or overreach himself (v.14a). V. 14b makes it clear that Paul sees himself as the first to have brought the gospel to Corinth. Thus he does not boast in what someone else has done. His hope is to make his own converts grow in the faith (v. 15).

Verse 16 shows that Paul has a larger goal as well: He wants to build up the Corinthians' faith so that he can go on beyond them, perhaps using them as a home base to preach in another field of service, though not where a claim has already laid and work has already begun. Paul saw it as his job to pioneer mission work in new areas. Paul then says that we should only boast in the Lord and the Lord's work, not in someone else's or our own apart from the Lord (v. 17), an allusion to Jer. 9:24. This reference will remind the Corinthians of the similar quotation in 1 Cor. 1:31. There the subject was the Corinthians' own boasting, but here the boasting of Paul's opponents is at issue. It is not the one who commends himself that is approved but rather the one that God approves (v. 18). Paul implies that his opponents are not so approved.[48]

---

45. Hence its later use of the collection of biblical books — the "canon."

46. E. A. Judge, in *New Docs. 1*, pp. 36-45 has provided evidence from the edict of Sotidius during the reign of Tiberius that *kanōn* could connote a measured area or a limited domain of service. It is used of the system of liturgical services, and 1 Clem. 1:3; 14:1 confirms that it could have the meaning "sphere of action or influence," "province," "limits." The translation "jurisdiction" best conveys both the idea of geographical limits and the idea of an area of service. If someone else intrudes on another's *kanōn*, they can be said to be out of bounds.

47. Cf. P. Bowers, "Paul and Religious Propaganda," *NovT* 22 (1980), pp. 316-23, here p. 317:

> It appears that for him mission had a distinctly spatial dimension, that it implied a sense of vocation deliberately to extend the gospel land by land, so that eventually he could survey his achievement in geographical terms, could pronounce his assignment through a certain range of territories completed, and could announce intentions to travel within the same vocation to new lands further on in the same direction (Rm. xv.17-24).

48. Cf. Danker's translation in *II Corinthians*, p. 160.

Thus in ch. 10 Paul has established his "bragging" rights, and the appropriate limits within which he can and will boast as a follower and agent of Christ who follows the injunction of Jer. 9:22-24. Christ, not Demosthenes or Isocrates or Cicero, is Paul's model for wise and persuasive behavior. Though a sage, he will follow Jeremiah's warning and will therefore boast in his foolishness, weakness, and poverty — all of which set him at odds with the way the Corinthians want their leaders to be and to boast.[49] He even insists on using the more offensive term "boasting" *(kauchēsis)* and its cognates rather than the usual language of self-praise used by Plutarch and others.[50] It is a mistake to detect just a psychological flavor to Paul's use of this language. For Paul the issue is fundamentally theological. In whom does one place one's trust and confidence? In whom may one properly boast?[51] As his quotation of Jeremiah shows, Paul plans to keep these questions steadily in view. It remains for him to execute his boast in the Fool's Discourse in a proper fashion.

49. C. K. Barrett, "Boasting *(kauchasthai ktl.)* in the Pauline Epistles," in *L'apôtre Paul. Personalité, style et conception du ministère* (Leuven: Leuven University, 1986), pp. 363-68, here pp. 364f.

50. Barrett, "Boasting," p. 363. The vast majority of Paul's uses of *kauchasthai* and its cognates are in 1 and 2 Corinthians — thirty-nine in 1 Corinthians and fifty-five in 2 Corinthians — with an especially high concentration of them in 2 Cor. 10–13. Because of the change in rhetorical tone between chs. 1–9 and chs. 10–13, there is also a shift in the connotation of these words. They are used mainly in a positive sense of proper pride and are not self-referential in chs. 1–9 (e.g., 1:12; 7:4-14), but are used with a pejorative and negative coloration in chs. 10–13, reflecting the tone of this part of the discourse in general. This is no sign of a separate letter, for we find both usages in 1 Corinthians, where there is only one letter (cf. 1:31 and 5:6).

51. Rightly Barrett, "Boasting," pp. 367f.

Argument V, Division 2: 11:1–12:10

FOOLISH THOUGHTS

The material in ch. 11 should be grouped with at least the first ten verses of ch. 12. Scholars debate the actual extent of the *Narrenrede* or "Fool's Discourse";[1] some say it begins at 11:1, some at 11:10, some at 11:21b. Here perhaps more than anywhere else in this letter we see Paul's rhetorical skills, including the use of *peristaseis,* rhetorical questions, irony, and invective. 11:21b-29 especially manifests a carefully crafted shape.[2]

Paul is at odds with his opponents not so much because they are offering "another gospel" (11:4) but because they do not accept his vision of ministry, that is, its cruciform, Christlike, and servant shape.[3] He deliberately lists his trials, troubles, and weaknesses to show what proper ministry is. He is a suffering sage. He has been in danger from "false brothers" (11:26), which may mean that his very life has been endangered by opponents who claimed to be Christians.[4] If so, the invective here is more than just for rhetorical effect. It may have been warranted and may testify to the seriousness of the opposition to Paul *among Christians.*[5]

From a rhetorical point of view, perhaps the most important feature of

---

1. For a detailed analysis of this material from the viewpoint of modern style criticism, cf. J. Zmijewski, *Der Stil der paulinischen Narrenrede* (Cologne and Bonn: Hanstein, 1978). Zmijewski agrees that 11:1–12:10 should be seen as a unit, with a subunit beginning at 11:21b, where Paul self-consciously takes up the mantle of the "fool."

2. See the chart in R. P. Martin, *2 Corinthians* (Waco: Word, 1986), p. 370.

3. Had theology been the main source of differences and problems, Paul would have been more than capable of mounting a theological comparison, but basically he does not do so here, unlike in Galatians 3–4. The endless studies trying to discover the "theology" that Paul opposes here are bound to be self-defeating.

4. Barrett suggested this in a lecture entitled "Paul the Controversialist" given at Ashland Theological Seminary. Since we probably should not lump all of Paul's opponents into one group (see above, pp. 343-50), we cannot be absolutely sure that those opposing Paul in Corinth had pursued such extreme means of getting Paul out of the way.

5. As we suggested at the outset of the discussion of 2 Corinthians, the opponents *in Corinth* were not Judaizers but Hellenized Jews enamored with rhetoric and other forms of *sophia,* but apparently also with the more pneumatic sort of experiences such as visions or miracles. See D. Kee, "Who Were the 'Super-Apostles' of 2 Corinthians 10–13," *Restoration Quarterly* 23 (1980), pp. 65-76.

this passage is its irony.[6] The terms *eirōneia* and *eirōn* often had more precise meanings in the Greco-Roman world than the derived words *irony* and *ironic* do in English. While *eirōneia* was saying one thing and meaning the opposite (cf. *Rhetorica ad Alexandrum* 1434a, 1441b23; Quintilian *Inst. Or.* 6.1.15), the *eiron* was mainly a self-deprecator, one who pretended to be less than he or she was.[7] Quintilian says that using irony or forms of *dissimulatio* is "the most effective of all means of stealing into people's minds and a very attractive device as long as we adopt a conversational rather than controversial tone" (*Inst. Or.* 9.1.29), which is certainly what Paul does here (vv. 7ff.).[8]

Irony was especially appropriate in contexts of invective and forensic oratory, hence its omnipresence in this Pauline discourse.[9] Since this is written irony, it must be conveyed by its content, not just by delivery or the *ēthos* of the speaker (*Inst. Or.* 8.6.54).[10] Quintilian says that there are even cases when a person's whole life is colored by irony, "as was the case with Socrates, who was called an ironist because he assumed the role of an ignorant man lost in wonder at the wisdom of others" (*Inst. Or.* 9.2.46).[11] Paul also sees his life as characterized by irony, but he is a suffering sage, not a declaimer, hence the catalogs of his apostolic experiences and the disclaimer about his oral rhetoric. A. B. Spencer suggests that one should be careful not to characterize Paul's

6. On Paul's use here of anti-Sophistic rhetoric to oppose the opponent's rhetoric, see W. Magass, "Theophrast und Paulus," *Kairos* 26 (1984), pp. 154-65, here p. 161.

7. Cf. C. Forbes, "Comparison, Self-Praise and Irony: Paul's Boasting and the Conventions of Hellenistic Rhetoric," *NTS* 32 (1986), pp. 1-30, here p. 10.

8. This is why some have seen the diatribe form in this material. Cf. T. Schmeller, *Paulus und die Diatribe* (Münster: Aschendorff, 1981), pp. 406ff. Quintilian actually seems to prefer open boasting to "that perverted form of self-praise that makes a millionaire say he is poor, a famous man describe himself as obscure, the powerful pose as weak, and the eloquent as unskilled and even inarticulate. But the most ostentatious kind of boasting takes the form of actual self-derision" (*Inst. Or.* 8.6.57-59).

9. Forbes, "Comparison, Self-Praise," p. 12.

10. Cf. J. A. Crafton, *The Agency of the Apostle: A Dramatistic Analysis of Paul's Responses to Conflict in 2 Corinthians* (Sheffield: Sheffield Academic Press, 1991), p. 38: "Rhetorical discourse is effective because it also evokes appropiate emotions, resonates with communal beliefs and values, indeed it integrates the various elements of human personality and experience into a single transaction." Paul's problem is that he does not want to resonate with the Corinthians' values and views about leaders. He wants rather to transform them, hence the resort to irony and parody.

11. In my critique of Betz (pp. 432-36 above), I do not deny that there are parallels between Paul in this passage and Socrates. It is just that the differences are more salient and important. G. A. Kennedy, *The Art of Rhetoric in the Roman World 300 B.C. to A.D. 300* (Princeton: Princeton University, 1972), p. 558, reminds us that "in the second sophistic the Socratic philosopher has apparently disappeared and we are left with a philosopher who uses oratory to expound his theories much like the older sophist, and a pure sophist who has no particular theories, but is interested in declamation." The second sophistic was already in its initial stages in A.D. 50.

tone here as sarcastic, but rather sardonic, for it is not sneering, caustic, or taunting but full of *pathos* over the apparent inconsistencies of his life.[12]

He warns his audience from the outset that what follows is a little foolishness (11:1), but he does not assume the full mantle of the "fool" until 11:21b.[13] There the irony becomes especially thick: He boasts in his sufferings and weaknesses, ironically using the form of the Emperor Augustus's *res gestae* to draw an analogy between his career and that most famous of leaders in the Roman Empire. Then he relates what happened to him in Damascus in a fashion that likely conjured up images in Roman Corinth of the *corona muralis,* a high military honor, only in reverse. He thus portrays how he fights his opponents, by being a suffering sage, parodying the images of what it means to be truly heroic in a culture saturated with Roman imperial propaganda and eschatology.[14] The Corinthians were still too enamored with these images of leadership that their culture, rather than the image of Christ, had long been feeding them.

The Damascus experience is followed by a third person boast about a great ecstatic experience and revelation that Paul received, but then he cheekily says that he is not permitted to relate what he heard (12:4)! He also received something else that he had not counted on, a "thorn in the flesh" to keep him from becoming too boastful, except of his weaknesses. How much more ironic could one get: Paul was a wounded healer (cf. v. 12), one who could not heal himself and whom God had chosen not to heal! This passage is incomprehensible unless one recognizes that while Paul is boasting, it is all clearly tongue-in-cheek.[15] The rhetorical intent of such a move was to ridicule the claims and boasts of his opponents indirectly so that the Corinthians would see how foolish *they* had been to listen to the opponents or to let these false ones take advantage of them (11:20).[16]

12. A. B. Spencer, "The Wise Fool (and the Foolish Wise): A Study of Irony in Paul," *NovT* 23 (1981), pp. 349-60.

13. So G. Holland, "Speaking like a Fool: Irony and Theology in 2 Corinthians 10–13," a paper given at a 1992 conference on rhetoric at Heidelberg, p. 16 in the distributed typescript.

14. See pp. 295-98 above on the imperial propaganda and eschatology.

15. As Holland, "Speaking like a Fool," p. 22, says, the content of this speech, not the boasting per se, makes it a fool's discourse.

16. Quintilian cautions that one must be careful how one uses irony because "it is a far more effective course to make your antagonist unpopular than to abuse him" (*Inst. Or.* 6.2.16). A good testimony to the tendency in Roman Corinth to be impressed by Sophistic rhetoric is the story of the young student of rhetoric from Corinth who came to visit Epictetus at his school in Nicopolis in Western Greece (*Diss.* 3.1.1-45) in the late first century A.D. dressed like a Sophist with his hair too lavishly done up and eyebrows plucked, wearing expensive robes. Epictetus tells the young man that this is no model to emulate if he wishes to be a good Corinthian citizen (3.1.34).

The heading for the material up to at least 12:10 is "a little foolishness" (**11:1**). Paul's point is not to confirm the Corinthians' already tarnished image of him but to expose his opponents for the bogus *apostoloi* they are and to make the Corinthians willing once again to "put up" with Paul. V. **2** has a metaphor drawing on the OT image of Yahweh's marriage to his people.[17] Paul here is playing the role of the groom's man or best man.[18] It is his job to deliver the bride pure and spotless to her one man — Christ.[19] The Corinthian Christians are already betrothed to Christ, but not yet married. The wedding will be in the future, apparently at the parousia.[20] Because they are betrothed to Christ, Paul jealousy guards them from other suitors, in this case, from those who would offer "another Jesus" (v. **4**). As God was jealous for the undivided loyalty of Israel, so also is Paul with the Corinthians. The imagery suggests moral corruption as well as other sorts of corruption.

Verse 3 expresses Paul's fear that just as the serpent deceived Eve with his cunning, this was also happening to the Corinthians. He characterizes the corruption as the antithesis of simplicity. Perhaps he sees his opponents as offering a more complicated gospel and image of Christ and of Christ's agents, which pales in comparison to the beauty and simplicity of his gospel and ministry. The tradition of the deception of Eve had come to be highly developed in the intertestamental period.[21] In some of this material,[22] the deception involves Eve being seduced by the serpent. Paul does not say this, but it may be implied. He is concerned with the corruption of the minds of his converts, which suggests mainly bad cognitive input.[23] V. **4** has an interesting triad: another Jesus, a different Spirit, and a different gospel. V. **4b** suggests that Paul

17. Cf. Hosea 1–3; Ezekiel 16; Isa. 50:1f.; 54:1-8; 62:5.

18. He is the helper and envoy of the groom, not of the bride. That is, he is again making it clear he is not the client of the Corinthians and that Christ is their ultimate Benefactor in a permanent reciprocity relationship. J. Neyrey, "Witchcraft Accusations in 2 Cor. 10–13: Paul in Social Science Perspective," *Listening* 21 (1986), pp. 160-70, is right in saying that the purity language in this passage shows once again that Paul is trying to increase the Corinthians' sense of the proper boundaries of the community, for its purity has been breached by the false apostles. "Paul . . . interprets the presence of rivals on his turf as a pollutant which has breached the social and individual bodies' boundaries and threatens a fatal corruption" (p. 166). On purity, see pp. 402-6 above.

19. Oxyrhynchus Papyrus 3177.2f. refers to female attendants of a deity called *hierai parthenoi*. More relevant here are the references to chastity requirements of women about to be married in *Ägyptische Urkunden aus den Museen zu Berlin. Griechische Urkunden* IV, 1050.22f.; 1051.31. Cf. the discussion in *New Docs. 1*, p. 71.

20. Cf. the later development of this image in Eph. 5:23ff.

21. Cf. *1 Enoch* 69:6; *2 Enoch* 36:6; *Apocalypse of Abraham* 23.

22. Cf. especially Babylonian Talmud *Yebamot* 103b, *'Aboda Zara* 22b, and *Šabbat* 146a.

23. But this could mean wrongheaded ideas about ministry and true leadership rather than other sorts of mental errors.

not only fears but also knows that the Corinthians are putting up with such bad information easily enough.

The major question that begins to come up in v. 5 is whether the "superlative *apostoloi*" (here) and the "false *apostoloi*" (v. 13) are one and the same. Martin, Barrett, and many scholars distinguish the two groups, but Barrett is right to argue that there must be some sort of relationship between them. One common conjecture is that the false apostles had received letters of recommendation from the superlative apostles in Jerusalem (from James?).[24] Though I formerly held this view, closer study of this passage has led me to abandon it for several reasons. First, there is no hint in chs. 10–13 or elsewhere in this letter that Paul is fundamentally at odds with Peter or James *in Corinth*. Second, if 3:1f. is a clue, then Paul's opponents needed letters of recommendation to the Corinthians, something that Peter or James would not likely have needed. When Paul speaks of them in 1 Corinthians, he assumes the Corinthians know well who they are and is happy to be numbered among them (1 Cor. 1:12; 15:5, 7).[25]

Third, when one understands the ironic flavor of this passage, 11:5 becomes a very plausible reference to the "false *apostoloi*" of v. 13.[26] It is *they* with whom Paul will draw an ironic comparison throughout this passage. He is not abruptly thrusting in another group of *apostoloi*. He does want his converts to see that he is in no way inferior to his rivals. But some Corinthian

---

24. C. K. Barrett, "Paul's Opponents in 2 Corinthians" and "ΨΕΥΔΑΠΟΣΤΟΛΟΙ (2 Cor. 11.13)," both in *Essays on Paul* (Philadelphia: Westminster, 1982), pp. 60-86 and 87-107; Martin, *2 Corinthians*, pp. 334ff.

25. This must count against the suggestion of M. Thrall, "Super-Apostles, Servants of Christ, and Servants of Satan," *JSNT* 6 (1980), pp. 42-57, that Paul, because of inadequate information from Titus, thought Peter might be among the intruders in Corinth. Thrall fails to see the "foolish" and rhetorical character of the whole argument, the ironic tone of the phrase "super apostles," and fails to reckon with the fact that Paul had to deal with the Corinthians' *own* conclusion that these new intruders were at least on a par with Paul. I find it unconvincing to argue that Paul would have called a group that included Peter "servants of Satan" and "bogus apostles." Matt. 16:23 is quite beside the point, since there Peter is in his pre-Christian days and without the Spirit. Cf. the critique by S. E. McClelland, "Super-Apostles, Servants of Christ, Servants of Satan: a Response," *JSNT* 14 (1982), pp. 82-87. Thrall is right, however, that 11:5 cannot be severed from 11:6 and so we must reckon with one group here, and that there is a dialectic character to this whole section since Paul refuses to compare himself with his rivals and then proceeds with the comparison. I see no evidence that Paul is mindful of any legitimate authority behind the opponents, but he must deal with how the Corinthians evaluate them.

One of the frequent appeals found in letters of recommendation was for patronage or financial support of some sort for the bearer, and so the false apostles may have come asking for funds from the outset. Cf. J. H. Elliott, "Patronage and Clientism in Early Christian Society," *Forum* 3 (1987), pp. 39-48, here p. 41.

26. So rightly F. Lang, *Die Briefe an die Korinther* (Göttingen: Vandenhoeck, 1986), p. 337: "super *apostoloi*" reflects the immoderate self-estimation of the opponents who saw themselves as pneumatic superstars.

Christians think and may be saying that he is, in fact, inferior. These words are not unthinkable, for Paul knew extreme situations called for extreme rhetoric. He freely admits that he has been driven to this comparison (cf. 12:11) due to the frame of mind of some of his converts in Corinth.

The opponents are probably *apostoloi* of congregations who have come bearing — and needing — letters of recommendation.[27] It appears that one person is the ringleader of the opposition in Corinth since Paul refers to "anyone" or "one" coming (*ho erchomenos*, v. 4) to Corinth. Chs. 3–4 may suggest that they were trading on their Jerusalem connections, but in light of the recent careful arguments of C. C. Hill this seems unlikely.[28] They were, nonetheless, touting their Jewishness.

Their criticism of Paul involved his oral presentation of the gospel. They argued that he was an amateur, untrained in words, which here likely means ornamental rhetoric (v. 6). This may explain the abundance of rhetorical devices here. Paul proves he is capable of more than passable rhetoric. An *idiōtēs* was not an "idiot" but an amateur or, as here, a person untrained in oral rhetorical performance.[29] Paul says that despite the form, the content is good. In 10:10 he has contrasted his writing and his public speaking. Here he contrasts his knowledge of rhetoric and his public speaking. As Winter points out, these contrasts reflect what 1 Cor. 2:3 says about how Paul appeared in Corinth, and this lack of skill in speaking was what his opponents called attention to.[30]

---

27. Furnish also thinks the false and super apostles are one and the same. Cf. his *II Corinthians* (Garden City: Doubleday, 1984), pp. 48-54, 502-5. Calling them super or superior apostles is Paul's parody of their pretensions.

28. 11:22a may suggest that they are from Israel or perhaps that they speak Hebrew, but nothing indicates they are from Jerusalem specifically. Cf. the discussion in Hill, *Hellenists and Hebrews: Reappraising Division within the Earliest Church* (Minneapolis: Fortress, 1992), pp. 158-78. I agree with his basic conclusions that the opponents are Jewish Christians but not Judaizers, that Paul does label them "super agents," that they are recognized in Corinth as some sort of *apostoloi,* and that the collection shows that it is not the mother *ekklēsia* Paul is fundamentally at odds with in the Corinthian correspondence, but rather this group of false ones whose connection to the Jerusalem *apostoloi* is doubtful at best. Cf. G. Strecker, "Die Legitimität des paulinischen Apostolates nach 2 Korinther 10–13," *NTS* 38 (1992), pp. 566-86, here pp. 570-73.

29. Philo *Agr.* 143, 159-60 clearly distinguishes among the *sophistēs*, the *idiōtēs*, and the ordinary person. The *idiōtēs* was not one who was untrained in rhetoric but could in fact be a student of a rhetorician or one who has graduated from a Sophist's school. Isocrates *Antidosis* 201-4 is even clearer that *idiōtēs* refers to one who, while trained in the schools of rhetoric, has not pursued a career as an orator. In short, Paul's admission that he is an *idiōtēs*, if it is not just for the sake of argument, is at most an admission that he is not a professional orator, Sophist, or declaimer. On this whole issue, cf. B. W. Winter, *Are Philo and Paul among the Sophists? A Hellenistic Jewish and a Christian Response to a First Century Movement* (dissertation, MacQuarrie University, 1988), pp. 225ff.

30. Winter, *Are Philo and Paul,* p. 229.

Apparently some were also complaining that Paul's humble or servant approach was despicable (vv. 7ff.).[31] The more well-to-do Corinthians likely had no high evaluation or appreciation for manual laborers like tentmakers.[32] Couple this with Paul's servant approach to ministry and there were surely some who saw Paul's approach as beneath a true *apostolos,* as demeaning. He is forced to compensate here with a Fool's Discourse. He must answer the fools according to their folly as Prov. 26:5 advises, "or they will be wise in their own eyes."[33]

Hamartia in v. 7 seems to mean "mistake" rather than "sin." Paul wanted the gospel of Christ to come to the Corinthians as a gift, not as goods for which they paid.[34] Some opposition was likely coming from wealthier Corinthian Christians who were used to being benefactors and would likely look down on manual workers and servants. V. 8 tells us that Paul "robbed" (this is meant tongue-in-cheek) in order not to burden the Corinthians. As we have argued in regard to chs. 8–9, Paul would not take certain kinds of support from the Corinthians because of the elitist, benefactor attitudes and obligations that would come with such support. Such attitudes kept the Corinthians from seeing the gospel as grace and Paul as *their* patron or bene-factor. They were tied too much into the conventional system of reciprocity to understand Paul's approach. "Other congregations" probably means Paul's other assemblies. He ran short while in Corinth, but fortunately the Mace-donians came and helped him out (v. 9). He adds that his policy of not taking support from the Corinthians will continue. He does not want his boast of a wage-free gospel to be stopped in the district of Achaia (v. 10).

In diatribal style, he forestalls an objection to his continued refusal of ongoing patronage (v. 11): It must not be interpreted to mean that he does

31. There seem to have been four major complaints: Paul's choice of working rather than accepting patronage, his appearance, his speech, and his reticence to boast. Cf. T. B. Savage, *Power through Weakness: A Historical and Exegetical Study of the Ministry in 2 Corinthians* (dissertation, Cambridge University, 1988), p. 63. All of these have to do with the normal expectations for both teachers and Sophists.

32. See above, pp. 208-9. This is the attitude of the more well-to-do, not the attitude of the workers and artisans themselves, who were often proud of their work. Cf. *ILS* 7422, 7427-49, 7627, 7682-84; Savage, *Power through Weakness,* p. 101. Paul's working with his hands was a deliberate step down the social ladder. Some in Corinth suffered from self-made-person-escapes-humble-origins syndrome.

33. Here Paul is hinting that he is pursuing a sapiential strategy counseled by earlier sages, that he himself is a sage, as will be further demonstrated by the *peristasis* to follow, and that 11:19 must be understood in light of Prov. 26:5. The Corinthians do fancy themselves wise, but Paul's discourse here will intimate that he believes they have acted like fools in regard to receiving and believing the false *apostoloi* and so only deserve a fool's discourse meant to shame them into seeing the error of their ways. On Paul as a sage, see B. Witherington, *Jesus the Sage: The Pilgrimage of Wisdom* (Minneapolis: Fortress, 1994), ch. 7.

34. On *opsōnion* (v. 8) meaning "wage" or "allowance," cf. *New Docs. 2,* p. 93.

not love the Corinthians (this very letter should be proof of that), but in any case God knows the real state of his heart. He wants to cut off any pretext for criticizing him, in particular in regard to the charge that he was defrauding the Corinthians by taking their money.

In v. 13 Paul goes on the offensive. The "bogus apostles"[35] are not just deceived but also deceivers and dishonest. They have transformed themselves into "*apostoloi* of Christ." While *metaschēmata* could mean "disguise," *eis* ("into") suggests the translation "transform." The point is that they are self-made *apostoloi*, not God-made, unlike Paul, and so claim the status dishonestly. Paul is willing to go so far as to call them "servants of Satan" (vv. 14f.). They behave like the Adversary, who transformed himself into an angel of light. This, too, draws on early Jewish traditions.[36] How much of this is a matter of rhetorical polemics meant to force the audience to reject the interlopers and how much is Paul's actual assessment of his opponents? The vehemence here is reminiscent of Galatians. The false ones only disguise themselves as servants of righteousness, but in the end they will be judged by their unrighteous and dishonest deeds.

Paul reminds his audience in v. 16 that he is not really foolish, that he is simply playing a role in order to make a point about himself and expose his opponents for what they truly are. V. 17 reiterates that this is not the real Paul; he is not speaking as the Lord might want, but desperate times call for desperate measures. He will boast in this particular matter alone, though he knows it is a boasting according to the flesh. In v. 18, as before, *kata sarx* seems to mean "according to fallen (sinful) inclinations," not just according to human or mortal inclinations.[37]

V. 19 amounts to biting irony: "Since you are so wise, you will no doubt gladly put up with foolishness." Then Paul shames his audience by showing how foolish they have already been by allowing people to enslave, devour,[38] or take advantage of them, to lift them up and even slap them on the face (v. 20). This sort of behavior was characteristic of Sophistic rhetors during and after Paul's day, and this suggests that the false ones were deliberately presenting themselves in that light.[39] V. 21a may mean that Paul

35. As Martin, *2 Corinthians*, p. 349, calls them.

36. Cf. *Life of Adam and Eve* 9:1, which speaks of Satan changing himself into the shining form of an angel and having a discussion with Eve.

37. See pp. 394-95 above.

38. "Devour" and possibly "enslave" suggest financial bilking.

39. Cf. Winter, *Are Philo and Paul*, pp. 243ff. On Sophistic boasting and verbal abuse of the audience, see Dio Chrysostom 8.9. On Sophists abusing each other in Corinth, see Philo *Det.* 32–34. It is significant that Philo contrasts Sophists and sages in *De Vita Contemplativa* 31, since Paul presents himself here as a sage. Even Quintilian says that there is a place for abusing one's audience, though the untrained orator is likely to do it too openly and too often, mistaking abuse for speaking freely (*Inst. Or.* 2.12.4). He also castigates the untrained orator for seeking "only themes that may beguile the ears of the public even at

says all this to shame them or less likely that he is ashamed even to mention such things.

The *peristasis* catalog that follows in vv. **21b-28** (or 23b-28) is to some extent a further development of the catalog in ch. 6, where Paul displayed evidence that God had empowered him as a sage and true agent of Christ to overcome considerable hardships. Here and in 6:8, 11f. Paul portrays himself as the foolish righteous sufferer whom God will vindicate. In 6:4f. and 11:23-28 he enumerates hardships, here an even longer list than before, to prove the greatness of his endurance.[40] The shift from *kagō* ("I also") in vv. 21b-22 to *hyper egō* ("I more so") in v. 23 followed by adverbs of excess suggests that Paul is comparing his own sufferings and hardships to those that the opponents claim to have endured.[41] Self-praise by sages and philosophers for endurance of hardships was exceedingly common in the Greco-Roman world, and thus we must reject Georgi's contention that Paul is not implying that the false *apostoloi* claimed that they had suffered.[42]

The difference between Paul and his adversaries was "in his *interpretation* of his hardships, not in the fact that he suffered and they did not. The difference is, he saw his weakness as the primary sphere for the manifestation of divine power, and they 'signs, wonders, and mighty works' (12:12)."[43] The false ones were claiming to be "servants of Christ,"[44] something Paul also claims in introducing both of these catalogs (6:4; 11:23).

Perhaps this label *diakonos*, "servant," as Hodgson suggests, leads Paul to

---

the cost of appealing to the most perverted tastes" (2.12.6) and then mentions the wild gestures of those who would advise an orator to "smite your hands together, stamp the ground, slap your thigh, your chest, your forehead, and you will go straight to the heart of the more common members of your audience" (2.12.10). Could it be that the so-called superlative *apostoloi* were themselves insufficiently trained in rhetoric, but like so many with a smattering of knowledge, pretended to be experts? 11:20 suggests that the Corinthians had very plebeian tastes in rhetoric.

40. Cf. J. T. Fitzgerald, *Cracks in an Earthen Vessel: An Examination of the Catalogue of Hardships in the Corinthian Correspondence* (Atlanta: Scholars, 1988), p. 204.

41. Rightly Fitzgerald, *Cracks*, p. 25.

42. Cf. D. Georgi, *The Opponents of Paul in Second Corinthians* (Philadelphia: Fortress, 1986), pp. 273ff.

43. *Ibid.*, p. 25, n. 95. Cf. S. K. Stowers, "Paul on the Use and Abuse of Reason," in *Greeks, Romans, and Christians,* ed. D. L. Balch, E. Ferguson, and W. A. Meeks (Minneapolis: Fortress, 1990), p. 274: "For him, the medium of his behavior as a missionary is part of the message. This prominently included his self-support, at which the Corinthians took offense. . . ."

44. As J. N. Collins, "Georgi's 'Envoys' in 2 Cor. 11:23," *JBL* (1974), pp. 88-96, shows, *diakonos* does not mean "envoy" as Georgi maintains, not even in Epictetus, though it sometimes could have the connotation "messenger." For a thoroughgoing refutation of W. Schmithals's thesis that Paul's opponents in Corinth are Gnostics, cf. L. D. McCrary, *Paul's Opponents in Corinth: An Examination of Walter Schmithals' Thesis in "Gnosticism in Corinth"* (dissertation, Southwestern Baptist Theological Seminary, 1985).

catalog occupational hardships undergone for his mission and for his converts in the style of the imperial *res gestae,* in which Augustus recounts his deeds as a public servant, beginning by identifying himself, then saying what he has done and undergone, and concluding with his acclamation by the Roman people as father of his country. Paul likewise begins with who he is (vv. 22f.) and goes on to his occupational hardships (vv. 23b-29), his humbling and exalting experiences (11:30–12:10), and his claim to the titles *apostolos* (12:11-13) and parent (v. 14).[45]

45. R. Hodgson, "Paul the Apostle and First-Century Tribulation Lists," *ZNW* 74 (1983), pp. 59-80.
  Some have argued that 11:23b-28 and 12:10 should be seen as separate catalogs, and this may be so, but it should be noted that as in the *res gestae* Paul continues to speak of datable experiences in 11:32f. and 12:1-10, and enumeration is seen also in 12:8 ("three times I besought"). Furthermore, the length of the *res gestae* exceeds what we find in 2 Cor. 11:23b–12:10 and includes a good deal more than just lists. For a transcript of the original in Greek and Latin, see V. Ehrenberg and A. H. M. Jones, *Documents Illustrating the Reigns of Augustus and Tiberius* (Oxford: Clarendon, 1955), pp. 1-31. The following excerpts follow R. K. Sherk's translation in *The Roman Empire: Augustus to Hadrian* (Cambridge: Cambridge University, 1988), pp. 41-50 (with Sherk's typographical indications of restored text removed):

> The accomplishments of the deified Augustus by which he subjected the whole world to the empire of the Roman People, and the expenses which he incurred for the state and the Roman People. . . .
> When I was nineteen years old, by my own deliberation and at my own expense, I raised an army by which I brought the Republic, oppressed by the domination of a faction, into a condition of freedom. For that reason the senate by honorary decrees enrolled me into its order in the consulship of Gaius . . . , assigning me consular position . . . and giving me imperium. . . .
> Wars on land and sea both domestic and foreign throughout the whole world I often waged and as victor I spared all citizens. . . . I captured six hundred ships, apart from those which were smaller than triremes.
> Twice I celebrated ovations and three curule triumphs, and I was acclaimed twenty-one times imperator. When the senate decreed more triumphs for me, all of them I declined. . . . Because of the things which I or legates of mine, acting under my auspices, accomplished successfully on land and sea, fifty-five times the senate decreed thanksgiving should be offered to the immortal gods. . . .
> I did not refuse in the great scarcity of grain, the superintendency of the grain-supply, which I administered in such a way that within a few days I freed the whole state from fear and immediate danger at my own expense and care. . . .
> To the Roman plebs man for man I paid out three hundred sesterces in accordance with the testament of my father and in my own name I gave each four hundred sesterces from the spoils of war when I was consul for the fifth time (29 BC). . . .
> I pacified the seas, freed it of pirates. In that war the slaves, who had fled from their masters and had taken up arms against the Republic, I captured about thirty thousand of them and turned them over to their masters for punishment. . . .
> I established colonies of soldiers in Africa, Sicily, Macedonia, the two Spains, Achaia, Asia, Syria. . . .
> In my sixth and seventh consulships (28-27 B.C.) after I had extinguished the civil wars and by the consent of all had acquired control of everything, I transferred

One of the social functions of both the imperial *res gestae* and Paul's catalog is public assertion of rightful authority over a group of people in view of the accomplishments and the things undergone on their behalf.[46] The difference is that Paul boasts in his weaknesses and his apparent defeats, while Augustus does the reverse. Paul and Augustus are similar in their attempts to show the great sacrifices they have made for their people. Since the *res gestae* was posted in various places in the provinces[47] in temples to Augustus, and in view of the status of Corinth as a Roman colony,[48] the Corinthians were probably familiar with the *res gestae* and would have recognized Paul's parody of the public standards by which leaders were normally judged to be great and legitimate.

Whatever his rivals may dare to boast about, Paul is about to do so as well. His first three boasts (v. 22) make it clear that the bogus agents boasted about their Jewish connections. This may have been important since some in Corinth had been converted out of the synagogue there, including the synagogue leader. "Hebrew" refers either to the native language or the outer identity or ethnic character of a person. "Israelite" has to do with one's spiritual allegiance. "Seed of Abraham" speaks of one's ancestry. Paul then says he is more *(hyper)* of a servant of Christ than his opponents are (v. 23a).

The catalog of woes or trials begins with v. 23b. The opponents may be engaging in gospel labor, but Paul more abundantly so. He has endured multiple imprisonments and beatings.[49] He says he was "in deaths" many times (v. 23). Perhaps some Jews, Christian or otherwise, have a contract out on him, but the phrase may simply mean that he was in mortal danger or at the point of death many times. Not only has he experienced the Jewish thirty-nine lashes five times,[50] he has also been beaten with Roman rods three times, something a Roman citizen should not have had to undergo, but such abuses

---

the Republic from my power to the discretion of the senate and the Roman People. In return for this service of mine by senatorial decree I was called Augustus . . . and a golden shield in the Curia Iulia was put in place, which the senate and the Roman People gave to me because of my courage, clemency, justice and piety . . .

When I was in my thirteenth consulship, the senate and the equestrian order and the Roman People as a whole called me father of my country. . . .

46. Though it has often been suggested, the parallels between Paul's catalog and the trials of Heracles (cf. Hodgson, "Paul the Apostle," pp. 78f.; Fitzgerald, *Cracks,* p. 7, n. 2) are less compelling than the parallels with the *res gestae* because Paul is waging war with adversaries in Corinth and has already used several military metaphors to display his intent.

47. The copy quoted above is from a temple of Roma and Augustus in Ancyra.

48. The establishment of colonies in Achaia is mentioned in the *res gestae,* and this makes it likely that it was posted in Corinth.

49. This fact is not mentioned in Acts.

50. This suggests that he accepted this Jewish discipline in order to get back into the synagogue and preach again, which in turn suggests that Paul did not understand his commission to limit him to evangelizing Gentiles.

were not unheard of (vv. 24f.). Once he was stoned, probably by a mob. Three times he was shipwrecked,[51] once spending a day and night in the ocean. He experienced dangers from flooding streams, from robbers,[52] and from fellow Jews, Gentiles, and even false Christians (v. 26). He engaged in extremely arduous work, and sleepless nights, hunger, and thirst were his companions (v. 27). He fasted many times, whether for religious purposes or of necessity, probably the latter. He has been cold and even naked. Furthermore, he feels the daily pressure of his ministerial responsibilities, his concern for all[53] the Christian assemblies (vv. 28f.). Whenever anyone was weak, Paul felt it; whenever anyone was scandalized or deliberately caused to stumble, Paul was burned up. He was totally absorbed in his work.

A Closer Look: Paul, Apostleship, and Social Networks ——————

One of the major theses used in evaluating early Christianity in this century has been the argument that Christianity developed from a charismatic and functional approach to leadership to a system of offices and titles as the early Christian movement became more and more institutionalized. Sometimes this thesis also sees this change in approach to leadership as part of a larger change from a sect or millenarian movement to an established "church." One of more recent variants of this same argument is the contention that the Jesus movement initially had an egalitarian character and at the hands of Paul and others became increasingly more hierarchical and patriarchal. There are problems with all these arguments, but they do bear witness to one discernible trend. Over the course of the first century there was growth and development of some forms of recognized leadership, eventually resulting in some positions being seen as both essential and official, while others faded out of existence.

Our particular concern here is with what existed in the congregations that Paul established. Here three major caveats to the earlier dominating thesis described above need to be stressed: (1) So far as I can tell, there is no evidence that Paul's communities were ever egalitarian, if by that one means nonhierarchical.[54] (2) At the same time,

51. Again Acts mentions only one shipwreck and it is from later in Paul's life than this letter.

52. This made delivery of the collection a dangerous task.

53. Probably this means all Pauline assemblies.

54. So rightly B. Holmberg, *Paul and Power: The Structure of Authority in the Primitive Church as Reflected in the Pauline Epistles* (Philadelphia: Fortress, 1980), p. 192, who concludes that

the numerous relationships of superordination and subordination that can be found in the Pauline texts are with few exceptions based neither on coercion nor on a utilitarian constellation of interests but on a belief in legitimacy shared by all parties. The asymmetric distribution of power that we can observe is justified by socially valid norms and beliefs concerning the legitimacy of this lack of symmetry. . . . All leadership in Paul's communities was not based on gender, race, or social status but on whether one was called and gifted by the Holy Spirit to perform certain tasks on a regular basis. (3) Several important studies have concluded in the last twenty years that the sharp distinction between charismatic and official approaches to leadership has been overdrawn. As U. Brockhaus has rightly pointed out, elements of institutional office such as permanence of position, titles, legitimation, authority, and compensation were issues even in the earliest of Paul's communities, though Paul does not dwell on such matters except when his authority and ministry are challenged, as in 2 Corinthians 10–13. Brockhaus's final conclusion that a strong distinction between charismatic and official functions in the Pauline communities is neither historically possible nor fully warranted is probably correct.[55] B. Holmberg's important work in this area has also led to the conclusion that while the primitive church should be viewed as one dominated by a form of charismatic authority,

> the Church must also be characterized as an institutionalized charismatic movement, since it exhibits elements of traditional and rational-legal authority. Even the founders of churches, such as Paul and Barnabas, refer to a common history and transmit a tradition, "the Gospel," containing a number of given elements of doctrine (christology, eschatology), cult (baptism, the Eucharist, the Lord's Day), and organization (the apostolate commissioned by Christ, the central role of the church in Jerusalem).[56]

> authority is considered as ultimately flowing from the same source, viz. the Founder of the Church, and this is recognized as being the basis for the legitimacy of the exercise of authority in the Church. This is why all local churches stand in relation to one another as part of one and the same Church.

On Paul's appeal to what is done "in all the Churches," see above, pp. 235-36.

55. U. Brockhaus, *Charisma und Amt. Die paulinische Charismenlehre aus dem Hintergrund der frühchristlichen Gemeindefunktionen* (Wuppertal: Theologischer Verlag R. Brockhaus, 1972), pp. 237f.

56. Holmberg, *Paul and Power*, p. 196. I reject the conclusions of J. H. Schütz, *Paul and the Anatomy of Apostolic Authority* (Cambridge: Cambridge University, 1975), who continues to overpress the distinctions of charisma and office and of legitimacy and authority. The distinction between Paul's apostolic call and his converting vision of the risen Christ will not work. Some of the more "charismatic" gifts did not die out in the first century, as is sometimes argued. Figures like Ignatius of Antioch and Cyprian of Carthage claimed prophetic inspiration as well as increasingly institutionalized roles. There was also the Montanist movement, which even a major figure like Tertullian got caught up in. Cf. now C. M. Robeck, *Prophecy in Carthage: Perpetua, Tertullian, and Cyprian* (Cleveland: Pilgrim, 1992).

Paul's definition of what was essential to qualify one as an *apostolos* of Christ and not just an agent of a congregation was having seen the risen Lord (1 Corinthians 15). There was, therefore, a built-in obsolescence to the apostolic office. When the witnesses had all died, one could transmit apostolic traditions but not the office. Perhaps this is one major reason that after the apostolic age there were many and varied attempts to define what were legitimate church offices and functions.

There is in the Pauline corpus, even in the Pastorals, no warrant for seeing *episkopoi* ("bishops") as successors of the apostles and bearers of apostolic authority. Even in Tit. 1:5-9 *episkopoi* seems to be a functional term defining a particular role of "oversight" that

A. J. Blasi's study has shown that while recognition is necessary for charisma to work, it is not sufficient. The identity of the authority figure is important, for unless the potential followers identify with him or her in some way, his or her authority will not be accepted. During Paul's time away from Corinth, his opponents had reconstructed his image, criticizing him in light of their idea of what a charismatic leader, a pneumatic apostle, a wise rhetor should look and act like. Not only was Paul's charisma questioned, but the authority that was related to it was impaired from working as it should have. Paul needed to reestablish his relationship with his converts, and he knew that "rhetoric, wisdom . . . , and insight are occasion-dependent." They work primarily if the *ēthos* of the speaker is accepted and trusted.[57]

With regard to the authority of *apostoloi* in the Pauline communities, there are several complicating factors. Paul and even his converts do not seem to have seen apostleship as a matter of "ascribed" or "achieved" authority, that is, authority that initially arose from the recognition of work done for those under its sway.[58] Paul does mention the "signs of apostleship" seen in him (12:12), but this is a matter of verification or proof of an already existing authority and legitimacy.

Obviously, without their voluntary recognition of his legitimacy, Paul cannot effectively function as the Corinthian Christians' *apostolos* without the use of force. His commitment to using rhetoric shows that his normal and preferred leadership style is to work by persuasion,[59] and even in 2 Corinthians 10–13 Paul is still striving to use that leadership style. He expects voluntary obedience and compliance (10:6), and only when he has it will he deal with the offenders,[60] presumably using some sort of spiritual power or force (cf. 10:11; 13:2, 10). This has led one scholar to conclude that "Paul's rhetorical style serves to mediate the paradox that the egalitarian social structure of Paul's churches is complemented by a hierarchial axis."[61] In Paul's view,

---

an elder *(presbyteros)* has. The description in 1 Tim. 3:1-7 of *episcopoi* suggests no connection with *apostoloi;* indeed it gives character requirements, not a job description. In short, while the Pastorals do reflect a stage in which more institutionalization seems to be at work than in Paul's early letters, they hardly warrant the label "early catholicism." There is nothing remotely close to the idea of the monarchical bishop, much less an idea of apostolic succession, and it is thus a mistake to date the Pastorals to the second century.

57. A. J. Blasi, *Making Charisma: The Social Construction of Paul's Public Image* (New Brunswick: Transaction, 1991), pp. 10ff.; the quotation is from p. 20.

58. Pace R. A. Atkins, *Egalitarian Community: Ethnography and Exegesis* (Tuscaloosa: University of Alabama, 1991), p. 134. Atkins's basic thesis is in part based on a misunderstanding of 1 Corinthians 12 as an anti-hierarchical argument while it is actually an anti-separatist or anti-factionalizing argument.

59. See pp. 44-48 above.

60. Presumably the false *apostoloi* and also their unrepentant Corinthian supporters.

61. N. R. Petersen, *Rediscovering Paul: Philemon and the Sociology of Paul's Narrative World* (Philadelphia: Fortress, 1985), p. 133. The question raised by this statement is: What does "egalitarian" mean? If it means that anyone could be gifted by the Spirit to assume a leadership role, that is correct, but if it means that anyone could and did lead or direct Paul's community since authority rested in the group as a whole, that is incorrect. Atkins, *Egalitarian Community,* is right in saying that it is "at the point of proximity to group boundary concerns (purity and identity) that Paul's appeals become commands" (p. 187).

his authority and hence his power comes from above, from Christ by means of the Holy Spirit, and is demonstrated by his words, deeds, lifestyle, and converts, not derived therefrom. This is why, for Paul, to question his authority is to question Christ. This in turn leads him to conclude that such questioning endangers the very Christian faith of his converts, since the link between Christ and Christ's agent is very close.

A much clearer fix on Paul's vision of apostleship and its social consequences can be derived by attempting to apply the theory of social networks to the discussion.[62] This would entail a detailed analysis of Paul's relationships, not only with his converts and opponents, but also with his coworkers, with other apostles of Christ, with agents of *ekklēsiai*, and especially with the "pillar" *apostoloi*. A helpful start has been made in this direction by N. R. Petersen, though he has confined himself in the main to Philemon.[63] More helpful is the exact graph of the whole of Paul's network that Atkins offers.[64] There is now a helpful collection of essays edited by L. Michael White on this subject, though they do not deal specifically with the issue of apostleship.[65] We have already pointed out that both social factors (such as who was the head of a home where the *ekklēsia* met) and spiritual gifts helped determine the structure of Paul's communities, including those in Corinth.[66] We also noted how the well-to-do Gentile males in the Corinthian congregation, who were causing Paul the most problems, had been inadequately socialized into the new community and so continued to apply their own pagan values to a variety of matters, including their religion. As White says, "Social bonds are often determinative of ideological attachment: 'faith constitutes conformity to the religious outlook of one's intimates'. . . ."[67]

Paul is seeking to change the primary socializing agent in his converts' lives by binding them more closely to each other (1 Corinthians) and to himself (2 Corinthians).[68] He is seeking to create a social and religious subunit in society.[69] He is also trying in 2 Corinthians to convince his converts to see his apostleship as entailing a sort of patronal-kinship relationship, by which Christ becomes the Corinthians' benefactor through Paul. The allusion to the *res gestae* is but one hint in this direction, as is the parent language in 12:14. Paul sees the increase of patronal structures paralleling

62. One helpful tool toward this end is analysis of Paul's use of kinship terms for relationships within his social network; cf. A. Funk, *Status und Rollen in den Paulusbriefen* (Innsbruck: Tyrolia, 1981), especially the charts on pp. 115ff.

63. Petersen, *Rediscovering Paul*, pp. 90ff.; Petersen's focus is on Paul's roles in general, not just on the character of apostleship.

64. Atkins, *Egalitarian Community*, pp. 106f.

65. L. M. White, ed., *Social Networks in the Early Christian Environment: Issues and Methods for Social History* (*Semeia* 56; Atlanta: Scholars, 1992).

66. See above, pp. 32-35 and 257-63.

67. White, "Finding the Ties that Bind: Issues from Social Description," in *Social Networks*, pp. 3-22, here p. 20 (quoting Stark and Bainbridge).

68. Cf. Atkins, *Egalitarian Community*, p. 61: "In order for the group to work or have substance, there must be a collection of individuals who give over some of their identity and independence explicitly or implicitly to the group."

69. I refrain from using the term "subculture," since Paul does not try to dictate all cultural values, only those that impinge on some fundamental Christian value, such as monotheism (as in 1 Corinthians 8–10).

the rise of the empire and is trying to offer his converts an alternative vision of how these sort of networks should work in the Christian community.

In this network Paul sees himself as the authorized agent of the Benefactor or, to put the matter metaphorically, as the "friend" of the groom (11:2). Since "patronage is a dyadic relationship between unequals that produces bonds of uneven exchange — loyalty for largesse,"[70] when Paul draws on patronal language to describe the role of the agent of Christ he is suggesting that it is inappropriate for him to receive patronage since he is the agent of the Patron, not the Corinthians' client. What he requires of them is loyalty and obedience, not monetary remuneration for his teaching. In view of his *res gestae*, Paul, like the emperor, ought to be honored: The Corinthians should boast of him. But Paul's experience, like that of patrons and clients, is that such relationships, being voluntary in origin, are fragile, and furthermore that when the agent of the Patron is absent, the clients are able and apparently willing to contract such semi-exclusive relationships with others (the false agents), only now as benefactors rather than as beneficiaries.

What this is all about is a struggle for status, power, and control. There are obviously some Corinthian Christians who want to be in the superior position in the social network, rather than allowing Paul his place there. "Benefactor-beneficiary and patron-client networks are operative in establishing and reinforcing the mutual status of persons involved. Balanced discharge of the obligations (expected behavior) . . . maintains and reinforces their respective powers."[71] Just as imperial patronal relationships were used to transform civic religion to serve Rome's new agenda,[72] so Paul is trying to transform patronal relationships in Corinth in order to better socialize his converts. He tries to get them to be more dependent on Christ by suggesting that they are already in a binding patronal relationship with Christ, one that obligates them to a new and different agenda from the one they are pursuing. He sees his own role as instructor (sage) and facilitator *(šāliaḥ)*, the agent of Christ.

It may be that one reason Paul's authority was compromised in Corinth was that many had come to view him simply as a teacher (like Epictetus, for example) and as a rather weak orator and were applying rhetorical and pedagogical criteria, not patronal criteria, in evaluating him. Hock demonstrates that one reason Epictetus had little success in transforming his students into Stoics is that they came to him with expectations different from his, hoping to gain only academic training, not a program for living a different sort of life. Epictetus's "free speech" alienated him from some he might have influenced, as was also true in Paul's case. Perhaps Paul, like Epictetus, had become isolated within his own social network, though for different reasons.[73] There-

---

70. White, "Social Networks: Theoretical Orientation and Historical Applications" in *Social Networks,* pp. 23-36, here p. 36.

71. H. Hendrix, "Benefactor/Patron Networks in the Urban Environment: Evidence from Thessalonica," in *Social Networks,* pp. 39-58, here p. 55.

72. *Ibid.,* p. 56.

73. In Paul's case the reasons were his absence from Corinth and the presence of alternative "apostles" there. The people that both Epictetus and Paul were having trouble with were in or near harbor towns, where the potential for outside influences was great. Cf. R. Hock, "'By the Gods, It Is My One Desire to See an Actual Stoic': Epictetus'

fore, to reassert his position and relationship with the Corinthians, he sends from among those with whom he still has a close bond a rhetorically adept coworker, Titus, and others, first with a painful letter and then with 2 Corinthians, in preparation for his own coming to renew his bond with his estranged converts. These sorts of considerations may lead to a fuller understanding of Paul's understanding of what it meant to be an *apostolos*.

Paul ends his list of hardships with a more detailed description of one particularly humiliating experience. 11:31-33 tells a tale that reveals both Paul's weakness and the way God providentially and miraculously helped him out of one scrape after another. Paul says that if he will boast, it will be in his weakness (v. 30), because he believes that God's power springs into action through such tribulations.[74] Where there is the wrong sort of pride and arrogance, there can be no divine power, for "the very existence of Christ's power in Paul depends on his humility and weakness."[75]

Paul first swears that he is not lying (v. 31).[76] The ethnarch of King Aretas was after Paul (v. 32). Already in the first few years of his ministry Paul was a marked man.[77] Acts 9:24f. tells the same tale, but from a slightly different angle, referring to Jews guarding the city and chasing Paul. In Acts the story is told as an example of Paul's and the early Christians' courage and cleverness; here he uses it as a sign of his weakness, boasting of what happens to him rather than of what he is able to accomplish.

One of the keys to understanding why Paul includes this apparently antiheroic tale is the Roman military honor called the *corona muralis,* the "wall crown." This was one of the highest military awards and was given to the

---

Relations with Students and Visitors in his Personal Social Network," in *Social Networks,* pp. 121-42.

74. Cf. Savage, *Power through Weakness,* p. 210. This is why Paul is not depressed or crushed by such occurrences.

75. *Ibid.,* p. 204. This may be one reason that the false apostles are labeled "servants of Satan" (11:14f.). They were arrogant and boastful of certain spiritual gifts or experiences, so Paul can only conclude that they received their power from the powers of darkness. Perhaps they claimed to perform miracles like Jesus, while Paul stresses following Jesus' moral example (10:1f.). Very little in 2 Corinthians gives us any clue as to what the false agents thought about the cross and other crucial matters.

76. This typical rhetorical device is another feature that leads Danker to see this speech as parallel to Demosthenes' *De Corona.* F. W. Danker, "Paul's Debt to the *De Corona* of Demosthenes: A Study of Rhetorical Techniques in Second Corinthians," in *Persuasive Artistry: Studies in NT Rhetoric in Honor of George A. Kennedy,* ed. D. F. Watson (Sheffield: Sheffield Academic, 1991), pp. 262-80, here pp. 279f.

77. Aretas's rule ended in A.D. 40. An ethnarch was a governor, here in charge of guarding the city of Damascus.

soldier who was first to scale the wall into an enemy city.[78] It was still being awarded in Paul's day, though to no one under the rank of centurion. Paul is saying that while the typical Roman hero is first up the wall, he is first down the wall![79]

In **12:1-10**, Paul continues his paradoxical boasting with tongue firmly in cheek. He now comes to "visions and revelations" (v. 1). Strictly speaking, the former are seen and the latter may be words, images, or something else sent or revealed to a person. In his discussion of *pathos* Quintilian says that there "are certain experiences that . . . the Romans call *visiones*, in which things absent are presented to our imagination with such extreme vividness that they seem to be actually before our very eyes. One who is sensitive to such impressions will have the greatest power over the emotions" (*Inst. Or.* 6.2.29f.). Like the Corinthians, Paul knows the emotional impact of such claims, especially on pneumatics. Thus he raises their expectations here, then teases them.[80]

In vv. **2-4** Paul says that his vision was a source of revelation, though he coyly says that he is not permitted to convey its contents.[81] Probably his opponents were claiming such experiences as a means of credentialing themselves. From 1 Corinthians it is apparent how interested the Corinthians were in things ecstatic. Paul puts the story of this revelation in the third person, following the rhetorical conventions in regard to inoffensive self-praise. He is a bit ashamed to be forced into having to do this, so he removes himself a step from this particular boast. This event happened some fourteen years prior to the writing of this letter, which puts it somewhere about 40 and 44 A.D. Certainly it was after his conversion, after the Damascus episode in 11:31-33,[82]

---

78. Cf. Polybius 6.39.5; Livy 6.20.8; 10.46.3; Aulus Gelius *Attic Nights* 5.6.16. A Corinthian statue of Tyche or Fortuna, the goddess of luck or fate, dating to the late first or early second century A.D., has a wall crown on its head. Cf. Furnish, *II Corinthians*, p. 542 and plate VIII; C. M. Edwards, "Tyche at Corinth," *Hesperia* 59 (1990), pp. 529-42. Paul's converts would have known of the convention and perhaps even the statue.

79. Cf. E. A. Judge, "Paul's Boasting in Relation to Contemporary Professional Practice," *Australian Biblical Review* 16 (1968), pp. 37-50, here p. 47; Furnish, *II Corinthians*, p. 542. There may be something to Holland's suggestion ("Speaking like a Fool," p. 25) that Paul may also have in mind OT providential rescues such as Josh. 2:8-15 or 1 Sam. 19:12. I doubt that this is the main thing in Paul's mind, however, in view of the military imagery earlier in his tribulation catalog and in 10:4f.

80. D. Marguerat, "2 Corinthiens 10–13. Paul et l'expérience de Dieu," *ETR* 63 (1988), pp. 497-519, plausibly suggests that Paul realized that with experientially oriented Corinthians it was not just the authenticity of his ministry that was on trial but also the very authenticity of his experience of God. On this latter more private matter, Paul shows a distinct reluctance to speak, both here and in 1 Corinthians 14.

81. On this episode, see the helpful articles by A. T. Lincoln, "Paul the Visionary," *NTS* 25 (1979), pp. 204-20, and H. Saake, "Paulus als Ekstatiker. Pneumatologische Beobachtungen zu 2 Kor. 12.1-10," *Biblica* 53 (1972), pp. 404-10.

82. Perhaps it happened while he was in the desert of Syrian Arabia.

and well before he ever came to Corinth. Like his revelation in 1 Corinthians 14 that he spoke in glossolalia more than all of them, the news of this experience may have come as a shock to the Corinthians. Why does Paul goes back so far to dredge up this example?

Acts records various visionary experiences of Paul, and Paul in Galatians 1 says he went up to Jerusalem by revelation, but that could mean that someone else received the revelation and told Paul of it. Some commentators have come to the conclusion that the date of the vision in 2 Corinthians 12 shows that such occurrences were rare in Paul's life. One could as easily conclude that Paul mentions this one because it was especially notable, not especially rare.[83] The careful parallel construction in vv. 2f. probably refers to one, not two, such incidents.[84]

Paul says twice that he does not know whether he was in or out of the body when he was "caught up." This may be significant in that a Greek or Roman would naturally think of such experiences as occurring out of the body, because of their dualistic understanding of the human person and because they did not usually regard the body as having any religious or eternal importance. Paul says he got as far as "the third heaven," which he also calls "paradise," a term from the Eden story that had come to be synonymous with what we call "heaven."[85] He is probably not suggesting there were any levels above the third heaven, for if he or his opponents or the Corinthians thought such a thing, this would not amount to much of a boast. In fact in early Jewish literature there was an interesting variety of opinions on the number of heavenly levels.[86] Paul's point may be that he got *all the way* to the third heaven. This was not a planned trip: He was caught up.

It is plausible, in view of the parallel with the pupils of Johanan ben Zakkai, Paul's near contemporary, that Paul is talking about the kind of experience here that later came to be identified as Merkabah mysticism (from the *merkābâ* or chariot-throne of Ezekiel's vision).[87] In the description of

83. Cf. Lincoln, "Paul the Visionary," pp. 204ff., who points out that 12:1 suggests that Paul originally intended to relate several such occurences.

84. Cf. Martin, *2 Corinthians*, pp. 396ff.

85. Cf. Jesus' words in Luke 23:43 and Rev. 2:7. Paradise and the third heaven are also equated in *2 Enoch* 8 and *Apocalypse of Moses* 37:5.

86. Three and seven were two of the favorite numbers, and five and ten also appear. Particularly interesting is the idea that the first level of heaven is the stratosphere (the heavens), the second level is outer space, where the constellations are, and the third level is the spiritual realm, what we would call heaven. Cf. Neh. 9:6; 1 Kgs. 8:27; 2 Chron. 2:6; 6:18; Ps. 148:4; A. T. Lincoln, *Paradise Now and Not Yet: Studies in the Role of the Heavenly Dimension in Paul's Thought with Special Reference to His Eschatology* (Cambridge: Cambridge University, 1981), pp. 77f. Perhaps this line of speculation began because the Hebrew word for heaven, *šāmayim* is plural.

87. Cf. also the *Testament of Levi* and the parables in *1 Enoch*.

some experiences of Merkabah mysticism it is said that the mystic, while experiencing exaltation, is attacked by demons or angels because he was not worthy to see the throne of God.[88] It is possible that the thorn in Paul's flesh (v. 7) was just such a messenger or supernatural being assaulting him.[89] But the text suggests that Paul's thorn persisted and was thus something other than a onetime experience that accompanied his ecstatic vision. More likely Paul cast this tale in light of his knowledge not of the Merkabah experiences but of apocalyptic experiences that did not necessarily involve Ezekiel's throne vision.

Paul heard "unutterable words" (v. 4). This he clarifies by saying that they were words he was not permitted to repeat, and not that they were unintelligible. The Corinthians would understand this in terms of their knowledge of the mystery religions. Some things were revealed only to special people at special times. Indeed, the deep secrets given to initiates in the mysteries have still not been disclosed, though at Pompeii and elsewhere we have found evidence of the secret rites.

Because Paul revealed this unrevealable revelation he was to be seen as a very special person, taken up by God to a special place, and given inside information. Therefore the Corinthians have badly underestimated him. But still they should not be enamored with such experiences, since they are not the most important criteria by which *apostoloi* are to be measured. Paul does not want them to overestimate him just because of an "excess" of revelations (v. 6).[90] This is an implicit rebuke against his opponents, who seem to have made some grandiose claims. Paul's preference is to boast in weaknesses and to always tell the truth (v. 5). Thus he has "foolishly" related a vision about which nothing can be revealed to the Corinthians, except that it happened.[91]

Verse 7 makes it clear that there was something else that God allowed to happen to Paul along with this heady experience. Betz may be right in saying that vv. 7-9 are a parody of a healing miracle story, in which a person prays for healing and God answers the prayer. Here the answer is no![92] God sent Paul a "thorn" or "stake" in the flesh, a "messenger of Satan," to prevent Paul

88. See the example in G. Scholem, *Major Trends in Jewish Mysticism* (New York: Schocken, 1973), pp. 52f.

89. So, e.g., R. M. Price, "Punished in Paradise: An Exegetical Theory in II Corinthians 12.1-10," *JSNT* 7 (1980), pp. 33-40.

90. Saake, "Paulus als Ekstatiker," p. 410, is right in saying that Paul is not referring here to the experience of glossolalia. He is recording something he heard and perhaps saw, not explaining something he spoke. On glossolalia, see pp. 274-81 above.

91. Cf. Holland, "Speaking like a Fool," p. 27.

92. Cf. H. D. Betz, *Der Apostel Paulus und die sokratische Tradition. Eine exegetische Untersuchung zu seiner 'Apologie' 2 Korinther 10–13* (Tübingen: Mohr, 1972), pp. 92f.

from becoming too elated over such revelations. In other words, it brought him right back down to earth.[93]

There is considerable debate as to whether we should take the dative of *sarx* as locative ("in the flesh") or as dative of disadvantage ("for the flesh"). If it is locative then Paul is probably referring to some sort of physical ailment, disease, or condition.[94] If one takes it as a dative of disadvantage, then "flesh" is used in a theological sense and the thorn attacked Paul's "sinful inclination." Paul does, of course, use "flesh" in this sense because the physical nature is the least redeemed portion of the believer in this life, and is accordingly the locus of most temptation.[95] Some have even thought that the thorn was Paul's opponents,[96] but the verb here means "batter" or "beat about the head," which certainly suggests something physical, and not mere opposition or temptation. Furthermore, we have already heard in this letter that the impression of Paul's physical presence was that he was weak.

God chose not to remove this problem from Paul despite repeated prayer.[97] We do not know what this illness or condition was, but there may be several clues in his letters. This letter intimates that it was something that affected the visual or less likely the oral impression Paul made on the Corinthians. A physical deformity is unlikely since we are not talking about something with which he was born. Rather, this is something that came on him and that he believed God might remove from him. Some have suggested that it was a speech impediment. This is possible, but surely the record of Acts suggests that Paul had no problems preaching. Even in Athens a few total strangers were impressed. This leaves us again with some sort of visually obvious, perhaps repulsive, disease or condition. It enfeebled Paul enough for him to be thought of as weak, but not enough to prevent him from traveling all over the empire and recovering from the disasters he has just listed. He may well have been a walking miracle, but the record suggests that he was basically in

93. J. W. McCant, "Paul's Thorn of Rejected Apostleship," *NTS* 34 (1988), pp. 550-72 proposes the novel thesis that the "thorn" was the Corinthians' rejection of Paul's apostleship. There are a host of reasons to reject this thesis, including the fact that it is not clear that the Corinthian church had simply or totally rejected Paul. There were notable troublemakers, but not rejection by the majority. Furthermore the parallels with Gal. 4:13f. are not to be dismissed lightly, even though they are not exact. Surely Paul's use of *sarx* ("flesh") here points to something physical, and a stake or thorn for the flesh is not the same as a pain in the heart.

94. So most commentators.

95. See pp. 394-95 above.

96. Cf. Num. 33:55; Ezek. 23:24 on foes as thorns.

97. The verb tense of "pleaded" suggests requests made and concluded in the past. Paul is not begging anymore; he takes God's answer to be no. This verb tense is also strongly against McCant's suggestion (see n. 93 above), since Paul is still concerned with and praying about the problem in Corinth.

robust health apart from this "thorn in the flesh." The text here suggests it was more of a nuisance than something that prevented Paul's ministry. It may be that the opponents had played up this malady to good effect: Paul is a sick miracle worker, a man who cannot even heal himself. Why should anyone believe him and his claims about God's power?

If the verb "beat about the head" is a meaningful clue, perhaps we may combine it with other clues. In Gal. 4:13 Paul says that it was because of a bodily ailment that he preached the gospel in Galatia and that his condition was a trial to them, though they did not scorn him. Then v. 15 says that they would have plucked out their eyes for him. Is this a mere figure of speech? Perhaps not. It is believable that Paul had some sort of eye disease. If he had impaired vision this might explain not only why he had traveling companions on his trips, but especially why Luke the physician seems to have been an important companion. This also makes sense of why Paul says that he signs his letters with a large signature (Gal. 6:11).

We are thus left with Paul the paradox: a visionary with bad eyes! What could he have seen in heaven anyway?[98] In any case some sort of visual impairment seems the best guess. It was a messenger of Satan, yet it was also from God, because God is ultimately in control. As Luther said, even the devil is God's devil.[99]

But it was not just that the thorn was sent to Paul. The Lord also told him that his grace was enough for Paul (v. 9). This grace was obviously strength to endure, not healing grace. Paradoxically enough, Christ's power is completed or comes to fullness in the midst of human weakness. When it is evident that Paul is weak, it will be equally evident that the power and miracles and conversions could not be coming from a human source but from Christ working in and through Paul. Thus weakness makes Paul most translucent so that one can see the source of the real power and light.

An interesting verb is used in v. 9. Paul says the power "made its home" in him, or "came to rest" on him. He is probably drawing on the image of the Shekinah coming down, the divine presence that conveys power. Because it has come on him, he is content with whatever weaknesses or verbal or physical abuse he has to undergo, because Christ is better revealed when it is apparent

98. Paul says that in the third heaven he *heard* things. Some have suggested that Paul had solar retinitis, the sort of thing one might get from staring at an eclipse. Are we being told that Paul was blinded by this experience, or at least partially so? If so, it is no wonder that he remembered it.

99. There may be something to the suggestion that here we have a nonmiraculous miracle story, in which paradoxically Paul *does* share an oracle from God. Cf. Lincoln, "Paul the Visionary," pp. 218f. This fits with the suggestion that God's power comes to completion in weakness. It was in his weakness that Paul received a late word from God, which he could, in fact, share with the Corinthians.

that the power and help are not coming from a human source (v. **10**). When he is weak, it is then that he is strong, because then he must rely totally on the Lord.[100]

Finally, it is possible, as McCant suggests, that Paul has patterned his description of his experience on the experience of Christ:

Christ faced a cross, Paul a stake or thorn;
Christ prayed three times for the suffering to pass, and so did Paul;
Jesus prayed "not my will but yours" while Paul received a revelation that
    God's grace would be sufficient *in* his weakness; and
the cross and the thorn had to be not only faced but actually endured.

Jesus was a suffering Messiah, so it is no wonder that his agent was a suffering *apostolos*.[101]

Paul hopes by the material in the Fool's Discourse to bring about a transvaluation of the Corinthians' values and of their criteria for apostles.[102] This required him to use irony, parody, invective, and paradox to make clear to his converts this message: *Things are not as they seem!*[103]

100. This passage has numerous implications for ministry. It shows that it is not always God's will to heal someone with a physical malady, for whatever reasons. The "health and wealth" gospel has overlooked not only the fact that there are occasions for suffering for Christ, but also that there are occasions when ordinary suffering is used by God for a higher good, including powerful witness to others. The theology that suggests that lack of healing necessarily means lack of faith has failed to reckon with numerous scriptural examples, including Paul's, and has failed to recognize that for early Christians, life in this body was seen as temporary and temporal. It was not something to be preserved at all costs, since a better life and a better body were coming in due course.

101. McCant, "Paul's Thorn," p. 571.

102. Rightly Holland, "Speaking like a Fool," p. 32.

103. Here the marriage of rhetorical device and intended social effect are quite close. The Corinthians are to see the paradox in their situation by properly reading the paradoxes in Paul's foolish discourse.

Argument V, Division 3: 12:11–13:4

CLOSING ARGUMENTS

In his closing arguments Paul will repeat several things that he has already stressed and will try to make clear that he has proven the *propositio* of this rhetorical discourse, that he is "not a peddler of God's word like so many" (2:17) and that Christ speaks in him. He resorts here to a technique called *amplificatio* as part of making an effective appeal to his audience's emotions. In *amplificatio* one deliberately uses for rhetorical effect a stronger or weaker word than is strictly warranted. Quintilian cites as an example calling a dishonest person a robber or saying that one who has been struck has been touched (*Inst. Or.* 8.4.1). Here Paul calls his refusal to be a burden (that is, to accept patronage) a "wrong" (12:13) and says that his refusal could be labeled "cunning" or "trying to take you in by deceit" (12:16). Probably this was a charge made against Paul by the opponents.

At this point Paul wishes to settle accounts with his primary audience, the Corinthians themselves, and desires to put them on the defensive, after he himself has been the defendant in all that came before in the discourse. He accomplishes this by turning the tables on them in 12:20 and reminding them of the faults that he has accused them of throughout the Corinthian correspondence, but especially in 1 Corinthians: quarreling, jealousy, factions, anger, arrogance, disorder, sexual sins, and failure to repent. His reference to impurity not yet repented of may allude to the matter discussed in the digression in 6:14–7:1, which in turn alludes to 1 Corinthians 8–10.

We have noted throughout this letter that while it primarily contains a forensic discourse, there are significant deliberative sections or elements, which serve the larger forensic purpose.[1] This is likewise true of this final argument, which is loaded with forensic language about self-defense, about God as judge, about the testimony of two witnesses, and about the demand for proof, but also includes deliberative elements. Sometimes the best defense is a good offense, and Paul wishes to put his audience on the defensive before he returns to Corinth.

12:20 prepares for the *peroratio* where Paul completely turns the tables

---

1. Thus one could call this an example of a mixed type of discourse, but I would suggest that that is not entirely apt, since the deliberative elements serve the larger purpose of defense of Paul and hence of reconciliation between Paul and his converts.

465

on the Corinthians by suggesting that instead of testing Paul and asking for proof that Christ speaks in him, they should test themselves. This is in part because he has stressed that they are what they are because he is what he is: If he is not a genuine *apostolos,* then neither have they genuinely been converted, since they came to faith through his preaching! On the other hand, if they are genuine Christians then they ought to be his letter of recommendation (3:2) and ought to defend him against his opponents.

The desired result of the whole letter is that the Corinthians cease putting Paul on trial, since they will end up convicting themselves of false faith in the process. It is a clever defense, and one that Romans 16 suggests finally worked.

12:11 indicates that Paul has finished his Fool's Discourse and is returning to normal sensible arguments. He stresses that he only undertook the Fool's Discourse because the Corinthians drove him to it. If they had taken Paul's part and defended or commended him (to the opponents?) he would not have had to do so himself. He claims that it should now be evident that he is in no way inferior to the so-called "superlative" *apostoloi.* Using irony, he claims that in nothing does he fall short of such agents, even though he is nothing in himself! The signs of an *apostolos,* which included "signs, wonders, and mighty works," that is, miracles, have been worked in and through him (v. 12).[2] The first of these terms (*sēmeia,* "signs") suggests the significance or symbolic power of miracles, the second their capacity to surprise and go beyond the ordinary, and the third their dynamic and powerful character. Paul is notably reluctant to talk about such deeds in his letters, perhaps because he, like his Master, did not see it as his essential commissioned task to perform miracles, but rather to preach the Good News (cf. Mark 1:32-39, especially v. 38). Miracles are performed as acts of compassion along the way, but are still secondary signs or proofs that Paul is an *apostolos.*[3]

Paul says that the only way he allowed the Corinthians to be inferior to the other (Pauline) congregations is in the matter of his support (v. 13). He then adds sarcastically, "Forgive me this wrong of not burdening you." There was an offense in what he did: He had violated the conventions of reciprocity and benefaction. His handling of money matters was a major sticking point,

2. Acts is replete with miracles performed by Paul and others, but Paul's letters are not. Yet we may point to 2 Cor. 6:6f.; Gal. 3:5; and Rom. 15:19. E. P. Sanders, *Paul* (Oxford: Oxford University, 1991), pp. 24f., also points to 1 Thess. 1:5. "Signs and wonders" is a frequent biblical pair, and in the Synoptics *dynameis* ("mighty works") is regularly used of Jesus' miracles.

3. It is interesting that Paul has not made miracles a major part of his defense up to this point and mentions them now at the end as an additional, almost supplementary, argument meant to remove all final doubt that he is an agent of Christ.

if not the the main one, that was alienating him from his converts.[4] He wanted to make clear to the proud Corinthians that he, or rather Christ through him, was the benefactor, and that they were the clients. Perhaps he wanted them to view him like the patron of a *collegia,* on which basis they should have commended and honored him.[5] He will allow them to play benefactor in relation to the collection for Jerusalem, but not in relation to him. It is money matters that prompt the paternal language that follows in v. **14**.[6]

Paul makes it clear that he is fully prepared to come to Corinth a third time. This makes good sense if our argument is correct that 2 Corinthians should be seen as a unity. The previous visits were the first, when a Christian congregation was first founded in Corinth, and then the so-called painful visit (chs. 1–2). Paul stresses again that he seeks them, not their possessions.[7] He also stresses the obligation of parents to children. At various points in the Corinthian correspondence Paul has made it clear that he would rather admonish than shame his spiritual children and give to them than take from them. But "although Paul is ready to spare the rod, he is not prepared to spoil the child,"[8] much less let others spoil them. Continuing with the economic metaphor, he says that he is ready to spend and be spent in their service (v. **15**). He asks them point blank, In view of how much I love you, will you love me less? Even if the answer is yes, Paul's attitude is "so be it." Like Christ, he is proactive, not just reactive, in his love.

Verse **16** must be seen as an example of *amplificatio* with an element of irony: "Of course you will accuse me of taking you in by deceit by such

4. See pp. 411-28 above.

5. Cf. R. MacMullen, *Roman Social Relations 50 B.C. to A.D. 284* (New Haven: Yale University, 1974), pp. 74-76, on inscriptions dedicated to patrons of such associations.

6. It is possible that Paul uses parental language because he is thinking of the patron-client relationship that was set up in the process of Roman adoption. One comes under the *patria potestas,* the authority of the adopting father, through a purchase. Cf. R. A. Atkins, *Egalitarian Community: Ethnography and Exegesis* (Tuscaloosa: University of Alabama, 1991), pp. 176ff. Thus Paul would be thinking of the Corinthians as Christ's adoptive sons and daughters, bought by means of Christ's death (cf. 13:4). Paul has already used this sort of language in exhorting the Corinthians in 1 Cor. 6:19f., and thus it would not be new to them here. Because they were converted and freed through Paul's ministry, he can claim to be their parent in a derivative sense. It was also true that a teacher was seen as *in loco parentis* (cf. Quintilian *Inst. Or.* 2.2.4); thus there may be more than one reason for Paul's use of this parental imagery.

7. As J. Murphy-O'Connor, *The Theology of the Second Letter to the Corinthians* (Cambridge: Cambridge University, 1991), p. 126, says, the phrase "I want you, not yours" sums up Paul's perspective on ministry. He wanted a loving relationship with his converts, not their patronal support. If this were the basic attitude of all ministers today, the modern *ekklēsia* would be much better off.

8. N. R. Petersen, *Rediscovering Paul: Philemon and the Sociology of Paul's Narrative World* (Philadelphia: Fortress, 1985), p. 130.

arguments. I am really cunningly getting you to support me by pretending that I do not want your support, all the while indirectly fleecing you through the funds you will give for the collection!" A perennial allegation against Sophists was that they were money-hungry and used deception to fleece people.[9] Isocrates, for instance, heaps scorn on the Sophistic practice of claiming to teach virtue while having their fees paid to a third party so that it would look like they were not charging anyone (*Against the Sophists* 5f.). This same sort of allegation was being made against Paul, and the third party in question was Titus, along with some of Paul's other coworkers (vv. 17f.).

It appears that the Corinthians had considerable confidence in Titus. Therefore Paul argues that neither Titus nor any other of his coworkers defrauded them. Why then should they suspect Paul, the leader of this group of workers?[10] He had lived and walked the same fine line, operating with the same spirit as the others have.

In v. **19** Paul says, "You will think that I have been defending myself to you for a long while now." In truth he has been, but he says that all this time he has been bearing witness to God, who is his real judge, and speaking in Christ, that is, speaking the truth, since he is in Christ. He thus implies that he does not have to answer to the Corinthians. Nonetheless, throughout this letter, so that his converts will know that he is genuine, he has been letting them listen in on his testimony or rendering of an account to God. He has done it all to build them up, not to tear them down.[11] Throughout, he has had their best interests at heart.

In vv. **20f.** Paul lists what he fears he will find when he comes back to Corinth. The first list (v. 20) is of social sins that divide the body of Christ, that separate an *apostolos* from his converts, and that generally cause havoc. The second list (v. 21) is of sexual sins. Both hark back to several problems dealt with in 1 Corinthians. Paul is afraid that the Corinthians have reverted to their old factious and immoral behavior.

In any case, he is not coming this third time so that God can again humiliate him in their presence as happened on his second, abortive, painful visit (v. 21a). Before he came with a glove; this time they may expect a hammer

---

9. Cf. B. W. Winter, *Are Philo and Paul among the Sophists? A Hellenistic Jewish and a Christian Response to a First Century Movement* (dissertation, MacQuarrie University, 1988), p. 230.

10. This is a form of the argument from the lesser to the greater.

11. This was one of the major purposes in the deliberative letter 1 Corinthians, but now Paul asserts that it has also been one of the purposes of 2 Corinthians as well. The close of this letter makes it clear that Paul still thinks the Corinthians are factious and so need to be built up and knit back together. Cf. I. Kitzberger, *Bau der Gemeinde* (Würzburg: Echter, 1986), p. 129. The major goal of reconciliation, however, could only be effected by Paul's defense of himself.

if he finds them in such a condition (13:2). He may have to mourn that they have not repented of their earlier sins (12:21).

Paul chooses to cite Deut. 19:15 at this point (**13:1**),[12] probably because Deuteronomy goes on (v. 16) to speak of malicious witnesses, in this case surely the false *apostoloi*, and (v. 19) to conclude that if malicious witnesses are shown to have testified falsely, then "You shall do to the false witness what the false witness meant to do to the accused. So you shall purge the evil from your midst." Those who knew the Hebrew Scriptures would likely catch a hint here of upcoming legal action against the offenders in Corinth.[13]

Are the "three witnesses" Paul's three visits? Is Paul saying that by his third visit he will establish his case? The context favors this view:[14] Paul is probably suggesting that he will hold court when he arrives.[15] He is turning the tables on his audience and preparing to put them on trial, just as he has been judged by them and has had to defend himself in this letter. Roman judicial proceedings included a preliminary hearing in which the facts of the case were determined and agreed on as the basis for the trial.[16] Paul may then be threatening to take forensic, but in-house, action against various Corinthians, perhaps the ones supporting the false *apostoloi*, unless they get their house in order.[17] The point is that when Paul comes he will not spare them, because he has warned them previously about their former sins and is warning them now in this letter as well (v. **2**).

The word *dokimē* in v. **3** is an important one as this letter approaches its close. It sometimes means "test" or "proof," that is, the result of a test. The cognate adjective can mean "approved," or its antonym "unapproved," describing therefore what has proven to be a failure. Paul is saying that the judicial action he will take against the offenders when he arrives will provide the

12. By way of Matt. 18:16; cf. 1 Tim. 5:19.

13. J. T. Fitzgerald, "Paul, the Ancient Epistolary Theorists, and 2 Corinthians 10–13," in *Greeks, Romans, and Christians*, ed. D. L. Balch, E. Ferguson, and W. A. Meeks (Minneapolis: Fortress, 1990), pp. 190-200, here p. 199, says that Paul will go on the witness stand to accuse the Corinthians, but it seems more likely that he sees himself as Christ's agent in this affair and thus as the judge.

14. Alternatively, Paul may be saying that this letter, the painful letter, and the first letter are three witnesses against the Corinthians. But this is unlikely since 1 Cor. 5:9 implies that there was yet another letter, for a total of four.

15. Among the stronger rhetorical proofs were the inartificial ones where one could appeal to a decision in an earlier document. See pp. 333-35 above.

16. Cf pp. 162-64 above.

17. He would be envisioning a trial *en ekklēsia*, like the one described in 1 Cor. 5:3f., in which he would take action against the real offenders. 2 Cor. 10:6 suggests that the offenders would be the Corinthian supporters of the opponents, or less probably the opponents themselves. Paul still seems to believe that most in Corinth will render obedience after this strong letter, and he can deal with the recalcitrants thereafter with the support of the majority.

ultimate proof, if it is still needed, that he is an authorized and empowered agent of Christ. The Jesus who speaks through Paul is not weak but strong in their midst.

In v. 4 Paul once again stresses the cruciform shape of his ministry based on Christ's life. Jesus was crucified when in the state of weak human flesh, but now he lives from the power of God. Similarly, though Paul came to them in his weakness, nonetheless when he comes again he will be alive with Christ by means of the power of God toward them.[18] Paul has transferred to his own ministry terms characterizing Christ's ministry: death, life, glory of God, and power, and thence has transferred them to the life of the Christian in general. This provided "a structure for that ministry, and a way in which it, or any other ministry claiming to represent the gospel, [could] be adequately evaluated."[19]

Paul's rhetorical strategy in this discourse has involved a considerable amount of risk. The combination of defense and exhortation or appeal has been necessary because "his authority is being tested to the same degree that the obedience of the others is being tested. If they obey, his authority is confirmed,"[20] and his defense will have achieved its ultimate goal — the reconciliation of Paul with his strange and estranged converts.

---

18. On Paul following the cruciform pattern of Christ's ministry, see S. Kraftchick, "Death in Us, Life in You: The Apostolic Medium," *Society of Biblical Literature 1991 Seminar Papers*, ed. E. H. Lovering (Atlanta: Scholars, 1991), pp. 618-37, here pp. 625ff.

19. *Ibid.*, p. 624.

20. Petersen, *Rediscovering Paul*, p. 142.

Peroratio: 13:5-10

The Last Harangue: The Defense Rests

The *peroratio* in a piece of forensic rhetoric will vary not only according to whether one is speaking for the defense or for the prosecution, but also according to whether the rhetor thinks that in the case at hand an emotional or a rational appeal would be best. The latter would normally amount to a brief rehearsal of the facts for the judge while the former could involve almost anything (Quintilian *Inst. Or.* 6.1.1f.). It was normal for the orator for the defense to make an emotional appeal, especially if the case had been difficult to defend. The *peroratio* was usually rather brief, lest one overtax the patience of the audience or draw one too many times on their emotional bank account.

Paul chooses to make a brief emotional appeal here, though he does mention the main aims of this whole discourse: to restore his former relationship with his converts and to make sure that they will endure in the faith and be finally judged as approved by God, though in Paul's view, their genuineness will only be shown if they recognize his. He has had to defend himself at every turn in this argument, but he makes clear that his major aim is not his own vindication and authentication but theirs.

The emotional character of the appeal is shown in that

for the self-confident Corinthians, nothing could be more emotional than being told they were in danger of being judged non-Christian,

Paul indicates that he prays for his converts and is more than willing to make the sacrifice of being weak so long as they are powerful in the faith,

like a good parent he does not want to be compelled to discipline his spiritual children, and he stresses that all he has said and done was to accomplish the aim in ministry that in 1 Corinthians he says that he always pursued for and with them — their building up and not their destruction.[1]

The Corinthians seek proof of the genuineness of Paul's apostleship, but Paul tells them to test themselves, to see if their own faith is genuine (v. 5). It was rhetorically appropriate in a *peroratio* to raise questions in order to force one's opponent or the audience to come up with some answers of their own (*Inst. Or.* 6.1.5). This Paul does, continuing to pursue the agenda of his final argument, which was to put the Corinthians themselves on the defensive. He has become the potential accuser rather than the defendant at the end of the letter. He knows that what ultimately works with these converts is an appeal to their own highest self-interest. Therefore, he sees it as his job not merely to soften them with an appeal to pity the defendant, the usual defensive move, but rather to rouse them to vigilance about their own spiritual status.[2] They must examine themselves to see if they are "in the faith." Here "faith" is used as a substantive, not unlike what we find in the Pastorals. Paul thus refers to genuine Christian faith, which involves theological, ethical, and social dimensions.

If they are genuine Christians, and they must test themselves to see if this is so, then ipso facto he is a genuine apostle, with Christ speaking through him (v. 6, cf. v. 3). He would rather not have to be "shown to be approved" as a real *apostolos* (v. 7), since that would mean he would have to come and exercise spiritual discipline among them. He would rather they repent and there be no such need for such a display of power. He would rather go on being weak in their midst (v. 9). His bottom line concern is not that he *appear* to be a genuine apostle — according to all the wrong criteria — but that the Corinthians do right, even if this requires that he appear to be a failure *(adokimoi).* He rejoices when he is weak but they are strong, and he prays for their restoration. This has been his goal in writing all this, their restoration, so that he does not have to treat them severely, as he did in the painful letter. His goal is to build up, not to tear down (v. 10).[3]

This letter, from start to finish, manifests the rhetoric of reconciliation.

---

1. On vv. 5-10 as a formal unit, see I. Kitzberger, *Bau der Gemeinde* (Würzburg: Echter, 1986), pp. 134f.

2. Quintilian tells us that the appeal that would carry the most emotional weight was the appeal to pity (*Inst. Or.* 6.1.23).

3. Kitzberger, *Bau der Gemeinde,* p. 134, suggests that this admonition to self-examination is the purpose of this letter, and to a degree he is right, but that is only a proximate aim along the way of producing the Corinthians' restoration, and thus their reconciliation with Paul. He is right, however, that v. 10 shows to the Corinthians that Paul believes he has from God the power to construct or deconstruct the community in Corinth.

But unlike 1 Corinthians, it is a matter of reconciliation between Paul and his converts. To this end, he has had to defend himself, attack his opponents, and exhort his converts to self-examination. He has attempted to remove one obstacle after another blocking his full reunion with the Corinthians, but by far the largest of these obstacles was the question of his own genuineness as an *apostolos* and the authenticity of his ministry. That subject he has had to dwell on repeatedly in this discourse. For that reason it rightly deserves to be called a forensic discourse, though with significant deliberative elements serving the larger forensic goals.

Closing Epistolary Greetings and Remarks: 13:11-13

PARTING SHOTS

It is striking that in Paul's forensic letters, such as 2 Corinthians or Galatians, he does not conclude on a convivial note with numerous personal remarks or greetings. Instead, in both Gal. 6:11-17 and here he continues to offer parting shots on some of his major themes right up to the final benediction(s). He begins with no thanksgiving in Galatians, and in 2 Corinthians he offers not a litany in thanksgiving form of things he was thankful for about the Corinthians but praise to God for God's work of comfort (1:3ff.). The rhetorical moves in both letters are similar in many ways and deserve further comparison. If it is true, as Mitchell urges, that one can tell much about the sort of rhetoric one is dealing with by how a discourse opens and closes,[1] then careful attention should be paid not only to the closing *peroratio* in each of these two letters, but also to the closing remarks, into which the *peroratio* spills over in both letters. In 2 Corinthians, this spilling over only amounts to a half verse, v. 11a, which serves as a summary of earlier appeals.

In v. 11 Paul urges the converts to rejoice.[2] They are also to amend their lives,

---

1. M. M. Mitchell, *Paul and the Rhetoric of Reconciliation* (Tübingen: Mohr, 1991), pp. 15ff.

2. *Chairete* could be a greeting and be put at the beginning of a letter (e.g., Jas. 1:1), but I see no evidence (pace C. K. Barrett, *The Second Epistle to the Corinthians* [New York: Harper and Row, 1973], p. 342) that it could mean "goodbye," especially not here where it is the first in a series of imperatives and deserves to be translated as such. Furthermore, the same verb has just been used in v. 9 to mean "rejoice," and, most telling, in 1 Thess.

encourage each other, be of the same mind, and live at peace. These remarks, like those in 12:20, harken back to the problems that Paul had to deal with in 1 Corinthians and suggest once again that such problems had not been put to rest. This view finds confirmation in Clement's letter to the Corinthians written in the last decade of the century, which manifests clear evidence that the Corinthians had still not entirely changed their stripes, being still a factious bunch.

Rhetorically, Paul's strategy is to continue putting the Corinthians on the defensive so that they will realize that they must get their house in order before Paul's return. Strangely, this is the only place in the Bible where we find the phrase "the God of love." The Corinthians are to be reconciled and treat each other as family,[3] hence the holy kiss (v. **12**).

2 Corinthians is too early to call the kiss a liturgical gesture, since Christians still met in homes and adopted and adapted family customs for their own use.[4] Klassen is right that the Christian kiss departs from similar first-century religious practices, especially because of the emphasis on the word "holy." It should "be seen in a living context of people who are building a new sociological reality rather than in restrictive eucharistic or liturgical terms."[5] Klassen also argues that Paul was the first popular ethical teacher to instruct members of a mixed social group to greet each other with a kiss when they met.[6] What this exhortation may show is that Paul expects his letter to be read in worship and to lead up to the climax of the service and the final benediction.

Paul's final benediction (v. **14**) mentions blessings that all three members of the Trinity bring: grace from Christ, love from God, and *koinōnia* of the Holy Spirit.[7] Paul does not elaborate a doctrine of the Trinity, but as a Jew he would not offer such a blessing in the name of anyone but the one God.

5:16 the same form is used to head a brief list of final exhortations. Cf. V. P. Furnish, *II Corinthians* (Garden City: Doubleday, 1984), p. 581; R. P. Martin, *2 Corinthians* (Waco: Word, 1986), p. 490. In Latin, *gaudete* was not exactly the same as *valete*. Finally, there is inscriptional evidence of *loipon* meaning "finally" followed immediately by an imperative. Cf. *New Docs. 4*, p. 67, where such an inscription is said to parallel 2 Cor. 13:11.

3. That only a majority were involved in approving discipline of the offender (2:6) is a sign that reconciliation among the Corinthian Christians was still needed.

4. On the holy kiss, see pp. 322-23 above and W. Klassen, "The Sacred Kiss in the NT: An Example of Social Boundary Lines," *NTS* 39 (1993), pp. 122-35.

5. Klaasen, "Sacred Kiss," p. 132. Kisses shared in the mystery cult groups showed the shared intimacy of the participants, and perhaps the gesture had a similar meaning in early Christianity. See pp. 191-95 above and W. Burkert, *Ancient Mystery Cults* (Cambridge: Harvard University, 1987), pp. 89-114.

6. Klaasen, "Sacred Kiss," pp. 126-30.

7. The last is either "sharing in common from" the Holy Spirit or "participation in" the Spirit, depending on whether "Holy Spirit" is objective genitive or, like "Jesus Christ" and "God," subjective genitive.

Trinitarian thinking in its rudiments is thus present in his letters.[8] Here the "economic" Trinity is in view, that is, the persons of God in their roles in relationship to believers. Paul implies that since the Godhead works together, surely he and his converts can do likewise, since God has blessed them greatly.

8. On Paul's christological monotheism, see B. Witherington, *Jesus the Sage: The Pilgrimage of Wisdom* (Minneapolis: Fortress, 1994), ch. 7.

Index of Modern Authors

Fiore, B.   136 n. 3, 168 n. 25

Fiorenza, E. S.   xiv n. 17, 34 n. 99, 232
   n. 5, 238 n. 27, 287, 288 n. 47, 319 n. 4

Fischer, J. E.   16 n. 39

Fitzgerald, J. T.   137 n. 4, 141 nn. 15 and
   17, 142 and n. 19, 143 n. 24, 329 n. 5,
   338, 339 n. 33, 370 n. 33, 387 nn. 6
   and 9, 388 and nn. 12 and 14, 393
   n. 5, 397 n. 22, 398 and n. 3, 399 nn. 5
   and 11, 436 n. 23, 438 n. 40, 450
   nn. 40 and 41, 452 n. 46, 469 n. 13

Fitzmyer, J. A.   237 and n. 25, 238

Fontenrose, J.   111 n. 13, 277 and nn. 13
   and 14, 278 and nn. 16, 18, and 19,
   279 nn. 21 and 22

Forbes, C.   280 n. 25, 282 n. 28, 375 n. 1,
   393 n. 3, 433 n. 15, 436 nn. 23 and 24,
   443 nn. 7 and 9

Ford, D. F.   333 and n. 21, 336, 338 and
   n. 31, 351 n. 62, 357 n. 3, 363 nn. 8
   and 9, 386 n. 1, 431 n. 6

Fox, R. L.   33 n. 94, 131 n. 2

Frid, B.   127 n. 26

Fridrichsen, A.   388 n. 14

Funk, A.   232 n. 4, 456 n. 62

Furnish, V. P.   132 n. 5, 272 n. 40, 331
   n. 15, 352 n. 63, p 365 n. 15, 373 n. 5,
   381 n. 20, 389 n. 15, 389 n. 15, 420
   n. 32, 423 n. 45, 447 n. 27, 459 nn. 78
   and 79, 475 n. 2

Gardner, P.   186 n. 1, 189 n. 13, 195
   n. 33, 199 n. 48, 200, 203 n. 2, 204
   n. 4, 218 n. 4, 219 nn. 7 and 9, 221
   and nn. 12 and 13, 223 n. 22, 226 n. 30

Garnsey, P.   193 nn. 5, 6, 8, and 9, 189
   n. 16, 190 n. 17, 259 n. 20, 260 nn. 21-23

Georgi, D.   4 n. 11, 314 n. 4, 343 n. 41,
   383 and n. 33, 413 n. 8, 420 n. 33, 423
   and n. 46, 424 and nn. 49 and 50, 425
   and nn. 53, 55, 57, 58, and 60, 427
   nn. 67 and 69, 436 n. 27, 450 and
   nn. 42 and 43

Gill, D. W. J.   33 nn. 92 and 94, 34 n. 98,
   189 n. 14, 233 n. 8, 234 n. 12

Gillman, J.   308 n. 64

Gooch, P. W.   199 n. 47

Goranson, S.   26 n. 74

Gordon, R.   222 n. 18

Goulder, M. D.   84 n. 6

Greenwood, D.   382 n. 27

Grelot, P.   381 n. 21

Grudem, W.   238 n. 26, 280 nn. 24 and
   27

Gundry, R. H.   307 n. 63

Guttierez, P.   138 n. 6

Güzlow, H.   181 n. 44

Hafemann, S.   366 n. 20, 367 and nn. 22
   and 24, 368, 369 n. 27, 370 n. 30, 373
   n. 4

Hanson. A. T.   379 n. 15

Harnack, A. von   264 n. 1

Harris, M.   298 n. 35, 308 and n. 65

Hartman, L.   124, 276 n. 10

Hay, D.   390, 410 n. 13

Hayes, J. W.   8 n. 18

Hays, R. B.   25 n. 72, 135 n. 16, 166
   n. 19, 380 n. 18, 381 n. 20, n. 22, 384
   n. 34

Heine, R.   271 n. 37

Heiny, S. B.   370 n. 31, 407 n. 2, 408
   nn. 2 and 3

Hemer, C. J.   2 n. 1, 5 n. 12, 361 n. 4

Hendrix, H.   457 nn. 71 and 72

Héring, J.   134 n. 12, 258 and n. 15, 308
   n. 64

Hill, C. C.   226 n. 30, 447 and n. 28

Hill, D.   280 n. 24

Hock, R. F.   11 n. 24, 19 n. 49, 20 n. 52,
   206 n. 14, 208 n. 18, 419 n. 24, 457
   and n. 73

Hodgson, R.   451 n. 45, 452 n. 46

Holladay, C. A.   264 n. 2, 265 n. 11, 266
   n. 13, 267 n. 20, 267 and n. 20, 268
   n. 26, 269 n. 27, 270 n. 34, 271 n. 35

Holland, G.   433 n. 14, 437 n. 30, 439
   n. 44, 444 nn. 13 and 15, 461 n. 91,
   464 n. 102

Holmberg, B.   xi n. 5, xv n. 18, 21 n. 56,
   453 n. 54, 454 and n. 56

Hooker, M. D.   86 n. 15, 140 and n. 14

Hopkins, K.   294 nn. 14 and 19

Horne, C. M.   124

Index of Scripture and Other Ancient Writings

OLD TESTAMENT

OTHER EARLY CHRISTIAN WRITINGS

PSEUDEPIGRAPHA